July 18–20, 2016
Darmstadt, Germany

**Association for
Computing Machinery**

Advancing Computing as a Science & Profession

WiSec'16

Proceedings of the 9th ACM Conference on

Security & Privacy in Wireless and Mobile Networks

Sponsored by:
ACM SIGSAC

In cooperation with:
ACM SIGMOBILE

Supported by:
NEC and NICER

Association for Computing Machinery

Advancing Computing as a Science & Profession

The Association for Computing Machinery
2 Penn Plaza, Suite 701
New York, New York 10121-0701

Notice to Past Authors of ACM-Published Articles
ACM intends to create a complete electronic archive of all articles and/or other material previously published by ACM. If you have written a work that has been previously published by ACM in any journal or conference proceedings prior to 1978, or any SIG Newsletter at any time, and you do NOT want this work to appear in the ACM Digital Library, please inform permissions@acm.org, stating the title of the work, the author(s), and where and when published.

ISBN: 978-1-4503-4270-4 (Digital)

ISBN: 978-1-4503-4615-3 (Print)

Additional copies may be ordered prepaid from:

ACM Order Department
PO Box 30777
New York, NY 10087-0777, USA

Phone: 1-800-342-6626 (USA and Canada)
+1-212-626-0500 (Global)
Fax: +1-212-944-1318
E-mail: acmhelp@acm.org
Hours of Operation: 8:30 am – 4:30 pm ET

Printed in the USA

Foreword

It is our great pleasure to welcome you to the 2016 ACM Conference on Security and Privacy in Wireless and Mobile Networks (WiSec'16), which takes place in Darmstadt, Germany. WiSec is the premier venue for research dedicated to all aspects of security and privacy in wireless and mobile networks, their systems, and their applications. In addition to the traditional ACM WiSec topics of physical, link, and network layer security, WiSec'16 has continued to solicit papers focusing on the security and privacy of mobile software platforms, usable security and privacy, biometrics, cryptography, and the increasingly diverse range of mobile or wireless applications such as Internet of Things, and Cyber-Physical Systems.

This year, WiSec received 71 complete paper submissions from around the world. Authors denoted 20 of these submissions as short papers, and no papers were reclassified during the reviewing process. There were many interesting and exciting papers. After a multiple round reviewing process, our program committee selected 13 full papers and 7 short papers for presentation and publication in the conference proceedings. These papers will be presented in a single track, along with a poster and demonstration session that will provide early results as well as mature and practical prototypes. New this year, we have made short public reviews for all accepted papers available on the conference website. Recognizing that no paper is perfect, we hope to provide the community with greater insight into the program committee's decision process.

In addition to the research papers presented at the conference, we have an exciting keynote to be delivered by Prof. Jean-Pierre Hubaux ("The Ultimate Frontier for Privacy and Security: Medicine"). Prof. Hubaux is one of the founders of WiSec.

For 2016, WiSec will be co-located with PETS, the 16th Privacy Enhancing Technologies Symposium. Our goal is to stimulate exchange and interaction with the privacy community. Furthermore, as part of the Security and Privacy Week 2016, nine additional conferences and workshops are taking place in Darmstadt, Germany, one of Europe's leading security research hotspots.

Putting together WiSec'16 was a team effort. We thank the authors for providing the content of the program. We are also very grateful to the program committee for their hard work reviewing all of the papers, as well as their efforts shepherding conditionally accepted papers and drafting public review summaries. We would also like to thank the demo chairs, Alexandra Dmitrienko and Bruce DeBruhl, who have compiled an exciting set of demonstrations. As well as Matthias Schulz as the finance chair, who ensured that WiSec is offering the best "bang for the buck". Additional thanks to the publication chairs, Daniel Steinmetzer and Adwait Nadkarni, and the webmaster, Jiska Classen. We also thank the publicity chairs and especially Wenjia Li, Matthias Schulz, and Max Maass for their efforts publicizing the conference. The local organization would not have been possible without the Security and Privacy Week 2016 team, including Jiska Classen, Verena Giraud, Matthias Schulz, Daniel Steinmetzer, and many other the student volunteers.

Finally, many thanks go to the LOEWE NICER priority project that helped in the organization of ACM WiSec as well as to the Network Laboratories, NEC Europe Ltd., Heidelberg, who act as a silver sponsor. WiSec is grateful to the ACM SIGSAC for their continuing sponsorship. We hope that you have a nice stay in Darmstadt, and find WiSec 2016 to be an enriching and enjoyable experience.

Matthias Hollick
WiSec'16 General Chair
Technische Universität Darmstadt

Panos Papadimitratos
WiSec'16 Technical
Program co-Chair
KTH

William Enck
WiSec'16 Technical
Program co-Chair
North Carolina State University

Table of Contents

Session 5: Cyber-security Physical Dimensions

Session 6: Mobile Malware and Spam Analysis

Session 7: IoT Security

Poster and Demo Session

WiSec 2016 Conference Organization

General Chair: Matthias Hollick (TU Darmstadt, Germany)

Program Chairs: Panos Papadimitratos (KTH, Sweden)
William Enck (NC State University, USA)

Publicity Chairs: Roberto Di Pietro (Nokia Bell Labs, Paris, France)
Wenjia Li (New York Institute of Technology, USA)

Publication/Registration Chairs: Daniel Steinmetzer (TU Darmstadt, Germany)
Adwait Nadkarni (NC State University, USA)

Poster/Demo Chair: Alexandra Dmitrienko (ETH Zürich, Switzerland)
Bruce DeBruhl (Cal Poly San Luis Obispo, USA)

Web Chair: Jiska Classen (TU Darmstadt, Germany)

Local Organization/ Arrangement Chair: Matthias Schulz (TU Darmstadt, Germany)

Finance Chair: Matthias Schulz (TU Darmstadt, Germany)

Steering Committee: Srdjan Capkun (ETH Zürich, Switzerland)
Ivan Martinovic (Oxford University, UK)
Cristina Nita-Rotaru (Purdue University, USA)
Ahmad-Reza Sadeghi (TU Darmstadt, Germany)
Patrick Traynor (University of Florida, USA)

Program Committee: Tuomas Aura (Aalto University, Finland)
Gildas Avoine (INSA Rennes, France)
David Barrera (ETH Zurich, Switzerland)
Mike Burmester (Florida State University, USA)
Kevin Butler (University of Florida, USA)
Levente Buttyan (Budapest University of Technology & Economics, Hungary)
Guohong Cao (Pennsylvania State University, USA)
Srdjan Capkun (ETH Zurich, Switzerland)
Claude Castelluccia (INRIA Rhone Alpes, France)
Hao Chen (University of California, Davis, USA)
Bruno Crispo (DistriNet - KULeuven, Belgium)
Emiliano De Cristofaro (University College London, UK)
Jing Deng (University of North Carolina at Greensboro)
Roberto Di Pietro (Nokia Bell Labs, Paris, France)
Wenliang Du (Syracuse University, USA)
Aurélien Francillon (EURECOM, France)
Sébastien Gambs (Université du Québec à Montréal, Canada)
Guofei Gu (Texas A&M University, USA)
Gerhard P. Hancke (City University of Hong Kong, China)

Program Committee (continued): Yih-Chun Hu (University of Illinois at Urbana-Champaign, USA)
Frank Kargl (Ulm University, Germany)
Sneha Kasera (University of Utah, USA)
Yongdae Kim (KAIST, Republic of Korea)
Loukas Lazos (University of Arizona, USA)
Zhenkai Liang (National University of Singapore, Singapore)
Long Lu (Stony Brook University, USA)
Keith Martin (Royal Holloway University of London, UK)
Ivan Martinovic (Oxford University, UK)
René Mayrhofer (Johannes Kepler University Linz, Austria)
Mahtab Mirmohseni (Sharif University of Technology, Iran)
Refik Molva (EURECOM, France)
Valtteri Niemi (University of Helsinki, Finland)
Guevara Noubir (Northeastern University, USA)
Damien Octeau (Google, USA)
Bart Preneel (KU Leuven and iMinds, Belgium)
Ahmad-Reza Sadeghi (TU Darmstadt, Germany)
Nitesh Saxena (University of Alabama at Birmingham, USA)
Reza Shokri (Cornell Tech/UTAustin, USA)
Kapil Singh (IBM T. J. Watson Research Center, USA)
Patrick Tague (Carnegie Mellon University, USA)
George Theodorakopoulos (Cardiff University, UK)
Patrick Traynor (University of Florida, USA)
Dirk Westhoff (Offenburg University of Applied Sciences, Germany)
Susanne Wetzel (Stevens Institute of Technology, USA)
Wenyuan Xu (Univ. of South Carolina, USA & Zhejiang Univ., China)
Heng Yin (Syracuse University, USA)
Sencun Zhu (Pennsylvania State University, USA)

Additional Reviewers:

Jagdish Achara	Markus Miettinen
Abhishek Anand	Manar Mohamed
Olabode Anise	Muhammad Muaaz
Christopher Becker	Ajaya Neupane
Ferdinand Brasser	Dorottya Papp
Henry Carter	Apostolos Pyrgelis
Rainhard Findling	Bradley Reaves
András Gazdag	Peter Riedl
Gabor Gulyas	Michael Roland
Thomas Hayes	Nolen Scaife
Grant Hernandez	Hocheol Shin
Michael Hölzl	Maliheh Shirvanian
Jialin Huang	Babins Shrestha
Mojgan Khaledi	Prakash Shrestha
Hongil Kim	Yunmok Son
Cedric Lauradoux	Dave 'Jing' Tian

WiSec 2016 Sponsor & Supporters

Sponsor:

In cooperation with:

Supporters:

The Ultimate Frontier for Privacy and Security: Medicine

Jean-Pierre Hubaux
EPFL

Abstract:

Personalized medicine brings the promise of better diagnoses, better treatments, a higher quality of life and increased longevity. To achieve these noble goals, it exploits a number of revolutionary technologies, including genome sequencing and DNA editing, as well as wearable devices and implantable or even edible biosensors. In parallel, the popularity of "quantified self" gadgets shows the willingness of citizens to be more proactive with respect to their own health. Yet, this evolution opens the door to all kinds of abuses, notably in terms of discrimination, blackmailing, stalking, and subversion of devices.

After giving a general description of this situation, in this talk we will expound on some of the main concerns, including the temptation to permanently and remotely monitor the physical (and metabolic) activity of individuals. We will describe the potential and the limitations of techniques such as cryptography (including secure multi-party computation), trusted hardware and differential privacy. We will also discuss the notion of consent in the face of the intrinsic correlations of human data. We will argue in favor of a more systematic, principled and cross-disciplinary research effort in this field and will discuss the motives of the various stakeholders.

Bio:

Jean-Pierre Hubaux is a full professor at the School of Information and Communication Sciences of EPFL. Through his research, he contributes to laying the foundations and developing the tools to protect privacy in tomorrow's hyper-connected world. He is focusing notably on network privacy and security, with an emphasis on mobile/wireless networks and on data protection, with an emphasis on health-related data and especially genomic data. He co-founded ACM WiSec in 2008 and chaired its steering committee during the first four years. Since 2007, he has been one of the seven commissioners of the Swiss FCC. He was recently appointed to the "Information Security Task Force", set up by the Swiss federal government. He has worked on the topic of genome privacy since 2011 and has designed related cryptographic solutions, in close collaboration with geneticists. He co-chaired the first workshop devoted to the topic (in Dagstuhl, Germany, in 2013). He is also a member of the "Genomics" task force set up by the Cantonal Ministry of Health. He is a Fellow of both IEEE (2008) and ACM (2010).

WiSec'16, July 18–20, 2016, Darmstadt, Germany.
ACM 978-1-4503-4270-4/16/07.
DOI: http://dx.doi.org/10.1145/2939918.2939939

Fingerprinting Wi-Fi Devices Using Software Defined Radios

Tien D. Vo-Huu   Triet D. Vo-Huu   Guevara Noubir

College of Computer and Information Science
Northeastern University
Boston, MA 02115
{tienvh|vohuudtr|noubir}@ccs.neu.edu

ABSTRACT

Wi-Fi (IEEE 802.11), is emerging as the primary medium for wireless Internet access. Cellular carriers are increasingly offloading their traffic to Wi-Fi Access Points to overcome capacity challenges, limited RF spectrum availability, cost of deployment, and keep up with the traffic demands driven by user generated content. The ubiquity of Wi-Fi and its emergence as a universal wireless interface makes it the perfect tracking device. The Wi-Fi offloading trend provides ample opportunities for adversaries to collect samples (e.g., Wi-Fi probes) and track the mobility patterns and location of users. In this work, we show that RF fingerprinting of Wi-Fi devices is feasible using commodity software defined radio platforms. We developed a framework for reproducible RF fingerprinting analysis of Wi-Fi cards. We developed a set of techniques for distinguishing Wi-Fi cards, most are unique to the IEEE802.11a/g/p standard, including scrambling seed pattern, carrier frequency offset, sampling frequency offset, transient ramp-up/down periods, and a symmetric Kullback-Liebler divergence-based separation technique. We evaluated the performance of our techniques over a set of 93 Wi-Fi devices spanning 13 models of cards. In order to assess the potential of the proposed techniques on similar devices, we used 3 sets of 26 Wi-Fi devices of identical model. Our results, indicate that it is easy to distinguish between models with a success rate of 95%. It is also possible to uniquely identify a device with 47% success rate if the samples are collected within a 10s interval of time.

1. INTRODUCTION

Wi-Fi is emerging as the primary medium for wireless Internet access. Cellular carriers are increasingly offloading their traffic to Wi-Fi Access Points (APs) to overcome capacity challenges, limited RF spectrum availability, cost of deployment, and keep up with the traffic demands driven by user generated content. Wi-Fi offloading is facilitated by 3GPP standards for Non-3GPP Access Networks Discovery and Roaming [1], IETF seamless USIM-based strong authentication and secure communication protocols such as EAP-SIM/AKA [10, 13]. Studies forecast a sustained 50% yearly growth in Wi-Fi offloading for many years to come [22, 23, 25]. This trend is paved by the increasing deployments of Hotspot 2.0 (HS2) Access Points enabled by seamless handover across networks implementing the IEEE 802.11u amendment [15]. Moreover, manufacturers of laptops and streaming devices, such as the Apple MacBook Pro and the Roku streaming player, are removing Ethernet ports and entirely relying on Wi-Fi, and several new variants of Wi-Fi are being developed to suit different environments (e.g., IEEE 802.11p for vehicular networking and IEEE 802.11af for TV white spaces).

The ubiquity of Wi-Fi and its emergence as a universal wireless interface makes it the perfect tracking device. The Wi-Fi offloading trend provides ample opportunities for adversaries to collect samples (e.g., Wi-Fi probes) and track the mobility patterns and location of users. The simplest way of tracking users consists of extracting the MAC address of probe packets periodically transmitted by Wi-Fi cards. This is known to be exploited by government agencies, marketing companies, and location analytics firms. In shopping malls for instance, companies such as Euclid Analytics state on their website that they collect "the presence of the device, its signal strength, its manufacturer (Apple, Samsung, etc.), and a unique identifier known as its Media Access Control (MAC) address." [8] to analyze traffic patterns of users over large spatio-temporal durations of time. Another example is by startup Renew, which installed a large number of recycling bins in London with capability to track users. This allows Renew to identify if the person walking by is the same one from yesterday, even her specific route, walking speed [6, 27]. While information about the activities of data analytics and advertizing firms is public by the nature of their business, little is known about governments and cyber-criminals Wi-Fi surveillance programs. The threats to privacy exploiting MAC address tracking triggered Apple to include a MAC address randomization feature in its iOS 8 release, receiving significant praise from privacy advocates [14]. Unfortunately, MAC address randomization is only the simplest and easiest to mitigate tracking techniques. Recent attacks demonstrated that it is feasible to infer Android devices routes using zero-permission sensors (i.e., gyroscope, accelerometers, and magnetometer) [18]. Such attack however focuses on devices in vehicles moving along roads and requires the installation of an App. On the other end of the spectrum, an adversary can potentially track a wireless device based on its physical layer characteristics. Variations in the fabrication process of silicon devices result in intrinsic random physical features that can potentially uniquely identify a device in a way difficult to compensate for or clone. The unique characteristics of the physical layer in wireless devices have even been considered for authentication purposes leading to the area of Physically Unclonable Func-

WiSec'16 , July 18–20, 2016, Darmstadt, Germany

© 2016 ACM. ISBN 978-1-4503-4270-4/16/07. . . $15.00

DOI: http://dx.doi.org/10.1145/2939918.2939936

tions (PUFs) [16, 19]. While researchers obtained mixed results with the use of physical charateristics of devices for authentication, the potential of fingerprinting for tracking devices is more serious. This is because, unlike in an authentication protocol where the authenticator needs a failure probability exponentially small in the security parameter, a tracking adversary only needs a reasonable probability to breach the privacy of users (e.g., if a given person is at home, office, cafe, entered a street). However, fingerprinting Wi-Fi devices is challenging. In this work, we develop a framework for investigating Wi-Fi devices fingerprinting, at various layers of the network stack and that enables reproducibility and analysis. Our goal is to provide both a solid theoretical and experimental foundation for understanding Wi-Fi devices fingerprinting. Our contributions can be summarized as follows:

- Our first step towards a methodical analysis of Wi-Fi fingerprinting was to develop a full implementation of a Wi-Fi stack for the popular Ettus USRP Software Defined Radio platform. Our platform can iteratively process RF signals and easily analyze a variety of features.

- Our platform extracts all the characteristics from the PHY, MAC, and Link layers that can be exploited for fingerprinting. For instance at the Physical layer, we extract the carrier frequency offset, the sampling frequency offset, transmitter turn on/off transients, scrambling seed.

- We analyzed the potential of each technique and their combination on a set of 93 devices spanning 13 different models including three sets of 26 cards each (from reputable manufacturers).

- We discovered new differentiating factors such as the common seed subsequences, the distributions of carrier and sampling frequency offsets through the Kullback-Leibler distance, and the envelop of frame transients.

In Section 2, we present how the key Wi-Fi features are extracted using our SDR receiver. Section 3, describes our device fingerprinting and classification techniques. Section 4, presents our testbed, evaluation methodology, and results. Finally, we summarize the related and conclusions.

2. FEATURE EXTRACTION

In order to characterize and fingerprint Wi-Fi devices, we develop our own Wi-Fi receiver [32] using Software Defined Radio [11] running on the popular Universal Software Radio Peripheral (USRP) [7]. Our receiver is able to decode transmissions of rate up to 54 Mbps[1]. Unlike with commercial Wi-Fi adapters, it is easy to extract physical characteristics of the Wi-Fi signal with our SDR receiver. To better explain and discuss the features that we use for fingerprinting, we first give a brief overview of the procedure of receiving Wi-Fi signal.

2.1 Wi-Fi Receiver using SDR

Our SDR Wi-Fi receiver block diagram is shown in Figure 1. The receiver consists of three main processing tasks: (1) baseband signal reception, (2) OFDM demodulation, and (3) data decoding. Except for the baseband signal reception handled in the USRP, the other two tasks are carried out on the host computer connected to the USRP.

---

[1] While there is an existing implementation of Wi-Fi receiver [2] on GNU Radio, it is not functional for rates beyond 18 Mbps.

Table 1: Features extracted from our fingerprinting system.

Feature	Extracted from
Scrambling seed	Descrambler
Sampling frequency offset	Channel Estimator
Carrier frequency offset	OFDM Synchronizer
Frame transient	OFDM Synchronizer

OFDM demodulation. After the USRP captures the Wi-Fi signal on its RF front end, it produces a stream of digitized complex samples. On the host computer, we look for the Wi-Fi packets in the digital samples based on the repeated patterns in the preamble of the Physical frame. During this phase, the carrier frequency offset (CFO) is also estimated to correct the mismatched clock between the receiver and transmitter. After that, the samples are transformed into the frequency domain for OFDM demodulation. In order to decode QAM-modulated transmissions, we developed a pilot-based phase tracking technique combined with a decision directed estimation technique to estimate and equalize the channel on individual data subcarriers. Through this method, we obtain the sampling frequency offset (SFO) used in fingerprinting, and also demodulate the complex samples into a binary data sequence.

Packet decoding. A chain of three decoding blocks is applied on the binary data sequence produced by the OFDM demodulator. First, it is deinterleaved to scatter possible bit errors and allow the convolutional decoder to correct the errors and decode the data. Finally, the original frame is recovered by the descrambler.

2.2 Fingerprinting Overview

As our Wi-Fi receiver is SDR-based, we can easily allow the extraction of various physical characteristics of the Wi-Fi signal. While features such as constellation error vectors, channel state information, decoding metrics, or transmit spectrum have been used for fingerprinting and achieved good performance in previous work (e.g., [4, 5] and references therein), we found that in our experiments, those features are more affected by the environment than by the device imperfection. We conjecture that the production quality has been improved since then, making devices more identical. In this work, we instead focus on 4 features listed in Table 1 for fingerprinting.

The main idea of our fingerprinting system is as follows. We capture the transmitted frames in the form of a digital signal, and decode them to extract Physical and MAC information. We group the recorded digital samples of frames based on the MAC addresses and perform the classification/characterization for each group. The classification is done by computing the likelihood between features extracted from the samples and features belonging to known Wi-Fi devices. It is worth noting that while existing machine learning algorithms (e.g., SVM) can be used for classification, it remains unclear how to tune parameters for achieving good accuracy. In this work, we design our own classification algorithms specically applied to the chosen physical features.

2.3 Extracting Scrambling Seed

According to the IEEE 802.11a/g standard, a Wi-Fi transmitter shall generate a new random scrambling seed for every transmission of a Physical Layer frame. However, not all chipset manufacturers follow the standard. Recent work [30] discovered that for some chipset manufacturers, scrambling seeds are generated in a free-wheeling mode with some specific shift distances which are used to distinguish the device models. In general, however, reverse engineering the seed generating algorithm is challenging as chipset manufacturers do not disclose their design. In our work,

4

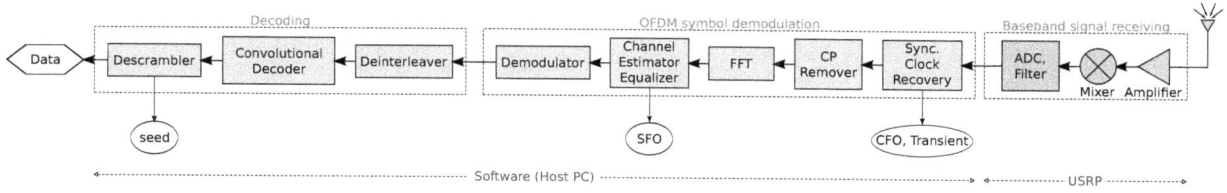

Figure 1: IEEE 802.11a/g SDR receiver block diagram with feature extraction capabilities.

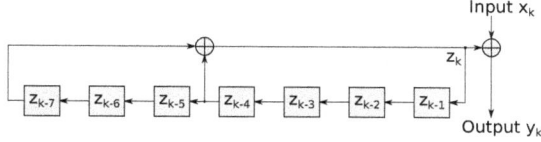

Figure 2: IEEE 802.11a/g scrambler structure.

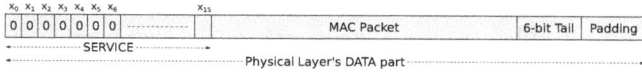

Figure 3: Prior to scrambling, the first 7 bits of SERVICE field in the Physical Layer's DATA part are set to zero.

we aim to design a generic classification technique that evaluates the likelihood of scrambling seed sequences based on the unique seed subsequences as seed signature. Our technique does not rely on the assumption that seeds are generated according to some shift distance, therefore it has the potential of distinguishing models that make use of their own algorithm for seed generation.

2.3.1 Recovering the Scrambling Seed

We briefly review the scrambling and descrambling processes defined in IEEE 802.11a/g/p.

Data scrambling. The binary data is scrambled by a special construction depicted in Figure 2, where a 7-bit linear feedback shift register (LFSR) produces the scrambled bit y_k at output by computing the exclusive-or (modulo-2 sum) of the input bit x_k and the LFSR feedback value z_k. The mathematical description of the scrambler in Figure 2 is given by

$$z_k = z_{k-4} \oplus z_{k-7}$$
$$y_k = x_k \oplus z_k \tag{1}$$

where x_k, y_k are the k-th input and output bits, while z_k represents the feedback of the shift register at that time. We can represent the shift register's content by either a binary sequence $z_{k-1} \ldots z_{k-7}$ or a single decimal value

$$s = z_{-1} \cdot 2^6 + \ldots + z_{-6} \cdot 2 + z_{-7}. \tag{2}$$

To prepare a packet for transmission, the transmitter prepends the packet by a 16-bit SERVICE field and appends it by tail and padding bits to create the DATA part of the Physical Layer frame (Figure 3). The LFSR is initialized with a new seed value s and the first seven bits of SERVICE field are set to zero, then the whole DATA part is scrambled.

Recovering transmitter's seed. As seen in Equation (1), since $y_k = x_k \oplus z_k$, we have $y_k \oplus z_k = x_k \oplus z_k \oplus z_k = x_k$. Consequently, an identical structure to the one described in Figure 2 is used for the descrambling process, where x_k and y_k switch roles. The unknown scrambling seed can be recovered by the receiver by relying on the fact that the first seven bits of the SERVICE field

prior to scrambling are $x_0 = \ldots = x_6 = 0$, resulting in a frame after scrambling having the first seven bits $y_0, \ldots, y_6$ of SERVICE field as $y_k = x_k \oplus z_k = z_k = z_{k-4} \oplus z_{k-7}$, specifically

$$
\begin{aligned}
y_0 &= z_{-4} \oplus z_{-7} & y_4 &= z_0 \oplus z_{-3} = y_0 \oplus z_{-3} \\
y_1 &= z_{-3} \oplus z_{-6} & y_5 &= z_1 \oplus z_{-2} = y_1 \oplus z_{-2} \\
y_2 &= z_{-2} \oplus z_{-5} & y_6 &= z_2 \oplus z_{-1} = y_2 \oplus z_{-1} \\
y_3 &= z_{-1} \oplus z_{-4}
\end{aligned} \tag{3}
$$

From the relations in Equation (3), the receiver can recover the transmitter's original seed s by first computing its bit values

$$
\begin{aligned}
z_{-1} &= y_6 \oplus y_2 & z_{-4} &= y_3 \oplus z_{-1} \\
z_{-2} &= y_5 \oplus y_1 & z_{-5} &= y_2 \oplus z_{-2} \\
z_{-3} &= y_4 \oplus y_0 & z_{-6} &= y_1 \oplus z_{-3} \\
& & z_{-7} &= y_0 \oplus z_{-4}
\end{aligned} \tag{4}
$$

then deriving s based on Equation (2).

2.3.2 Seed Patterns

In this subsection, we study the characteristics of seed sequences generated by Wi-Fi devices. We first define the seed pattern $P = (s_1, \ldots, s_k)$ as a sequence of seed values s_i corresponding to *consecutive* Physical Layer frames (regardless of frame types) sent by a transmitter. We emphasize that the consecutiveness is a required property in the definition of seed pattern. If a frame is lost in the middle, we observe two separate seed patterns. Based on experimental results, we identify the following classes of seed patterns generated by commercial Wi-Fi devices.

- *Fixed:* The same seed value is used for all transmitted frame: $P = (s, s, \ldots, s)$.

- *Incremental:* Seed value is incremented after every transmitted frame: $P = (s, s+1, \ldots, s+k)$. Due to lost packets, a seed sequence may contain multiple incremental patterns.

- *Repeated pattern:* A group of seed values is repeated for some number of times. After that, a new group of seed values is selected and repeated in the same manner. The sequence may be observed as $P_1, \ldots, P_1, P_2, \ldots, P_2, \ldots$.

- *Pseudo-random:* Seed values are pseudo-randomly generated: $P = (s_1, \ldots, s_k)$ for random s_i and large k.

Characteristics. While seed patterns such as fixed or incremental can be easily recognized by observing a few seed values, the repeated and pseudo-random patterns are less trivial to understand. Based on experiments of multiple transmissions from different Wi-Fi models, we found the following characteristics of non-trivial seed sequences.

- *Non-zero:* Zero is never used by any device as a scrambling seed. This is also advised by the standard to avoid sending biased data stream.

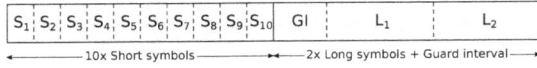

Figure 4: IEEE 802.11a/g/p preamble consists of 10 short symbols and 2 long symbols prepended with an extended guard interval (GI).

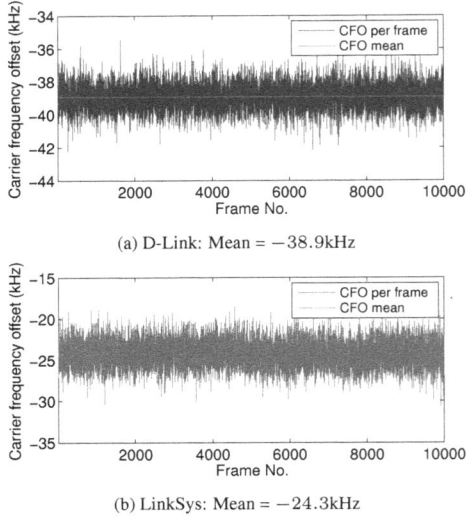

(a) D-Link: Mean = -38.9kHz

(b) LinkSys: Mean = -24.3kHz

Figure 5: Estimated CFO between our SDR Wi-Fi receiver and commercial Wi-Fi adapters: D-Link WDA-1320 and LinkSys WMP54G.

- *Uniform:* For a long enough transmission, seed distribution is actually uniform. This property indicates that a good classification algorithm should not solely rely on seed distribution to distinguish them.

- *Retransmission sensitive:* For some Wi-Fi chipsets, a retransmission can terminate the ongoing seed pattern and start a different pattern. This implies that those chipsets take into account the state of retransmission. In the classifier, the algorithm should be able to distinguish this pattern behavior due to retransmissions.

Later in Section 3.1, we discuss our method for classifying the device based on these scrambling seed characteristics.

2.4 Extracting Frequency Offset

The high spectral efficiency of IEEE 802.11a/g/p systems heavily relies on the subcarrier orthogonality, which allows the adjacent subcarriers to overlap each other to increase the bandwidth efficiency. However, the trade-off that OFDM systems make is that they are very sensitive to factors impacting the carrier orthogonality. One notable factor is the carrier frequency offset (CFO) caused by the typical slight frequency difference between the transmitter and receiver crystal oscillators, which directly impacts the downconversion of the RF signal to baseband signal. The effect of CFO is the shift of the subcarriers in the frequency domain, resulting in the loss of orthogonality at the receiver. Another factor, which received less attention in the community but also greatly reduces the OFDM signal quality, is the sampling frequency offset (SFO) due to the unsynchronized sampling rate between the two RF front ends [21, 29]. The SFO causes the constellation symbols to rotate in the frequency domain. In typical low-cost RF devices, downconversion and sampling tasks are driven by the same clock. Therefore, CFO and SFO are both usually present in OFDM communications.

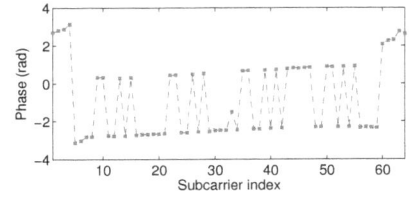

Figure 6: SFO causes phase shift across subcarriers, making phase of the constellation symbols (indicated in Red color) increasing (or decreasing).

In our fingerprinting system, we also exploit these factors to distinguish between Wi-Fi devices.

2.4.1 Carrier Frequency Offset

Due to the presence of a carrier frequency offset θ, every transmitted time-domain symbol s_n at discrete time n is rotated with a phase offset $n\theta$ and seen at the receiver as $r_n = s_n e^{jn\theta}$. In other words, the CFO makes the signals rotate in the time-domain. In order to avoid loss of orthogonality of subcarriers, the CFO must be compensated before the signal is transformed into the frequency domain. We estimate the CFO based on the special structure of the preamble, which consists of two parts: the first part comprises 10 identical short symbols, and the second part is composed of 2 identical long symbols (Figure 4). The repeated preamble symbols lead to an efficient estimation of CFO [26] as follows.

Estimation. Let us focus on short preamble symbols each containing $L = 16$ samples. For every time instant n, we compute the auto-correlation of r_n at lag L as $A = \sum_{k=0}^{L-1} r_{n+k+L} r_{n+k}^*$, where $*$ denotes the complex conjugate. When the frame preamble $\{p_n\}$ is found in the received signal, i.e., $r_n = p_n e^{jn\theta}$, we obtain

$$
\begin{aligned}
A &= \sum_{k=0}^{L-1} p_{n+k+L} e^{j(n+k+L)\theta} \left(p_{n+k} e^{j(n+k)\theta} \right)^* \\
&= \sum_{k=0}^{L-1} |p_{n+k}|^2 e^{jL\theta}
\end{aligned}
\tag{5}
$$

where the second equality is due to the repeated property of preamble symbols $p_{n+k+L} = p_{n+k}$. The CFO value θ is readily estimated as $\theta = \frac{\angle A + m2\pi}{L}$, for some integer m. In practice, since θ is typically smaller than the bandwidth of a subcarrier, m can be safely chosen to be $m = 0$ and hence, $\theta = \frac{\angle A}{L}$. In our SDR Wi-Fi receiver, we estimate the CFO using the following steps: (1) We use short preamble symbols to obtain a coarse estimate $\hat{\theta}$, and correct the rest of the signal with $\hat{\theta}$; (2) Now since the long preamble symbols are also repeated twice, we apply the same approach to compute the fine estimate $\tilde{\theta}$ based on the long preamble symbols, each consisting of $L = 64$ samples. Finally, we derive the final estimated CFO value $\theta = \hat{\theta} + \tilde{\theta}$. Figure 5 shows an example of a CFO recorded in our testbed, which fluctuates around a mean value due to noise in the environment. It is also noted that different Wi-Fi transmitters may create different CFO distributions at the receiver as observed with the LinkSys and D-Link adapters in the above example.

2.4.2 Sampling Frequency Offset

To observe the sampling frequency offset effect, we look into the transformation between the frequency and time domains of the signal. Let $d_1, \ldots, d_N$ be the data symbols on N subcarriers in an OFDM symbol period. For IEEE 802.11a/g/p, $N = 64$. The sender performs the Inverse Fourier Transform on data symbols to obtain

(a) D-Link WDA-1320

(b) LinkSys WMP54G

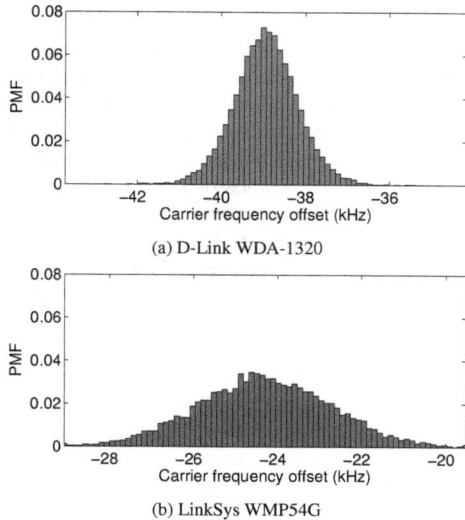

Figure 7: Histogram of CFO: D-Link vs. Linksys.

the time-domain signal $s_n = \mathcal{F}_n^{-1}(d_k) = \sum_{k=1}^{N} d_k e^{j2\pi kn/N}$ and transmits s_n to the receiver. To simplify the notations, we assume the carrier frequency offset has been compensated and the channel noise is negligible. However, due to the mismatched sampling rate between two RF front ends, the receiver obtains the time-domain samples as $r_n = s_{n(1+\epsilon)}$, where $\epsilon = (f_R - f_S)/f_S$ denotes the relative SFO between the transmitter's sampling frequency f_S and the receiver's sampling frequency f_R [28, 29]. Applying the Fourier Transform on r_n, the receiver obtain the subcarrier symbols $\hat{d}_k = \mathcal{F}_k(r_n)$. By the time-shifting rule, we can rewrite $\hat{d}_k$ as

$$\hat{d}_k = \mathcal{F}_k(s_{n(1+\epsilon)}) = \mathcal{F}_k(s_n)e^{j2\pi kn\epsilon/N} = d_k e^{j2\pi kn\epsilon/N}. \quad (6)$$

It can be seen that due to the sampling frequency offset ϵ the receiver obtains the rotated version of the original data symbols. Moreover, the phase shift $2\pi kn\epsilon/N$ is proportional to the subcarrier index k and OFDM symbol index $\lfloor n/N \rfloor$. Figure 6 shows an example of a slightly increasing phase shift along the subcarrier indices in an OFDM symbol. This leads to our pilot-aided SFO estimation method described in the following.

Estimation. In IEEE 802.11a/g, four pilot subcarriers are inserted equally in between the data subcarriers to assist the channel estimation at the receiver. We use the pilot symbols for SFO estimation as follows. Let p_i be the known pilot symbol, and k_i be the index of the i-th pilot carrier ($i = 1, 2, 3, 4$). According to Equation (6), the received pilot symbols in the m-th OFDM symbol (note that $m = \lfloor n/N \rfloor$) are $\hat{p}_{k_i} = p_{k_i} e^{j2\pi k_i m\epsilon}$.

We compute $A_m = \prod_{i=1}^{4} \hat{p}_{k_i} = A e^{j2\pi Km\epsilon}$, where $A = \prod_{i=1}^{4} p_{k_i}$ and $K = \sum_{i=1}^{4} k_i$ are constants. Similarly, we obtain $A_{m+1} = A e^{j2\pi K(m+1)\epsilon}$ for the $(m+1)$-th OFDM symbol. Now, the SFO can be estimated by $\epsilon = \angle(A_{m+1} A_m^*)$, where $*$ indicates the complex conjugate. In our SDR Wi-Fi receiver, to reduce the variations due to noise, we compute the average SFO over multiple OFDM symbols within each frame and use it for fingerprinting purpose.

2.5 Extracting Frame Transient

The last physical feature that we use for fingerprinting is the signal transient at the start and the end of each transmitted frame. The signal transient is defined as the portion of the time-domain signal in this duration, in which the transmitted signal envelope changes

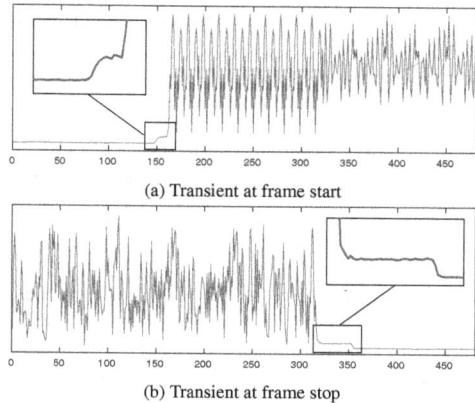

(a) Transient at frame start

(b) Transient at frame stop

Figure 8: Signal transients at the start and the stop of a frame transmitted by the Panda Ultra Wireless dongle.

from one stable energy level to another stable energy level. Figure 8a shows an example of the transient observed at the beginning of a frame transmission by the Panda Ultra Wireless dongle, in which the received signal starts to increase from the noise level and finally reaches a stable level after a few preamble samples. The transient at the end of this frame is shown in Figure 8b, where the signal energy drops to the noise level a few samples after the last sample of the frame.

While the IEEE 802.11 standard only requires a maximum period of $2\mu s$ for the signal transient (both at the frame's start and stop periods), no specific behavior of the transient is defined. As a result, the concrete signal shape in such periods is device specific primarily characterized by the hardware manufacturing process and its imperfections (which can be unique across devices of the same model). We exploit these signal transients to identify the devices.

We obtain the signal transient feature for each frame as follows. First, we identify each frame based on its special preamble (Figure 4). In our fingerprinting system, both frame identification and carrier frequency offset estimation (cf. Section 2.4.1) are performed at the same time. Without loss of generality, each detected frame is assumed to start from time 0 and stop at time L with L denoting the number of samples contained in the frame. By parsing the Physical Header, we can determine L. We obtain the frame's transient feature as the composition of the start and stop transients, which are sequences of samples captured in the following time durations:

- *Start transient:* $(r_{-T_1}, \ldots, r_{T_2})$,

- *Stop transient:* $(r_{L-T_3}, \ldots, r_{L+T_4})$,

where T_1, T_2 are the number of samples on the left and right of the first preamble sample, and T_3, T_4 are similarly defined with respect to the last sample of the frame.

3. DEVICE FINGERPRINTING

3.1 Seed classification

While optimal solutions for seed sequence classification deserve a more in-depth study, we are interested in a fast algorithm for finding a suboptimal classification of Wi-Fi devices. Our main idea for classifying Wi-Fi devices is to compute the likelihood of the scrambling seed sequences based on the common subsequences. We first define the likelihood between two seed patterns as follows.

DEFINITION 1 (LIKELIHOOD OF SEED PATTERNS). *Given two seed patterns $P = (s_1, \ldots, s_k)$ and $Q = (t_1, \ldots, t_m)$, let $\mathrm{LCS}(P, Q)$ be the longest common subsequence found in P and Q. The likelihood between P and Q is defined as*

$$\mathcal{L}(P, Q) = \begin{cases} \frac{|\mathrm{LCS}(P,Q)|}{\min(|P|,|Q|)} & if \, |\mathrm{LCS}(P,Q)| \geq n \\ 0 & otherwise \end{cases}$$

where $|\cdot|$ denotes the number of seeds contained in a sequence, and n is the likelihood threshold.

The pattern likelihood defined above has the property that for any patterns P and Q, if they are equal to each other or one is a subsequence of the another, then $\mathcal{L}(P, Q) = 1$, otherwise $\mathcal{L}(P, Q) \leq 1$. When $\mathcal{L}(P, Q)$ is close to 1, P and Q are more similar. By including $\min(|P|, |Q|)$ in the formula, we capture such scenarios, where a frame loss may cause a pattern to become a sub-pattern of the another. In such cases, they are considered similar according to the definition. The threshold n is used to control the likeliness decision region. We derive $n = 3$ based on experiments.

Finding seed patterns. As mentioned previously, the seed sequence used by a transmitter observed at the receiver may not comprise values belonging to consecutive frames due to various reasons such as frame loss, frames being incorrectly decoded, or simply the receiver missing the transmitted frame. In order to properly collect the seed patterns, we apply the following rules for processing the received seed values. Let s_{i-1} be the last seed retrieved from the packet trace. We accept s_i as the next seed in the same pattern, if

- $\mathrm{MSEQ}_i = \mathrm{MSEQ}_{i-1} + 1$ and $\mathrm{RETX}_i = $ false; or
- $\mathrm{MSEQ}_i = \mathrm{MSEQ}_i$ and $\mathrm{RETX}_i = $ true,

where MSEQ_i is the value in Sequence Number field of the i-th MAC data frame, and RETX_i is the Retry flag in Frame Control field, indicating whether the corresponding frame is retransmitted. If none of the above conditions holds, we consider that some frames might be missing in between, and therefore, s_i will start a new pattern. Based on the above rules, we can construct from the received seeds sequence multiple sets of patterns: $\mathcal{S} = \{P_1, \ldots, P_k\}$.

Algorithm. We now define the likelihood between two sets of seed patterns as follows.

DEFINITION 2 (PATTERN SETS LIKELIHOOD). *Given two sets of seed patterns $\mathcal{S} = \{P_1, \ldots, P_k\}$ and $\mathcal{R} = \{Q_1, \ldots, Q_m\}$, their likelihood is defined as*

$$\mathcal{L}(\mathcal{S}, \mathcal{R}) = \frac{1}{k} \sum_{i=1}^{k} \max_j \mathcal{L}(P_i, Q_j).$$

The likelihood between two pattern sets also has the property that $\mathcal{L}(\mathcal{S}, \mathcal{S}) = 1$ and $\mathcal{L}(\mathcal{S}, \mathcal{R}) \leq 1$ for any $\mathcal{S}$ and $\mathcal{R}$. This is the basis for our classification algorithm, in which we compute the likelihood between a given set of seed patterns retrieved from a transmitter and a reference set of seed patterns of known Wi-Fi devices. The outcome will be a known Wi-Fi device, which maximizes the likelihood. Our algorithm is given as follows.

ALGORITHM 1 (SEED CLASSIFICATION). *Given N sets of seed patterns $\mathcal{S}_1, \ldots, \mathcal{S}_N$ generated by known Wi-Fi devices, a Wi-Fi transmitter with seed pattern $\mathcal{S}$ is classified to be in class n^* using the following steps:*

1. *For each pattern set $\mathcal{S}_n$, compute $\mathcal{L}(\mathcal{S}, \mathcal{S}_n)$.*

2. *Return $n^* = \arg\max_{n=1\ldots N} \mathcal{L}(\mathcal{S}, \mathcal{S}_n)$.*

3.2 Frequency Offset Classification

While carrier frequency offset (CFO) and sampling frequency offset (SFO) are two distinct features that we use for our fingerprinting system, they are similar from the classifier's point of view. In this subsection, we focus on the classification techniques for the CFO only. The same approach can be directly applied to the SFO.

First, to study the CFO characteristics, we carried out an experiment to collect CFO values corresponding to every received frame from the same transmitter. Figure 5a shows the estimated CFO values between our SDR Wi-Fi receiver and a D-Link WDA-1320 Wi-Fi transmitter. It can be seen that the CFO fluctuates around a mean value of -38.9kHz (roughly 12.5% of the subcarrier bandwidth). The fluctuation is not only caused by the interference in the wireless medium, but also by the internal noise inside the RF front ends. For comparison, we perform a similar measurement for a Linksys WMP54G Wi-Fi transmitter, whose CFO values are shown in Figure 5b. Although the fluctuations of two devices look similar, their mean CFO values are different, which implies that they can be distinguished solely based on the mean CFO. This is the main idea of our first approach for frequency offset classification, specified in Algorithm 2.

ALGORITHM 2 (MEAN FREQUENCY OFFSET CLASSIFICATION). *Given N sets of carrier frequency offsets $\omega_1, \ldots, \omega_N$ corresponding to N known Wi-Fi devices, we identify a Wi-Fi transmitter as the n^* device by the following steps:*

1. *Compute the transmitter's average frequency offset θ over m received frames: $\theta = \frac{1}{m} \sum_{i=1}^{m} \theta_i$.*

2. *Compute $D(\theta, \omega_n) = |\theta - \omega_n|$ for each Wi-Fi device n.*

3. *Return $n^* = \arg\min_n D(\theta, \omega_n)$.*

As shown later in Section 4, this approach can achieve good results for a small set of devices. However, in our testbed evaluation with a large set of devices, we found that many devices can have quite close CFO values, resulting in misclassification. This motivates us to improve the accuracy by studying the distribution of CFO values. First, we compute the probability mass function of the CFO based on CFO values extracted from all received frames. Figures 7a and 7b illustrates an example of CFO histograms for the D-Link WDA-1320 and Linksys WMP54G adapters. In order to justify the difference between two distributions, we use a symmetric variant of the Kullback-Leibler (KL) divergence as the evaluation metrics. Specifically, the symmetric KL divergence between two distributions P and Q is computed by

$$D_{\mathrm{KL}}(P, Q) = \frac{1}{2} \sum_{i=1}^{B} \left(P_i \log \frac{P_i}{Q_i} + Q_i \log \frac{Q_i}{P_i} \right) \quad (7)$$

where B is the number of discrete values two distributions can take (i.e., the number of bins in the histogram of the distribution).

We note that the KL divergence is only defined for non-zero probability distribution, i.e., $P_i > 0$ and $Q_i > 0$ for all $i = 1 \ldots B$. This requirement, however, may not be satisfied by the CFO distributions for two reasons: (1) Since we build the histogram of CFO based on measurement results, there might exist an empty bin leading to zero probability in that bin; (2) CFO distributions of two devices may only partially overlap or completely not overlap, resulting in the existence of such bins whose probabilities are not non-zero for both distributions. To solve these issues, we perform the following two steps prior to the KL divergence computation:

1. Translate the distribution to the origin, i.e., compute the mean of CFO values and subtract it from all CFO values before computing the probability mass function.

2. Replace zero-probability with non-zero ε-probability ($\varepsilon > 0$ and $\varepsilon \ll 1$).

Our algorithm for identifying a transmitter based on the frequency offset distribution is described in Algorithm 3.

ALGORITHM 3 (F.O. DISTRIBUTION CLASSIFICATION). *Given N sets of frequency offset distributions $Q_1, \ldots, Q_N$ belonging to N known Wi-Fi devices, the task of identifying a Wi-Fi transmitter comprises the following steps:*

1. *Compute the transmitter's frequency offset distribution P.*

2. *Translate P to the origin, replace $P_i = \varepsilon$ for all $P_i = 0$, and recompute P to obtain a proper distribution.*

3. *Compute $D_{KL}(P, Q_n)$ for all $n = 1 \ldots N$.*

4. *Return $n^* = \arg\min_n D_{KL}(P, Q_n)$.*

3.3 Frame Transient Classification

Our frame transient classification is based on the observation that while the signal emitted from the same Wi-Fi transmitter might exhibit differences during the transient periods across the transmitted frames, unique signatures can be obtained via averaging on multiple frames. In our fingerprinting system, we use the amplitude of transient samples as the transmitter's signature.

Let $(r_{i,1}, \ldots, r_{i,T})$ denote the sequence of $T = T_1 + T_2 + T_3 + T_4$ samples containing both start and stop transients of an i-th frame (cf. Section 2.5). The transient $\mathbf{a} = (a_1, \ldots, a_T)$ of a device is obtained by taking the average of sample amplitude over m detected frames: $a_k = \frac{1}{m} \sum_{i=1}^{m} |r_{i,k}|$ for $k = 1 \ldots T$. As we are only interested in the shape of the transient (i.e., the relative change of amplitude across samples), we eliminate the effect of absolute received power by normalizing the samples such that $\sum_{k=1}^{T} a_k = 1$. The similarity of two devices is now computed based on the difference between their transient signatures $\mathbf{a}$ and $\mathbf{a}'$ as follows:

$$D(\mathbf{a}, \mathbf{a}') = \sum_{k=1}^{T} |a_k - a_k'|.$$

Algorithm 4 summarizes our frame transient classification.

ALGORITHM 4 (FRAME TRANSIENT CLASSIFICATION). *Given N sets of transient signatures $\mathbf{a}_1, \ldots, \mathbf{a}_N$ corresponding to N known Wi-Fi devices, we identify a Wi-Fi transmitter as follows:*

1. *Compute the transmitter's transient $\mathbf{a}$ over m received frames.*

2. *Compute $D(\mathbf{a}, \mathbf{a}_n)$ for all $n = 1 \ldots N$.*

3. *Return $n^* = \arg\min_n D(\mathbf{a}, \mathbf{a}_n)$.*

3.4 Combined Classification

To improve the overall accuracy of our fingerprinting system, we combine the above individual features by linearly adding the similarity scores obtained from each feature and classify the devices based on the total score. We note that while the scrambling seed likelihood metric approaches 1 when the seed sequences are similar, the scores produced by other features converge to 0 if devices are alike. Therefore, for integration into the combined classification, we convert the scrambling seed likelihood into the seed score (distance) by computing $D(\mathcal{S}, \mathcal{R}_n) = 1 - \mathcal{L}(\mathcal{S}, \mathcal{R}_n)$. The combined metric is then derived as the sum of weighted individual scores with the weights denoted in Table 2.

Table 2: Features and weights used in the combined method for model classification and device identification.

Feature	Model classification	Device identification
CFO mean value	$\alpha_M = 0.4$	$\alpha_M = 0.3$
CFO distribution	$\alpha_D = 0.2$	$\alpha_D = 0.2$
SFO mean value	$\beta_M = 0.2$	$\beta_M = 0.2$
SFO distribution	$\beta_D = 0$	$\beta_D = 0.1$
Scrambling seed	$\gamma = 0.05$	$\gamma = 0$
Transient	$\tau = 0.45$	$\tau = 0.25$

ALGORITHM 5 (COMBINED CLASSIFICATION). *Given N Wi-Fi devices with known profiles for the feature set of scrambling seed, mean and distribution of carrier and sampling frequency offset, and frame transient, we identify a Wi-Fi transmitter as follows:*

1. *Compute the signatures sig_f of the tested Wi-Fi transmitter (as in Algorithms 1 to 4) for each feature f.*

2. *Compute the score $D_n = \sum_{f \in Features} w_f D_f(sig_f, profile_f)$ for all $n = 1 \ldots N$.*

3. *Return $n^* = \arg\min_n D_n$.*

4. FINGERPRINTING TECHNIQUES PERFORMANCE EVALUATION

4.1 Setup and Methodology

We report on our experimental results for a total 93 Wi-Fi devices of 13 different models, including 6 PCI adapters, 85 USB adapters, and 2 smartphones. Table 3 summarizes all the devices used in our testbed. Our general setup consists of a TP-Link N600 Access Point serving as the base station, and a desktop computer as a wireless transmitter using 91 Wi-Fi devices, among which 6 PCI adapters are directly attached to the computer through PCI slots, and the other 85 USB adapters are connected through USB hubs (Figure 9). For experiments with two smartphones, we associate them to the Access Point and use them as wireless transmitters. On the other side, the Access Point is also connected via the its Ethernet network interface to another desktop computer used as the receiver. We use the *iperf* traffic generator to transmit packets, each of 1500 bytes, between the transmitter and receiver. We carry out the experiments in our lab environment during daily hours, where traffic from other regular Wi-Fi users and human movement are also present. We place no constraint on location of the testbed nodes, and they can be dynamic (e.g., phone held in moving hand while transmitting). Our Wi-Fi testbed experiments were carried out on channel 11 with 20 MHz bandwidth.

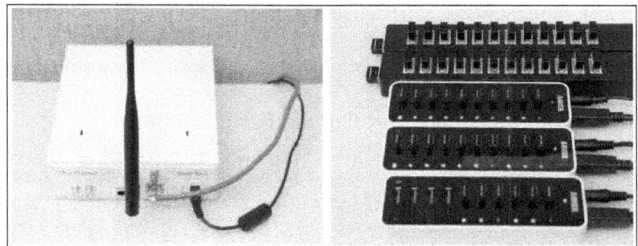

Figure 9: Our testbed consists of a custom made SDR Wi-Fi receiver (left), and 93 Wi-Fi transmitters (right) including 85 Wi-Fi dongles connected to the PC via USB hubs, 6 PCI adapters and 2 phones.

In order to capture the wireless communications for fingerprinting, we run our SDR Wi-Fi sniffer on an Ettus USRP N210 with

Table 3: Wi-Fi devices in our evaluation.

	Model	Quantity	Chipset	Type
1	D-Link WDA-1320	2	Atheros AR2413	PCI
2	Linksys WMP54G	2	Ralink RT2560	PCI
3	TP-Link TL-WN751ND	2	Atheros AR9227	PCI
4	Cisco Linksys AE2500	26	Broadcom BCM43236	USB
5	Panda Ultra Wireless	26	Ralink RT5370	USB
6	TP-Link TL-WN725N	26	Realtek RTL8188CUS	USB
7	Belkin F7D1102	2	Realtek RTL8188CUS	USB
8	Edimax EW-7811Un	2	Realtek RTL8188CUS	USB
9	TP-Link TL-WN321G v4	1	Ralink RT2070	USB
10	TP-Link TL-WN722N	1	Atheros AR9271	USB
11	TP-Link TL-WN821N v4	1	Realtek RTL8192CU	USB
12	Apple iPhone 5	1	Broadcom BCM4334	Phone
13	Nokia Lumia 635	1	Snapdragon 400	Phone
	Total	93		

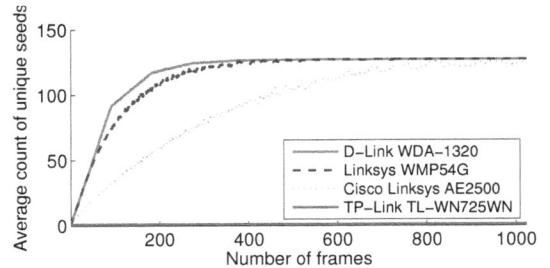

Figure 10: Comparison of seed generating strategies applied by different Wi-Fi adapters. The Y-axis shows the average number of unique seeds counted in every group of consecutive frames specified by the X-axis.

SBX v3.0 daughterboard. Our Wi-Fi sniffer captures and performs signal processing on the overheard transmissions. During the decoding of Physical Layer frames, we extract the scrambling seeds, carrier and sampling frequency offsets belonging to every frame. Based on the MAC address in each frame, we group the extracted features together and run the fingerprinting algorithms to identify them. The rationale behind grouping based on MAC address is that even though the transmitter can modify his MAC address, it remains the same during the transmission session. We classify the transmitter based on features collected over multiple frames of the transmission. We note that we also use the features of frames with incorrect checksums as they still contain valuable information for classification purpose (as opposed to user data payload which might be uninteresting when corrupted). Moreover, by grouping frames of the same MAC address together, the chance of errors is lower (otherwise we would not see the same address field), and hence the Physical Layer features are more precise with high probability.

Our evaluation consists of extensive experiments over the span of three weeks. Using our SDR Wi-Fi receiver, we collected digital samples and extracted features from each of the 93 Wi-Fi transmitters for at least five different periods of time per day. Each transmission session is carried out in various time durations, ranging from 1 to 100 seconds. We use data collected on the first day as fingerprint profiles and each of the other days as tests.

4.2 Identifying Chipsets by Scrambling Seed

We first evaluate our scrambling seed classification algorithm on all the Wi-Fi devices in our testbed. Using the device profiles recorded on the first day, we compute the likelihood of scrambling seed sequences between the profiles and the tests. Our first observation is that any two devices with chipsets made from the same manufacturer have similar seed patterns during their transmissions. This is explained by the fact that since the scrambling seed sequence is produced by the baseband chipset, the generated seeds are independent of the device brand name, but they are chipset manufacturer specific.

Looking further into the difference in seeds generating mechanisms by different chipsets, we present both the average and the standard deviation of the likelihood between any two models summarized in Table 4. It is an interesting fact that all four chipset manufacturers of our experimental Wi-Fi devices develop their own seed generation completely different from each other, which fall into four classes we defined in Section 2.3. The Realtek chipsets always use a special value 124 as the scrambling seed, while Qualcomm Atheros chooses to increment the seed after every transmitted frame regardless of whether it is retransmitted. Although Broadcom and Ralink generate somewhat random seeds, their strategies are different.

To illustrate the difference in seed generation, we conduct another experiment as follows. We select 4 Wi-Fi adapters (D-Link WDA-1320, Linksys WMP54G, Cisco Linksys AE2500, TP-Link TL-WN725N) corresponding to 4 baseband chipset brands (Atheros, Ralink, Broadcom, Realtek, respectively). In the trace of scrambling seed sequence extracted from each adapter, we count the number of unique seeds generated by the chipset over multiple groups of n consecutive frames, and take the average over those groups. We repeat this step for each value of n from 1 to 1024 and achieve an overall picture of how frequently new seeds are generated by different chipsets, shown in Figure 10. We can observe that, seed generating strategies applied by chipset manufacturers can be distinguished clearly by the curves separation. Even though seeds generated by Atheros (incremental) and Ralink (random) are completely different, they are more similar in terms of seed diversity within small periods of transmitted frames. It is also easily seen that Realtek chipsets use only one seed value for all frames, illustrated by the horizontal line. In contrast, though Broadcom BCM43236 generated seeds are random, they differ from the Ralink strategy. To understand how it produces seeds, we investigate the trace and found that Broadcom BCM43236 tends to "reuse" seeds for some number of frames. For example, we select a range of consecutive frames and read the corresponding seed values as follows: 76, 93, 108, 25, 108, 25, 79, 104, 79, 108, 93, 108, 93, 108, 25, 41, 79, 104, 79, 104, 85, 116, 35, 113, 124, 113, 35, 113. We can immediately see that seed values 93, 108, 25, 79, 104 are repeated after a few transmitted frames. This pattern is in fact quite common in the seed sequence generated by Cisco Linksys AE2500 adapter, and that is also illustrated by the slowly increasing average count of unique seeds over consecutive frames, shown in Figure 10.

Moreover, Broadcom seems to apply different seed randomizing mechanisms for different chip generations. This can be seen from the low likelihood between Apple iPhone 5 and Cisco Linksys AE2500 in Table 4. Table 5 summarizes the scrambling seed generating mechanisms discovered during our experiments. We conclude that based on analyzing the scrambling seed sequence received from the transmitter, we can reveal its chipset brand. When this is combined with other techniques, one can narrow down the fingerprinting and classification of a device.

4.3 Frequency Offset Fingerprint

As seen from Section 4.2, we can classify the Wi-Fi devices into different categories with respect to their baseband chipsets. Our goal in this subsection is to further differentiate the devices within the same category based on the frequency offsets extracted from every frame of the transmission.

First, we study the potential of using the average frequency offsets for differentiating the Wi-Fi device models. For this purpose,

Table 4: Average and standard deviation of scrambling seed likelihood (%) between different Wi-Fi adapter models.

	Model	1	2	3	4	5	6	7	8	9	10	11	12	13
D-Link WDA-1320	1	61±2	0	55±2	0	0	0	0	0	0	58±.5	0	0	1±.6
Linksys WMP54G	2	0	71±3	0	0	48±4	0	0	0	49±3	0	0	2±.8	32±2
TP-Link TL-WN751ND	3	55±2	0	63±5	0	0	0	0	0	0	61±3	0	0	0
Cisco Linksys AE2500	4	0	0	0	88±1	0	0	0	0	0	0	0	0	0
Panda Ultra Wireless	5	0	48±4	0	0	80±4	0	0	0	83±4	0	0	8±3	77±4
TP-Link TL-WN725N	6	0	0	0	0	0	100	100	100	0	0	100	0	0
Belkin F7D1102	7	0	0	0	0	0	100	100	100	0	0	100	0	0
Edimax EW-7811Un	8	0	0	0	0	0	100	100	100	0	0	100	0	0
TP-Link TL-WN321G v4	9	0	49±3	0	0	83±4	0	0	0	83±5	0	0	6±2	69±5
TP-Link TL-WN722N	10	58±.5	0	61±3	0	0	0	0	0	0	58±7	0	0	0
TP-Link TL-WN821N v4	11	0	0	0	0	0	100	100	100	0	0	100	0	0
Apple iPhone 5	12	0	2±.8	0	0	8±3	0	0	0	6±2	0	0	27±5	18±7
Nokia Lumia 635	13	1±.6	32±2	0	0	77±4	0	0	0	69±5	0	0	18±7	71±10

(standard deviation is omitted when zero)

Table 5: Scrambling seed generation methods by Wi-Fi devices.

Class	Model	Seed type
A	Belkin N150, Edimax EW-781Un TP-Link TL-WN725N, TP-Link TL-WN821N	fixed = 124
B	D-Link WDA-1320, TP-Link TL-WN751ND, TP-Link TL-WN722N	incremental
C	Cisco Linksys AE2500	repeated
D	Apple iPhone 5	random
E	Linksys WMP54G, Panda Ultra Wireless, TP-Link TL-WN321G, Nokia Lumia 635	random

(a) CFO.

(b) SFO.

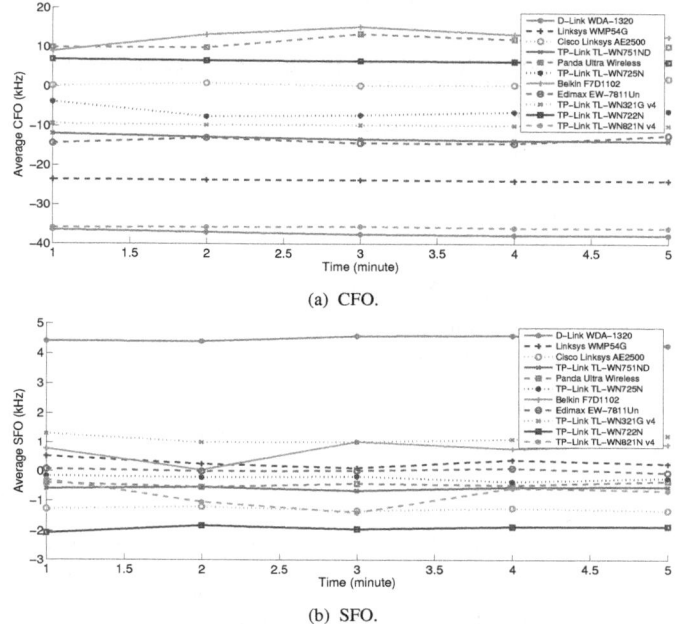

Figure 11: Average CFO and SFO of different Wi-Fi devices measured per one-minute transmission during the span of 5 minutes.

we select one device per model in Table 3 and extract the carrier and sampling frequency offsets from every received frame belonging to the same transmitter. To see how the frequency offset changes over a short time, we capture 1 second of the transmission for each device, and repeat this 5 times, each 1 minute after the previous one. The average CFO and SFO are shown in Figure 11.

CFO based distinguishing. We observe that the CFO can be quite different for devices of the same chipset. As an example, Belkin F7D1102 and Edimax EW-7811Un (both use identical chipset Realtek RTL8188CUS) have CFO around 10kHz and −10kHz, respectively. On the contrary, the Belkin's CFO is very close to the Panda Ultra's despite that they use different chipsets. If we repeat the experiment for 20 times and apply Algorithm 2 for all devices, we obtain the average correct detection rate of 17% with the standard deviation of 2%.

SFO based distinguishing. The average SFO values of the experimented devices, as seen from Figure 11b, are much closer to each other. In the above experiment, we also perform the average SFO based classification and observe that there is a drop of average correct detection rate to 9% with the standard deviation of 2%. This can be explained by the SFO of devices being in a much smaller vicinity, resulting in lower detection accuracy.

4.4 Transient Fingerprint

Using the set of 93 devices, we extract the start and stop transients of each frame and apply Algorithm 4 to classify the devices. The results in Table 6 show that most device models can be recognized with a high probability. There are, however, exceptions that the TP-Link TL-WN722N Wi-Fi dongle and the Apple iPhone5 are not correctly classified in all experiments. In fact, they are misclassified to TP-Link TL-WN725N. In the next evaluation, we show that despite individual techniques do not achieve high accuracy, the combined classification can improve significantly the results.

4.5 Device Identification

To evaluate the classification accuracy for a large set of devices, we perform an extensive experiment, in which we collect the scrambling seed, frame transients, CFO and SFO values from all Wi-Fi devices in our testbed. The extracted features of tested devices are collected from 20 experiments during three weeks. For each transmitter, we apply Algorithms 1 to 5 as the classification methods for identifying *both* the models and the devices themselves. We use the weights specified in Table 2. Note that in case of device identification, we set the scrambling seed weight to 0 since the scrambling seed sequence is produced in the same manner by devices of the same chipset, and as a result, negative impact can be created if the scrambling seed is included in the scoring metric. The results are reported in Table 7, where the outcomes are averaged out over 20 experiments.

First, we see that for the model identification task, even the worst-performance task, the classification based on scrambling seed, can still achieve an accuracy of 87%. The combined method can successfully recognize the device model with a high probability of roughly 95%. The most interesting results are the device identification capability of our fingerprinting system. By exploiting all physical features supported in our system, we can trace the identity of almost half (47%) of the Wi-Fi devices in the testbed.

Table 6: Model identification results for 93 devices using transient classification method.

Model	Model Identification Accuracy (%)
D-Link WDA-1320	100
Linksys WMP54G	100
TP-Link TL-WN751ND	75
Cisco Linksys AE2500	99
Panda Ultra Wireless	91
TP-Link TL-WN725N	97
Belkin F7D1102	75
Edimax EW-7811Un	88
TP-Link TL-WN321G v4	100
TP-Link TL-WN722N	0
TP-Link TL-WN821N v4	75
Apple iPhone 5	0
Nokia Lumia 635	50

Table 7: Fingerprinting results on 93 devices with different classification methods.

Method	Model identification (%)	Device identification (%)
CFO mean value	55±7	17±2
CFO distribution	55±6	10±2
SFO mean value	61±4	9±2
SFO distribution	25±1	1±.1
Scrambling seed	87±1	6±1
Transient	92±1	26±3
All combined	**95±1**	**47±3**

5. RELATED WORK

Previous work considered several approaches to fingerprint and identify radio devices, as well as techniques to prevent cloning and spoofing. Some early work considered the characteristics of the MAC and higher layers of devices. These characteristics where used to detect the location and even the identity of users [20]. For instance, in a conference event hosted on the West coast, overhearing a probe request with id "MIT", is indicative that that a person from MIT might be at the conference, as his Wi-Fi device is trying to associate with an AP of the MIT campus. The assumption that the MAC Sequence number cannot be manipulated by an adversary was used to propose techniques to detect spoofing [12]. Other work, investigated the use of Time of Probe request frames from STA [9]. They measured the received time of those Probe Request frames, and analyzed the interval between them. The goal of this study is to identify different driver behaviors in terms of implementation of the MAC protocol. This work exploits the fact that the standard does not specify the step-by-step behavior for sending the MAC frames (like Probe Requests).

The general problem of uniquely identifying RF devices based on their physical characteristics has been studied for various security applications including authentication and prevention of wormhole attacks as part of the area of Physically Unclonable Functions (PUFs) [16, 19]. Early work demonstrated that it is possible to fingerprint and uniquely identify the CC1000 radios of 10 Cricket Motes operating at 433MHz with an average accuracy of 70% [3]. This work focused on several features of the transient signal of the CC1000 radio. It opened the door for various applications of fingerprinting both in terms of adversarial use such as the potential of invading privacy, and defensive use such as preventing spoofing and wormhole attacks in wireless sensor networks. More recent work investigated the fingerprinting of USRP transceivers using preamble-based identification [24]. This work experimented with seven different USRPs and used a machine learning algorithm (kNN). The paper claims that for each USRP receiver, it is possible to identify the transmitter based on the recorded samples. It is, however, difficult to justify the accuracy of this technique in practice, because during the evaluation the nodes were static. This

means that each pair of USRPs has a unique channel with different multipath and RSSI and the system might be mostly identifying the channel. It is unclear how such techniques would perform if the nodes are relocated, or if the environment is changed.

Prior work on fingerprinting Wi-Fi devices investigated the second-order cyclic features of OFDM signals [17]. This work looked at the spectral cross-correlation of the signal based on the assumption that signals of most of communication systems today have periodicity, such as modulated sinusoidal carrier, and cyclic prefix. However, the devices locations were static and it is unclear if this technique too fingerprinted the channel or the devices and how it would perform when the devices are relocated. Moreover, their experiments were performed for a relatively small set of 6 devices.

The closest and best performing related work on fingerprinting Wi-Fi devices considered a combination of frequency offset, transients, and constellation errors for IEEE802.11b cards. A performance accuracy of 99% was reported for a matching of two recordings. While they experimented with a relatively large number of devices (138), all the devices were located in the stable, static and RF-insulated Orbit Lab environment (almost no noise, stable temperature) [4]. It is unclear if this impressive performance is due to the stability of laboratory environment between the two runs (e.g., absence of noise boosted the performance of error vector magnitude or stable laboratory temperature led to a stable CFO), or to other unknown factors. Since then no other work (see [5] and references therein) was able to reproduce these results so far.

Our work, not only provides a framework for repeatable experimentation with Wi-Fi fingerprinting on a low-cost flexible hardware/software platform, it also devised new features (e.g., scrambling seed) and techniques (Kullback-Leibler divergence) across the various blocks of an RF transceiver chain. We achieved high accuracy for Wi-Fi model classification. While our results for device identification reduce to almost half, we believe that further improvements are possible on our platform such as a more careful analysis of the scrambling seed algorithm and the per-carrier frequency domain RF front end characteristics, or using directional antennas to scan and focus on different directionns [31].

6. CONCLUSION

We developed a set of techniques for RF fingerprinting Wi-Fi devices. Our techniques span several blocks of a Wi-Fi receiver. Our results indicate that identifying Wi-Fi devices is possible (with results spanning 44%-50%), and potentially feasible with hardware implementation of lower cost than Wi-Fi chipsets. Further, improvements of the proposed techniques are also possible, for example with more careful analysis and reverse engineering of scrambling seed algorithms, CFO and SFO patterns. Through this work, we hope that the research community can build on our results and tools to better understand the potential and privacy-invasion risks emanating from Wi-Fi devices fingerprinting.

Acknowledgements. This material is based upon work supported by the National Science Foundation under Grant No. NSF/CNS-1409453.

References

[1] 3GPP TS 24.312. Access Network Discovery and Selection Function (ANDSF) Management Object (MO). http://www.3gpp.org/DynaReport/24312.htm, 2014.

[2] B. Bloessl, M. Segata, C. Sommer, and F. Dressler. Decoding IEEE 802.11a/g/p OFDM in Software using GNU Radio. In *19th ACM International Conference on Mobile Comput-*

ing and Networking (MobiCom 2013), Demo Session, pages 159–161, Miami, FL, October 2013. ACM.

[3] K. Bonne Rasmussen and S. Capkun. Implications of radio fingerprinting on the security of sensor networks. In *Security and Privacy in Communications Networks and the Workshops, 2007. SecureComm 2007. Third International Conference on*, pages 331–340, Sept 2007.

[4] V. Brik, S. Banerjee, M. Gruteser, and S. Oh. Wireless device identification with radiometric signatures. In *Proceedings of the 14th ACM International Conference on Mobile Computing and Networking*, MobiCom '08, pages 116–127, New York, NY, USA, 2008. ACM.

[5] B. Danev, D. Zanetti, and S. Capkun. On physical-layer identification of wireless devices. *ACM Comput. Surv.*, 45(1):6:1–6:29, Dec. 2012.

[6] S. Datoo. This recycling bin is following you. http://qz.com/112873/this-recycling-bin-is-following-you/, Quartz, August 2013. Accessed: May, 2015.

[7] Ettus Research. USRP: Universal software radio peripheral.

[8] Euclid Analytics. Privacy statement. http://euclidanalytics.com/about/privacy-statement/. Accessed: May, 2015.

[9] J. Franklin, D. McCoy, P. Tabriz, V. Neagoe, J. Van Randwyk, and D. Sicker. Passive data link layer 802.11 wireless device driver fingerprinting. In *Proceedings of the 15th Conference on USENIX Security Symposium - Volume 15*, USENIX-SS'06, Berkeley, CA, USA, 2006. USENIX Association.

[10] Free Forfait Mobile. FreeWiFi secure EAP-SIM. http://mobile.free.fr/assistance/261.html, August 2010.

[11] GNU. Gnu radio. http://www.gnuradio.org.

[12] F. Guo and T.-c. Chiueh. Sequence number-based mac address spoof detection. In A. Valdes and D. Zamboni, editors, *Recent Advances in Intrusion Detection*, volume 3858 of *Lecture Notes in Computer Science*, pages 309–329. Springer Berlin Heidelberg, 2006.

[13] H. Haverinen and J. Salowey. Extensible Authentication Protocol Method for Global System for Mobile Communications (GSM) Subscriber Identity Modules (EAP-SIM). RFC 4186 (Informational), January 2006.

[14] L. Hutchinson. iOS 8 to stymie trackers and marketers with mac address randomization. http://arstechnica.com/apple/2014/06/ios8-to-stymie-trackers-and-marketers-with-mac-address-randomization/, June 2014. Accessed: May, 2015.

[15] IEEE. IEEE 802.11 Interworking with External Networks. http://standards.ieee.org/findstds/standard/802.11u-2011.html.

[16] S. Katzenbeisser, Ünal Kocabaş, V. Rožić, A.-R. Sadeghi, I. Verbauwhede, and C. Wachsmann. PUFs: Myth, fact or busted? a security evaluation of physically unclonable functions (pufs) cast in silicon. In *Cryptographic Hardware and Embedded Systems-CHES, Springer*, 2012.

[17] K. Kim, C. Spooner, I. Akbar, and J. Reed. Specific emitter identification for cognitive radio with application to ieee 802.11. In *Global Telecommunications Conference, 2008. IEEE GLOBECOM 2008. IEEE*, pages 1–5, Nov 2008.

[18] S. Narain, T. D. Vo-Huu, K. Block, and G. Noubir. Inferring location and traffic patterns without permissions using side-channels. In *Proceedings of IEEE Symposium on Security and Privacy*, 2006.

[19] NXP. PUF - physical unclonable functions protecting next-generation smart card ics with sram-based pufs. http://www.nxp.com/documents/other/75017366.pdf, 2013.

[20] J. Pang, B. Greenstein, R. Gummadi, S. Seshan, and D. Wetherall. 802.11 user fingerprinting. In *Proceedings of the 13th Annual ACM International Conference on Mobile Computing and Networking*, MobiCom '07, pages 99–110, New York, NY, USA, 2007. ACM.

[21] T. Pollet, P. Spruyt, and M. Moeneclaey. The BER performance of OFDM systems using non-synchronized sampling. In *Global Telecommunications Conference, 1994. GLOBECOM '94. Communications: The Global Bridge, IEEE*, pages 253–257 vol.1, Nov 1994.

[22] Qualcomm. 3G LTE Wifi offload framework: Connectivity Engine (CnE) solution, July 2013. http://www.qualcomm.com/media/documents/3g-lte-wifi-offload-framework.

[23] M. Ramsay. Wi-Fi offload rising amid soaring data traffic. http://www.wirelessweek.com/News/2012/07/technology-WiFi-Offload-Rising-Amid-Soaring-Data-Traffic/, July 2012.

[24] S. U. Rehman, K. W. Sowerby, and C. Coghill. Analysis of impersonation attacks on systems using RF fingerprinting and low-end receivers. *Journal of Computer and System Sciences*, 80(3):591 – 601, 2014. Special Issue on Wireless Network Intrusion.

[25] B. Rooney. Data-hungry 4G users gorge on Wi-Fi, report finds. http://blogs.wsj.com/tech-europe/2013/09/19/data-hungry-4g-users-gorge-on-wi-fi-report-finds/, September 2013.

[26] T. Schmidl and D. Cox. Robust frequency and timing synchronization for OFDM. *Communications, IEEE Transactions on*, 45(12):1613–1621, Dec 1997.

[27] Z. M. Seward and S. Datoo. City of london halts recycling bins tracking phones of passers-by. http://qz.com/114174/city-of-london-halts-recycling-bins-tracking-phones-of-passers-by/, Quartz, August 2013. Accessed: May, 2015.

[28] M. Sliskovic. Carrier and sampling frequency offset estimation and correction in multicarrier systems. In *Global Telecommunications Conference, 2001. GLOBECOM '01. IEEE*, volume 1, pages 285–289, 2001.

[29] M. Sliskovic. Sampling frequency offset estimation and correction in OFDM systems. In *Electronics, Circuits and Systems, 2001. ICECS 2001. The 8th IEEE International Conference on*, volume 1, pages 437–440, 2001.

[30] M. Vanhoef, C. Matte, M. Cunche, L. Cardoso, and F. Piessens. Why MAC Address Randomization is not Enough: An Analysis of Wi-Fi Network Discovery Mechanisms. In *ACM AsiaCCS*, Xi'an, China, May 2016.

[31] T. D. Vo-Huu, E.-O. Blass, and G. Noubir. Counter-jamming using mixed mechanical and software interference cancellation. In *Proceedings of the Sixth ACM Conference on Security and Privacy in Wireless and Mobile Networks*, WiSec '13, pages 31–42, New York, NY, USA, 2013. ACM.

[32] T. D. Vo-Huu, T. D. Vo-Huu, and G. Noubir. SWiFi: An Open Source SDR for Wi-Fi Networks High Order Modulation Analysis. Technical report, 2015.

Defeating MAC Address Randomization Through Timing Attacks

Célestin Matte[†], Mathieu Cunche[†], Franck Rousseau[‡], Mathy Vanhoef[Ⅱ]
[†]Univ Lyon, INSA Lyon, Inria, CITI, France,
[‡]Grenoble Alpes, Grenoble Institute of Technology, LIG, France, [Ⅱ]iMinds-Distrinet, KU Leuven

ABSTRACT

MAC address randomization is a common privacy protection measure deployed in major operating systems today. It is used to prevent user-tracking with probe requests that are transmitted during IEEE 802.11 network scans. We present an attack to defeat MAC address randomization through observation of the timings of the network scans with an off-the-shelf Wi-Fi interface. This attack relies on a signature based on inter-frame arrival times of probe requests, which is used to group together frames coming from the same device although they use distinct MAC addresses. We propose several distance metrics based on timing and use them together with an incremental learning algorithm in order to group frames. We show that these signatures are consistent over time and can be used as a pseudo-identifier to track devices. Our framework is able to correctly group frames using different MAC addresses but belonging to the same device in up to 75% of the cases. These results show that the timing of 802.11 probe frames can be abused to track individual devices and that address randomization alone is not always enough to protect users against tracking.

CCS Concepts

•Networks → Network privacy and anonymity; •Security and privacy → *Mobile and wireless security;*

Keywords

Security; Privacy; 802.11; Tracking; MAC address randomization

1. INTRODUCTION

Wi-Fi devices are periodically sending frames containing a unique identifier (the MAC address) which can be leveraged to track the owners of those devices. As a countermeasure against tracking, MAC address randomization is becoming an industry standard and is being deployed in most major

This work is partially funded by Région Rhône-Alpes's ARC7.
ACM acknowledges that this contribution was authored or co-authored by an employee, contractor or affiliate of a national government. As such, the Government retains a nonexclusive, royalty-free right to publish or reproduce this article, or to allow others to do so, for Government purposes only.
WiSec'16, July 18-22, 2016, Darmstadt, Germany

DOI: http://dx.doi.org/10.1145/2939918.2939930

OSes: iOS since version 8 [9], Windows 10 [10], Android 6.0 [1] and Linux kernel 3.18 [5].

Recently, Vanhoef et al. [10] showed that probe requests contain enough information to form a fingerprint of a device, even without a reliable link-layer identifier. In the present paper, we use even stronger conditions: we suppose that we don't have access to data-link layer information, except the randomized MAC address. In other words, we go further than this previous paper, supposing the previously demonstrated flaws were fixed, and devices stopped adding identifying information in probe requests.

Instead, we study the feasibility of tracking devices based on timing information only. More particularly, we exploit the fact that the frames sent by Wi-Fi devices follow regular patterns that can be used for time-based fingerprinting [3].

The difficulty of such a technique, compared to classical fingerprinting [3], is that we only have a small number of frames to fingerprint a device. In many implementations, random MAC addresses change after a small number of frames have been sent. As a result, we can only gather a small amount of information for each random MAC address. Our solution has to work with this small quantity of information, and has to be reliable at the same time. Besides, as we do not know the number of devices communicating, we cannot build a database of devices before the attack, we have to restrict ourselves to incremental learning methods. Thus, we have to build an hybrid attack that can reliably cluster frames from an unknown number of devices.

This work makes the following contributions. First, we show that the time-based signature is consistent over time, making it a possible pseudo-identifier of a device. Then, we propose an algorithm able to defeat MAC address randomization, in the sense that we are able to group frames from the same device despite the use of random MAC addresses. This attack only relies on timing information and is able to reach an accuracy of up to 75%.

The paper is organized as follows. Section 2 introduces some background information. Section 3 details our algorithm and its various components and parameters. Section 4 presents the results of the tests of our solution, and discusses the efficiency of its parameters. Section 5 concludes the paper.

2. BACKGROUND

2.1 Probe requests

In order to discover 802.11 networks, devices frequently send probe request frames. These frames contain enough

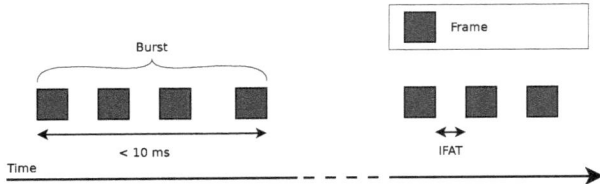

Figure 1: Transmission sequence of frames with Inter-Frame Arrival Time (IFAT) and burst that is a group of frames sent by a device within a time window smaller than 10 ms.

information to identify a device in many cases [10]. For most devices, frames are sent in groups within a small timeframe (less than 10ms), each frame of the group containing a different searched network name (SSID). Such groups of frames are called *bursts* (see Figure 1).

2.2 MAC address randomization schemes

Linux supports MAC address randomization, and lets the driver or firmware generate per-burst random MAC addresses. Indeed, only recent firmware allow for changing the MAC address at each burst but because manufacturers are slow in updating the firmware of Wi-Fi devices, most Linux devices change their MAC address at most every few bursts [5]. As a result, most Linux devices change their MAC address at most every few bursts. The default duration for a random MAC address in `wpa_supplicant` is 60 seconds.

MAC address randomization is supported by iOS since version 8. Randomization is limited to probing and only happens under specific conditions: the device has to be unassociated and in sleep mode [7]. We observe different kinds of behaviour with an iPad 2 running iOS 9.1: the device usually changes its MAC address every few bursts (2-4 bursts), and sometimes changes it for every burst. The conditions for these different behaviors to happen are still to be determined.

Some implementations, such as the one in Windows 10 [6] or the one used in the privacy-oriented Linux distribution Tails do not change the MAC address regularly for Wi-Fi service discovery. Windows 10 changes the MAC address when the device connects or disconnects from a network, and when it is restarted. For such implementations, tracking is trivial since the device identifier does not change during a tracking session.

To sum up, with current implementation of randomization, the same MAC address is used over at least one burst and can cover multiple consecutive bursts.

2.3 Related work

Franklin *et al.* showed that the wireless driver of Wi-Fi-enabled devices can be fingerprinted using the inter-arrival time of the probe requests [3]. They did not discuss the efficiency of their method to distinguish individual devices. As a single driver is used by a great number of devices, being able to distinguish between devices adds a level of precision necessary for tracking.

Freudiger performed an extensive study of Wi-Fi probe requests [4]. The author showed how often certain devices send such frames. He discovered that the number and the frequency of probe requests sent by a device depend on their number of known networks, which hints at the possibility to more precisely fingerprint devices. More specifically, bursts

of probe requests are sent with different timings depending on the number of configured networks. He also showed that MAC address randomization can be defeated using sequence numbers.

Wiedersheim *et al.* proposed a method to break pseudonym in Inter-Vehicular Networks [11]. Using a technique called Multiple Hypothesis Tracking, they reached accuracy of almost 100% to track vehicles changing their pseudonym every 10 seconds and sending one beacon message per second. This algorithm makes a strong use of the position of the devices, which is unknown in our case (or at best very imprecise with RSSI), since we only have a single sensor.

Pang *et al.* showed how *implicit identifiers* can be used to track devices and discussed how it rendered pseudonyms insufficient to prevent tracking [8]. They studied several link-layer fields used by associated devices and used a naive Bayes classifier to distinguish between those devices. As we focus on unassociated devices, we do not have access to most of these fields.

2.4 Threat model

We consider an attacker able to monitor the wireless signals in the vicinity of the target, using one off-the-shelf Wi-Fi card. Such an attacker can thus only monitor one channel at a single location. We make this strong assumption so as to show that the location information is not necessary to track devices. This attacker has access to the timing information and the MAC address of each probe request frame, but not more. We make this assumption to consider a situation where the information leakage in Wi-Fi passive discovery has been fixed, as the latter has already been shown to allow device tracking [10].

The goal of this attacker is to distinguish the signals of all devices in range from the crowd even though they use MAC address randomization, and to track individual devices among extended periods of time.

This simple attacker model can be further extended by considering advanced techniques and using several sensors. Adding the location information obtained by different sensors would improve the accuracy of our algorithm.

This attacker model is complementary to the one used in [11], which focuses on location information to track vehicles using pseudonyms. In fact, both attacks could be combined to defeat pseudonymization.

3. DEFEATING RANDOMIZATION USING TIMING

We present an attack grouping probe requests together based on the sending device despite the use of a changing link-layer identifier. To do so, we use a timing-based method, which considers inter-frame arrival time (IFAT) between frames using the same MAC address. We compute signatures for each group of frames using the same MAC address and compare these signatures using custom distances.

3.1 Terminology

We introduce the following definitions:
- a *burst* is a group of probe request frames sent by a device within 10ms,
- a *burst set* is a group of bursts sent with the same (possibly random) MAC address,
- an *alias* of a MAC address is another (random) MAC address used by the same device,

16

Algorithm 1: Random MAC breaking

Input: $\mathcal{G}$: groups of burst sets, grouped by MAC
      address
      t: distance threshold
      d: a distance function
Returns: $\mathcal{A}$: dictionary of aliases

$\mathcal{A} \leftarrow \emptyset$
$\mathcal{D} \leftarrow \emptyset$ // Database of signatures
foreach $\mathcal{B} \in \mathcal{G}$ **do**
    $\mathcal{S} \leftarrow$ signature($\mathcal{B}$)
    $d_{min} \leftarrow min(d(\mathcal{S}, \mathcal{S}')$ where $\mathcal{S}' \in \mathcal{D})$
    if $d_{min} < t$ **then**
        $\mathcal{A}[\mathcal{B}.mac] \leftarrow \mathcal{A}[\mathcal{S}'.mac]$
    else
        $\mathcal{A}[\mathcal{B}.mac] \leftarrow \mathcal{B}.mac$
    end
    $D \leftarrow \mathcal{D} \cup \mathcal{S}$
end
---
return $\mathcal{A}$

- Inter-Frame Arrival Time (IFAT) is the time difference between two frames.

Also, *randomization* will be used as short for *MAC address randomization* throughout the paper.

3.2 Frame grouping algorithm

Our algorithm takes as input a capture of probe requests and outputs a mapping between the frames and a set of identifiers. Ideally, each identifier should correspond to a distinct device and its associated frames. The mapping is obtained by grouping together frames that appear to originate from the same device based on timing information. More particularly, our algorithm relies on timing-based distances and on an incremental learning algorithm customized to fit the constraints of our use case.

We build a database of time-based signatures for the different MAC addresses, as described in [3]. We divide time into discrete timeframes of equal size (bins). For each group G of frames using the same MAC address, we calculate the inter-frame arrival time (IFAT) between each pair of consecutive frames. We then calculate the ratio and mean value of IFATs in each bin, which constitutes the signature $\mathcal{S}(G)$ for group G. For G, let P_b^G be the percentage of frames in a bin b, and M_b^G the mean IFAT value in bin b. Let $\mathcal{B}$ be the set of all possible bins, the signature $\mathcal{S}$ of group G is given by:

$$\mathcal{S}(G) = \{P_b^G, M_b^G | b \in \mathcal{B}\}$$

For each burst set, we calculate the distance between the signature of this group and every other known signature. If at least one of these distances is below a given threshold t, we choose the MAC address of the signature yielding minimal distance, and consider the two MAC addresses to belong to the same device. Otherwise, we estimate the MAC address to belong to a new device. We add the signature of the new burst set to the database.

We consider two options for this algorithm:
- online: try to group burst sets with previous burst sets only (as described in Algorithm 1).
- offline: try to group burst sets with any burst set

3.3 Distance

The previous algorithm relies on a distance metric in order to group frame together. In this section, we introduce several timing-based distance metrics derived from the one originally introduced by Franklin *et al.* [3].

3.3.1 Franklin's distance

The first considered distance is a modification of the one used by Franklin to fingerprint device drivers. We modify Franklin's distance formula so that it respects the symmetric propriety of a distance. Instead of multiplying the difference of the means by the percentage of a single device, we multiply by the mean of the percentages of both devices.

The distance between two burst sets A and B is based on their signatures. We calculate the distance $D1_{AB}$ using the following formula:

$$D1_{AB} = \sum_{b \in \mathcal{B}} (|P_b^B - P_b^A| + \frac{(P_b^A + P_b^B)}{2} * |M_b^B - M_b^A|)$$

Percentages and means are set to 0 if the bin is empty.

As our distance uses inter-frame arrival time, single frames cannot be considered. We choose to ignore them.

3.3.2 Adding inter-burst set arrival time

As opposed to previous work, the number of frames on which the fingerprint can be computed is limited to a small number of bursts because the MAC address is changed periodically (see section 2). To deal with this reduced amount of information, we extend the previous distance by considering inter-arrival time between the compared burst. The underlying assumption is that bursts exhibit a temporal regularity.

Assuming a group B is composed of frames seen later than those of group A, we calculate the IFAT between the last frame of A and the first one of B: $\text{IFAT}_{AB} = B.first - A.last$. We then check if this IFAT exists in the signature $\mathcal{S}(A)$. If this is not the case, we consider the distance to be $+\infty$. Otherwise, we look at the percentage p of the signature of the IFAT's bin. We multiply the distance by $1 - p$.

So, if we call $D2_{AB}$ this new distance:

$$D2_{AB} = \begin{cases} +\infty & \text{if } \text{IFAT}_{AB} \notin S_A \\ (1 - P_b^A) * D1_{AB} & \text{otherwise} \end{cases}$$

In our algorithm, two burst sets with infinite distance will never be grouped as they are assumed to have very few chance to come from the same device.

3.3.3 Hybrid distance

Because of frame losses and delays in burst transmissions, the previous distance metric may lead to a large amount of false negatives. Therefore, we introduce D3, which constitutes a trade-off between D1 and D2: instead of giving an infinite value, we multiply D1 by a constant C (the choice of the value of this constant is discussed in section 4.8). In other words:

$$D3_{AB} = \begin{cases} C * D1_{AB} & \text{if } \text{IFAT}_{AB} \notin S_A \\ (1 - P_b^A) * D1_{AB} & \text{otherwise} \end{cases}$$

As a result, this distance favors groups of frames having a coherent IFAT with the current group, but seeks to group frames even if no group with coherent IFAT is found.

3.4 Knowledge-keeping algorithm

Our algorithm groups burst sets together, and stores these relationships in an internal structure. It does not use previous knowledge about aliases to group new-coming burst sets, so as not to spread error to further grouping guesses. In concrete terms, a new burst set is compared to each previous burst set. It can thus be compared to several burst sets from a device.

Another way to proceed would be to use previous knowledge of which burst sets are assumed to belong to the same device by creating meta-groups of frames. Signatures of these meta-groups would include more frames, making the results possibly more accurate. A new burst set is then compared once to each known device.

3.5 Nearest neighbors method

We consider an improvement of our algorithm by borrowing the approach of the k-nearest neighbors (k-NN) algorithm. When trying to group a burst set S with other burst sets, we compute the distances with all other burst sets. Instead of grouping S with the burst sets which yields the lowest distance, we have a look at the k burst sets which yield the lowest distances, and group S with the burst set which is most present within those k burst sets.

With this modified algorithm, groups of frames from random MAC addresses will score a low distance with all the previous groups from the same device, and should then have a better chance to be classified correctly.

4. EXPERIMENTS AND RESULTS

We first evaluate our distances in order to find the most efficient one to estimate if two groups of frames come from the same device or from different ones. We then proceed to improve the efficiency of our solution by overviewing the impact of the different parameters: distance threshold, size of the bins for the distance.

4.1 Dataset

In order to estimate our solution, we use a real-world dataset free of random MAC addresses. This dataset of more than 120 000 probe requests sent by over 550 devices was collected in our laboratory, over a period of 6 days.

We transform it into a dataset containing devices changing their MAC addresses every p bursts of probe requests. For evaluation purpose, the resulting dataset keeps a trace of which probe requests come from the same device despite MAC address randomization. This allows us to keep the ground truth data.

We generate a trace having 100 among the 550 devices using random MAC addresses for burst sets of 4 bursts.

4.2 Distance metric evaluation

In order to evaluate the efficiency of our distance, we calculate the distances between burst sets from the same devices, as well as the distances between burst sets from different devices. We then compare those two groups of distances in order to see if our distance metric can be used to identify if two burst sets come from the same device or from different ones. We only do this for $D1$, as $D2$ and $D3$ will fail to evaluate non-consecutive burst sets properly since they use inter-burst arrival time.

Results can be seen in Figure 2. We observe that bursts from distinct devices have a larger distance than the bursts

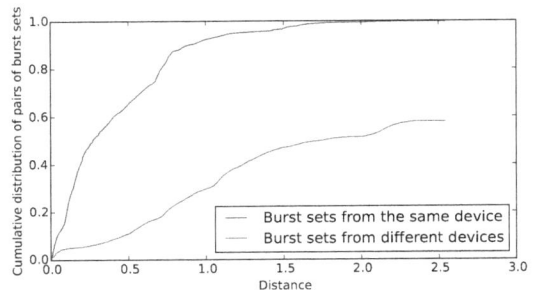

Figure 2: Cumulative distribution of the distance $D1$ for pairs of burst set from the same device and from distinct devices.

from the same device, which confirms the utility of this distance for our attack.

4.3 Stability of the distance over time

In this section, we study the stability of the considered distance over time in order to confirm that our algorithm can work to track a device over an extended period of time. To do so, we compute the distance between groups of frames sent by the same device at distinct time intervals.

We consider several time differences between 1 minute and up to 50 days. For each of them, we select 50 devices for which frames separated by this time difference ($\pm 10\%$) are available in our dataset. We take two groups of 1 minute of these frames at each extremity of the time difference and compute the distance between these groups. In order to have data covering an extended time period, we use the Sapienza dataset [2] as it covers 50 days, a longer time period than our own. Thanks to this dataset, we can calculate the consistency of the distance over long time periods.

The results are shown on figure 3. We observe an increase of less than 50% even after 50 days, which seems low enough to allow tracking devices over a long time period. Values reached by the distance even after 50 days still make a difference of 49% between the two kinds of burst sets in figure 2 (42% in the worst case), while the average distance for burst sets with 1 minute of time interval make a difference of 61%.

In our dataset and experimental conditions, we do not observe the probable IFAT deviation mentioned by Freudiger [4], observed when disabling Google services on Android.

4.4 Performance metrics

We evaluate the performances of the proposed algorithm based on a number of metrics: accuracy, true positive rate and false positive rate.

We define the accuracy metrics as being the ratio of correct decisions made by our algorithm. We define a correct decision as being either:

- a burst set using a random MAC address correctly grouped with another burst set from the same device;
- a burst set from a device not using a random MAC address not grouped with any other burst sets (i.e. a group of frames from a device using a normal MAC address is not grouped with frames from another device).

Accuracy in itself does not provide information about the

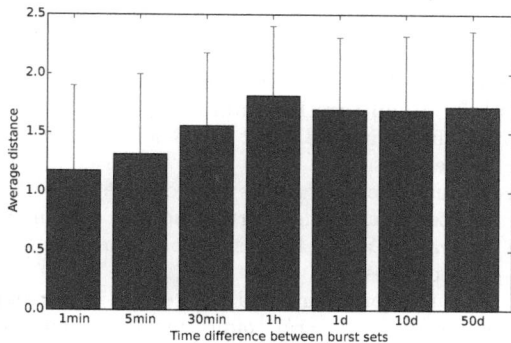

Figure 3: mean and standard deviation of the distance w.r.t. time difference between groups of frames.

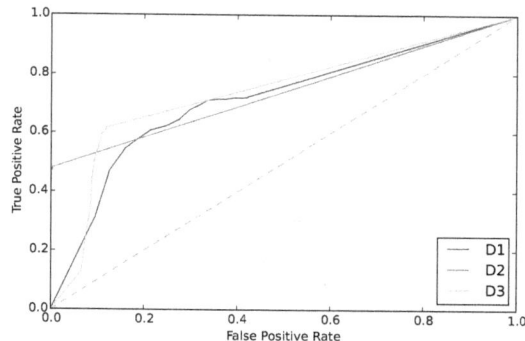

Figure 4: ROC curve of the three distances, over the range of threshold values.

kinds of errors made by the algorithm. For that purpose, we define two supplementary metrics:

- True positive rate (TPR): number of burst sets from devices using random MAC addresses correctly grouped together, over the number of burst sets from devices using random MAC addresses,
- False positive rate (FPR): number of burst sets incorrectly grouped with burst sets from other devices, over the total number of burst sets.

TPR gives a better insight about positive results related to devices using random MAC addresses only. FPR shows the ratio of undesirable errors made by the algorithm (burst sets from different devices grouped together). In an attack, a false positive may lead to a device being taken for another one. As a result, the actual device may not be detected, while the other device may be missed. Nevertheless, such errors will only be significant if they appear on a long number of successive burst sets, as they could be detected by human judgement or a filtering algorithm otherwise.

4.5 Performances as a function of the threshold

We plot the performance of our algorithm with the 3 distances as a function of the distance threshold t, summarized in a ROC curve (Figure 4). With distance $D1$, we observe a maximum for the accuracy metrics for $t = 0.4$, with accuracy $= 62.7\%$. Increasing the distance threshold then increases both true positive and false positive rates.

With distance $D2$, our false positive rate stays close to 0. Thanks to this, we can afford higher values of t, for which the FPR stays much smaller than 1%. However, our TPR is not as good as with distance $D1$, and our algorithm fails to find the original MAC address for more than half groups of frames using random MAC addresses. With distance $D1$, we could succeed for more than 70% of such groups, at a cost of a high FPR.

Further investigations show that higher values of t (such as 10) do not modify the results anymore. As a result, with distance $D2$, the value of t can be taken arbitrarily high for optimal results.

As expected, distance $D3$ appears to be a good trade-off between $D1$ and $D2$: results values for TPR and FPR lie between those of $D1$ and $D2$.

4.6 Knowledge-keeping algorithm evaluation

We evaluate our knowledge-keeping algorithm (see section 3.4) on our 3 distances.

As this method is more prone to error accumulation, it is not surprising that the best results are given by distance $D2$, which yields almost no false positive. Distance $D3$ becomes victim of this error accumulation for high values of t, due to a higher FPR, and sees an accuracy drop of about 8%. Performances for distance $D1$ are definitely worse, with a fall in accuracy of about 18%. Performances for distance $D2$ are almost equal with both strategies (the difference is less than 0.01%).

To sum up, the knowledge-keeping algorithm does not improve performances but has the potential to make them drop in some cases.

4.7 Influence of the parameters

In order to improve the results of the algorithm, we evaluate the influence of several parameters on its efficiency: size of the bins, number of future bursts.

4.7.1 Temporal granularity/Size of the bins

To build our signatures for the MAC addresses, we discretize time by forming bins of fixed size. We vary the size of these bins used to calculate the distance between groups of frames, from $1\mu s$ to $1s$. What appears is that the size of the bins does not matter much, as long as it is bigger than a threshold of $50ms$ to $300ms$, depending on the distance used. bins smaller than this threshold result in a lower accuracy. The best results are obtained with bins of size $670ms$ which an accuracy of 76.2%. Tests for higher values (1 to 5s) do not yield better results.

4.7.2 Number of future bursts

We attempt to use our algorithm with harder conditions: instead of considering all frames with the same MAC address to build signatures, we only take the first N bursts in time, with N from 1 to 5. The aim of this harder condition is to see if our algorithm can be used in near real-time, where the amount of information is reduced to a small timeframe.

Results are presented in Figure 5. Not fetching bursts of probe requests in the future yields a drop of 40% in the accuracy of our algorithm. Actually, no probe request with a random MAC address is classified correctly ($TPR = 0$). The

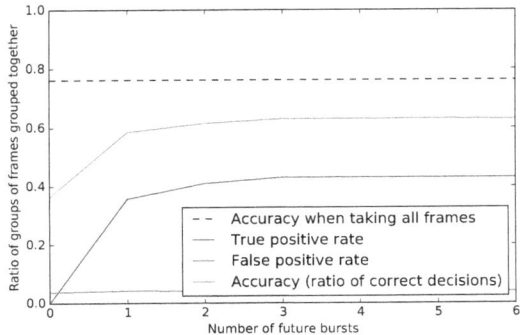

Figure 5: Influence of the number of future bursts fetched for distance $D2$.

Table 1: Results of the attack with the best parameters and options.

Distance	Accuracy	TPR	FPR
D1	66.8%	74.1%	24.3%
D2	**77.2%**	64.0%	**0.6%**
D3	71.8%	**75.2%**	17.5%

accuracy of 40% is only due to probe requests not using random MAC addresses not being grouped with other frames. This shows that our algorithm fails to classify groups of only one burst of frames. With two groups of frames or more, results become usable with a drop in accuracy of less than 20%. Above 4 groups of bursts, results don't vary since we simulate devices using random MAC addresses by randomizing groups of 4 bursts.

4.8 Other parameters and options

This section ends the discussion about the tested parameters. We evaluate the effectiveness of the two options presented in section 3.2. We observe an increase of 2 to 3% for the 3 distances with the offline algorithm.

We evaluate our k-NN method (see section 3.5) with the 3 distances. 1-NN corresponds to the default behaviour, where we only consider the closest group of frames. Results show that this method is not more efficient for any value of k greater than 1: tests on the values of k from 2 to 10 on the 3 distances yield a ratio decrease of 1 to 30%.

For the choice of the constant used for distance $D3$, we calculate accuracy, TPR and FPR for various values of this constant, ranging from 1 to 100. 10 appears to be the best choice for this constant as it maximizes accuracy.

4.9 Results summary

Our estimated best parameters are: $t = 0.4$ for distance $D1$, $t = 2.0$ for distances $D2$ and $D3$, bins of size 670ms, offline algorithm, not using the knowledge-keeping algorithm. With these parameters, we obtain results presented in Table 1. $D2$ appears to yield both the best accuracy and the lowest FPR, whereas $D3$ yields the best TPR. Depending on the conditions, $D2$ or $D3$ may be considered the best distance metric.

5. CONCLUSION

In this work, we presented an attack capable of tracking Wi-Fi devices over time despite the use of MAC address randomization mechanisms. Our timing-based attack is able to successfully group together frames originating from the same device, but having a distinct MAC address pseudonym in 77.2% of the cases.

This new class of attack shows that owners of Wi-Fi devices are exposed to tracking. Furthermore, it demonstrates that the content of Wi-Fi frames is not even necessary in order to track devices.

Based on our observations and the results of our experiments, we can devise several countermeasures that would reduce the effectiveness of the attack presented in this paper. First, changing the MAC address more often, e.g. every burst or every frame, has the potential to reduce the trackability of devices, as the amount of information for fingerprinting will be limited to a few frames. Then, since our attack relies on temporal pattern, a simple countermeasure would be to break those patterns by introducing some random delays between probes and between bursts.

6. REFERENCES

[1] Android 6.0 changes. Retrieved from https://developer.android.com/about/versions/marshmallow/android-6.0-changes.html, 2015.

[2] M. V. Barbera, A. Epasto, A. Mei, S. Kosta, V. C. Perta, and J. Stefa. CRAWDAD dataset sapienza/probe-requests (v. 2013-09-10). Retrieved 10 November, 2015, from, http://crawdad.org/sapienza/probe-requests/20130910, Sept. 2013.

[3] J. Franklin, D. McCoy, P. Tabriz, V. Neagoe, J. V. Randwyk, and D. Sicker. Passive data link layer 802.11 wireless device driver fingerprinting. In *Usenix Security*, volume 6, 2006.

[4] J. Freudiger. How talkative is your mobile device?: an experimental study of Wi-Fi probe requests. In *Proceedings of the 8th ACM Conference on Security & Privacy in Wireless and Mobile Networks*. ACM, 2015.

[5] E. Grumbach. iwlwifi: mvm: support random MAC address for scanning. Linux commit `effd05ac479b`.

[6] C. Huitema. Experience with mac address randomization in windows 10, 2015.

[7] B. Misra. ios8 mac randomization – analyzed! http://blog.mojonetworks.com/ios8-mac-randomization-analyzed/, 2014.

[8] J. Pang, B. Greenstein, R. Gummadi, S. Seshan, and D. Wetherall. 802.11 user fingerprinting. In *MobiCom*, pages 99–110. ACM, 2007.

[9] K. Skinner and J. Novak. Privacy and your app. In *Apple Worldwide Dev. Conf. (WWDC)*, June 2015.

[10] M. Vanhoef, C. Matte, M. Cunche, L. Cardoso, and F. Piessens. Why MAC Address Randomization is not Enough: An Analysis of Wi-Fi Network Discovery Mechanisms. In *AsiaCCS*, May 2016.

[11] B. Wiedersheim, Z. Ma, F. Kargl, and P. Papadimitratos. Privacy in inter-vehicular networks: Why simple pseudonym change is not enough. In *Wireless On-demand Network Systems and Services (WONS)*, pages 176–183. IEEE, 2010.

Profiling the Strength of Physical-Layer Security: A Study in Orthogonal Blinding

Yao Zheng
Complex Networks & Security
Research Laboratory
Virginia Polytechnic Institute
and State University
zhengyao@vt.edu

Matthias Schulz
Secure Mobile Networking Lab
Technische Universität
Darmstadt
mschulz@seemoo.tu-
darmstadt.de

Wenjing Lou
Complex Networks & Security
Research Laboratory
Virginia Polytechnic Institute
and State University
wjlou@vt.edu

Y. Thomas Hou
Complex Networks & Security
Research Laboratory
Virginia Polytechnic Institute
and State University
thou@vt.edu

Matthias Hollick
Secure Mobile Networking Lab
Technische Universität
Darmstadt
mhollick@seemoo.tu-
darmstadt.de

ABSTRACT

Physical layer security for wireless communication is broadly considered as a promising approach to protect data confidentiality against eavesdroppers. However, despite its ample theoretical foundation, the transition to practical implementations of physical-layer security still lacks success. A close inspection of proven vulnerable physical-layer security designs reveals that the flaws are usually overlooked when the scheme is only evaluated against an inferior, single-antenna eavesdropper. Meanwhile, the attacks exposing vulnerabilities often lack theoretical justification. To reduce the gap between theory and practice, we posit that a physical-layer security scheme must be studied under multiple adversarial models to fully grasp its security strength. In this regard, we evaluate a specific physical-layer security scheme, *i.e.* orthogonal blinding, under multiple eavesdropper settings. We further propose a practical "ciphertext-only attack" that allows eavesdroppers to recover the original message by exploiting the low entropy fields in wireless packets. By means of simulation, we are able to reduce the symbol error rate (SER) at an eavesdropper below 1% using only the eavesdropper's receiving data and a general knowledge about the format of the wireless packets.

Keywords

physical-layer security, information-theoretic security analysis, orthogonal blinding, cryptanalysis, ciphertext-only attack

WiSec'16 , July 18-22, 2016, Darmstadt, Germany

© 2016 ACM. ISBN 978-1-4503-4270-4/16/07. . . $15.00

DOI: http://dx.doi.org/10.1145/2939918.2939933

1. INTRODUCTION

Physical-layer security has been a long-standing security area that achieves confidentiality for data transmissions by exploiting the two fundamental characteristics of the wireless medium, which are *broadcast* and *superposition*. By stirring transmitted signals with synthesized noise, physical-layer security schemes can effectively corrupt the eavesdropper's reception and achieve secure communication in a broadcast system [1]. While theoretical study shows that this design philosophy holds a lot of promise, several practical physical-layer security schemes proposed for multiple input multiple output (MIMO) systems have been proven insecure over time. For instance, friendly jamming, proposed by Gollakota *et al.*, applying jamming techniques to prevent unauthorized access to implantable medical devices [2] or camouflage the transmission of a secret key [3], was later proven to be vulnerable when an attacker strategically places her antenna array to discern and cancel the jamming signals [4, 5]. Another example is orthogonal blinding [6], proposed by Anand *et al.*, which thwarts a eavesdropper by injecting artificial noise into channels orthogonal to the intended receiver's channels. The scheme was recently shown to be vulnerable against a multi-antenna eavesdropper with capabilities similar to those of the transmitter [7, 8]. In [7], the eavesdropper attacks orthogonal blinding by training an adaptive filter through known data symbols to separate transmitted signals from artificial noise.

The swift development of attack methods toward physical-layer security schemes has raised concerns about its practicality. The reasons behind those prompt attack methods are usually tri-fold: (1) The actual secrecy rate attained by a physical-layer security scheme can be significantly lower than the secrecy capacity of the MIMO wire-tap channel, and may depend on the MIMO configurations of the transmitter, the receiver, and the eavesdropper. (2) The evaluation of a physical-layer security scheme has been focusing on a single-antenna eavesdropper [3, 6] due to technology constrains, which lead to inconclusive results. For instance, in [6], the scheme considers the eavesdropper to be limited by singular antenna methods due to constrains of mobile devices. (3) While the assumption of a single-antenna eavesdropper might be realistic in the past, the rapid advancement of MIMO technology quickly obviates such an assumption by increasing the number of antennas for average devices.

To that end, we argue that physical-layer security schemes must be scrutinized under multiple MIMO configurations in order to gain comprehensive insights about their security strength and lifespan as the technology progresses. In this paper, we provide an extensive evaluation framework for physical-layer security by associating theoretical analysis with practical attack method under multiple MIMO configurations. In particular, we focus on profiling the security strength of orthogonal blinding based physical-layer security schemes. To identify vulnerabilities, we derive and compare the secrecy rates attained by orthogonal blinding under different MIMO configurations. Based on the theoretical analysis, we further present an attack showcase that allows a multi-antenna eavesdropper to effectively recover the transmitted data solely using the received signal. Our attack corresponds to the "ciphertext-only attack" model in cryptanalysis, where the eavesdropper exploits the nonuniform statistical profile of the transmitted data to infer its content.

Our results emphasize that, unlike conventional approaches such as contemporary cryptography, the level of information protection provided by a physical-layer security scheme is a dependent variable affected by practical conditions. A scheme that performs reasonably well against a single-antenna eavesdropper can have zero security incentive against a multi-antenna eavesdropper. In addition, the randomness of the input data, or the lack thereof, can deteriorate the performance of a physical-layer security scheme as well. In our case, it is the extremely regularized wireless packets that exposes a potential vulnerability of orthogonal blinding that is otherwise concealed. Our contributions in this paper are the followings:

- We provide an intuitive framework to study the security strength of orthogonal blinding based physical-layer security by comparing the secrecy capacity of the wire-tap channel with the secrecy rate attained by the scheme.

- We correlate the theoretical results with a cryptographic attack scenario, *i.e.* ciphertext-only attack. We show that the entropy contained in wireless packets is insufficient to prevent a powerful adversary from launching a brute force ciphertext-only attack toward orthogonal blinding.

- We design a practical, ciphertext-only attack scheme that allows an adversary to recover the transmitted data by exploiting the low entropy fields in wireless packets without knowing any transmitted data a priori.

- We implement our attack in MATLAB and evaluate its performance through extensive simulations.

In what follows, we show the motivation of our work by reviewing the theoretical foundation of physical-layer security in Sec. 2. In Sec. 3 we present the system model and the method of orthogonal blinding used for secure transmission. We analyze the performance of orthogonal blinding under various MIMO configurations using in Sec. 4. In Sec. 5, we channel our analysis results into a practical attack and present our ciphertext-only attack method against orthogonal blinding. We demonstrate our attack in Sec. 6. Finally, we discuss our findings in Sec. 7 and conclude in Sec. 8.

2. BACKGROUND

The theoretical foundation of physical-layer security was laid by Aaron Wyner, when he introduced the concept of the wire-tap channel [9] in 1975. In a basic wire-tap channel model, there are three terminals, one transmitter, one receiver, and one eavesdropper. The transmitter encodes a message M and broadcast it. Through the broadcast channel, the receiver and the eavesdropper observe Y and Z respectively. The goal is to exploit the channel such that the receiver can recover M from Y while the the eavesdropper cannot recover M from Z. Subsequent work extended this result to a basic Gaussian channel [10], that better models wireless communication systems. In the original framework, the channel must have two properties to permit secure communication: (1) Soundness: the error rate between transmitter and the receiver is asymptotically zero. (2) Completeness: the communication rate between the transmitter and the receiver is asymptotically zero. There two properties are formally defined by the *secrecy capacity*, which represent the maximum secrecy rate at which Alice and Bob can communicate while Eve receives an arbitrarily small amount of information.

Wyner's original treatment inspires a flourishing area of research, which studies characterizations of physical-layer security for more complex wireless communication systems. In particular, there are several works that aim to derive the secrecy capacity of a MIMO wire-tap channel by extending a basic Gaussian wire-tap channel to the case when the terminals have multiple antennas [11, 12]. One of the important result from these works is that the attainable secrecy rate can be greatly affected by the ratio of eavesdropping antennas to transmitting antennas. The result, while significant, is not widely adapted when evaluating physical-layer security schemes in practice due to its complexity.

In parallel with the theoretical research, several practical physical-layer security schemes have been proposed in the literature. An interesting family of them is based on orthogonal blinding [6], otherwise known as masked beamforming. The idea of orthogonal blinding is to simultaneously transmit the message to the intended receiver's channel while transmitting synthesized noise in the orthogonal subspace to interfere with the eavesdropper's reception. Based on empirical measurements, these schemes have been shown to be effective against a single-antenna eavesdropper. However, due to lack of evaluation under other MIMO configurations, especially in the multi-antenna eavesdropper regime, these schemes are often found to be vulnerable when facing powerful eavesdroppers. For instance, in [7, 8], Schulz et al. presented an attack toward [6] under an multi-antenna eavesdropper setting. In [13], Tung et al. showed two active, single-antenna attacks toward MIMO systems protected by orthogonal blinding.

Despite its flaws, we still find orthogonal blinding an interesting case in physical-layer security designs, due to its practical assumption about the knowledge of channel state information (CSI). Specifically, The scheme performs reasonably well against a single-antenna eavesdropper even if the sender and the receiver have no knowledge the eavesdropper's channel, a quality desirable among physical layer security schemes. In addition, the weakness of orthogonal blinding against a multi-antenna eavesdropper is representative as mobile terminals progress from singular antenna to multiple antennas. To better understand its limitations, and limitations of physical-layer security schemes in general, we see a compelling reason to study the strength and weakness of orthogonal blinding, since the notions of secure and insecure are never absolute, and vary by the capabilities of the attacker and defender. Only by determining the boundary inbetween, we can better assess the usefulness of a security method. Unlike previous work that focus on specific attack method, our study aims to provide an intuitive framework for physical-layer security that incorporates both theoretical and practical machinery.

3. SYSTEM MODEL

In this section, we describe the communication system, the channel model and the secure transmission method. Our subject to study is based on MIMO transceivers using orthogonal frequency-division multiplexing (OFDM), a prevalent wireless technology adapted in 802.11ac Wi-Fi standard [14]. Using OFDM, we can split wide-band channels into narrow sub-channels to counter the problem of intersymbol interference (ISI) and channel fading. It allow us to describe the CSI using a linear model. Through MIMO, we allow the transmitter to apply orthogonal blinding based physical-layer security to protect data transmission. Our analysis focus on the case of slow fading, where the transmitted data block is short compared to the coherence time of the fading. But the result can be extended to the case of fast fading channels.

3.1 Communication System

Consider a multi-user MIMO-OFDM system, as shown in Fig. 1, with one transmitter Alice, $\mathcal{A}$ with $n_\mathcal{A}$ antennas, one receiver Bob $\mathcal{B}$ with $m_\mathcal{B}$ antennas, and one eavesdropper Eve $\mathcal{E}$ with $m_\mathcal{E}$ antennas. Due to OFDM, the downlink CSI from Alice's j-th antenna to a receiver's i-th antenna can be characterized by a single complex number per subcarrier in the frequency domain, *i.e. channel coefficient* $H_{i,j}[k] \in \mathbb{C}$. The full CSI can be represented by a three dimensional array, $H \in \mathbb{C}^{m \times n_\mathcal{A} \times k}$, in which the third dimension represents the number of sub-channels. The CSI of the k-th sub-channel is a two dimensional matrix, $H[k] \in \mathbb{C}^{m \times n_\mathcal{A}}$. At the k-th sub-channel, the relationship between the received signal, $R[k] \in \mathbb{C}^{m \times *}$, and the transmitted signal, $D[k] \in \mathbb{C}^{n_\mathcal{A} \times *}$, can be expressed as:

$$R[k] = H[k] \cdot D[k] + \mathcal{N}, \quad (1)$$

where $\mathcal{N} \in \mathbb{C}^{m \times *}$ represents additive white Gaussian noise. A specific CSI is only valid within the channel coherence time. Beyond that, a new CSI must be estimated to abstract the channel. A common approach for Alice to obtain CSIs of each receiver is through direct feedback from the receiver. For that, Alice broadcasts well known pilot symbols to all receivers. Each receiver then divides the reception by the pre-known pilot symbols to obtain its own CSI and reports it back to the Alice. Finally, the input $D[k]$ must satisfy the power constraint

$$\mathbf{E}\left[\|d[k]\|^2\right] \le P, \quad (2)$$

where $d[k]$ represents a column in $D[k]$.

3.2 Secure Transmission

One of the key benefits of a multi-user MIMO-OFDM system is to avoid cross-talking and eavesdropping through transmitter-side precoding. As the eavesdropper, Eve attempts to overhear the message Alice sends to Bob. If Eve is *honest*, she would faithfully report her CSI, $H_\mathcal{E} \in \mathbb{C}^{m_\mathcal{E} \times n_\mathcal{A} \times k}$, to Alice. To secretly communicate with Bob, Alice can transmit within the null-space of Eve's CSI. Specifically, Alice precodes the transmitting data using the pseudo inverse of the block matrix consisting of Bob's and Eve's CSI,

$$D[k] = \begin{pmatrix} H_\mathcal{B}[k] \\ H_\mathcal{E}[k] \end{pmatrix}^H \left(\begin{pmatrix} H_\mathcal{B}[k] \\ H_\mathcal{E}[k] \end{pmatrix} \begin{pmatrix} H_\mathcal{B}[k] \\ H_\mathcal{E}[k] \end{pmatrix}^H \right)^{-1} \begin{pmatrix} D_\mathcal{B}[k] \\ D_\mathcal{E}[k] \end{pmatrix}, \quad (3)$$

where $H_\mathcal{B} \in \mathbb{C}^{m_\mathcal{B} \times n_\mathcal{A} \times k}$, $D_\mathcal{B} \in \mathbb{C}^{m_\mathcal{B} \times * \times k}$ and $D_\mathcal{E} \in \mathbb{C}^{m_\mathcal{E} \times * \times k}$ represent Bob's CSI and the transmitted signal intended for Bob and Eve. The precoding scheme, known as zero-forcing beamforming, prohibits cross-talk by nullifying the interference caused by other concurrent transmissions.

If Eve is *dishonest*, she may choose to not report her CSI or report fake CSI to Alice. In case Eve's CSI cannot be trusted, Alice must change her communication strategy. To still achieve confidentiality, Alice transmits artificial noise, $AN \in \mathbb{C}^{(n_\mathcal{A} - m_\mathcal{B}) \times * \times k}$, in the null-space of Bob's CSI to mislead Eve. For each sub-channel, Alice finds a random matrix, $H_r[k] \in \mathbb{C}^{(n_\mathcal{A} - m_\mathcal{B}) \times n_\mathcal{A}}$ that is orthonormal to $H_\mathcal{B}[k]$. To compute $H_r[k]$, Alice uses the projection matrix,

$$H_\mathcal{B}^H[k](H_\mathcal{B}[k]H_\mathcal{B}^H[k])^{-1}H_\mathcal{B}[k] \quad (4)$$

and a complex random uniform matrix, $\hat{H}_r[k] \in \mathbb{C}^{(n_\mathcal{A} - m_\mathcal{B}) \times n_\mathcal{A}}$. Alice subtracts the projected image of $\hat{H}_r[k]$ from $\hat{H}_r[k]$,

$$\hat{H}_r[k] - \hat{H}_r[k] \cdot \left(H_\mathcal{B}^H[k](H_\mathcal{B}[k]H_\mathcal{B}^H[k])^{-1}H_\mathcal{B}[k] \right) \quad (5)$$

and normalizes the result to obtain $H_r[k]$. Prior to transmitting, Alice precodes the data for Bob and artificial noise using the pseudo inverse of the block matrix consisting of $H_\mathcal{B}[k]$ and $H_r[k]$,

$$D[k] = \begin{pmatrix} H_\mathcal{B}[k] \\ H_r[k] \end{pmatrix}^H \left(\begin{pmatrix} H_\mathcal{B}[k] \\ H_r[k] \end{pmatrix} \begin{pmatrix} H_\mathcal{B}[k] \\ H_r[k] \end{pmatrix}^H \right)^{-1} \begin{pmatrix} D_\mathcal{B}[k] \\ AN[k] \end{pmatrix}. \quad (6)$$

Since the artificial noise in the null-space of Bob's CSI, it degrades Eve's channel and leaves Bob's channel unaffected.

In both cases (with the honest and with the dishonest eavesdropper), the overall communication system is modeled by a wire-tap channel model

$$\begin{pmatrix} R_\mathcal{B}[k] \\ R_\mathcal{E}[k] \end{pmatrix} = \begin{pmatrix} H_\mathcal{B}[k] \\ H_\mathcal{E}[k] \end{pmatrix} \cdot D[k] + \mathcal{N}, \quad (7)$$

where the channel between Alice and Bob is the main channel, and the channel between Alice and Eve is the wire-tap channel. The linear precoding allows Alice to thwart eavesdroppers by inhibiting information leakage due to the cross-talk in a MIMO-OFDM system. Physical-layer security systems like this were proposed as an alternative or as an extension to high-layer encryption since the overhead of such an approach is small and no pre-shared secret is required. However, in Sec. 4 we show that the secrecy level of the scheme varies depending on the assumptions about Eve.

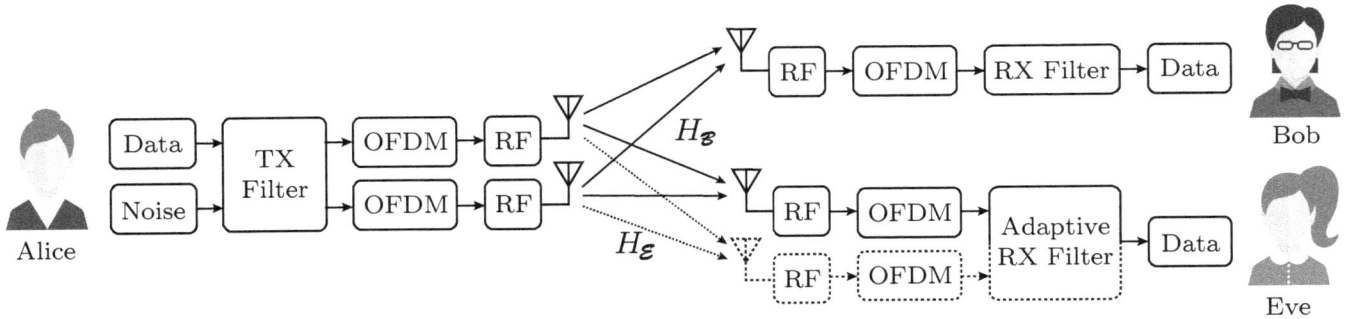

Figure 1: Our system model illustrating the transmitter Alice, the intended receiver Bob and the eavesdropper Eve.

4. SECURITY PROFILING

Here we present a comprehensive security evaluation of orthogonal blinding under different MIMO configurations. For convenience, we restrict our attention to two typical cases: (1) *inferior eavesdropper*: $m_{\mathcal{B}} + m_{\mathcal{E}} < n_{\mathcal{A}}$; (2) *superior eavesdropper*: $m_{\mathcal{B}} \leq n_{\mathcal{A}} \leq m_{\mathcal{E}}$. In both cases, we consider $H_{\mathcal{B}}$, $H_{\mathcal{E}}$, and H_r to be full rank. We further categorize our result based on the eavesdropper's behavior: (1) Eve is *honest* and faithfully reports her CSI. (2) Eve is *dishonest* and chooses to not report her CSI or report fake CSI. Finally, we profile the security strength of the scheme based on the soundness and completeness of the security system. Analogous to a logical proof, we consider the system to be sound if the wire-tap channel supports secure communication, *i.e.*, it has a positive secrecy capacity. We consider the system to be complete if the communication protocol can achieve the optimal capacity. The overall analysis results are summarized in Table 1. Our result is based on a MIMO Gaussian wire-tap channel but can be extend to other channel types with orthogonal blinding.

4.1 Preliminary

Here we review properties of generalized singular value decomposition (GSVD) in preparation for our analysis. The GSVD is a matrix decomposition that simultaneously diagonalizes a pair of matrices. In particular, by applying GSVD, we can transform Eq. 7 into a diagonal form,

$$\begin{pmatrix} \tilde{R}_{\mathcal{B}}[k] \\ \tilde{R}_{\mathcal{E}}[k] \end{pmatrix} = \begin{pmatrix} \Sigma_{\mathcal{B}}[k] \\ \Sigma_{\mathcal{E}}[k] \end{pmatrix} \cdot \tilde{D}[k] + \tilde{\mathcal{N}}, \qquad (8)$$

Table 1: Summary of security profiling.

Eve shares …	**Honest** … correct CSI	**Dishonest** … incorrect or no CSI
Inferior $m_{\mathcal{B}} + m_{\mathcal{E}} < n_{\mathcal{A}}$	sound; complete	unsound; incomplete
Superior $m_{\mathcal{B}} \leq n_{\mathcal{A}} \leq m_{\mathcal{E}}$	sound; incomplete	unsound; incomplete

where

$$\Sigma_{\mathcal{B}}[k] = \begin{array}{c} s \\ r \end{array} \begin{pmatrix} \overset{q-r-s}{0} & \overset{s}{\mathbf{D}_{\mathcal{B}}} & \overset{r}{0} \\ 0 & 0 & \mathbf{I} \end{pmatrix} \qquad (9)$$

$$\Sigma_{\mathcal{E}}[k] = \begin{array}{c} q-r-s \\ s \end{array} \begin{pmatrix} \overset{q-r-s}{\mathbf{I}} & \overset{s}{0} & \overset{r}{0} \\ 0 & \mathbf{D}_{\mathcal{B}} & 0 \end{pmatrix}, \qquad (10)$$

are two block diagonal matrices with

$$\mathbf{D}_{\mathcal{B}} = \text{diag}(\alpha_1, \ldots, \alpha_s), \quad \mathbf{D}_{\mathcal{E}} = \text{diag}(\beta_1, \ldots, \beta_s). \qquad (11)$$

The values, q, r, and s, correspond to the dimension of the subspaces of the entire wire-tap channel, the sub-channels that go only to the Bob, and the subspaces that go to both the Bob and Eve. The generalized singular values are defined as

$$\sigma_i = \frac{\alpha_i}{\beta_i}, \quad i = 1, 2, \ldots, s. \qquad (12)$$

4.2 Inferior, Honest Eavesdropper

Consider the first scenario that Eve reports her CSI honestly and is *inferior* to Alice in terms of number of antennas, *i.e.* $m_{\mathcal{B}} + m_{\mathcal{E}} < n_{\mathcal{A}}$. Since $H_{\mathcal{E}}$ is full rank, *i.e.* rank$(H_{\mathcal{E}}) = m_{\mathcal{E}} < n_{\mathcal{A}}$, we have $r > 0$, $s \geq 0$[1] in Eq. 9 and Eq. 10. Hence, the sub-channels that allow Alice to securely communicate with the Bob are: (1) The r sub-channels that solely go to the Bob and (2) The subset of $s' < s$ sub-channels that go to both Bob and Eve and have σs greater than one. The wire-tap channel's secrecy capacity is positive. Because Alice has full knowledge of the channel, she can achieve the secrecy capacity by transmitting through the top $m_{\mathcal{B}}$ of the $r + s'$ viable sub-channels with proper wiretap codes. The security of the system is therefore sound and complete.

4.3 Superior, Honest Eavesdropper

Consider the second scenario that Eve reports her CSI honestly and is *superior* to Alice in terms of number of antennas, *i.e.* $m_{\mathcal{B}} \leq n_{\mathcal{A}} \leq m_{\mathcal{E}}$. Observe that rank$(H_{\mathcal{E}}) = n_{\mathcal{A}}$, and we have $r = 0$ and $s = m_{\mathcal{B}}$ in Eq. 9 and Eq. 10. Hence, the sub-channels that allow Alice to securely communicate with Bob are the subset of $s' < s$ sub-channels that go to

---

[1]Technically, we have $r \geq 0$ and $s \geq 0$. However, unless $H_{\mathcal{B}}$ is extremely unfortunate, we can assume $r > 0$.

both Bob and Eve and have σs greater than one. The wiretap channel's secrecy capacity is not guaranteed to be positive. Formally, the secrecy capacity of this scenario is [12]

$$\sum_{j:\sigma_j \geq 1} \log \sigma_j^2, \tag{13}$$

which is only positive if

$$\sigma_{\max} > 1. \tag{14}$$

Given that Alice has full knowledge of the channel, she can achieve the secrecy capacity of the wire-tap channel by transmitting through the top $m_{\mathcal{E}}$ of the s' sub-channels with proper wiretap codes. The security of the system is therefore unsound but complete.

4.4 Inferior, Dishonest Eavesdropper

Consider the third scenario that Eve reports her CSI dishonestly and is *inferior* to Alice in terms of number of antennas, *i.e.* $m_{\mathcal{B}} + m_{\mathcal{E}} < n_{\mathcal{A}}$. The secrecy capacity of the wire-tap channel is the same as what we show in Sec. 4.2. Since Alice does not know Eve's CSI, She cannot identify the sub-channels that support secure transmission. Instead, Alice transmits artificial noise in the null space of $H_{\mathcal{B}}[k]$. It is equivalent to Alice randomly selecting $m_{\mathcal{B}}$ sub-channels from the total $r + s$ sub-channels, and hoping to avoid the ones that have σs smaller or equal to one. Obviously, Alice's choice is, in general, suboptimal. However, the probability for Alice to avoid unsuitable sub-channels is nondiminishing,

$$0 < \binom{m_{\mathcal{B}}}{m_{\mathcal{B}} + m_{\mathcal{E}}} \leq \binom{m_{\mathcal{B}}}{r + s - s'} \leq 1, \tag{15}$$

when Eve is inferior,*i.e.*,

$$m_{\mathcal{B}} \leq r + s - s' \leq m_{\mathcal{B}} + m_{\mathcal{E}}. \tag{16}$$

Hence, orthogonal blinding can guarantee that the *stochastic* secrecy loss of the wire-tap channels is at most $\binom{m_{\mathcal{B}}}{m_{\mathcal{B}} + m_{\mathcal{E}}}$ of the optimal secrecy capacity. The security of the system is therefore sound but incomplete.

4.5 Superior, Dishonest Eavesdropper

Consider the last scenario that Eve reports her CSI dishonestly and is *superior* to Alice in terms of number of antennas, *i.e.* $m_{\mathcal{B}} \leq n_{\mathcal{A}} \leq m_{\mathcal{E}}$. The secrecy capacity of the wire-tap channel is the same as what we show in Sec. 4.3. However, when Alice applies orthogonal blinding, the the probability for Alice to avoid unsuitable sub-channels can be arbitrarily close to zero,

$$0 \leq \binom{m_{\mathcal{B}}}{r + s - s'} \leq 1, \tag{17}$$

When Eve is superior, *i.e.*,

$$r + s - s' = s - s' \leq m_{\mathcal{B}}. \tag{18}$$

Therefore, Alice's choice can be arbitrarily far from optimal. The security of the system is therefore neither sound nor complete.

5. CIPHERTEXT-ONLY ATTACK

The previous information theoretic analysis give us an overall picture about the security level of the physical-layer security system against eavesdroppers with different capabilities. In particular, when facing a superior, dishonest eavesdropper, the security system is unsound and incomplete, which renders it vulnerable to various attacks. In [7], Schulz *et al.* demonstrated that the system is subject to attack analogous to a known-plaintext attack in the cryptography domain. In this work, we extend that idea and show that the system is also vulnerable to attack analogous to a ciphertext-only attack by exploiting the low entropy fields in wireless packets.

5.1 Entropy Analysis

We can compare the physical-layer security system to a cryptography system, where the transmitted data, $D_{\mathcal{B}}[k]$, equals to the plaintext, $\mathcal{M}^2$, Eve's received data, $R_{\mathcal{E}}[k]$, equals to the ciphertext, $\mathcal{C}$, and Bob's CSI, $H_{\mathcal{B}}[k]$, equals to the key, $\mathcal{K}$. By using sufficiently many antennas, Eve can effectively weaken the secure communication between Alice an Bob and be able to decode a nonvanishing fraction of any sent message. From a cryptographic perspective, it is analogous to the case when $H(\mathcal{M} \mid \mathcal{C})$ is arbitrarily small, and the system is not cryptographically secure due to the nonzero mutual information between $\mathcal{C}$ and $\mathcal{M}$.

Due to the linearity of the precoding mechanism, we have

$$H(\mathcal{K} \mid \mathcal{M}, \mathcal{C}) = H(\mathcal{K} \mid \mathcal{C}) - H(\mathcal{M} \mid \mathcal{C}) = 0.$$

Eve, therefore, can uniquely identify the key from the ciphertext if the entropy of the plaintext is low,

$$H(\mathcal{K} \mid \mathcal{C}) = H(\mathcal{M} \mid \mathcal{C}) \leq H(\mathcal{M}).$$

Intuitively, $H(\mathcal{M} \mid \mathcal{C})$ is upper bounded by $H(\mathcal{M})$. Hence, a smaller $H(\mathcal{M})$ decreases the unicity distance of the cryptographic system, which reduces the amount of ciphertext needed to learn the key. When Eve knows the exact plaintext, we have $H(\mathcal{M}) = 0$, and the attack model reduces to a known-plaintext attack as shown in [7].

Note that this vulnerability is unique to the orthogonal blinding based physical-layer security schemes. In a strong cryptography system, the adversary should not be able to learn the key, $\mathcal{K}$, from the cyphertext, $\mathcal{C}$, even if the entropy of the plaintext, $\mathcal{M}$, is low. However, the coding method of orthogonal blinding is complete deterministic and linear, which makes it vulnerable to various cryptography attacks.

Of course, the requisite of breaking orthogonal blinding with ciphertext-only attack is the existence of some low entropy segments in the plaintext. To investigate the likeliness of low entropy data, we analyzed WiFi frames. Thereto, we captured 10^5 raw frames with a minimal length of 103 bytes using a MacBook Pro in monitor mode in our office environment. We observed up to 123 individual MAC addresses in management frames with correct FCSs. For each byte, starting at the MAC header, we calculated the entropy and divided by 8 bits/byte to get the *information efficiency*.

The results are illustrated in Fig. 2. In the MAC header (bytes 1 to 24 resp. 32 (enc.)), we observe high entropy at the sequence number field (bytes 23 to 24), medium entropy at the destination MAC address field (bytes 5 to 10) and low entropy in the beginning (vendor fields) of the transmitter and source MAC addresses (bytes 11 to 14 and 17 to 20). Those medium and low entropy fields significantly reduce

---

^{2}In practice, $\mathcal{M}$ refers to the part of the transmitted data Eve uses to launch the attack.

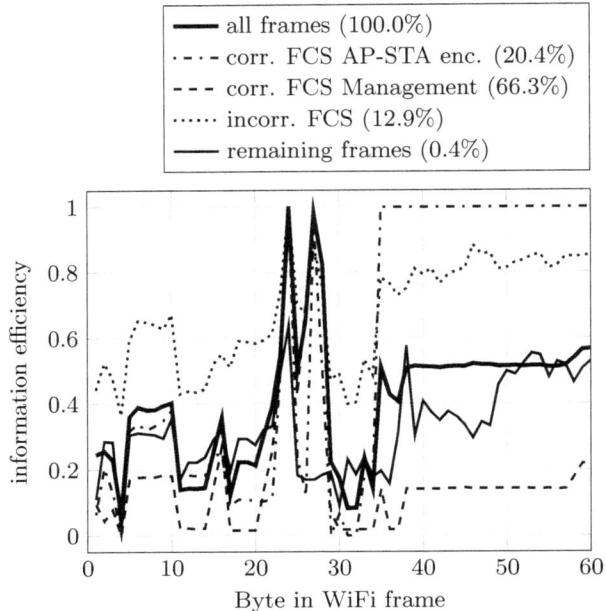

| all frames (100.0%) |
| corr. FCS AP-STA enc. (20.4%) |
| corr. FCS Management (66.3%) |
| incorr. FCS (12.9%) |
| remaining frames (0.4%) |

Figure 2: Information efficiency measurement for different bytes in Wi-Fi frames.

Eve's search space while training her receive filter presented in this work, while the high entropy fields are useless for us. Regarding the payload section (starting roughly at byte 36), encrypted frames offer the highest amount of entropy, while management frames have a very low entropy considering receptions with correct FCSs. In case of damaged frames, indicated by incorrect FCSs, the entropy increases which renders those frames less useful for our filter training.

5.2 Adversary Model

In [7], Schulz *et al.* present a known-plaintext attack against orthogonal blinding, in which Eve trains an adaptive filter, $F_{\mathcal{E}} \in \mathbb{C}^{m_{\mathcal{B}} \times m_{\mathcal{E}} \times k}$, using known plaintext and the corresponding ciphertext to separate the data from artificial noise,

$$\begin{pmatrix} D[k] \\ \mathrm{AN}[k] \end{pmatrix} = F_{\mathcal{E}}[k] \cdot R_{\mathcal{E}}[k].$$

The attack requires Eve to know the exact plaintext during training. Based on our analysis, we see that physical-layer security is limping when operating against superior eavesdropper and handling low entropy input. Hence, we can relax the adversary model to a ciphertext-only attack, where Eve knows only $R_{\mathcal{E}}$ and has a general knowledge about the format of the wireless packets. We shall see that, even in such a scenario, Eve can still successfully train the adaptive filter by locating the low entropy fields in the unknown plaintext.

5.3 Attack Algorithm

Here we present how Eve can launch the ciphertext-only attack by formulating and solving an optimization problem. From our previous entropy analysis, we see that the transmitted data is bound to have low entropy fields either in the header of the physical-layer or in the headers of the higher layers. In particular, consider that the transmitted data can

be divided into three parts

$$D_{\mathcal{B}}[k] = \begin{pmatrix} \overset{\leftarrow}{D}_{\mathcal{B}}[k] & \bar{D}_{\mathcal{B}}[k] & \vec{D}_{\mathcal{B}}[k] \end{pmatrix},$$

where $\overset{\leftarrow}{D}_{\mathcal{B}}[k]$ and $\bar{D}_{\mathcal{B}}[k]$ contain low entropy, and $\vec{D}_{\mathcal{B}}[k]$ contains high entropy. In practice, $\overset{\leftarrow}{D}_{\mathcal{B}}[k]$ and $\bar{D}_{\mathcal{B}}[k]$ represents the low entropy fields in various headers, and $\vec{D}_{\mathcal{B}}[k]$ represents the payload. The three-way partition is analogous to the training, validating and testing set in machine learning. Correspondingly, Eve's reception can be divided into three parts,

$$R_{\mathcal{E}}[k] = \begin{pmatrix} \overset{\leftarrow}{R}_{\mathcal{E}}[k] & \bar{R}_{\mathcal{E}}[k] & \vec{R}_{\mathcal{E}}[k] \end{pmatrix},$$

where $\overset{\leftarrow}{R}_{\mathcal{E}}[k]$, $\bar{R}_{\mathcal{E}}[k]$, and $\vec{R}_{\mathcal{E}}[k]$ are the corresponding superposition of data and artificial noise.

To launch the attack, Eve aims at finding $F_{\mathcal{E}}$ to minimize

$$\|F_{\mathcal{E}}[k]R_{\mathcal{E}}[k] - D_{\mathcal{B}}[k]\|_F^2.$$

However, since Eve does not know $D_{\mathcal{B}}$, the problem appears to be unsolvable. Instead, Eve may attempt to solve an alternative problem,

$$\begin{array}{ll} \text{minimize} & \mathrm{H}\left(F_{\mathcal{E}}[k]\left(\overset{\leftarrow}{R}_{\mathcal{E}}[k] \quad \bar{R}_{\mathcal{E}}[k]\right)\right) \\ \text{subject to} & F_{\mathcal{E}}[k]F_{\mathcal{E}}^H[k] \succ 0 \\ & \mathbf{E}\left(F_{\mathcal{E}}[k]\vec{R}_{\mathcal{E},c}[k]\vec{R}_{\mathcal{E},c}^H[k]F_{\mathcal{E}}^H[k]\right) \geq G \end{array}, \quad (19)$$

where the objective function gives the entropy of the decoded data, $\vec{R}_{\mathcal{E},c}[k]$ represents each column in $\vec{R}_{\mathcal{E}}[k]$, and G is the average modulation gain. The constrains prevent any trivial solution such as $F_{\mathcal{E}}[k] = \mathbf{0}$. Intuitively, if the filter is optimal, the objective function gives the entropy of $\left(\overset{\leftarrow}{D}_{\mathcal{B}}[k] \quad \bar{D}_{\mathcal{B}}[k]\right)$. Otherwise, the residual noise should increase the total entropy.

Unfortunately, since entropy is a concave function, it can be shown that Eq. 19 is NP-hard [15]. To still solve the problem, Eve may exploit the low entropy fields and apply a greedy hill climbing approach. Let $\{\overset{\leftarrow}{d}_{\mathcal{B}}[k]\}$ be a set of frequent columns in $\overset{\leftarrow}{D}_{\mathcal{B}}[k]$[3]. Eve cycles through the columns in $\overset{\leftarrow}{R}_{\mathcal{E}}[k]$ and iteratively update the filter by randomly sampling $\overset{\leftarrow}{d}_{\mathcal{B}}[k] \in \{\overset{\leftarrow}{d}_{\mathcal{B}}[k]\}$ and solving

$$\text{minimize} \quad \|F_{\mathcal{E}}^{i+1}[k]\overset{\leftarrow}{R}_{\mathcal{E},c}[k] - \overset{\leftarrow}{d}_{\mathcal{B}}[k]\|_2^2 + \|F_{\mathcal{E}}^{i+1}[k] - F_{\mathcal{E}}^i[k]\|_2^2, \quad (20)$$

where the proximal operator $\|F_{\mathcal{E}}^{i+1}[k] - F_{\mathcal{E}}^i[k]\|_2^2$ is used to confine the solution close to the previous filter and within the feasible region. There are two possible outcomes for such update: (1) Eve's guess is correct and the update moves the current filter closer to the optimal one. (2) Eve's guess is incorrect and the update moves the current filter farther from the optimal one or outside of the feasible region. Eve can check which outcome it is by applying the filter to $\bar{R}_{\mathcal{E}}[k]$ and comparing the resulting entropy, $\mathrm{H}\left(F_{\mathcal{E}}^{i+1}[k]\bar{R}_{\mathcal{E}}[k]\right)$. If the entropy decreases, Eve accepts the update and vise versa. Note that Eve's guesses do not need to fully match the actual plaintext. Due to the robustness of Eq. 20, Eve can make progress as long as a majority of symbols in her guesses match the plaintext. Once the algorithm converges, Eve can apply the filter to $\vec{R}_{\mathcal{E}}[k]$ to obtain the content of the payload.

---

[3]In practice, low entropy fields may occupy multiple columns or a fraction of columns. The iterative approach still applies since Eve knows the beginning of the packet through pilot symbols, and is able to locate the low entropy fields.

6. EXPERIMENTAL EVALUATION

Here, we present the performance of the ciphertext-only attack against orthogonal blinding. In Sec. 6.1 we briefly review the simulation parameters we use for our experiments. We consider three parameters that could affect the attack algorithm, i.e., channel signal-to-noise ratio (SNR), Alice's noise-to-data ratio (NDR), and information efficiency of the transmitted data. In Sec. 6.2, we show the signal reception at Bob's side under a variety of channel SNR and NDR. In Sec. 6.3, we show the convergence behavior and effectiveness of our attack algorithm. In Sec. 6.4, we discuss how the attack algorithm performs against blinded data with different information efficiency. In Sec. 6.5 and Sec. 6.6, we analyze the effect of channel SNR and Alice's NDR. Finally, we summarize our finding in Sec. 6.7.

6.1 Technical Parameters

As we described in Sec. 3, our three nodes Alice, Bob and Eve are multi-antenna nodes using OFDM transmitters. In particular, our evaluation setup considers Alice and Eve having two antennas, and Bob having one. We use synthetic wireless packets with predefined information efficiency as transmitted data. To create the synthetic packets, we randomly generate a set of 16-bit binary vectors and perform rejection sampling to collect samples that have H distinct values. This way, the corresponding wireless packets have an overall information efficiency of H/16. To transmit the data, We use OFDM to split a 40 MHz wide additive white Gaussian noise (AWGN) channel into 64 equally spaced sub-channels. The OFDM frames consist of pilot symbols for channel sounding and 500 data symbols for each sub-channel.

We use normalized quadrature phase shift keying (QPSK) as our primary modulation scheme. To generate the data symbols for each sub-channel, we encode the synthetic wireless packets trough a 2 bit Gray code encoder, and modulate the gray codes into QPSK data symbols. We assign every 8 successive data symbols to one sub-channel such that every sub-channel carries a parallel string of packets. To measure the effect of Alice's artificial noise, we vary the ratio between artificial noise and transmitted data signal, i.e. NDR. Since Alice's total transmit power is fixed, a higher NDR reduces the amount of power to transmit the data signal,

$$\frac{1}{\text{NDR}+1}\left(\frac{D[k]}{\text{NDR}\cdot\text{AN}[k]}\right).$$

To measure the effect of channel noise, we also vary the channel's SNR referenced by Alice's transmit power. Finally, we use Eve's symbol error rate (SER) to measure the progress and performance of the attack algorithm. The following results are based on 50 Monte Carlo simulations for each configuration.

6.2 Bob's Signal Reception

To evaluate the performance of our ciphertext-only attack, We first show Bob's SER under orthogonal blinding. As shown in Fig. 3, Bob's SER is affected by both the channel's SNR and Alice's NDR. As Alice increases the NDR, she dedicates more power to transmit the artificial noise instead of data symbols, which increases Bob's SER. As the channel's SNR decreases, the channel noise also increases Bob's SER. Note that under the same setting as in Fig. 4, where

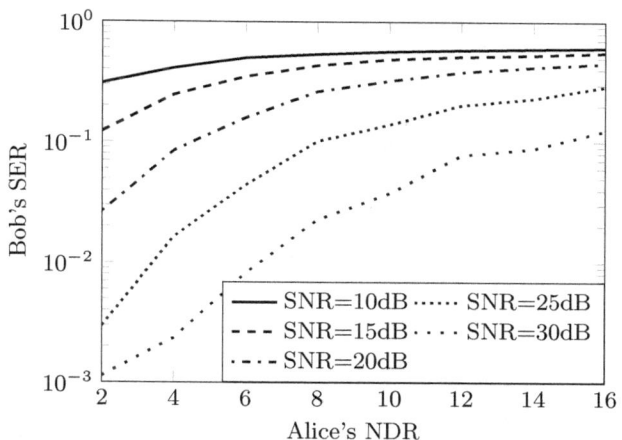

Figure 3: Bob's SER over Alice's NDR for different SNRs.

NDR = 4 and SNR = 30 dB Bob can achieve an average SER of 1.1×10^{-3}.

6.3 Convergence Behavior

In Fig. 4, we show how Eve's SER reduces over the number of iterations. Since the performance of the hill climbing algorithm varies with the initial conditions, the result is obtained by averaging over 50 Monte Carlo simulations. From Fig. 4, we see that minimizing the entropy of the decoded message serves as a good searching oracle. When the information efficiency equals 0.4, the hill climbing algorithm is able to converge within 5 iterations[4], which corresponds to 40 symbols in the received data. Due to the robustness of the least-square solution and proximal operator, Eve can always make progress as long as her guesses are not completely wrong. When the algorithm converges, Eve can reduce her SER to approximately 0.1. Note that the result is achieved without knowing the exact plaintext symbols transmitted by Alice. Yet, the SER achieved through ciphertext-only attack is only 1.3% higher than the SER achieved through the optimal filter, $H_{\mathcal{B}}^{\dagger}[k]$.

6.4 Effect of Information Efficiency

In Fig. 5, we illustrate how information efficiency of the training data affects the algorithm's rate of convergence and Eve's SER. The information efficiency practically correlates to Eve's guessing space. A high information efficiency reduces the probability for Eve to obtain a correct guess. In addition, a high information efficiency reduces the number of accidental matching symbols when Eve's guess is wrong. Due to the two factors, the algorithm's rate of convergence increases as the information efficiency increases. In our simulation, when the information efficiency increases from 0 to 0.6, the algorithm's rate of convergence increases from 1 iteration to 17 iterations. However, the information efficiency has no dramatic effect toward Eve's optimal SER. The reason is because, unlike channel SNR and NDR, the information efficiency does not introduce additional noise into Eve's reception. In our simulation, when the information efficiency increases from 0 to 0.6, Eve's SER merely increases by 3.1%.

[4] We define the algorithm convergence as the iteration when the objective value is within 10% of the optimal value.

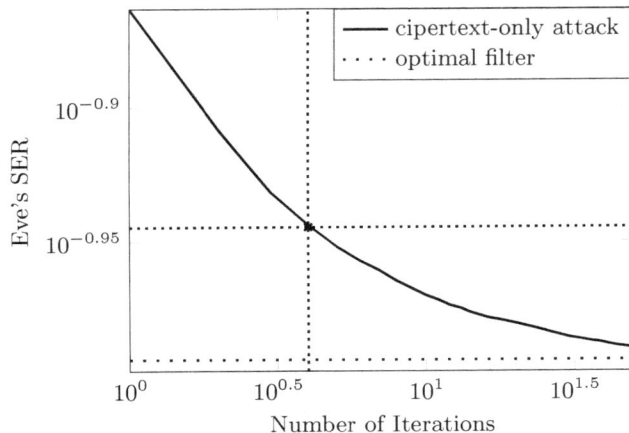

Figure 4: Eve's SER over the number of iterations. SNR = 30 dB; NDR = 4; information efficiency = 0.4. The dotted line marks Eve's SER when applying the optimal filter.

6.5 Effect of Channel Noise

In Fig. 6, we illustrate how channel SNR affects the algorithm's rate of convergence and Eve's SER. By increasing the channel noise, we can decrease the channel SNR, which affects both Eve and Bob. As shown in Fig. 3 and Fig. 5, a low channel SNR increase Bob's SER as well as Eve's optimal SER during the ciphertext-only attack. In our simulation, when the channel SNR decreases from 30 dB to 10 dB, Eve's optimal SER increases from 0.11 to 0.54. The channel SNR also affects algorithm's rate of convergence since low channel SNR reduces the algorithm's sensitivity. When the channel SNR is low, there is a high chance that the transmitted data is distorted even without orthogonal blinding. Therefore, the algorithm tends to quickly converge to a high SER instead of slowly converging to a low SER. In our simulation, when the channel SNR efficiency decreases from 30 dB to 10 dB, the rate of convergence decreases from 10 iterations to 4 iterations.

6.6 Effect of Artificial Noise

In Fig. 7, we show how Alice's NDR affects the performance of the attack algorithms. Same as Bob's signal reception, Eve's SER decreases as Alice increases her NDR. The reason is because the high NDR reduces the amount of power to transmit the data signal. In our simulation, when Alice's NDR increases from 2 to 10, Eve's optimal SER increases from 0.09 to 0.21. However, Alice's NDR has little effect on the algorithm's rate of convergence. In our simulation, when Alice's NDR increases from 2 to 10, the algorithm's rate of convergence stays between 8 to 10 iterations.

6.7 Summary

In Table 2, we summarize the findings of our experiments. In particular, when Eve is powerful and dishonest, she can effectively reduce her SER using the ciphertext-only attack. By minimizing the entropy of the decoded message, our hill climbing method allows Eve to estimate the channel between Alice and Bob, and find the optimal filter to separate the data and the artificial noise within 20 iterations. Our method can handle a wide range of channel SNR, Alice's

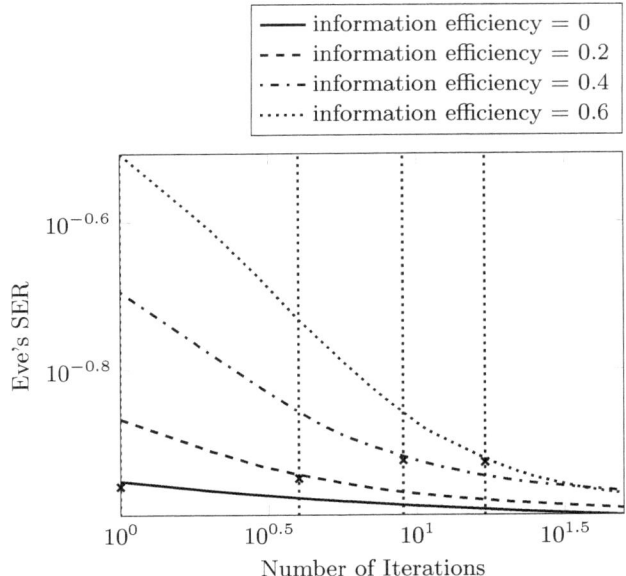

Figure 5: Eve's SER over the number of iterations. SNR = 30 dB; NDR = 4; various information efficiencies.

NDR, and a variety of transmitted data with different information efficiency. The only side channel knowledge that Eve uses to breach the system is a general knowledge about the format of the wireless packets.

7. DISCUSSION

In the previous sections, we analyzed the security level of orthogonal blinding under different MIMO configurations. Our attack showcase further proves that orthogonal blinding vulnerable against ciphertext-only attack launched by multi-antenna eavesdropper. We now reflect on the limitation of physical-layer security in general and discuss how our analysis framework can be applied to other physical-layer security schemes.

Unlike higher-layer security measures, physical-layer security approaches are usually "keyless" methods that operate within the principles of wireless communication. The sole purpose of communication is to allow receivers to recover the transmitted message as much as possible. Hence, the operations applied at transmitter's side must be reversible by the receiver. In addition, the wireless medium only permits linear combination between various signals. These two prior conditions significantly limits the level of confusion and diffusion a physical-layer security method can achieve. In fact, most physical-layer security methods do not employ any one-way operation, but rely on interference to thwart the eavesdropper. As a result, the strength of physical-layer security methods is bound to be lower that higher-layer security measures, such as encryption.

Despite of its limitations, physical-layer security may still achieve "practical security" depending on its application scenarios. For instance, we have shown that a user cannot use orthogonal blinding to transmit long, regular messages with low information efficiency. However, the method is still relatively secure when it transmits random bits in short burst, given that the length of the bit string is smaller than the number of transmitting antennas. Such feature can be

Table 2: Summary of the major findings in simulations.

Experiment	Section	Conclusion
Convergence behavior	Sec. 6.3	The algorithm is able to converge within 10 iterations (160 symbols) and achieves comparable SER as the optimal filters.
Effect of information efficiency	Sec. 6.4	A high information efficiency increases the algorithm's rate of convergence but does not affect Eve's optimal SER.
Effect of channel noise	Sec. 6.5	A low channel SNR increases the algorithm's rate of convergence and Eve's optimal SER.
Effect of artificial noise	Sec. 6.6	A high NDR increases Eve's optimal SER but does not affect the algorithm's rate of convergence.

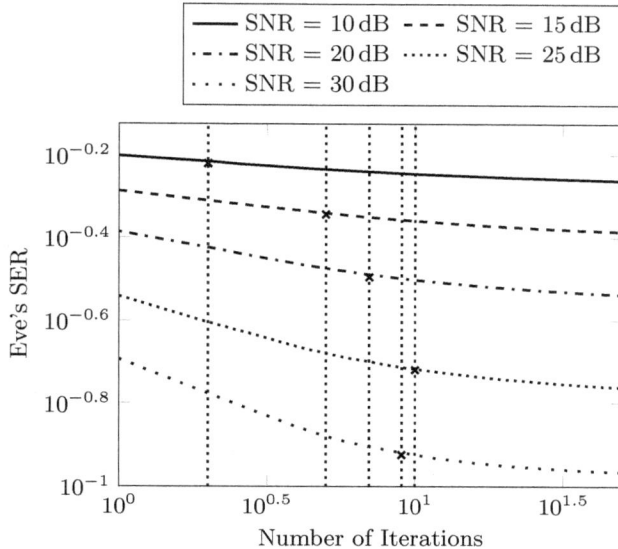

Figure 6: Eve's SER over the number of iterations, NDR = 4; information efficiency = 0.4; various SNRs.

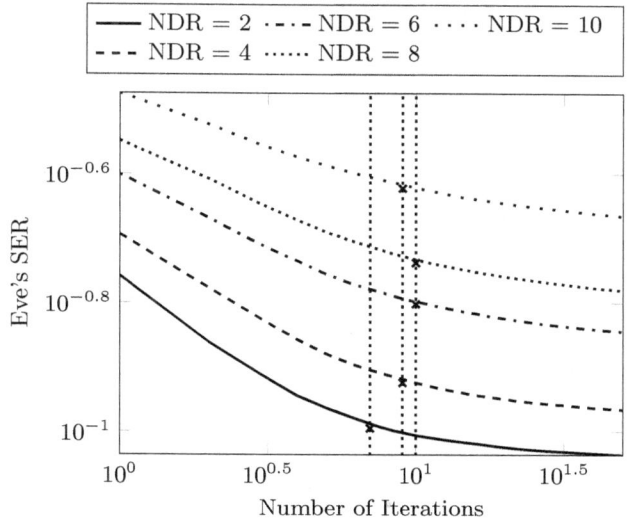

Figure 7: Eve's SER over the number of iterations. SNR = 30 dB; information efficiency = 0.4; various NDRs.

found useful in key exchange protocols. However, these application scenarios can only be identified after a thorough security analysis, which physical-layer security designer often neglect to do.

In our framework, we mainly rely on information theoretic analysis to determine the secrecy levels of linear precoding based physical-layer security method. The technique can also be extended when assessing physical-layer security schemes in general. The reason is because the obfuscation functions employed by physical-layer security are relatively simple and easy to handle mathematically. In most cases, these functions are linear or affine in nature, which makes theoretical analysis an ideal tool to determine the correlation between the received signal and the transmitted signal. Moreover, by categorizing eavesdroppers according to their capacities, we can better analyze the secrecy level of a physical-layer security method and provide a clearer picture about the its strength and weakness. For future work, we aim to apply our framework upon other physical-layer security schemes to help identify the application scenarios that are within their limitations.

8. CONCLUSION

In this work, we studied the strength of physical-layer security by means of theoretical analysis and practical attack. we evaluated a specific physical layer security scheme, *i.e.* orthogonal blinding, under multiple eavesdropper settings. We identified the weakness of orthogonal blinding by channeling the concepts from information theory into cryptanalysis. We discovered that, due to the linearity and the low entropy contents in the transmitted data, the system is vulnerable against attack equivalents to the "ciphertext-only attack" in the cryptography domain against a multi-antenna eavesdropper. We presented a practical attack method that allows eavesdroppers to recover the original message by exploiting the low entropy fields in wireless packets. By means of simulation, we demonstrated the effectiveness of the attack by reducing the eavesdropper's SER below 1% using only the eavesdropper's receiving data and a general knowledge about the wireless packets.

Acknowledgment

This work has been funded by the German Research Foundation (DFG) in the Collaborative Research Center (SFB) 1053 "MAKI – Multi-Mechanism-Adaptation for the Future Internet", by LOEWE CASED, and BMBF/HMWK CRISP. Zheng and Hou's work was partially supported by the National Science Foundation under grants CNS-1446478, CNS-1405747, CNS-1443889, and CNS-1343222. Lou's work was supported by (while serving at) the National Science Foundation. Any opinion, findings, and conclusions or recommendations expressed in this material are those of the author(s) and do not necessarily reflect the views of the National Science Foundation.

References

[1] Xiangyun Zhou, Lingyang Song, and Yan Zhang. *Physical layer security in wireless communications*. Crc Press, 2013.

[2] Shyamnath Gollakota et al. "They can hear your heartbeats: non-invasive security for implantable medical devices". In: *ACM SIGCOMM Computer Communication Review* 41.4 (2011), pp. 2–13.

[3] Shyamnath Gollakota and Dina Katabi. "Physical layer wireless security made fast and channel independent". In: *INFOCOM, 2011 Proceedings IEEE*. IEEE. 2011, pp. 1125–1133.

[4] Nils Ole Tippenhauer et al. "On limitations of friendly jamming for confidentiality". In: *Security and Privacy (SP), 2013 IEEE Symposium on*. IEEE. 2013, pp. 160–173.

[5] Daniel Steinmetzer, Matthias Schulz, and Matthias Hollick. "Lockpicking Physical Layer Key Exchange: Weak Adversary Models Invite the Thief". In: *Proceedings of the 2015 ACM Conference on Security and Privacy in Wireless Mobile Networks*. WiSec '15. 2015.

[6] N. Anand, Sung-Ju Lee, and E.W. Knightly. "STROBE: actively securing wireless communications using Zero-Forcing Beamforming". In: *Proc. INFOCOM'12*. 2012, pp. 720–728.

[7] Matthias Schulz, Adrian Loch, and Matthias Hollick. "Practical Known-Plaintext Attacks against Physical Layer Security in Wireless MIMO Systems". In: *Proc. NDSS'14*. 2014.

[8] Yao Zheng et al. "Highly Efficient Known-Plaintext Attacks Against Orthogonal Blinding Based Physical Layer Security". In: *IEEE Wireless Communications Letters* 4.1 (Feb. 2015), pp. 34–37.

[9] Aaron D Wyner. "The wire-tap channel". In: *Bell System Technical Journal, The* 54.8 (1975), pp. 1355–1387.

[10] S. Leung-Yan-Cheong and M. Hellman. "The Gaussian wire-tap channel". In: *IEEE Transactions on Information Theory* 24.4 (July 1978), pp. 451–456.

[11] Ashish Khisti and Gregory W Wornell. "Secure transmission with multiple antennas I: The MISOME wiretap channel". In: *Information Theory, IEEE Transactions on* 56.7 (2010), pp. 3088–3104.

[12] Ashish Khisti and Gregory W Wornell. "Secure transmission with multiple antennas—Part II: The MIMOME wiretap channel". In: *Information Theory, IEEE Transactions on* 56.11 (2010), pp. 5515–5532.

[13] Yu-Chih Tung et al. "Vulnerability and Protection of Channel State Information in Multiuser MIMO Networks". In: *Proceedings of the 2014 ACM SIGSAC Conference on Computer and Communications Security*. CCS '14. 2014.

[14] The Institute of Electrical and Inc. Electronic Engineers. "IEEE Standard 802.11-2013". English. In: *IEEE Standard for Information technology* (2013).

[15] Mladen Kovacevic, Ivan Stanojevic, and Vojin Senk. "On the hardness of entropy minimization and related problems". In: *Information Theory Workshop (ITW),*

Interleaving Jamming in Wi-Fi Networks

Triet D. Vo-Huu   Tien D. Vo-Huu   Guevara Noubir

College of Computer and Information Science
Northeastern University
Boston, MA 02115, USA
{vohuudtr|tienvh|noubir}@ccs.neu.edu

ABSTRACT

The increasing importance of Wi-Fi in today's wireless communication systems, both as a result of Wi-Fi offloading and its integration in IoT devices, makes it an ideal target for malicious attacks. In this paper, we investigate the structure of the combined interleaver/convolutional coding scheme of IEEE 802.11a/g/n. The analysis of the first and second-round permutations of the interleaver, allows us to design deterministic jamming patterns across subcarriers that when de-interleaved results in an interference burst. We show that a short burst across carefully selected sub-carriers exceeds the error correction capability of Wi-Fi. We implemented this attack as a reactive interleaving jammer on the firmware of the low-cost HackRF SDR. Our experimental evaluation shows that this attack can completely block the Wi-Fi transmissions with jamming power less than 1% of the communication (measured at the receiver) and block 95% of the packets with less than 0.1% energy. Furthermore, it is at least 5 dB and up to 15 dB more power-efficient than jamming attacks that are unaware of the Wi-Fi interleaving structure.

1. INTRODUCTION

The broadcast nature of the wireless medium makes it vulnerable to two types of major attacks *denial of service*, and *information leakage*. Designing countermeasures to wireless DoS attacks before they become widespread is very important for both military and commercial applications. Due to a series of recent incidents, the FCC has stepped up its education and enforcement effort [11], rolled out a new jammer tip line (1-855-55NOJAM), and issued several fines [12]. At the same time jammers are becoming a commodity and are growing in sophistication and convenience of use and deployment. Beyond degrading a critical communication infrastructure, wireless DoS can also be the prelude to more sophisticated attacks where the adversary deploys rogue infrastructure [6]. Evidence of such attacks in the real world started emerging in the recent years [13, 33].

Within the wireless ecosystem, Wi-Fi (IEEE 802.11) has emerged as the defacto primary technology for connecting devices to the Internet. This manifests itself first in the increasing Wi-Fi offloading

of mobile traffic, caused by the limited ability of cellular ISPs to scale to applications demands, and second in the integration of Wi-Fi in a variety of low-cost Internet of Things (IoT) and Machine to Machine (M2M) devices.

In this work, we are interested in investigating the most efficient, yet practical, jammer against IEEE 802.11a/g/n physical layer. We analyzed the structure of the combined interleaver/convolutional coding scheme of 802.11a/g/n, and observed two key properties: (1) the coded bits' deterministic and predictable interleaving pattern common to all frames, and (2) the interleaving is deterministic across OFDM subcarriers. Further analysis, of the first and second round permutations of the interleaver, allows us to design jamming patterns across subcarriers that when de-interleaved results in an interference burst. We show that a short burst across carefully selected subcarriers exceeds the convolutional code error correction capability. The 802.11 OFDM interleaving across subcarriers makes interleaving attacks highly practical. In order to evaluate the efficiency of this attack, we developed an experimental testbed that enables a systematic comparison of various types of IEEE 802.11 jamming attacks. We implemented a reactive jammer that specifically targets 802.11a/g/n frames. This jammer runs as part of the firmware of the low-cost HackRF One and achieves a response time of less than $30\mu s$. Using a tested including our HackRF-based jammer, off-the-shelf Wi-Fi cards transmitter/receivers, and also our own Wi-Fi SDR receiver [39], we investigated several interleaved jamming techniques (including single and multi OFDM symbols) and compared them to whole band jamming and pilot jamming. We show that interleaving jamming is 5-15 dB more efficient than the most efficient known techniques. In the absolute, we show that an adversary can destroy over 95% of the packets with an energy cost less than three orders of magnitude in comparison to the communicating nodes; blocking all communication requires less than two order of magnitude energy in comparison the communication nodes. Interleaving jamming can be combined with attacks on rate adaptation [25, 27], and potentially with other attacks [32], and can be embedded in traditional Access Points firmware [4]. Besides understanding the threat of such attacks against IEEE 802.11a/g/n, interleaving jamming can also be used for spatial access control [4, 18], as well as in other IEEE 802.11 OFDM systems. We summarize our contributions as follows:

- We analyze IEEE 802.11a/g/n physical layer (modulation, coding, interleaving) for OFDM. We discover that the deterministic combined first/second round permutation when combined with multi-carrier coding in OFDM, enables efficient interleaving jamming attacks.

- We developed a reactive jammer using the low-cost HackRF One SDR platform that can realize the interleaving jamming

WiSec'16 , July 18–20, 2016, Darmstadt, Germany

© 2016 ACM. ISBN 978-1-4503-4270-4/16/07. . . $15.00

DOI: http://dx.doi.org/10.1145/2939918.2939935

Table 1: Relations between Rate [Mbps], Modulation and Coding Scheme, Interleaving size m [bits] and Number of bits per subcarrier b [bits]

Rate	MCS	b	m	Rate	MCS	b	m
6	BPSK 1/2	1	48	24	16-QAM 1/2	4	192
9	BPSK 3/4	1	48	36	16-QAM 3/4	4	192
12	QPSK 1/2	2	96	48	64-QAM 2/3	6	288
18	QPSK 3/4	2	96	54	64-QAM 3/4	6	288

attack in real time. This jammer is implemented in the HackRF firmware and has a response time of $30\mu s$ making it practical even for high rates short packets.

- We demonstrate that the interleaving jamming attack can significantly degrade and even block Wi-Fi communications at an energy cost of 2 to 4 orders of magnitude less than the communicating nodes (not even accounting for the additional benefits of being reactive and/or combining with impact on rate adaption). We also show the interleaving jammer is 5-15 dB more efficient than existing Wi-Fi attacks (including pilot jamming). The performance evaluation is carried both on our custom made Wi-Fi receiver and commercial Wi-Fi cards.

2. IEEE 802.11 PHYSICAL LAYER INTERLEAVING

In this section, we briefly overview the interleaving mechanism used at the Physical Layer in OFDM-based IEEE 802.11 networks. Figure 1 illustrates a packet transmission flow carried out at the Physical Layer. The interleaving mechanism is performed by the Interleaver component as part of the Encoding phase. The goal of interleaving is to improve the receiver's capability of correcting bursty errors that might happen due to channel distortions during the signal propagation. The principle of interleaving is to scatter the bursts of errors by separating bits in a small vicinity to larger distances and vice versa. Specifically, the interleaving process defined in the IEEE 802.11 standard first divides the coded bit sequence produced by the convolutional encoder into multiple same-size groups. The number of bits per group, or the *interleaving size*, depends on the Modulation and Coding Scheme (MCS) specified in the RATE field of the Physical Header. More precisely, let b be the number of bits per subcarrier (BPSC), i.e., the number of bits transmitted per constellation point, the interleaving size m is determined by $m = 48b$ (cf. Table 1). Within each group of m bits, the interleaving process is performed in two rounds of permutations.

First-round permutation: The purpose of the first-round permutation is to scatter adjacent coded bits into non-adjacent subcarriers in order to counter interference affecting multiple adjacent subcarriers. This permutation is performed by

$$K' = (K \bmod 16)\frac{m}{16} + \lfloor K/16 \rfloor,$$

where $K, K' = 0, \ldots, m-1$ are the positions of a bit before and after the first-round permutation, respectively. Intuitively, this permutation is thought as if the m-bit input group was arranged in a matrix of 16 rows and $(m/16)$ columns, where bits are stored in column-major order, then the positions of m output bits were read in row-major order. Figure 2 illustrates an example of first-round permutation for BPSK modulation ($m = 48$).

Second-round permutation: The second-round permutation's purpose is to shuffle adjacent coded bits within every subcarrier in order to avoid biased distortion that might occur on the same bit of multiple constellation points. The permutation rule is defined by

the following formula

$$K'' = s\lfloor \frac{K'}{s} \rfloor + (K' + m - \lfloor 16\frac{K'}{m} \rfloor) \bmod s,$$

where $s = \max(b/2, 1)$. Note that for BPSK and QPSK modulations, where $s = 1$, the second-round permutation has no effect (i.e., interleaving BPSK and QPSK data is equivalent to first-round permuting only). For 16-QAM and 64-QAM modulations, the second-round permutation is interpreted as cyclically shifting each half of a constellation point. The number of bits shifted is either 0 or 1 for 16-QAM, and either 0, 1, or 2 for 64-QAM, dependently on the subcarrier index. Figure 3 shows all possible permutations for the second round.

We observe from the above Wi-Fi interleaving rule that while the first-round permutation separates adjacent bits into two different subcarriers, the second round permutes bits within the same subcarrier. This can be viewed as an outer permutation followed by an inner permutation.

3. INTERLEAVING JAMMING

In this section, we study the effectiveness of the interleaving structure defined by IEEE 802.11 from the viewpoint of an adversary, and based on that, we propose an efficient jamming strategy. We will later show in Section 5 that it can significantly degrade the performance of Wi-Fi and even block it at very low energy cost.

3.1 Understanding the Interleaving Pattern

First, we illustrate the operation of the interleaver, using as an example rate 54 Mbps, which used 64-QAM modulation and a convolutional code with rate 3/4. According to the interleaving rule described in Section 2, the interleaving table (mapping results after two rounds of permutations) is constructed and partially shown in Figure 4, in which each data subcarrier (DSC) carries 6 bits. Note that for the indexing of DSCs, since the interleaving is performed only on the data subcarriers, we index the DSCs from 0 to 47, skipping the pilot and null subcarriers[1].

We emphasize that while the transmission rate can vary across packets according to the channel state (by means of rate adaptation algorithms), each individual packet is transmitted using one constant rate for all of the OFDM symbols. Therefore, the same interleaving table is used for every group within a packet. For instance, when a 1500-bytes packet is transmitted at 54 Mbps, it contains 58 groups of 288 bits, each of which corresponds to one OFDM symbol. All the OFDM symbols are interleaved in the same manner.

In Figure 4, each square represents a bit after interleaving, while its numeric content indicates the original bit position before interleaving. For instance, the first 6 squares contain bits originally located at positions 0, 16, 32, 48, 64, and 80. By the first-round permutation, any two bits carried by the same subcarrier symbol are originally from those positions whose difference is a multiple of 16. By the second-round permutation, bits of each half of a subcarrier can be rotated, e.g., $(1, 17, 33) \rightarrow (17, 33, 1)$. An important pattern is observed that the coded bits at original positions $0, 1, 2, 3, 4, \ldots$ are interleaved into new positions $0, 20, 37, 54, 74, \ldots$, respectively corresponding to DSC $0, 3, 6, 9, 12, \ldots$, which are separated at distances of multiples of 3. Interestingly, this property does not only hold for rate 54 Mbps, but also holds for all non-BPSK modulations, as stated in Theorem 1.

[1]The 20 MHz of Wi-Fi channel is divided into a total 64 subcarriers, among which 48 subcarriers are used for data transmission, 4 pilot subcarriers are inserted among DSCs for channel estimation, and the remaining 12 null subcarriers are used as guards to avoid inter-channel interference.

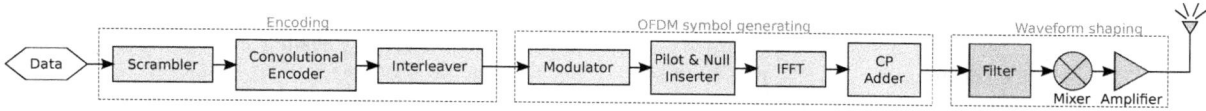

Figure 1: A packet transmission flow consists of three phases: (1) in the Encoding phase, the PSDU (Physical Service Data Unit) received from the MAC Layer is transformed into a sequence of coded bits with a certain amount of redundancy for error correction, then the coded bit sequence is embedded into the Physical Frame with an appropriate Physical Header and payload padding; (2) in the second phase, OFDM (Orthogonal Frequency Division Multiplexing) symbol signals are generated by a series of digital signal processing operations on the Physical Frame; and (3), finally the Wi-Fi signals are upconverted to the channel's carrier frequency and transmitted by the RF front end.

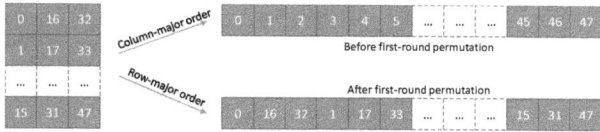

Figure 2: First-round permutation for BPSK modulation ($m = 48$).

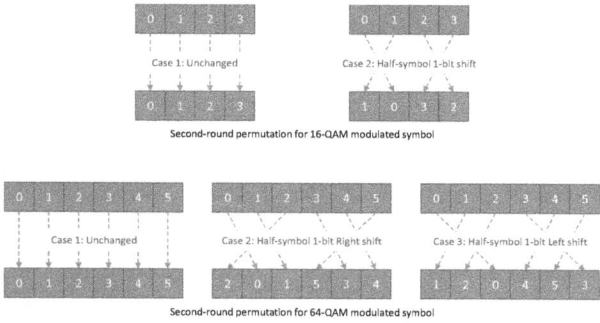

Figure 3: Second-round permutation for 16-QAM and 64-QAM modulations. Depending on the subcarrier index, this permutation can rotate every half-symbol by 0, 1, or 2 bits.

Figure 4: Interleaving table for a 64-QAM transmission. A data packet is divided into multiple same-size groups. In each group of 288 bits, every 6 bits are embedded into one data subcarrier (DSC). The shaded squares indicate the adjacent bits in the original data packet are now interleaved into DSCs separated by distances of multiples of 3.

THEOREM 1. *For IEEE 802.11 non-BPSK transmissions, adjacent bits at positions K and $K + 1$ in the original coded data sequence, where $K \notin \{\frac{1}{3}m - 1, \frac{2}{3}m - 1\}$, are interleaved into separate data subcarriers, whose distance (in the spectrum) is a multiple of 3.*

PROOF. We adopt the notations introduced in Section 2, where K, K', K'' are respectively bit positions prior to interleaving (K), after the first-round permutation (K'), and after the second-round permutation (K''). Also let $M(x) = \lfloor \frac{x}{b} \rfloor$ denote the index of the DSC carrying the bit at position x.

We consider two adjacent bits at positions K and $K + 1$ in the coded data sequence (output of the convolutional encoder) prior to interleaving. After interleaving, these bits will be transmitted by subcarriers $M(K'')$ and $M((K + 1)'')$. In the following, we investigate the relation between $M(K')$ and $M((K+1)')$ after the first permutation. Recall that $m = 48b$, we consider two cases:

Case 1: If $K + 1 \neq 0 \mod 16$, then $\lfloor (K+1)/16 \rfloor = \lfloor K/16 \rfloor$, and we obtain

$$(K + 1)' = ((K + 1) \mod 16)\frac{m}{16} + \lfloor (K + 1)/16 \rfloor$$
$$= K' + \frac{m}{16} = K' + 3b.$$

The subcarrier index is then derived as $M((K + 1)') = \lfloor (K' + 3b)/b \rfloor = M(K') + 3$, i.e., the adjacent bits at positions K and $K + 1$ are permuted into DSCs of distance 3.

Case 2: If $K + 1 = 0 \mod 16$, then $\lfloor (K+1)/16 \rfloor = \lfloor K/16 \rfloor + 1$, $K = 15 \mod 16$, and

$$(K + 1)' = ((K + 1) \mod 16)\frac{m}{16} + \lfloor (K + 1)/16 \rfloor$$
$$= \lfloor K/16 \rfloor + 1 = K' - (K \mod 16)\frac{m}{16} + 1$$
$$= K' - 45b + 1.$$

The subcarrier carrying the bit originally at position $K + 1$ is $M((K + 1)') = \lfloor \frac{K'+1}{b} \rfloor - 45$. We see that if $K' \neq -1 \mod b$, then $\lfloor (K'+1)/b \rfloor = \lfloor K'/b \rfloor$, and $M((K+1)') = M(K')-45$, in which case adjacent bits K and $K+1$ are permuted into subcarriers of distance 45. For example, Figure 4 shows that two adjacent bits originally at positions $K = 15$ and $K + 1 = 16$ are now located in DSC $M(K') = 45$ and $M((K + 1)') = 0$. Similar patterns are observed for bits at original positions $K = 31, 47, 63, \ldots$, except when $K = 95$ and $K = 191$, the distance becomes 44.

In fact, we show that there are only two values of K that result in adjacent bits K and $K + 1$ being moved to two DSCs with distance of 44. This subcase happens when both conditions $K+1 = 0 \mod 16$ and $K' = -1 \mod b$ hold. First, as $K + 1 = 0 \mod 16$, we write $K = 16k + 15$ for some integer k, then express $K' = (K \mod 16)\frac{m}{16} + \lfloor K/16 \rfloor = 45b + \lfloor K/16 \rfloor = 45b + k$. Next, due to the second condition $K' = -1 \mod b$, i.e., $45b + k =$

$-1 \mod b$, it is required that $k = qb-1$ for some integer q. Finally, combining the above requirements, we obtain $K = 16(qb - 1) + 15 = qm/3 - 1$. Given the constraint $0 \leq K \leq m - 1$, these conditions are satisfied by only two values of K: $K = m/3 - 1$ or $K = 2m/3 - 1$.

Since the second-round permutation shuffles the bits only within each data subcarrier, $M(K'') = M(K')$ and $M((K + 1)'') = M((K + 1)')$, i.e., the mapping between DSCs and bits after the first-round permutation is not altered by the second-round permutation. Therefore, we only need to investigate the bit-subcarrier mapping after the first permutation.

In summary, except for $K = m/3 - 1$ and $K = 2m/3 - 1$, adjacent bits at positions K and $K + 1$ will be interleaved into data subcarriers separated by a distance of multiple of 3. $\square$

Using Theorem 1, one can derive which subcarriers will carry the adjacent bits, and how far they are after the interleaving process. From the point of view of the adversary, however, the reverse mapping is desired, that determines in case of some particular subcarriers being jammed, which bits are destroyed and whether they are adjacent to each other. This reverse mapping is provided by Theorem 2 as follows.

THEOREM 2. *For IEEE 802.11 non-BPSK transmissions, any two data subcarriers, whose distance is either 3 or 45, always consist at least two bits originally located adjacently in the coded data sequence.*

PROOF. The proof for this theorem is derived directly from Theorem 1. Let K and L be the positions of two bits before interleaving. Under the theorem's assumption, either $M(L'') = M(K'') + 3$ or $M(L'') = M(K'') - 45$ holds.

If $M(K'') \neq M((m/3 - 1)'')$ and $M(K'') \neq M((2m/3 - 1)'')$, then by Theorem 1, we have $K \neq m/3-1$ and $K \neq 2m/3-1$. Now, due to the assumption of distance 3 or 45, we conclude $L = K + 1$. In other words, the data subcarriers $M(K'')$ and $M(L'')$ consist of bits originally at positions K and $K + 1$.

If $M(K'') = M((m/3-1)'')$ or $M(K'') = M((2m/3-1)'')$, then letting $\hat{K} = K - 1$ and $\hat{L} = L - 1$, we have $M(\hat{K}'') = M(K'')$ and $M(\hat{L}'') = M(L'')$. By similar arguments above, we have $\hat{L} = \hat{K} + 1$. We conclude that the data subcarriers $M(\hat{K}'')$ and $M(\hat{L}'')$ carry bits originally at positions $\hat{K}$ and $\hat{K} + 1$, or equivalently $M(K'')$ and $M(L'')$ consist positions $K - 1$ and K.

Consequently, the two data subcarriers with distance 3 or 45 always contain at least two bits originally adjacent to each other. $\square$

3.2 The Interleaving Jamming Strategy

Theorem 2 imply that if two data subcarriers separated by distance 3 (or 45) are not correctly decoded at the receiver, there will be two adjacent bit errors in the bit sequence fed to the convolutional decoder. In general, a sequence of n consecutive bit errors is created when interference is caused to a group of n DSCs separated by distances that are multiples of 3. As the design of IEEE 802.11 standard has mainly focused on protecting the communications against non-malicious interference, the specified interleaving structure is only sufficient for dealing with typically random noise in the environment, where only a few of subcarriers at random positions are defective at a given time, and is adequate for a repeating worst-case scenario. Against multi-carrier malicious interference, according to the pattern we identified, the Wi-Fi interleaving process is unable to prevent bursts of bit errors, making the convolutional codes ineffective. Exploiting this property, we devise an *interleaving jamming* strategy as follows.

DEFINITION 1 (INTERLEAVING JAMMING). *Interleaving jamming is a multi-carrier jamming strategy that generates interference on data subcarriers $i, i + 3, i + 6, \ldots, i + 3(n - 1)$, where i is any starting data subcarrier, and n is the number of subcarriers targeted for jamming.*

In Section 5 we evaluate the effectiveness of this interleaving jamming attack and the impacts of parameters i and n.

4. INTERLEAVING JAMMER DESIGN

In this section, we describe the design of the interleaving jammer that we use to demonstrate the efficiency of this attack against Wi-Fi communications. The jammer is implemented on the low-cost HackRF One software defined radio [16]. In order to enable real-time jamming, we design our jammer to be capable of quickly detecting the transmitted frames and reactively jamming with a variable duration pulse without the need of decoding the whole packet.

4.1 Frame Detection

The frame detection is based on the special format of preamble at the beginning of every transmitted frame. Specifically, the IEEE 802.11a/g/n preamble comprises two parts: short preamble and long preamble. Our frame detection relies on the short preamble, which contains 10 repeated patterns, each of which consists of 16 samples. We emphasize that while the short preamble in the IEEE 802.11n Greenfield mode is different from a/g modes, the repetition of 10 patterns is still preserved. Our detection technique described below is, therefore, able to detect frames transmitted in all modes.

The main idea of frame detection is based on the auto-correlation property of the short preamble. Let $\mathbf{p} = (p_1, p_2, \ldots, p_L)$ be a time-domain pattern of $L = 16$ samples repeated 10 times in the short preamble. At the receiver, we obtain the received signal r_n as a sample sequence consisted of preamble and data parts of transmitted frames separated by the inter-frame spacing (IFS).

$$\{r_n\} = \underbrace{\ldots\ldots\ldots}_{\text{inter-frame spacing}}, \underbrace{\hat{p}_1, \ldots, \hat{p}_L, \hat{p}_{L+1}, \ldots, \hat{p}_{2L}, \ldots}_{\text{preamble starting with 10 short patterns}}, \underbrace{\ldots, \hat{x}_k, \ldots}_{\text{data}}$$

Let A_n denote the correlation between two consecutive L-sample chunks, and E_n be the energy of the current chunk at each time n: $A_n = \sum_{k=0}^{L-1} r_{n+k+L} r_{n+k}^*$, $E_n = \sum_{k=0}^{L-1} |r_{n+k}|^2$. Due to the auto-correlation property of the preamble, the ratio $|A_n/E_n|$ exceeds a high threshold value when the preamble is found at time n, otherwise it remains low. Specifically, a frame is detected, if $|A_n/E_n| \geq \alpha$. We determine the parameter α based on our testbed experiments, in which $\alpha \in [0.8, 0.9]$ results in best detection.

In practice, false detection may occur due to several reasons. First, the low noise floor E_n, especially when the channel is idle, may unexpectedly result in a high ratio $|A_n/E_n|$. Moreover, if the data part of the transmitted signal contains a repetition of exactly 16 samples, the above condition can also be triggered. To reduce the false positive detection rate, we include into the frame detection two additional mechanisms: power squelch, and plateau detection.

Power squelch: Based on the energy of the signal received during two consecutive chunks, we can quickly differentiate between the channel idle states and transmission activities, thus mitigating the false detection rate due to noise. Specifically, a transmission is identified at time n when $E_n/E_{n-L} > \beta$. In our experiments, β can be chosen between 3 and 25, for which transmission activities are detectable with high accuracy. We note that as the power squelch is an energy-based detection, it does not distinguish Wi-

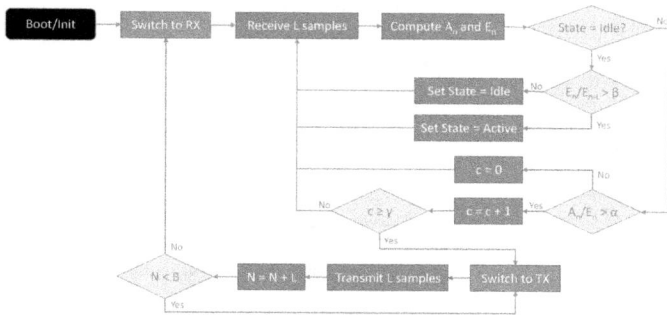

Figure 5: Flow chart of our jammer prototype.

Fi and non-Wi-Fi packets. Wi-Fi packets are recognized by the plateau detection described as follows.

Plateau detection: Based on the auto-correlation of short preamble symbols, a high ratio $|A_n/E_n|$ indicates two repeated patterns to be found. Since repetitions in other parts of the received signal might also result in a high ratio, we increase the detection confidence by requiring the appearance of multiple repeated patterns in a row. The frame is believed to be present in the received signal when the count c of consecutive repeated patterns exceeds a threshold γ. Specifically, if $|A_{n_1}/E_{n_1}| \geq \alpha, \ldots, |A_{n_c}/E_{n_c}| \geq \alpha$ for $c \geq \gamma$, $n_i = n_1 + (i-1)L$, then the frame is detected. We use $\gamma = 4$ in our prototype, as we found that it leads to the best detection performance.

4.2 Real-time Jamming

The HackRF, on which we build the jammer, is a software defined radio capable of capturing wireless signals, converting them to digital samples and transferring them to a computer for the remaining steps of the receiver chain (including signal processing and data decoding). On the reverse direction, the HackRF takes generated samples from the PC and emits the analog signals using the radio RF front end. While this architecture provides flexibility for developing a variety of useful radio applications, the latency due to sample transfer between the HackRF and the PC over USB 2.0 is in orders of milliseconds, which significantly exceeds the requirements of real-time jamming that needs to quickly react within orders of microseconds. For instance, a 1500-byte TCP packet length is approximately $250\mu s$ at 54 Mbps.

To overcome the timing issue, we modified the HackRF firmware such that all functionalities required for the real-time interleaving jamming are done on the HackRF itself without interacting with the PC. In other words, samples are not transferred over the USB link, but are handled by the HackRF's micro-controller, which also takes care of controlling the radio to transmit jamming signals.

Figure 5 shows the flow chart of our custom firmware developed for the interleaving jamming prototype on HackRF. The whole radio application, including frame detection and interference generation, is implemented on the NXP LPC4320 micro-controller on the HackRF One's board. The jammer can switch between RX (receiving) and TX (transmitting) modes. Initially at the system boot, the device is set to RX mode in order to listen to the channel for detecting IEEE 802.11 frames. During the listening phase, the micro-controller periodically captures and processes every $L = 16$ samples at a time. The frame detection efficiency heavily relies on the computation of auto-correlation A_n and energy E_n of the chunks of samples. Using the SIMD instructions supported by the ARM Cortex-M4 processor, we achieve both A_n and E_n in a total 128 CPU cycles. As the HackRF's micro-controller is set to run at 204 MHz, it takes roughly $0.64\mu s$ to process each 16 samples, or $0.04\mu s$ per sample. Combining with the remaining operations in the flow chart, the frame detection's running time is close to $0.05\mu s$ per sample, which is the upper-bound required for real-time processing Wi-Fi signals transmitted at 20 MHz.

When a frame is detected, the device switches to the TX mode for transmitting the jamming signal. As interleaving jamming is a multi-carrier jamming attack, the interference is generated in the frequency domain such that each selected subcarrier contains random noise (while the rest are nulled), then the signal is transformed into the time domain for transmitting. To avoid the FFT computation burden, we do not generate the interference on the fly. Instead, we store pre-generated samples in memory and subsequently use them for jamming. Furthermore, we also optimize the TX/RX switching operation in order to minimize the switching time and improve the responsiveness of the jammer. To destroy a frame, it is sufficient to jam a small portion of the frame. The length of the jamming burst, denoted B, is configurable by the adversary from the PC. Immediately after completing the transmission of the B multi-subcarrier interference samples, the jammer turns back to the RX mode to detect the next frames.

5. PERFORMANCE EVALUATION

To evaluate the efficiency of the interleaving jamming attacks on Wi-Fi communications, we compare it with other types of multi-carrier jamming attacks (cf. Table 2), which are categorized based on the number and pattern of subcarriers selected by the adversary.

Our metrics for the attack efficiency is the Packet Error Rate (PER) observed at the receiver. For a fair comparison between jamming strategies, the packet error rate is evaluated based on the transmitted signal to jamming power ratio (SJR) as measured on the receiver. Our general setup consists of a pair of transmitter and receiver, which are desktop computers equipped with off-the-shelf Wi-Fi cards. The transmitter constantly sends UDP packets to the receiver. The jammer sits nearby to monitor the channel and accordingly jam all detected packets. All experiments are carried out on a 20 MHz communication of channel 11.

The performance of Wi-Fi communications is dependent on various factors such as the interference level, transmission rate, and channel access mechanisms. To quantify the impact of jamming only, we control the testbed experiments as follows. First, we verify that the natural noise in the environment is at least 40 dB lower than the Wi-Fi transmitted signal power, therefore it barely affects the reception rate at the receiver. We use the performance obtained in normal conditions without jamming as the baseline for comparison of jamming efficiency. Specifically, if T_{JAM} and T_{NOJAM} denote the number of correct packets seen at the receiver under jammed and unjammed conditions, the PER is calculated as PER $= \frac{T_{\mathrm{JAM}}}{T_{\mathrm{NOJAM}}}$.

As adaptive transmission rates can result in instable throughput and error rate, we disable the rate adaptation and set a constant transmission rate for each experiment. At the receiver, we run Wireshark in monitor mode to obtain the Physical and MAC layer information of the received packets. In monitor mode, however, the receiver might observe multiple copies of a frame due to unicast re-

Table 2: Jamming attacks investigated in our evaluation.

Attack	Jammed subcarriers
Single jamming	1 single DSC
Range jamming	Set of adjacent DSCs
Whole-band jamming	Whole Wi-Fi channel
Pilot jamming	Pilot subcarriers
Interleaving jamming	Multiple DSCs (cf. Definition 1)

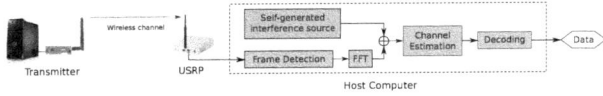

Figure 6: Self-jamming setup: Transmitter (D-Link WDA-1320 Wi-Fi adapter) broadcasts packets on the wireless channel. The receiver is a USRP connected to a Host Computer for receiving transmitted packets with self-generated interference.

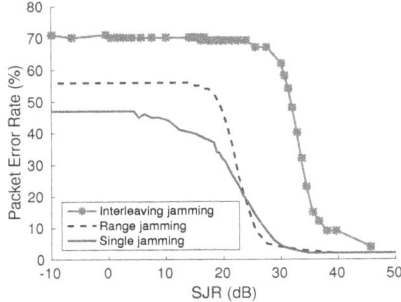

Figure 7: Impact of narrow-band jamming: Single jamming on DSC 0; Range jamming on DSC 0, 1, 2; Interleaving jamming on DSC 0, 3, 6.

transmissions[2], leading to inaccurate throughput results. To avoid this issue, we configure the transmitter to send packets in broadcast mode, therefore disabling the retransmissions.

In each experiment, we gradually decrease the jamming power, while fixing the transmitter's power at a regulated transmit power, to have the SJR varying between 0 dB and 50 dB. For each value of SJR, results are collected every 1 s in the total duration of 10 s per run, and the mean PER is accordingly computed. We note that since UDP transmissions have no flow control and are broadcast at fixed rate, the short duration of 10 s per run is sufficient for us to obtain stable results. In the following, we study the jamming impact in different scenarios, from ideal to realistic jamming attacks.

5.1 Preliminary Results on SDR Receiver

We consider an ideal jamming signal generator, in which no real jammer is running, but the receiver jams itself during the packet reception process. The motivation and implications of this model is that the constraints of a practical adversary (e.g., timing, energy, detection accuracy, hardware capability, etc.) can be eliminated, with the additional advantage of being able to repeat experiments and apply different jamming techniques to exactly the same received RF signals. Specifically, in this scenario (cf. Figure 6), while the transmitter remains the same as in the general setup (i.e., transmitter is a commercial Wi-Fi card), the receiver is an SDR Wi-Fi receiver that we have developed [39] on a USRP device [10]. It is also able to inject self-generated interference into the samples sequence (received over the air) before decoding the data. In [39], we verified that this custom receiver has a reception performance comparable to commercial Wi-Fi cards, therefore allowing us to readily evaluate the impact of jamming using this self-jamming setup. In this first set of experiments, we transmit 1500-byte UDP packets at a fixed rate of 54 Mbps. The self-generated interference is added to the whole duration of each packet, except for Section 5.1.4, where we only add the interference to a few first OFDM symbols of each packet. We call the former *long-burst* jamming, and the latter *short-burst* jamming. To refer to the burst length, we use the notation s as

---

[2]In IEEE 802.11 MAC protocol, up to 12 retransmissions are triggered for an unacknowledged frame in unicast mode.

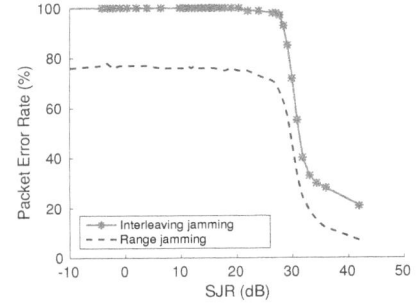

Figure 8: Impact of jamming with 7 subcarriers: Range jamming on DSC 0 to 6; Interleaving jamming on DSC 0, 3, 6, 9, 12, 15, 18.

the size of burst in number of OFDM symbols, which is computed by $s = B/80$, where B is the burst length in number of samples, previously introduced in Section 4.2. In Sections 5.1.1 to 5.1.3, long-burst jamming is considered with burst length corresponding to $s = 58$ (covering the whole packet).

5.1.1 Narrow-band Jamming

First, we evaluate the impact of narrow-band jamming, where the jamming signal covers only a few subcarriers. Three types of attacks are considered: (a) *Single-carrier jamming* at DSC 0, (b) *Range jamming* at DSC 0, 1, 2, and (c) *Interleaving jamming* at DSC 0, 3, 6. The impact on performance of the Wi-Fi link between the transmitter and receiver is shown in Figure 7. We note that to achieve PER of 40%, the Single-carrier jamming attack requires at least 15 dB more jamming power in comparison with the Interleaving jamming strategy. Interestingly, the Range jamming strategy creates slightly less harm (PER 10%) than Single-carrier jamming when the SJR is higher than 25 dB. It can be explained by the fact that spreading the jammer power over multiple subcarriers weakens the interference in individual subcarriers. In this case, since the jammer is not aware of the interleaving pattern, these low-power individual jamming subcarriers cannot effectively cooperate to destroy the packets. In contrast, with the same low power constraint, the Interleaving jamming is able to corrupt 70% of transmitted packets at the same SJR of 25 dB.

Now we look at the lower SJR conditions (less than 20 dB). Although all three jamming strategies have considerable impacts on the PER (more than 40%), there are specific PER thresholds such that a higher degradation of performance cannot be achieved by increasing jamming power. This is explained by the narrowband jamming constraint, which leaves a large enough portion of data subcarriers intact so that the depth-6 convolutional code is able to correct the errors introduced by the interference. In this experiment, the PER threshold for Single-carrier jamming, Range jamming, and Interleaving jamming are 48%, 56%, 70%, respectively.

Aiming to achieve higher jamming impact, we configure the jammer to jam on more subcarriers. In particular, we compare the Range jamming and Interleaving jamming with 7 subcarriers, where the former attack jams on DSC 0 to 6, while the latter jams on DSC 0, 3, 6, 9, 12, 15, 18. Figure 8 shows that at high SJR around 30 dB, there is a little difference (roughly 2 dB) in the required jamming power between Range jamming and Interleaving jamming strategies that block up to 50% of packets. In contrast to the previous jamming attacks with 3 DSCs, there is now no clear advantage of Interleaving jamming over Range jamming at low-power jamming. The reason is that on one hand the Range jamming on DSC 0 to 6 now also covers DSC 0, 3, 6, so it can effectively destroy three consecutive bits in the original data sequence, thus creating more

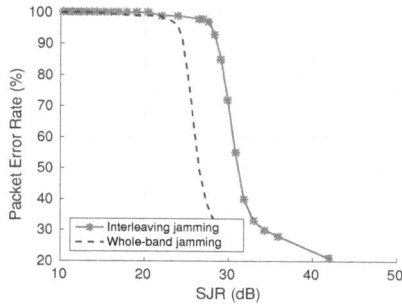

Figure 9: Comparison between Interleaving jamming on DSC 0, 3, 6, 9, 12, 15, 18 and Whole-band jamming on 20 MHz of Wi-Fi channel.

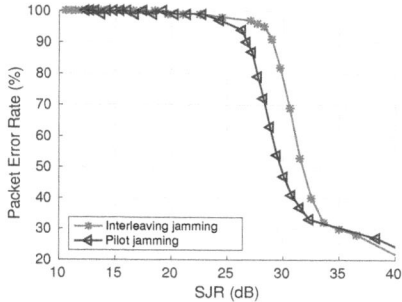

Figure 10: Comparison of performance impact by jamming on pilot subcarriers and Interleaving jamming on 7 data subcarriers.

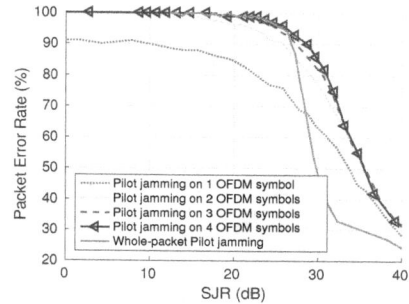

Figure 11: Impact of short-burst jamming on pilot subcarriers.

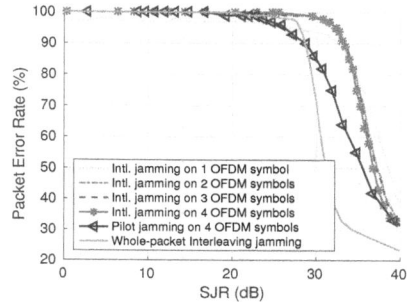

Figure 12: Impact of short-burst Interleaving jamming.

impact than the previous Range jamming on DSC 0 to 2. On the other hand, Interleaving jamming with expanded number of DSCs from 3 to 7 only adds little impact due to low power constraint. However, at SJR lower than 20 dB, the Interleaving jamming can now destroy all transmitted packets, while the Range jamming still lets 20% of packets through. This implies the superiority of Interleaving jamming in completely blocking Wi-Fi packets.

5.1.2 Whole-band vs. Interleaving Jamming

To further understand and quantify the efficiency of Interleaving jamming, we compare its performance to the Whole-band jamming. The results in Figure 9 show that to achieve the same jamming impact, the Whole-band jamming requires about 5 dB more power than the Interleaving jamming on DSC 0, 6, 9, 12, 15, 18.

5.1.3 Jamming on Pilot Subcarriers

In IEEE 802.11, pilot subcarriers are located among the data subcarriers, and used for channel estimation and equalization. Interference mitigation for pilot subcarriers is, therefore, very important for the robustness of OFDM systems [9, 26, 34]. In this subsection, we compare the impact of Pilot jamming and Interleaving jamming. For Pilot jamming, all four pilot subcarriers are jammed. For Interleaving jamming, we select to jam on DSC 0, 3, 6, 9, 12, 15, 18 similarly as in previous experiments. Figure 10 shows that Pilot jamming results in a slightly less impact (roughly 2 dB less power efficiency) than Interleaving jamming. It is noted that both are more efficient than Range jamming and Whole-band jamming.

5.1.4 Short-burst Jamming

We have so far investigated long-burst jamming scenarios. To obtain more insight about the effectiveness of the interleaving jamming strategy, we now perform another series of experiments, in which the subcarriers are jammed for a short duration spanning few

OFDM symbols within each packet. In this subsection, we study the two most efficient jamming strategies observed above: short-burst Pilot jamming and short-burst Interleaving jamming.

First, we compare the performance of the Wi-Fi transmissions under Pilot jamming of different jamming burst lengths. Specifically, the first s OFDM symbols within every packet are jammed, with $s = 1, 2, 3, 4$ for short-burst jamming scenarios and $s = 58$ for whole-packet jamming. We can see from Figure 11 that jamming only one OFDM symbol of every packet appears as the least efficient burst, while jamming the whole packet does not result in high efficiency. We find that Pilot jamming on 3, 4 OFDM symbols results in the highest attack efficiency, which can corrupt over 80% of the packets at SJR = 30 dB and 99% at SJR = 20 dB.

Now we carry out a similar experiment to study the impact of the short-burst Interleaving jamming strategy, in which burst lengths $s = 1, 2, 3, 4$ are considered. For the sake of comparison, the packet error rates caused by the Interleaving jamming on the whole packet and Pilot jamming on the first 4 OFDM symbols are also included in the results shown in Figure 12.

First, we observe that in contrast to short-burst Pilot jamming strategies, the short-burst Interleaving jamming strategies can block over 95% of packets by using a burst of only 1 OFDM symbol. Interestingly, this attack uses a jamming power as low as 0.1% (30 dB less than) the transmitted signal power. Moreover, when the burst length is increased to span the duration of 2, 3, or 4 OFDM symbols, the adversary can block 99% of the transmitted packets at the jamming power level of 0.1% of the transmitter's power. In comparison with short-burst Pilot jamming, the short-burst Interleaving jamming is at least 5 dB more power efficient at PER of 90%. The gap of 5 dB is also observed at all PERs when compared to whole packet Interleaving jamming.

In summary, our preliminary results on the Wi-Fi SDR-based receiver setup show that the most efficient jamming attack against Wi-Fi communications is the short-burst Interleaving jamming.

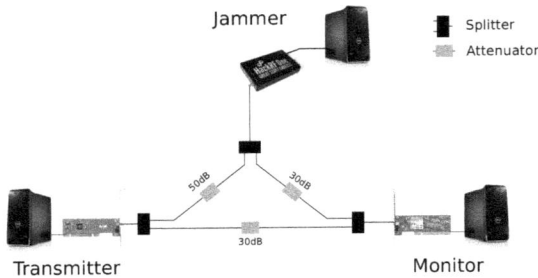

Figure 13: Experiment setting: (a)TX: D-Link WDA-1320; (b)RX: TP-Link TL-WN751ND; (c)Jammer: HackRF

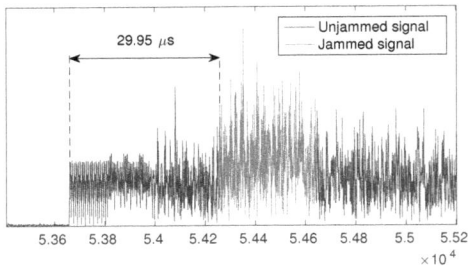

Figure 14: HackRF jammer's response time is $29.95\mu s$.

5.2 Impact of Practical Jammer on Commercial Wi-Fi Cards

Based on the insights gained in Section 5.1, we now evaluate the impact of Interleaving jamming attacks on commercial Wi-Fi cards. In this case, the jammer is implemented on the HackRF One SDR firmware (as described previously). The HackRF device continuously listens to the Wi-Fi channel and jams every detected packet. First, we carry out the experiments in a testbed with controlled attenuation in order to minimize interference from external sources such as other simultaneously ongoing Wi-Fi communications. Our testbed, illustrated in Figure 13, consists of three nodes: the transmitter broadcasting data, the receiver operating in monitor mode for measuring the reception performance, and the jammer running on the HackRF One device. Both the transmitter and receiver consist of commercial off-the-shelf D-Link WDA-1320 Wi-Fi adapters. Three nodes are connected by a triangular topology with attenuators that emulate the path loss in a typical wireless channel. Similarly to Section 5.1, 1500-byte packets are broadcast at 54 Mbps on 20 MHz of channel 11, unless otherwise stated. For each experiment, the configurations of jamming attack (including the number and pattern of jammed subcarriers, jamming power, burst length) are controlled from the PC connected to the HackRF One through a USB port. We emphasize that this USB connection is only used for configuring the jammer. The detection and jamming tasks are handled in real-time by the HackRF itself. Our metric is again the PER with respect to the SJR, in which the latter is computed based on the received signal power obtained at every value of the HackRF One's transmit gain. To verify that these experimental results are not specific to this D-Link card, we also changed the receiver to use a different Wi-Fi adapter manufacturer/model, TP-Link TL-WN751ND, and repeated all experiments. We observe that the results obtained in the two sets of experiments are very similar. Therefore, in the subsequent subsections, we report the results from the TP-Link TL-WN751ND receiver only (for graph readability).

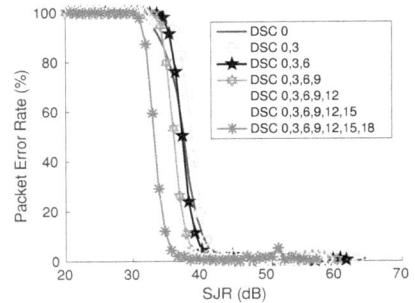

Figure 15: Effect of number of DSCs on attack efficiency of short-burst Interleaving jamming.

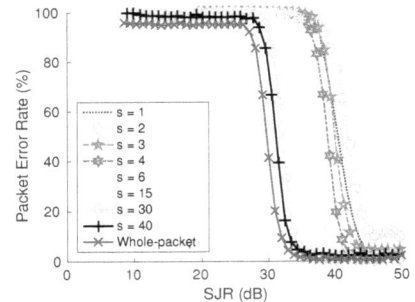

Figure 16: Interleaving jamming with different burst lengths s (measured as the duration of s OFDM symbols).

5.2.1 Response Time

In practice, the attack efficiency does not only depend on the detection capability, the jamming pattern and power, but also on the response time of the jammer, which is the duration between the time of receiving the first sample of a frame and the time of emitting the first jamming sample. To evaluate the response time of the HackRF jammer, we configure the jammer to apply the maximum power and use our custom Wi-Fi receiver as described in Section 5.1 to receive the transmitted packets. We note that in this experiment, self-jamming is disabled and the receiver simply captures all received samples. For each detected frame, we locate the first jamming sample by looking at an increase in the signal envelope.

Figure 14 illustrates this process, and shows that the response time is $29.95\mu s$, approximately the duration of 7.5 OFDM symbols. By repeating the experiment, we find that the average response time is around $30\mu s$ with insignificant variance. Furthermore, it is also invariant to all attack configurations tested in our evaluation. Since each frame contains a preamble of 4 OFDM symbols and a Physical header of 1 OFDM symbol, this response time implies that the jammer can successfully jam a MAC frame of at least 3 OFDM symbols. Our rough estimation suggests that a small UDP packet containing only 6 bytes of payload and 64 bytes of header (including UDP, IP, LLC, MAC headers) can be jammed by our HackRF implementation if the packet is transmitted at 54 Mbps. In case of TCP transmissions, the hit probability is even higher, because small data chunks are typically combined into one big chunk (Nagle algorithm). Consequently, our jammer can effectively destroy most of the traffic in Wi-Fi networks.

5.2.2 Effect of Number of Subcarriers

We evaluate the effectiveness of Interleaving jamming by the number of DSCs selected for jamming. The jamming pattern is configured to $0, 3, \ldots, 3(n-1)$ for $n = 1 \ldots 7$. The adversary

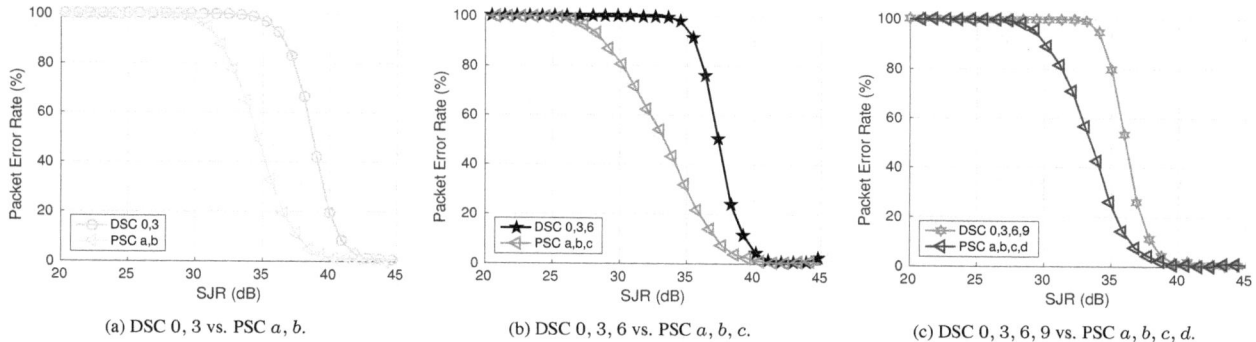

(a) DSC 0, 3 vs. PSC a, b. (b) DSC 0, 3, 6 vs. PSC a, b, c. (c) DSC 0, 3, 6, 9 vs. PSC a, b, c, d.

Figure 17: Comparison between Interleaving jamming and Pilot jamming (both have short burst length $s = 4$).

uses a fixed burst length of $s = 4$ OFDM symbols. Figure 15 shows that jamming on two DSCs 0 and 3 is the most effective attack that can create a PER of 20% at SJR of 40 dB (i.e., the jamming power is only 0.01% of the transmitted signal power). When the SJR decreases to 35 dB (i.e., the jamming power increases to 0.03% of the transmitter's power), the PER rises to 95%. We also observe that jamming on more DSCs tends to decrease the attack efficiency, because less power is distributed to each individual subcarrier. Nevertheless, even the weakest jamming pattern with 7 DSCs can still block all packets (PER = 100%) at SJR = 30 dB.

5.2.3 Short-burst Interleaving Jamming

In this experiment, we study the impact of the jamming burst length on the performance of the Wi-Fi link. We fix the pattern of jammed subcarriers to be DSC 0, 3 and vary the burst length from $s = 1$ OFDM symbol to $s = 58$ (the total number of OFDM symbols contained in a 1500-byte packet transmitted at 54 Mbps). It is seen in Figure 16 that the burst length of $s = 2$ results in the most powerful jamming attack, whereas extending the jamming period gradually reduces the efficiency. We notice that the efficiency gap between the best and worst attacks is up to 12 dB. These results also match with those of SDR-receiver self-jamming experiments (Figure 12), in which $s = 2$ appears to be the most efficient one. This indicates that very short jamming bursts are sufficient for an effective attack, whereas jamming in more time simply wastes the energy without achieving more impact.

5.2.4 Interleaving vs. Pilot Jamming

Recall that in Section 5.1, we discovered that the two most effective attacks among those investigated are Interleaving jamming and Pilot jamming, among which the former outperforms the latter by around 2 dB in case of whole-packet jamming, and around 5 dB in case of short burst jamming. To see whether the advantage of Interleaving jamming holds with the HackRF jammer against commercial receivers, we compare these two attacks in different scenarios, where we change the number of jammed subcarriers from 2 to 4. The following cases are evaluated: (a) DSC 0, 3 vs. PSC a, b; (b) DSC 0, 3, 6 vs. PSC a, b, c; (c) DSC 0, 3, 6, 9 vs. PSC a, b, c, d, where the locations of pilot subcarriers (PSC) are specified by IEEE 802.11 as in Table 3.

Table 3: Pilot subcarrier (PSC) and data subcarrier (DSC) locations.

Pilot subcarrier	Location
PSC a	between DSC 4 and 5
PSC b	between DSC 17 and 18
PSC c	between DSC 29 and 30
PSC d	between DSC 42 and 43

Figure 17 shows that Interleaving jamming attacks outperform Pilot jamming, despite the fact that both jam on the same number of subcarriers. At PER around 95%, the efficiency gap is at least 10 dB (Figures 17a and 17c) and up to 15 dB (Figure 17b).

5.2.5 Impact on Coding Rates

So far, the experiments we carried out were performed for the transmission rate 54 Mbps, which uses the highest coding rate of 3/4. In this subsection, we evaluate the jamming impact on lower coding rates of 2/3 and 1/2. Specifically, we configure the transmitter to use three different rates: 54 Mbps, 48 Mbps and 24 Mbps corresponding to coding rates 3/4, 2/3 and 1/2, respectively (cf. Table 1). In this experiment, we again compare the attack efficiency between Interleaving and Pilot jamming, both of which are short-burst jamming ($s = 4$) on 2 subcarriers (DSC 0, 3 vs. PSC a, b).

We see from Figure 18 that at any transmission rate, Interleaving jamming is more power efficient than Pilot jamming. While at 24 Mbps (coding rate of 1/2), only $2 - 3$ dB are gained by Interleaving jamming, the gap increases to 10 dB for higher transmission rates. The implication is that when less redundancy is produced in the coded data sequence, Interleaving jamming is very effective to destroy the packets due to the vulnerability of the interleaver structure in IEEE 802.11.

5.2.6 Over the Air Experimental Results

In this experiment, we evaluate the impact of Interleaving jamming in an open environment, where the wireless channel can be affected by other factors such as parallel communications, channel distortions, fading, or multipath effect. We perform this experiment by removing all the RF cables and attenuators between all nodes. The transmitter, receiver, and jammer are within 2 metres range of each other. Since our HackRF jammer does not parse each detected frame, it may also jam packets coming from external Wi-Fi transmitters during the experiment. On the receiver end, however, we only count the correctly received packets originated from our transmitter and use this statistic to compute the results shown in Figure 19. For comparison, we also carry out the experiment for the Pilot jamming strategy. Both attacks are short-burst of length $s = 4$ and jam on two subcarriers: DSC 0, 3 for Interleaving jamming and PSC a, b for Pilot jamming. The Wi-Fi transmission is configured to operate at a fixed rate of 54 Mbps.

Figure 19 shows that Interleaving jamming destroys about 95% of packets at SJR = 30 dB, which is a slight drop in comparison with Figure 18, where it blocks all packets at the same SJR. Nevertheless, the Interleaving jamming in wireless environment is still more power efficient than Pilot jamming by roughly 8 dB.

In summary, our practical jammer with Interleaving jamming

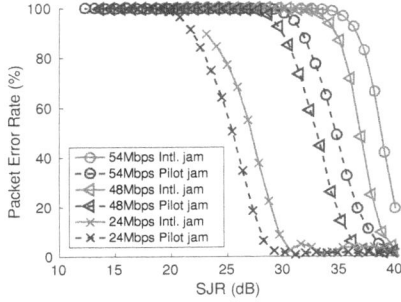

Figure 18: Comparison between Interleaving and Pilot jamming in different coding rates.

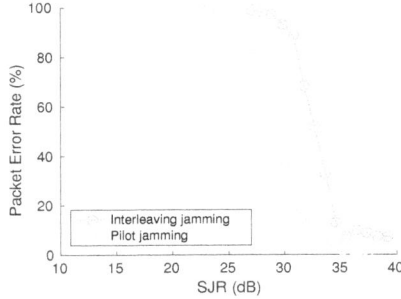

Figure 19: Comparison between Interleaving and Pilot jamming in wireless environment.

strategy is significantly effective against Wi-Fi communications. It can block 95% of transmitted packets by using a jamming power equal to 0.1% of the transmitter's power.

6. COUNTERMEASURES

As Wi-Fi protocol is not designed to combat malicious interference, protecting the communications against Interleaving jamming attacks requires modifications to the standard. One possible approach is to randomize the interleaving mapping cryptographically such that only the transmitter and receiver, who share a common secret, can understand and the de-interleave the received sequence, therefore preventing the adversary from generating jamming patterns that result into interference bursts post de-interleaving [38]. An alternative short-term solution that can reduce the practicality of interleaving jamming consists of making the interleaving structure dependent on the IEEE802.11 frame (e.g., scrambling seed), and permute both over time and frequency subcarriers.

7. RELATED WORK

Over the last few years, the wireless community made significant progress characterizing the potential of smart-jamming attacks against general wireless systems and IEEE 802.11 in particular. A variety of attack and mitigation techniques were developed including reactive jammers [37, 40], channel adaptation [14, 15, 17, 42], keyless spread spectrum [5, 21, 22, 35], broadcast and control channels resiliency [1, 8, 29, 31, 36], MAC resiliency [2, 7, 19, 24], and even communication through silence [30, 41].

In the context of Wi-Fi, previous work demonstrated the feasibility of building reactive jammers [4], understanding IEEE 802.11 MAC and Link layer vulnerabilities [3, 25, 27], and spatial access control [4, 18], but only limited work investigated the vulnerabilities of Wi-Fi that are specific to its physical layer.

The potential existence of interleaving jammers against communication systems was first conjectured in the time domain in our previous work [20]. In the same paper, the jamming efficiency against IEEE 802.11a was estimated for such attacks that target the whole OFDM symbol but did not investigate the unique characteristics of the interleaver. In this work, we demonstrate that interleaving jamming attack is practical in the frequency domain and is even much more power efficient by destroying sub-OFDM symbols with a careful selection of subcarriers.

Other recent works [23, 28, 32] have demonstrated jamming attacks on IEEE 802.11a preambles, which aim to disturb the synchronization mechanism at the receiver, leading to incorrect packet decoding. Based on the reported results in [32], where the optimal frequency offset attack achieved a bit error rate (BER) of 0.5 at short-lived samples' SJR of 1.46 dB, our rough computation suggests that this could be roughly equivalent to blocking all packets at an average SJR of 21.46 dB (for 1500-byte UDP packets). In contrast, the OFDM symbol timing attack [23], which generates fake preambles to deceive the receiver, achieved a similar performance at SJR around 12.5 dB. While it is difficult to give a direct comparison (as the previous work did not report the attack performance in a real Wi-Fi system with important components such as encoding, interleaving), our real Wi-Fi experiments indicate that the proposed interleaving jamming was able to destroy all packets at an average SJR of at least 25 dB and up to 32 dB.

Regarding the timing requirement for the attacks, frequency and timing synchronization jamming requires fast hardware and software solutions in order to perform the responsive jamming within the very short duration of the preambles (e.g., 16 us for 20 MHz), therefore limiting the practicality of such attacks on low cost radios. In contrast, the interleaving jamming can be performed on any sub-OFDM symbol, making the attack easier for the adversary. Another condition for the frequency offset attack [32] is that the adversary needs to measure and estimate the frequency offset between the transmitter and receiver (based on data/ack exchange) before the attack can be performed. Moreover, when multiple transmitter-receiver pairs are present with different frequency offsets, it is difficult for the adversary to properly perform the attack, as the source of the current frame is only known after the MAC header is decoded.

8. CONCLUSION

We devised a new jamming strategy that exploits the IEEE 802.11 interleaving mechanism in order to actively introduce burst errors to the Wi-Fi receiver's convolutional decoder resulting in a significant impact on the Wi-Fi link performance. Our short-burst Interleaving jamming strategy can destroy more than 95% of the transmitted packets by using a jamming power equal to only 0.1% of regular transmitted signal power. When the jamming power is increased to the fraction of 1%, our strategy can completely block all packets. In comparison with jamming strategies that are unaware of the interleaving structure, we can achieve the same jamming impact with at least 5 dB and up to 15 dB more power efficiency. We note that this attack can be combined with other techniques (e.g., targeting the rate adaptation mechanism) for higher efficiency and stealth. We also demonstrated that the Interleaving jamming is practical enough for implementation on a low-cost SDR platform such as the HackRF One.

Acknowledgements. This material is based upon work supported by the National Science Foundation under Grant No. NSF/CNS-1409453.

References

[1] G. N. A. Chan, X. Liu and B. Thapa. Broadcast control channel jamming: Resilience and identification of traitors. In *IEEE International Symposium on Information Theory (ISIT)*, 2007.

[2] B. Awerbuch, A. W. Richa, and C. Scheideler. A jamming-resistant MAC protocol for single-hop wireless networks. In *Proceedings of the 27th ACM Symposium on Principles of Distributed Computing*, PODC'08, pages 45–54, 2008.

[3] E. Bayraktaroglu, C. King, X. Liu, G. Noubir, R. Rajaraman, and B. Thapa. On the performance of IEEE 802.11 under jamming. In *INFOCOM*, pages 1265–1273, 2008.

[4] D. S. Berger, F. Gringoli, N. Facchi, I. Martinovic, and J. B. Schmitt. Gaining insight on friendly jamming in a real-world IEEE 802.11 network. In *7th ACM Conference on Security & Privacy in Wireless and Mobile Networks, WiSec'14, Oxford, United Kingdom, July 23-25, 2014*, pages 105–116, 2014.

[5] A. Cassola, T. Jin, G. Noubir, and B. Thapa. Efficient spread spectrum communication without pre-shared secrets. *IEEE Transactions on Mobile Computing*, 2013.

[6] A. Cassola, W. Robertson, E. Kirda, and G. Noubir. A practical, targeted, and stealthy attack against wpa enterprise authentication. NDSS, 2013.

[7] S. Chang, Y. Hu, and N. Laurenti. Simplemac: a jamming-resilient mac-layer protocol for wireless channel coordination. In *The 18th Annual International Conference on Mobile Computing and Networking, Mobicom'12, Istanbul, Turkey, August 22-26, 2012*, pages 77–88, 2012.

[8] J. T. Chiang and Y. Hu. Cross-layer jamming detection and mitigation in wireless broadcast networks. In *Proceedings of the 13th Annual International Conference on Mobile Computing and Networking, MOBICOM 2007, Montréal, Québec, Canada, September 9-14, 2007*, pages 346–349, 2007.

[9] A. Coulson. Narrowband interference in pilot symbol assisted ofdm systems. *Wireless Communications, IEEE Transactions on*, 3(6):2277–2287, Nov 2004.

[10] Ettus Research. Universal Software Radio Peripheral.

[11] FCC. FCC enforcement bureau steps up education and enforcement efforts against cellphone and gps jamming, 2013.

[12] FCC. FCC fines jammers, 2013.

[13] FCC. Marriott hotels fined $600,000 by FCC for jamming Wi-Fi hotspots, October 2014.

[14] K. Firouzbakht, G. Noubir, and M. Salehi. On the capacity of rate-adaptive packetized wireless communication links under jamming. In *Proceedings of the Fifth ACM Conference on Security and Privacy in Wireless and Mobile Networks*, WISEC '12, 2012.

[15] K. Firouzbakht, G. Noubir, and M. Salehi. On the performance of adaptive packetized wireless communication links under jamming. *IEEE Transactions on Wireless Communications*, 13(7), 2014.

[16] Great Scott Gadgets. Hackrf one. https://greatscottgadgets.com/hackrf/.

[17] L. Jia, X. Liu, G. Noubir, and R. Rajaraman. Transmission power control for ad hoc wireless networks: throughput, energy and fairness. In *Proceedings of IEEE Wireless Communications and Networking Conference, 2005*, 2005.

[18] Y. S. Kim, P. Tague, H. Lee, and H. Kim. A jamming approach to enhance enterprise wi-fi secrecy through spatial access control. *Wireless Networks*, 21(8):2631–2647, 2015.

[19] M. Li, I. Koutsopoulos, and R. Poovendran. Optimal jamming attacks and network defense policies in wireless sensor networks. In *INFOCOM*, 2007.

[20] G. Lin and G. Noubir. On link layer denial of service in data wireless lans. *Wireless Communications and Mobile Computing*, 5(3):273–284, 2005.

[21] A. Liu, P. Ning, H. Dai, Y. Liu, and C. Wang. Defending DSSS-based broadcast communication against insider jammers via delayed seed-disclosure. ACSAC'10.

[22] S. Liu, L. Lazos, and M. Krunz. Time-delayed broadcasting for defeating inside jammers. *IEEE Trans. Dependable Sec. Comput.*, 12(3):351–365, 2015.

[23] C. Mueller-Smith and W. Trappe. Efficient ofdm denial in the absence of channel information. In *MILCOM 2013 - 2013 IEEE Military Communications Conference*, pages 89–94, Nov 2013.

[24] R. Negi and A. Perrig. Jamming analysis of MAC protocols. Technical report, Carnegie Mellon University, 2003.

[25] G. Noubir, R. Rajaraman, B. Sheng, and B. Thapa. On the robustness of IEEE 802.11 rate adaptation algorithms against smart jamming. In *Proceedings of the fourth ACM conference on Wireless network security*, WiSec '11, pages 97–108, New York, NY, USA, 2011. ACM.

[26] S. Ohno, E. Manasseh, and M. Nakamoto. Preamble and pilot symbol design for channel estimation in ofdm systems with null subcarriers. *EURASIP Journal on Wireless Communications and Networking*, 2011(1), 2011.

[27] C. Orakcal and D. Starobinski. Jamming-resistant rate adaptation in wi-fi networks. *Performance Evaluation*, 75-76, 2014.

[28] M. J. L. Pan, T. C. Clancy, and R. W. McGwier. Phase warping and differential scrambling attacks against ofdm frequency synchronization. In *2013 IEEE International Conference on Acoustics, Speech and Signal Processing*, pages 2886–2890, May 2013.

[29] R. D. Pietro and G. Oligeri. Freedom of speech: thwarting jammers via a probabilistic approach. In *Proceedings of the 8th ACM Conference on Security & Privacy in Wireless and Mobile Networks, New York, NY, USA, June 22-26, 2015*, pages 4:1–4:6, 2015.

[30] R. D. Pietro and G. Oligeri. Silence is golden: Exploiting jamming and radio silence to communicate. *ACM Trans. Inf. Syst. Secur.*, 17(3):9:1–9:24, 2015.

[31] C. Pöpper, M. Strasser, and S. Capkun. Anti-jamming broadcast communication using uncoordinated spread spectrum techniques. *IEEE Journal on Selected Areas in Communications*, 28(5):703–715, 2010.

[32] H. Rahbari, M. Krunz, and L. Lazos. Security vulnerability and countermeasures of frequency offset correction in 802.11a systems. In *2014 IEEE Conference on Computer Communications, INFOCOM 2014, Toronto, Canada, April 27 - May 2, 2014*, pages 1015–1023, 2014.

[33] B. Schneier. Fake cell phone towers across the US, Sep. 2014.

[34] A. Stamoulis, S. Diggavi, and N. Al-Dhahir. Intercarrier interference in mimo ofdm. *Signal Processing, IEEE Transactions on*, 50(10):2451–2464, Oct 2002.

[35] M. Strasser, C. Pöpper, S. Capkun, and M. Cagalj. Jamming-resistant key establishment using uncoordinated frequency hopping. In *2008 IEEE Symposium on Security and Privacy (S&P 2008), 18-21 May 2008, Oakland, California, USA*, pages 64–78, 2008.

[36] P. Tague, M. Li, and R. Poovendran. Mitigation of control channel jamming under node capture attacks. *IEEE Trans. Mob. Comput.*, 8(9):1221–1234, 2009.

[37] T. D. Vo-Huu, E.-O. Blass, and G. Noubir. Counter-jamming using mixed mechanical and software interference cancellation. In *Proceedings of the Sixth ACM Conference on Security and Privacy in Wireless and Mobile Networks*, WiSec '13, pages 31–42, New York, NY, USA, 2013. ACM.

[38] T. D. Vo-Huu and G. Noubir. Mitigating rate attacks through crypto-coded modulation. In *Proceedings of the 16th ACM International Symposium on Mobile Ad Hoc Networking and Computing*, MobiHoc '15, pages 237–246, New York, NY, USA, 2015. ACM.

[39] T. D. Vo-Huu, T. D. Vo-Huu, and G. Noubir. Swifi: An open source sdr for wi-fi networks high order modulation analysis. Technical report, 2015.

[40] M. Wilhelm, I. Martinovic, J. B. Schmitt, and V. Lenders. Short paper: reactive jamming in wireless networks: how realistic is the threat? In *Proceedings of the Fourth ACM Conference on Wireless Network Security, WISEC 2011, Hamburg, Germany, June 14-17, 2011*, pages 47–52, 2011.

[41] W. Xu, W. Trappe, and Y. Zhang. Anti-jamming timing channels for wireless networks. In *Proceedings of the First ACM Conference on Wireless Network Security, WISEC 2008, Alexandria, VA, USA, March 31 - April 02, 2008*, pages 203–213, 2008.

[42] W. Xu, W. Trappe, and Y. Zhang. Defending wireless sensor networks from radio interference through channel adaptation. *TOSN*, 4(4), 2008.

Trust The Wire, They Always Told Me!
On Practical Non-Destructive
Wire-Tap Attacks Against Ethernet

Matthias Schulz,
Patrick Klapper, Matthias Hollick
Secure Mobile Networking Lab
TU Darmstadt, Germany
{mschulz,pklapper,mhollick}
@seemoo.tu-darmstadt.de

Erik Tews
School of Computer Science
University of Birmingham
United Kingdom
erik@datenzone.de

Stefan Katzenbeisser
Security Engineering Group
TU Darmstadt
Germany
katzenbeisser@seceng.
informatik.tu-darmstadt.de

ABSTRACT

Ethernet technology dominates enterprise and home network installations and is present in datacenters as well as parts of the backbone of the Internet. Due to its wireline nature, Ethernet networks are often assumed to intrinsically protect the exchanged data against attacks carried out by eavesdroppers and malicious attackers that do not have physical access to network devices, patch panels and network outlets. In this work, we practically evaluate the possibility of *wireless* attacks against *wired* Ethernet installations with respect to resistance against eavesdropping by using off-the-shelf software-defined radio platforms. Our results clearly indicate that twisted-pair network cables radiate enough electromagnetic waves to reconstruct transmitted frames with negligible bit error rates, even when the cables are not damaged at all. Since this allows an attacker to stay undetected, it urges the need for link layer encryption or physical layer security to protect confidentiality.

1. INTRODUCTION

Since the late 1980s, Ethernet has been the dominant wired network technology. As of today, it connects all kind of networked devices in home and enterprise networks. Also for industrial machine-to-machine communication, EtherCAT [3] interconnects devices in the domain of process automation to exchange real-time control messages. Ethernet variants such as IEEE 802.3bw are targeting automotive applications.

Despite constant evolution in terms of performance and application-specific solutions, the security of Ethernet installations is rarely questioned. Due to the wireline nature, Ethernet networks are often assumed to intrinsically protect data transmissions from attackers in close proximity that do not have physical access to the end-systems, the wiring and switching closets, or network outlets. In this paper, we challenge this assumption and investigate eavesdropping attacks against Ethernet. We assume an attacker in close proximity to Ethernet cables, who operates non-destructively, not physically tampering with the cable. Our goal is to demonstrate in how far Ethernet is prone to wireless eavesdropping and that an attacker getting close enough to an Ethernet cable is able to extract private information without damaging the cable.

Even though Wi-Fi transmissions are generally encrypted, hence, hard to eavesdrop, the backhaul network is still wired and, most importantly, often not secured by link-layer encryption. Additionally, access to network cables is often as easy as opening a removable floor or a hung ceiling where cables are installed in many companies. Cutting those cables to place physical wire-taps is effective but also conspicuous. Hence, in this work, we focus on non-destructive (*wireless*) eavesdropping attacks against cable-based networks, using wireless near field probes.

That information leak by electromagnetic radiation (EMR) was discovered by Bell Labs in the 1940s and documented under the name TEMPEST in [1]. In the following years, countermeasures were designed. Bell Labs proposed to apply shielding against radiation of magnetic fields, filtering against signal leakage through power and signal lines, and masking against radiated signals. Budget-limited consumer products usually do not implement any of those countermeasures and are therefor vulnerable to those attacks.

The purpose of this work is to demonstrate how information can be extracted from Ethernet networks based on twisted-pair cables with different degrees of shielding. To summarize, our contributions are as follows:

- we capture and analyze signals radiated by Ethernet cables

- we implement an software-defined radio (SDR)-based Ethernet eavesdropper and evaluate its performance

- we discuss countermeasures against our attack.

We structure this work as follows: In Sec. 2 we present the system and attack model, followed by background information in Sec. 3 and the experimental setup in Sec. 4. Then, we describe the implementation of our eavesdropper in Sec. 5, present our practical evaluation in Sec. 6, followed by a discussion in Sec. 7 and countermeasures against our attack in Sec. 8. Finally, we conclude the paper with related work in Sec. 9 and a conclusion in Sec. 10.

WiSec'16 , July 18-22, 2016, Darmstadt, Germany

© 2016 ACM. ISBN 978-1-4503-4270-4/16/07. . . $15.00

DOI: http://dx.doi.org/10.1145/2939918.2940650

2. SYSTEM AND ATTACK MODEL

In our system model, we consider an Ethernet link consisting of twisted-pair cables, an optional patch panel and two connected devices. In general, these can be any kind of device with an Ethernet port, such as computers, machine control units, or switches. For our experiments, we consider two directly interconnected computers that exchange information over this Ethernet link, as illustrated in Fig. 1.

Our attacker's intend is eavesdropping on the information transmitted over the Ethernet link. We assume that the attacker can get close to the cable to install probes that capture wireless signals. The attacker is, however, not allowed to damage the cable itself, for example, by opening the cable to attach mechanical wire taps.

3. BACKGROUND

We start with an introduction into the IEEE 802.3 physical layer with respect to waveforms and cable types to better follow the attack and countermeasures sections in this paper.

3.1 IEEE 802.3 waveforms

For this work, we focus on Ethernet standards using twisted-pair cables. Depending on transmission speed, IEEE 802.3 defines different modulation schemes. For 10 Mbps (10BASE-T, 802.3i) Manchester encoding is used on two twisted wire pairs. It encodes bits in transitions between two voltage levels. This allows easy clock extraction and robust signal decoding, but doubles the bandwidth requirements. For 10 Mbps with 1 bit per symbol, a bandwidth of 20 MHz is required. 100BASE-TX (802.3u) increases the transmission speed by a factor of ten by increasing the bandwidth to 125 MHz, while simultaneously using a more bandwidth efficient MLT-3 line encoding than Manchester coding. In combination with 4B5B block coding, speeds of 100 Mbps can be reached with 20 percent overhead for error correction coding. 1000BASE-T (802.3ab) increases its speed by using four wire pairs simultaneously, transferring 250 Mbps on each of them. To keep the 100BASE-TX's bandwidth of 125 MHz, a five level pulse amplitude modulation (PAM-5) is used in combination with more efficient forward error correction (FEC), that leads to less than 14 percent overhead. Eavesdropping 1000BASE-T is especially complicated as four simultaneous transmissions need to be separated.

3.2 Differential signaling over twisted-pairs

In 802.3 systems, twisted pair cables are used and fed by differential signals. These signals allow to eliminate interfering signals that couple equally into both wires. On the receiver side, subtracting both signals of a wire pair from each other, amplifies the differential signal components, while reducing the common-mode interfering signals. To additionally reduce the interference between wire pairs, signal emissions should be avoided. This is achieved by twisting wire pairs. In [16], Stolle shows that perfectly balanced twisted-pair cables with optimal terminations do not radiate differential signals traversing the wires. Common-mode signals, on the other hand, are radiated. In theory wireless eavesdropping in such a perfect setting is therefor not possible. As a wireless eavesdropper, we rely on receiving radiations, hence we aim at imperfections in practical wires as well as the effect of longitudinal conversion loss, that allows the conversion of differential-mode to common-mode signals due to asymmetries in a cable.

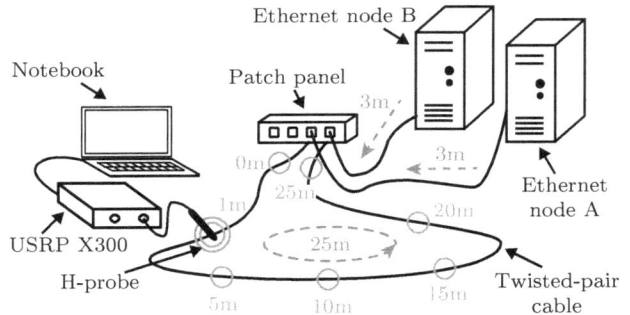

Figure 1: Lab environment for the eavesdropping attack evaluation

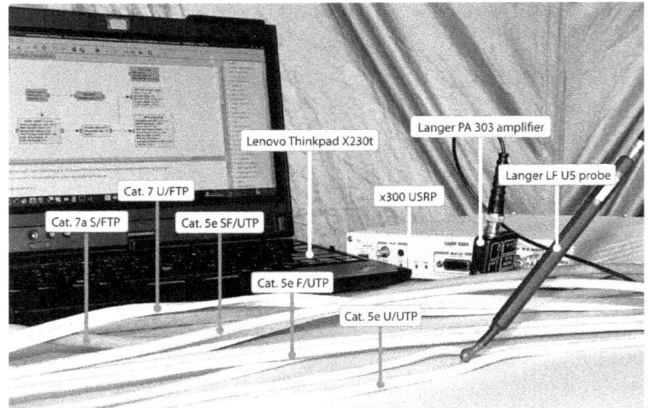

Figure 2: Lab environment including the cables under test, the Universal Software Radio Peripheral (USRP) and the H-field probe.

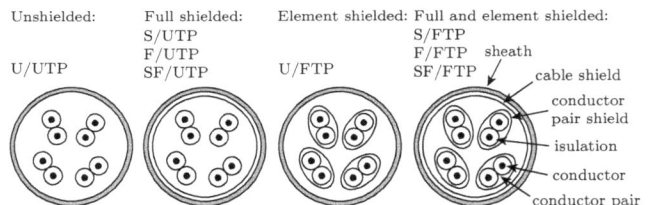

Figure 3: Differently shielded twisted-pair cables

3.3 Shielding

To additionally reduce the emission of electromagnetic radiation, different kinds of cable shieldings are used. The International Electrotechnical Commission (IEC) defines the naming scheme a/bTP in [10] to describe the overall shielding (a) and the individual shielding of twisted pairs (b) as unscreened (U), foil screened (F) or braid screened (S). In this work, we focus our analysis on U/UTP (patch cable, Cat. 5e), F/UTP, SF/UTP (both installation cables, Cat. 5e), U/FTP (flat cable, Cat. 7) and S/FTP (installation cable, Cat. 7) cables (see Fig. 2 and Fig. 3).

4. EXPERIMENTAL SETUP

In this work, we attack the wire link between two Ethernet participants that are connected via twisted-pair cables according to different shielding standards. The setup is illustrated in Fig. 1 and 2. The two participants under test are Ethernet nodes A and B. To coordinate our experiments and to evaluate eavesdropped frames, we used a notebook that is connected to a USRP X300, which is a SDR with sampling rates of up to 200 M Samples per second. That is sufficient for 10BASE-T but not for 100BASE-TX and 1000BASE-T.

To capture emissions of a cable without damaging it, we tried wide-band antennas for electromagnetic compatibility (EMC) measurements, magnetic-loop antennas, as well as magnetic near-field probes[1]. We evaluated the ability to capture signals with a spectrum analyzer and realized that only the near-field probes were able to capture enough signal power for further analysis. Even though 100BASE-TX and 1000BASE-T signals were observable the bandwidth limitation of 50 MHz of our near-field probes were not sufficient to capture with 125 MHz bandwidth required for faster standards. Due to these hardware restraints, we focus our analysis in this work on 10BASE-T and leave faster standards for future work.

5. IMPLEMENTATION

In this section, we describe the implementation of the eavesdropper for 10BASE-T signals. The same components are required 100BASE-TX but with higher bandwidth requirements. For 1000BASE-T four receive paths are needed to separate the signals that are simultaneously transmitted over four wire pairs. This system is comparable to a 4×4-MIMO system in wireless communications. Focusing on 10BASE-T, we decided to use a USRP X300 with BasicRX daughterboard that allows direct sampling of received signals. We use the USRP's digital down-converter to convert the received Ethernet signal into a complex baseband signal, which we process in GNU Radio on a notebook, as illustrated in Fig. 4. Here our *Ethernet Decoder Sink* is used to decode Ethernet signals and store the result in pcap files or forward them to Wireshark.

An exemplary frame capture is illustrated in Fig. 6 with a clearly visible preamble at the left, followed by the start frame delimiter (SFD), which marks the beginning of the Medium Access Control (MAC) header. Our decoder performs an energy detection to find the start of a frame. To reduce noise during idle periods, a squelch block is used. As soon as a frame is recognized, we count samples above and below a given threshold and thereby detect the preamble bits. Counting samples allows us to automatically extract the clock signal so that our decoder works independent of the sampling frequency, which equals 20 MHz in our setup with a down-conversion center frequency of 10 MHz. The preamble detection runs, until the SFD is found indicating the start of a frame. The frame bits are decoded according to the extracted clock signal.

6. EVALUATION

In the following, we present the challenges of our analysis, the preparation of the experiments as well as a performance evaluation. The main challenge of eavesdropping Ethernet frames without damaging the cable is the low amount of longitudinal conversion loss, that converts differential-mode

[1] As H-probe, we use the Langer EMV low-frequency magnetic near-field probe LFU5 together with a 30 dB preamplifier Langer EMV PA303.

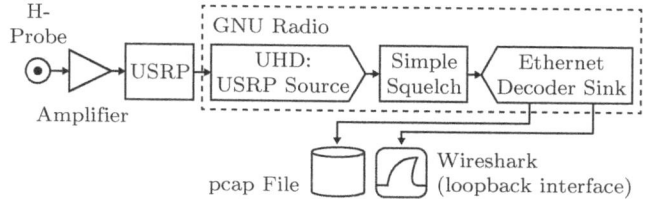

Figure 4: Diagram illustrating our eavesdropper implementation. The USRP captures signals from a probe and passes them to a computer to extract the transmitted frames.

Figure 5: Near Field/H-Probe used to capture the radiated electromagnetic fields around an Ethernet cable.

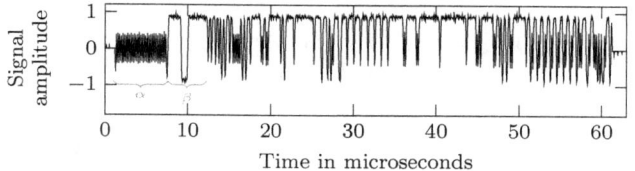

Figure 6: Received frame after down-conversion with $f_c = 10$ MHz. The preamble with SFD is clearly visible on the left (α), followed by the MAC address 00:00:FF:00:00:00 (β).

signals into common-mode signals. The more precise and uniform the twisting of the wires, the less signals can be captured. If shielding is used, less signal power can be collected by an antenna or near-field probe to perform a successful attack, which limits the distance between attacker and cable.

In all of our experiments, we evaluated cables with different shielding, as described in Sec. 3.3, namely: U/UTP, F/UTP, SF/UTP, U/FTP and S/FTP cables. As most of these cables are installation cables, we took 25 meters of each of them and attached both ends to a patch panel. Each end of a cable under test is connected to a computer using an S/FTP patch cable, as illustrated in Fig. 1. On each of the cables under test, we placed an H-probe, as illustrated in Fig. 2. An optimal placement of the probe matters, as the radiated fields are small and only receivable in the near vicinity of a cable, which means between zero to two centimeters away from the cable. This constraint has the upside of being able to eavesdrop on a cable bundle by precisely selecting which cable or even wire-pair to listen to. For example, we observed that optimizing the probe placement to receive signals from one node leads to a significant reduction in signal energy from the other node, that uses different wire-pairs to transmit. Hence, we suggest using two probes to allow individual optimizations for full-duplex eavesdropping. In addition, this result shows that it is possible to differentiate between emissions of different wire-pairs, which is the foundation of eavesdropping on 1000BASE-T that simultaneously uses four wire-pairs. In another experiment, we moved the probe along the cable, but the measurements showed no crucial variations in receivable signal energy.

A much greater effect on the eavesdropping performance has the shielding of the cables. In Fig. 7 and 8 we, hence, focus on the measurement of the signal-plus-noise-to-noise ratio ((S+N)/NR) for different cable types. The results in Fig. 8 are based on the analysis of 700 Ethernet frame transmissions with random payload. We choose to use the (S+N)/NR as the received frames are always superpositioned by noise. To get (S+N)/NR measurements, we took the average power during a frame transmission and divided it by the average power of a long noise sample which did not contain any Ethernet signal transmission.

7. DISCUSSION

In this section, we interpret the measurements and discuss their influence on our eavesdropping results, also with regard to 100BASE-TX and 1000BASE-T. As illustrated in Fig. 8, the (S+N)/NR of completely unshielded cables (U/UTP) is very high (roughly 40 dB) and allows frame decodings with low error rates (see Fig. 8). Fig. 7a shows the recording of a Manchester signal (10BASE-T). The noise margin is sufficiently high, that even decoding MLT-3 (100BASE-TX) or PAM-5 (1000BASE-T) should lead to low error rates. Cables with only shielding around each twisted pair (U/FTP), as well as, those cables with only shielding around all twisted pairs have a medium (S+N)/NR of roughly 20 dB. Nevertheless, it is sufficient to receive more than 60 percent of 10BASE-T frames without any bit errors (valid FCS). The strongest shielded cable contains a foil shield around each twisted pair, as well as, an additional braid shield around all pairs (S/FTP). This combination reduces the (S+N)/NR to under 10 dB, which makes it hard to even correctly differentiate a frame transmission from noise.

In the following we focus on the types of errors that occurred. Instead of considering bit error rates, we evaluated if our receiver implementation can (a) correctly detect a frame, and (b) extract the frame without any bit errors, which was checked by validating the frame check sum (FCS). The results are presented in Fig. 9. The trend of increasing reception errors at cables with more shielding is clearly observable. While our implementation reliably detects the existence of all frames on the wire for U/UTP, U/FTP, F/UTP and SF/UTP cables, only half of the transmitted frames are detected on S/FTP. Regarding error-less frame decodings, for U/UTP cables, more than 70 percent of the transmitted frames are received without errors. This rate drops down to roughly 50 percent on SF/UTP cables and vanishes for S/FTP cables. We already predicted the result of the latter by analyzing the (S+N)/NRs above and considered it unlikely to decode those Ethernet frames without any error due to the high amount of noise power compared to the available signal power.

We additionally evaluated the different reasons for unsuccessful frame decodings and illustrate the results in Fig. 10. Here, we consider three types of errors (a) invalid frames, (b) undetected SFD, and (c) undetected frames. *Invalid frames* contain frames that were correctly detected but decoded with bit errors. This is the main error reason for cables having up to SF/UTP shielding. This error rate increases for heavier shielded cables. In the case of S/FTP cables, it is also responsible for more than 60 percent of the

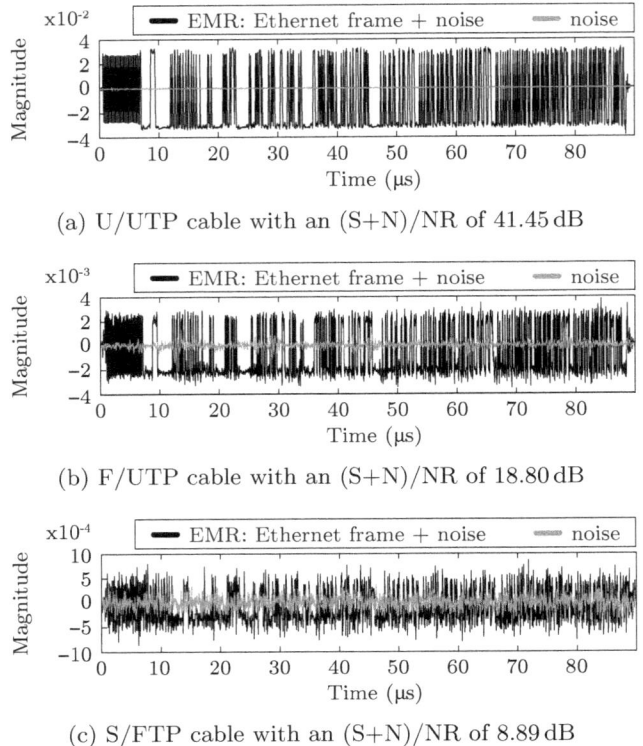

(a) U/UTP cable with an (S+N)/NR of 41.45 dB

(b) F/UTP cable with an (S+N)/NR of 18.80 dB

(c) S/FTP cable with an (S+N)/NR of 8.89 dB

Figure 7: Observed waveforms of the same Ethernet frame and noise. Due to shielding, the signal amplitude reduces which results in decreased signal-to-noise ratios.

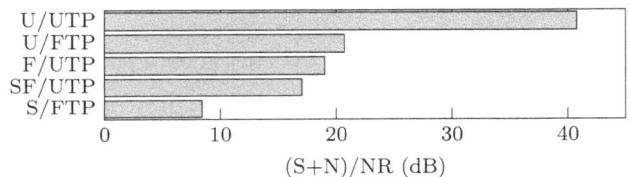

Figure 8: Comparison of the (S+N)/NRs of different twisted-pair cable types

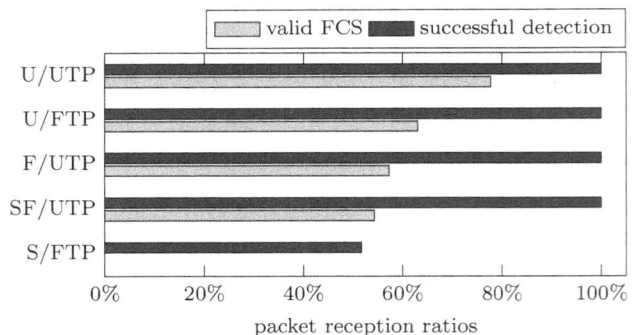

Figure 9: Ratios describing how many packets were correctly detected and how many were decoded with a correct FCS.

frame errors that are not caused by *undetected frames*, which did not trigger the energy detector. The remaining reasons for errors in the case of S/FTP cables are *undetected start frame delimiters*. Those errors occur, if a frame is detected,

46

but no SFD is found. Those errors are negligible for the less shielded cables.

Concluding the discussion, we demonstrated that it is indeed possible to launch a non-destructive attack on Ethernet transmissions by simply attaching a wireless H-field probe to the outside of an Ethernet cable. Especially unshielded cables are very vulnerable to this attack, but also the U/FTP, F/UTP, and SF/UTP cables allow to achieve error-less frame decodings of at least half of the frames transmitted. Only S/FTP cables helped to avoid the error-free decoding with out implementation. Nevertheless, even though error-free receptions might not be possible, one can at least use our eavesdropper to decode frames with certain bit error rates and thereby extract partially correct information.

8. COUNTERMEASURES

As the eavesdropping attack described above is concerning, in this section we present possible countermeasures. The only way to avoid an eavesdropper from getting direct access to the exchanged plaintext information is to use encryption. End-to-end encryption between two communicating end points would be optimal, however, not all applications support it. IPSec in transport mode and encapsulating security payload (ESP) could address this problem by providing end-to-end encryption. However, it comes with a high management overhead, particularly if used across security domains. A more suitable solution to avoid eavesdropping would be link-layer encryption, that is transparent to upper layer protocols in all Ethernet installations. 802.1AE or MACsec is a standard that provides confidentiality and integrity on the link layer, which helps to avoid eavesdropping attacks on the payload. Nevertheless, MAC addresses of the communicating stations are still exchanged in plaintext, so that attackers can create statistics about who communicates with whom in a local network.

One way to reduce the risk of eavesdropping is to use network cables with a maximum amount of shielding in the whole network, for example, Cat. 7 S/FTP cables. However, these cost roughly 2.4 times more[2] than simple Cat. 5e U/UTP cables. Due to budget limitations the latter one might be preferable, even though it lowers the security of the whole network installation by allowing eavesdropping attacks.

An additional defense against eavesdropping is the introduction of a "masking" signal (following the terminology of the TEMPEST paper [1]). Using this additional signal, one can hide the existence of an information signal. On Ethernet's physical layer, only differential-mode signals carry information that are evaluated by a receiver. Solely due to the longitudinal conversion loss that converts differential-mode to common-mode signals, Ethernet frames are radiated and can be received with a wireless device. To mask the radiation, one could inject random common-mode signals with a spectral mask of Ethernet signals. An eavesdropper would fail to extract the actual data frames if their power is sufficiently lower than the "masking" signal. Though possible, the radiation of a masking signal might not comply with electromagnetic compatibility requirements.

---

[2]Based on the price of 49.99 EUR/100 m of Cat. 7 S/FTP and 20.69 EUR/100 m of Cat. 5e U/UTP cables.

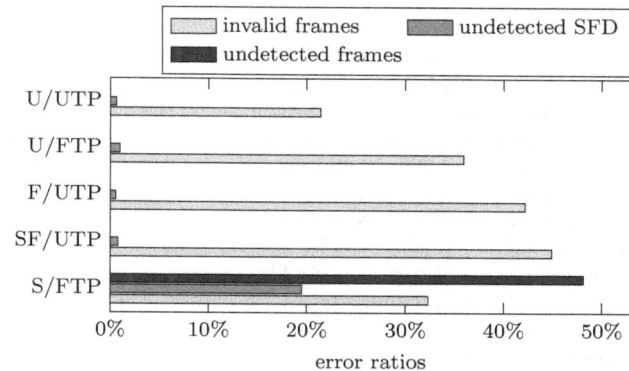

Figure 10: Reasons for unsuccessful frame detections for different cable types.

9. RELATED WORK

This work mainly relates to research in the domain of wireless eavesdropping and side-channels, the radiation characteristics of twisted pair cables and countermeasures against presented attacks. In the following we give an overview of those domains. TEMPEST attacks in our field of interest rely on electromagnetic emanations that leak confidential information to an eavesdropper. Those attacks were implemented for many different categories of devices. In the area of attacks against displays Van Eck uses cathode ray tube (CRT) radiations to reproduce screen content in [20]. This attack is extended by Kuhn by intercepting emitted light in [13]. He also investigated the security of flat-panel displays in [11]. Hayashi et al. present an approach to reconstruct display images of tablets using SDRs in [9]. Besides displays, various wired devices are attackable. The security of RS-232 cable radiations, for example, is investigated by Peter Smulders in [15]. Vuagnoux et al. attack wired and wireless keyboards in [21]. Another prominent area for TEMPEST attacks are power lines. In [4], Degauque et al. demonstrate that unintentional power line radiations can be eavesdropped to listen to communication systems. Electromagnetic interference (EMI) of television sets also leaks information about their display content according to Enev et al. [5]. Signature based EMI attacks are described in [8] by Gulati et al. who also use SDRs. Especially for side-channel attacks against cryptosystems, electromagnetic emanations can be used to extract RSA keys according to Genkin et al. [6]. Enforced emanations through memory access patterns are also usable for data exfiltration as presented by Zajić et al. in [22].

Very relevant for this work are analyses of twisted-pair cable based systems. According to Murai et al. twisted-pair cables in an imbalanced system radiate electromagnetic fields [14]. In [16], Stolle analyzes the electromagnetic coupling of twisted-pair cables. Grassi et al. make differential-mode to common-mode conversions responsible for electromagnetic radiations [7].

Besides attacks, also countermeasures against TEMPEST are presented in the literature. While Van Eck relies on metal shielding in [20], Hayashi et al. propose transparent conductive shielding films to protect tablet computers [9]. An evaluation of conventional countermeasures is given by Suzuki et al. in [17, 19, 18]. Kuhn et al. reduce monitor emanations using software-based techniques [12, 2].

10. CONCLUSION

As a wired system, Ethernet is often considered immune to attackers operating wireless and eavesdropping network traffic is only possible by attaching a probe to the wires of a cable or a connector. In this paper, we have shown that this assumption is not correct and eavesdropping traffic is possible without leaving any traces on the cable for 10BASE-T Ethernet. We have also shown that this attack will likely also succeed for 100BASE-TX Ethernet and possibly also for faster modes of operations. The success rate of the attack depends on the shielding of the cable. Cat.7 S/FTP provides good protection against eavesdropping while all weaker shielding such as Cat.5e SF/UTP, Cat.5e F/UTP, Cat.7 U/FTP and Cat.5e U/UTP result in a higher success rate. To provide an adequate protection against such adversaries, better shielded cables should be deployed and whenever possible, link layer encryption should be used. Just protecting the physical access to network cables such as locking them in a cabinet or in a small plastic conduit without shielding is not sufficient.

11. ACKNOWLEDGMENTS

This work has been funded by the German Research Foundation (DFG) in the Collaborative Research Center (SFB) 1053 "MAKI – Multi-Mechanism-Adaptation for the Future Internet", by LOEWE CASED, and by BMBF/HMWK CRISP.

12. REFERENCES

[1] TEMPEST: A signal problem.

[2] R. Anderson and M. Kuhn. Soft Tempest - An Opportunity for NATO, 1999.

[3] I. E. Commission et al. IEC 61158: Digital data communications for measurement and control-Fieldbus for use in industrial control systems, 2003.

[4] P. Degauque, P. Laly, V. Degardin, and M. Lienard. Power line communication and compromising radiated emission. In *Proceedings of the International Conference on Software, Telecommunications and Computer Networks – SoftCOM'10*, pages 88–91, 2010.

[5] M. Enev, S. Gupta, T. Kohno, and S. N. Patel. Televisions, Video Privacy, and Powerline Electromagnetic Interference. In *Proceedings of the 18th ACM Conference on Computer and Communications Security – CCS'11*, pages 537–550, 2011.

[6] D. Genkin, L. Pachmanov, I. Pipman, and E. Tromer. Stealing Keys from PCs using a Radio: Cheap Electromagnetic Attacks on Windowed Exponentiation. In *Proceedings of the Cryptographic Hardware and Embedded Systems Workshop – CHES'15*, pages 207–228, 2015.

[7] F. Grassi, G. Spadacini, and S. Pignari. The Concept of Weak Imbalance and Its Role in the Emissions and Immunity of Differential Lines. *IEEE Transactions on Electromagnetic Compatibility*, 55:1346–1349, 2013.

[8] M. Gulati, S. Ram, and A. Singh. An in Depth Study into Using EMI Signatures for Appliance Identification. In *Proceedings of the 1st ACM Conference on Embedded Systems for Energy-Efficient Buildings – BuildSys'14*, pages 70–79, 2014.

[9] Y. Hayashi, N. Homma, M. Miura, T. Aoki, and H. Sone. A Threat for Tablet PCs in Public Space: Remote Visualization of Screen Images Using EM Emanation. In *Proceedings of the 21st ACM SIGSAC Conference on Computer and Communications Security – CCS'14*, pages 954–965, 2014.

[10] IEC. Information technology – generic cabling for customer premises, Sep 2002.

[11] M. Kuhn. Electromagnetic Eavesdropping Risks of Flat-panel Displays. In *Proceedings of the 4th International Conference on Privacy Enhancing Technologies – PETS'04*, pages 88–107, 2005.

[12] M. Kuhn and R. Anderson. Soft Tempest: Hidden Data Transmission Using Electromagnetic Emanations. In *Proceedings of the 2nd Information Hiding Workshop – IHW'98*, pages 124–142, 1998.

[13] M. G. Kuhn. Optical time-domain eavesdropping risks of CRT displays. In *Proceedings of the 23rd IEEE Symposium on Security and Privacy – IEEE S&P'02*, pages 3–18, 2002.

[14] K. Murai, N. Hasebe, and I. Yokoyama. Analysis of the induced voltage on a twisted pair cable in an electromagnetic field. *Electronics and Communications in Japan*, 82:32–44, 1999.

[15] P. Smulders. The Threat of Information Theft by Reception of Electromagnetic Radiation from RS-232 Cables. *Computer Security*, 9:53–58, 1990.

[16] R. Stolle. Electromagnetic coupling of twisted pair cables. *Selected Areas in Communications, IEEE Journal on*, 20(5):883–892, 2002.

[17] Y. Suzuki and Y. Akiyama. Jamming technique to prevent information leakage caused by unintentional emissions of PC video signals. In *Proceedings of the IEEE International Symposium on Electromagnetic Compatibility – IEEE EMC'10*, pages 132–137, 2010.

[18] Y. Suzuki, M. Masugi, H. Yamane, and K. Tajima. Countermeasure Technique for Preventing Information Leakage Caused by Unintentional PC Display Emanations. In *Proceedings of the IEEE International Symposium on Electromagnetic Compatibility – IEEE EMC'09*, pages 9–12, 2009.

[19] Y. Suzuki†, M. Masugi, K. Tajima, and H. Yamane. Countermeasures to Prevent Eavesdropping on Unintentional Emanations from Personal Computers. *NTT Technical Review*, 6, 2008.

[20] W. van Eck. Electromagnetic Radiation from Video Display Units: An Eavesdropping Risk? *Computer Security*, 4:269–286, 1985.

[21] M. Vuagnoux and S. Pasini. Compromising Electromagnetic Emanations of Wired and Wireless Keyboards. In *Proceedings of the 18th Conference on USENIX Security Symposium – USENIX SSYM'09*, pages 1–16, 2009.

[22] A. Zajic and M. Prvulovic. Experimental Demonstration of Electromagnetic Information Leakage From Modern Processor-Memory Systems. *IEEE Transactions on Electromagnetic Compatibility*, 56:885–893, 2014.

Exploiting Data-Usage Statistics for Website Fingerprinting Attacks on Android

Raphael Spreitzer, Simone Griesmayr, Thomas Korak, and Stefan Mangard
Graz University of Technology, IAIK, Austria
raphael.spreitzer@iaik.tugraz.at

ABSTRACT

The browsing behavior of a user allows to infer personal details, such as health status, political interests, sexual orientation, etc. In order to protect this sensitive information and to cope with possible privacy threats, defense mechanisms like SSH tunnels and anonymity networks (e.g., Tor) have been established. A known shortcoming of these defenses is that website fingerprinting attacks allow to infer a user's browsing behavior based on traffic analysis techniques. However, website fingerprinting typically assumes access to the client's network or to a router near the client, which restricts the applicability of these attacks.

In this work, we show that this rather strong assumption is not required for website fingerprinting attacks. Our client-side attack overcomes several limitations and assumptions of network-based fingerprinting attacks, e.g., network conditions and traffic noise, disabled browser caches, expensive training phases, etc. Thereby, we eliminate assumptions used for academic purposes and present a practical attack that can be implemented easily and deployed on a large scale. Eventually, we show that an unprivileged application can infer the browsing behavior by exploiting the unprotected access to the Android data-usage statistics. More specifically, we are able to infer 97% of 2 500 page visits out of a set of 500 monitored pages correctly. Even if the traffic is routed through Tor by using the Orbot proxy in combination with the Orweb browser, we can infer 95% of 500 page visits out of a set of 100 monitored pages correctly. Thus, the READ_HISTORY_BOOKMARKS permission, which is supposed to protect the browsing behavior, does not provide protection.

Keywords

Mobile security; side-channel attack; website fingerprinting; data-usage statistics; mobile malware

1. INTRODUCTION

Mobile devices, like smartphones and tablet computers, are widely employed and represent an integral part of our everyday life. Due to this tight integration, these devices store and process sensitive information. In order to protect this data as well as the users' privacy, appropriate mechanisms must be implemented. For instance, the Android operating system relies on two fundamental security concepts, namely the concept of sandboxed applications and a permission system. Sandboxing is ensured by the underlying Linux kernel by assigning each application a unique user ID (UID). This means that an application's resources can only be accessed by this application itself, whereas applications running in parallel on the same device do not gain direct access to other applications. The permission system ensures that applications must explicitly request specific permissions for dedicated resources, for example, access to the GPS sensor or the Camera, which might harm the users' privacy.

Although Android relies on the two concepts of sandboxing and permissions, applications running in parallel on the same device are still able to gain information about other applications by exploiting shared resources. Examples are the list of installed applications, the memory footprint of applications, the data-usage statistics, and also the speaker status (speaker on/off). Even though this information seems to be innocuous, sensitive information can be inferred as has been demonstrated by Jana and Shmatikov [22] and Zhou et al. [44]. Studies like these do not exploit specific vulnerabilities of applications but investigate and demonstrate weaknesses of fundamental security concepts on mobile devices. In order to advance the field of mobile security and to protect the user's privacy, a thorough understanding regarding the limitations of fundamental security concepts is required.

In this work, we study the information leakage of the publicly available data-usage statistics on Android. More specifically, Android-based smartphones track the amount of incoming/outgoing network traffic on a per-application basis. This information is used by data-usage monitoring applications to inform users about the traffic consumption. However, while this feature might be helpful to stick to one's data plan and to identify excessive data consumptions of applications, we show that this seemingly innocuous information allows to infer a user's visited websites. Thereby, we demonstrate that the READ_HISTORY_BOOKMARKS permission, which is intended to protect this sensitive information, is actually useless as any application without any permission at all is able to infer visited websites rather accurately.

The exploitation of observed "traffic information" to infer visited websites is known as website fingerprinting [21, 37]. Thereby, an attacker aims to match observed "traffic information" to a previously established mapping of websites and

WiSec'16, July 18–22, 2016, Darmstadt, Germany.

© 2016 Copyright held by the owner/author(s). Publication rights licensed to ACM.
ISBN 978-1-4503-4270-4/16/07...$15.00

DOI: http://dx.doi.org/10.1145/2939918.2939922

their corresponding "traffic information". Most of the investigations in this area of research consider an attacker who sniffs the traffic information "on the wire". This means that the attacker needs to be located on the client's network or on the ISP's router near the client. However, as Android allows an attacker to capture the required data directly on the smartphone without any permission, we show that an attacker is not required to be located somewhere on the victim's network. Hence, the rather strong assumption of a network-based attacker is not required for website fingerprinting attacks. Furthermore, our attack is invariant to traffic noise of other applications—one of the major drawbacks of network-based attacks—as Android captures these statistics on a per-application basis. Compared to existing website fingerprinting attacks, we significantly reduce the computational complexity of classifying websites as we do not require a dedicated training phase, which sometimes requires several hundred CPU hours [38, 39]. Instead, we rely on a simple yet efficient classifier.

Based on our observations, we developed a proof-of-concept application that captures the data-usage statistics of the browser application. With the acquired information in a closed-world setting of 500 monitored websites of interest, we are able to classify 97% of 2 500 visits to these pages correctly. The fact that not even Tor on Android (the *Orbot*[1] proxy in combination with the *Orweb*[2] browser) is able to protect the user's page visits clearly demonstrates the rather delicate issue of this fundamental design flaw.

1.1 Further Security Implications

We stress that the presented attack can be combined with related studies to obtain even more sophisticated attack scenarios. For instance, sensors employed in mobile devices—including the accelerometer, the gyroscope, and also the ambient-light sensor—have been shown to be exploitable in order to infer the user's keyboard inputs without any permission (cf. [1, 3, 31, 34, 36, 41]). In combination with such sensor-based keyloggers, our attack would allow an adversary to determine when a user visits a specific website and to gather login credentials for specific websites. Such an attack does not only endanger the users' privacy but also allows for large-scale identity theft attacks. Thus, OS developers need to deal with this problem in order to prevent users from such severe privacy threats and identity thefts.

1.2 Contribution

The contributions of this work are as follows. First, we investigate the information leakage through the data-usage statistics published by the Android OS. Based on this investigation, we provide an adversary model for a realistic attack scenario that allows for large-scale attacks against the browsing behavior of smartphone users. Furthermore, we discuss how to capture the required information and we show how to infer the browsing behavior with a high accuracy, including a setting where traffic is routed through the anonymity network Tor. We compare our results with existing fingerprinting attacks and show that our attack (1) outperforms these attacks in terms of accuracy, (2) can be deployed significantly easier than existing attacks, and (3) is more efficient in terms of computational complexity. Hence, our attack can be easily deployed on a large scale.

---

[1]https://guardianproject.info/apps/orbot
[2]https://guardianproject.info/apps/orweb

1.3 Outline

The remainder of this paper is organized as follows. In Section 2, we introduce website fingerprinting and related work. In Section 3, we discuss the feature of data-usage statistics captured by the Android OS and how this information relates to the actual transmitted TCP packets. Based on these observations, we outline the adversary model and possible attack scenarios in Section 4 and we discuss our chosen attack approach in Section 5. We extensively evaluate the results in Section 6 and discuss possible countermeasures in Section 7. Finally, we conclude this work in Section 8.

2. BACKGROUND AND RELATED WORK

Website fingerprinting can be considered as a supervised machine-learning problem, namely a classification problem. The idea is to capture the "traffic signature" for specific websites—which are known to the attacker—during a training phase. The "traffic signature" consists of specifically chosen features like unique packet lengths, packet length frequencies, packet ordering, inter-packet timings, etc. In order to capture this information, the attacker loads different websites and observes the resulting "traffic signature", which is usually done somewhere on the network. During the attack phase, an observed "traffic signature" can be classified according to the previously trained classifier.

Most related work in the context of website fingerprinting attacks operate in the closed-world setting. In contrast to the open-world setting, the closed-world setting assumes that the victim only visits a specific set of monitored websites. Furthermore, most fingerprinting attacks assume a passive attacker, although studies considering an active attacker also exist [19]. In contrast to passive attackers, active attackers can influence the transmitted packets, e.g., by delaying specific packets. Thus, active attacks rely on stronger assumptions of the attacker's capabilities.

Subsequently, we summarize related work according to the exploited information and how this information is gathered. We start with attacks that require access to the victim's network trace or to the ISP's router near the victim. Afterwards, we continue with remote adversaries and finally we discuss the exploitation of shared resources on the victim's device, which is the category of attacks our work belongs to.

2.1 On the Wire

Back in 2002, Hintz [21] mentioned that encrypted traffic does not prevent an adversary from inferring a user's visited website. In fact, the simple observation of the amount of transferred data—which is not protected by means of SSL/TLS (cf. [30])—allows an adversary to infer the visited website. Similarly, Sun et al. [37] mentioned that the observation of the total number of objects and their corresponding lengths can be used to identify websites, even if the content itself is encrypted.

While early studies [21,37] exploited the actual size of web objects, a more recent study [27] focused on the exploitation of individual packet sizes. Such fingerprinting attacks have been demonstrated to work against the anonymity network Tor [6,35,39] and also against WEP/WPA encrypted communication as well as IPsec and SSH tunnels [2,28]. Recently, also evaluations of different attacks and countermeasures under different assumptions have been done [5,24].

Instead of inferring specific websites, Chen et al. [7] extracted illnesses and medications by observing the sequence of packet sizes. Similarly, Conti et al. [8] inferred a user's interaction with specific Android applications, e.g., *Gmail*, *Twitter*, and *Facebook*, based on the transmitted packets. In order to eavesdrop on the transmitted packets, they routed the network traffic through their specifically prepared server.

2.2 Remote

Timing attacks on the browser cache [14, 26] can be used to infer whether or not a user visited a specific website before. More specifically, by measuring the loading time of a specific resource, an attacker can determine whether it was served from the browser's cache or not. Similarly, CSS styles of visited URLs can be used to determine the browsing behavior [23]. Gong et al. [15, 16] even demonstrated that fingerprinting can be done remotely when given the victim's IP address. Therefore, the attacker sends ping requests to the user's router and computes the round-trip time, which correlates with the victim's HTTP traffic. Another remote exploitation has been demonstrated by Oren et al. [33], who showed that JavaScript timers can be used to distinguish between memory accesses to the CPU cache and the main memory, which allows for so-called cache attacks via JavaScript. Based on these precise JavaScript timers, they were able infer page visits to a set of 8 websites. Similarly, Gruss et al. [17] exploited so-called page-deduplication attacks to infer page visits to a set of 10 websites.

2.3 Local

In 2009, Zhang and Wang [42] exploited the /proc file system to infer inter-keystroke timings and argued that the privacy risks of the /proc file system need to be investigated further. This has been done, for instance, by Jana and Shmatikov [22] who demonstrated the possibility to fingerprint websites based on the browser's memory footprint, which is available via the /proc file system. In addition, Zhou et al. [44] demonstrated that the data-usage statistics of Android applications can be used to infer the user's activities within three Android applications, namely *Twitter*, *WebMD*, and *Yahoo! Finance*. Later, Zhang et al. [43] exploited the data-usage statistics of an Android-based Wi-Fi camera to determine when the user's home is empty.

Even though Zhou et al. [44] and Zhang et al. [43] started the investigation of the information leakage through the data-usage statistics on Android devices for specific applications, a detailed study regarding the applicability of this information leakage to infer websites has not been done yet. Compared to the work of Jana and Shmatikov [22] who exploit the memory footprint of the browser application for website fingerprinting attacks, we demonstrate a significantly more accurate attack by exploiting the data-usage statistics.

3. ANDROID DATA-USAGE STATISTICS

Android keeps track of the data usage in order to allow users to stick to their data plan. This accounting information is available through the public API as well as through the /proc file system. More specifically, the `TrafficStats` API as well as `/proc/uid_stat/[UID]/{tcp_rcv|tcp_snd}` provide detailed information about the network traffic statistics on a per-UID basis. Since every Android application is assigned a unique UID, these traffic statistics are gathered on a per-application level. In order to observe the data-usage statistics of an application, e.g., the browser, the correspond-

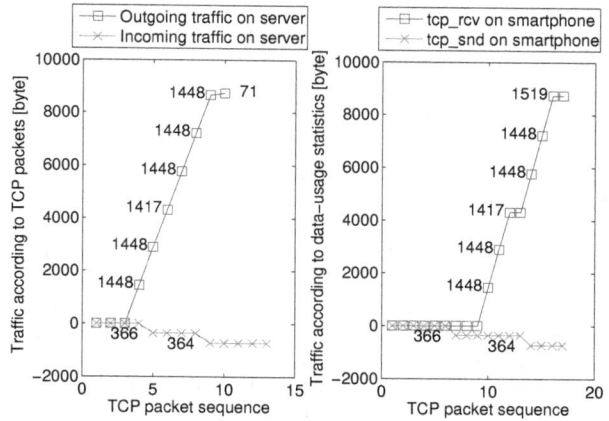

Figure 1: TCP packet lengths according to `tcpdump` and data-usage statistics on the smartphone.

ing UID is required. This information can be retrieved via the `ActivityManager` API for all running processes.

Subsequently, we investigate the information leakage of the data-usage statistics in more detail. We study the information leakage for browser applications considering a standard setting and in case the traffic is routed through the Tor network. Furthermore, we also investigate the information leakage depending on the network connection. Finally, we discuss our observations regarding the API support for the data-usage statistics and we discuss a mechanism to circumvent the `REAL_GET_TASKS` permission, which is required on Android Lollipop to retrieve the list of running applications.

3.1 Usage Statistics in a Controlled Scenario

For a first experiment, we set up a local server hosting a website and we launched `tcpdump` to dump all incoming and outgoing TCP packets on this server. Furthermore, we launched the browser application on one of our test devices (a Samsung Galaxy SIII) and retrieved its UID. We navigated to the website hosted on our server and monitored `tcp_snd` and `tcp_rcv` for a period of ten seconds with a sampling frequency of 50 Hz.

Figure 1 illustrates the accumulated TCP packet lengths (left) and the data-usage statistics on the Android smartphone (right). We indicate the outgoing traffic on our server as well as the incoming traffic on the smartphone above the x-axis. Similarly, we indicate the incoming traffic on our server as well as the outgoing traffic on the smartphone below the x-axis. For the sake of readability, we removed measurement samples where the traffic statistics did not change, i.e., we removed consecutive samples where the `tcp_rcv` and `tcp_snd` values did not change. Furthermore, we labeled each TCP packet with the corresponding packet length in both plots. The left plot shows the generated TCP packets according to our website. The first three outgoing packets (1448, 1448, 1417) correspond to the HTML page itself and the following packets (1448, 1448, 1448, 71) correspond to the retrieval of the embedded image. Interestingly, the data-usage statistics on the Android smartphone (right) corresponds to these TCP packet lengths, except for the last two packets (1448, 71), which are observed as one "large" packet (1519=1448+71) instead of two separate packets.

The same observation also holds for the incoming traffic on the server and the outgoing traffic on the smartphone, which are indicated below the x-axis. The corresponding TCP packet lengths can be observed in the outgoing data-usage statistics (366, 364).

The plots in Figure 1 illustrate the observed TCP packet lengths when loading the website for the first time, i.e., without any data being cached. When visiting the website for the second time, the traffic signature slightly changes. More specifically, the second part of the packet sequence (1448, 1448, 1448, 71) is missing as the embedded image is not requested anymore. However, some packet lengths remain the same, regardless of whether the website is cached or not.

Sampling Frequency. Zhou et al. [44] reported to be able to observe single TCP packet lengths with a sampling frequency of 10 Hz most of the time. We performed experiments with higher sampling frequencies but also observed the aggregation of multiple TCP packet lengths as one "larger" packet from time to time. A more detailed investigation of specific browser implementations—which is beyond the scope of this paper—might reveal further insights regarding the missed TCP packet lengths and might allow to pick up every single TCP packet properly. Nevertheless, even with some TCP packet lengths being accumulated into one observation, we can successfully exploit this side channel with a sampling frequency between 20 Hz and 50 Hz.

3.2 Usage Statistics for Real Websites

In order to investigate the information leakage for real websites, we developed an application that performs the following actions. First, we launch the browser and retrieve its UID. Then, we load three different websites (google.com, facebook.com, and youtube.com) and monitor tcp_snd and tcp_rcv for a period of ten seconds. The resulting plots can be seen in Figure 2. According to the notion of Jana and Shmatikov [22], these measurements are *stable*, meaning that these observations are similar across visits to the same page, and also *diverse*, meaning that these observations are dissimilar for visits to different pages. Hence, this plot confirms our previous observation that the data-usage statistics can be used to distinguish websites. A similar plot can be obtained from the tcp_snd file, i.e., the outbound network traffic, but has been omitted due to reasons of brevity.

3.3 Usage Statistics in the Tor Setting

Background on Tor. Before we investigate the information leakage of the data-usage statistics in case the network traffic is routed through the Tor network, we start with some background information on Tor. The major design goal of Tor [10] is "to frustrate attackers from linking communication partners" by considering an attacker who can, for instance, observe the network traffic. Therefore, a user runs a so-called onion proxy that is responsible for handling connections from user applications (e.g., the browser), fetching directories (e.g., known onion routers), and establishing circuits (paths) through the network. Such circuits consist of multiple onion routers—which are connected by means of a TLS connection—and are updated periodically. However, establishing such circuits is a costly action that takes some time, which is why multiple TCP streams share one circuit. The onion proxy accepts TCP streams from user applications (browsers) and forwards the data in fixed-size cells (512 bytes) through the TLS connection to the Tor network.

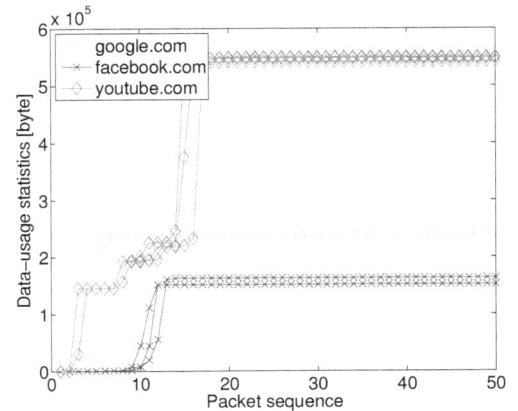

Figure 2: Data-usage statistics for the inbound traffic of three samples per website.

Information Leakage. In order to investigate the information leakage for traffic routed through the Tor network, we installed the Orweb browser and the corresponding Orbot proxy. The Orweb browser represents the user application and the Orbot proxy represents the onion proxy that handles connections from the Orweb browser and forwards the data to the Tor network. Since websites take longer to load, we increased the time for sampling the data-usage statistics to 20 seconds. As Tor on Android relies on two different applications, i.e., the Orweb browser and the Orbot proxy, we investigated the information leakage for both applications. While the Orweb browser communicates with the Orbot proxy only, the Orbot proxy communicates with the browser as well as the Tor network. Thus, the data-usage statistics for the Orbot proxy are slightly higher. However, both applications revealed the exact same behavior, i.e., the data-usage statistics yield stable and diverse plots, which can be exploited for website fingerprinting attacks. We also installed Firefox 42.0 and configured it to use the Orbot proxy. Repeating the experiment yields the same result, i.e., the data-usage statistics gathered for Firefox allow us to perform website-fingerprinting attacks even if Firefox is configured to route the network traffic through the Tor network. We stress that this is not a vulnerability of Tor or any browser but a fundamental weakness of the Android OS.

Even though data is sent through the Tor network in fixed-size cells (512 bytes), the data-usage statistics leak enough information to perform website fingerprinting attacks. We do not even need to extract complex features as in case of network-based fingerprinting attacks. Instead, the simple yet efficient observation of the data-usage statistics allows us to infer the user's visited websites as if the browser accesses the website directly (cf. Section 3.2).

3.4 Usage Statistics for Mobile Connections

The above performed experiments have been carried out with WLAN connections. For the sake of completeness, we also performed experiments with mobile data connections to be sure that we observe the same information leakage when the device is connected, e.g., via the 3G wireless network. The results confirmed our initial observations regarding the data-usage statistics also for mobile connections.

Table 1: Test devices and configurations

Device	OS	Browser/Orbot
Acer Iconia A510	Android 4.1.2	Chrome 44.0
Alcatel One Touch Pop 2	Android 4.4.4	Browser 4.4.4 (default browser)
Nexus 9	Android 5.1.1	Chrome 40.0
Samsung Galaxy SII	Android 2.3.4	Internet 2.3.4 (default browser)
Samsung Galaxy SII	Android 2.3.4	Orweb 0.7 and Orbot 13.0.4a
Samsung Galaxy SII	Android 2.3.4	Firefox 42.0 and Orbot 13.0.4a
Samsung Galaxy SIII	Android 4.3	Internet 4.3 (default browser)

3.5 API and /proc Support

Table 1 summarizes our test devices and their corresponding configurations. On most of these devices, we accessed the corresponding files within the /proc file system to retrieve the data-usage statistics. However, on the Alcatel One Touch Pop 2, the uid_stat file does not exist within the /proc file system, yet the TrafficStats API returned the accumulated bytes received (getUidRxBytes([uid])) and transmitted (getUidTxBytes([uid])) for a given UID. Similarly, on the Samsung Galaxy SIII, we always retrieved 0 when querying the TrafficStats API, but still we were able to read the data-usage statistics from the /proc file system.

To summarize our investigations, on some devices an attacker needs to rely on the /proc file system, while on others the attacker needs to rely on the TrafficStats API. However, all test devices showed the same information leakage through the data-usage statistics.

REAL_GET_TASKS Permission in Lollipop. Since Android Lollipop (5.0), the REAL_GET_TASKS permission is required to retrieve all running applications via ActivityManager.getRunningAppProcesses(). However, one can bypass this permission by retrieving a list of installed applications via PackageManager.getInstalledApplications(). The returned information also contains the UID for each of the installed applications. Now, instead of waiting for the browser application to show up in the list returned via getRunningAppProcesses(), the malicious application can also wait for the tcp_rcv file to be created, which indicates that the application with the given UID has been started. Another alternative to retrieve all running applications is the unprivileged ps command. Thus, even on Android Lollipop, our malicious service can be implemented without any suspicious permission and is still able to wait in the background for the browser application to start.

4. ADVERSARY MODEL AND SCENARIO

Traditional website fingerprinting attacks consider a *network attacker* who is located somewhere on the victim's network. As illustrated in Figure 3, the adversary observes the encrypted communication between a client and a proxy (or similarly the encrypted communication between the client and the Tor network). In contrast, we consider an attacker who managed to spread a malicious application through a popular app market like *Google Play* or the *Amazon Appstore*. The malicious application running in unprivileged mode represents a *passive* attacker that observes the incoming and outgoing traffic statistics for any target application, e.g., the browser. Figure 4 illustrates this attack scenario for traffic routed through the Tor network. In this case, the user browses the web with the Browser application (e.g., Orweb) and the traffic is routed through the Tor network by means of a dedicated Proxy (e.g., Orbot). However, our attack

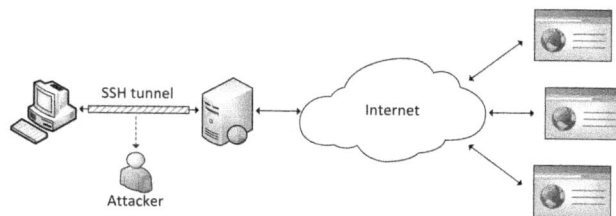

Figure 3: Traditional website fingerprinting attack considering a network attacker.

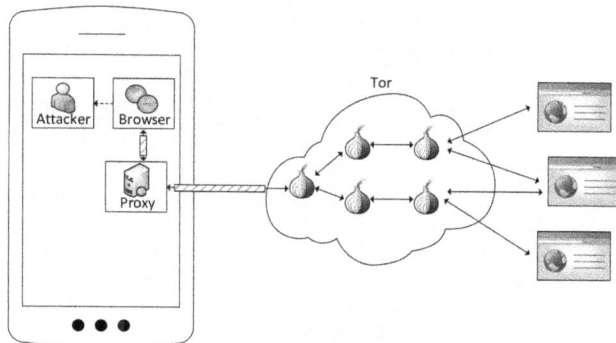

Figure 4: Client-side website fingerprinting attack exploiting side-channel information.

works analogously in case the browser connects to websites directly. Furthermore, our attack also works against the Proxy application, as has been discussed in Section 3.3.

According to the notion of Diaz et al. [9], our attacker is passive as it cannot add, drop or change packets. However, this also means that our attacker is lightweight in terms of resource usage as it runs in the background and waits for the browser application to start. Below we describe two possible attack scenarios, one where the training data is gathered on dedicated devices and another one where the attack application gathers the training data directly on the device under attack. Note that the INTERNET permission is not required at all due the following reasons. Since Android Marshmallow (6.0), the INTERNET permission is granted automatically[3] and below Android 6.0, ACTION_VIEW[4] Intents can be used to access the Internet via the browser without this permission.

Since the application neither requires any suspicious permission nor exploits specific vulnerabilities except accesses to publicly readable files and the Android API, the sanity checks performed by app markets (e.g., Google Bouncer) will not detect any malicious behavior. Thus, the application can be spread easily via available app markets. Based on the presented adversary model and the low effort to spread such a malicious application, there is a significantly higher attack potential than in previous fingerprinting attacks. Furthermore, as discussed in Section 1.1, an attacker could combine website fingerprinting attacks with sensor-based keyloggers to launch large-scale identity theft attacks.

---

[3] http://developer.android.com/guide/topics/security/normal-permissions.html

[4] http://www.leviathansecurity.com/blog/zero-permission-android-applications

4.1 Possible Attack Scenarios

In order to exploit the information leakage, we consider two different attack scenarios.

Scenario 1. For this scenario we assume that the malicious application does not capture the required training data on the device itself. Instead, a more powerful adversary gathers the training data on specifically deployed devices. The application only waits for the browser to start, gathers the traffic information, and sends the gathered data to the remote server that infers the visited websites. In order to match the device name of the attacked device with the training devices, the `android.os.Build` API can be used.

Scenario 2. For this scenario we assume that the malicious application captures the required training data directly on the device. Therefore, it triggers the browser to load a list of websites, one after each other, via the `ACTION_VIEW` Intent. While the browser loads the website, the malicious application captures the traffic statistics from `tcp_rcv` and `tcp_snd`, which then acts as training data. After collecting the required training data, the application waits in the background until the unsuspecting user opens the browser and starts browsing the web. Then, the application gathers the traffic statistics from `tcp_rcv` and `tcp_snd` again, and matches the collected information against the previously established training data to infer the visited websites.

A technicality that needs to be solved in case of scenario 2 is that users should not notice the gathering of the training data. For that purpose, we note that Zhou et al. [44] demonstrated the possibility to (1) wait for the screen to dim before launching the browser, and (2) to close the browser after loading the website. Thereby, the user does not observe any suspicious behavior, even though the application launches the browser application in the foreground. However, the main drawback of this approach is that the device might switch to sleep mode and pause all activities, which means that gathering the training data takes some time.

4.2 Assumptions

According to Wang et al. [38], existing fingerprinting attacks rely on two assumptions. We briefly summarize these assumptions and argue why our attack approach is more realistic than existing fingerprinting attacks.

1. *The attacker knows the start and end of a packet trace.* This assumption is based on the observation that users take some time to load the next webpage. We justify this assumption by arguing that we are able to determine when the browser starts. Thus, we are able to observe the first trace. Afterwards, we assume that the user takes some time to load the next page.

2. *The client does not perform any other activity that can be confused with page-loading activities, for example, a file download.* Hayes and Danezis [18] pointed out that it is highly unlikely that an attacker will be able to gather traffic information without background traffic, which limits the applicability of existing website fingerprinting attacks. However, Android captures the data-usage statistics on a per-application basis and, thus, our approach is invariant to network activities of other applications. For instance, our attack also works in case an e-Mail app, WhatsApp, or any other app fetches updates in the background while the user browses the web. In contrast, it is highly unlikely that the network traffic on the wire does not contain any background traffic.

Another thing that needs to be clarified is the browser's caching behavior. For our experiments, we do not clean the cache before loading a page as we assume that adversaries might be interested in identifying frequently visited websites of a user. If users frequently visit specific websites, then these sites are most probably already cached. Still, specific parts of the TCP packets are equal between cached and non-cached pages, as has been discussed in Section 3.1. Our experiments with the Orweb browser use the default settings, meaning that caching of websites is disabled. Thus, we provide insights for both settings of the caching behavior.

5. ATTACK DESCRIPTION

Based on the presented adversary model and attack scenarios, we now describe the attack in more detail. First, we discuss how to gather the required traffic statistics for a set of monitored websites. Afterwards, we describe the employed classifier to infer the visited websites.

5.1 Gathering Traffic Signatures

The list of monitored websites might, for example, be chosen according to specific interests like political interests, sexual orientation, illnesses, or websites that are supposed to be blocked. For our evaluation, we decided to use popular websites among different categories according to `alexa.com`. The fact that Tor browsers, e.g., Orweb, do not cache pages, leads to the realistic scenario that an adversary wants to monitor landing pages (cf. [18]). Thus, we consider our chosen setting for the evaluation as being realistic.

Algorithm 1 summarizes the basic steps to establish the required training data denoted as traffic signature database T. The algorithm is given a list of monitored websites W, the desired number of samples per website n, a profiling time τ, and a sampling frequency f. For each website $w_i \in W$, the algorithm loads this website within the browser. While the browser application loads the website w_i, we gather the data-usage statistics f times per second for a period of τ seconds. Each tuple (w_i, t_i), which is denoted as one *sample* for a specific website w_i, is added to T. These steps are repeated until n samples have been gathered for each website. Finally, the algorithm returns the traffic signature database T.

Algorithm 1: Gathering training samples.

Input: List of monitored websites W, number of samples per website n, profiling time τ, sampling frequency f

Output: Traffic signature database T

Launch browser application and retrieve its UID
repeat *n times*
    foreach *website w_i in W* **do**
        simultaneously
        Launch website w_i in browser
        while *profiling time τ not passed* **do**
            f **times per second**
            read `tcp_rcv` and append to t_{IN}
            read `tcp_snd` and append to t_{OUT}
        end
        $t_i \leftarrow \{t_{IN}, t_{OUT}\}$
        Add tuple (w_i, t_i) to T
    end
end

5.2 Classification

The traffic signature database T requires only minor pre-processing before the actual classification. More specifically, we removed samples of websites that did not load, i.e., we removed tuples (w_i, t_i) from T where all entries in t_i are 0. Furthermore, if $n-1$ samples for a specific website are removed, we remove the remaining sample as well. We justify this as follows. If this single remaining sample of a specific website is used for training, then it cannot be used for evaluation purposes. Similarly, if we do not have a single sample for training, then this site will never be classified correctly.

We use the Jaccard index as a metric to determine the similarity between two websites. In case of our measurement samples, the Jaccard index as defined in Equation 1 compares two traces t_1 and t_2 based on unique and distinguishable packet lengths.

$$\text{Jaccard}(t_1, t_2) = \frac{|t_1 \cap t_2|}{|t_1 \cup t_2|} \qquad (1)$$

We consider the traces of the inbound and outbound traffic separately. Hence, our classifier aims to find the maximum similarity for a given trace $t_A = \{t_{IN_A}, t_{OUT_A}\}$ compared to all traces $t_i = \{t_{IN_i}, t_{OUT_i}\}$ within the previously established traffic signature database T. We illustrate this similarity measure in Equation 2.

$$\begin{aligned}\text{Sim}(t_A = \{t_{IN_A}, t_{OUT_A}\}, t_i = \{t_{IN_i}, t_{OUT_i}\}) = \\ \text{Jaccard}(t_{IN_A}, t_{IN_i}) + \text{Jaccard}(t_{OUT_A}, t_{OUT_i})\end{aligned} \qquad (2)$$

Based on this similarity metric, we implemented our classifier as outlined in Algorithm 2. The algorithm is given a list of monitored websites W, a traffic signature database T, and the signature t to be classified. As T contains multiple samples (w_i, t_i) for one website, we compute the similarity of t with all these traffic signatures t_j with $1 \leq j \leq n$ corresponding to a specific website w_i. Afterwards, we compute the average similarity with all these traces for this specific website w_i. Finally, we return the website w_i with the highest average similarity s_i compared to the given trace t.

Algorithm 2: Classification algorithm.

Input: List of monitored websites W, traffic signature database T, traffic signature t

Output: Website w

foreach *website w_i in W* **do**
  Retrieve all samples $(w_i, t_1), \ldots, (w_i, t_n) \in T$
  $s_i = \text{avg}(\text{Sim}(t_1, t), \ldots, \text{Sim}(t_n, t))$
  Add tuple (w_i, s_i) to S
end
Return $(w_i, s_i) \in S$, s.t. s_i is maximized

Compared to network-based fingerprinting attacks, our attack relies on a simple yet efficient classifier. We do not need a dedicated training phase that requires several hundred CPU hours for some network-based fingerprinting attacks (cf. [38, 39]). Still, the testing time of our classifier is comparable to existing fingerprinting attacks and yields highly accurate results as will be discussed in Section 6.5.

6. EVALUATION AND RESULTS

We now evaluate the classification rate for a standard browser application and continue with a setting where the

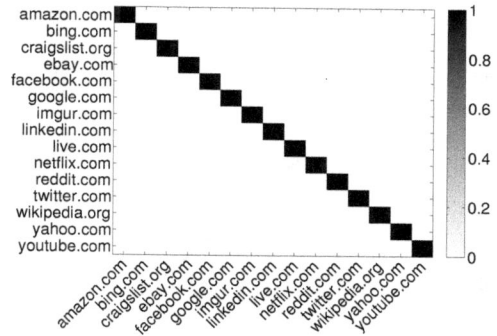

Figure 5: Confusion matrix for the 15 most popular websites in the US.

Table 2: Google websites that have been merged

google.co.in	google.co.jp	google.de
google.co.uk	google.com.br	google.fr
google.ru	google.it	google.es
google.ca	google.com.mx	google.com.hk
google.com.tr	google.co.id	google.pl
google.com.au	google.co.kr	googleadservices.com

traffic is routed through the Tor network. We also investigate how the classification rate decreases over time and we evaluate the scalability of our attack for larger sets of monitored websites. Finally, we compare our results to related work. All experiments in this section have been performed with data-usage statistics captured via WLAN connections.

6.1 Intra-Day Classification Rate

For our first experiment, we took the 15 most popular websites in the US according to `alexa.com` and we gathered $n = 5$ samples for each of these websites to establish the signature database T. In order to estimate the performance of our classifier, we performed a leave-one-out cross validation. Thus, for each sample $(w_i, t_i) \in T$, we removed this sample (one at a time) from the traffic signature database T, and called the classification algorithm (Algorithm 2) with the traffic signature database $T \setminus (w_i, t_i)$ and the traffic signature t_i to be classified.

Figure 5 illustrates the resulting confusion matrix. We indicate the ground truth along the y-axis and the inferred website along the x-axis. Since each of the five page visits to each of these 15 websites has been classified correctly, we achieve a classification rate of 100%. More specifically, each sample (w_i, t_i) has been classified correctly considering the traffic signature database $T \setminus (w_i, t_i)$ for training the classifier.

If we have a look at the 100 most popular websites globally, then we observe a classification rate of 89% for a total of 500 page visits. After further investigations of the resulting confusion matrix, we noticed that several misclassifications occur because `google*.*` pages have been misclassified among each other. For example, `google.es` has been misclassified as either `google.fr`, `google.it`, or `google.pl`. Nevertheless, we do not aim for a detailed classification of different Google domains and, hence, we merged all websites as shown in Table 2 to be classified as `google.com`.

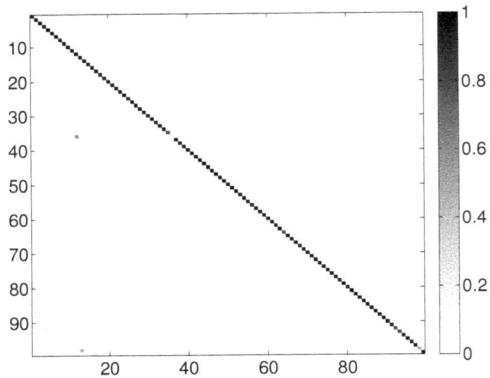

Figure 6: Confusion matrix for the 100 most popular websites globally with *google*.** pages merged.

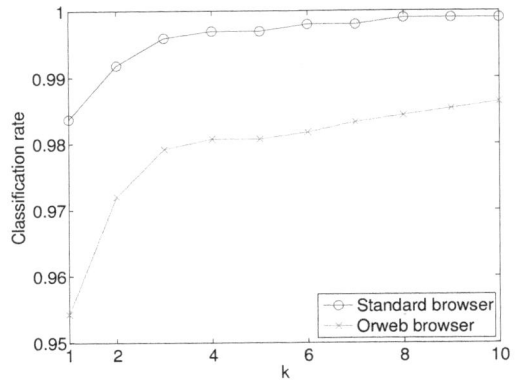

Figure 7: Classification rates considering the k most probable websites returned from the classifier.

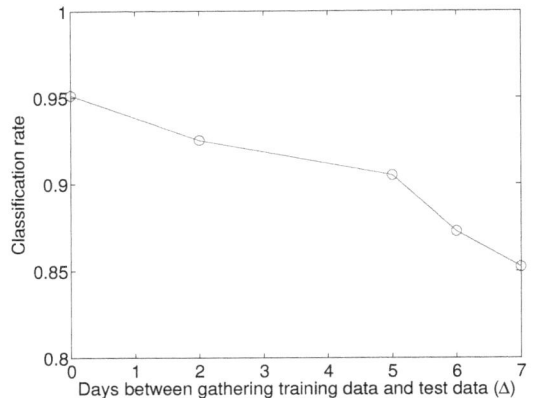

Figure 8: Decreasing accuracy for samples captured Δ days after the training data.

Performing the classification again, we achieve a classification rate of 98% for these 500 page visits. The corresponding confusion matrix can be seen in Figure 6. Merging these Google websites leads to a total of 9 misclassified websites among these 500 page visits, with `mail.ru` at index 36 being the most commonly misclassified website (4 times).

6.2 Classification Rate for Tor

We also evaluated our attack for traffic routed through Tor. Therefore, we gathered $n = 5$ samples for the top 100 websites in the US by capturing the data-usage statistics of the Orweb browser, but we used a profiling time of 20 seconds as websites accessed via Tor take more time to load. Again, we performed a leave-one-out cross validation resulting in a classification rate of 95% for these 500 page visits.

If we instruct the classifier to return a set of k possible websites, which are sorted according to their probability for being the correct one, then the success rate steadily increases with the number of websites k taken into consideration. As can be seen in Figure 7, taking the two most probable websites ($k = 2$) into consideration, we achieve a classification rate of 97% and taking the three most probable websites ($k = 3$) into consideration yields a classification rate of 98%. Similar classification rates can be observed for the standard Android browser where the traffic is not routed through Tor. Although the standard browser yields slightly better classification rates, we did not observe significant differences between the classification rates when accessing websites directly and when accessing websites via Tor.

Security Implications. Even though browsers (e.g., Orweb or "private/incognito" modes) do not store the browsing history and the network traffic is protected against specific attacks while being routed through the Tor network, an unprivileged application can infer the user's browsing behavior for monitored websites. Thus, the `READ_HISTORY_BOOKMARKS` permission does not protect the user's privacy and even routing the network traffic through Tor provides a false sense of privacy for Android users. Furthermore, given the fact that Orweb disables JavaScript and Flash by default, users do not use Orweb to access sites that heavily rely on these techniques. Hence, attackers explicitly targeting Tor users can significantly reduce the set of monitored websites, which increases the success rate. However, we do not blame the browsers for these security implications but the Android OS.

6.3 Inter-Day Classification Rate

We also performed experiments with an outdated training set. In order to do so, we used Orweb to collect measurement samples for the top 100 websites in the US a few days after gathering the training data. The evaluation in Figure 8 shows that the accuracy decreases rather slowly. For test data that has been gathered on the same day as the training data ($\Delta = 0$), 95% of all page visits can be inferred. Using the same data to classify 500 page visits captured two days later ($\Delta = 2$) still yields a classification accuracy of 93%. Testing measurement samples captured after five days ($\Delta = 5$) yields a classification accuracy of 91%. Even data gathered one week later ($\Delta = 7$) achieves a classification rate of 85%. Hence, even slightly outdated training data allows to infer websites accurately.

This slowly decreasing classification rate allows an adversary to keep the traffic signature database T for some time, meaning that the adversary does not need to update the database for the monitored websites on a daily basis. Thereby, the attacker's effort and workload can be reduced significantly, which leads to more practical attacks. Furthermore, this also indicates that the training samples can be gathered after the actual attack samples, which represents another advantage for the attacker (cf. [27]).

Table 3: Websites with the highest number of misclassifications in the inter-day setting

Δ	Website	# misclassifications
2 days	ask.com	5 times
2 days	twitch.tv	5 times
2 days	cnn.com	3 times
5 days	bbc.com	5 times
5 days	indeed.com	5 times
5 days	nytimes.com	5 times
5 days	twitch.tv	5 times
5 days	espn.go.com	4 times
6 days	bbc.com	5 times
6 days	indeed.com	5 times
6 days	nytimes.com	5 times
6 days	twitch.tv	5 times
6 days	espn.go.com	4 times
7 days	bbc.com	5 times
7 days	bleacherreport.com	5 times
7 days	indeed.com	5 times
7 days	nytimes.com	5 times
7 days	twitch.tv	5 times
7 days	xfinity.com	5 times
7 days	homedepot.com	4 times

Table 3 shows the worst websites (according to their classification accuracy) in case the attack samples are captured Δ days after the training data. As news sites tend to change frequently, it is not surprising that the classification rate decreases for such websites. Based on this observation, an attacker can selectively rebuild the training set for frequently changing websites like news portals, while the training data for more static websites can be kept for a longer period. We point out that we did not employ any measures to ensure that we exit Tor with a specific country IP. Instead, every time we gathered new test samples, we reconnected to the Tor network by restarting the Orbot proxy. Nevertheless, the classification rates indicate a high success rate even with a training set that is not completely up to date.

6.4 Scalability for Larger World Sizes

In order to investigate the scalability of our attack for a larger set of monitored websites, we consider the top 500 websites. However, we did not route the network traffic through Tor as this would have taken significantly longer. Our results indicate that we are able to classify 97% of 2 500 page visits out of a set of 500 monitored websites.

6.5 Comparison with Related Work

As our attack only requires an unprivileged Android application, it is easier to perform than wiretapping attacks where the attacker observes TCP packets on the victim's network. Considering the ease of applicability, the computational performance of the classifier, and the classification rates, our attack outperforms existing fingerprinting attacks.

Table 4 provides a comprehensive comparison of website fingerprinting attacks in the closed-world setting. For each attack, we present the attacker or the exploited information in column 2. Column 3 indicates the caching behavior of the browser. Column 4 shows the employed classifier. For the sake of brevity, we do not list the exact features that are used for classification purposes, but we refer the interested reader to the corresponding works. Column 5 shows the attacked countermeasure, where "none" refers to

no specific countermeasure, "SSH tunnel" means that the client hides its network traffic through a proxy where the encrypted communication between the client and the proxy is observed, and "Tor" means that the traffic is routed through the anonymity network Tor. As most website fingerprinting attacks consider a closed-world setting, we state the number of monitored websites in column 6. Furthermore, we indicate the accuracy within the last column.

The only works in Table 4 that exploit client-side side-channel information are the work of Jana and Shmatikov [22] as well as ours. To be more precise, Jana and Shmatikov do not exploit information that relates to the TCP packet lengths. Instead, they exploit the memory footprint of the browser while rendering the monitored website. However, our approach of exploiting the data-usage statistics allows a significantly more accurate inference of visited websites.

Compared to wiretapping attacks against the anonymity network Tor, we observe that our approach of exploiting client-side information leaks yields mostly better results. Though, the works of Wang and Goldberg [39] and Wang et al. [38] achieve a rather similar classification accuracy. For instance, on a set of 100 monitored websites, they achieve a classification accuracy of 91% [39] and 95% [38], respectively. However, training their classifiers, which are based on the optimal string alignment distance and a weighted k-NN, takes a significant amount of time (608 000 CPU seconds [39]). This, however, is not feasible for every attacker. As our classifier does not require a training phase, we significantly reduce the computational effort. Our test algorithm scales linearly with the number of monitored websites and the corresponding samples, i.e., $\mathcal{O}(|W| \cdot n)$. A naive implementation of our classifier (Algorithm 2)—without any specific optimizations—in Matlab takes a testing time of about 0.4 seconds on an Intel Core i7-5600U CPU for a set of 100 monitored websites and 5 samples per website. This testing time is comparable to the testing time of 0.7 seconds reported by Wang and Goldberg [39], but in contrast to their work we do not require an expensive training phase.

Wiretapping vs. Side-Channel Observations. The subtle difference between observing traffic information on the wire and the side-channel information of the data-usage statistics requires further considerations. In the wiretapping scenario it is impossible to miss single packets, whereas in in the side-channel scenario the attacker might miss single packets which are then observed as one "large" packet due to the accumulation of TCP packets within the data-usage statistics. However, wiretapping attacks against Tor need to rely on the observation of padded packets only, whereas we also observe unpadded packets due to the separation of the browser and proxy application on the smartphone.

To summarize this comparison, we consider it easier to deploy a malicious application than to wiretap the victim's network, but we trade the exact observation of single TCP packet lengths (or padded packets in case of Tor) for a slightly less accurate side-channel observation. The most significant advantage of our attack is that it only requires an unprivileged Android application and a simple (yet efficient) classifier. Thus, in contrast to wiretapping attacks, the presented attack can be deployed on a large scale. In addition, our client-side attack overcomes many limitations and assumptions of network-based fingerprinting attacks that are considered unrealistic, i.e., it is invariant to background traffic and does not require expensive training phases.

Table 4: Comparison of website fingerprinting attacks in the closed-world setting

Work	Exploited information	Caching	Classifier	Countermeasure	# websites	Classification rate
Ours	Client-side data-usage statistics	Enabled	Jaccard index	None	500	**97%**
Jana and Shmatikov [22]	Client-side memory footprint	Enabled?[a]	Jaccard index	None	100	35%
Cai et al. [6]	TCP packets captured via tshark	Disabled	Damerau-Levenshtein distance	SSH tunnel	100	92%
Herrmann et al. [20]	Client-side tcpdump	Disabled	Naive-Bayes classifier	SSH tunnel	775	96%
Liberatore and Levine [27]	Client-side tcpdump	Disabled	Jaccard index	SSH tunnel	500	79%
Liberatore and Levine [27]	Client-side tcpdump	Disabled	Naive-Bayes classifier	SSH tunnel	500	75%
Ours	Client-side data-usage statistics	Disabled	Jaccard index	Tor	100	**95%**
Herrmann et al. [20]	Client-side tcpdump	Disabled	Multinomial Naive-Bayes classifier	Tor	775	3%
Cai et al. [6]	TCP packets captured via tshark	Disabled	Damerau-Levenshtein distance	Tor	100	84%
Panchenko et al. [35]	Client-side tcpdump	Disabled	Support vector machines	Tor	775	55%
Wang and Goldberg [39]	TCP packets[b]	Disabled	Optimal string alignment distance[c]	Tor	100	91%
Wang and Goldberg [39]	TCP packets[b]	Disabled	Levenshtein distance	Tor	100	70%
Wang et al. [38]	TCP packets[d]	Disabled	k-nearest neighbour[e]	Tor	100	95%

[a]We are not sure whether caching has been disabled for the Android browser.
[b]They parsed TCP packets to obtain the underlying Tor cells but did not specify how to obtain the TCP packets.
[c]Training took 608 000 CPU seconds.
[d]They used the same data set as in [39].
[e]The computational complexity of the training phase is similar to [39] (cf. footnote c).

7. DISCUSSION OF COUNTERMEASURES

We now provide an overview of existing countermeasures. However, most of these countermeasures have been proposed to mitigate wiretapping attacks and, thus, we discuss the relevance of these defense mechanisms against our attack.

7.1 Existing Countermeasures

Traffic Morphing. Wright et al. [40] suggested traffic morphing, which requires the cooperation of the target web server or proxy as well as the browser. Each packet from a website is padded or split in such a way that the traffic information of the actual website matches the traffic information of a different website. As a result, an attacker observing the traffic information will most likely misclassify this website.

HTTPOS. A browser-based defense mechanism denoted as HTTP or HTTPS with Obfuscation (HTTPOS) has been proposed by Luo et al. [29]. HTTPOS focuses on changing packet sizes and packet timings, which can be done, for instance, by adding bytes to the referer header or by using the HTTP range option to fetch specific portions of websites.

BuFLO. Dyer et al. [11] presented Buffered Fixed-Length Obfuscator (BuFLO) that sends fixed-length packets at fixed intervals for a fixed amount of time. While the authors claim that BuFLO significantly reduces the attack surface, it is rather inefficient in terms of bandwidth overhead. Again, BuFLO requires the cooperation of the involved proxies. Cai et al. [4] proposed an extension denoted as Congestion-Sensitive Buffered Fixed-Length Obfuscator (CS-BuFLO).

Glove. Nithyanand et al. [32] proposed Glove, which tries to cluster similar websites according to pre-selected features. Based on these clusters, transcripts of packet sizes (denoted as super-traces) are computed, which are later transmitted whenever a page in the corresponding cluster is loaded. This super-trace is obtained by inserting, merging, splitting, and delaying packets. The major drawback of Glove is that the traces must be updated regularly, which is rather expensive.

7.2 Discussion

The above mentioned countermeasures aim at preventing website fingerprinting attacks. Nevertheless, network-level defenses do not provide effective countermeasures against client-side attacks. For instance, if the traffic is routed through the Tor network, then the traffic might be protected on the network. However, unless the browser itself is actively involved in these defense mechanisms, these countermeasures do not provide protection against client-side attackers. We demonstrated this by exploiting the data-usage statistics of browser applications that route the traffic through the Tor network. Furthermore, application-level defenses like HTTPOS might prevent such attacks at first glance, but Cai et al. [4] already demonstrated that a network attacker can circumvent this countermeasure. Besides, many network-level defenses add a significant overhead in terms of bandwidth and data consumption, which is impractical for mobile devices with a limited data plan. We consider further investigations regarding the effectiveness of countermeasures against client-side attacks as an interesting open research problem. Furthermore, new proposals for countermeasures should consider mobile devices.

Client-Side Countermeasures. Besides these proposed countermeasures, which mostly target network-level attackers, fixing fundamental design flaws of Android should be considered as absolutely necessary. Zhou et al. [44] suggested two permission-based approaches. The first one is a new permission that allows applications to monitor the data-usage statistics. The second one is to let applications define how data-usage statistics should be published. We, however, do not consider these approaches as viable countermeasures for the following reasons. First, many users either do not pay attention to the requested permissions or they do not understand the meaning of these permissions (cf. [13, 25]). Second, the permission system also confuses developers which leads to overprivileged applications [12]. Besides, developers might not be aware that the data-usage statistics of their application leaks sensitive information and, thus, should impose restrictions on how to publish these statistics.

A more general approach to prevent such side-channel attacks has been suggested by Zhang et al. [43]. The basic idea of their approach is that an application (*App Guardian*) pauses/stops suspicious background processes when the application to be protected (principal) is executed. This idea sounds quite appealing but still struggles with unsolved issues like a proper identification of malicious processes.

A first solution to defend against such attacks would be to update these statistics according to a more coarse-grained granularity. We stress that data-usage statistics capturing single TCP packet lengths represents a significant threat. Updating data-usage statistics in a more coarse-grained interval, e.g., on a daily basis, should suffice for users to keep an eye on their data consumption. Future work might come up with more advanced countermeasures and the above outlined approach of *App Guardian* [43] definitely follows the right direction towards the prevention of such attacks. Still, we urge OS developers to address this issue immediately.

8. CONCLUSION

In this work, we investigated a new type of client-side website fingerprinting attack that exploits the data-usage statistics published by Android. We argue that incognito/private browsing modes, the `READ_HISTORY_BOOKMARKS` permission, and even routing the network traffic through Tor provides a false sense of privacy for smartphone users. Even though the browser itself does not store any information about visited websites and the traffic is protected while being routed through Tor, the data-usage statistics leak sensitive information. We demonstrated that any application can accurately infer a user's visited websites without any suspicious permission. Hence, the `READ_HISTORY_BOOKMARKS` permission—which is supposed to protect a user's browsing behavior—is actually irrelevant as it does not provide protection.

Compared to existing website fingerprinting attacks, our attack can be deployed significantly easier and allows for more accurate classifications of websites. The ease of applicability allows even less sophisticated attackers to perform accurate website fingerprinting attacks on a large scale, which clearly proves the immense threat arising from this information leak. As a user's browsing behavior reveals rather sensitive information, we urge the need to address this issue on the operating system level. Furthermore, due to the simple (yet accurate) classification algorithm, real-time detection of the user's browsing behavior in combination with sensor-based keyloggers allows for large-scale identity theft attacks which must be prevented by all means.

Acknowledgment

This work has been supported by the Austrian Research Promotion Agency (FFG) and the Styrian Business Promotion Agency (SFG) under grant number 836628 (SeCoS) and in part by the European Commission through the FP7 program under project number 610436 (project MATTHEW).

9. REFERENCES

[1] A. J. Aviv, B. Sapp, M. Blaze, and J. M. Smith. Practicality of Accelerometer Side Channels on Smartphones. In *Annual Computer Security Applications Conference – ACSAC 2012*, pages 41–50. ACM, 2012.

[2] G. D. Bissias, M. Liberatore, D. Jensen, and B. N. Levine. Privacy Vulnerabilities in Encrypted HTTP Streams. In *Privacy Enhancing Technologies – PET 2005*, volume 3856 of *LNCS*, pages 1–11. Springer, 2005.

[3] L. Cai and H. Chen. TouchLogger: Inferring Keystrokes on Touch Screen from Smartphone Motion. In *USENIX Workshop on Hot Topics in Security – HotSec*. USENIX Association, 2011.

[4] X. Cai, R. Nithyanand, and R. Johnson. CS-BuFLO: A Congestion Sensitive Website Fingerprinting Defense. In *Workshop on Privacy in the Electronic Society – WPES 2014*, pages 121–130. ACM, 2014.

[5] X. Cai, R. Nithyanand, T. Wang, R. Johnson, and I. Goldberg. A Systematic Approach to Developing and Evaluating Website Fingerprinting Defenses. In *Conference on Computer and Communications Security – CCS 2014*, pages 227–238. ACM, 2014.

[6] X. Cai, X. C. Zhang, B. Joshi, and R. Johnson. Touching from a Distance: Website Fingerprinting Attacks and Defenses. In *Conference on Computer and Communications Security – CCS 2012*, pages 605–616. ACM, 2012.

[7] S. Chen, R. Wang, X. Wang, and K. Zhang. Side-Channel Leaks in Web Applications: A Reality Today, a Challenge Tomorrow. In *IEEE Symposium on Security and Privacy – S&P 2010*, pages 191–206. IEEE Computer Society, 2010.

[8] M. Conti, L. V. Mancini, R. Spolaor, and N. V. Verde. Analyzing Android Encrypted Network Traffic to Identify User Actions. *IEEE Transactions on Information Forensics and Security*, 11:114–125, 2016.

[9] C. Díaz, S. Seys, J. Claessens, and B. Preneel. Towards Measuring Anonymity. In *Privacy Enhancing Technologies – PET 2002*, volume 2482 of *LNCS*, pages 54–68. Springer, 2002.

[10] R. Dingledine, N. Mathewson, and P. F. Syverson. Tor: The Second-Generation Onion Router. In *USENIX Security Symposium 2004*, pages 303–320. USENIX, 2004.

[11] K. P. Dyer, S. E. Coull, T. Ristenpart, and T. Shrimpton. Peek-a-Boo, I Still See You: Why Efficient Traffic Analysis Countermeasures Fail. In *IEEE Symposium on Security and Privacy – S&P 2012*, pages 332–346. IEEE Computer Society, 2012.

[12] A. P. Felt, E. Chin, S. Hanna, D. Song, and D. Wagner. Android Permissions Demystified. In *Conference on Computer and Communications Security – CCS 2011*, pages 627–638. ACM, 2011.

[13] A. P. Felt, E. Ha, S. Egelman, A. Haney, E. Chin, and D. Wagner. Android Permissions: User Attention, Comprehension, and Behavior. In *Symposium On Usable Privacy and Security – SOUPS 2012*, page 3. ACM, 2012.

[14] E. W. Felten and M. A. Schneider. Timing Attacks on Web Privacy. In *Conference on Computer and Communications Security – CCS 2000*, pages 25–32. ACM, 2000.

[15] X. Gong, N. Borisov, N. Kiyavash, and N. Schear. Website Detection Using Remote Traffic Analysis. In *Privacy Enhancing Technologies – PET 2012*, volume 7384 of *LNCS*, pages 58–78. Springer, 2012.

[16] X. Gong, N. Kiyavash, and N. Borisov. Fingerprinting Websites Using Remote Traffic Analysis. In *Conference on Computer and Communications Security – CCS 2010*, pages 684–686. ACM, 2010.

[17] D. Gruss, D. Bidner, and S. Mangard. Practical Memory Deduplication Attacks in Sandboxed Javascript. In *European Symposium on Research in Computer Security – ESORICS 2015*, volume 9326 of *LNCS*, pages 108–122. Springer, 2015.

[18] J. Hayes and G. Danezis. Better Open-World Website Fingerprinting. *CoRR*, abs/1509.00789, 2015.

[19] G. He, M. Yang, X. Gu, J. Luo, and Y. Ma. A Novel Active Website Fingerprinting Attack Against Tor Anonymous System. In *Computer Supported Cooperative Work in Design – CSCWD 2014*, pages 112–117. IEEE, 2014.

[20] D. Herrmann, R. Wendolsky, and H. Federrath. Website Fingerprinting: Attacking Popular Privacy Enhancing Technologies with the Multinomial Naïve-Bayes Classifier. In *Cloud Computing Security Workshop – CCSW*, pages 31–42. ACM, 2009.

[21] A. Hintz. Fingerprinting Websites Using Traffic Analysis. In *Privacy Enhancing Technologies – PET 2002*, volume 2482 of *LNCS*, pages 171–178. Springer, 2002.

[22] S. Jana and V. Shmatikov. Memento: Learning Secrets from Process Footprints. In *IEEE Symposium on Security and Privacy – S&P 2012*, pages 143–157. IEEE Computer Society, 2012.

[23] A. Janc and L. Olejnik. Web Browser History Detection as a Real-World Privacy Threat. In *European Symposium on Research in Computer Security – ESORICS 2010*, volume 6345 of *LNCS*, pages 215–231. Springer, 2010.

[24] M. Juárez, S. Afroz, G. Acar, C. Díaz, and R. Greenstadt. A Critical Evaluation of Website Fingerprinting Attacks. In *Conference on Computer and Communications Security – CCS 2014*, pages 263–274. ACM, 2014.

[25] P. G. Kelley, S. Consolvo, L. F. Cranor, J. Jung, N. M. Sadeh, and D. Wetherall. A Conundrum of Permissions: Installing Applications on an Android Smartphone. In *Financial Cryptography – FC 2012*, volume 7398 of *LNCS*, pages 68–79. Springer, 2012.

[26] B. Liang, W. You, L. Liu, W. Shi, and M. Heiderich. Scriptless Timing Attacks on Web Browser Privacy. In *Dependable Systems and Networks – DSN 2014*, pages 112–123. IEEE, 2014.

[27] M. Liberatore and B. N. Levine. Inferring the Source of Encrypted HTTP Connections. In *Conference on Computer and Communications Security – CCS 2006*, pages 255–263. ACM, 2006.

[28] L. Lu, E. Chang, and M. C. Chan. Website Fingerprinting and Identification Using Ordered Feature Sequences. In *European Symposium on Research in Computer Security – ESORICS 2010*, volume 6345 of *LNCS*, pages 199–214. Springer, 2010.

[29] X. Luo, P. Zhou, E. W. W. Chan, W. Lee, R. K. C. Chang, and R. Perdisci. HTTPOS: Sealing Information Leaks with Browser-side Obfuscation of Encrypted Flows. In *Network and Distributed System Security Symposium – NDSS 2011*. The Internet Society, 2011.

[30] B. Miller, L. Huang, A. D. Joseph, and J. D. Tygar. I Know Why You Went to the Clinic: Risks and Realization of HTTPS Traffic Analysis. In *Privacy Enhancing Technologies – PET 2014*, volume 8555 of *LNCS*, pages 143–163. Springer, 2014.

[31] E. Miluzzo, A. Varshavsky, S. Balakrishnan, and R. R. Choudhury. Tapprints: Your Finger Taps Have Fingerprints. In *Mobile Systems – MobiSys 2012*, pages 323–336. ACM, 2012.

[32] R. Nithyanand, X. Cai, and R. Johnson. Glove: A Bespoke Website Fingerprinting Defense. In *Workshop on Privacy in the Electronic Society – WPES 2014*, pages 131–134. ACM, 2014.

[33] Y. Oren, V. P. Kemerlis, S. Sethumadhavan, and A. D. Keromytis. The Spy in the Sandbox: Practical Cache Attacks in JavaScript and their Implications. In *Conference on Computer and Communications Security – CCS 2015*, pages 1406–1418. ACM, 2015.

[34] E. Owusu, J. Han, S. Das, A. Perrig, and J. Zhang. ACCessory: Password Inference Using Accelerometers on Smartphones. In *Mobile Computing Systems and Applications – HotMobile 2012*, page 9. ACM, 2012.

[35] A. Panchenko, L. Niessen, A. Zinnen, and T. Engel. Website Fingerprinting in Onion Routing Based Anonymization Networks. In *Workshop on Privacy in the Electronic Society – WPES 2011*, pages 103–114. ACM, 2011.

[36] R. Spreitzer. PIN Skimming: Exploiting the Ambient-Light Sensor in Mobile Devices. In *Security and Privacy in Smartphones & Mobile Devices – SPSM@CCS*, pages 51–62. ACM, 2014.

[37] Q. Sun, D. R. Simon, Y. Wang, W. Russell, V. N. Padmanabhan, and L. Qiu. Statistical Identification of Encrypted Web Browsing Traffic. In *IEEE Symposium on Security and Privacy – S&P 2002*, pages 19–30. IEEE Computer Society, 2002.

[38] T. Wang, X. Cai, R. Nithyanand, R. Johnson, and I. Goldberg. Effective Attacks and Provable Defenses for Website Fingerprinting. In *USENIX Security Symposium 2014*, pages 143–157. USENIX Association, 2014.

[39] T. Wang and I. Goldberg. Improved Website Fingerprinting on Tor. In *Workshop on Privacy in the Electronic Society – WPES 2013*, pages 201–212. ACM, 2013.

[40] C. V. Wright, S. E. Coull, and F. Monrose. Traffic Morphing: An Efficient Defense Against Statistical Traffic Analysis. In *Network and Distributed System Security Symposium – NDSS 2009*. The Internet Society, 2009.

[41] Z. Xu, K. Bai, and S. Zhu. TapLogger: Inferring User Inputs On Smartphone Touchscreens Using On-board Motion Sensors. In *Security and Privacy in Wireless and Mobile Networks – WISEC 2012*, pages 113–124. ACM, 2012.

[42] K. Zhang and X. Wang. Peeping Tom in the Neighborhood: Keystroke Eavesdropping on Multi-User Systems. In *USENIX Security Symposium 2009*, pages 17–32. USENIX Association, 2009.

[43] N. Zhang, K. Yuan, M. Naveed, X. Zhou, and X. Wang. Leave Me Alone: App-Level Protection against Runtime Information Gathering on Android. In *IEEE Symposium on Security and Privacy – S&P 2015*, pages 915–930. IEEE Computer Society, 2015.

[44] X. Zhou, S. Demetriou, D. He, M. Naveed, X. Pan, X. Wang, C. A. Gunter, and K. Nahrstedt. Identity, Location, Disease and More: Inferring Your Secrets from Android Public Resources. In *Conference on Computer and Communications Security – CCS 2013*, pages 1017–1028. ACM, 2013.

Can Android Applications Be Identified Using Only TCP/IP Headers of Their Launch Time Traffic?*

Hasan Faik Alan
Department of Computer Science
UNC - Chapel Hill, NC, USA
alan@cs.unc.edu

Jasleen Kaur
Department of Computer Science
UNC - Chapel Hill, NC, USA
jasleen@cs.unc.edu

ABSTRACT

The ability to identify mobile apps in network traffic has significant implications in many domains, including traffic management, malware detection, and maintaining user privacy. App identification methods in the literature typically use deep packet inspection (DPI) and analyze HTTP headers to extract app fingerprints. However, these methods cannot be used if HTTP traffic is encrypted. We investigate whether Android apps can be identified from their launch-time network traffic using only TCP/IP headers. We first capture network traffic of 86,109 app launches by repeatedly running 1,595 apps on 4 distinct Android devices. We then use supervised learning methods used previously in the web page identification literature, to identify the apps that generated the traffic. We find that: (i) popular Android apps can be identified with 88% accuracy, by using the packet sizes of the first 64 packets they generate, when the learning methods are trained and tested on the data collected from same device; (ii) when the data from an unseen device (but similar operating system/vendor) is used for testing, the apps can be identified with 67% accuracy; (iii) the app identification accuracy does not drop significantly even if the training data are stale by several days, and (iv) the accuracy does drop quite significantly if the operating system/vendor is very different. We discuss the implications of our findings as well as open issues.

Keywords

Network Traffic Analysis; Android Apps; Privacy

1. INTRODUCTION

The problem of identifying applications, by analyzing just the TCP/IP network traffic they generate, has received significant attention in the literature over the past decade and a half. This is for two compelling reasons. First, the ability

---

*This material is based upon work supported by the National Science Foundation under Grant No. CNS-1526268.

WiSec'16 , July 18-20, 2016, Darmstadt, Germany
© 2016 ACM. ISBN 978-1-4503-4270-4/16/07... $15.00
DOI: http://dx.doi.org/10.1145/2939918.2939929

to identify client applications from network traffic is tremendously useful in several domains—including malware detection, traffic management, network capacity planning, as well as, understanding the degree of user privacy leakage [1–4]. Second, with growing adoption of encryption and compression, as well as stronger Internet privacy legislation, HTTP payloads are increasingly becoming inaccessible to traffic monitors [5, 6]—consequently, analysis that relies on only TCP/IP headers is most useful.

The above trends have been well recognized in the literature on web page identification. Indeed, significant leaps have been made over the past several years in accurately identifying from TCP/IP headers, which web pages are being visited by a web client [4, 7, 8]. However, there has been little work in the domain of identifying mobile apps. While there has been some preliminary evidence collected using 40-70 apps [9, 10], there has been no comprehensive study of the identifiability of apps. Given the exponential rise of mobile app usage [11], we address this need in this paper. Specifically, we present the following key innovations:

- *Data Collection:* We set up 4 different Android devices (2 tablets and 2 phones) and select 1,595 most popular apps that use networking, as well as are compatible with all 4 devices. We then repeatedly run these apps over a duration of 25 days, and capture network traffic across 86,109 app launches. To the best of our knowledge, this is the largest data set considered to date.

- *Identifiability Evaluation:* Since mobile apps use mostly HTTP/HTTPS for networking [12], we next select learning algorithms and features that have worked well in the past for identification of web pages in web traffic. Specifically, we consider the packet sizes found in the initial launch time traffic of mobile apps, and evaluate three classifiers from the web page identification literature. We find that the mobile apps in our dataset do generate distinctive TCP/IP traffic, and just 32-64 initial packets from their launch time traffic can be used to identify them with up to 88% accuracy.

- *Robustness Evaluation:* The large number of app launches included in our data set also enables us to consider the impact on identification accuracy of several factors, including the training set size, frequency of training, app updates, and device differences. We find that the app identification accuracy does not drop significantly, even if the training data is stale by several days. However, when data from an unseen device is used for testing, the identification accuracy drops to around 67% (with similar operating system/vendor) or to even around 28% (with very different operating system/vendor).

2. DATA COLLECTION

For data collection, we use 4 different Android devices (Table 1) and capture the network traffic generated by running 1595 apps on them. In the remaining of this section, we explain how we determined the 1595 apps that we experimented with and how we captured the network traffic of these apps. We also describe the dataset we collected.

Table 1: Android Devices

ID	Device	Type	Android Version
S7	Samsung Galaxy Tab 4 7.0	tablet	4.4.2
S4	Samsung Galaxy S4 mini	phone	4.4.4
N5	Nexus 5	phone	6.0.1
N7	Nexus 7	tablet	6.0.1

App Selection There are around 2 million apps on Google Play, the Android application distribution platform [13]. We rely on the GooglePlayAppsCrawler.py project [14] to identify the 2000 most popular (most installed) free apps as of November 2015. We next identify the subset of these apps that are compatible with all 4 of our devices. The Google Play page for a given app lists all compatible devices used by the same account—using this, we determined that 1655 of the above 2000 apps are compatible with all of our devices.

The goal of this paper is to study identifiability of apps from the network traffic they generate. We analyze the Android application package files of the above 1655 apps to find that 1595 of these explicitly request network access by using the "android.permission.INTERNET" permission—we consider all of these apps in our study. Please note that the above permission is necessary but not sufficient for an app to generate network traffic [15]—an app may simply not use networking even though it has the permission.

Network Traffic Capture We use a USB WiFi adapter in access point (AP) mode to provide Internet connectivity for multiple Android devices. We capture the network traffic on the AP interface using tcpdump [16], while running apps on the devices. We capture only the first 100 bytes of network packets, which contain TCP/IP headers.

Android Debug Bridge (ADB) is a command line tool that allows us to communicate with Android devices [17]. It provides commands for performing several tasks such as installing, starting and stopping, and uninstalling an app. We use ADB commands and automate the process of capturing the network traffic of an app while the app is running concurrently on multiple devices. First, we install the same app on each of the devices. We then start tcpdump for network traffic capture and run the app for 20 seconds on the devices. Finally, we stop tcpdump and uninstall the app from the devices. We repeat this process for each of the apps to be analyzed. We log the times when an app was started and stopped, and the IP address of the device that the app was running on.

We extract the network traffic generated by an app while it is running on a specific device using the information available in the logs. We consider all of the TCP connections that were initiated between start and stop times of the app and are associated with the IP address of the device that the app was running on.

Dataset We conducted 14 data collection sessions, which lasted over 25 days (Table 2). In each session, we ran each of the 1,595 apps for 20 seconds on all of our 4 devices using the methodology described above. To minimize interfering traffic, we had disabled the automatic updates of apps and Android OS—after the 7th session, we manually updated the 515 apps that had a new version and conducted 7 additional data collection sessions using the latest versions of the apps. In total 86,109 successful app launches were performed, and network traffic was generated in 83,606 of them.

3. TRAFFIC FEATURES & CLASSIFIERS

We model the app identification problem as a multi-class supervised machine learning problem. A supervised machine learning algorithm is first trained with samples each in the form of a pair (x, y) where x and y are the feature vector and the class of a sample, respectively. The algorithm is then expected to predict the class of an unseen sample given its feature vector. In our problem, app launches are the samples, and the app package names are used as the classes of the samples. The feature vector belonging to an app launch is extracted from the TCP/IP headers of the packets generated during the launch.

Why Do We Consider Packet Sizes of App Launch Time Traffic? Many apps use networking immediately upon their launch for several reasons. They retrieve new ads from ad-networks or send information to analytics services. They also perform app specific communication—for example, an email app may check for new emails when it is launched. Results established previously in the field of non-mobile traffic classification suggest that, packet sizes observed within such launch time traffic may yield good feature sets for app identification. Specifically, [18] shows that the first few packets of TCP flows can be used to classify Internet applications into categories such as Web, FTP, and Games. More relevantly, [8] shows that web page identification can be performed solely using packet sizes.[1]

Classifiers Considered We select three methods from the web page identification literature that have been shown to achieve high accuracies using packet sizes. These methods mainly differ in the way feature vectors are extracted from packet sizes and the classification algorithms used, and are briefly summarized below (in chronological order).[2]

Method 1 (Sun et al. [19]): This method first groups contiguous incoming or outgoing packets within a TCP connection into "bursts". Given a traffic sample, incoming burst sizes are extracted from TCP connections and each of them are rounded to the nearest 32 bytes. A traffic sample is considered as a multiset of burst sizes. Similarity between two samples is measured using Jaccard's coefficient ($Sim(X,Y) =$

---

[1]The server IP addresses may seem to be a tempting feature to rely on. However, in our pilot studies we attained a lower accuracy (60-65%) compared to the methods that we discuss later (88%), when we use a bag-of-words model with the frequencies of IP addresses found in a traffic sample. Furthermore, using the packet sizes and IP addresses together did not improve the accuracies we attain by using only the packet sizes. This may be because many apps use the same third party services such as advertisement and analytics services.

[2]We only consider TCP packets with a payload.

Table 2: Dataset Summary

session	start	end	duration (days)	Days Since Beginning	Nexus 5		Galaxy S4		Galaxy Tab 4		Nexus 7	
					S	N	S	N	S	N	S	N
1	01/30 06:13	01/31 12:26	1.3	0.0	1552	1547	1555	1486	1522	1486	1539	1533
2	01/31 13:50	02/01 20:21	1.3	1.3	1563	1558	1558	1505	1541	1533	1564	1561
3	02/02 13:22	02/03 19:17	1.2	3.3	1566	1560	1555	1496	1539	1532	1564	1560
4	02/03 20:57	02/05 11:12	1.6	4.6	1560	1557	1553	1495	1538	1528	1559	1555
5	02/06 16:15	02/07 20:23	1.2	7.4	1466	1348	1455	1315	1444	1329	1465	1350
6	02/08 14:13	02/09 21:14	1.3	9.3	1492	1488	1488	1429	1467	1454	1491	1489
7	02/10 13:44	02/12 00:57	1.5	11.3	1490	1475	1486	1395	1468	1445	1492	1476
8	02/13 20:18	02/15 03:41	1.3	14.6	1550	1543	1539	1473	1522	1519	1551	1544
9	02/15 08:40	02/17 00:23	1.7	16.1	1567	1558	1549	1442	1533	1523	1566	961
10	02/17 18:57	02/19 00:03	1.2	18.5	1566	1562	1558	1492	1549	1535	1564	1556
11	02/19 00:23	02/20 07:36	1.3	19.8	1565	1555	1558	1324	1550	1545	1565	1561
12	02/20 10:11	02/21 15:03	1.2	21.2	1567	1562	1556	1491	1552	1545	1567	1559
13	02/21 17:46	02/22 22:46	1.2	22.5	1567	1563	1558	1498	1551	1542	1567	1563
14	02/23 01:03	02/24 13:52	1.5	23.8	1565	1553	1559	1455	1550	1541	1566	1556

Notes. S: Successful app launches. N: App launches that generated network traffic.

$\frac{X \cap Y}{X \cup Y}$). A test sample is identified by finding the most similar sample among the training samples.

Method 2 (Liberatore et al. [8]): Given a traffic sample, packet sizes are extracted. Minus sign is used to represent incoming packet sizes. A traffic sample is considered as a multiset of packet sizes. The Gaussian Naive Bayes classifier is used for classification.

Method 3 (Herrmann et al. [7]): Given a traffic sample, multisets of packet sizes are extracted as in Method 2. Term frequency - inverse document frequency transformation and normalization are applied to feature vectors. The Multinomial Naive Bayes classifier is used for classification.

4. EVALUATION

In this section, we use the methods described in Section 3 to evaluate the identifiability of the apps in our dataset.

App Identification From Launch Time Traffic The number of packets generated by an app during launch time depends on the Internet speed and the application logic of the app. Two reasons motivate us to minimize the number of packets used for app identification. First, less number of packets to process means less computational resource requirements for an identification method. Second, and more importantly, a user may start performing actions in an app such as tapping buttons or entering text immediately after the user interface of the app is available. Such actions may generate additional network traffic which would add noise to the launch time traffic of the app. By minimizing the number of packets considered as launch time traffic, we ensure that there will be minimal interference from user actions.

To find the minimum number of packets to consider as launch time traffic, we train the methods multiple times, varying the number of packets used. We consider only those apps that generated network traffic every time when they were launched in the first 7 sessions (i.e., 28 times) to ensure that there are equal number of app launch samples from each app—there were 1046 such apps. We first use the 20920 samples from the first 5 sessions for training the methods. We then use the 4184 samples from the 6th session for validation and determine when the methods perform best. Figure 1a plots the validation accuracies of the methods. We find that the accuracies of the methods increase significantly as larger number of initial packets are used by them. However,

the gain in accuracy seems to taper down considerably after 32-64 packets are considered.

Another consideration that should drive the choice of number of packets to use is whether the apps are likely to generate these many packets quickly. As explained before, the goal is to minimize the user action interference on the traffic. To investigate this issue, we consider the apps that generated network traffic every time when they were launched in the first session. There are 1384 such apps, yielding 5536 app launches. We find that more than 8 packets were generated in the 99% of these launches (see Fig. 1b) and the median time to generate 64 packets is under 5 seconds (see Fig.1c[3]). Based on these findings, in the rest of this paper, we decide to limit the launch time network traffic of apps to the first 64 packets they generate.

After determining the optimal number of packets to use as 64, we train the methods using the first 6 sessions (25104 app launches of 1046 apps) and test them on the 7th session (4184 app launches).[4] We obtain app identification accuracies of 87%, 82% and 74% for the methods Herrmann, Liberatore and Sun, respectively. An identification accuracy of 87% is significantly high, given that there are 1046 different apps (i.e., classes) that each of the 4184 app launch samples can be identified as.

How Much Training Data is Needed? We achieved a high identification accuracy above when we use the first 6 sessions for training and the 7th session for testing. We next study the impact of using smaller training sets on the accuracy. For this purpose, we train the methods using the most recent k sessions, where k ranges from 1 to 6, and test them on the 7th session. Figure 2a plots the identification accuracy versus the sessions used for training. We find that the methods do benefit from using multiple sessions for training. However, the contribution of each added session decreases. In particular, even when only the 6th session is used for training, Herrmann yields 80% identification accuracy. Furthermore, the performance of all three

---

[3]The boxes extend from the lower to upper quartile; median and mean are shown with line and square respectively (using matplotlib).

[4]Please note that in order to measure the generalization of the methods, we test them on samples unseen during training and validation.

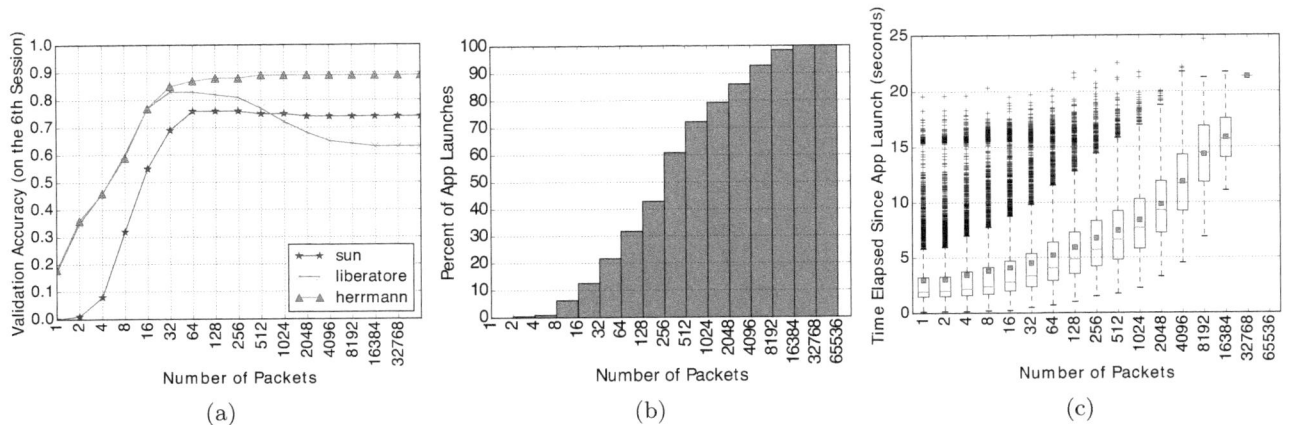

Figure 1: (a) Validation for Tuning Number of Packets; (b) Cumulative Histogram of Packets Per App Launch (Session 1); (c) Box Plot of Time Taken to Generate Certain Number of Packets (Session 1)

methods hardly improves once more than 4 sessions are used for training. These findings suggest that *app identification methods can sustain a high level of accuracy by keeping only a small number of most recent sessions for training, in this experiment 4, and discarding the older ones.*

How Frequently Do the Classifiers Need to Be Retrained? To answer this question, we use *one* of the first 6 sessions for training, and the 7th session for testing—Figure 2b plots the accuracy of each method. The best identification accuracy is achieved when the 6th session, the most recent session which contains samples just 2 days older than the test session, is used for training. The accuracies of the methods decrease gradually when older sessions are used for training—when samples that are 6 days older are used, the accuracy drops by only around 3%. The lowest accuracy (5-7% drop in accuracy for all methods) is attained when the first session, which contains samples 11 days older than the test samples, is used for training. These results indicate that launch time traffic of apps does change over time—however, the decrease in accuracy is not severe for samples collected within the past week. This allows us to collect training samples several days before testing.

How Do App Updates Impact Identification Accuracy? Mobile apps are regularly updated—app updates may impact the nature of launch time traffic as well. To study this issue, we updated the apps in our data set after the 7th session (515 of the apps had a new version). We then tested the methods using each of the sessions from 7 to 14 to investigate the effect of app updates—we trained the methods using the most recent 6 sessions before each test session. In this scenario, the 7th session is the only test session which contains samples from the original versions of the apps.

Since this evaluation involves all 14 sessions, we select the apps considered slightly differently—this is necessitated in part by the 9th session, in which Nexus 7 lost Internet connectivity and only 961 apps generated network traffic (Table 2). Specifically, we consider the apps that generated network traffic in at least 3 of the 4 launches in each of the 14 sessions—there are 1177 such apps. Figure 2c plots the accuracies of the methods, as a function of the test session.

We find that the accuracies of the methods drop at the 8th session (by 5% for Herrmann) and then gradually increase on subsequent sessions. The reason is that the training set does not contain any launch samples from the new versions of the apps when we use the 8th session for testing. However, when we use the subsequent sessions for testing, the training set contains more and more samples from the new versions of the apps (since we use the most recent sessions for training). This result suggests that apps need to be updated regularly and *identification methods should be retrained with samples from the latest versions of the apps to keep them accurate over time.*

How Do Device Differences Impact Identification Accuracy? There are over 24000 distinct Android devices [20]. It is not feasible to run apps on each of these devices for the purpose of training an app identification method. Thus, we evaluate the methods with samples from a device that is unseen during training. For comparison, we also test them using samples from the same device. In all of these scenarios, we use the samples from the first 6 sessions for training and the 7th session for testing. Table 3 summarizes the experiments, and shows the respective accuracy of each method.

We find that the methods perform significantly better when they are trained and tested using the samples from the same device (see highlighted rows in Table 3)—Herrmann yields 88% identification accuracy, on average. The methods also perform better when both training and testing sets contain different devices but with a similar vendor/OS (Nexus/Android 6.0.1 or Samsung/Android 4.4.x).[5] However, when a similar vendor/OS is not included in the training set, the performance drops quite significantly (to around 28%)—compare the rows with a star.

To further investigate the vendor/OS differences, we downgrade the OS version of N7 (6.0.1) to the OS version of S7 (4.4.2). We collect new app launch samples. We use the samples from S7 for testing. The classification accuracies are 38%, 67% and 88%, when Herrmann is trained on samples from N5 (different OS & device), N7 (same OS & different

---

[5] The Nexus devices have the same Android version and the Samsung devices have very similar versions (see Table 1).

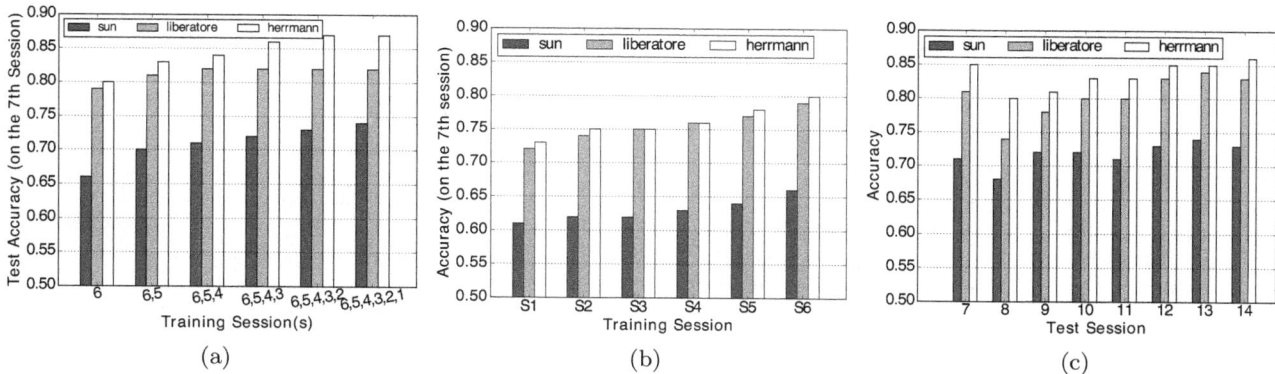

Figure 2: Evaluation of the methods, effect of: (a) training set size, (b) time, and (c) app updates on the accuracies

Table 3: Device Differences

test	training	herrmann	liberatore	sun
N5	N5	0.90	0.89	0.52
* N5	N7	0.66	0.59	0.47
* N5	S4	0.28	0.18	0.33
* N5	S7	0.28	0.14	0.33
N5	N7,S4,S7	0.70	0.61	0.49
N7	N5	0.67	0.58	0.45
N7	N7	0.88	0.88	0.49
N7	S4	0.26	0.16	0.28
N7	S7	0.29	0.15	0.30
N7	N5,S4,S7	0.68	0.59	0.47
S4	N5	0.29	0.13	0.28
S4	N7	0.27	0.13	0.28
S4	S4	0.84	0.81	0.39
S4	S7	0.66	0.59	0.39
S4	N5,N7,S7	0.71	0.64	0.42
S7	N5	0.27	0.13	0.34
S7	N7	0.29	0.15	0.35
S7	S4	0.67	0.62	0.45
S7	S7	0.88	0.88	0.52
S7	N5,N7,S4	0.71	0.61	0.50

Notes. N5, N7, S4, S7: see Table 1

device), and S7 (same OS & device), respectively. This result confirms that OS version and device have a significant impact on the accuracy. There are at least two approaches to address this issue. First, we can enumerate major Android OS versions and collect app launch samples from the devices running these OS versions to train an accurate classifier. Second, we can identify and use only those features that are robust across different devices.

It is critical to understand the significance of this observation—most of the past work on web page identification does not consider the impact of client diversity on the performance of identification methods. Our evaluation suggests that different devices (with different vendors/OS) do produce traffic features that may differ significantly. Consequently, *if an app identification method is biased towards a device or an Android version, it may perform poorly in the real world.*

5. DISCUSSION ON FUTURE WORK

When the app launch samples from same device is used for training and testing, we have found that apps can be identified with significantly high accuracy. Can this performance be improved further? It is likely that it can, especially since we have only evaluated with features and classification methods considered by others for web page identification. However, at 88% accuracy, there is only so much room for

improvement of the accuracy itself. What is even more interesting is to investigate whether the identifiability of mobile apps is robust to other challenges. We identified one of these, robustness to differences across devices and operating systems, before. We identify some more below.

Web page identification experiments in the literature are conducted in laboratory conditions by logging start and end times of web page loads. Similarly, we log the exact start and stop times of apps during our data collection and consider only the network packets generated during this time interval for app identification. However, given a real world traffic trace, it is not easy to detect the start of web page loads or app launches in it. This problem is still being considered as unsolved and left as a future work in the web page identification literature as well as in this paper [4, 8]. In addition, an app may have already been launched before joining a network. In this case, it is not possible to capture the launch time network traffic of the app.

We show that the packet size based traffic analysis methods developed for webpage identification can also be used for app identification. Similarly, the countermeasures in the literature such as the ones that hide the packet sizes by padding can be used to preserve privacy of users. Nine such methods are analyzed in [21].

Our data collection methodology can be improved by using a VPN app that captures the traffic generated by other apps on the same device. Such an app is presented in [9]. In this context, there are VPN apps in Google Play that are used by millions of people. A VPN app developed with the explicit intent of collecting training data (or maliciously), can capture TCP/IP headers of network packets and label them with the apps generating them. A dataset collected in this way will contain app launch samples from many distinct devices. An app identification method trained using this dataset will be more robust to device/OS differences.

The ability to identify apps from launch time traffic can also help with classifying subsequent (non launch time) traffic—indeed, after identifying the launch of an app from the first 64 packets, subsequent packets are likely to belong to the same app. This heuristic can be used to extract labeled network traces of apps from a traffic trace collected in the wild—such datasets would be valuable for future traffic analysis research.

6. RELATED WORK

Dai et al. [12], Xu et al. [22], Yao et al. [23], and Miskovic et al. [24] analyze HTTP headers to extract string patterns that identify apps. Such strings are generally used by third party Ads or analytics services to assign unique identifiers to apps. However, as mentioned by the same studies [22, 23], such deep packet inspection methods cannot be used when an app encrypts is HTTP traffic using the TLS protocol.

Two recent studies have provided some preliminary evidence on the identifiability of mobile apps without using HTTP headers. Specifically, Le et al. [9] present a VPN app for capturing the network traffic of apps installed on a device and use 40 apps to conduct a pilot app identification study with the data collected using their VPN app. Qazi et al. [10] integrate an app identification method based on packet sizes to a Software Defined Networking (SDN) platform, and use it to study identifiability of 70 apps. In this paper, we collect a comprehensive data set by considering 1,595 mobile apps, multiple devices, and 86,109 app launches—we also evaluate three methods from the web page identification literature.

Stöber et al. [25] show that the identity of a smartphone that a combination of 14 specific apps are installed on, can be determined with 90% probability from the background 3G network traffic generated by the apps. In [26], network traffic generated when certain user actions are performed in 7 apps is studied. It is shown that a user action such as sending an email or opening chat can be identified with more than 95% accuracy when the app generating the traffic (e.g., Gmail) is known. This work can be considered as complementary to our paper. After identifying an app from its launch time network traffic, a method trained to differentiate between user actions performed within the app can be used on the subsequent network traffic.

7. CONCLUSIONS

In this paper, we study the identifiability of Android apps from the TCP/IP headers of their launch time network traffic. We first conduct a data collection study in which we capture launch time network traffic of 1595 apps, repeatedly over time and across distinct devices. We then formalize the concept of app launch time traffic by limiting the number of packets considered for app identification using validation. We use supervised learning methods from the web page identification literature to identify the apps that generated the launch time traffic samples. Our results show that when the methods are trained and tested using the samples collected on the same device, apps can be identified from their launch time network traffic with 88% accuracy. This finding has significant implications for domains that can benefit from app identification. However, there are several open issues that need to be addressed before such methods can be used in the real world.

References

[1] A. Callado et al. "A survey on internet traffic identification". In: *Communications Surveys & Tutorials, IEEE* 11.3 (2009), pp. 37–52.

[2] S. Chen et al. "Side-channel leaks in web applications: A reality today, a challenge tomorrow". In: *Security and Privacy (SP), 2010 IEEE Symposium on*. IEEE. 2010, pp. 191–206.

[3] W. Zhou et al. "Detecting repackaged smartphone applications in third-party android marketplaces". In: *Proceedings of the second ACM conference on Data and Application Security and Privacy*. ACM. 2012, pp. 317–326.

[4] B. Miller et al. "I know why you went to the clinic: Risks and realization of https traffic analysis". In: *Privacy Enhancing Technologies*. Springer. 2014, pp. 143–163.

[5] D. C. Sicker, P. Ohm, and D. Grunwald. "Legal issues surrounding monitoring during network research". In: *Proceedings of the 7th ACM SIGCOMM conference on Internet measurement*. ACM. 2007, pp. 141–148.

[6] A. M. White et al. "Clear and Present Data: Opaque Traffic and its Security Implications for the Future." In: *NDSS*. 2013.

[7] D. Herrmann, R. Wendolsky, and H. Federrath. "Website fingerprinting: attacking popular privacy enhancing technologies with the multinomial naïve-bayes classifier". In: *Proceedings of the 2009 ACM workshop on Cloud computing security*. ACM. 2009, pp. 31–42.

[8] M. Liberatore and B. N. Levine. "Inferring the source of encrypted HTTP connections". In: *Proceedings of the 13th ACM conference on Computer and communications security*. ACM. 2006, pp. 255–263.

[9] A. Le et al. "AntMonitor: A System for Monitoring from Mobile Devices". In: *Proceedings of the 2015 ACM SIGCOMM Workshop on Crowdsourcing and Crowdsharing of Big (Internet) Data*. ACM. 2015, pp. 15–20.

[10] Z. A. Qazi et al. "Application-awareness in SDN". In: *ACM SIGCOMM Computer Communication Review*. Vol. 43. 4. ACM. 2013, pp. 487–488.

[11] "Cisco Visual Networking Index: Global mobile data traffic forecast update, 2015-2020". In: *White Paper* (2015).

[12] S. Dai et al. "Networkprofiler: Towards automatic fingerprinting of android apps". In: *INFOCOM, 2013 Proceedings IEEE*. IEEE. 2013, pp. 809–817.

[13] *Number of available Android applications - AppBrain*. http://www.appbrain.com/stats/number-of-android-apps. (accessed February 13, 2016).

[14] M. Lins. *MarcelloLins/GooglePlayAppsCrawler*. https://github.com/MarcelloLins/GooglePlayAppsCrawler. (accessed February 7, 2016).

[15] *Connecting to the Network | Android Developers*. http://developer.android.com/training/basics/network-ops/connecting.html. (accessed February 13, 2016).

[16] *TCPDUMP/LIBPCAP public repository*. http://www.tcpdump.org/. (accessed February 13, 2016).

[17] *Android Debug Bridge | Android Developers*. http://developer.android.com/tools/help/adb.html. (accessed February 13, 2016).

[18] Y.-s. Lim et al. "Internet traffic classification demystified: on the sources of the discriminative power". In: *Proceedings of the 6th International COnference*. ACM. 2010, p. 9.

[19] Q. Sun et al. "Statistical identification of encrypted web browsing traffic". In: *Security and Privacy, 2002. Proceedings. 2002 IEEE Symposium on*. IEEE. 2002, pp. 19–30.

[20] *Android Fragmentation Report August 2015 - OpenSignal*. http://opensignal.com/reports/2015/08/android-fragmentation/. (accessed February 13, 2016).

[21] K. P. Dyer et al. "Peek-a-boo, i still see you: Why efficient traffic analysis countermeasures fail". In: *Security and Privacy (SP), 2012 IEEE Symposium on*. IEEE. 2012, pp. 332–346.

[22] Q. Xu et al. "Automatic generation of mobile app signatures from traffic observations". In: *Computer Communications (INFOCOM), 2015 IEEE Conference on*. IEEE. 2015, pp. 1481–1489.

[23] H. Yao et al. "SAMPLES: Self Adaptive Mining of Persistent LExical Snippets for Classifying Mobile Application Traffic". In: *Proceedings of the 21st Annual International Conference on Mobile Computing and Networking*. ACM. 2015, pp. 439–451.

[24] S. Miskovic et al. "AppPrint: automatic fingerprinting of mobile applications in network traffic". In: *Passive and Active Measurement*. Springer. 2015, pp. 57–69.

[25] T. Stöber et al. "Who do you sync you are?: smartphone fingerprinting via application behaviour". In: *Proceedings of the sixth ACM conference on Security and privacy in wireless and mobile networks*. ACM. 2013, pp. 7–12.

[26] M. Conti et al. "Analyzing Android Encrypted Network Traffic to Identify User Actions". In: *Information Forensics and Security, IEEE Transactions on* 11.1 (2016), pp. 114–125.

Slogger: Smashing Motion-based Touchstroke Logging with Transparent System Noise

Prakash Shrestha
University of Alabama at
Birmingham
Birmingham, Alabama
prakashs@uab.edu

Manar Mohamed
University of Alabama at
Birmingham
Birmingham, Alabama
manar@uab.edu

Nitesh Saxena
University of Alabama at
Birmingham
Birmingham, Alabama
saxena@cis.uab.edu

ABSTRACT

Recent research shows that it is possible to infer a user's touch-screen inputs (e.g., passwords) on Android devices based on inertial (motion/position) sensors, currently freely-accessible by any Android app. Given the high accuracies of such touchstroke logging attacks, they are now considered a significant threat to user privacy. Consequently, the security community has started exploring defenses to such side channel attacks, but the suggested solutions are either not effective (e.g., those based on vibrational noise) and/or may significantly undermine system usability (e.g., those based on keyboard layout randomization).

In this paper, we introduce a novel and practical defense to motion-based touchstroke leakage based on *system-generated, fully automated* and *user-oblivious* sensory noise. Our defense leverages a recently developed framework, SMASheD, that takes advantage of the Android's ADB functionality and can programmatically inject noise to various inertial sensors. Although SMASheD was originally advertised as a malicious app by its authors, we use it to build a defense mechanism, called *Slogger* ("Smashing the logger"), for defeating sensor-based touchstroke logging attacks. Slogger transparently inserts noisy sensor readings in the background as the user provides sensitive touchscreen input (e.g., password, PIN or credit card info) in order to obfuscate the original sensor readings. It can be installed in the user space without the need to root the device and to change the device's OS or kernel.

Our contributions are three-fold. *First*, we introduce Slogger, identifying a novel, benign use case of SMASheD that can defeat touchstroke logging attacks. *Second*, we design and implement the Slogger app system that can be used to protect sensitive touchscreen input from leaking away. *Third*, we comprehensively evaluate Slogger against state-of-the-art touchstroke detection and inference attacks. Our results show that Slogger can significantly reduce the level of touchstroke leakage to the extent these attacks may become unworkable in practice, without affecting other benign apps. We also show that the leakage can be minimized even when attacks utilize a *fusion* of multiple motion-position sensors.

WiSec'16 , July 18-22, 2016, Darmstadt, Germany
© 2016 ACM. ISBN 978-1-4503-4270-4/16/07. . . $15.00
DOI: http://dx.doi.org/10.1145/2939918.2939924

CCS Concepts

•**Security and privacy** → **Malware and its mitigation; Side-channel analysis and countermeasures; Mobile platform security;**

Keywords

Side-channel attacks, mobile security, Android

1. INTRODUCTION

Sensors are becoming an inevitable part of mobile and wireless computing. With mobile devices coming readily equipped with multiple, low-cost sensors and mobile OS platforms adding full software support for developing applications using these sensors, there is an enormous growth in the adoption of mobile devices.

Different varieties of sensors are available on the current generation of mobile devices, such as smartphones and tablets, including: user input sensor (touchscreen and hardware buttons), audio-visual sensors (microphone and camera), and inertial or motion-position sensors (e.g., accelerometer, gyroscope and magnetometer). The mobile apps that are based on these sensors have seen a widespread deployment in many domains ranging from entertainment, navigation and transportation (e.g., [12]) to elderly care (e.g., [4, 7]) and safety (e.g., [24]). In addition, mobile device sensors are used to build a wide range of security/privacy applications, including those geared for authentication and authorization (e.g., [9, 10, 19]).

Since mobile sensors provide potentially sensitive information about the host device, the device's user or the device's surroundings, protecting sensor data from abuse by malicious applications becomes paramount. Consequently, most mobile platforms have established a sensor security access control model. Specifically, Android, one of the most popular mobile OSs and the subject of this paper, follows a model where *read access* to many sensitive sensors is very restrictive (e.g., an app can only read its *own* touchscreen input data) or requires special install-time permissions granted by the user (e.g., to access microphone or camera).

However, the read access to most other sensors, including inertial sensors, is not restricted within this model because Android may not consider these sensors as explicitly sensitive. This openness in the Android sensor security architecture to the inertial sensors has given rise to a potentially significant threat of *motion-based side channel attacks*. Especially, an interesting line of recent research [17, 23] has shown that it is possible to infer a user's touch-screen inputs on Android devices (deemed sensitive, and protected by Android's security model), such as passwords, based on these "globally accessible" inertial sensor measurements. The primary intuition behind these attacks is that the movement and positional changes introduced by hitting a key on the device's touchscreen are correlated with the key itself and can thus be exploited to make an inference of the key. These attacks generally follow a two-step process. The first step is *touchstroke detection*, that is, finding the start and end of the tap event based on the motion sensor readings. The second step is *touchstroke inference*, that is, inferring the pressed key based on the motion sensors readings during the touch event detected in the first step. (These attacks are reviewed in Section 2.)

Given the high accuracies of such touchstroke logging attacks [17, 23], they may now be considered a significant threat to user privacy. For example, as shown in prior research, user's PINs or passwords can be extracted with high success rates. Naturally, the security community has responded by studying defenses to such side channel attacks. However, the suggested solutions are either not effective, such as the one based on vibrational noise created by the mobile phone's vibration motor [17], and/or may significantly compromise the usability of the system, such as the one based on keyboard layout randomization [20, 22]. We analyze the limitations of prior defense mechanisms in Section 3.

In this paper, we introduce a novel and practical defense to motion-based touchstroke leakage based on *system-generated*, *fully automated* and *user-oblivious* sensory noise. Our defense leverages a recently developed framework, SMASheD ("Sniffing and Manipulating Android Sensor Data") [16], that takes advantage of the Android's ADB (Android Debugging Bridge) functionality and can programmatically sniff and inject noise to various inertial sensors. Although SMASheD was originally advertised as a malicious app by its authors [16], we use it to build a defense mechanism, called *Slogger* ("Smashing the logger"), for defeating sensor-based keystroke logging attacks. Slogger transparently inserts noisy sensor readings in the background as the user provides sensitive touchscreen input (e.g., password, PIN or credit card info) in order to obfuscate the original sensor readings. It does so without impacting other benign apps that rely upon original sensor readings.

Our Contributions: We believe that our work brings forth the following contributions to the field of mobile and wireless security:

1. *Defensive Use of a Malicious Tool*: We identify a novel, benign use case of the SMASheD framework that can be used to defeat touchstroke logging attacks. We believe that turning an existing malicious approach into a defensive tool could be valuable to the advancement of science.

2. *Design and Implementation of Slogger*: We provide the design and implementation of the Slogger app system that can be used to protect sensitive touchscreen input from leaking away using the motion-based side channel attacks. Slogger works in the background and is completely transparent to the user and other benign apps. It can be installed in the user space like any other ADB app, without the need to root the device and to change the device's OS or kernel. Our design and implementation details are presented in Section 4.

3. *Recreation of Prior Attacks and Evaluation of Slogger*: We comprehensively evaluate Slogger against state-of-the-art touchstroke detection and inference attacks. To achieve this goal, we first present a re-implementation and evaluation of the prior attacks in independent settings. Our results show that Slogger can significantly reduce the level of touchstroke leakage to the extent these attacks may become completely unworkable in practice. We also demonstrate that Slogger may not cause any negative effects to other benign apps that rely upon sensor measurements while the user provides sensitive input (e.g., the pedometer and fall detection apps). Our re-validation of prior attacks is described in Sections 2.2 and 2.3. Our evaluation of Slogger is presented in Section 5.

4. *Evaluation against Fusion of Sensors*: We show that the touchstroke leakage based on motion sensors can be greatly increased by utilizing a *fusion* of multiple motion sensors. That is, we propose new attacks that achieve much higher accuracies than the existing attacks employing only single sensor (accelerometer alone). Importantly, we further show that Slogger can still minimize this leakage thereby defeating even these powerful attacks. The details of this part of the work are presented in Section 5.3.

2. BACKGROUND

Several research works have been proposed that utilize motion-based side-channel attack to log the user's touchscreen input (e.g., passwords) [17, 23]. The general approach of these motion-based touchstroke logging attacks consists of two steps. The first step is *touchstroke detection*, that is, finding the start and end of the tap event based on the motion sensor readings. The second step is *touchstroke inference*, that is, inferring the pressed key based on the motion sensors readings during the touch event detected in the first step. Most of the recent work focuses on the second step, in which the attacker extracts the features from the sensor readings and employs one of the standard machine learning techniques to infer the pressed key. Intuitively, if we can block one or both of these two steps, it is possible to defend against such attacks. To show that our proposed defense mechanism – *Slogger* – works well against both touchstroke detection as well as inference attacks, we implemented one of the state-of-the-art touchstroke detection algorithms, as implemented in the TapLogger [23], and one of the state-of-the-art touchstroke inference algorithm, called ACCessory [17].

In this section, we first present the general threat model that most of the motion-based side-channel touchstroke logging attacks have considered. Then, we provide a brief review of TapLogger and ACCessory , and independently re-create and re-validate both attacks. Next, we present SMASheD [16], a framework that has been proposed to inject sensors events for malicious purposes, that we used to build our *Slogger* defense system. Throughout our work, we use Samsung S4 with sampling frequency of 100Hz.

2.1 Threat Model

As mentioned earlier, motion-based side-channel touchstroke logging attacks consist of two steps: *touchstroke detection* and *touchstroke inference*. Each of these steps first needs to learn the patterns (basically extract the features) of the touchstrokes based on the motion sensor measurements. Later, they utilize the learned touchstrokes motion pattern to detect and to infer the touchstrokes. Both steps in motion-based touchstrokes logging attacks have two phases:

1. **Training Phase:** In this phase, the touchstroke logging model acquires the touchstroke information such as the timestamps of the touch pressed and released events, the coordinates of the touchstroke on the screen and the motion sensor measurements during the touchstroke event to learn the motion pattern corresponding to a touchstroke. This model assumes that the adversary fools the user to install and use a malicious application that stealthily collects this information. The malicious application can be, for example, a gaming application, such as *HostApp* used by TapLogger, that requires the user to tap on various positions of the screen. The adversary then utilizes the collected information to extract the features and learn the pattern of the touchstrokes.

2. **Testing Phase:** In this phase of the attack, the malicious application runs in the background, and records sensor measurements stealthily whenever user starts entering the sensitive input. Using the learned knowledge in the training phase, the touchstroke logging model attempts to detect and infer the touchstrokes.

The model presented above is in line with the general threat model that motion-based side-channel touchstroke logging attacks have assumed in their work, such as TapLogger [23], ACCessory [17], TextLogger [18], and TouchLogger [3].

Slogger aims to defend such attacks by injecting noise into the sensors files. Slogger threat model also consider attackers with more capabilities, such as those who try deliberately to remove the injected noise, or trying to infer the keystrokes over multiple rounds of sniffing the sensors data.

2.2 TapLogger: Review and Re-Validation

Xu et al. [23] developed "TapLogger" to infer a user's tap inputs to a smartphone by utilizing the accelerometer and orientation sensors. First, TapLogger learns the motion change patterns of tap events. Later, TapLogger uses the learned pattern to infer the occurrence of tap events and the tapped positions on the touchscreen. TapLogger shows that tap events have a unique pattern in terms of the changes in the accelerometer readings, which can be utilized in detecting the occurrence of taps. This information along with the orientation sensor readings and the screen layout can be utilized to infer the user input.

We re-implemented the tap event detection algorithm, *Tap-detector*, as described in [23]. Tap-detector calculates the square sum of accelerometer readings, $SqSum = x^2 + y^2 + z^2$, which represents the force induced on the smartphone while typing. During the training phase, as the user is tapping on the attacker's trojan app, the start and end of the tapping event can be identified by the timestamps in which Motion.Event.ACTION_DOWN and Motion.Event.ACTION_UP events are received, respectively. Tap-detector first extracts the $SqSum$ corresponding to the tap events. Then, it extracts several features to describe the tap event: the peak and trough of the readings minus base, difference and time gap between the peak and the trough, and the standard deviation of the entire tap event. After the user performs multiple taps, Tap-detector learns the range between the lower and upper extremes of each of the features and utilizes these ranges to detect tapping events later.

In our study, we do not use TapLogger 's tap inference algorithm. This is because TapLogger employs the orientation sensor measurements for touchstroke inference attacks. Orientation sensor is a software-based sensor that derives its data from accelerometer and geomagnetic field sensor which is deprecated starting from Android 2.2 (API Level 8) [1]. Even if Orientation sensor were to be used, Slogger can still defeat it since it can insert noise to both accelerometer and geomagnetic field sensor from where this sensor derives its data.

Validation: To validate our implementation, we trained our implementation of Tap-detector with 1200 taps, and tested it against another 100 taps. We tested our implementation with 5 sets of these 100 taps. These taps were collected in a similar setting as documented in the TapLogger paper [23], i.e., the phone is held by one hand and the key on touchscreen is pressed by index finger of the other hand. Tap-detector was able to get the precision of 88.31%, recall of 84.02% and F-measure of 85.97%, which is very close to the one reported in the TapLogger paper. Given these validation results, we later (in Section 5.1) evaluate our Slogger defense system against Tap-detector.

2.3 ACCessory: Review and Re-Validation

Owusu et al. [17] provided the design and implementation of an Android application, ACCessory, which demonstrates that accelerometer can be used as a side channel attack to infer short sequence of touchstroke on a smartphone soft keyboard, and machine learning techniques can be employed to infer input like password.

ACCessory has two collection modes: area mode and character mode. In the area mode, the screen was divided into regions, and the task was to infer the tapped regions at different granularities level (i.e., 2, 4, or 8). In particular, the goal of the area mode was to evaluate the inference accuracy at varying levels of granularity. The authors determined that splitting the screen into eight regions and classifying individual region keys separately yields the best average key accuracy of approximately 24.5%. The purpose of the character mode of collection was to extend the attack to inferring a sequence of entered text, in contrast to a per-key inference, in order to reconstruct typed passwords.

We re-created the area mode collection of ACCessory to later evaluate the performance of our proposed defense. We designed an Android application for area mode collection similar to the one described in [17] that consists of 10x6 array of buttons that completely cover the entire screen of the smartphone. As the application runs, it starts recording every new updated accelerometer reading. Each record contains accelerometer measurement and timestamp for the accelerometer measurement. The same application also monitors the key-pressed and key-released touch events as they are dispatched by each button and the coordinates of the button pressed on the touchscreen to establish ground truth for the analysis. As in the ACCessory design, we first use the linear interpolation technique to obtain consistent sampling interval throughout the dataset. The average sampling rate of our device's accelerometer is 100 Hz. We then compute $SqSum$ and extract the features that describe a tap event in a particular region of the screen. The features used to describe a tap event in a particular region of the screen, as described in ACCessory and used in our implementation, are shown in Table 1. Random Forest algorithm is then used to obtain the per key inference accuracy corresponding to each of the regions granularity.

We note that it was important for us to evaluate our Slogger system against touchstroke inference, even if Slogger could perfectly defeat touchstroke detection. This is because the attacker may employ various strategies other than utilizing the sensor measurements to perform tap detection which may be more accurate. For instance, attacker may surreptitiously monitor the process's shared memory size while the device's keyboard app is being used, and uses it to infer the tap events [18]. It is also possible that the attacker is recording a video of user typing on touch enabled devices, which may be utilized to detect the touchstroke events [21]. To this end, to evaluate our defense against touchstroke inference attacks, given touchstroke detection has been launched successfully, we implemented the area mode collection of ACCessory and tested with our proposed defense mechanism, Slogger.

Validation: To validate our implementation, we consider the setting which is similar to the one used in the ACCessory paper, i.e., the device is held by both hands in the landscape orientation, and thumbs are used to enter the text. Similar to ACCessory, with this setting, we collected data corresponds to about 1200 key presses, where each key receives about 20 presses. Using stratified 10-fold cross-validation, our implementation was able to achieve 90.02% of accuracy for two region splits (i.e., for two halves of the screen) which is in line with the result reported in the ACCessory work. When considering the higher level of granularity, our implementation was able to achieve 68.73% for 4 regions, and 10.93% for

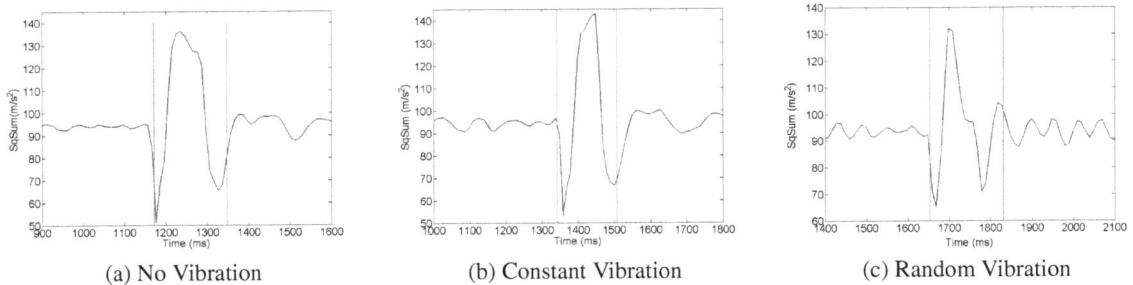

(a) No Vibration   (b) Constant Vibration   (c) Random Vibration

Figure 1: Negligible effect of vibrational noise on a stream of accelerometer readings while pressing a key on phone's touchscreen.

Table 1: List of features used to describe accelerometer stream values for a tap inference. Dimensional features (D) are computed separately for each dimension (x, y, z) as well as for $SqSum$ of acceleration. Meta features (M) describe the window features of acceleration stream and are calculated only once per feature vector [17].

Feature	Description	D/M
RMS	The Root-Mean-Square Value	D
RMSE	The Root-Mean-Square Error	D
Min	The Minimum Value	D
Max	The Maximum Value	D
AvgDeltas	The average sample-by-sample change	D
NumMax	The number of local peaks	D
NumMin	The number of local crests	D
TTP	The average time from a sample to a peak	D
TTC	The average time from a sample to a crest	D
RCR	The RMS cross rate	D
SMA	The Signal Magnitude Area	D
Total Time	The Total Time of the window	M
Window Size	The number of samples in the window	M

60 regions while ACCessory reported more than 80% for 4 regions and 24.5% for 60 regions. We attribute these differences to use of a different device in our experimental set-up. We used a Samsung Galaxy S4 phone, while ACCessory experiments were done with an HTC ADR6300. These two devices differ in screen sizes: S4 has a larger screen (136.6 mm x 69.8 mm) than HTC ADR6300 (117.5 mm x 58.5 mm). The larger the screen size, the higher will be the motion generated noise while typing, which may have contributed to lower accuracies in our case.

2.4 SMASheD Framework

SMASheD [16] is a framework that can be used for sniffing and manipulating Android sensor data. SMASheD leverages ADB to install a service on an Android device with shell privileges. Specifically, the installed service would have privileges to read from and write to the Android device sensors files (i.e., the files corresponding to position, motion and environmental sensors as well as user input sensors: touch screen and hardware buttons).

SMASheD framework consists of a service, two scripts, and an Android application. The service is responsible to read from and write to the sensors files. The two scripts are used to push the service from a PC to an Android device and run it. This way the service will be granted all the shell privileges. The Android application is an application that monitors the device status. For example, it checks which applications are installed on the device and which applications are running in the foreground, and according to its desired purpose, it sends read or write requests to the SMASheD service.

In [16], Mohamed et al. provided various functionalities that SMASheD can achieve given its capabilities in attacking various sensing-based authentication and authorization applications. That

is, the original use case of the SMASheD framework was malicious in nature. In our paper, we utilized the SMASheD framework for a novel benign use case, specifically defending against touchstroke logging attacks. We propose Slogger – a defense based on SMASheD's sensor event injection functionality in an attempt to mitigate well-researched attacks that utilize motion sensors for touchstroke detection and inference. Slogger injects negligible sensor events such that the benign apps are not affected and injects sensor events only when the user is entering sensitive information like a password.

3. LIMITATIONS OF KNOWN DEFENSES

In this section, we discuss and analyze various possible defenses against touchstroke detection and keystroke inference attacks that have been suggested in prior research, and argue for their ineffectiveness.

Vibrational Noise: One of the possible strategies to mitigate the sensor-based touchstroke detection and inference attack, as pointed in [17], is to automatically initiate the phone vibration while the input is being provided to the phone. However, authors did not perform detailed evaluation of this intuitive strategy. To this end, we set out to evaluate the strategy of creating vibrational noise to defend against sensor-based side-channel attack. We considered two different types of vibrational noise: *(1) Constant Vibration*, and *(2) Random Vibration*. In the Constant Vibration mode, the phone is programmed to vibrate constantly over the time with same vibrational intensity as the user provides the input to the phone, whereas in the Random Vibration mode, the phone vibrates with a random pattern, i.e., the phone vibrates for some random duration, pauses for a random duration and then vibrates again, repeating this process while the user provides input to the device.

We evaluated whether the creation of such vibrational noise has significant effects on the motion sensors that may mitigate the keystroke information leakage. We recorded the accelerometer measurements when a key is being pressed, while holding the phone with one hand and pressing with index finger of another hand, in presence of both types of vibrational noise. Figure 1 represents a $SqSum$ plot of accelerometer measurements in presence and absence of the two types of vibrational noise. Specifically, Figure 1(a) represents a scenario where there is touchstroke event without any vibration (i.e., in the absence of the defense). In this case, the $SqSum$ of the stream of accelerometer can be used to detect the touchstroke event and later on detected touchstroke signal can be analyzed to infer the touchstroke. Figure 1(b) and 1(c) represent the scenarios with constant vibration and random vibration, respectively. The figures clearly show that, although both types of vibrations have some effect on the stream of accelerometer measurements corresponding to the touchstroke event, they do not offer significant contribution to hide the touchstroke event from the stream of accelerometer readings. That is, touchstrokes are still clearly distinguishable and would be subject to inference. This analysis therefore demonstrates that vibrational noises generated by the phone's vibrational motor do not have significant effect on the accelerometer measurements and is ineffective in defending against sensor-based touchstroke logging attack, contrary to what was assumed by the ACCessory authors.

Keyboard Layout Randomization: In the motion-based key inference attack, the goal of the attacker is to learn the key pressed on the screen to learn sensitive information such as PIN, password, or even email content. By statistical analysis of motion sensor measurements, the attacker can determine the position of the touchstroke on the screen. Since the layout of the keyboard or number pad on standard devices is typically public knowledge, the keyboard layout is known to the attacker. Once the attacker determines the position of the touchstroke on the screen, with the knowledge of keyboard layout, he can map touchstroke position with keyboard/number pad layout and find out the actual key pressed on the screen.

If the layout information is kept secret from the attacker, even if the attacker knows the touchstroke position on the screen, it may fail to determine the actual key pressed and thus the information leakage can be eliminated. Song et al. [22] have proposed the idea of randomizing the layout of keyboard to hide the layout information from the attacker so that attacker could not figure out which key has been pressed even if he could find the exact tap position.

Though the idea of randomizing the layout have a sound potential to defend against motion based touchstroke inference attack, it may not be practical. Randomizing the keyboard layout significantly increases the time taken by the user to enter the text, as the user would need to search for the keys in the randomized keyboard layout every time rather than using his knowledge about the keyboard layout to locate the keys. Thus, this approach would significantly compromise the usability of the system [20] and would not be a viable defense the users can deploy.

Motion Shielding: One possible strategy to defeat motion-based touchstroke logging attacks is motion shielding. As proposed in [15], the use of phone cases, such as the one made up of leather or rubber, can minimize the motion generation, which in turn can potentially minimize the information leakage. However, this approach requires the phone cases to be highly shock absorbent and thick. Thin leather/rubber cases may reduce the motion leakage by absorbing certain amount of motion, but there may still be some motion leakage that the high resolution accelerometers can still record, which can be used by an attacker to infer the actual keys. Moreover, many users may not be willing to use such specialized phone cases due to cost or convenience reasons.

Permission Restriction to On-Board Sensors: As suggested in [2, 15, 17], on-board sensors, such as accelerometer and gyroscope, should be considered sensitive to user's privacy and therefore special security permissions must be required to gain access to such sensors. This approach, however, requires users to have a good understanding of the security model, and relies upon the users to read and understand the app's permission dialog while installing the app. This approach requires cognitive effort from the user and may not work in practice as shown by many studies [8, 13].

Sensor Access Control: Another approach as suggested in [2, 15] to mitigate the sensor-based touchstroke logging attack is the modification of mobile devices' operating systems to pause the motion sensors when sensitive input operation is being performed. This approach would make it impossible for an attacker to correlate the sensor data with the keyboard taps. However, there are several applications that run in background all the time (e.g., pedometer applications), and withholding such applications from gaining access to the sensors, or requiring manual shut down before performing any sensitive operation by the user, would greatly reduce the applicability of this approach.

Reduced Sampling Rate: Varying the sensor sampling rate can reduce the accuracy of touchstroke detection as well as touchstroke inference. Higher the sampling rate, the better the tap inference performance because more sensor samples are available to capture each tap's measurements that can model the tap effectively. Increasing the sampling rate improves the inference accuracy [15, 17]. Conversely, reducing the sampling rate can reduce the effect of touchstroke inference attack [14]. However, such approach may have undesirable effect on several legitimate applications running in the background (e.g., pedometer). Furthermore, there exist some sophisticated machine learning techniques that work well even with sampling frequency as low as 20Hz [2].

4. SLOGGER DESIGN AND IMPLEMENTATION

Our defense mechanism Slogger aims to cloak the motion-based touchstroke logging attacks with the use of internal, programmatic noise which is completely transparent to the user. We follow the implementation of the SMASheD framework [16] to realize our Slogger system. We added an initialization phase, in which Slogger learns the range of the sensor values corresponding to the user's typing style. When the user installs Slogger on her device, the user is asked to type on her device in all the settings (i.e., holding a phone in hand, or keeping phone on a surface of table and typing), and the minimum and the maximum values of all the axes for all the position sensors are computed. These values are later used to set the range of the values of the injected noise. This step is performed by the user only once. In our experiment, we used Samsung S4 which has only accelerometer and gyroscope as hardware position sensors. The rest of the position sensors (i.e., gravity, linear acceleration and orientation) are calculated based on the readings of the hardware position sensors.

We implemented the Slogger application such that whenever a user launches the application that we use for our data collection, Slogger sends inject request to the Slogger server, when the user closes the application Slogger sends stop request to Slogger server. The application that we developed for our analysis purpose can be updated such that it sends the inject request whenever the keyboard is running or whenever the user is entering any sensitive data.

Slogger server locates the files corresponding to accelerometer and gyroscope in "/dev/input/" folder. Slogger server has a socket, that keeps listening for requests. When Slogger server gets a start request, it injects random values in both the accelerometer and gyroscope that are in the range between the pre-calculated maximum and minimum values. After injecting sensor events in both the accelerometer and gyroscope sensors, it waits for a random amount of time between 7 and 12 milliseconds. Slogger server keeps on injecting till it receives a stop request.

Slogger is installed in the Android device in a similar way as described in [16]. A script is used to push the Slogger server and another script to "/data/local/temp/" folder on the Android device, then run the other script which is responsible for running the Slogger server. Like SMASheD, Slogger does not require the phone to be rooted.

Evaluation Scenarios: We implemented our system in accordance with the following three scenarios later used to evaluate Slogger against touchstroke logging attacks:

- *Slogger Absent*: In this scenario, we assume that the touch enabled device has not implemented any defense mechanism, in particular Slogger, against touchstroke logging attack. So, both training and testing phases of the touchstroke logging attacks (as described in Section 2.1) use normal (noise-free) stream of sensor measurements. We consider this scenario as the baseline scenario to evaluate the impact of our defense mechanism against the touchstroke logging attack.

- *Slogger Present, Attacker Trained with Non-Noisy Data*: In this scenario, we assume that Slogger has been activated on the touch-enabled devices. We also assume that it has been implemented in a way that it works with only a subset of applications that the system or the user thinks are sensitive, and the user has marked the malicious application collecting the training data as non-sensitive (i.e., unprotected by Slogger). Here, the training phase of the touchstroke logging attack uses regular (non-noisy) stream of sensor measurements while the testing phase uses the noisy stream of sensor measurements containing the Slogger injected noise.

- *Slogger Present, Attacker Trained with Noisy Data*: Similar to our second scenario, we assume that Slogger has been implemented on the touch-enabled devices in a way that it works with only a subset of applications that system or user thinks are sensitive. We also assume that the user has marked the malicious application collecting training data as a sensitive application. In such setting, Slogger noise injection will be activated when the user interacts with the malicious application. In this scenario, both the training and the testing phases use stream of sensor measurements with Slogger injected noise.

5. EXPERIMENTS AND EVALUATION

In this section, we present our experiment to evaluate the impact of Slogger against touchstroke detection based on the *Tap-detector* algorithm described in Section 2.2, followed by the impact of Slogger against touchstroke inference methodology explained in Section 2.3. Then, we show that even if fusion of multiple (motion/position) sensors is used for the touchstroke inference attack, Slogger serves as a viable defense. We also show that Slogger does not have a significant impact on any other common benign applications that utilizes motion sensors.

For our evaluation, we built an Android application with two view layouts. The first view layout consists of a number pad as described in TapLogger experiments that portray a standard number pad on a smartphone. Standard number pad on a smartphone usually contains 12 keys: 10 keys for (0 - 9) numbers, and the remaining two are '∗' and '#'. The second view layout consists of 10x6 array of buttons covering the entire screen, as described in ACCessory experiments. The first layout is used to collect data set to investigate the impact of Slogger against touchstroke detection while the second layout is used to collect data set to investigate the impact of Slogger against touchstroke inference. The data set includes measurement of various motion sensors (accelerometer, linear acceleration, gyroscope, gravity, and rotation sensor) and log of touch events. Since all the sensors that are being recorded are tri-axial, each sensor record includes three values corresponding to the three axes and the timestamp of the record. Each record in the touch event log includes the timestamp of key-pressed or key-released event as they are dispatched by each button and the coordinates of the touch event that facilitates the establishment of the ground truth in the subsequent analysis.

We performed the experiments in normal scenario (i.e., Slogger Absent scenario) and the defensive scenario with Slogger in two different settings (i.e., when the attacker is trained with or without the noisy data). In all the experiments, we collected key presses data samples from one of the researchers involved in this study.

5.1 Slogger against Touchstroke Detection

In this experiment, we evaluate Slogger against one of the state-of-the-art touchstroke detection attacks, Tap-detector presented in (Section 2.2).

5.1.1 Data Collection

For evaluation purposes, we collected 1200 samples of key presses such that each key receives 100 touchstrokes using the number pad view layout of our application. These samples were used to train the Tap-detector system. Then, we collected 5 sets of 100 key presses to test Tap-detector, and the detection accuracy is computed by averaging the accuracies for these 5 sets. All the touchstroke samples were collected using the same setting as considered in the TapLogger experiments, i.e., phone is held by one hand and the keys on touchscreen are pressed by the index finger of the other hand. We conducted this experiment twice, one without activating Slogger, the normal scenario, and another with Slogger running in background, the defensive scenario.

5.1.2 Results

The result of Tap-detector in the normal and the defensive scenarios with Slogger are summarized in Table 2. In the absence of Slogger, Tap-detector successfully detects the touchstrokes with accuracy (F-measure) of 85.97%, which is in line with the result reported in [23]. Considering the second scenario, where Tap-detector is trained with regular stream of sensor readings while it is supplied with Slogger injected stream of sensor readings to detect the touchstroke event, Tap-detector is not able to detect any of the touchstrokes. The features that Tap-detector extracts from each window of the stream of accelerometer readings to predict the touchstroke events are now no longer present in the touchstroke signal because the touchstroke signal has been completely obfuscated by the noise injected by Slogger. Figure 2 clearly explains the impact of Slogger in accelerometer readings that completely prevent Tap-detector from detecting any of the touchstrokes. Even when both of the training and the testing sensor readings are collected while Slogger is activated (i.e., the attacker was trained with noisy data), the accuracy of Tap-detector dropped by a considerable amount, from 85.97% (normal scenario) down to 32.20%.

Table 2: Results of Tap-detector in three different scenarios: Slogger Absent, and two different defensive scenarios with Slogger.

Scenarios	Precision	Recall	F-measure
Slogger Absent	88.31%	84.01%	85.97%
Slogger Present, Attacker Trained with Non-Noisy Data	0	0	N/A
Slogger Present, Attacker Trained with Noisy Data	38.07%	27.93%	32.20%

5.2 Slogger against Touchstroke Inference

In this experiment, we evaluate Slogger against one of the state-of-the-art touchstroke inference attacks, ACCessory (presented in Section 2.3).

5.2.1 Data Collection

There are several ways in which users hold their phones and several typing styles that users employ while providing input to the phone device. Addressing all possible phone holding patterns and

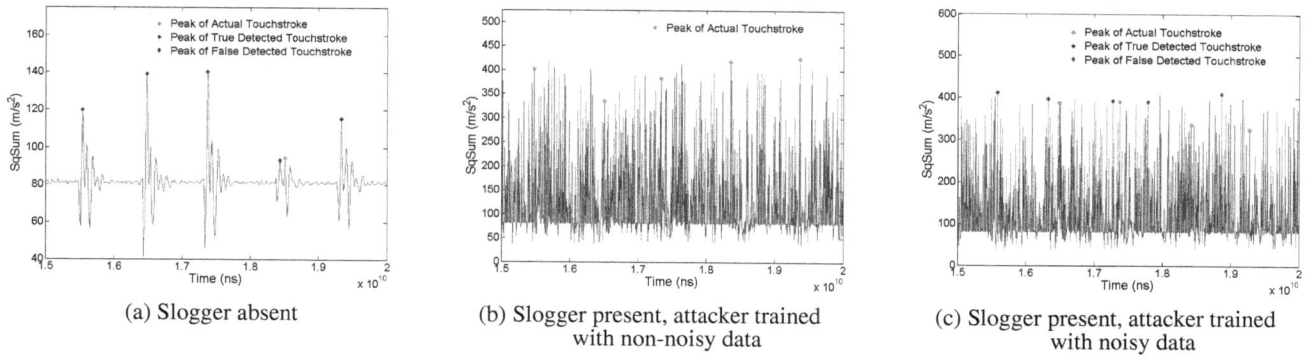

| (a) Slogger absent | (b) Slogger present, attacker trained with non-noisy data | (c) Slogger present, attacker trained with noisy data |

Figure 2: $SqSum$ plot of Accelerometer signal and results of Tap-detector in three different scenarios.

typing styles is not a feasible endeavor. Rather, in our study, we consider two realistic, commonly used phone holding settings:

- *In Hand*: In this setting, user holds the touch-enabled device using both of his hands in the landscape orientation, and provides the input to the device using the thumbs of both of these hands (similar to the setting used in [17]).

- *On Surface*: In this setting, touch-enabled device is placed on a smooth surface (e.g. a table) and the user types using the index finger of his dominant hand.

We collected 1200 samples of key presses using 10x6 buttons view layout such that each key receives 20 key presses. These samples were used to train the touchstroke inference model. Then, 5 sets of 100 key presses were collected and the inference accuracy was computed by averaging the inference accuracies over these 5 set of samples. We repeated this experiment for both the *In Hand* and *On Surface* settings in both normal and defensive scenarios.

5.2.2   Results

We evaluated Slogger against the touchstroke inference attack in all the scenarios described in Section 4. The results are summarized in Figure 3 and Figure 4.

Slogger Absent: Figure 3 shows the inference accuracy in the absence of defense system in two different settings, *In Hand* and *On Surface*. The results show that the touchstroke inference accuracy is more than 90% (compared to 50% for a random guessing attack) on average for 2 region splits (i.e., for two halves of the screen) in both the settings. For the eight-region granularity of the screen, inference accuracy drops to 45.4% in the *In Hand* setting and to 56.2% in the *On Surface* setting. Intuitively, it is obvious that increasing the granularity level of screen regions decreases the inference accuracy (but is significantly higher than random guessing accuracy of 25%). Further increasing regions granularity to 60 regions, the inference accuracy substantially drop to 17.8% in case of the *On Surface* setting and to 10.2% for the *In Hand* setting (compared to 1.67% for a random guessing attack). From Figure 3, we can find that the inference accuracy is higher in the *On Surface* setting than in the *In Hand* setting for all the granularity levels. We believe that the reason behind this is the higher amount of movement-based noise generated on the phone when it is held in hand than when it is placed on a smooth surface (table) where the phone typically remains stationary.

Slogger Present, Attacker Trained with Non-Noisy Data: Figure 3 shows that in the presence of our defensive mechanism and when the attacker is trained with non-noisy data, inference accuracy significantly drops below the random guessing accuracy. For

instance, inference accuracy drops to 35.5% (random being 50%) for two halves of the screen, and to 7% (random being 12.5%) for 8 regions while for 60 regions, it drops to 0.6% (random being 1.67%).

Since the inference model is trained with regular (non-noisy) stream of touchstroke signal and is supplied with totally obscured signal of touchstroke for inference that it has never encountered (in the presence Slogger), it does not know how to predict the touchstrokes. Therefore, it gives a prediction much worse than a random prediction model. Thus, Slogger serves to provide a strong defense system against sensor-based touchstroke inference attack that enforces the inference model to behave worse than a random prediction model under all granularity level of screen areas.

Slogger Present, Attacker Trained with Noisy-Data: Figure 4 also shows the inference accuracy when the inference model is trained and tested with the stream of sensor readings that contain noise inserted by Slogger. This model seems to reduce the impact of noise in dropping the inference accuracy, as it may learn the pattern taking into account of the noises. However, the noise injected by Slogger is randomly generated as described in Section 4, the touchstroke inference model still could not learn the touchstroke features well.

In the *On Surface* setting, Slogger is able to reduce the inference accuracy to nearly random in all level of regions granularity. For instance, for two halves of the screen areas, when enabling the Slogger system, the inference accuracy drops to 56.5%, for 8 regions the inference accuracy drops to 15.8%, and it drops to 1.5% for 60 regions granularity of screen areas.

In the *In Hand* setting, inference accuracy of touchstroke inference model is reduced by nearly or more than 20% in almost all level of regions granularity. For 16 and 60 regions granularity level, inference accuracy drops to, nearly random accuracy, 10.4% and 2.6%, respectively.

5.3   Slogger against Sensor Fusion

As the attacker can gain unfettered access to all the motion/position sensors on an Android device in a similar way as access to the accelerometer sensor, the attacker can utilize other sensors or a combination of sensors to enhance the inference accuracy. In this section, we first show that such a *fusion* of sensors can significantly improve the accuracy of touchstroke inference, and then evaluate the impact of Slogger against this powerful fusion attack.

5.3.1   Data Collection

We used the same data set that we collected to evaluate Slogger against touchstroke inference attack in the previous subsections. To

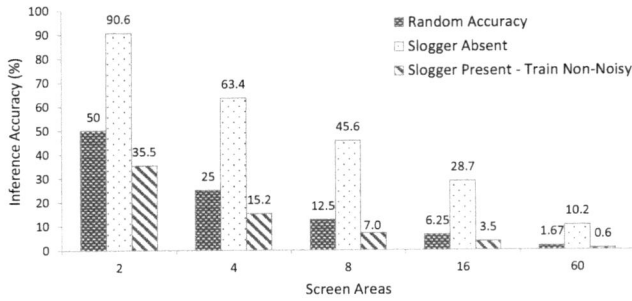

(a) In Hand

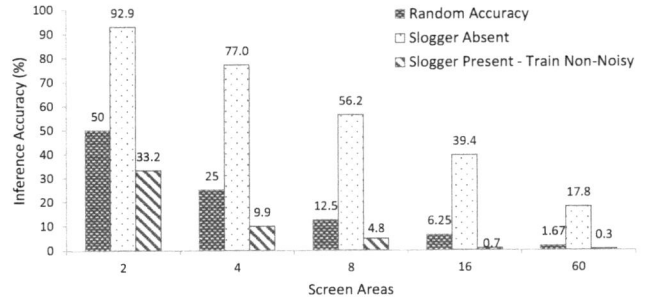

(b) On Surface

Figure 3: Touchstroke inference accuracy for different screen region granularity in the *Slogger Absent* scenario and the *Slogger Present, Attacker Trained with Non-Noisy Data* scenario.

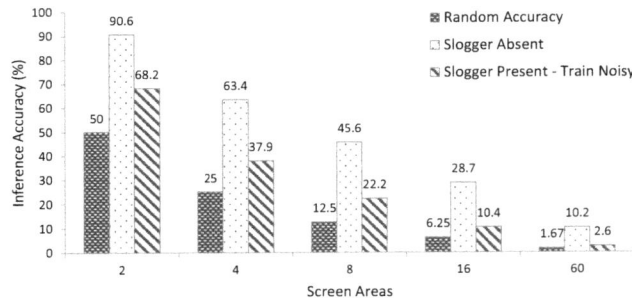

(a) In Hand

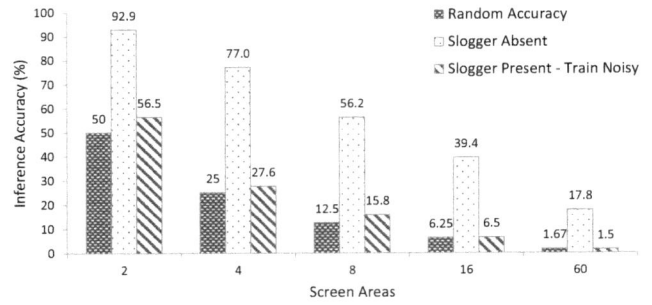

(b) On Surface

Figure 4: Touchstroke inference accuracy by screen region granularity in the *Slogger Absent* scenario and the *Slogger Present, Attacker Trained with Noisy Data* scenario.

recall, earlier we considered the touchstroke inference attack based only on accelerometer sensor readings while now we consider the *fusion* of various motion sensors enhancing the touchstroke inference attack. The motion sensors used in our study are accelerometer, linear acceleration, gravity, gyroscope, and rotation.

5.3.2 Results

We extracted the same set of features for each of the motion sensors that we used for the accelerometer sensor. Out of all possible combination of sensors, we noted the sensor combinations which yield the maximum inference accuracy for each of the regions granularity levels in both the *In Hand* and *On Surface* settings separately. The results are shown in Table 3. As we can see, the accuracies resulting from the fusion are higher compared to the accelerometer only case.

In Slogger defensive scenarios, we evaluated the reduction in the maximum inference accuracy of the inference model while employing the fusion of multiple sensors. Results are shown in Figure 5. In the first scenario, where inference model is trained with regular stream of sensor readings and tested against Slogger injected stream of sensor readings, inference accuracies drop significantly below the random guessing inference. In the second scenario, where both the training and the testing stream of signals have Slogger injected noises, Slogger is able to reduce the maximum inference accuracy to nearly random inference in case of the *On Surface* setting, while in the *In Hand* setting, Slogger is able to reduce the accuracy by more than 25%, which is a significant degradation in the inference accuracy. This analysis shows that even if fusion of multiple sensors were to be used for the touchstroke inference attack, Slogger is still able to effectively defend against such attack.

5.4 Impact of Slogger on Benign Applications

Since Slogger works by injecting sensory noise, one natural question is whether it can have an adverse effect on benign applications that rely upon the sensor data. To this end, we performed an experiment to study the impact of Slogger on benign application. We tested Slogger with one of the Android applications, pedometer[1], in two different settings, *In Hand* and *On Surface*. Pedometer primarily records the number of steps the user has walked as well as the distance covered, walking time and speed per hour. When the phone was placed on a surface, while the pedometer and Slogger applications were running in the background, the step count as shown by the application was affected. However, when phone was held in hand in a similar setting, the step count was not affected. This is because the range of values of noise that Slogger injects is similar to the user typing movements. So, when the phone is placed on the surface, the difference between the injected values and the readings generated by the hardware sensors becomes high, contrary to the case when the phone was in hand, that fools the pedometer application to count it as a step. It is important to note that Slogger does not inject noise all the time, rather it is activated only when sensitive input is being provided by the user. Typically, in a real-world scenario, the user enters the sensitive input while holding the phone in hand - the scenario in which Slogger does not have noticeable impact on the benign applications such as Pedometer. We further tested Slogger with other benign apps, such as "fall detection" [2] and "shake to clear notes" [3], and confirmed that Slogger injection did not affect these apps.

---

[1]Pedometer – https://goo.gl/RFB64p

[2]FADE: fall detector – https://goo.gl/YFIsO0

[3]Any.do: To-Do List, Task List – https://goo.gl/7oIHZN

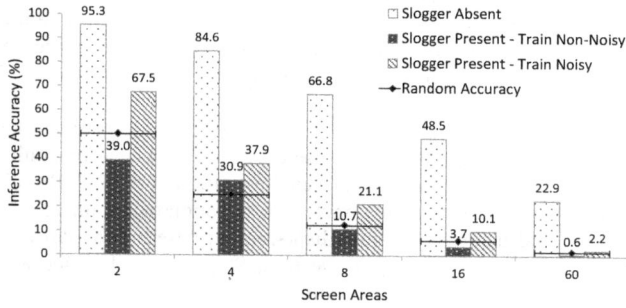

(a) In Hand

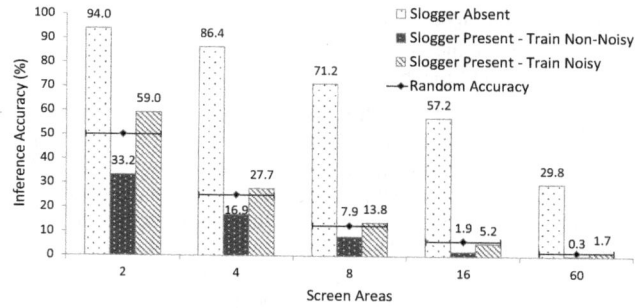

(b) On Surface

Figure 5: Touchstroke inference accuracy by screen region granularity of *fusion of sensors* in presence and absence of Slogger.

Table 3: Maximum touchstroke inference accuracy gained for various regions granularity as a result of *Fusion of Sensors*, and respective sensor combination.

	Screen Areas	Accelerometer Only – Accuracy	Fusion – Maximum Accuracy	Sensor Combination Yielding Maximum Accuracy
In Hand	2	90.62%	95.34%	accelerometer, linear acceleration, gyroscope, gravity, rotation
	4	63.41%	84.62%	linear acceleration, gyroscope, gravity
	8	45.56%	66.83%	linear acceleration, gyroscope, gravity
	16	28.71%	48.51%	linear acceleration, gyroscope, gravity
	60	10.20%	22.91%	linear acceleration, gyroscope, gravity
On Surface	2	92.88%	94.01%	linear acceleration, gyroscope
	4	77.04%	86.42%	linear acceleration, gyroscope, rotation
	8	56.21%	71.25%	linear acceleration, gyroscope, gravity, rotation
	16	39.35%	57.12%	linear acceleration, gyroscope, gravity, rotation
	60	17.78%	29.78%	linear acceleration, gyroscope, rotation

6. DISCUSSION AND FUTURE WORK

Summary of Analysis: Our evaluation demonstrates that Slogger is able to defeat both the touchstroke detection and touchstroke inference steps, and hence it can defeat sensor-based touchstroke inference attack as a whole.

In both of the attack scenarios, *Attacker Trained with Non-Noisy data*, and *Attacker Trained with Noisy-Data*, Slogger is able to defeat the touchstroke detection attack. In the first attack scenario, the noise injected by Slogger completely prevented *Tap-detector* to detect any of the touchstrokes present in the sensor signal, while in the second attack scenario, Slogger is able to significantly reduce the detection accuracy down to as low as 32%. The touchstroke inference attack is also undermined by considerable amount with Slogger noise injection. Slogger is able to drop the inference accuracy nearly as low or even lower than the random guessing accuracy in almost all the scenarios. One exception is the *'In Hand', Attacker Trained with Noisy-Data* scenario, where detection accuracy still dropped significantly, by more than 20%.

In a realistic keylogging attack, where the attacker has to combine the touchstroke detection and inference steps, the error in the detection step propagates to the inference step, which would further lower the overall inference accuracy. This is because if the inference algorithm works with wrongly detected tap regions, the accuracy of inference model will degrade considerably. Even if we assume a scenario where the attacker achieves the highest possible accuracies in both of these steps (32% in touchstroke detection and 68.2% for touchstroke inference step for two-halved regions) in presence of Slogger, the overall inference accuracy becomes 21.76%, which is far below than the random guessing inference for two-halved regions.

Further, even if fusion of multiple sensors is used for touchstroke inference attack, which usually enhances the inference accuracy,

Slogger is still able to effectively defend against such an attack.

All these results show that Slogger serves to provide an effective defense mechanism against sensor-based touchstroke logging.

Deliberate Noise Filtering: We argue that removing the noise injected by Slogger is a challenging task. First, Slogger injects the noise at random intervals, and the attacker cannot gain access to the sensor files and therefore there is no way that the attacker can get the information as to when the noise is injected. Second, the injected noise does not have a profile as it is random and therefore there is no way the attacker can try to reproduce the noise and then remove it from the signal. Third, the injected noise sometimes overwrites the original sensor values (or part of them), so any method that tries to delete part of the signal will delete some of the original readings as well and therefore degrade the original signal. Finally, the injected noise values lie within the range of the values corresponding to the user typing.

Touchstroke Inference over Multiple Rounds: We performed an experiment to check if the attacker can infer the touchstrokes after sniffing the accelerometer readings multiple times while the user is pressing the same sequence of buttons (e.g., in case of a PIN or password typed during each login attempt) in the (10 × 6 button grid). In our experiment, the user pressed on a sequence of 8 buttons for 20 times, while the phone is left on a surface, and we recorded the corresponding accelerometer readings. Then, for each button in the sequence, we predicted the pressed button as the one that got predicted in the majority of the trials. Without noise injection, the attack succeeded in predicting all the pressed regions (for 2 regions screen granularity), 6 out of 8 (for 4 regions screen granularity), and 5 out of 8 (for 60 regions screen granularity). In contrast, when Slogger was activated, the attack could only predict 5 out of the 8 for (2 regions screen granularity), 1 out of the 8 for (4 regions screen granularity) and 0 out of 8 for (60 regions screen granularity). The results of this study show that Slogger is an effective mechanism for even defending such a multi-round, powerful attack. Since the injected noise is random, every time the attack inferred different touchstrokes in presence of Slogger.

Slogger to Defeat Other Side-Channel Attacks: Other side channel attacks based on motion sensors have been proposed in prior research, including location tracking and device fingerprinting. Location tracking side-channel attack, named "ACComplice", was presented in [11]. ACComplice is a malware that can track the location information of the users based on the accelerometer data. It uses the accelerometer readings to infer the trajectory and the starting point of the user who is driving. A device fingerprinting attack, called AccelPrint, was presented in [6]. The attack shows that each accelerometer has unique fingerprints which can be exploited for tracking users. These fingerprints are due to the hardware imperfections inculcated during the sensor manufacturing process, which makes every sensor chip respond to the same motion stimulus in a different way. Both these attacks are reviewed in detail in the next section. We believe that Slogger can be utilized in defeating such attacks given its ability to inject sensor events. To defend against ACComplice, Slogger can inject noisy accelerometer data to the system whenever a user is driving at random or specific intervals of time. To defend against AccelPrint, Slogger can inject accelerometer events with values similar to the accelerometer data used by AccelPrint to fingerprint the phone. However, this approach may also affect the benign apps which use sensor data for different purposes. Hence, Slogger should only inject negligible sensor events such that the benign apps are not affected and/or inject sensor events for only a short period of time (like in the Slogger defense against touchstroke logging attacks). Further work will be needed to test the viability of this defense mechanism.

7. OTHER RELATED WORK

In the current Android security model, motion, position and environmental sensors are considered *insensitive* resources – any app can read these sensors without any security permissions. However, many researchers have shown that many sensitive information about the user can be inferred only by monitoring these benign-looking sensors (especially the motion sensors), and thereby compromising the user privacy.

In this paper, we explored the effectiveness of, and defense against, touchstroke detection and touchstroke inference based on motion sensors by re-implementing two of the state-of-the-art attacks - Tap-detector [23] and ACCessory [17].

Another side channel attack for touchstroke logging is presented in [2]. They presented an attack based on accelerometer data to learn user's PIN/password or Android's pattern unlock while the user is unlocking her smartphone. This attack system uses machine learning techniques to infer four-digit PINs and password patterns. Since the accelerometer data is varied by subtle tilts and shifts, the approach normalizes the data, extracts 774 different features based on signal processing and polynomial fitting techniques, and then feeds these features to a classifier. It is worth noting that Slogger would affect the accuracy of such attack, as it injects random values in the accelerometer sensor.

Another interesting type of side-channel attack is motion-based location tracking. Han et al. in [11] presented "ACComplice", a malware which can track the location information of the users based on the accelerometer data. ACComplice uses the accelerometer readings to infer the trajectory and the starting point of the user who is driving, and thereby compromising the user privacy. ACComplice first tries to infer the trajectory based on accelerom-

eter readings and then associates that trajectory to the most likely location on a map. One of the main challenges of this system is to deal with "drifting error". The drifting error occurs as the position of vehicle at time t depends upon the position at time $t-1$ and the displacement occurred at the time interval $[t-1, t]$. Also, the drifting error aggregates over time. In order to estimate the location accurately, Han et al. use a probabilistic dead reckoning method called Probabilistic Inertial Navigation "ProbIN". ProbIN treats sensor measurements only as observation of the underlying motion and maps the vehicle displacement based on a statistical model. As discussed in prior section, Slogger may be used as a defense system to address this attack.

Further, Marquardt et al. [14] showed that it is possible to infer key presses on a regular keyboard using motion sensor of a phone when the phone is placed two inches away. They developed an spying application, (sp)iPhone, that records and interprets the surface vibrations sensed by the phone's accelerometer to predict what was typed on the keyboard.

Moreover, a few sensor and device fingerprinting attacks have been proposed based on motion sensors. "AccelPrint" presented in [6] showed that each accelerometer has unique fingerprints which can be exploited for tracking users. These fingerprints are due to the hardware imperfections inculcated during the sensor manufacturing process, which makes every sensor chip respond to the same motion stimulus in a different way. They argued that the differences in responses across accelerometers are negligible for the higher level apps such that it does not affect their performance. The analysis of these negligible differences showed that these fingerprints emerge with consistency and can even be somewhat independent of the stimulus that generates them. To get the stimulus, they use the period when the vibration motor is turned on. In order to remain stealthy, the developed malware does not turn on the vibration motor itself, but rather waits for some other apps/event to turn the vibration motor on. The malware also uses the accelerometer data to detect this vibration.

Another fingerprinting attack is presented by Das et al. in [5] utilizing accelerometer and gyroscope sensors readings. Moreover, Das et al. presented two mitigation mechanisms, one is based on sensors calibration and the other is based on obfuscating the anomalies by injecting random noise. Both of the methods have shown decreased in the accuracy of the fingerprinting and shown to be promising to defeat device fingerprinting based on motion sensors imperfections. However, the authors did not show how to implement such mitigation mechanisms without modifying the operating system or the device manufacture. We believe that Slogger can serve as a viable defense to such attacks at the app level alone (i.e., without changing the OS or the kernel).

8. CONCLUSIONS

We presented Slogger, a practical defense to the problem of motion-based touchstroke logging attacks applicable to current Android devices. The Slogger app can be installed on the device easily using the ADB workaround (just like typical screenshot apps), without requiring to root the device or make any changes to the Operating System. Once installed, Slogger can protect the touchscreen input to any app by obfuscating the motion/position sensor readings with randomly generated noisy readings. It works invisibly in the background without affecting the user or other benign apps that need to use the raw sensor measurements. Slogger also boasts to defeat powerful and sophisticated attackers who may combine multiple sensors readings or use deliberate noise filtering mechanisms to infer the touchstrokes provided by the user.

Acknowledgements

This work is partially supported by National Science Foundation (NSF) grants: CNS-1209280 and CNS-1526524.

References

[1] A. Al-Haiqi, M. Ismail, and R. Nordin. Keystrokes inference attack on android: A comparative evaluation of sensors and their fusion. *Journal of ICT Research and Applications*, 7(2):117–136, 2013.

[2] A. J. Aviv, B. Sapp, M. Blaze, and J. M. Smith. Practicality of accelerometer side channels on smartphones. In *Proceedings of the 28th Annual Computer Security Applications Conference*, pages 41–50. ACM, 2012.

[3] L. Cai and H. Chen. Touchlogger: Inferring keystrokes on touch screen from smartphone motion. *HotSec*, 11:9–9, 2011.

[4] J. Dai, X. Bai, Z. Yang, Z. Shen, and D. Xuan. Perfalld: A pervasive fall detection system using mobile phones. In *Pervasive Computing and Communications Workshops (PERCOM Workshops)*, 2010.

[5] A. Das, N. Borisov, and M. Caesar. Exploring ways to mitigate sensor-based smartphone fingerprinting. *arXiv preprint arXiv:1503.01874*, 2015.

[6] S. Dey, N. Roy, W. Xu, R. R. Choudhury, and S. Nelakuditi. Accelprint: Imperfections of accelerometers make smartphones trackable. In *NDSS*. Citeseer, 2014.

[7] S.-H. Fang, Y.-C. Liang, and K.-M. Chiu. Developing a mobile phone-based fall detection system on android platform. In *Computing, Communications and Applications Conference*, ComComAp, 2012.

[8] A. P. Felt, E. Ha, S. Egelman, A. Haney, E. Chin, and D. Wagner. Android permissions: User attention, comprehension, and behavior. In *Proceedings of the Eighth Symposium on Usable Privacy and Security*, page 3. ACM, 2012.

[9] M. Frank, R. Biedert, E. Ma, I. Martinovic, and D. Song. Touchalytics: On the applicability of touchscreen input as a behavioral biometric for continuous authentication. *IEEE Transactions on Information Forensics and Security*, Jan 2013.

[10] H. Gascon, S. Uellenbeck, C. Wolf, and K. Rieck. Continuous authentication on mobile devices by analysis of typing motion behavior. In *Sicherheit*, 2014.

[11] J. Han, E. Owusu, L. T. Nguyen, A. Perrig, and J. Zhang. Accomplice: Location inference using accelerometers on smartphones. In *Communication Systems and Networks (COMSNETS), 2012 Fourth International Conference on*, pages 1–9. IEEE, 2012.

[12] S. Hemminki, P. Nurmi, and S. Tarkoma. Accelerometer-based transportation mode detection on smartphones. In *ACM Conference on Embedded Networked Sensor Systems*, SenSys. ACM, 2013.

[13] P. G. Kelley, L. F. Cranor, and N. Sadeh. Privacy as part of the app decision-making process. In *Proceedings of the SIGCHI Conference on Human Factors in Computing Systems*, pages 3393–3402. ACM, 2013.

[14] P. Marquardt, A. Verma, H. Carter, and P. Traynor. (sp) iphone: decoding vibrations from nearby keyboards using mobile phone accelerometers. In *Proceedings of the 18th ACM conference on Computer and communications security*, pages 551–562. ACM, 2011.

[15] E. Miluzzo, A. Varshavsky, S. Balakrishnan, and R. R. Choudhury. Tapprints: your finger taps have fingerprints. In *Proceedings of the 10th international conference on Mobile systems, applications, and services*, pages 323–336. ACM, 2012.

[16] M. Mohamed, B. Shrestha, and N. Saxena. Smashed: Sniffing and manipulating android sensor data. In *Conference on Data and Application Security and Privacy*, 2016.

[17] E. Owusu, J. Han, S. Das, A. Perrig, and J. Zhang. Accessory: password inference using accelerometers on smartphones. In *Proceedings of the Twelfth Workshop on Mobile Computing Systems & Applications*, page 9. ACM, 2012.

[18] D. Ping, X. Sun, and B. Mao. Textlogger: inferring longer inputs on touch screen using motion sensors. In *Proceedings of the 8th ACM Conference on Security & Privacy in Wireless and Mobile Networks*, page 24. ACM, 2015.

[19] F. Roesner, T. Kohno, A. Moshchuk, B. Parno, H. J. Wang, and C. Cowan. User-driven access control: Rethinking permission granting in modern operating systems. In *IEEE Symposium on Security and Privacy (SP)*, 2012.

[20] Y. S. Ryu, D. H. Koh, B. L. Aday, X. A. Gutierrez, and J. D. Platt. Usability evaluation of randomized keypad. *Journal of Usability Studies*, 5(2):65–75, 2010.

[21] D. Shukla, R. Kumar, A. Serwadda, and V. V. Phoha. Beware, your hands reveal your secrets! In *Proceedings of the 2014 ACM SIGSAC Conference on Computer and Communications Security*, pages 904–917. ACM, 2014.

[22] Y. Song, M. Kukreti, R. Rawat, and U. Hengartner. Two novel defenses against motion-based keystroke inference attacks. *arXiv preprint arXiv:1410.7746*, 2014.

[23] Z. Xu, K. Bai, and S. Zhu. Taplogger: Inferring user inputs on smartphone touchscreens using on-board motion sensors. In *Proceedings of the fifth ACM conference on Security and Privacy in Wireless and Mobile Networks*, pages 113–124. ACM, 2012.

[24] C.-W. You, N. D. Lane, F. Chen, R. Wang, Z. Chen, T. J. Bao, M. Montes-de Oca, Y. Cheng, M. Lin, L. Torresani, and A. T. Campbell. Carsafe app: Alerting drowsy and distracted drivers using dual cameras on smartphones. In *Mobile Systems, Applications, and Services*, MobiSys, 2013.

Don't Touch that Column: Portable, Fine-Grained Access Control for Android's Native Content Providers

Aisha Ali-Gombe, Golden G. Richard III, Irfan Ahmed and Vassil Roussev
Department of Computer Science, University of New Orleans
New Orleans, Louisiana, USA
aaligomb@uno.edu, golden@cs.uno.edu, irfan@cs.uno.edu, vassil@cs.uno.edu

Abstract

Android applications access native SQLite databases through their Universal Resource Identifiers (URIs), exposed by the Content provider library. By design, the SQLite engine used in the Android system does not enforce access restrictions on database content nor does it log database accesses. Instead, Android enforces read and write permissions on the native providers through which databases are accessed via the mandatory applications permissions system. This system is very coarse grained, however, and can allow applications far greater access to sensitive data than a user might intend.

In this paper, we present a novel technique called *priVy* that merges static bytecode weaving and database query rewriting to achieve low-level access control for Android native providers at the application level. *priVy* defines access control for both database schema and entities and does not require any modifications to the underlying operating system and/or framework code. Instead, it provides a new Controller stub which is statically woven into the target application and a Controller interface for setting access levels, thus making it accessible and easily adoptable by average users. We provide an evaluation in terms of the resilience of applications to instrumentation as well as static and runtime instrumentation overhead. In our testing, *priVy* incurs an average of 1032 additional method calls or joinpoints created and it takes an average of 15 seconds to recompile an app and imposes virtually no runtime overhead.

1. INTRODUCTION

Smartphone technology has not only revolutionized our telephony experience, but has successfully integrated a vast amount of personal data, including our address books, calendars, diaries, pictures, etc. onto a single device. From a security perspective, the ease and convenience provided by this integration can have disastrous consequences, serving as a single point of exposure for a tremendous amount of personal data if not properly managed.

WiSec'16 , July 18-22, 2016, Darmstadt, Germany

© 2016 ACM. ISBN 978-1-4503-4270-4/16/07. . . $15.00

DOI: http://dx.doi.org/10.1145/2939918.2939927

Access to data and resources on Android systems is regulated by two important concepts, specifically, the permissions model and application sandboxing. Third party applications are required to make explicit requests for permissions at installation time and while this mechanism provides a general idea of what an application can access on a device, it does not provide the ability to institute fine-grained control over sensitive data. Essentially, it's an all-or-nothing model under which the user has to approve all permissions or abort the installation of the application. Perhaps more disturbing is that the approved permission(s) remain a right of the installed application as long as it remains on the phone.

Android extends this model to cover structured data stored in SQLite databases. However, it does not separate roles and privileges on the database, nor does it protect content data at the schema or entity levels. In fact, it does very little to protect the privacy of the stored user data and its associated metadata. Such a wide level of access is tantamount to giving the application administrative rights over the target provider. For example, this system does not distinguish accesses to a contact's phone number from the email and physical addresses. Other important information like the "last time contacted" as well as account type and names are also easily accessible with a simple READ permission. Similarly, write permission on the contacts provider allows an application to insert, delete and modify any contact at will. The application can also create groups and make them invisible. Such "perceived" benign access however can lead to malicious contacts been created and synched to restricted groups in major accounts like Google.

Looking at the bigger picture, the privacy violation scales beyond the device user alone. It also exposes data associated with third parties to the prying eyes of malware and other privacy-violating applications. For instance, clearly mapped information like phone numbers, email and physical addresses provide sufficient information about third parties that they could be used to support targeted advertisement, social engineering, surveillance, and physical attacks

Furthermore, due to the interconnectivity of the different providers and their data, we have found the current approach to result in various forms of inferential permission leaks. Other security breaches like denial of service due to malformed SQL data are also possible.

To reduce the propensity of these problems and provide users with additional control over the Android content providers, Mutti et al [16] proposed an integration of SQLite and SELinux. Based on context security, this system enforces fine grain access control at the lowest level in the database. Unfortunately, the solution requires extensive changes in the operating system code to accommodate the security context schema table and its corresponding library code. Given how long it takes for Android to effect changes and for manufacturers to integrate such solutions on existing systems, techniques that require extensive OS modifications are not viable, practical options for an average user.

To solve these problems, we developed a new technique that enforces access restrictions, query-rewriting and database access logging via static bytecode weaving. Our system, called *priVy*, does not require any change to the Android kernel and middleware. Furthermore, *priVy* does not treat SQLite databases as a single information store with a single set of access permissions; instead, it enforces restrictions for different schema and entity levels by re-implementing content provider library code using instrumentation at the application level, based on user-provided access restrictions. The new weaved checking code forces the application to access only user-approved schema or entities, while maintaining application integrity.

Contributions Our techniques provide the following unique features:

- *More control over data*: *priVy* provides schema and entity level access control for Android content providers through method hooking, access constraint enforcement, and query re-writing.

- *Portability*: Our scheme does not require changes to the Android kernel and/or framework code, for maximum usability.

- *Efficiency and Usability*: Aside from minimal instrumentation overhead and better control over user data, the use of *priVy* is virtually transparent.

The rest of the paper is organized as follows: Section 2 presents background on SQLite and Android content providers; Section 3 provides an overview of possible threats and vulnerabilities on the content provider; Section 4 details the design of *priVy*; Section 5 and 6 presents the implementation and evaluation of our work respectively; Section 7 reviews the related literature followed by section 8 that concludes the paper.

2. BACKGROUND

2.1 SQLite Databases

SQLite is a single-user relational database management system (RDMS) used for storing structured data. Unlike a traditional RDMS, SQLite is a server-less database engine that stores data in normal files. It manages access and concurrency based on direct file reads and writes and operating system-level file locks, respectively. SQLite is lightweight and efficient and requires little configuration, making it the database engine of choice on many operating systems, such as Android and Apple's iOS.

2.2 Android Native Providers

Android offers built-in native content providers that store a variety of user data maintained by the system. Each is associated with at least one SQLite database that contains various tables, columns and entities. Some of the Android native providers are: Contacts, CallLog, VoiceMail, Browser, Settings, Media and Dictionary.

These providers together with the content resolver provide the basis for Android CRUD (Create, Read, Update, Delete) operations, corresponding to SQL insert, query, update and delete operations on database objects. The chain of events for data access occurs at two levels. At a high level, access begins with the resolver object invocation of one of the CRUD functions, passing at least a *Uri* parameter, which identifies the location of the required data. Other parameters for CRUD functions include column name(s), a WHERE clause, and order information. The resolver validates the *Uri* and then passes the request to its provider. The provider performs permission checks and if the requesting application has the required permissions, it uses the function parameters to construct an appropriate *SQLiteStatement*.

At a lower level, the SQLiteStatement is passed to the native content provider through the binder parcel. The native library translates the parcel and sends the request to the database engine, which then performs syntax and semantic checks, expansion and code generation. The result is sent back through the same route. In the case of read operations, a database *Cursor* is returned, For write operations, an integer indicating the number of entries affected is returned.

As discussed above, each of the CRUD operations triggers permission checks by the content provider. Queries are protected by READ permission while insert, delete, and update are guarded by WRITE permission. However, these coarse-grained permissions do not distinguish database roles for applications or privileges for individual database items. A simple READ permission allows access to all the tables, column and rows in the entire database, while a simple WRITE permission allows manipulation or deletion of any database entities.

3. THREATS AND VULNERABILITIES

The coarse-grained access control for databases under Android has serious security and privacy implications. In our preliminary research, we analyzed the contacts database and explored some issues associated with providing arbitrary applications with READ and WRITE access to this database.

3.1 Security Implications

Denial of Service: We explored a vulnerability with account types based on a malformed SQL statement that can crash the *acore* process, resulting in denial of service on the phone. A malicious app with WRITE permission can create a new contact without the user's knowledge under the "com.google" account type with a malformed account-name which contains a SQL terminator ";". The system will accept the malformed account name at the time of insertion, but after a while, Android will try to synchronize and delete bad account names. When this occurs, the malformed account-name will trigger a SQL exception in the SELECT statement and crash both the contacts application and the *acore* process. This key process is designed to automatically restart after it is killed, however, the malformed name will cause it to die once again. The repeated restart followed by crash of *acore* results in a denial of service attack on the phone and the only solution is to delete the entire contacts database, causing a loss of all local contacts if the user has no backups at hand.

Permission Leak: We also discovered that applications with the READ-CONTACTS permission can infer the user accounts on a device without requesting the GET-ACCOUNT permission. If a contact belongs to an account, the account name will be written alongside the contact in the RAW-CONTACTS table. And since there is no restriction on schema or column, an application can read the account name and type for all the contacts on the phone.

Malicious Contact: Finally, an application with WRITE access to the contacts can add a new contact under a particular account and group without restriction. When that account is synced, the contact gets pushed on to the server. This becomes a serious problem if, for example, the contact is pushed into an important work group that shares confidential information or if a contact's email address is secretly updated, to facilitate a targeted attack.

3.2 Privacy Concerns

Applications with appropriate coarse-grained permissions can read clearly mapped data containing names, phone numbers, email and physical addresses, and even IM status. This data can clearly distinguish an individual and be used for annoying advertisement or targeted social engineering attacks. Worse, information such as "last time contacted" can provide inferential information about call logs without having the CALL-LOG permission.

3.3 Forensic Concerns

With WRITE permission, update, insert, and delete database operations can be performed by an application with very little data available to support attribution, since Android produces no audit logs associated with database operations. This is primarily because SQLite is a single user system and is not designed to keep track of who performs what operations on a system. For forensics investigation, this makes it very hard to ascertain if a particular entry in the database is added or updated by the user or by a malicious application.

4. SYSTEM DESIGN

Our goal is to define low-level access controls for Android's native content providers and enforce these access controls for third party applications. This will ensure that users have tight control over read/write accesses on sensitive data for instrumented applications.

priVy is comprised of two components, a Controller app and Controller stub. The Controller app is an independent application running in a different process that registers an instrumented application and sets up and manages its access levels. The stub provides the weaved code that forces the instrumented app to verify access levels at startup, enforce access constraints, perform query-rewriting as necessary, and effect database auditing. The architecture of *priVy* is illustrated in Figure 1.

4.1 Controller Stub

Our approach uses the AspectJ instrumentation framework [14] to insert and enforce fine level access verification, query re-writing and database auditing for Android's native providers. AspectJ is an aspect-oriented programming (AOP) extension developed specifically for Java that allows cross-cutting concerns defined as aspects to be statically weaved into either raw Java source code or a compiled class. Our system employs a well known AspectJ compiler called *ajc* [1] to perform the application repackaging of Android binaries with our specially crafted, modularized aspects. Unlike most instrumentation libraries, AspectJ can perform highly optimized code injection at runtime, making it an ideal choice for our system. It can manipulate parameters, return values, and target objects, and new code can be inserted to run alongside or replace an existing method implementation based on some static or runtime condition.

In aspect-oriented programming, a *joinpoint* is an identifiable construct within program execution, e.g., a method call, while a *pointcut* is a program element which defines a joinpoint via a signature pattern. These signatures can contain *modifier, type, id* or *throw* patterns. The weaving process in static instrumentation creates and manages joinpoints based on these predefined signatures at compilation time. When a certain joinpoint is reached at runtime, AspectJ executes the encapsulated analysis routine called the *advice* defined for it. In *priVy*, this contains the newly inserted policy and query-rewriting code.

Depending on the cross cutting concern, signatures can be made very broad using wildcards or specific with direct package names, return types and parameter types. In *priVy*, we designed signatures for Android packages related to data access on SQLite databases. The three most important are *Database, Content Provider and Resolver*. The database package hosts the main SQLite database object and corresponding methods to query it in raw form. It also provides the *Cursor* interface for reading the results of database queries. It is important to note that Android does not support direct raw access for databases associated with an application with a different *uid*. Access to such data can only be provided via the *Uri* of the target Content provider. The provider classes expose data of one app to the code executing in a different process.

Generic AspectJ advices were then developed around the methods in the relevant classes from the packages discussed above. These advices are encapsulated in an aspect which is then statically recompiled into an Android binary. The result is the same Android binary extended with our controller stub. This static instrumentation process intercepts the resolver CRUD functions and inserts the controller code where necessary. As mentioned in Section 2, direct access to native databases is completely prohibited by Android and access is only available through the exposed native content. Thus, it is relatively convenient for us to develop specific signatures corresponding to only the resolver and provider packages.

As shown in Table 1, insertion operations can be performed in three different ways, either via a single insert, bulk insert, or using a content provider operation. Delete, update, and query operations can each be performed in two different ways. Our signatures take into account all these and we target the respective joinpoints accordingly.

AOP exposes three different ways to weave the checking code, either as "before", "after" or "around" advice. The "before" advice inserts new code before the joinpoint, thus its execution precedes that of the joinpoint. The "after" advice prepends the code beneath the joinpoint's code, while the "around" advice inserts it within the joinpoint's implementation. With the exception of adding auditing log entries, where code is inserted using "after" advice, all other code that performs constraint checks and query-rewriting uses "around" advice, which can perform code injection in the middle of method execution and allows manipulation of target object, parameter(s) and return value. This enables us to generate the correct return values in case a query is

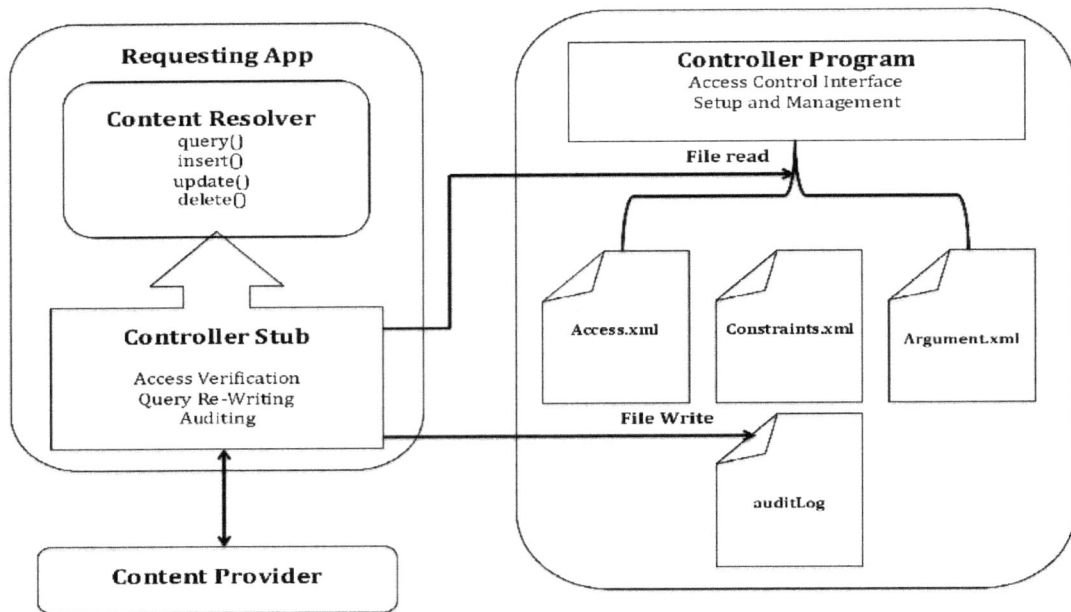

Figure 1: *priVy's* System Architecture.

blocked or restricted. It also allows us to enforce constraints and reflectively perform new method invocation on an already created object residing in memory.

4.1.1 Access Verification

At runtime, when the instrumented app begins execution, the controller stub performs the access verification as illustrated in Figure 1. It reads and parses the assigned access control for the target application from the world readable, shared preferences XML file for the controller app. It sets up the global variables for the access level, schema, and column as well as entity privileges for each provider. The global variables are used by the CRUD operation's joinpoint to determine how the method call will proceed when invoked.

The CRUD function's access level can be ALL_ALLOW, ALL_BLOCK and RESTRICT. The ALL_ALLOW access level, as the name implies, does not impose sanctions on the joinpoint and simply allows it to proceed with its original parameters. ALL_BLOCK, on the other hand, completely blocks the execution of a joinpoint. For ALL_BLOCK, our controller stub must ensure that the query is actually blocked while not affecting application stability. We are able to achieve this by ensuring the affected functions return appropriate values as shown in Figure 2 for Query joinpoint. Specifically, depending on the type of access functions, different actions must be taken:

1. Query and Insert: We transform the given *Uri* parameter of the function into an *Entity Uri* with appended zero. For queries, the system proceeds with this special entity *Uri* which in turn will force the return of an empty cursor with at least header information. For insert operations, the entity *Uri* gets returned and the parameters are discarded.

2. Update and Delete: Functions performing update and

delete operations expect an integral return type indicating how many rows were affected. We simply return 0, indicating that no rows were affected and thus the program will continue to execute smoothly.

The RESTRICT option regulates access to database schema, column and entities. In a relational database, a schema represents a logical group of objects. In this paper we restrict the schema definition to the database tables available through the content *Uri*, e.g., the contact table in "Contacts.db" or the events table in "Calendar.db". Also, we logically include all objects in a table that can be grouped by the same MIME types, like emails, phone numbers, and addresses, as different schemas.

Thus, the schema restriction ensures an app only queries from the approved tables or MIME type(s). Since most of these MIME types have individual Uris assigned to them through the *CommonKind Uri*, their schema restriction must ensure a entity restriction on the main table as well. The controller stub makes a decision to ALLOW, BLOCK or REWRITE the query based on the schema restriction established by the user. For example, if a user has a schema restriction set up to only allow access to email information and and the app requests both email and phone numbers, *priVy* must re-write the query such that only the email table gets projected on the SQL statement. Furthermore, restrictions can be imposed on database columns so that certain columns are prohibited from being viewed by apps, e.g., account-type and name, or an entity based on a column value.

Aside from the two mandates mentioned above for BLOCK option, a third condition becomes necessary here, specifically, that *priVy* must ensure that any other part of the application that depends on the return value of the function does not crash. This is mostly an issue with query functions, because they return a cursor and the program may have been designed to access a particular column which may not

Table 1: Joinpoints Picked by *priVy*'s Pointcut Signatures

Target Object	Insert	Update	Query	Delete
Content Resolver	insert(..)	update(..)	query(..)	delete(..)
Content Resolver	bulkInsert(..)			
ContentProviderOperation	newInsert(..)	newUpdate(..)	newAssertQuery(..)	newDelete(..)

```
pointcut getCurObj(Uri uri, String[] Projection,
    String Selection, String[] Selection_Args):
    call(*..*Cursor* *..*.query(..))
    || call(*..*Cursor* *..*.*Query(..)))
    && args(uri, Projection, Selection,
    Selection_Args,..) && NotNewLogger();

Object around(Object tar, Uri uri, String[] Projection,
    String Selection, String[] Selection_Args):
    target(tar) && getCurObj(uri, Projection,
    Selection, Selection_Args){
    //...
    //...
    ContentValues cont = getAccess();//From SharedPrefs
    if (cont.containsKey(uri.getAuthority())){
        start = System.nanoTime();
        String level =
        cont.get(uri.getAuthority()).toString();
        if (level.equals("ALL_ALLOW")){
            ret = proceed(tar, uri, Projection,
            Selection, Selection_Args);
        }else if (level.equals("ALL_BLOCK")){
            ret = proceed(tar, getEntityUri(uri),
            Projection, Selection, Selection_Args);
        }else if (level.equals("RESTRICT")) {
            checkSRestrict(..);//Schema Restriction
            //...
            checkCRestrict(..);//Column Restriction
            //...
            checkERestrict(..);//Entity Restriction

        }else{

        }
    }
}
```

Figure 2: Advice on a Query Joinpoint that Shows How the Controller Stub Performs Access Verification

```
// qSRestrict contains list of restricted Uri
public Uri checkSRestrict(ArrayList<String> qSRestrict,
    Uri uri, ContentResolver resolver){
    if (qSRestrict.contains(resolver.getType(uri))){
        uri= getEntityUri(uri);
    }else{
        //...
    }
    //...
}
```

Figure 3: Schema Restriction Check on a Query Function

column-level access restriction, the Controller stub executes *checkCRestrict* function and re-writes the query based on the following rules;

1. **If projection is not null** - the stub checks for the intersection of the *projected column(s)* and the restricted column(s) and then removes them from the projection list as shown in Figure 4.

2. **If the prohibited column is the only column to be projected** - the function will be blocked completely. This is because exchanging the prohibited list with null will return all the columns including the prohibited ones.

3. **If projection is null** - For query, the stub checks the intersection of the columns of the *return cursor* and the restricted column(s). If found, the intersected column(s) are removed and the query continues with the remaining column as shown in Figure 5. For Update and Insert, restricted column are prevented from database write thus key sets of the content values are compared against the restricted column and removed if there is an intersection. Delete operations do not require column projection.

```
if (Projection!=null){
    if(myMap.keySet().contains(resolver.getType(uri))){
        String val = myMap.get(resolver.getType(uri));
        for(String str: Projection){
            if(!(resolver.getType(uri)+str).equals
                (resolver.getType(uri)+val)){
                newProj.add(str);
            }
        }finProj = newProj.toArray(new
        String[newProj.size()]);
    }else{
        finProj= Projection;
    }
}
```

Figure 4: Column-level Restriction with Not-Null Projection

be available due to restrictions. To solve this problem, we instrument all the functions that access cursor information directly. The advice on these joinpoints tests if the column requested is available and if it isn't, the column will return a empty string. This has proven to work well in practice to ensure that applications do not crash due to the imposed access restrictions.

4.1.2 Query Re-Writing

Android creates a proper SQLstatement after the request has passed the permission checks. Since our system operates at the highest level, we rewrite the intended query by altering and/or supplying new CRUD function argument(s). These functions contains *Uri, Projection, Selection Selection-Arguments* and *Content Values* parameters.

In SCHEMA restriction, *priVy* compares the query Uri with the restricted schema, if matched, the query is simple blocked otherwise the system allows it to execute. The code snippet is shown in Figure 3.

The query-rewriting module is triggered when the initial query is projected on column(s) and/or entities outside its access restriction. In a query function a projection argument can take an array of column names or null (indicating all rows in a table should be returned). Armed with the

Selection and Selection-Arguments indicate the WHERE clause column(s) and value(s). The user can restrict access on some predefined values, e.g., to certain account types, whitelisted contacts, etc. For the most part, we don't test or nullify these arguments, but rather we enforce the new

```
if (ret instanceof Cursor){
    Cursor cur =(Cursor)ret;
    if(cur.getCount()>0){
        String[] pNames = cur.getColumnNames();
        if(myMap.keySet().contains
            (resolver.getType(uri))){
            String val =
                myMap.get(resolver.getType(uri));
            for(String str: pNames){
                if(!(resolver.getType(uri)
                    +str).equals(resolver.getType
                    (uri)+val)){
                    newProj.add(str);
                }
            }finProj = newProj.toArray(new
                String[newProj.size()]);

        }else{
            finProj= null;
        }
    }
}
```

Figure 5: Column-level Restriction with Null Projection

specification by concatenating our restriction to an already established WHERE clause. For instance, an application might be restricted to only query contacts from account-type *"com.google"* and we simply ensure that this is enforced by influencing the WHERE clause. If this restriction involves only one entity, the controller stub appends it with an "AND" operator to the function's WHERE clause, if not null. If the WHERE clause is null, however, the stub then substitutes the null with the new restriction, and the function proceeds with this new value. On the other hand, the situation is more challenging when there are more than one entity restriction and it applies to different tables (e.g., account type (Raw_Contacts) and lookup key (Contacts)). In typical SQL we can perform complex joins on the different tables. However, on content providers such operations are very limited. To solve this, we extract the primary key (and foreign key where necessary) from each of the tables and use them as the parameter(s) for the target query's WHERE clause as shown in 6.

```
public String checkERestrict(Uri uri, ContentResolver resolver){
    String finSel= null;
    if (uri.getAuthority().contains("contacts")){
        // for each entity restriction,
        // getContactIds(..) gets its primary key column.
        //The intersection of the results is return in fin
        String fin = getContactIds(resolver);
        if(fin!=null){
            if(uri.equals(ContactsContract.Contacts.
                CONTENT_URI)){
            finSel = ContactsContract.Contacts._ID +
                " IN ( "+fin+" )";
            }else if (uri.equals(ContactsContract.Data.
                CONTENT_URI)){
                finSel = ContactsContract.Data.
                    RAW_CONTACT_ID + " IN ( "+fin+" )";
            }else{
                finSel = ContactsContract.
                RawContactsEntity.CONTACT_ID + " IN (
                "+fin+" )";
            }
        }
    }
    return finSel;
}
```

Figure 6: Code Snippet Showing Entity Restriction for Contacts Provider

For example, consider the query "_ID from contacts WHERE

lookup key = value" and the query "_ID and RAW_CONTACT_ID from raw_contacts WHERE account_type = value". The intersection of _ID and RAW_CONTACT_ID in these query results will be the new WHERE clause for the target CRUD operation.

For delete and update functions, a developer may or may not supply the WHERE clause and/or its argument. According to a user's preferences, our system can enforce restrictions on when and where delete operations can occur by reflectively invoking a new delete function within the joinpoint on the target object. After it returns, the new return value is supplied as the return value of the joinpoint's advice as shown in Figure 7.

```
pointcut deleteInst(Uri uri):call(* *..*.delete(..))
    && NotNewLogger() && args(uri,..);

Object around(Uri uri, ContentResolver tar):
    deleteInst(uri) && target(tar){
    if (access.containsKey(uri.getAuthority())){
        //
        }else if (level.equals("RESTRICT")){
        ContentResolver resolver = null;
        if (tar instanceof ContentResolver){
            resolver = (ContentResolver)tar;
        }
        if (resolver!=null){
            //check Schema Restriction
            uri = checkSRestrict(qSRestrict,
                uri, resolver);
        }
        if (!uri.toString().contains("/0")){
            Log.d(uri.toString(), "here3");
            //check Entity Restriction
            String finSel = checkERestrict(uri,
                resolver);
            if(finSel!=null){
                //populate selection
            }
        String[] selArgs = (String[])args[2];
        Object[] params = new Object[]{uri,
            sel, selArgs};
        Class clazz = thisJoinPoint.getSignature().
            getDeclaringType();
        //Reflectively Recreate Delete
        //function with new selection and
        //return number of rows deleted
        try {
            String methName = thisJoinPoint.
            getSignature().getName();
            Class[] paraTypes
                =getMeth(thisJoinPoint);
            Method method
                =clazz.getDeclaredMethod(methName,
                paraTypes);
            ret = method.invoke(tar, params);
            delRet= true;
        }catch (Exception e){
            //
        }
        }
    //
    }
    return ret;
}
```

Figure 7: Code Snippet Showing Query Re-writing for Delete Function

4.1.3 Database Auditing

Currently, Android does not provide any form of auditing on the native provider. As discussed in Section 2, applications are considered individual users with different user IDs. It is important to keep track of which applications perform which actions on system resources, especially since these applications are typically created by different developers and may manipulate the same data with few restrictions.

In our prototype implementation of *priVy*, we introduce auditing using a file attached to the Controller app called

```
after(Uri uri, String[] Projection, String Selection,
    String[] Selection_Args) returning (Cursor ret):
    getCurObj(uri, Projection, Selection, Selection_Args){
    //...
    if (ret.getCount()>0 ){
        String vals=null;
        StringBuilder stb = new StringBuilder();
        if(Projection!=null){
            for(String str: Projection){
                stb.append(str);
                stb.append(",");
            }
        }
        vals = stb.toString();
        String args=null;
        stb = new StringBuilder();
        if(Selection_Args!=null){
            for(String str: Selection_Args){
                stb.append(str);
                stb.append(",");
            }
        }
        args = stb.toString();
        String audit = "Time"+Long.toString(System.nanoTime())
        +" Uri "+uri.toString() +" Values "+vals + "Selection"
        +Selection + " Selection_Args "+ args+
        thisJoinPoint.getSignature().getDeclaringTypeName()+
        "."+thisJoinPoint.getSignature().getName();
        Log.d("R-DAC","Query Audit- "+audit);
        //…
    }
}
```

Figure 8: Instrumentation Code Snippet for Auditing Query Operations

the auditLog. We implement this by injecting the auditing function after the CRUD function has executed and returned a desired result. For insert, an "after" advice will request for the returned *Uri* and then parse it get the row id. This package name, row id, together with Uri name, Content Values and time stamp are written to the auditLog file.

On update, the return value is the number of rows affected rather than the *Uri*. Thus, we need a global variable to keep track of the row lookup ids (rowid) affected by the update function. We use this global rowid, together with package name, Uri name, Selection and its Arguments (if any), Content Values and time stamp as an audit file entry. This also applies for Delete operations. Query operations return a Cursor, thus we keep the audit of the query parameters as well as the number of rows in the cursor. We do not track the IDs of the columns because it may or may not be part of the projection list. The code snippet for auditing query operations is shown in Figure 8.

Apart from its major objectives, our controller stub further checks for malformed strings in arguments passed to the CRUD function. This is important so as to prevent the *denial of service* attack mentioned in Section 3. This functionality checks for special characters in the content value(s) of an insert or update function. It then triggers warning to the user and he/she can opt to remove such special character.

4.2 Controller App

The controller app running on a separate process coordinates the content provider restrictions for targeted applications. Our aspects are written as generically as possible to integrate into any Android app as well as work for all the native providers. The controller app provides an interface for choosing the access levels and further access restric-

tions on schema, column or entity, thus saving the cost of re-instrumentation in case changes need to be made. This significantly improves the usability of our approach.

When an application is installed, the user needs to register it with the controller. Its user interface (UI) exposes the available access level/restrictions for the user to choose from. After selection, the values is set for the target application in a shared preferences XML file maintained by this controller app. The Controller stub queries these files at runtime. The controller app maintains three different XML files for the access level, constraints, and the arguments, as shown in Figure 1.

1. Access.xml - this file contains entries for all registered instrumented apps. It takes the concatenation of package name, provider names and CRUD function name as the key which is also the record identifier *RID*, while the value contains the access level as ALL_ALLOW, ALL_BLOCK or RESTRICT. Listing 1 shows an example of key:value pair in Access.xml file.

2. Constraint.xml - If the access level is set to RESTRICT, the schema, column or entity constraint has to be provided. This constraint is registered in constraint.xml. Its entries are the RID as provided in Access.xml file and the values are the constraints separated by commas as shown in Listing 2. Empty brackets indicate there is no constraint on the element. The SCHEMA constraint has to take complete Uri string names, while the COLUMN and ENTITY constraints contains the Uri and column name, each of which can have zero or more constraints.

3. Argument.xml - As mentioned above, the ENTITY constraints are enforced in the WHERE clause of the SQLStatement. Thus for each entry in the Constraint.xml file that contains a record for an ENTITY constraint, there must exist a record in the Argument.xml file that provides the argument value(s). For example, if Constraint.xml contains a record as shown in Listing 2, the Argument.xml file will have a corresponding record as shown in Listing 3. This constraint ensures an app is restricted from querying contacts WHERE account_type is *"com.google"*.

Listing 1: Entry in Access.xml

```
key - com.bbm:contacts:query:
value <RESTRICT>
```

Listing 2: Entry in Constraint.xml

```
key - com.bbm:contacts:query:
value < SCHEMA(),
    COLUMN(vnd.android.cursor.dir/contact:
        display_name),
    ENTITY(vnd.android.cursor.dir/raw_contacts:
        account_type)
    >
```

Listing 3: Entry in Arugument.xml

```
key - com.bbm:contacts.query:
value < ENTITY((vnd.android.cursor.dir/raw_contacts:
        account_type) :com.google)>
```

Apart from creating and managing access verification information, the controller app also manages the auditLog file.

5. IMPLEMENTATION

We implemented the prototype of our approach in Python, Java and AspectJ as the weaving framework. The Controller app is written as a standalone Android application with three shared preference files that store the access level, constraints, and its arguments for an instrumented app. This app does not require any permissions to install. For the Controller stub, the instrumentation process is implemented using Python scripts which automate application unpacking, repacking and signing, while the weaving aspect is written using Java/AspectJ.

Android apps are shipped as a single zip file called an *apk*, which contains the main *classes.dex* file and other resource files. The classes.dex is a highly optimized compressed file that contains the Dalvik bytecode which is parsed and interpreted by the Dalvik Virtual machine at runtime. It is created by removing redundant information from the app's compiled Java classes. The AspectJ framework, on the other hand, does not understand the Dex file format. Thus, to weave-in the Controller stub, we need to unpack from Dex to Java class files.

The automated instrumentation processing makes use of an open source Dalvik translator called *"dex2jar"* [3] for the unpacking, repackaging, and app signing. This processing is set up on a Linux system with Java and "ajc" compilers installed and the AspectJ library and the Android SDK on its class-path. The weaving module takes the unpacked classes as input which after recompilation executes the repackaging and resigning modules, respectively.

We developed generic aspects that can be woven into any Android application to enforce access control on any of the Seven native providers. However we limited our testing and evaluation to contacts and calendar providers. These two providers contain valuable and sensitive data for both the device user and any third party associated with the user. According to [9], the contact information is by far the biggest privacy concern of all the sensitive data found on smartphones. The contacts provider exposes different kind of data via its numerous Uris. These data are contained in three tables (Contacts, Raw_Contacts, Data) under the contacts database, while the calendar provider on the other exposes five tables (Calendars, Events, Attendees, Reminders, Instance) from the calendar database through its URIs.

Our aspect has a total of 11 pointcuts which corresponds to the 9 method calls as shown in Table 1, one pointcut for application context, and one for the aspect itself. It also has a total of 16 advices for these pointcuts and numerous Java-related methods that help the functionality of the advices.

6. EVALUATION

The target of our evaluation covers two main objectives; Overhead and Application Crash. *priVy* is developed as a User-centric solution with the aim of providing a reliable means of securing and restricting access to native database objects. The goal is to ensure *priVy* works on a diverse group of applications with minimal overhead. More so, we want to ensure the instrumented app does not crash as a result of the weaved controller stub.

We downloaded the top 350 applications from Google Play [2] and choose 76 apps with read/write permission to either the contacts or calendar providers. Our samples are instrumented and repackaged with new sign-in keys. We assess their static overhead in terms of weaving time and number of joinpoints created.

We also measure the runtime overhead, which is the time it takes to execute each of our joinpoint's advice. We developed a test application that triggers all the advices in our aspect (since most of the sample apps trigger only one or two of them) and measured their execution time. Finally we evaluate app crashes by executing each of the instrumented applications. Our testbed is a Samsung tablet running on the Android 4.4.2 kernel. It has some saved contacts under the device's main gmail account, local phone numbers, and others imported from one extra exchange account.

6.1 App Execution

We then test run all the 76 instrumented apps on a three round testing (total 228 execution) on the test bed and examined them for app crashes that can be directly linked to the instrumentation stub. The testing involves changing the different access levels - ALL_ALLOW, ALL_BLOCK and RESTRICT. Each app is manually installed, executed and profile created for those requiring one. We interact with them using touch events, text inputs, and various system events like calls. The testing period for each app ranges between 15 to 20 minutes, depending on the initial setup required by the app.

In the first round of testing, we set the access policies for all the 76 apps to ALL_ALLOW. Our first observation is five apps (Chase, SendHub, All State, BlueBird, Citizens) fail to execute or connect to their server in the first round of testing. An examination into these groups revealed that mostly they are vendor apps like mobile banking. Such apps, for security reasons, do not execute when the signature changes or have broken resources. They fail to execute not because of our instrumentation stub but because of a change in the application file, thus we eliminate these from further testing.

The second group of seven apps (Sirma Bible, Docusign, Autodesk, FaithComesbyHearing, Zillow, Backgrounds, Jiffy) did not make any attempt to query the contacts or calendar database, even though they requested READ and/or WRITE permission. Thus, they were eliminated too.

The final group executed correctly in all the 3 rounds of testing. We randomly change different combination of access restrictions that will trigger the query re-writing module during the manual execution and check for app failure. Within the execution period, we observed that all the 64 apps in this group invoked one or more of our joinpoints. For instance, the BBM app requested READ CONTACT permission and it also asks users explicitly for access to contacts on the setup window. When we BLOCK all contacts, it was not able to access any. Similarly for RESTRICT, it was only able to view contacts from the gmail account. This is the same for other apps like KIK, Pinterest, Mr. Number, AVG AntiVirus, AutoCard, Vine etc. The Sunrise app uses the calendar provider to manage and organize events. We successfully limited the events that can be viewed by this app based on Event_ID.

We have observed that $\approx 82\%$ of the apps in our sample perform only database read (query) even though 60% of them request both READ and WRITE permissions.

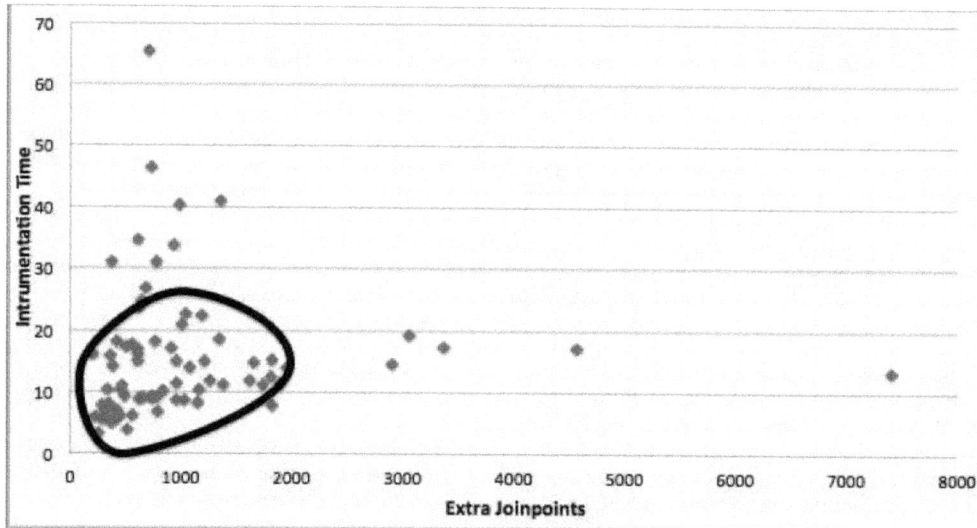

Figure 9: Relationship Between Instrumentation Time and Extra Joinpoints

6.2 Static Overhead

Instrumentation entails weaving new code into a binary and optimization becomes essential in order to avoid bloating the existing code. Specifically, the nature of pointcut signatures can have adverse effects on the number of joinpoints to be created and wildcards that designate all (*) either in the parameter(s), names, or return type broaden the scope of joinpoint matching. As mentioned in section 3, Android has restricted native database access to very few libraries, and as such we avoided using wildcards where necessary and used more specific signatures instead.

In this test, we measured the time it takes to perform bytecode weaving as well as the number of joinpoints that are created. The bytecode weaving involves class parsing, joinpoint matching and insertion of advices for every class on the jar path as specified by the weaving aspect. On average it takes 15 seconds weaving time on our test platform to process each sample app, with the highest and lowest being 65.5 and 3.3 seconds respectively. The plot in figure 9 showed no correlation between instrumentation time and the number of joinpoints created. Nevertheless, we can see from the cluster that almost all the apps are weaved in less than 30 seconds. Manual investigation into the packages of the outlier applications indicates they contain a very large number of classes, thus requiring more time for the compiler to parse and match the joinpoints. Overall, we find the instrumentation time to be very acceptable as the maximum is slightly above 60 seconds.

In AspectJ weaving, for every matched joinpoint, the compiler adds a call to its corresponding advice. This is in addition to any Aspect-specific and Java-based method attached to the aspect class. Based on our sample set, we recorded an average of 1032 joinpoints created, with the highest being 7407 and the lowest 199. We find our joinpoint's overhead of approximately 1000 is on the high side considering there are about 16 advices. On investigation we find the pointcut that gets *application context* is the culprit. Though not part of the main functionality of our aspect, this pointcut serves as a helper that assigns context into the aspect's global context variable.

The Aspect class in not part of the traditional Android API and thus cannot instantiate a context. On the other hand, our advices requires it to get a ContentResolver for nested SQLstatements and the processing of ContentProviderOperations functions. Thus, we created this pointcut around the *onCreate* method of every Activity to get its context. This ensures at every point during the app's execution, a context is available to the aspect class. We find this method to be very reliable since even if one activity dies, the next activity will provide the needed context for the aspect, but not necessarily efficient.

6.3 Runtime Overhead

In this evaluation, we examined the impact of the introduced code on the app performance on the device at runtime. This is measured as the extra time it takes to run the advice on a joinpoint. Our advices verify access levels and enforce restrictions where necessary.

As mentioned in section 3, *priVy* provides three access levels, and when the access level is set to RESTRICT, zero or more schema, column and entity restrictions can be enforced. Thus, considering all this criteria, we expect different possible combinations for each of the CRUD function. It is important to note that this runtime overhead remains the same irrespective of the application executing because the advice code does not change. However, it is only affected by the access level and constraints enforced by the user. The more constraints there are, the more instructions are traversed and the greater the size of the SQLstatement.

To make this experiment possible we develop a testing app that triggers all our joinpoints and we run it many times with different combinations as shown in Table 2.

Each point on the table represents the average time in nanoseconds (ns) required to execute each CRUD function based on at least one restriction.

ALL_BLOCK and ALL_ALLOW incurs zero runtime overhead to process thus these are excluded from table. The times are computed by Java's *System.nanoTime()*. We set the start time at the beginning of the "around" advice execution and an end time at the beginning of its "after" advice. This ensures we take the time after the method has returned

Table 2: *priVy*'s Average Runtime Overhead Given Various Access Restrictions

Restrictions	Insert (ns)	Update (ns)	Query (ns)	Delete (ns)
1 Schema	59	40	64	47
1 Column	53	45	62	50
1 Entity	23	38	92	54
1 Schema , 1 Column	57	48	58	49
1 Schema , 1 Entity	76	47	70	69
1 Column , 1 Entity	74	50	73	67
1 Schema, 1 Column , 1 Entity	62	70	75	54
Average	57.71	48.29	70.57	55.71

and before the next instruction. The difference between the start and the end time is the runtime overhead per joinpoint.

Our experiments indicates it takes an average of 70.57 nanoseconds to execute the joinpoint on update, 55.71 for delete, 48.29 for insert, and 57.71 for query, with imposed restrictions. Overall our joinpoints take an average of 58.07 nanoseconds to execute any of their advice.

Since the static overhead gave us an average of 1032 joinpoints created, our instrumentation can incur a maximum runtime overhead of 0.06 milliseconds if all the joinpoints are executed in a single app. We find this overhead to be negligible and not be noticeable by users.

6.4 Access Policies

The access policies exposed by our Controller app enable users to protect the security and privacy of their devices and its data.

For instance, entity restriction can help protect devices from adding malicious contact on protected account types such as google.com or exchange. The entity restriction is set with an appropriate argument e.g., "com.google". Denial of service attacks due to malformed SQL can also be checked and special characters removed in the content values of an insert or update function.

Both Schema and Column restrictions can help reduce the exposure of clearly mapped data, e.g., enforcing schema restrictions on an email Uri can block a target app with access to Contacts from mapping contacts phone numbers and their email addresses. However, to attain absolute protection for some chosen contacts, the user can set up entity restrictions on individual names, IDs or groups. This will completely safeguard whole record(s).

Column restrictions can also protect permission leaks. As mentioned in Section 3, enumerating account names and types can give apps access to all accounts on the system just like those provided by *getAccount* permission. Thus, a user can set a policy to restrict these columns. This policy can further be optimized by enforcing entity restriction such that apps can access only their account name and types.

6.5 Limitation

priVy performs instrumentation via application repackaging and thus depends on the fact that the app will be correctly translated before and after instrumentation. However this may not be true for apps with:

1. Anti-repackaging techniques that detect and crash the translation process, often detected at compilation time. To deal with such problems, we use a well documented and widely used open source utility *dex2jar*. So far

we have not encountered this issue, but it remains a possibility.

2. Signature verification that detects changes in the developer's original signature at runtime. Such an app may not necessarily crash but will fail to either render its activity or connect to its server. We have encountered some of these apps, which are mostly banking applications. Support for such applications is outside the scope of our research.

7. LITERATURE REVIEW

7.1 Android SQLite

The sensitivity of data and the disastrous effect of its breach has led RDBMSs to evolve over the years, incorporating different levels of security granularity at schemas, column and entity level. SE-PostgreSQL [15] for instance integrates PostgreSQL with SELinux such that every database object has a security context indicating its privilege and attributes. Oracle's virtual private database [10] and INGRES [22] on the other hand support fine grained access through runtime query modification. SQLite is an RDBMS which by design is a server-less jumbo file attached to an application. Its security layer is completely provided by the Android OS through the READ/WRITE permission system on the file. Although the file is protected from unauthorized access, privileges on the individual objects (schema, column, entities) are not segregated. SE-SQLite [16] like SEPostgreSQL is developed by integrating SELinux into Android SQLite. It provides low-level access control on database schema and tuples. Our work, though very much related in objective, differs completely in implementation. Theirs integrated the access policies on the database engine, while we enforced the access constraints at the application level by hooking the CRUD method calls and forcing query-rewriting where necessary. Our system does not require flashing a customized ROM, thus it is a more accessible and easily deployable solution.

7.2 Instrumentation

Instrumentation has been a vital tool for enforcing secure policies on Android systems both in static and dynamic contexts. Largely due to ease of application repackaging, static bytecode weaving at the application level has gained a lot of significance. Dr. Android [13] retrofits Android permissions using bytecode instrumentation. Capper [25] tracks sensitive information flow from source to sink while RetroSkeleton [8] enforces various flexible security policies at runtime. Appguard [4] and [5] both provides customizable user-policies through on-the-device application repackaging.

Most of these solutions have the same aim of reducing permissions associated with an Android app in general, whereas *priVy* is very specific to access control on SQLite database and its objects of which permission control alone cannot achieve.

Dynamically, FireDroid [19] and NJAS [7] use ptrace to attach their policy monitor to the target process. In both of these solutions, security policies are defined at a lower level by re-mapping the system calls to higher level API calls. Android PIN project also supports dynamic binary instrumentation. TISSA [26], Aurasium [24] Apex [17], all developed different security policies mostly with respect to reducing permissions by extending the Android framework. COMPAC [23] segregates permissions within the components of an application. AdDroid [18] segregates advertisement and the Android framework by introducing new advertisement APIs and permissions while AdSplit [20] executes the advertisement code in a different process.

ASM [11], SEAndroid [21], MockDroid [6] and AppFence [12] are operating system-centric solutions that developed integrated security policies at the kernel and Dalvik code. While the security policies suggested above can be used to either allow or deny access to the database file, that cannot address the issue of access control on the database object.

8. CONCLUSION

In this paper we presented *priVy*, a user-centric approach to enforcing object level privilege on Android native providers. Currently, database objects are not treated differently from their main source, meaning when access is granted to a SQLite database file, that access extends to all the objects encapsulated within it. The native databases contains enormously important data that should not be lumped together as a single entity, hence our motivation to segregate their access control. Our system *priVy* is designed to guarantee a user's privacy is secured in an accessible and highly usable way. It does not require operating system extensions nor does it tamper with the framework code, making it a much more practical solution than its contemporaries like SE-SQLite.

priVy leverages static bytecode instrumentation to weave in controlling code in database CRUD functions. The controller stub ensures only user approved schema, column, and/or entities are accessed by an instrumented application. When these CRUD operations are intercepted, the attached stub performs access level verification, query-rewriting where necessary, and proceeds with the function execution. It also performs database auditing when the attached app accesses any of the encapsulated objects. Our evaluation results demonstrated *priVy* incurs a minimal overhead of 15 seconds instrumentation time and a very negligible execution time overhead.

ACKNOWLEDGMENT
This work was partially funded by the NSF grant, CNS #1409534.

9. REFERENCES

[1] The aspectjtm development environment guide.
[2] Google play.
[3] pxb1988/dex2jar.
[4] BACKES, M., GERLING, S., HAMMER, C., MAFFEI, M., AND VON STYP-REKOWSKY, P. Appguard–enforcing user requirements on android apps. In *Tools and Algorithms for the Construction and Analysis of Systems*. Springer, 2013, pp. 543–548.
[5] BARTEL, A., KLEIN, J., MONPERRUS, M., ALLIX, K., AND LE TRAON, Y. Improving privacy on android smartphones through in-vivo bytecode instrumentation. Tech. rep., uni. lu, 2012.
[6] BERESFORD, A. R., RICE, A., SKEHIN, N., AND SOHAN, R. Mockdroid: Trading privacy for application functionality on smartphones. In *Proceedings of the 12th Workshop on Mobile Computing Systems and Applications* (New York, NY, USA, 2011), HotMobile '11, ACM, pp. 49–54.
[7] BIANCHI, A., FRATANTONIO, Y., KRUEGEL, C., AND VIGNA, G. Njas: Sandboxing unmodified applications in non-rooted devices running stock android. In *Proceedings of the 5th Annual ACM CCS Workshop on Security and Privacy in Smartphones and Mobile Devices* (New York, NY, USA, 2015), SPSM '15, ACM, pp. 27–38.
[8] DAVIS, B., AND CHEN, H. Retroskeleton: Retrofitting android apps. In *Proceeding of the 11th Annual International Conference on Mobile Systems, Applications, and Services* (New York, NY, USA, 2013), MobiSys '13, ACM, pp. 181–192.
[9] FERREIRA, D., KOSTAKOS, V., BERESFORD, A. R., LINDQVIST, J., AND DEY, A. K. Securacy: An empirical investigation of android applications' network usage, privacy and security. In *Proceedings of the 8th ACM Conference on Security & Privacy in Wireless and Mobile Networks* (New York, NY, USA, 2015), WiSec '15, ACM, pp. 11:1–11:11.
[10] HEIMANN, J., AND NEEDHAM, P. White paper :the virtual private database in oracle9ir2 - understanding oracle9i security for service providers. Tech. rep., Oracle Corporation, 2002.
[11] HEUSER, S., NADKARNI, A., ENCK, W., AND SADEGHI, A.-R. Asm: A programmable interface for extending android security. In *23rd USENIX Security Symposium (USENIX Security 14)* (San Diego, CA, Aug. 2014), USENIX Association, pp. 1005–1019.
[12] HORNYACK, P., HAN, S., JUNG, J., SCHECHTER, S., AND WETHERALL, D. These aren't the droids you're looking for: Retrofitting android to protect data from imperious applications. In *Proceedings of the 18th ACM Conference on Computer and Communications Security* (New York, NY, USA, 2011), CCS '11, ACM, pp. 639–652.
[13] JEON, J., MICINSKI, K. K., VAUGHAN, J. A., FOGEL, A., REDDY, N., FOSTER, J. S., AND MILLSTEIN, T. Dr. android and mr. hide: Fine-grained permissions in android applications. In *Proceedings of the Second ACM Workshop on Security and Privacy in Smartphones and Mobile Devices* (New York, NY, USA, 2012), SPSM '12, ACM, pp. 3–14.
[14] KICZALES, G., HILSDALE, E., HUGUNIN, J., KERSTEN, M., PALM, J., AND GRISWOLD, W. Getting started with aspectj. *Commun. ACM 44*, 10 (Oct. 2001), 59–65.
[15] KOHEI, K. Security enhanced postgresql, 2013.

[16] MUTTI, S., BACIS, E., AND PARABOSCHI, S. Sesqlite: Security enhanced sqlite: Mandatory access control for android databases. In *Proceedings of the 31st Annual Computer Security Applications Conference* (New York, NY, USA, 2015), ACSAC 2015, ACM, pp. 411–420.

[17] NAUMAN, M., KHAN, S., AND ZHANG, X. Apex: Extending android permission model and enforcement with user-defined runtime constraints. In *Proceedings of the 5th ACM Symposium on Information, Computer and Communications Security* (New York, NY, USA, 2010), ASIACCS '10, ACM, pp. 328–332.

[18] PEARCE, P., FELT, A. P., NUNEZ, G., AND WAGNER, D. Addroid: Privilege separation for applications and advertisers in android. In *Proceedings of the 7th ACM Symposium on Information, Computer and Communications Security* (New York, NY, USA, 2012), ASIACCS '12, ACM, pp. 71–72.

[19] RUSSELLO, G., JIMENEZ, A. B., NADERI, H., AND VAN DER MARK, W. Firedroid: Hardening security in almost-stock android. In *Proceedings of the 29th Annual Computer Security Applications Conference* (New York, NY, USA, 2013), ACSAC '13, ACM, pp. 319–328.

[20] SHEKHAR, S., DIETZ, M., AND WALLACH, D. S. Adsplit: Separating smartphone advertising from applications. In *Presented as part of the 21st USENIX Security Symposium (USENIX Security 12)* (Bellevue, WA, 2012), USENIX, pp. 553–567.

[21] SMALLEY, S., AND CRAIG, R. Security enhanced (se) android: Bringing flexible mac to android. In *NDSS* (2013), vol. 310, pp. 20–38.

[22] STONEBRAKER, M., AND WONG, E. Access control in a relational data base management system by query modification. In *Proceedings of the 1974 annual conference-Volume 1* (1974), ACM, pp. 180–186.

[23] WANG, Y., HARIHARAN, S., ZHAO, C., LIU, J., AND DU, W. Compac: Enforce component-level access control in android. In *Proceedings of the 4th ACM Conference on Data and Application Security and Privacy* (New York, NY, USA, 2014), CODASPY '14, ACM, pp. 25–36.

[24] XU, R., SAÏDI, H., AND ANDERSON, R. Aurasium: Practical policy enforcement for android applications. In *Proceedings of the 21st USENIX Conference on Security Symposium* (Berkeley, CA, USA, 2012), Security'12, USENIX Association, pp. 27–27.

[25] ZHANG, M., AND YIN, H. Efficient, context-aware privacy leakage confinement for android applications without firmware modding. In *Proceedings of the 9th ACM Symposium on Information, Computer and Communications Security* (New York, NY, USA, 2014), ASIA CCS '14, ACM, pp. 259–270.

[26] ZHOU, Y., ZHANG, X., JIANG, X., AND FREEH, V. W. Taming information-stealing smartphone applications (on android). In *Proceedings of the 4th International Conference on Trust and Trustworthy Computing* (Berlin, Heidelberg, 2011), TRUST'11, Springer-Verlag, pp. 93–107.

Shatter: Using Threshold Cryptography to Protect Single Users with Multiple Devices

Erinn Atwater and Urs Hengartner
Cheriton School of Computer Science
University of Waterloo
{erinn.atwater, urs.hengartner}@uwaterloo.ca

ABSTRACT

The average computer user is no longer restricted to one device. They may have several devices and expect their applications to work on all of them. A challenge arises when these applications need the cryptographic private key of the devices' owner. Here the device owner typically has to manage keys manually with a "keychain" app, which leads to private keys being transferred insecurely between devices – or even to other people. Even with intuitive synchronization mechanisms, theft and malware still pose a major risk to keys. Phones and watches are frequently removed or set down, and a single compromised device leads to the loss of the owner's private key, a catastrophic failure that can be quite difficult to recover from.

We introduce Shatter, an open-source framework that runs on desktops, Android, and Android Wear, and performs key distribution on a user's behalf. Shatter uses threshold cryptography to turn the security weakness of having multiple devices into a strength. Apps that delegate cryptographic operations to Shatter have their keys compromised only when a threshold number of devices are compromised by the same attacker. We demonstrate how our framework operates with two popular Android apps (protecting identity keys for a messaging app, and encryption keys for a note-taking app) in a backwards-compatible manner: only Shatter users need to move to a Shatter-aware version of the app. Shatter has minimal impact on app performance, with signatures and decryption being calculated in 0.5s and security proofs in 14s.

1. INTRODUCTION

With breaches of personal data becoming a daily occurrence, and in the wake of the Snowden revelations of mass government spying [18], consumer interest in strong cryptography to protect their data and transactions is at an all-time high. In particular, end-to-end cryptography allows users to obtain strong privacy and authentication properties for their communications without the need to trust any intermediate parties. However, there are numerous unsolved challenges standing in the way of incorporating such protections into traditional user-facing products [7, 16, 32]. Whitten and Tygar [40] showed in their seminal paper "Why Johnny Can't Encrypt" that major usability flaws prevent users from widely adopting PGP email encryption software. A significant aspect of this is requiring users to interact manually with a keychain; the concept of managing keys is not an intuitive one for most non-technical users.

Using end-to-end encryption necessitates the creation and handling of long-term identity keys for each user, with both a private component that must be handled with care, and a public component that must be distributed to and verified by others. Usability literature has widely revealed that the average computer user is not comfortable managing such keys manually, and necessitated placing trust in third parties instead (such as the public key infrastructure, or intermediate message-routing services). These key management problems include distributing one's public keys (and only the public keys) to communication peers, as well as protecting private keys from adversaries while also enabling access to them from any location the user wishes to use their software. While the former is being addressed by other researchers [25], we are interested in tackling the latter.

The most recognizable form of this problem is posed by users wishing to use the same software on multiple different devices. For example, it is common for users to own at least a smartphone and a personal computer; other common devices include tablets, work computers, smartwatches, a variety of Internet of Things devices, and access to various cloud computing services. In order for a user to authenticate themselves with a consistent identity across all devices, or read their encrypted messages from any location, they need to share access to secret keys that are intended to remain secure and moved around as little as possible. If any single device with access to these keys is stolen or compromised by malware, the data on every device becomes vulnerable and the key itself must be revoked (a costly process). The keys can be partially protected—for example, with a password entered by the user—but they are still vulnerable to attacks such as pulling them from memory while in use, phishing, or offline password cracking. Although practitioners have developed some partial solutions to this problem [1, 19, 35], we believe a more promising approach lies in using threshold cryptography to distribute cryptographic operations across the user's very devices that are creating the problem in the first place.

In this scenario, the user is able to perform actions requiring private keys from any of their devices, but the theft of a single device (or more, up to some user-defined threshold number) does not result in the loss of the private key. For example, identity authentication mechanisms in communication platforms such as instant messaging and email typically rely on digital signatures generated from the user's private key. If a single copy of that private key is stolen, the user must generate a new key for themselves, inform everyone they communicate with that the old key has been compromised, and somehow securely distribute the new key to everyone. If the signature were generated using threshold cryptography, however, then no individual device contains the private key any longer – it contains a *share* of the key. Even if a device is compromised by sophisticated malware that initiates these threshold signature operations on behalf of the user, the user will notice the unsolicited requests on her uncompromised devices and simply reject them. Furthermore, even if the user's devices automatically acquiesced to such requests (for the sake of convenience), the attacker would not actually gain the private key *itself*, and the requests generated by the attacker must still show up in the logs of the other devices. We are not simply distributing cryptographic *keys* across devices – we are distributing the cryptographic operations themselves. In this case, the attacker would obtain digital signatures for some number of messages, but still not possess the private key to generate more after the user has noticed the compromise (which is easily visible in the logs of all other, uncompromised devices).

Our work makes the following contributions:

- We show that using threshold cryptography is a viable way of allowing users to distribute private keys and cryptographic operations amongst their many devices, while leveraging what was once a vulnerability into protection against device theft.

- We provide Shatter, the first (to our knowledge) free and open-source [1] cross-platform framework for easily managing private keys on multiple devices, and providing threshold cryptographic protections to applications using strong cryptography.

- We demonstrate how Shatter can be used to protect identity keys in the ChatSecure instant messaging app, and encryption keys in the OmniNotes note-taking app.

- We show that Shatter-compatible apps can be used with existing communication platforms without requiring non-Shatter users to adopt our new software wholesale (or even being made aware that it exists), facilitating easy adoption.

We define our version of the multi-device problem in Section 2 as well as how the use of threshold cryptography addresses it. Section 3 describes Shatter, our framework for providing protections of threshold cryptography to end-user applications. We have integrated Shatter with two example Android applications, and this integration is described in Section 4. A performance evaluation is provided in Section 5. Related work is discussed in Section 7, and Section 8 concludes.

---

[1] https://crysp.uwaterloo.ca/software/shatter/

2. PROBLEM SETTING

This section describes the multi-device problem as we seek to address it. Section 2.1 describes the problem itself, and Section 2.2 enumerates the properties our ideal solution would have. Section 2.3 describes how threshold cryptography can be employed as a solution, and Section 2.4 walks through a real-world example. Section 2.5 defines the threat model we use for this paper.

2.1 The multi-device problem

As discussed above, it has become common for users to own and even carry several different computing devices at a time. Cryptographic keys that are traditionally stored on a user's sole computer are now needed from each of these devices. In order for a user to authenticate themselves with a consistent identity across all devices, or read their encrypted messages from any location, they need to share access to secret keys that are intended to remain secure and moved around as little as possible. The keys can be partially protected with e.g. a password entered by the user, but they are still vulnerable to attacks such as pulling them from memory while in use, phishing, or offline password cracking.

The simplest approach to solving this problem is simply to sync private keys between devices, protected during transport with, for example, the user's password for logging into the software. However, this solution engenders a new set of problems. For example, if a user transfers their private key to their smartphone, and the phone is subsequently stolen or lost, the user's key has been compromised for all the devices they were using it on. They are required to revoke the lost key, generate a new one, update all their remaining devices with the new one, and communicate the revocation and new key to all parties they are in contact with. Protecting the keychain with a password, as mentioned above, does not change this scenario in the event that the keychain is somehow compromised.

Another approach is to use multiple keys, such as the case with "manual" threshold schemes[2]: a different identity key is generated for each of the user's devices, and remote parties must be made aware of all of them (or a hierarchical scheme could be used to issue keys from a central dealer). This approach also has its problems. For one, it exposes details of how a user uses their individual devices to the recipient (such as whether they are currently sending an email from their phone, instead of their workstation). For another, a stolen device still results in a stolen key that must be revoked. It also places a burden on the communication partner: they must now run software that is compatible with the multi-key scheme chosen by the sender, in order to encrypt each message to all the user's devices simultaneously (or to verify more complex conditions such as "require at least three signatures on all messages", as discussed below). This is a significant barrier to real-world deployment, as it necessitates all members of a communication system to upgrade and adopt the system. Group signature schemes, where one device generates a signature on behalf of all the devices in the group [3], can solve several of these issues, but not all of them; primarily, they are still vulnerable to the problem of single stolen devices.

---

[2] http://crypto.stackexchange.com/q/15520

2.2 Goals

To motivate our own work, we must first consider other various potential solutions to the multi-device problem. Below, we enumerate various approaches to performing digital signature operations for the same user on multiple devices. Encryption, depending on implementation, tends to have the same single/multiple device cooperation properties, and requires remote parties to encrypt for multiple keys in schemes where a single key is not somehow distributed amongst devices.

Per-device keys The user has an independently generated key on each of their devices.

Key sync The user generates a single key and copies it to their other devices.

Manual thresholding As per-device keys, but the user also embeds a "policy" in each signature, instructing verifiers to look for multiple signatures (from the user's other devices) on each message.

Personal PKI As 'key sync', but the user also has a single "master" key, stored on one device, which signs the keys on each other device. This can also be used in combination with 'manual thresholding'.

Group signatures Group signature schemes allow any one member of a group to sign messages on behalf of the entire group. These schemes present a single public key to the world, but each member has a unique "share" of the private key.

Secret-shared keys As 'key sync', but a threshold secret sharing scheme is used to protect the private key. Whenever it is required for a cryptographic operation, a user-defined threshold number t of their n devices ($t \leq n$) work together to recover the original private key.

Threshold cryptography As 'secret-shared keys', but the private key is not regenerated for normal operations (signature generation). Instead, the cryptographic operation itself is distributed amongst the t user devices. This is our approach, as described above.

Figure 1 summarizes the properties provided by each of these schemes, which are defined as follows:

Backwards compatibility The scheme can be used to communicate with people who are using unmodified software. Schemes are listed as "potentially" having this property if a modified version of the original cryptography algorithm is required.

Weak theft resistance If only $0 < x < t$ devices are compromised, the long-lived private keys remain uncompromised and do not need to be revoked (as long as devices do not automatically participate in requests from other devices).

Strong theft resistance If only $0 < x < t$ devices are compromised, the long-lived private keys remain uncompromised and do not need to be revoked (even if devices do automatically participate in requests from other devices). For example, in the secret-shared keys scheme, a single request is all the attacker needs to perform in order to recover the private key.

Only one active device The scheme does not require multiple devices to be powered on and in communication with each other in order to perform a necessary operation (initial enrolment and revocation do not count for this purpose).

Device anonymity The remote party cannot distinguish which of the user's devices were used to perform an operation.

Single public key Remote parties only see a single public key representing the user, and do not need to consider others when performing signature verification or encryption.

No master device / CA All of the devices are treated equally; there is no device that acts as a single point of failure.

2.3 Proposed solution

This work proposes using threshold cryptography to aid in solving the problems with sharing a single cryptographic identity across multiple devices. Threshold cryptosystems are usually presented as $(t, n)-$threshold algorithms, where n parties are initially enrolled in a system, but any subset of size $t < n$ can subsequently work together to perform the corresponding operation (typically decryption, or creation of a digital signature).

Traditionally, threshold cryptography schemes have been designed with organizations in mind: the authority to perform some action (such as "launch missiles") is split amongst high-ranking officials, and several of them must act in unison in order to carry out said action. The rising prevalence of individual users possessing multiple computing devices for their own personal use, however, leads to an opportunity to adapt such schemes for the single-user setting. Using threshold schemes to distribute secrets, or the ability to perform signing/decryption operations with a combination of devices working in unison, solves many of the problems with the schemes enumerated above. Theft of a (single) device no longer necessitates revoking the key; the user simply has to use a coalition of the remaining devices in their possession to recover the original secret key, and they can generate new shares without distributing one to the affected device. It can also be implemented in a manner entirely application-agnostic and invisible to the communication partner (as long as threshold versions of the cryptographic algorithms used in the original application exist). Corresponding parties do not need to upgrade their software, and indeed do not even need to be aware that the user is generating signatures or performing decryption in a distributed manner. The drawback to this approach is that it now requires multiple devices (a user-configurable threshold) to be powered on and accessible to each other, be it by proximity or over the Internet. This inconvenience can be mitigated by providing many forms of interconnection between devices, and creating software that runs on a wide variety of platforms. In this way, the user simply has to set the threshold number t to something that is convenient for them and their particular set of devices (which can be as low as only two devices), many of which are left powered on at all times anyway.

Going forward, we are interested in the applications of both threshold signature and threshold encryption algorithms. Signatures are frequently used as components to provide

	Backwards compatibility	Weak theft resistance	Strong theft resistance	Only one active device	Device anonymity	Single public key	No master device / CA
Per-device keys	●	◐	-	●	-	-	●
Key sync	●	-	-	●	●	●	●
Manual thresholding	-	●	●	-	-	-	●
Personal PKI, thresholding	-	◐	-	-	◐	●	-
Personal PKI, no thresholding	-	◐	-	●	◐	●	-
Group signatures	◐	-	-	●	●	●	●
Secret-shared keys	●	●	-	-	●	●	●
Threshold cryptography	◐	●	●	-	●	●	●

● = provides property; ◐ = could provide property, depending on implementation; - = does not provide property

Figure 1: Attributes provided by various solutions or proposed solutions to the multi-device problem

authentication to security protocols, including email (e.g., PGP and S/MIME), instant messaging (e.g., OTR and Text-Secure), and authentication itself (e.g., FIDO and SQRL). Encryption is used to provide confidentiality to user communications (e.g., email), backend communications (e.g., software updates), and user data-at-rest (e.g., password managers). Each of these applications would interact with threshold versions of their cryptography in (sometimes subtly) different ways, posing their own questions, all of which must be answered by the framework we define.

2.4 Walked-through example

To illustrate how this solution would work in practice, let us consider the example of a user Alice using an instant messaging app to talk to her friend, Bob. Alice has three devices: a smartphone, a laptop she uses for school, and a desktop at her home. Alice's first step is to install Shatter on each of her devices. After installation is complete, the three devices discover each other through her home network and ask if she would like to add them all to her personal set of devices. She agrees, and decides to set the threshold t to two. Upon doing so, one of the devices generates a new public/private keypair and splits the private key into three shares. It distributes a share to each of Alice's devices, keeping one for itself, and then erases the original private key from its memory. Finally, Alice installs a Shatter-compatible version of the IM app onto her smartphone.

Later, Alice is traveling and has only her phone with her. Bob, who is using a normal version of the IM app and has never heard of Shatter, tries to initiate a secure conversation with her. The IM app uses digital signatures for authentication, so it sends a request for a signature to the Shatter process running on the phone. Shatter prompts Alice to accept the request via a notification on her phone, and also connects to her desktop and laptop over the Internet to request participation. Although Alice has left her laptop running at home, she has it configured to show a prompt requiring her to approve incoming requests. Her desktop, however, is configured to automatically accept all requests, and so the Shatter process on the phone communicates with the desktop to generate a threshold signature and returns it

to the IM app. On Bob's end, he sees that a secure connection has been established without knowing anything unusual happened, and proceeds to chat with Alice.

After their conversation, Alice sets her phone down on a table in a coffee shop and accidentally leaves it behind. When she gets home, she realizes it is gone. If someone at the coffee shop were to pick up her phone and try to initiate a new conversation with Bob, it would only be possible because Alice has configured her desktop to automatically accept requests, and Alice would be able to look at the request log on her other two devices to see that it had happened. Even if the thief were aware that Shatter was installed on the phone and accessed its control panel, they would be unable to obtain Alice's private key – it is not stored on the phone, it is not regenerated in the process of creating a threshold signature, and neither the desktop nor the laptop will agree to regenerate the key without explicit user authorization.

At home, Alice is able to see whether or not her phone was used to perform any privileged operations. She then accesses the Shatter control panel on her desktop, and initiates a revocation of the smartphone. The revocation request appears on her laptop, which she accepts, and the laptop sends its secret share to the desktop, where they are recombined to recover the original private key. The desktop then creates a new set of secret shares for only the desktop and laptop. It sends a courtesy message to Shatter running on the smartphone (if it is able to reach it over the Internet) alerting it to the revocation. It is not imperative that this notification reaches the smartphone, however – the desktop and laptop will no longer accept signature requests from the smartphone. Indeed, even if the same thief were to then steal Alice's laptop, now possessing two of her devices, he would still be unable to recover her private key. Despite having two of Alice's three devices in such a situation, Alice was able to revoke the phone's keys first, essentially starting a new epoch the moment she did so.

Alice then purchases a new phone, installs Shatter and the IM app on it, and enrols it with her desktop and laptop using a similar recover-and-reshare process as used for revocation. This process does not change her public key, and she is able to initiate new secure conversations with Bob without him having any way of knowing she had lost a key share.

2.5 Threat model

Our threat model is primarily restricted to less than some user-specified threshold t of that user's n devices being compromised by colluding adversaries. "Compromise" for our purposes is defined to include physical theft, privileged malware running on the device, and remote code execution. In the event that $x \geq t$ devices are compromised, private keys are able to be regenerated by the adversary and should be considered lost by the user.

In this threat model, two considerations must be made for damage mitigation and recovery in the event of device compromise. The first is in the case of data recovery by the user: in the event that $t \leq x \leq n - t$, any data protected by the private key should be considered compromised, but it is possible for the user to recover that data as well. However, for $x > n - t$, the user will no longer be able to recover the private data. For example, if an application is designed to protect a user's personal notes with threshold encryption, both the user and the adversary would have access to the notes with $t \leq x \leq n-t$; with $x > n-t$ only the adversary has access to the notes. In our threat model, another consideration is for the harm possible by $x < t$ devices being compromised when some of the user's other devices automatically participate in threshold operations. In this instance, the adversary is limited to performing the pre-designed cryptographic operations but cannot obtain the long-lived private keys of the user. This creates a window of opportunity wherein the adversary can cause harm by imitating the user (such as accessing plaintext or impersonating the user), but results in a user-auditable log of operations performed. It also does not preclude the user from subsequently revoking the lost device and continuing to use the same private keys.

We also consider the case of using untrusted cloud providers as participants in the user's threshold scheme. Such a cloud provider would accept threshold participation requests from the user's devices prerequisite on the user authentication with the service through some separate mechanism (which may be persistent, e.g. "stay logged in" cookies). Third-party cloud services should be barred from initiating requests (by having the user's devices ignore requests generated by cloud services), and should require re-authentication from the user before participating in key recovery operations. The user should not add more than one third-party service to their group of threshold participants, as collusion between two or more such services cannot be prevented and would compromise the scheme as described above. However, cloud services acting as part of the user's device group provide an always-on party that can participate in threshold cryptographic operations, and can even allow users with only a single internet-connected device (e.g., a smartphone) to gain the protections afforded by our solution by setting $t = n = 2$.

3. SHATTER ARCHITECTURE

Shatter's primary component is a library that implements various threshold cryptography protocols, as well as providing convenience functions and platform-specific operations for easily incorporating the library into client applications. It contains a daemon that can be run by client applications, although this daemon is intended to be run by a dedicated

Shatter app, with client apps in turn communicating with the dedicated app to have it perform operations on their behalf. This software pattern allows users to use multiple client applications while only having to maintain their device configuration in a single location. Figure 2 illustrates this organization and how the components interact with each other. The following sections give an overview of the architecture and role of the individual components themselves.

3.1 Crytographic algorithms

The first threshold algorithm we have implemented is a (t, n)-Threshold-DSA signature scheme proposed by Gennaro et al. [14]. DSA was chosen as it provides the authentication in most OTR (Off-The-Record messaging) protocol implementations, which we later aim to provide threshold cryptography support to. OTR uses end-to-end cryptography to give instant messaging protocols authentication, encryption, and deniability [6]. The Gennaro scheme consists of six rounds that can be performed in parallel by all of the participating devices, each either broadcasting their result for the round when complete or, in the case of the last two rounds, sending it to the initiating device. This means that the algorithm runs in time independent of the values of t or n. Some of the interim calculations in the protocol are performed under additively homomorphic encryption, in order to hide secret information from other participants. There is some choice available as to precisely which encryption scheme is used.

The second threshold algorithm implemented is the Damgaard-Jurik (t, n)-threshold version of Paillier's additively homomorphic encryption algorithm [10]. This algorithm provides the properties required of the encryption algorithm used as a component of the Gennaro signature algorithm. For convenience, we also make the algorithm available for general-purpose use to other Shatter applications. For example, one of our example applications in Section 4 uses it to encrypt the contents of a user's personal notes.

3.2 libShatter

The library provides the actual implementation of the threshold cryptography protocols, as well as classes for facilitating network communication between clients, loading and storing configurations, and a variety of other functions useful to client applications. It is implemented in Java (targetting versions 1.7+), and is thus easily portable to all major desktop platforms. It also compiles to an Android app library, allowing it to be easily imported and used in any Android app.

libShatter consists of the following major components:

ThresholdAgent: Daemon that performs the core operations of a threshold cryptography operation, as well as device management. The ThresholdAgent daemon is responsible for managing network connections (via delegation to the NetworkAgent, below), incoming packets, and any received or pending requests. Client applications are intended to instantiate a ThresholdAgent thread and register a callback handler with it in order to implement any operations they require. For example, a client application would register a ConfigEventListener to take over loading/storing any configuration changes required by the daemon (such as changing keys or enrolled devices). It would register a SignatureEventHandler in order to be notified of new requests for distributed operations (to which it should respond by ei-

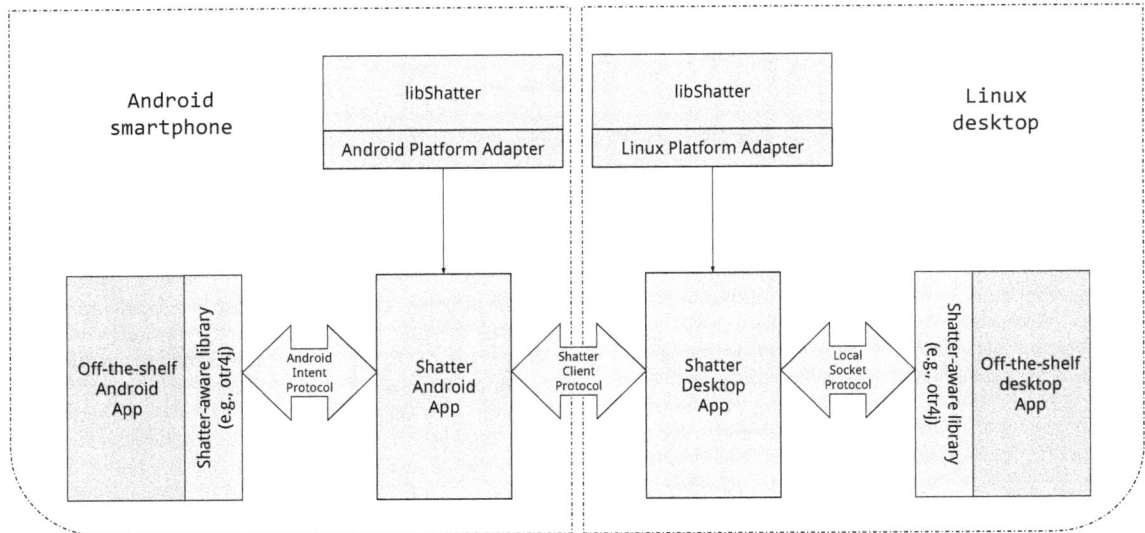

Figure 2: High-level architecture of the Shatter library. Android Wear devices run a Shatter client similar to the Android implementation (left), while Windows and OSX machines use an analogous setup to the linux example (right).

ther agreeing or declining to participate), progress updates, and the result of completed threshold operations.

NetworkAgent: Daemon that manages connections to the user's other devices, and performs all network communication between them. Currently, the NetworkAgent finds other devices by periodically broadcasting a multicast message advertising its presence to other devices on the local network, and keeping track of recent advertisements from other like devices. These advertisements contain the device identity (for determining if it is part of the user's personal set of devices), as well as instructions for which address and port it listens for messages on. It is also responsible for providing transport layer encryption, and authenticating messages received from other devices. Currently, this is done using client-authenticating TLS.

The NetworkAgent listens on this port for incoming connections, reads a single JSON-formatted message from the initiating party, and closes the connection. The JSON message is then passed back to the ThresholdAgent for processing. Although incurring some additonal overhead by not using long-lasting connections, this pattern means that the application is not weak in the presence of poor-quality network conditions or roaming users, which is frequently the case in mobile environments. Finally, while the NetworkAgent currently operates only via local network connections, it is architected in such a way that new network modalities can easily be dropped-in. For example, future network adapters might allow connecting devices over Bluetooth, or via a third-party or user-hosted cloud server as a proxy to allow easy firewall piercing and long-distance roaming (we are currently developing both of these options). The Multicast classes can be replaced with any program that advertises and finds other active devices; the LocalServer class with anything that receives JSON-formatted messages; and finally a PacketSendHelper with anything that allows sending JSON-formatted messages to an address compatible with the two Server classes.

Platform Adapters: Package containing adapters for platform-specific operations. This includes a set of convenience classes for manipulating and storing persistent configuration information with a uniform interface on various platforms. There is also an implementation of several BroadcastReceivers to be used by Android apps. Android apps simply need to add this receiver to their manifest files, and it will listen for Shatter-specific broadcast intents from other apps. It also registers event handlers with the ThresholdAgent when instantiated, allowing it to communicate the result of threshold operations back to the app that made the original request.

Crypto: Package containing the actual implementations of cryptographic protocols (although not the network protocols, which are done by ThresholdAgent). These operations are called by ThresholdAgent in order to perform threshold DSA operations, as well as (currently) distributed and non-distributed Paillier operations. It also contains miscellaneous convenience utilities, such as a central class for generating secure random numbers. For non-threshold operations (such as DSA verification and storing DSA keys/parameters), it imports SpongyCastle as a dependency (SpongyCastle is a full version of the BouncyCastle cryptography library, with its namespaces changed in order not to conflict with the pared-down version of BouncyCastle included with Android).

3.3 Shatter desktop app

This is the reference implementation for a Shatter client application. It is implemented in Java as an interactive command-line application, and allows making all possible calls to ThresholdAgent, displaying and responding to requests, and maintaining configurations using flat files. The source code for the application shows how a developer need only implement a thin UI that binds to the various exposed API functions: it primarily consists of a switch statement driving a menu displaying the available API calls, and several methods designed to handle the callbacks required

96

for it to act as both a ThresholdEventListener and ConfigEventListener.

3.4 Shatter Android app

In addition to replicating the basic driver functionality of the desktop application, the Android app acts as the host service for the ThresholdAgent for all other apps on the device. This provides a central device management interface for the user, who may have multiple distributed apps installed on their phone. Apps that want to perform distributed operations communicate with the central app via intents. The app itself communicates with any other Shatter clients (desktop or Android) to perform requested operations, and communicates the result back to the requestor via intents.

3.5 Device group management

Any number of Shatter-compatible apps can connect to a single instance of a Shatter client application, giving the user the convenience of only have to manage their devices from one place. The Shatter client takes care of group formation, new device enrolment, and old/lost device revocation. Initial formation of a group involves showing the user all discovered devices, asking which ones should be included in the group, generating a set of key shares for the group, and asking the user to securely pair each of the devices in order to receive those shares. Currently, the user has two choices for secure pairing: scanning a QR code, or verifying a displayed code on both screens (both of which contain a cryptographic hash of the public key for the central device, allowing the devices to authenticate each other from then on). For both revocation and enrolment, the user must gather at least the threshold number of the devices in their group together. The process is initiated on one device, which then sends the request to the other devices in the group. The user must accept this request (Shatter clients should never accept these requests automatically) on each other device, which causes them to send their shares directly to the initiating device. The shares are then combined to recover the original private key, which can then be used to generate a new set of shares (plus or minus the targeted device).

4. MOBILE APPLICATIONS

To demonstrate the feasibility of adding support for our library to end-user applications, we added Shatter support to two open-source Android apps: one which provides off-the-record messaging with strong participant identity verification, and one which allows a user to write and store arbitrary plaintext notes on their device. Screenshots of the Shatter client and Shatter-compatible apps are presented in Figure 3.

4.1 ChatSecure

We added Shatter support to ChatSecure[3], an app by The Guardian Project that allows the user to connect to arbitrary Jabber servers, and optionally to use Off-the-Record (OTR) messaging over them. In the OTR protocol, parties in a conversation authenticate each other once (at the beginning of the conversation) by way of DSA signatures. The implementation of OTR used by ChatSecure is called **otr4j**,

which is originally developed and maintained by Jitsi, an open-source videochat and IM application.

We replaced calls to sign() in otr4j with a request for a distributed DSA signature from the Shatter app. This required a slight refactoring of the library – it originally expected signature operations to complete near-instantaneously, and thus simply blocked on calls to the method. This was replaced with a request+callback pattern, so the encryption resumes once the user has assembled the requisite number of other devices and permitted them to generate a signature. The refactoring was accomplished by adding new message types to the otr4j incoming message handler, and putting the OTR engine into a "waiting for callback" state in the meantime. Thus even though calls to the sign() method may be made on the main thread, they will return immediately without causing the UI to hang.

4.2 OmniNotes

We also added Shatter support to OmniNotes v5.1.3[4], the most popular open-source Android note-taking application at the time of this writing. OmniNotes supports very basic (password-keyed) encryption on a per-note basis, which we improve by generating strong random keys and protecting them with a threshold encryption scheme.

OmniNotes' default encryption behaviour is to display a prompt for the user to enter their password whenever opening a "locked" note. We removed the text field from this prompt and replaced it with a call to Shatter asking to decrypt the symmetric encryption key for the current note (encrypted keys are stored prepended to encrypted notes, as is typical with hybrid encryption). This effectively turns the password prompt into a loading screen for the note, while the Shatter client sends requests to the user's other devices requesting their participation. When the decryption is completed, the callback closes the loading screen and supplies the decrypted text of the note to be displayed.

We note that, if the user's other devices are accessible and configured to automatically participate in decryption requests, the final experience is actually *easier* with Shatter. Whereas previously the user had to stop, remember, and type their password, they now have to wait only a second or two for a loading screen (see Section 5). It also provides significantly stronger encryption for the user's notes. Previously, all notes were protected with a single key derived from a password that generally needs to be simple enough for users to remember. With Shatter support, each note has a different, randomly-generated 128-bit key.

5. EVALUATION

This section provides an evaluation of the algorithms currently implemented by Shatter. It should be noted that performance is generally particular to the cryptographic algorithms being used, and not the implementation itself.

5.1 Procedure

We ran our threshold signature and decryption algorithms on a desktop running Ubuntu 14.04 with an AMD FX-6100 3.3GHz 6-core processor, Nexus 5 smartphones running Android 5.1.1, and a Moto 360 smartwatch running Android Wear v5.0.1. These devices can be combined in any permu-

---

[3] https://chatsecure.org/

[4] https://play.google.com/store/apps/details?id=it.feio.android.omninotes

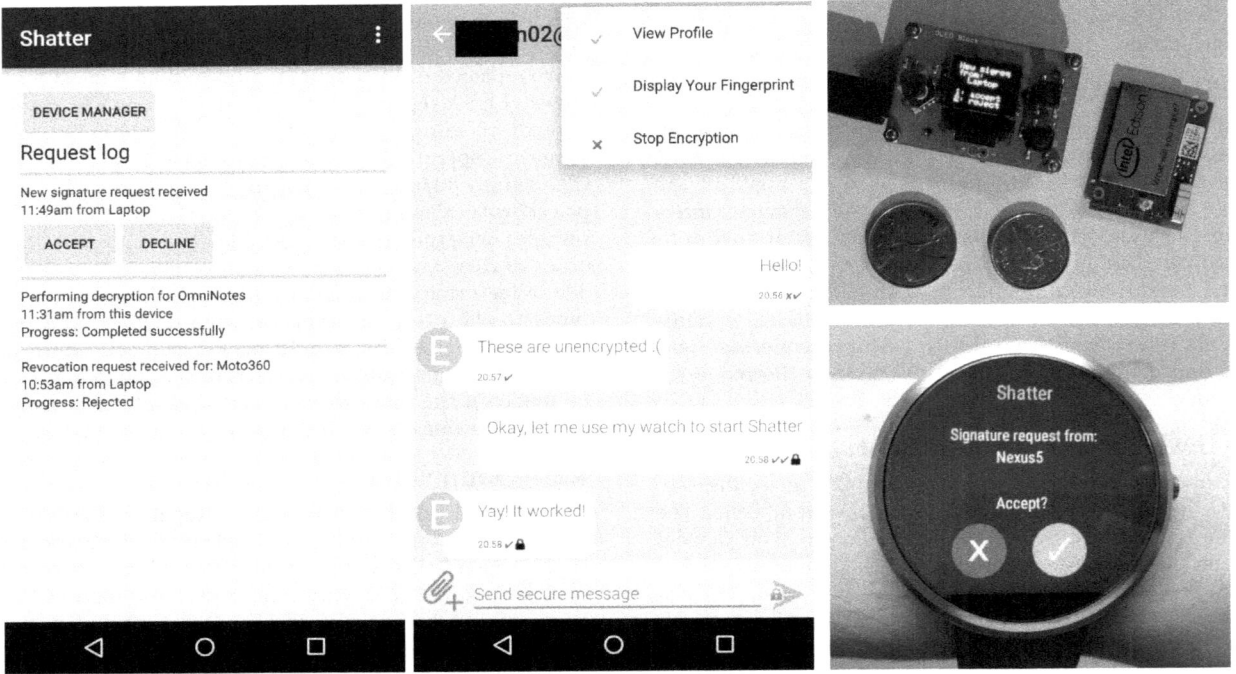

Figure 3: The Shatter client app for Android (left); Shatter-aware ChatSecure conversation with a non-Shatter aware remote participant (middle); Shatter client running on an Intel Edison with OLED display (top-right); Shatter client running on a Moto 360 (bottom-right).

tation; we restrict our evaluation to all-desktop, all-phone, and all-unique (that is, phone-watch-desktop) configurations with $n = t = 3$. As mentioned above, the performance of both algorithms is independent of the number of devices participating. Although the desktop clients are run on the same machine, in practice each instance runs on a single core and so the performance slowdown on our 6-core machine is negligible. We provide numbers both with and without checking of the zero-knowledge proofs that the algorithms require in order to detect malicious parties, but not in order to proceed with functionality. If an app is able and willing to provide latent detection of adversaries, it can get away with deferring the checking of proofs until the actual result has been computed, and the user will experience a shorter interruption.

Computation times are averaged across 20 runs of the algorithm. These times include some periods of network transmission, but this is performed over a local network and is negligible. The timer is started once a threshold number of devices have agreed to participate in a threshold operation, and stopped once the result has been calculated and delivered to the application requesting it. We use DSA parameters of $L = 1024, N = 160$, chosen to correspond to ChatSecure's DSA parameters, with the Paillier parameters being derived from the DSA parameters to preclude needing to use a block cipher mode of encryption.

5.2 Results & observations

Table 1 shows the computation time needed to perform threshold signing and decryption operations. Both signatures and decryption can be calculated in a quarter of a second on all devices. If proofs cannot be deferred, decryp-

tion needs several seconds extra while signatures need up to fourteen seconds extra.

We believe the delays are acceptable if proofs do not need to be verified immediately. In the event that the app does require up-front verification, the longer delay for signatures is mitigated by the fact that signatures tend to be performed only for infrequent operations. They only need to be calculated once at the beginning of a new OTR session with a friend, and this is done immediately before the user typically sends a "hello" message and waits for the recipient to notice it. Another common use of signatures is on outgoing emails; in this scenario, users are already accustomed to waiting a short period of time for an email to be sent (and indeed, Gmail currently suggests adding an artificial delay of ten seconds or more in order to provide "undo" functionality to sending mail [8]). Decryption only needs to be performed in OmniNotes when a note is first opened and, as we note in Section 4.2, this can actually result in a *shorter* delay for the user. Encryption is performed when closing/saving notes, and does not need to be distributed since Damgaard-Jurik is a public-key encryption algorithm.

As discussed in Section 3.1, we implemented a (t, n)-Threshold-DSA signature scheme designed by Gennaro et al. because it was necessary to find a threshold equivalent of the DSA algorithm in order to be backwards compatible with existing OTR apps. In analyzing the performance of our implementation, we found the homomorphic encryption and decryption operations dominate the computation time. As we outline in Section 3, the major calculations involved in this particular threshold signature scheme are performed under homomorphic encryption. This dominating factor, as well as the ratio of encryption to decryption time, is ap-

Device, role	No proofs	Proofs
Signature, 3 desktops	0.243 (0.01)	10.8 (1.09)
Signature, 3 phones	0.509 (0.01)	12.0 (1.09)
Signature, all unique	0.543 (0.02)	13.2 (1.11)
Decryption, 3 desktops	0.118 (0.01)	0.822 (0.10)
Decryption, 3 phones	0.249 (0.01)	1.941 (0.11)
Decryption, all unique	0.261 (0.01)	2.479 (0.11)

Table 1: Performance numbers, broken down by device combination ("all unique" means phone-watch-desktop). Average times are given in seconds, with standard deviations in parentheses. "No proofs" refers to the time to complete *before checking* the deferrable zero-knowledge proofs (see text for discussion).

proximately consistent with the analysis in Paillier's original paper [27].

Gennaro et al.'s scheme also requires several rounds wherein a partial computation by one device is broadcast to the other participants, and the broadcast from all other participants must be received before continuing with the computation. This results in t messages being sent in parallel a total of six times in sequence, with most messages being 4kB and the largest being 16kB (including transport encryption). The scheme also *uses* the Damgaard-Jurik threshold encryption scheme twice as a sub-operation, and therefore its computation time can never be lower than that of the encryption scheme by itself. For our threshold decryption scheme, however, backwards-compatibility with other communication partners is not a concern and so we can make use of any algorithm we wish. We chose to re-use our implementation for convenience and to demonstrate the utility of our crypto library; in the future, we will investigate using more appropriate algorithms for apps like OmniNotes.

6. LIMITATIONS

Shatter's protections only apply within the limitations of the threat model defined in Section 2.5. If an adversary compromises more than the user-defined threshold t of that user's devices, they are able to regenerate any private keys protected with threshold cryptography. Shatter does not allow the user to set $t = 1$, which would be essentially the same as not using Shatter at all. We do not consider application security vulnerabilities in our implementation to be in scope; however, we note that even an exploit allowing device compromise still only results in a *share* of a private key being stolen, and the attacker will still need to compromise t or more devices in order to defeat Shatter.

Our ability to provide backwards compatibility with remote communication partners is limited to apps using protocols for which there is a threshold version of any cryptographic algorithms relying on private keys available. In our current implementation, these are the DSA/ECDSA signature scheme and the Paillier homomorphic encryption scheme. Threshold cryptography is an active area of research, however, and threshold versions of many popular algorithms have already been published.

Shatter also introduces a requirement for t of the user's devices to be online and accessible to each other (e.g. over the internet) whenever the user wishes to perform an operation relying on their private keys. The user is expected to

pick a value of t that is realistic for their normal usage (e.g., it would be annoying to pick $t = 3$ when one of the user's devices is a laptop that they typically leave off). We help mitigate this inconvenience by supporting as many communications protocols as possible, making it easy to add new ones, and implementing new ones ourselves as we are able to. We also aim to support as many platforms as possible, with our current Java implementation easily running on Windows, Linux, Mac OSX, Android, and Android Wear (with an iOS implementation currently under development).

7. RELATED WORK

The idea of using threshold cryptography between a single user's cooperating devices has been proposed before. In 1979, Blakley et al. systematized the set of threats posed against storage of sensitive private keys [5]. While one of the authors later worked on using threshold cryptography to help defend against some of these threats [4], it was two decades later before Desmedt et al. proposed using threshold cryptography to protect keys stored on "things that think" (contemporarily, Internet of Things devices) [11]. Desmedt et al. did not go so far as to offer comprehensive guidelines on how this should be implemented, however; they merely suggested that a set of standards should be developed to allow a wide variety of different devices and different applications to interoperate. These recommendations built on earlier work outlining the threat model addressed by threshold cryptography schemes in general [20], discussing how it might be adapted to the personal device scenario. The earlier work remains relevant, however, in that it contains suggestions and schemes that are applicable to our work (such as methods of identifying misbehaving devices, and key rotation schemes that reduce the damage done in the event of a compromised share). Papers building on Desmedt et al.'s work have investigated protocols for securing the underlying communication between devices, focusing on such goals as adding and removing devices from the threshold group securely [29] or preventing eavesdroppers from tracking the user via their device signatures [38]. More recent work has focused on applications (as do we), using threshold schemes to protect keys used for unlocking a device [39] or evaluating the usability of various pairing schemes [22].

The key difference between the work in this section and our proposed work is a lack of focus on real-world deployment issues. All of the aforementioned papers focus on using ordinary secret sharing to protect a secret key, and thus lack desirable properties as discussed in Section 2.1. They have no thought given to backwards compatibility or theft protection against malware, which requires modifying applications to perform distributed cryptographic operations and, in some cases, creating new cryptographic operations themselves. With one exception [22], they also tend to ignore the usability outcomes of their proposals, whereas we are interested in facilitating a smooth experience for both users of our software and the developers themselves.

The thread of work by Peeters et al. resembles our work most closely, in that they are also interested in applications of threshold things that think. In 2008, they presented an adaptation of Shoup's threshold RSA encryption algorithm [33] intended to be run on things that think [30] (including a proof-of-concept implementation). In a 2012 PhD thesis, Peeters discussed some of the ideas outlined herein, and presented proposals for storing secret shares on devices without secure storage [28, 34]. The thesis also discussed methods of securely pairing devices [29], and presented a proposal using the location information available on devices with a GPS [31, 36]. Stajano presented the Pico/Picosiblings system in 2011 [37]. Picosiblings are IoT devices intended to be worn by a user, which use threshold cryptography to authenticate the user to remote services. This application is similar to proposals like FIDO / SQRL, but using threshold cryptography to offer theft-resistance. Although Stajano does not explicitly consider Picosiblings as a solution to the multi-device problem (only one device, the Pico, is intended to permit user interaction), it is trivial to envision how such a solution might be incorporated into the existing work. Finally, Gennaro et al. present an algorithm and software for distributing Bitcoin wallets across multiple devices with threshold cryptography [14]. Their work is discussed extensively in Section 3, as our current work implements their proposed threshold-DSA algorithm.

Other researchers have proposed solutions to the multi-device problem with alternative methods to threshold cryptography. For example, Sinclair and Smith described a method of sharing PKI credentials (signing keys) to mobile devices, reducing the impact of stolen / compromised devices [35]. Their work essentially uses personal PKI to issue "proxy" (short-lived) certificates from a master certificate on a central workstation. As we discussed in Section 2, this approach does not solve problems such as having to revoke stolen signing keys, and reveals details of the user's device usage to correspondents. Some researchers propose using multiple devices for novel two-factor authentication mechanisms, such as proximity detection [9, 21] or using a mobile phone to authenticate on an untrusted (public) terminal [26]. In the latter scheme, a trusted third party server is used to establish what is essentially a VNC connection via an untrusted terminal, while authenticating to it using the phone's internet connection (and issuing temporary credentials to the untrusted device). While not directly addressing the problems we are facing, this work contains interesting and useful discussion of the design issues that arise with such two-factor authentication schemes on mobile devices.

Farb et al. [12] considered making personal key management and distribution easier for smartphone users. While we are working toward similar goals of user-friendliness and easy adoption, they did not consider the case of users with multiple devices. Other researchers have proposed protocols for *multiple* users in proximity to communicate anonymously [17, 23, 24], and we are investigating using similar schemes for the single-user setting in order to decrease potential side-channel privacy invasions. Geambasu et al. [13] presented Keypad, a filesystem which stores per-file keys on a remote server. This provides some of the properties of our OmniNotes app, such as remotely revoking access from lost devices and creating a guaranteed audit log, but is not as flexible in terms of combining multiple devices (which may be local, thus not necessitating an internet connection).

There has been some non-academic work on sharing private keys between a user's personal devices, but these rarely incorporate threshold cryptography and tend to rely on simply encrypting the private key and uploading it to a third-party synchronization service. Such is the case with White-out.io, which generates a long random password for the user and requires them to write it down and manually enter it into their devices during configuration [19]). Apple iMessage, a widely-deployed instant messaging platform, uses another of the approaches discussed in Section 2.1. Users have a separate keypair generated for each of their devices, and key distribution is done by sending all of the user's public keys from Apple's central server (and encryption by encrypting to *all* of the user's devices) [2]. Gil summarized common community approaches to this problem in 2014 [15].

8. CONCLUSION

In this work, we presented Shatter, a free and open-source library and set of applications for providing threshold cryptographic protections to desktop and Android apps. As opposed to making users copy private keys to each of their multiple devices, introducing a significant weakness to device theft and compromise, we instead leverage this multitude of devices to provide significant protection against a variety of adversaries. Shatter allows app developers to easily perform distributed signature and encryption operations, by communicating with a central application that takes care of enrolment and revocation of the user's other devices. We showed that Shatter has acceptable overhead in the context of two real-world applications—ChatSecure and OmniNotes—and that threshold cryptography is, indeed, a feasible method of distributing and protecting "keys" across a user's different devices.

Shatter and its source code are available now, and are under active development by our lab. Ongoing work includes adding support for more cryptographic algorithms, improving the user experience to make it desirable by everyday device owners, and adding support for new technologies such as Bluetooth LE and new Internet of Things platforms.

9. ACKNOWLEDGEMENTS

We thank the anonymous reviewers for their helpful comments. This work is supported by funding from the Natural Sciences and Engineering Research Council of Canada, the Ontario Research Fund, and a Google Focused Research Award.

10. REFERENCES

[1] Overview of projects working on next-generation secure email. https://github.com/OpenTechFund/secure-email. Accessed Feb 2015.

[2] Apple Inc. iOS security. https://www.apple.com/business/docs/iOS_Security_Guide.pdf, June 2015.

[3] M. Bellare, D. Micciancio, and B. Warinschi. Foundations of group signatures: Formal definitions, simplified requirements, and a construction based on general assumptions. In *Advances in Cryptology – Eurocrypt 2003*, pages 614–629. Springer, 2003.

[4] B. Blakley, G. Blakley, A. H. Chan, and J. L. Massey. Threshold schemes with disenrollment. In *Advances in Cryptology – CRYPTO'92*, pages 540–548. Springer, 1993.

[5] G. R. Blakley. Safeguarding cryptographic keys. In *the National Computer Conference*, volume 48, pages 313–317, 1979.

[6] N. Borisov, I. Goldberg, and E. Brewer. Off-the-record communication, or, why not to use PGP. In *2004 ACM Workshop on Privacy in the Electronic Society*, pages 77–84. ACM, 2004.

[7] P. Bright and D. Goodin. Encrypted e-mail: How much annoyance will you tolerate to keep the NSA away? *Ars Technica*, June 2013.

[8] A. Chowdhry. Gmail's 'Undo send' option officially rolls out. *Forbes*, June 2015.

[9] M. D. Corner and B. D. Noble. Zero-interaction authentication. In *8th Annual International Conference on Mobile Computing and Networking*, pages 1–11. ACM, 2002.

[10] I. Damgård and M. Jurik. A generalisation, a simplification and some applications of Paillier's probabilistic public-key system. In *Public Key Cryptography*, pages 119–136. Springer, 2001.

[11] Y. Desmedt, M. Burmester, R. Safavi-Naini, and H. Wang. Threshold things that think (T4): Security requirements to cope with theft of handheld/handless internet devices. In *Symposium on Requirements Engineering for Information Security*, 2001.

[12] M. Farb, Y.-H. Lin, T. H.-J. Kim, J. McCune, and A. Perrig. Safeslinger: Easy-to-use and secure public-key exchange. In *19th Annual International Conference on Mobile Computing & Networking*, pages 417–428. ACM, 2013.

[13] R. Geambasu, J. P. John, S. D. Gribble, T. Kohno, and H. M. Levy. Keypad: An auditing file system for theft-prone devices. In *Sixth Conference on Computer Systems*, EuroSys '11, pages 1–16, New York, NY, USA, 2011. ACM.

[14] R. Gennaro, S. Goldfeder, and A. Narayanan. Threshold-optimal DSA/ECDSA signatures and an application to Bitcoin wallet security. In *14th International Conference on Applied Cryptography and Network Security*. Springer, 2016.

[15] D. L. Gil. Multiple devices and key synchronization. https://github.com/coruus/zero-one/blob/master/multidevice-keysync.markdown, 2014.

[16] M. Green. The daunting challenge of secure e-mail. *The New Yorker*, November 2013.

[17] B. Greenstein, D. McCoy, J. Pang, T. Kohno, S. Seshan, and D. Wetherall. Improving wireless privacy with an identifier-free link layer protocol. In *Sixth International Conference on Mobile Systems, Applications, and Services*, MobiSys '08, pages 40–53, New York, NY, USA, 2008. ACM.

[18] G. Greenwald, E. MacAskill, and L. Poitras. Edward Snowden: The whistleblower behind the NSA surveillance revelations. *The Guardian*, 2013.

[19] T. Hase. Secure PGP key sync – a proposal. https://blog.whiteout.io/2014/07/07/secure-pgp-key-sync-a-proposal/, 2014.

[20] A. Herzberg, S. Jarecki, H. Krawczyk, and M. Yung. Proactive secret sharing or: How to cope with perpetual leakage. In *Advances in Cryptology – CRYPT0'95*, volume 963 of *Lecture Notes in Computer Science*, pages 339–352. Springer Berlin Heidelberg, 1995.

[21] A. Kalamandeen, A. Scannell, E. de Lara, A. Sheth, and A. LaMarca. Ensemble: Cooperative proximity-based authentication. In *8th International Conference on Mobile Systems, Applications, and Services*, pages 331–344. ACM, 2010.

[22] F. M. A. Krause. Designing secure & usable Picosiblings. https://www.cl.cam.ac.uk/~fms27/papers/2014-Krause-picosiblings.pdf, 2014. Masters thesis.

[23] M. Lentz, V. Erdélyi, P. Aditya, E. Shi, P. Druschel, and B. Bhattacharjee. SDDR: Light-weight, secure mobile encounters. In *23rd USENIX Security Symposium*, pages 925–940, 2014.

[24] Y.-H. Lin, A. Studer, H.-C. Hsiao, J. M. McCune, K.-H. Wang, M. Krohn, P.-L. Lin, A. Perrig, H.-M. Sun, and B.-Y. Yang. Spate: Small-group PKI-less authenticated trust establishment. In *7th International Conference on Mobile Systems, Applications, and Services*, MobiSys '09, pages 1–14, New York, NY, USA, 2009. ACM.

[25] M. S. Melara, A. Blankstein, J. Bonneau, E. W. Felten, and M. J. Freedman. CONIKS: Bringing key transparency to end users. In *24th USENIX Security Symposium*, pages 383–398, Aug. 2015.

[26] A. Oprea, D. Balfanz, G. Durfee, and D. Smetters. Securing a remote terminal application with a mobile trusted device. In *20th Annual Computer Security Applications Conference*, pages 438–447, Dec 2004.

[27] P. Paillier. Public-key cryptosystems based on composite degree residuosity classes. In *Advances in Cryptology – EUROCRYPT'99*, pages 223–238. Springer, 1999.

[28] R. Peeters. Security architecture for things that think. http://www.cosic.esat.kuleuven.be/publications/thesis-202.pdf, 2012. Ph.D. thesis.

[29] R. Peeters, M. Kohlweiss, and B. Preneel. Threshold things that think: Authorisation for resharing. In J. Camenisch and D. Kesdogan, editors, *iNetSec 2009 – Open Research Problems in Network Security*, volume 309 of *IFIP Advances in Information and Communication Technology*, pages 111–124. Springer Berlin Heidelberg, 2009.

[30] R. Peeters, S. Nikova, and B. Preneel. Practical RSA threshold decryption for things that think. In *3rd Benelux Workshop on Information and System Security*, 2008.

[31] R. Peeters, D. Singelée, and B. Preneel. Threshold-based location-aware access control. *Mobile and Handheld Computing Solutions for Organizations and End-Users*, pages 20–36, 2013.

[32] S. Sheng, L. Broderick, C. Koranda, and J. Hyland. Why Johnny still can't encrypt: Evaluating the usability of email encryption software. In *2006 Symposium On Usable Privacy and Security - Poster Session*, 2006.

[33] V. Shoup. Practical threshold signatures. In *19th International Conference on Theory and Application of Cryptographic Techniques*, EUROCRYPT'00, pages 207–220, Berlin, Heidelberg, 2000. Springer-Verlag.

[34] K. Simoens, R. Peeters, and B. Preneel. Increased resilience in threshold cryptography: sharing a secret with devices that cannot store shares. In *Pairing-Based Cryptography-Pairing 2010*, pages 116–135. Springer, 2010.

[35] S. Sinclair and S. Smith. PorKI: Making user PKI safe on machines of heterogeneous trustworthiness. In *21st*

Annual Computer Security Applications Conference, pages 10 pp.–430, Dec 2005.

[36] D. Singelee, R. Peeters, and B. Preneel. Toward more secure and reliable access control. *IEEE Pervasive Computing,* (3):76–83, 2012.

[37] F. Stajano. Pico: No more passwords! In *Security Protocols XIX,* volume 7114 of *Lecture Notes in Computer Science,* pages 49–81. Springer Berlin Heidelberg, 2011.

[38] O. Stannard and F. Stajano. Am I in good company? A privacy-protecting protocol for cooperating ubiquitous computing devices. In *Security Protocols XX,* volume 7622 of *Lecture Notes in Computer Science,* pages 223–230. Springer Berlin Heidelberg, 2012.

[39] Q. Staórd-Fraser, G. Jenkinson, F. Stajano, M. Spencer, C. Warrington, and J. Payne. To have and have not: Variations on secret sharing to model user presence. In *2014 ACM International Joint Conference on Pervasive and Ubiquitous Computing: Adjunct Publication,* pages 1313–1320. ACM, 2014.

[40] A. Whitten and J. D. Tygar. Why Johnny can't encrypt: A usability evaluation of PGP 5.0. In *8th USENIX Security Symposium,* SSYM'99, pages 14–14, Berkeley, CA, USA, 1999.

Vibreaker: Securing Vibrational Pairing with Deliberate Acoustic Noise

S Abhishek Anand
University of Alabama at Birmingham
anandab@uab.edu

Nitesh Saxena
University of Alabama at Birmingham
saxena@uab.edu

ABSTRACT

Pairing between wireless devices may be secured by the use of an auxiliary channel such as audio, visuals or vibrations. A simple approach to pairing involves one of the devices initiating the transmission of a key, or keying material like a short password, over the auxiliary channel to the other device. A successful pairing is achieved when the receiving device is able to decode the key without any errors while the attacker is unable to eavesdrop the key.

In this paper, we focus on the security of the vibration channel when used for the key transmission. As shown in some recent work, sending the keying material over a clear vibrational channel poses a significant risk of an acoustic side channel attack. Specifically, an adversary can listen onto the acoustic sounds generated by the vibration motor of the sending device and infer the keying material with a high accuracy. To counteract this threat, we propose a novel pairing scheme, called *Vibreaker* (a "Vibrating speaker"), that involves active injection of acoustic noise in order to mask the key signal. In this scheme, the sending device artificially injects noise in the otherwise clear audio channel while transmitting the keying material via vibrations. We experiment with several choices for the noise signal and demonstrate that the security of the audio channel is significantly enhanced with Vibreaker when appropriate noise is used. The scheme requires no additional effort by the user, and imposes minimum hardware requirement and hence can be applied to many different contexts, such as pairing of IoT and implanted devices, wearables and other commodity gadgets.

1. INTRODUCTION

The wireless communication (Bluetooth, WiFi or RFID) is easy to eavesdrop and manipulate, and therefore a fundamental security objective is to secure this communication channel. "Pairing" is a term commonly used to refer to the operation of bootstrapping secure communication between two wireless devices, resistant against eavesdropping and man-in-the-middle attacks. Pairing is generally a hard problem due to the lack of a global infrastructure enabling devices to share an on- or off-line trusted third party, a certification authority, a PKI or any pre-configured secrets.

A well-researched approach to pairing is to leverage an auxiliary channel, also called an out-of-band (OOB) channel, which is governed by the users operating the devices. Examples of OOB channels include audio, visual, and vibrational channels. Unlike the radio communication channels, OOB channels are "human-perceptible", i.e., the underlying transmission/reception can be perceived by one or more human senses. In other words, a user can validate the intended source of an OOB message and an adversary can not manipulate the OOB messages in transit (although he can eavesdrop). Prior research refers to such an authenticated OOB communication as A-OOB [1]. Using these protocols, a multitude of pairing methods based on a large variety of A-OOB channels have been proposed, as surveyed in [3].

Pairing protocols are challenging to implement on constrained devices that lack a good quality output interfaces (e.g, a speaker, display), input interfaces (e.g., keypads), or receivers (e.g., microphone, camera), and may not be physically accessible. Limited computational resources are also a limiting factor for establishing A-OOB channel on such devices. An alternative pairing approach involves the use *secret as well as authenticated* OOB channels (termed AS-OOB [1]). In this approach, the adversary is not only assumed to be incapable of manipulating OOB communication but also can not eavesdrop upon it.

Several prior proposals, including [2, 6], have taken the AS-OOB approach to pairing. The IMD Pairing scheme of [2] uses a low-frequency audio channel to pair an RFID tag – attached to an IMD (Implanted Medical Device) – with an authorized RFID reader. Basically, the tag generates a random key and broadcasts it to the reader which listens to it from a close distance (e.g., a microphone is placed in close proximity to the patient's chest in case of a cardiac implant). The PIN-Vibra method for pairing [6] uses an automated vibrational channel to pair a personal RFID tag with a mobile phone. The phone generates a PIN and transmits it to (an accelerometer-equipped) tag through its vibrations, while the user presses the phone against the tag. (The same channel is later used by the phone to authenticate to (or activate) the tag).

However, both of these pairing schemes have been subject to acoustic eavesdropping attacks and shown to be vulnerable [1]. The work of [1] demonstrated highly accurate attacks on IMD pairing (which uses direct acoustic signals), and PIN-Vibra (in which the acoustic signals are a by-product of the vibration – a side channel). These attacks serve to call the security of the whole AS-OOB model to pairing into question.

In this paper, we set out to enhance the security of the simple AS-OOB approach to pairing by cloaking the acoustic leakage underlying such schemes. In particular, we focus on a representative instance of vibrational pairing, the PIN-Vibra scheme, and aim to obfuscate the sounds created by the vibration motor of the sending device (the phone). The idea is to selectively jam the acoustic chan-

WiSec'16 , July 18-22, 2016, Darmstadt, Germany

© 2016 ACM. ISBN 978-1-4503-4270-4/16/07... $15.00

DOI: http://dx.doi.org/10.1145/2939918.2939934

nel leakage by having the sending device produce deliberate sounds that would mask the sounds produced by the vibration motor.

Our Contributions: We propose a practical defense mechanism, called *Vibreaker*, against acoustic side channel attacks in vibrational pairing (PIN-Vibra), and evaluate its security against several attack vectors. The main contributions of this paper are summarized below.

1. *Design and Implementation of the Defense*: We build Vibreaker, a viable defense system that utilizes masking signals to mitigate vibration pairing side channel attacks. The defense system is designed to be a part of the device that is the source of acoustic leakage, which would be the phone in our case study. The intuition behind our defense model is to actively cloak the acoustic leakage emanating from the phone's vibration motor with other sounds that would be played back by the phone in the background. In this model, the insertion of acoustic noise only impacts the acoustic eavesdropper but does not at all affect the capability of the device which is receiving and decoding the vibrations (e.g., an RFID tag or possibly another phone).

2. *Evaluation of Security*: We evaluate the security of the Vibreaker system by testing its ability to reduce the accuracy of the acoustic side channel attack that we recreated in the initial step of our research by preventing the adversary from gaining usable information about the transmitted PIN (or any short content). In particular, we test two masking signals: white noise and sounds generated by the vibrations against the acoustic side channel attack. We also examine their performance against noise reduction techniques aimed at filtering out the masking signals. Our results show both types of masking signals to be effective against curbing the existing eavesdropping attack.

2. BACKGROUND AND RELATED WORK

2.1 A-OOB Pairing of Constrained Devices

A-OOB pairing of constrained wireless devices is challenging due to a number of reasons. Several prior pairing methods are based on bidirectional automated device-to-device (dtd) A-OOB channels (e.g., [3]). Such dtd channels require both devices to have transmitters and corresponding receivers (e.g., IR transceivers), which may not exist on constrained devices. In settings, where dtd channel(s) do not exist (i.e., when at least one device does not have a receiver), pairing methods can be based upon device-to-human (dth) and human-to-device (htd) channel(s) instead (e.g., based on transfer of numbers [7]). However, establishing such channels on constrained devices may also not be feasible.

One solution to the above problem is to use only unidirectional communication (from device A to B), but have the user transfer the result of pairing shown on B over to A, as shown in [5]. This, however, may lead to a critical security failure – a user may accept the pairing on A even though B indicates otherwise, as shown via the usability studies in [3]. (This is referred to as a *fatal* human error [3] which translates into a man-in-the-middle attack).

Another possible approach is based on manual comparison of audiovisual OOB strings over synchronized device-to-human (dth) channels, as shown in [3]. This would only require the two devices to be equipped with low-cost transmitters, such as LED(s) (and two buttons). However, the security of these approaches rely upon the decision made by the user and is prone to fatal human errors, as demonstrated in [3]. Even worse, a user who is in a rush to connect her devices may simply "accept" the pairing, without having to correctly take part in the decision process [3].

2.2 PIN-Vibra: AS-OOB Vibrational Pairing

Personal (passive) RFID tags (found, e.g., in access cards, e-passports, licenses) are increasingly becoming ubiquitous. Similar to other personal devices, personal RFID tags often store valuable information privy to their users, and are likely to get lost or stolen. However, unlike other personal wireless devices, such information can be easily be subjected to eavesdropping, relay attacks and unauthorized "reading", and can lead to owner tracking.

User authentication to an RFID device would allow a user to control when and where her RFID tag can be accessed and thus help solve some of the aforementioned problems. A road-block in developing an RFID user authentication mechanism is the lack of any input or output interfaces on RFID tags (RFID devices were not meant to interact with their users and vice-versa) and a somewhat atypical usage model (users often place RFID tags in their wallets and might not be in direct contact with them).

In [6], authors present PIN-Vibra, a novel approach for user authentication to RFID tags. PIN-Vibra leverages a pervasive device such as a personal mobile phone, motivated by its ubiquity. It uses the mobile phone as an authentication token, forming a unidirectional AS-OOB tactile communication channel between the user and her (accelerometer-equipped) RFID tags. Pairing of (and later authenticating to) an RFID tag requires the user to simply touch her vibrating phone with the tag or object carrying the tag (e.g., a wallet); the phone encodes a short PIN into vibrations which are read by the tag's accelerometer and decoded.

The security of PIN-Vibra relies on secrecy of the underlying vibrational channel, i.e., an adversary who is not in close physical contact with the phone should not be able to learn the transmitted PIN. In [1], the authors investigated the feasibility of eavesdropping the PIN-Vibra vibrational channel. In particular, they demonstrated how the acoustic emanations associated with a vibrating mobile phone can be eavesdropped upon from a short distance with off-the-shelf microphones. In Section 3, we will recreate and re-validate this attack, which will serve as a pre-requisite for the evaluation of our proposed defense Vibreaker to defeat this attack.

3. PIN-VIBRA ATTACK RECREATION

In this section, we provide the details of the vibration pairing scheme PIN-Vibra and show its vulnerability against an eavesdropping adversary over the audio channel.

3.1 PIN-Vibra Details

In the vibration pairing scheme, the transmitter (a phone or a smart device) encodes the keying material into a series of vibrations through its vibration motor. The receiver, also a smart device equipped with an accelerometer reads the vibrations and decodes the transmitted information with the help of the accelerometer. For successful decoding of the vibrations by the receiver, both devices need to be in contact with each other.

For our work, we implement the scheme proposed in [6]. We use four digit PINs as the data to be transmitted using a simple time interval based ON-OFF encoding mechanism. The PIN is treated as a decimal number and converted to its 14 bit binary equivalent. A preamble "110" is added at the beginning of the binary representation of the PIN to denote the start of the transmission bringing the total bit length of the sequence to 17 bits. Each '1' bit in the bit sequence is encoded into a vibration lasting for 200ms and each '0' bit is encoded as a silence period of 200ms. The total time to transmit a 17 bit sequence is therefore estimated to be $17 \times 200ms = 3.4s$.

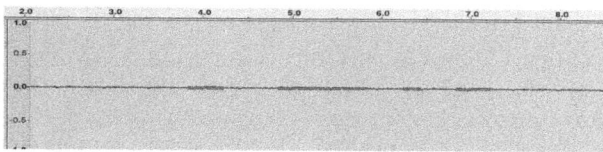

(a) Raw Audio Signal

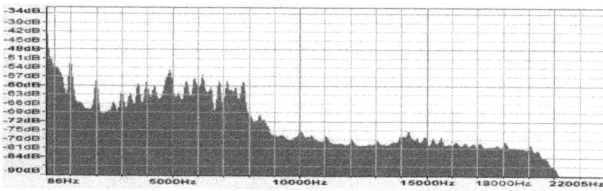

(b) Amplitude vs Frequency

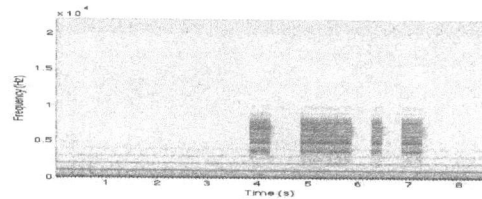

(c) Spectrogram of the Acoustic Leakage

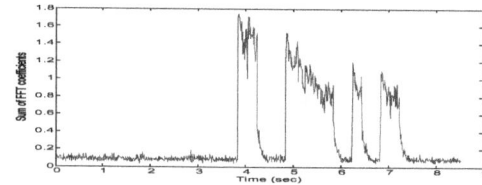

(d) Sum of the FFT coefficients for Acoustic Leakage

Figure 1: Acoustic Characterstics of the Vibration for PIN "4562"

3.2 Threat Model

We follow a similar threat model as that of [1] where the adversary is able to eavesdrop on the devices in communication from a distance (10cm or more). This implies that while the adversary does not have access to the device's microphone, it can use a covert listening device for eavesdropping. Since the adversary is at a distance from the pairing devices, the listening device can be hidden in the surrounding environment. After recording, the adversary can process the recording offline for decoding the pairing key from the eavesdropped signal.

The environment is supposed to be quiet, devoid of any interfering background noise that lets the adversary eavesdrop on the vibration sounds with the best possible quality. The listening device could be any off the shelf recording devices available in the market that provide a decent recording quality. Thus, we have a realistic eavesdropping scenario in a clean environment with a moderate capability adversary.

3.3 Eavesdropping Attack Model

In any vibration based scheme, the bits are encoded into a series of vibrations. While the vibrations seem to be barely audible, an examination of the audio spectrum of the vibrations from a close distance reveals significant acoustic leakage in a particular frequency band.

For our experiment, we used Motorola Droid X2 android based phones as both the transmitter and the receiver. We also utilized a PC microphone to eavesdrop on the audio produced during bit transmission due to vibrations. Audio processing was done offline using Matlab software.

Figure 1a represents the raw audio signal captured during the vibration of the phone. The figure confirms the assumptions that the amplitude of the acoustic leakage from the vibrations is very low. However, upon examining the frequency spectrum in Figure 1c, the acoustic leakage from the vibrations seems to stretch from 3.5 kHz to 8.3 kHz. The power of the frequency spectrum appears to be consistently high in the frequency range 6.8 kHz to 7.8 kHz in both a normal scenario Figure 1d and on a dampened surface Figure 2. We therefore restrict the attack to this frequency band and use it in our evaluation as it seems to be the optimal one from the point of view of the attacker.

The first step to recover the transmitted data from the acoustic leakage involves the detection of the beginning of the transmission. Hence, we search for the preamble "110" in the eavesdropped audio signal. To detect a valid bit in the audio signal, we transform

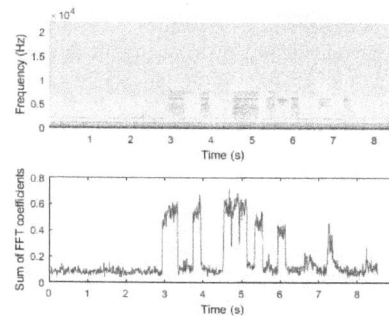

Figure 2: Spectrum Analysis on a Dampening Surface

the recorded audio signal from the time domain to the frequency domain by performing a Fast Fourier Transformation (FFT) of the signal using the *spectrogram* function of Matlab. We used a hamming window of size 441 samples with an overlap of half of the window size. Then, we sum up the FFT coefficients of the signal at each time instance in the frequency band 6.8 kHz - 7.8 kHz. The results obtained are similar to Figure 1d.

Once, we have calculated the sum of the FFT coefficients, we determine a threshold value above which we consider a vibration to have begun. This threshold value can be set as the maximum value of the sum of the FFT coefficients and can be reduced by 10% each time until the audio signal is correctly decoded.

As mentioned in the description of the vibration pairing scheme, each vibration lasts for a period of 200ms. We therefore divide the signal into audio bins of 200ms and find the average power in each bin. If the average power in the bin is more than the pre-defined threshold, we decode the corresponding bit as '1' otherwise '0'. Since the first three bits should be "110" as the preamble for a valid transmission, we continue checking the bits until we get a valid preamble. Once a valid preamble is found, we begin decoding the bits until all remaining 14 bits have been decoded.

We test our eavesdropping attack on ten random PINs using the above setup with the recordings done at a distance of 15cm. The attack was successful with 100% accuracy thereby demonstrating that communication using vibrations is highly susceptible to an acoustic eavesdropping adversary. This result confirms the results of the attack scheme proposed by Halevi et al. [1].

In the above discussed scenario, the two devices are assumed to be in contact during the transmission. We also studied other

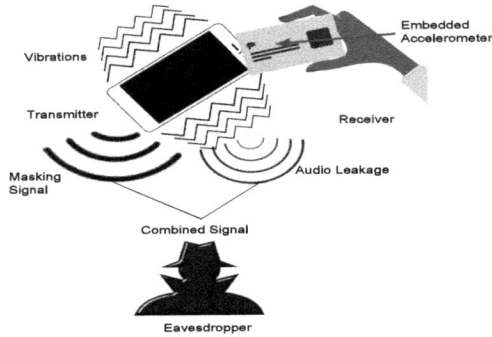

Figure 3: Defense Model Setup

scenarios where the transmitting device may be resting on a wallet (communicating with an RFID tag inside the wallet) or on an audio dampening surface (a thick layering of cloth). The results from the frequency spectrum analysis of the eavesdropped signal (Figure 2) show that even though the surface muffles the vibration sounds, it is still possible to decode the bits by lowering the threshold according to the obtained sum of FFT coefficients.

4. DEFENSE

In the previous section, we described an eavesdropping attack on pairing through vibrations. Now, we will briefly explore some potential defense mechanisms that could be used to mitigate this class of attack and follow it with the design of Vibreaker, the defense scheme proposed in this paper.

4.1 Defense Background

The acoustic side channel attacks on vibration pairing exploit the leaked audio that is generated due to the vibrations of the device. In order to prevent an adversary from gaining any useful information from the audio leakage, the vibration sound should be either canceled or masked with the help of another sound. In case of masking, the adversary has to filter out the masking signal in order to recover the audio signal and extract the keying material from it.

Signal cancellation usually involves introducing another signal having similar features (frequency characteristics and amplitude level) as the signal to be canceled but having opposite phase. Signal masking requires introducing a signal that contains all the frequencies of the signal to be masked and an amplitude level equal to or more than that of the signal to be masked. With the masking signal, we try to distort the original signal to an extent that the resultant signal has entirely different features from the original signal.

4.1.1 Audio Leakage Cancellation

Roy et al. [4] examined the possibility of canceling the sound of vibration (termed SoV) by creating an "anti-noise" signal on the transmitter's end. The challenges of creating an anti-noise signal involve an estimation of the surface in contact with the phone, the phase of the SoV signal and the limited real-time audio processing capabilities offered by the Android platform.

For estimating the effect of the surface on which the device has been placed, they transmitted a short preamble and recorded the resulting SoV. The FFT of the SoV was examined to look for the strongest overtones that are combined to create the "anti-noise" signal. For phase alignment, Ripple transmitter increases the sampling frequency of the "anti-noise" signal keeping track of the phase difference of the "anti-noise" and SoV and switching it back to its original value when the phase difference is minimum.

There exist multiple issues with this approach if we try to implement the scheme in our communication model. Our model is focused on short message exchange between two devices like pairing or authentication. Hence, a simple ON/OFF scheme is sufficient for all of our purposes. Since we implement our model on Android based smartphones, computationally exhaustive signal processing tasks such as calculating FFT for creating an "anti-noise" signal take more time than the entire duration of communication that is as mentioned in Section 3 is only 3.4s.

After combining the "anti-noise" signal with the SoV, the frequency domain of the reduced sound still remains unchanged though the amplitude is reduced significantly. However, a powerful adversary could scrutinize the frequency spectrum of the reduced sound looking for frequency footprints of the SoV. This can potentially reveal some information about the transmitted bits to the adversary.

If we do not consider the duration of the communication as a limiting factor by artificially increasing it via an addition of a preamble to the actual PIN, cancellation of audio signal may yet prove to be capable of mitigating the acoustic side channel attack. However, in this work, we restrict ourselves to the examination of easy to generate and computationally light signal masking technique.

4.1.2 Audio Leakage Masking

Signal masking mechanism borrows its motivation from a very common problem in signal communications where the presence of noise in the environment corrupts the signal. If the signal to noise ratio (SNR) is low, it becomes hard to differentiate the signal from the encompassing noise. We utilize this idea to intentionally introduce noise (referred as masking signal) during the vibration of the device so that it corrupts the audio leakage from the vibration to an extent that it becomes indistinguishable from the masking signal.

As the strength of the defense mechanism depends on the difficulty of the adversary's task in filtering out the masking signal from the eavesdropped signal, we test out some types of masking signal that can be deployed to defend against eavesdropping attack. We also evaluate the effectiveness of these signals in masking the audio leakage and the difficulty of filtering these signals from the eavesdropped signal to recover partial or full audio signal (SoV).

4.2 Vibreaker Design and Setup

Vibreaker is designed to generate a masking signal that obscures the audio leakage in a fashion that makes it hard for the adversary to extract any information about the transmitted data. In order to accomplish this task, we test different types of sounds that could potentially be the masking signal and evaluate their security against an adversary as defined in Section 3.

In our setup for testing Vibreaker, the transmitter and the receiver are positioned similar to the attack recreation model where the devices are in contact. The transmitter transmits data by vibrating in a certain pattern that is decoded by the receiver. In addition, the transmitter is also equipped with speakers that emit the masking signal while the transmission is in progress. This ensures that any eavesdropping adversary will receive the combined signal (a mix of the audio leakage from vibrations and the masking signal) from which it would be difficult to recover the transmitted information. Figure 3 details the overview of the Vibreaker model.

5. EVALUATION OF THE DEFENSE

In this section, we will evaluate the efficiency of some types of masking signals against the attack setup described in Section 3. We will also investigate the prospect of filtering out the masking signals by the adversary and test if the resultant signal contains any relevant information about the transmitted data.

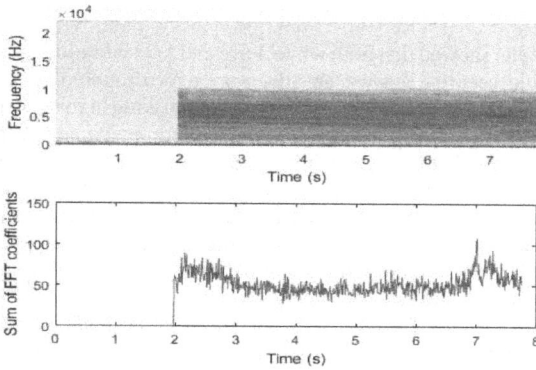

Figure 4: White Noise Masking Spectrum

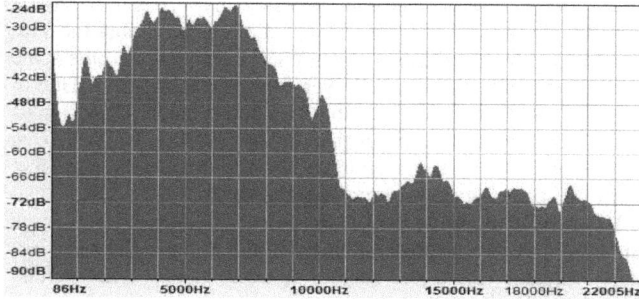

Figure 5: Amplitude vs Frequency for the White Noise

5.1 White Noise as Masking Signal

White noise is defined as a random signal having a constant power spectral density. White noise is constantly present in the environment for example the humming sound emanating from air conditioning units. It has also been used for sound masking in offices by suppressing other distracting sounds. Here, we use the white noise as the base level candidate signal for masking. It is not a sophisticated signal and can easily be generated. Filtering the white noise signal is fairly simple, but the process of filtering also affects the quality of the recovered signal. Since white noise has an equal distribution over all of the frequency spectrum, trying to filter it out also filters out the frequencies where the white noise overlaps with the frequency spectrum of the original signal (audio leakage from the vibrations).

Experimental Setup: We use the *wgn* function of Matlab to generate a 10 second sample of white Gaussian noise at a sampling frequency of 44.1 kHz. White Gaussian noise is a good approximation of real world white noise and hence sufficient for our intentions. We then apply a frequency filter to the noise sample to make sure that the white noise remains in the same frequency band as the audio leakage.

Once we have generated the white noise sample, we play it in the background while the phone vibrates. To make sure that the white noise suppresses all the audio leakage, we introduce a delay in the phone vibration at the beginning such that the phone starts vibrating only after the white noise has begun playing in the background.

Observations: To study the effectiveness of the white noise as a masking signal, we consider an adversary snooping at a distance of 15cm using the attack recreated in section 3.

Our observations for the recording done at a distance of 15cm (Figure 4) show that white noise completely masks the audio leakage from the vibrations. In addition, nothing can be learned about the vibrations in the frequency domain even after obtaining FFT of the eavesdropped signal. Apart from covering the spectrum in

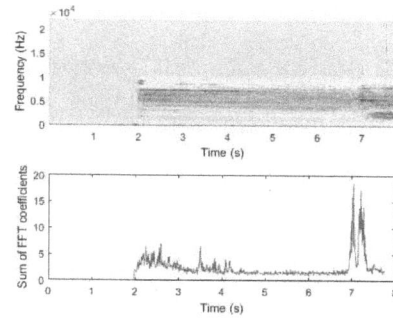

Figure 6: Signal Features for PIN "4562" after filtering the White Noise

which the audio leakage from the vibrations lie, the sound level of the white noise as shown in Figure 5 is more than twice than that of vibrations alone (Figure 1b) thereby easily suppressing the leakage.

Filtering the Masking Signal: For filtering the white noise, we use the *noise reduction* effect from Audacity software that allows us to select a small sample of noise as the noise profile and apply it to the whole signal for noise reduction. We used a noise reduction level of 15dB and a sensitivity value of 6 to get the best results for our scenario. Figure 6 shows the frequency spectrum of the captured audio signal after filtering out the noise.

The frequency spectrum in Figure 6 does not reveal any information about the audio leakage from the vibration. This effect is due to complete cloaking of the audio leakage by the white noise. Since vibration sounds are not loud, the attenuation of the audio leakage at the attacker's eavesdropping device makes it infeasible to extract any information from the recorded signal. In Figure 6, the plot of the sum of FFT coefficient vs time does not contain any vibration peaks. Hence, our attack would be unable to identify the vibration periods leading to a 0% success rate.

5.2 Vibration Noise as Masking Signal

Our next choice of masking signal is a close representation of the audio leakage itself. We pre-record a clip of the sound generated during the vibration and try to confuse the attacker by masking the audio leakage from the vibrations with the pre-recorded vibration noise (henceforth referred as fake vibrations).

Experimental Setup: We generate a random sequence of numbers and encode them as vibrations using the same protocol as PIN-Vibra [6]. However, in order to make sure that the fake vibrations completely overlap with the actual vibrations, we reduce the duration of silence from 200ms to 100ms between the vibrations. The resultant vibration sequence is recorded offline and stored for use as the masking signal.

When the user initiates the protocol for sending the PIN via vibrations, the device in addition to vibrating also begins playing the stored masking signal in the background. We adjust the timings of the masking signal such that it always begins playing at the approximately the same time as the vibrations. The adversary is presumed to be eavesdropping at a distance of 15cm.

Observations: The results show that fake vibrations are able to mask the audio leakage from the device's vibration. It is nearly impossible to distinguish between the fake vibration signals and the audio leakage by looking at the frequency spectrum. The FFT measure also shows only the response from the fake vibrations indicating that audio leakage has completely been masked.

Filtering the Masking Signal: We apply the same filtering process that was used for filtering out the white noise. Since sounds of fake vibration differ from actual vibration sound due to imper-

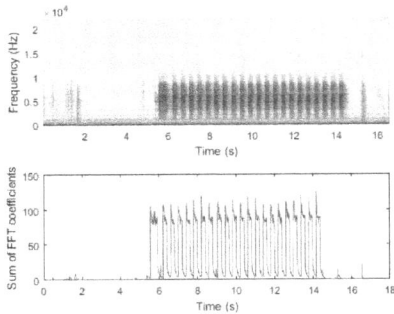

Figure 7: Signal Features for PIN "4562" in presence of Fake Vibrations

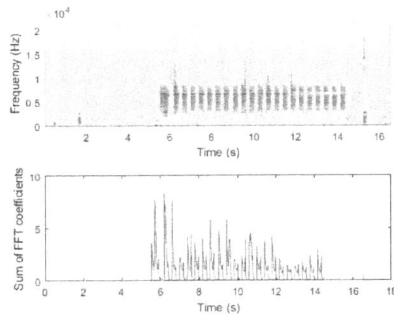

Figure 8: Signal Features for PIN "4562" after filtering Fake Vibrations

fect reproduction by the speakers, we (as an attacker) listen to the eavesdropped audio signal and select the part that is believed to be the fake vibrations. The selected part of the audio is used as the noise profile and applied to the full length of the eavesdropped audio signal for filtering the fake vibrations.

The results (Figure 8) after the filtering process reveal no additional information about the audio leakage from the vibration of the device. In the plot of the sum of FFT coefficient vs time (Figure 8), there does not exist a threshold that could differentiate between real and fake vibrations. Hence, our attack fails to decode the correct PIN leading to 0% success rate. Thus fake vibrations also serve a an efficient masking signal for obfuscating the vibration sounds.

Effect on the Receiver: We believe that the proposed defense mechanism does not affect the communication between the pairing devices because the the data transfer is through vibrations. Vibreaker relies on audio signal for masking the audio leakage. Receiver is using accelerometer to learn the real vibrations, fake vibrations is just sound and, as mentioned above, would have no effect on accelerometer readings.

6. CONCLUSION AND FUTURE WORK

In this paper, we explored possible ways to mitigate an acoustic side channel attack on vibration based pairing interactions. In particular, we focused our investigation on PIN-Vibra instance of vibrational pairing [6] and recreated the side channel attack on this pairing model, as earlier reported in [1].

We introduced Vibreaker, a novel defense mechanism to mitigate acoustic side channel attacks against PIN-Vibra by active injection of masking signal in the environment. The purpose of the masking signal was to obfuscate the acoustic leakage generated by the vibrations of the transmitting device. We studied some audio signals as candidates for masking the acoustic leakage and evaluated the security offered by them against the recreated attack.

Our results showed that both white noise and fake vibration sounds offer viable security against an adversary eavesdropping on the acoustic side channel leakage. Both types of masking signals were able to hide the acoustic leakage from an eavesdropping adversary making it difficult to distinguish between the masking signal and the acoustic leakage. We also studied the effect of noise filtering mechanism against Vibreaker and found out that even if the adversary tries to filter out the masking signal using noise reduction technique, it may not help the adversary in recovering any useful information from the eavesdropped signal.

A possible avenue for future work would be to evaluate the performance of Vibreaker against more powerful attackers who may use triangulation techniques based on multiple, strategically placed, audio recording devices or more powerful and direction oriented microphones. We believe that Vibreaker may be able to thwart such attacks due to the sources of audio leakage (vibration motor) and audio noise (speakerphone) being embedded to the same device (transmitter), essentially very close to each other. Due to the same reason, it would be viable to generate the masking signals at the receiving device (rather than the transmitting device). This may be useful when the transmitting device does not have a speaker while the receiving device is equipped with one.

However, while using the FFT features of the audio leakage was enough to create a successful attack in the absence masking signals, Vibreaker would also need to be tested against other sophisticated attacks that may utilize machine learning and feature classification (using FFT or MFCC) to detect vibration sounds in the eavesdropped signal. Another consideration may be to develop a stricter attack model where the distance of attacker is 0cm from the transmitter, or the attacker has a very powerful microphone, e.g., a parabolic microphone.

While Vibreaker transmission process is very short (less than 4 seconds), insertion of masking sounds may have an impact on the usability of the process. We believe that the use of fake vibration sounds may be less distracting to the users compared to white noise, since fake vibration sounds aim to match the sounds of the vibration itself. A formal usability study may need to be conducted to evaluate and compare the distraction effects of various masking signals in the Vibreaker system.

7. REFERENCES

[1] T. Halevi and N. Saxena. On pairing constrained wireless devices based on secrecy of auxiliary channels: the case of acoustic eavesdropping. In *ACM CCS*, 2010.

[2] D. Halperin, T. S. Heydt-Benjamin, B. Ransford, S. S. Clark, B. Defend, W. Morgan, K. Fu, T. Kohno, and W. H. Maisel. Pacemakers and implantable cardiac defibrillators: Software radio attacks and zero-power defenses. In *IEEE Symposium on S&P*, 2008.

[3] R. Kainda, I. Flechais, and A. W. Roscoe. Usability and security of out-of-band channels in secure device pairing protocols. In *SOUPS*, 2009.

[4] N. Roy, M. Gowda, and R. R. Choudhury. Ripple: Communicating through physical vibration. In *NSDI*, 2015.

[5] N. Saxena, J.-E. Ekberg, K. Kostiainen, and N. Asokan. Secure device pairing based on a visual channel. In *IEEE S&P*, 2006.

[6] N. Saxena, M. B. Uddin, J. Voris, and N. Asokan. Vibrate-to-unlock: Mobile phone assisted user authentication to multiple personal RFID tags. In *Percom*, 2011.

[7] E. Uzun, K. Karvonen, and N. Asokan. Usability analysis of secure pairing methods. In *USEC*, 2007.

Constructive and Destructive Aspects of Adaptive Wormholes for the 5G Tactile Internet

Christian T. Zenger[1,2], Jan Zimmer[2], Mario Pietersz[1,2],
Benedikt Driessen[1,2], and Christof Paar[2]
[1]PHYSEC GmbH, Universitätsstr. 150, 44801 Bochum, Germany
{christian.zenger, mario.pietersz, benedikt.driessen}@physec.de
[2]HGI, Ruhr-University Bochum, Germany
{jan.zimmer, christof.paar}@rub.de

ABSTRACT

In this work, we constructively combine *adaptive wormholes* with *channel-reciprocity based key establishment* (CRKE), which has been proposed as a lightweight security solution for IoT devices and might be even more important for the 5G Tactile Internet and its embedded low-end devices. We present a new secret key generation protocol where two parties compute shared cryptographic keys under narrow-band multi-path fading models over a delayed digital channel. The proposed approach furthermore enables distance-bounding the key establishment process via the coherence time dependencies of the wireless channel. Our scheme is thoroughly evaluated both theoretically and practically. For the latter, we used a testbed based on the IEEE 802.15.4 standard and performed extensive experiments in a real-world manufacturing environment. Additionally, we demonstrate adaptive wormhole attacks (AWOAs) and their consequences on several physical-layer security schemes. Furthermore, we proposed a countermeasure that minimizes the risk of AWOAs.

1. INTRODUCTION

We are in the midst of a collective movement towards the Internet of Things (IoT). Myriads of resource-constrained network nodes will communicate with each other, forming a wide spectrum of applications. A large number of IoT systems will be sensitive, e.g., automotive controllers, medical devices, SCADA systems, and many other cyber-physical systems. It is thus paramount that future IoT applications are equipped with security mechanisms.

A considerable portion of IoT devices can be characterized as resource-constrained platforms. Due to the fact that cheap platforms often do not provide true random number generators (TRNGs)—or efficient mechanisms for the statistical evaluation of randomness—and no secure storage for keys, security concepts based on pre-shared secrets or asymmetric cryptography do not fit very well. Furthermore,

the calculation of discrete modular exponentiations or point multiplications on an elliptic curve is $\mathcal{O}(n^3)$ where n is the size of the desired key. Enabling dynamic encryption keys on low-end devices is, therefore, still one of the most difficult challenges.

Channel-reciprocity based key establishment (CRKE) is a practice-oriented secret-key agreement mechanism and part of the *physical layer security* (PHYSEC) family [9]. Recently, CRKE has been proposed as a potential lightweight solution for low-end IoT devices due to its linear complexity [38, 47, 49]. CRKE's low complexity results in low latency, which is one key-requirement for the Tactile Internet. Enabling the Tactile Internet is a main objective of the 5G Initiative [4]. The Tactile Internet is another paradigm shift lying ahead; it is motivated by the idea of controlling real and virtual objects in real-time via tactile feedback. A breakthrough is immanent once the latency of communication systems becomes low enough to enable round trip delays (from the input device through the network and back) of approximately 1 ms [13]. Areas in our life in which the Tactile Internet will have an important impact are health and care, education and sports, traffic, free-viewpoint video, smart grid, as well as robotics and manufacturing.

While promising in terms of latency, running CRKE over a purely digital channel (e.g., the Internet) was not possible so far. This changes when *adaptive wormhole attacks* (AWOA) are used in a constructive manner, as will be demonstrated later. Adaptive wormholes were introduced in theory as a potential attack against hidden wormhole detection mechanisms [23]. The attacker tricks the channel-based wormhole detection mechanism of two parties to believe they are communicating directly using the same physical channel. To do so, an adaptive wormhole works as a relay[1] that reactively adapts the transmission signal to manipulate channel estimations. Wormhole attacks are especially critical for distance-bounded applications (e.g., where a specified transmission range is used as a trust boundary), routing protocols of MANETs, and for CRKE as well. However, we identified adaptive wormholes as a security primitive which might have constructive applications, especially for IoT and low-latency technology such as 5G.

WiSec'16, July 18–20, 2016, Darmstadt, Germany.
© 2016 ACM. ISBN 978-1-4503-4270-4/16/07. . . $15.00
DOI: http://dx.doi.org/2939918.2939923

---

[1]We note that relay attacks have been similarly applied in mobile ad-hoc networks (MANET), where they are known as wormhole attacks [17].

In this paper, we make the following contributions:

- We attacked two wormhole detection mechanisms and ten CRKE systems and present evaluation results.

- To the best of the author's knowledge, we present the first adaptive wormhole attack implementation.

- We present a new protocol that connects adaptive wormholes with CRKE. The wormhole is used to bridge digital channels for key establishment over the Internet and allows to achieve perfect forward secrecy based on a pre-distributed secret.

Prior work, as well as our prototypes are based on the popular IEEE 802.15.4 standard, frequently used in short-range industrial wireless sensor networks. We performed an extensive measurement campaign in a real-world industrial environment.

2. BACKGROUND

In this section, we characterize properties of a narrowband wireless channel and introduce constructions based on these.

2.1 Wireless Channel Primitives

The design of PHYSEC mechanisms, hidden wormhole attacks, as well as of wormholes detection mechanisms are based on features of the physical wireless channel. Therefore, we summarize three important properties of a radio channel, which can be assumed to be given in indoor environments.

2.1.1 Symmetry

The first key feature of a wireless channel is its symmetry, which can be exploited and utilized. Without taking noise, interference, and non-linear components into account, this symmetry relies on the principles of *antenna reciprocity* [33] and *channel reciprocity* [42]. In other words, the channel between A and B behaves similarly for transmissions from A to B and B to A. While antenna reciprocity is high and constant, a symmetric observation by A and B is only given if both channel measurements are done within a short period. This period is called *coherence time* and is highly dependent on the environment and movement within the transmission range. For most practical channels, these reciprocity properties hold and are easily observed [2].

2.1.2 Diversity

The second property of a radio channel is its spatial decorrelation or *channel diversity*: If uniformly distributed scatterers are given and channel variations occur, such as, due to moving scatterers, transmitters or receiver nodes, the spatial decorrelation is determined by a zero-order Bessel function. Here the first zero crossing of the correlation is given after approx. $\lambda/2$, where λ is the wavelength of the carrier signal [8]. Therefore, the correlation between a channel shared by A and B and a channel between A and C exhibits a distance-dependent behavior (cf. Fig. 1). However, an open research question is how the channel (de-)correlation behavior looks like if the requirements are not fully given (e.g., scatterers are not uniformly distributed). We do not tackle this question in this work, we rely on recent work showing that passive attacks are highly environment specific and only rarely successful [29, 20, 12, 47].

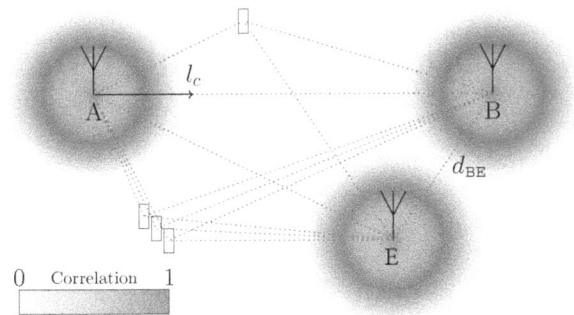

Figure 1: Simplified channel model: The spatial channel (de-)correlation versus distance is illustrated for each node. Further, because of the complex, time-varying environment, all channels are independent.

2.1.3 Randomness

The third key feature is the randomness of a radio channel. A complex and dynamic environment leads to unpredictable wave propagation effects, such as diffraction, scattering, and reflection. As a result, channel measurements between two parties A and B are location-specific, reciprocal, and time-varying. A wireless channel can thus serve as entropy source for cryptographic solutions. However, this requires a secure modus operandi in the case of entropy loss as well as a thorough evaluation of the physical source of randomness. Depending on the application, on-line statistical testing is an essential ingredient in order to detect statistical defects during runtime [48].

2.2 Channel-Reciprocity Based Key Extraction

As mentioned above, an alternative approach to key agreement is based on PHYSEC, which exploits physical features of wireless communication. In particular, the inherent randomness of the wireless medium can be utilized to establish a shared secret. This approach is referred to as CRKE and is characterized by three parties A, B, and E which observe a *discrete memoryless source* (DMS). The observations of A and B are assumed to contain mutual information, which is not or only partly shared with E. Entropy not shared with E is called the secret-key capacity of the DMS. Furthermore, it is assumed that the DMS is not predictable or malleable in a way that E can guess $A's$ and $B's$ observations. See Figure 1 for the general model.

The approach is based on the quasi-simultaneous measurement of the wireless channel by A and B. Afterwards, measurements are post-processed, quantized, and error corrected in order to remove noise and interferences. The resulting entropy is collected and utilized as a shared symmetric key. Besides providing shared randomness, the scheme is also inherently secure to attacks. If E's distance to both legitimate nodes is large enough, her observation of the channel is uncorrelated with the observations of A and B and thus an attack is not possible.

The general feasibility of the approach has been reported by extensive prior work [37, 26, 44, 32, 5, 6, 29, 20, 31, 27, 3, 46, 14, 29, 45, 50, 41, 43]. The first practice-oriented protocol for the unconditionally secure extraction of a symmetric key over public wireless fading channels was introduced by

Tope et al. [37] in 2001. Based on his approach, many protocols for key extraction have been proposed. One CRKE family is based on received signal strength indicators (RSSIs) [5, 6, 29, 20, 31, 27, 3, 46]. RSSI-based systems are very attractive because virtually every wireless communication interface provides RSSI values on a per packet basis. Another family exploits the channel impulse response (CIR) as a more general estimate [14, 29, 45, 50]. Other variants are based on channel phase randomness [41] or frequency hopping [43]. Mathur et al. [29] and Jana et al. [20] included brief thoughts on potential attacks in their proposals. Simple countermeasures against spoofing attacks by active adversaries were introduced by Mathur et al. [29] and Ye et al. [45]. There has also been some work that deals with temporal correlation of samples, such as principal component analysis [10], beamforming [28] or linear prediction [30].

2.3 (Adaptive) Wormhole Attacks

In many use cases (e.g., remote keyless entry systems, MANET routing protocols, or future Tactile Internet applications) correctly estimating the distance of two communication parties is crucial. In the absence of such possibilities, a wormhole attacker can trick two communication parties into believing they are close, when in fact they are not. These attacks exploit the flawed assumption that the ability to wirelessly communicate with a party guarantees its proximity.

Jain et al. [19] proposed a technique which exploits the reciprocity of RSSIs in order to detect wormhole attacks. Specifically, the property being leveraged is that, when two nodes communicate through a wormhole, their channel measurements will be uncorrelated with high probability. The approach is based on key extraction schemes with relaxed requirements (because no cryptographic key needs to be established). Krentz et al. build upon this with their own variant for 6LoWPAN, which uses channel hopping and randomized transmission powers [23]. They furthermore describe an AWOA that aims to be undetectable by past detection algorithms including Krentz et al.'s scheme itself.

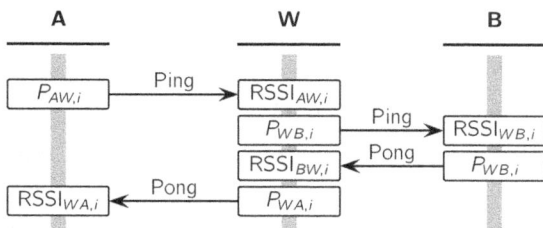

Figure 2: The adaptive wormhole attack, which was introduced by Krentz et al. [23].

The basic scenario is shown in Figure 2. The goal for an attacker is to recreate equal (or highly correlated) RSSI measurements for A and B so that a wormhole attack cannot be detected. Equal transmission power $P_{AB,i} = P_{BA,i}$ is assumed here. There is a relationship $RSSI = P - L$, with P being transmission power and L path loss. Path loss is the reduction in power density of an electromagnetic wave as it propagates through space. This is a function of the travel distance of the wave as well as of fluctuations due to large-scale and small-scale fading. We define that $L_{1,i}$ and $L'_{1,i}$ is the path loss from A to W, and vice versa. Further,

we define that $L_{2,i}$ and $L'_{2,i}$ is the path loss from B to W, and vice versa. This leads to the following equations:

$$RSSI_{WA,i} - RSSI_{WB,i} = P_{WA,i} - P_{WB,i} - L'_{1,i} + L_{2,i}$$
$$RSSI_{AW,i} - RSSI_{BW,i} = P_{AW,i} - P_{BW,i} - L_{1,i} + L'_{2,i}$$

Due to channel reciprocity we can assume that $L_{1,i} \approx L'_{1,i}$ and $L_{2,i} \approx L'_{2,i}$, thus:

$$RSSI_{WA,i} - RSSI_{WB,i} \approx RSSI_{AW,i} + P_{WA,i} - P_{AB,i}$$
$$- RSSI_{BW,i} - P_{WB,i} + P_{BA,i} \quad (1)$$

Now the i'th PONG is forwarded by W with the transmission power $P_{WA,i}$ chosen as:

$$P_{WA,i} = P_{WB,i} + RSSI_{BW,i} - RSSI_{AW,i}. \quad (2)$$

Combining Equation 1 and 2 we get the results $RSSI_{WA,i} \approx RSSI_{WB,i}$, which leads to the wormhole being undetected (Jain et al.'s channel reciprocity metrics show high values, which results in false negatives). The attack was designed to attack routing protocols of IPv6-based WSNs. However, it can also be used to attack future latency (or hop count) critical network, novel remote keyless entry systems as well as CRKE schemes.

2.4 Evaluation Metrics

Throughout this paper, we use the Pearson correlation, mutual information and the secret-key rate as evaluation metrics for achievable security levels.

2.4.1 Pearson correlation

The Pearson correlation provides a measure of linear dependency between two data series. For PHYSEC, it was introduced for the analysis of coherence time behavior as well as for analyses of the performance of quantization schemes. Correlation values are between -1 and 1, where 1 refers to absolute correlation, 0 to no correlation, and -1 to perfect inverse correlation. Given a finite collection of N pairs (x_i, y_i) we use the following estimator:

$$\rho_{xy} = \frac{\sum_{i=0}^{N-1} (x_i - \bar{x})(y_i - \bar{y})}{\sqrt{\sum_{i=0}^{N-1} (x_i - \bar{x})^2} \sqrt{\sum_{i=0}^{N-1} (y_i - \bar{y})^2}}, \quad (3)$$

where $\bar{x} = \frac{1}{N} \sum_{j=0}^{N-1} x_j$ and $\bar{y} = \frac{1}{N} \sum_{j=0}^{N-1} y_j$ are the sample means of x_i and y_i, respectively.

2.4.2 Mutual Information

Mutual information is a general metric for the dependency between two random variables. It is a function of joint and marginal probability densities. We utilize a k-nearest neighbor estimator (kNNE) to estimate the mutual information, which is based on the idea and implementation of Kraskov et al. [22]. For a measure of the joint density, the estimator computes the distance between a tuple of samples and its kth-nearest neighbors. A similar approach is provided for the marginal densities. We use the mutual information estimator also to estimate the entropy $H(X) = I(X; X)$.

2.4.3 Secret-Key Rate

Based on the mutual information metric, a lower bound on the secret-key capacity of a channel in the source-model can be applied under the following conditions:

1. The joint probability density function is known a priori at all channel end-points.

2. Alice and Bob exchange messages over an authenticated, public channel with unlimited communication capacity, e.g., over the Internet.

3. Eve remains passive at all times.

Subsequently, the asymptotic bound is given by

$$C_{sk}(X;Y;Z) \geq I(X;Y) - \min[I(Y;Z), I(X;Z)],$$

since the process is stationary [1].

The lower bound $R_{sk}(X;Y;Z)$ is evaluated by estimations based on a finite number of measured samples and gives the secret-key capacity of a channel.

3. AWOUR - ADAPTIVE WORMHOLE BASED UNTRUSTED RELAY

In this section, we introduce the *Adaptive WOrmhole based Unstrusted Relay* (AWOUR) protocol for secret-key establishment. With this novel protocol, fresh key material (or joint entropy not shared with others) can be established between two authenticated devices over two-way, untrusted relayed, and delayed channels (TW-UR-DC). To do so, the mechanism utilizes CRKE and adaptive wormholes. Additionally, the scheme enforces a maximum delay which makes it interesting for distance bounding applications. The approach is particulary suitable for embedded devices without a secure clock or applications where the physical distance between both parties is important.

AWOUR is based on the time dependent amount of reciprocity between bidirectional measurements. The reciprocity can be estimated using the Pearson correlation. Furthermore, the minimum correlation required to perform CRKE can be determined [48]. In this context, the duration between channel measurements by the two communication partners is defined as the coherence time. As we show later in this section, the channel can be interpreted as a stationary random process with *adjustable coherence times*.

3.1 Protocol

The goal of the protocol is to continuously generate fresh secret keys, known only to A and B, in order to achieve *perfect forward secrecy* (PFS). However, A and B do not share the same physical channel. Instead, A communicates with W_1 and W_2 with B via a reciprocal channel. W_1 and W_2 are the two end-points of a wormhole, connected with each other over a delayed digital channel, see Figure 3. The protocol requires a previously distributed symmetric key k_0, known to only A and B. This key is assumed to be established during an earlier phase, e.g., when both devices were in proximity and executed a PHYSEC-based pairing protocol.

The general protocol works like this: Initially, A and B use k_0 and a public constant c_0 to generate a sequence of random power levels:

$$f_1(k_0, 0) = \{P_{A,0}, P_{A,1}, ...\} \quad \text{and}$$
$$f_1(k_0, c_0) = \{P_{B,0}, P_{B,1}, ...\} \quad \text{with} \quad c_0 \neq 0.$$

Care needs to be taken that these values are in the set $\mathbb{P} \subset Z$ of power levels supported by the participating devices, i.e., $P_{AW_1,i}, P_{BW_2,i} \in_R \mathbb{P}$.

For each pair $(P_{AW_1,i}, P_{BW_2,i})$ and $0 \leq i < N$ the parties A and B can execute a Ping-Pong protocol to extract shared entropy from the local channels between A and W_1 and W_2 and B. For this, A uses power level $P_{AW_1,i}$ and sends a Ping to W_1 over the reciprocal channel. W_1 measures $RSSI_{AW_1,i}$ and relays it (together with the message) to W_2 over the digital channel. W_2 uses power level $P_{W_2B,i} = f_2(RSSI_{AW_1,i})$ and sends the Ping to B where $RSSI_{W_2B,i}$ is measured. On the way back, B sends Pong to W_2 using $P_{BW_2,i}$. W_2 measures $RSSI_{BW_2,i}$ and relays it to W_1 with $P_{W_1A,i} = f_2(RSSI_{BW_2,i})$. Finally, the Pong reaches A, where $RSSI_{W_1A,i}$ is measured.

The previously introduced relationship $RSSI = P - L$ leads to the following equations:

$$RSSI_{AW_1,i} = P_{AW_1,i} - L_{1,i} \qquad (4)$$
$$RSSI_{BW_2,i} = P_{BW_2,i} - L_{2,i} \qquad (5)$$

We also have the following:

$$
\begin{aligned}
RSSI_{W_1A,i} &= P_{W_1A,i} - L'_{1,i} \\
&= f_2(RSSI_{BW_2,i}) - L'_{1,i} \\
RSSI_{W_2B,i} &= P_{W_2B,i} - L'_{2,i} \\
&= f_2(RSSI_{AW_1,i}) - L'_{2,i}
\end{aligned}
$$

If we define $\mathbb{R} \subset \mathbb{Z}$ as the range of RSSI values measurable by the participating devices, then we have

$$f_2 : \mathbb{R} \to \mathbb{P},$$

i.e., a mapping from RSSIs to power levels. We define $RSSI_{W_1,max}, RSSI_{W_2,max}$ as the maxima of the actually occuring RSSIs for W_1 and W_2 and $RSSI_{W_1,min}, RSSI_{W_2,min}$ as the respective minima, i.e.,

$$RSSI_{W_1,min} \leq RSSI_{AW_1,i} \leq RSSI_{W_1,max},$$
$$RSSI_{W_2,min} \leq RSSI_{BW_2,i} \leq RSSI_{W_2,max},$$

for all $0 \leq i < N$. Assuming that

$$|RSSI_{W_1,max} - RSSI_{W_1,min}| + 1 \leq |\mathbb{P}| \quad \text{and}$$
$$|RSSI_{W_2,max} - RSSI_{W_2,min}| + 1 \leq |\mathbb{P}|$$

holds (and $\mathbb{P}$ and $\mathbb{R}$ are consecutive), we can say that

$$P_{W_2,i} = f_2(RSSI_{AW_1,i}) \approx RSSI_{AW_1,i} + c_1 \quad \text{and}$$
$$P_{W_1,i} = f_2(RSSI_{BW_2,i}) \approx RSSI_{BW_2,i} + c_2$$

holds as well, where c_1 and c_2 are public constants. If A or B may move the constants may change over time.

Combining all this—and given that A knows $P_{BW_2,i}$ and B knows $P_{AW_1,i}$ due to shared knowledge of k_0—we find that due to

$$RSSI_{W_1A,i} - P_{BW_2,i} - c_2 = -L_{2,i} - L'_{1,i} \quad \text{and} \quad (6)$$
$$RSSI_{W_1B,i} - P_{AW_1,i} - c_1 = -L_{1,i} - L'_{2,i} \qquad (7)$$

both have access to a common entropy source not shared with others. A and B can then use this entropy source to establish keys with well-known CRKE protocols. We discuss the results of 10 different approaches from the literature in Section 4.5. To hold the pre-shared authenticity, the key k_0 could be used in the derivation of the final session key.

(a) Protocol view.

(b) Model view.

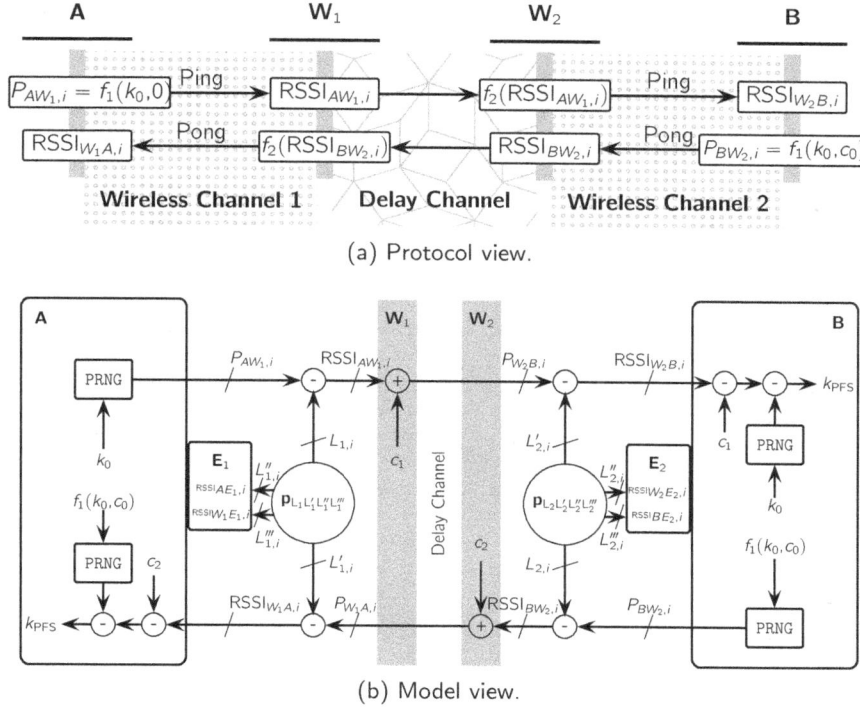

Figure 3: AWOUR protocol for secret key generation over a digital channel.

3.2 Security Analysis

The goal of an adversary Oskar O is to obtain either the key k_{PFS} directly or information about the path losses $L_{1,i} \approx L'_{1,i}$ and $L_{2,i} \approx L'_{2,i}$ such that he can reconstruct the key.

Denial of service attacks are not considered.

3.2.1 Untrusted Wormhole (UW)

The untrusted wormhole (UW) attacker O_{UW} has full access to $RSSI_{AW_1,i}$ (Eq. 4) and $RSSI_{BW_2,i}$ (Eq. 5). However, $P_{A,i}$ and $P_{B,i}$ are independent and unknown to O_{UW}, furthermore $L_{1,i}$ and $L_{2,i}$ are uncorrelated and unpredictable as well. Therefore, the attacker cannot extract the secret channel parameters $L_{1,i}$ and $L_{2,i}$ out of the measured values.

3.2.2 Passive Eavesdropper (PE)

Both bidirectionally communicating devices (here A and W_1 as well as W_2 and B) are using the channel-reciprocity to access the common entropy ($L_{1,i}$ and $L_{2,i}$). The attackers O_{PE_1} and O_{PE_2} are able to measure these values:

$$
\begin{aligned}
RSSI_{AE_1,i} &= P_{AW_1,i} - L''_{1,i}, \\
RSSI_{W_1E_1,i} &= P_{W_1A,i} - L'''_{1,i}, \\
RSSI_{BE_2,i} &= P_{BW_2,i} - L''_{1,i}, \\
RSSI_{W_2E_2,i} &= P_{W_2B,i} - L'''_{1,i}.
\end{aligned} \tag{8}
$$

where L'' and L''' are their observations (cf. Fig. 3). Because $L_{1,i}$ and $L_{2,i}$ are independent, their secret-key capacity can be estimated separately. Due to spatial diversity, complex environments, and random physical processes within the transmission ranges, we assume that the secret-key rate is larger than zero. Therefore, secret-key extraction is assumed to be possible. Furthermore, the attackers need

to perform the eavesdropping attack simultaneously at both locations.

Existing literature provides different analyses with varying results for passively eavesdropping on CRKE [32, 5, 6, 29, 20, 31, 46, 14, 29, 43]. Successful attacks—attacks with low secret-key rate due to observation—have in common that special-cases need to be created and a *sweet spot* position for attacker's antenna need to be found.

3.2.3 Known Key₀ (KK₀) Attacker

For the O_{KK_0} attacker we assume a rather strong attacker, who can extract the pre-shared secret k_0 before the re-keying/entropy collection protocol starts. Key extraction per se is a realistic attack because it is easy to dump the memory of low-end devices without secure storage. The attacker's goal is still to obtain the new secret key, instead of performing an impersonating attack. O_{KK_0} is of course able to reproduce the pseudo random variables $P_{AW_1,i}$ and $P_{BW_2,i}$. However, without further knowledge (e.g., $RSSI = P - L$) he is not able to guess either the key k_{PFS} or path losses, e.g., L_1 and L_2, because P and L are independent. Since the pre-shared trusted relationship between the nodes is broken at this point, attacks on the authenticity can be carried out by a MitM attack. However, the attack is different to the previous discussed, since the MitM exchanges different keys with each party and only relays information as required.

3.2.4 UW-KK₀ Attacker

Next we consider the attacker O_{UW-KK_0}, combining the capabilities of O_{KK_0} and O_{UW}. This is a rather strong attacker because he has to extract k_0 directly after its establishment and simultaneously gets access to a wormhole gateway before sufficient entropy was collected. Zenger et al. [48]

have shown that 128 bit keys, which are verified by a NIST on-line entropy estimation suite [7], can be established within 58 s, therefore this time window is very narrow.

With knowledge of k_0 the attacker can reproduce $P_{AW_1,i}$ and $P_{BW_2,i}$, then he measures $RSSI_{AW_1,i}, RSSI_{BW_2,i}$ and can thus extract $L_{1,i}$ and $L_{2,i}$ (see Eq. 4 and Eq. 5). Because the mutual information $I(L_1, L_1')$ and $I(L_2, L_2')$ is high per definition, the attacker can thus obtain the key k_{PFS} (see Eq. 6 and Eq. 7).

4. IMPLEMENTATION AND EVALUATION

In this section, we describe a use cases driven evaluation of adaptive wormholes. In Section 4.1, we present a test environment that corresponds to a real-world environment as much as possible in order to minimize the risk of environment-specific failures not being found during testing. Our contribution is really the prototyping of the adaptive wormhole system for the random source of interest (wireless channels), the evaluation of the random process involved, and the presentation of results for several CRKE-quantization schemes. Our prototype testbed is presented in Section 4.2. In Section 4.3 and Section 4.4, we describe properties of the random sources, and real-world restrictions of the testbed. In Section 4.5, we provide results of the AWOA as well as results and discussion for our proposed secret key generation system.

4.1 Use Case and Environment

We address an example application which requires PFS: sensor readings for industrial automation. Confidentiality of sensor readings is important because they contain information about the intellectual property of its operators. Furthermore, integrity of sensor data needs to be protected against manipulation by saboteurs.

We executed our experiments in a 400 qm production hall equipped with housing manufacturing tools and robots for metal processing. Three kinds of industrial sensors are already in use: electrical energy measuring sensors, air pressure sensors, and cooling lubricant consumption sensors. Sensor readings are currently transported via cable and used to control and improve manufacturing processes.

For several reasons, future sensors will provide their readings wirelessly. For example, wireless sensors have a unique advantage over traditional sensors. They enable the mounting at almost any position and drastically simplify installation. Upgrading existing manufacturing facilities with wired sensors is a hassle today: the installation requires drilling new holes and running wires across the facility, which is typically avoided at all costs. Furthermore, cable ducts require advanced fire protection and further qualifications, which, again, is expensive and takes time.

In the facility at hand, wireless communication systems are used for the communication between Programmable Logic Controllers (PLCs) of different machines and a PCL head control. Our testbed systems as well as the PLC communication system use the 2.4 GHz ISM band, however, the channels are not overlapping. Our testbed gateway A is positioned next to the head control gateway (cf. Figure 9 (g)). The head control gateway forwards sensor reading via wire to the head control. Six testbed nodes B_k are located at across the facility, close to actual sensors.

4.2 Testbed to measure Joint Stationarity

We perform bidirectional, narrow-band short-range channel measurements on 2.4 GHz (wavelength 12.5 cm) based on the IEEE 802.15.4 standard. We use Texas Intruments CC2530 modules to access the physical layer and combine them with Raspberry PI 2 devices, where the higher-levels of our measurement logic are implemented. The IEEE 802.15.4 standard is suited for energy-constrained device, such as mobile sensors and electronic keys. The CC2530 is a SoC designed for 20-years battery life and compatibility to network layer standards for resource-constrained devices: Zig-Bee, WirelessHART, and 6LoWPAN. WirelessHART, and 6LoWPAN are network standards which were introduced for industrial applications. The CC2530 is built around the 8051 processor with 8-bit data paths. Furthermore, it is equipped with a proprietary 5 mm × 12 mm *Meandered Inverted-F antenna* (MIFA) which provides good performance with a small form factor. The platform and antenna design is widely used in commercial products and suited for systems where ultra-low power consumption is required.

In order to establish common channel probing, the gateway W periodically sends data frames to receivers B_k and waits for acknowledgments. When receiving a probe, all devices extract RSSI values and, thus, can measure a channel-dependent sequence over time. We perform N reciprocal measurements v_i between W and nodes $B_0, B_1, ..B_5$, each of these producing a set of six tuples

$$v_i = \{ \quad (RSSI_{WB_0,i}, RSSI_{B_0W,i}),$$
$$(RSSI_{WB_1,i}, RSSI_{B_1W,i}), ...\}$$

where $RSSI_{WB_0,i}$ denotes value for the channel between W and B_0 on B_0's side, whereas $RSSI_{B_0W,i}$ denotes the result of the quasi-simultaneous measurement at W's end.

The CC2530 provides 7-bit RSSI values within the range of $-100\,dBm$ to $20\,dBm$ and, further, transmission power levels between $-25\,dBm$ and $3\,dBm$, both with $1\,dBm$ resolution. Note than only 16 different power levels are documented[2], however, we figured out that more transmission power levels are configurable by using intermediate values of the official transmission power register settings. IEEE 802.15.4 transceivers provide software and hardware acknowledgments, which are used in our setup for the PONGS. The round trip time (RTT) of the PING-PONGS is ≈3.5 ms using software and ≈1 ms for hardware acknowledgments. As we will see later, the RTT is crucial for achieving highly correlated measurements. However, through the use of software acknowledgment frames a reactive transmission power adoption is possible.

We obtain a complete set $\mathbf{v_i}$ for every sampling interval. The setup is able to adapt the interval between two PING-PONGS down to $T_s = 6.25ms$. However, we use a sampling interval of $T_s = 50ms$, if it is not otherwise specified. Further, the protocol ensures that gateway and end-device can probe the channel within a probing duration $T_p \approx$ 1 msec using hardware acknowledgments. The gateway and all six nodes extract the common randomness $RSSI_{WB_k,i}$ and $RSSI_{B_kW,i}$ from a time-varying channel. Since we aim for meaningful and reproducible results, we have to create an environment which provides joint stationarity to the random process. Therefore, with a distance of 10 cm to gateway's antenna, we deploy a curtain of 30×30 cm aluminum strips

---

[2]http://www.ti.com/tool/cc2531emk

114

that continuously rotates at ≈ 0.1 rotations per second, cf. Figure 9 (h).

However, continuous rotation itself inserts a deterministic component into the channel which is illustrated in Figure 4. It shows that the mutual information decays rapidly and vanishes after four samples, corresponding to approximately 400 ms. However, due to the continuously rotating curtain of aluminum strips, we discover strong stochastic dependencies after 96 samples, corresponding to approximately 9.6 seconds. To solve this problem, we randomize the direction and angle intervals of the rotating curtain. We applied five different speed levels as summarized in Table 2. Figure 4 shows that no strong stochastic dependencies are given anymore for random rotation.

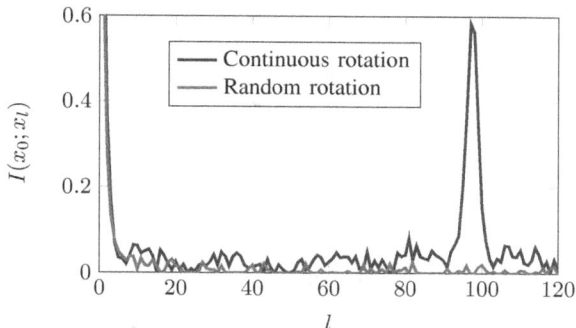

Figure 4: Self-dependence of RSSI values with respect to time delay. Setup is equipped with curtain of aluminum strips, rotating either continuously or randomly.

Next we analyzed six simultaneous measurements using different sensor positions. The results we present are representative for the different speed levels of the randomized curtain as well as for different transmission power levels. For the latter, the average receiving power of course changes. The probability density function of the received RSSI values are Rayleigh distributed. The mean value of the measurements differs due to the sensor testbed's positions. For this experiment, the randomized curtain runs at a mean angular-speed of 1.047 rad/s. We use transmission power levels of 3 dBm for the best case and -25 dBm for the worst case. The mutual information as well as the Pearson correlation ρ between channel measurements $RSSI_{WB_k,i}$ and $RSSI_{WB_l,i}$, with $k, l \in \{0, 1, ..5\}$ and $k \neq l$, of different sensor nodes are always low ($\rho_{max} = 0.17$), which demonstrates the channel's spatial diversity with almost independent measurement results. The mutual information and Pearson correlation between PING-PONGS ($RSSI_{WB_k,i}$ and $RSSI_{B_kW,i}$) is high due to channel reciprocity ($\rho_{max} = 0.94$). The secret-key rate is positive for both transmission power levels. While for the best case more than 3 Bit can be extracted securely, for the worst case it is only 0.8 Bit. Detailed results are summarized in Table 1.

4.3 Coherence Time of the Channel

To estimate the channel reciprocity behavior over time, we sampled the channel with the highest possible rate of our testbed, which is $r_s = T_s^{-1} = 160$ bidirectional packets per second. Then we calculated the Pearson correlation between the original and the delayed samples. We re-

Table 1: Worst case results of measurements using constant transmission power.

	$TX = 3$ dBm	$TX = -25$ dBm
$H(X) = H(RSSI_{WB_k})$	4.4096 bit	1.9844 bit
$H(Y) = H(RSSI_{B_kW})$	4.3943 bit	2.1897 bit
$H(Z) = H(RSSI_{WE})$	3.7004 bit	2.3337 bit
$I(X;Y)$	3.2876 bit	0.8543 bit
$I(X;Z)$	0.1169 bit	0.0397 bit
$I(Y;Z)$	0.1201 bit	0.0474 bit
$R_{sk}(X,Y,Z)$	3.1707 bit	0.8146 bit

peated the experiment for different speeds (on average) levels of the aluminum strips based random process generator. The correlation versus sampling delays is illustrated in Figure 5. It shows that the reciprocity steadily decreases as probing delays increase. The (de-)correlation courses (slope of the curves) clearly demonstrate the relationship between the coherence time and the chosen speed level. For example, we identified the two coherence times $t_{c,\rho=0.9}$ and $t_{c,\rho=0.8}$ for cross-correlations of $\rho(X, X_{delayed}) = 0.9$ and $\rho(X, X_{delayed}) = 0.8$, respectively. In Table 2, we summarize the coherence time results for all five speed levels. For

Table 2: Coherence time results.

Speed levels [rad/s]	$t_{c,\rho=0.9}$ [ms]	$t_{c,\rho=0.8}$ [ms]
$v_0 = 1.047$	21	62
$v_1 = 0.572$	42	142
$v_2 = 0.393$	61	156
$v_3 = 0.298$	142	294
$v_4 = 0.241$	177	397

$t_{c,\rho=0.8}$, the results show that a 62 ms probing delay in the 1.047 rad/s speed level is equivalent to a 142 ms probing delay in the 0.572 rad/s speed setup, as well as equivalent to a 397 ms probing delay in the 0.241 rad/s speed setup. Therefore, results confirm the intuition that the speed levels of the randomized generator influence coherence times of the resulting measurements.

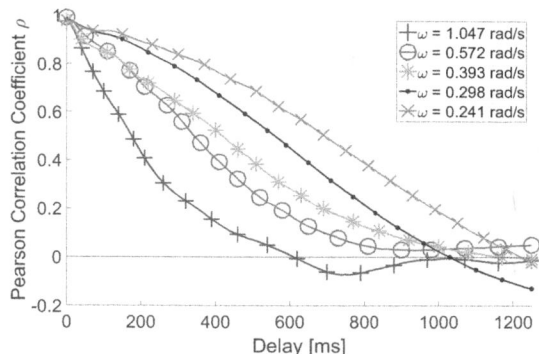

Figure 5: Correlation ρ versus sampling delay.

4.4 Adaptive Wormholes

Next, we analyze the performance of the AWOA in the testbed environment, where small-scale and large-scale fading effects as well as noise and interference occur. We performed different experiments to create and analyze adaptive wormholes across six sensor testbeds. Unfortunately, we were not able to sufficiently reduce the process time duration of the communication stacks between the first wormhole transceiver and the second one to make the system real-time capable. However, we describe a method how adaptive wormholes can still be evaluated for such applications.

For the performance analyses of the AWOUR protocol, we simulated the real-time adaptivity of the wormhole between both wormhole ends. The CC2530 testbeds provide 29 different power levels: $\{-25, ..., 3\}$ dBm. We generated six independent sensor-gateway series $\mathbf{v}_k^{TX_{S_k}, TX_{G_k}}$ applying all possible 29×29 transmission power combinations, with $k \in \{0, 1, ...5\}$. The results allow us to include potential non-linear effects of both channels, of the transmission unit, and of the receiver unit, into the evaluation. The transmission power of G_k is TX_{G_k} and for S_k it is TX_{S_k}. Therefore, the received RSSI values of the receiving party are based on the transmission power level of the transmitting party: $\mathbf{v}_k^{TX_{G_k}, TX_{S_k}} := \left(RSSI_{G_k S_k}^{TX_{G_k}}, RSSI_{S_k G_k}^{TX_{S_k}} \right)^T$. One sensor-gateway realization series can be represented by the matrix

$$\mathbf{v}_k^{TX_{G_k}, TX_{S_k}} = \begin{bmatrix} \mathbf{v}_k^{-25,-25} & \mathbf{v}_k^{-25,-24} & \cdots & \mathbf{v}_k^{-25,3} \\ \mathbf{v}_k^{-24,-25} & \ddots & & \mathbf{v}_k^{-24,3} \\ \vdots & & & \vdots \\ \mathbf{v}_k^{3,-25} & \mathbf{v}_k^{3,-24} & \cdots & \mathbf{v}_k^{3,3} \end{bmatrix}.$$

For statistical reasons, each measurement representation contains $2 \cdot 100\,000$ RSSI values and, therefore, each series contains 135.2 million RSSI values. We used combinations of these individual sensor-gateway channels in the testbed to simulate the PING-PONG protocols between A and W_1 and W_2 and B.

Next, we want to address the physical limitations of our testbed. Because the actual transmission power range is limited to 29 distinct levels, the result of Equation 2 needs to be within this range to perform optimally. However, this is not always given. For example, in the case of creating a wormhole between two devices the average transmission power would be:

$$\begin{aligned} P_{WA,i} &= P_{WB,i} + RSSI_{WB,i} - RSSI_{WA,i} \\ &= 0\,\text{dBm} - 45\,\text{dBm} - (-90\,\text{dBm}) \\ &= 45\,\text{dBm}. \end{aligned}$$

Unfortunately, this power level cannot be reached with our low-cost testbed, even though this is not a principal problem in itself (it can be done with special hardware).

The worst case scenario is given if one party would be very close to the wormhole, e.g., $RSSI_{WB,i} = 0\,\text{dBm}$, and the other far away, e.g., $RSSI_{WA,i} = -90\,\text{dBm}$. Now the required transmission power is $P_{WA,i} = -90\,\text{dBm}$, which is, again, out of the possible range for our testbed. For such scenarios the adaptive wormhole attacker or the AWOUR wormhole needs to be within a comfort distance. In Figure 6 such a comfort zone is shown. With regard to the IEEE 802.15.4 standard we estimate the link budget for receiver power (and the corresponding distances) for optimal wormhole performance. To do so, we fix the sum of transmitter output power, transmitter and receiver antenna gain, as well as transmitter and receiver losses (mismatching etc.) to an on average value of $-20\,\text{dBm}$. Then Friis equation for

path loss is applied $L_{FS} = 20\log(\frac{4\pi d}{\lambda})$, where L_{LS} is the free space path loss, λ is the wavelength of the carrier, and d is the distance between transmitter (victim) and receiver (attacker).

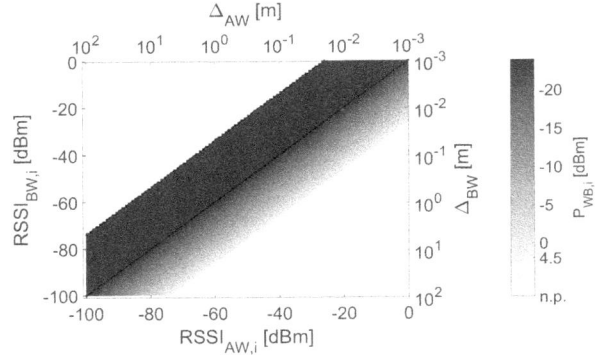

Figure 6: RSSI ranges of $RSSI_{BW,i}$ and $RSSI_{AW,i}$ to perform the AWOA optimally.

The linear relationship between transmission power and the corresponding RSSI value is of importance for the quality of the adaptive wormhole attacker and the AWOUR wormhole, as well. Figure 7 illustrates four different joint distributions of RSSI values of a $\mathbf{v}_{WB,i}$ measurement. The differences between the measurement sets are the transmission power levels we have used. The chosen power values are $\{-25, -12, -5, 3\}$ dBm. The resulting mean RSSI values are $\{-83, -73, -66, -56\}$ dBm. The variance of the error distribution over all measurements is 2.35. The figure also shows that the correlation is high, which is clearly visible by observing how little the results are spread out vertically within one set of measurements for a fixed power level.

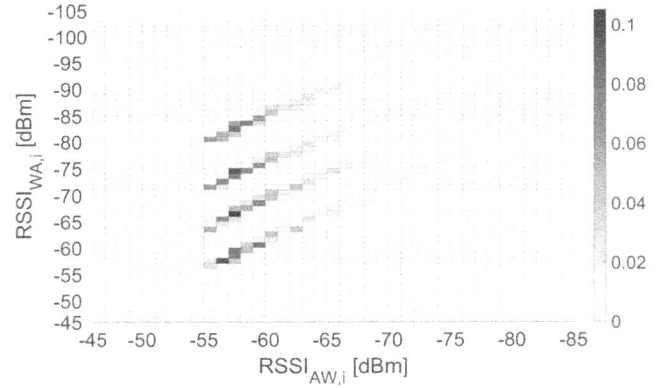

Figure 7: Joint distribution of $RSSI_{WA,i}$ and $RSSI_{AW,i}$ for four different reactively adopted transmission power levels of $P_{WA,i}$.

Next, we analyze the performance of recovering the channel profiles using single-side random transmission power. Therefore, we estimate the mutual information $I(X; Y)$ between $X = RSSI_{W_1A}^{TX=const.}$ and $Y = RSSI_{AW_1}^{TX=random} - P_{W_1A}^{random}$. The average $I(X; Y)$ for randomly chosen transmission power levels is 2.5906. Compared to the best for a constant power level we lose ≈ 0.7 bit of mutual information; and win ≈ 1.7 bit compared to the worst case results. To analyze the capabilities of an attacker to separate the components, e.g., $P_{AW_1,i}$ and $L''_{1,i}$ of the $Z = RSSI_{E,i}^{TX=random}$ he received, we estimate the mutual information $I(X;Z)$ and $I(Y;Z)$ as well as the secret-key rate $R_{sk}(X;Y;Z)$. With $I(X;Z) = 0.1983$ bit and $I(Y;Z) = 0.9544$ bit the secret-key rate is 2.3923 bit.

Finally, we analyzed the performance of the AWOA. Compared to our previous analyses the second channel L_2 added an additional error due to non-perfect reciprocity. The results show that the correlation $\rho(RSSI_{W_1A,i}, RSSI_{W_2B,i})$ (using the wormhole) is 0.91 and, therefore, only slightly lower than the correlation of $\rho(RSSI_{W_2B,i}, RSSI_{BW_2,i})$ (using the reciprocal channel measurements by direct link), which is 0.94. The mutual information between A and B is 1.8678 bit. Compared to the results of measurements using single-side, random transmission power reduces the mutual information by 0.7228 bit. Assuming a passive eavesdropper trying to attack the key generated using the adaptive wormhole, the scheme achieves a secret-key rate of R_{sk} of 1.3452 bit. This is 1.0471 bit less than using single-side random transmission powers.

For the performance evaluation of the AWOUR protocol we use two independent measurement series of $\mathbf{v}_{G_k,S_k,i}^{TX1,TX2}$ for wireless communication channels. The Pearson correlation between $RSSI_{W_1A,i}^{TX=adap.}$ and $RSSI_{W_2B,i}^{TX=adap.}$ is 0.8. The average entropy is $H(RSSI_{W_1A}^{TX=adap.}) = 4$. The mutual information of the shared key material is $I(-L_1-L'_2; -L'_1-L_2) = 1.015$. By introducing a passive eavesdropper into one of both channel, we achieve a secret-key rate of $R_{sk} = 0.4894$. The results show that the AWOUR protocol is capable to perform secret-key establishment using narrowband multipath fading channel.

Figure 8 shows exemplary the *probability density function* (PDF) of the overall measured RSSI values (dotted line). This PDF is composed out of several PDFs. These PDFs correspond to six different transmission power levels, which is only an exemplarly subset. With this information the corresponding entropy (or uncertainty of an O_{UW} attacker) can be calculated. Determining the amount of entropy and the corresponding secrecy rate is left for future work.

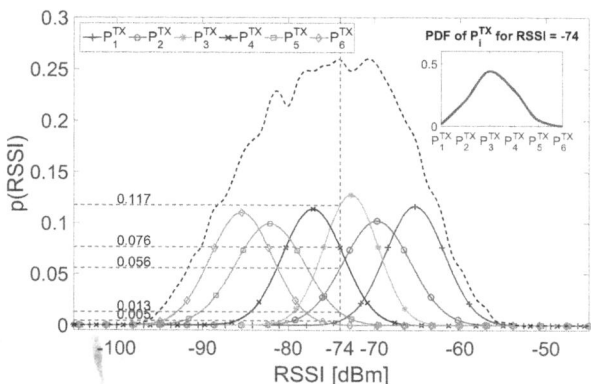

Figure 8: Probability density functions of measured RSSI values per transmission power level.

4.5 Good News and Bad News

In this section, we first utilize the adaptive wormhole mechanism to attack PHYSEC protocols and then show results of our AWOUR protocol using CRKE. We start attacking wormhole detection mechanisms suggested in [23] and CRKE systems. In the latter case, A and B want to agree on a key which is established by using correlated channel profiles. To do so, the first step is to quantize the channel profiles. Then error correction is applied, and later on privacy amplification (hashing). The literature provides a large number of proposals for quantization schemes. We implemented 10 different quantization schemes from the literature, which were recently introduced for CRKE schemes. We additionally implemented three straight forward quantization schemes, using mean, median, and Lloyd-Max thresholds. We analyzed the performance using reciprocal measurements with constant transmission power and compare these with the resulting channel measurements of attacked adaptive wormhole end devices.

The results of the analyses of the quantization schemes are summarized in Table 3. Generally CRKE systems are designed to handle a worst case BER[3] by applying error correction mechanism. Depending on the correction (or detection) capability the maximum BER is given. For example if the code is capable to correct 0.1 bit disagreement the schemes of Tope et al. [37], Aono et al. [5], Mathur et al. [29], Jana et al. [20] (single-bit version), Hamida et al. [14], Wallace et al. [40], and Ambekar et al. [3] are all fully attackable by adaptive wormholes.

Note that Jain et al. [19] applied in his wormhole detection protocol the quantization scheme of Azimi et al. [6] for deriving a bit sequence. The authors utilized classical CRKE for channel-reciprocity verification. Krentz et al.'s [23] detection scheme requires pre-shared secrets for the exchange of measured channel profiles. Then the Pearson correlation coefficient is calculated and a judgement is made. The thresholds for judgement is 0.93. The correlation results demonstrate that the AWOA achieves cross-correlations between 0.86 and 0.96. Therefore, the scheme in [23] is successfully attackable. We achieve false-negative judgment of 22.3%. Jain et al. [19] propose that a BER of ≤ 0.3 concludes the absence of an adversary. The quantization scheme used here gives a BER of 0.0523 with the constant transmission power and a BER of 0.1310 for the adaptive wormhole. Therefore, we achieve false-negative judgement of 100%. Note, the wormhole attack can be easily prevented by increasing the RTT. Therefore, the correlation, mutual information, and efficiency of the system decreases.

The CRKE results using the AWOUR protocol are summarized in Table 3. Due to the low correlation of 0.8 between $-L_1-L'_2$ and $-L'_1-L_2$ not all quantization schemes are suitable. Four scheme which are designed to be extremely robust provide BERs lower than 0.05. Those schemes are the ones of Aono et al. [5], Mathur et al. [29], Jana et al. [20], and Ambekar et al. [3].

---

[3]The *bit error rate* (BER) indicates the percentage of bits that are in disagreement between the initial key material of two parties. BER is evaluated after quantization by the relation: $BDR = \frac{b_e}{b}$ where, b_e is the number of bits in the sequence that disagree and b is the length of the initial key.

Table 3: BER of quantization schemes using Reciprocal Channel (RC) profiles, profiles separated by an AWOA and profiles extracted using AWOUR.

Name	BER_{RC}	BER_{AWOA}	BER_{AWOUR}
Mean th.	0.0482	0.1174	0.1836
Median th.	0.0878	0.2133	0.2427
Lloyd-Max	0.0788	0.1504	0.2883
Tope et al. [37]	0.0019	0.0437	0.1590
Aono et al. [5]	0.0001	0.0046	0.0156
Azimi et al. [6]	**0.0523**	**0.1310**	**0.2258**
Mathur et al. [29]	0.0	0.0076	0.0037
ASBG [20]	0.0	0.0156	0.0481
ASBG-MB [20]	0.0564	0.1203	0.2157
Hamida et al. [14]	0.0920	0.0937	0.4550
Wallace et al. [40]	0.0229	0.0978	0.1967
Patwari et al. [31]	0.0984	0.2335	0.2567
Ambekar et al. [3]	0.0001	0.0033	0.0008

5. RELATED WORK

5.1 Wormholes

Wormholes are realized in different ways. A hidden wormhole is implemented by two nodes which do not participate in the attacked networks. They relay the unchanged traffic between nodes (or networks) which were formerly unreachable. Participating [21] or exposed [23] wormholes are implemented between two legitimate network participants which relay traffic through an out-of-band link.

An established wormhole can be the basis for a number of different other attacks. Tsao et al. [39] discussed sinkhole where the attacker pretends to provide a high-quality route to a communication party and in fact either is not able to forward or knowingly drops all incoming data. As well, Tsao et al. proposed the wormhole as a potential means for selective forwarding attack where the attacker forwards only a subset of the incoming data to all nodes or only forwards incoming data to a subset of all nodes. A wormhole attacker is also able to manipulate selective packages if no further security measures such as encryption and/or authentication is applied. Using wormholes with short lifetime, an attacker is able to run rushing attacks [18] against routing protocols.

To detect or prevent wormholes, multiple schemes were introduced in the past [34, 15, 21, 19, 24]. These techniques can be categorized into three major aspects: (1) Topology, round-trip-time or routing based, (2) hardware-based, and (3) channel(-reciprocity) based countermeasures. For exposed wormholes, Khan et al. [21] introduced a Merkle-tree based wormhole prevention method. Other detection mechanisms which rely on detecting topology or routing anomalies are found in [34, 15]. However, they are either vulnerable to selective forwarding or short wormholes [24]. Chen et al. [11] proposed an approach to detect wormholes using channel measurements and delays. However, this approach may be vulnerable to a low-latency wormhole, e.g., realized by a fast out-of-band connection. Jain et. al [19] proposed a detection mechanism which is based on the reciprocity of RSSI measurements between nodes. As this approach does have issues with false positives and negatives [24], Krentz et al. proposed a scheme called "Secure Channel REciprocity-based WormholE Detection (SCREWED)"

which utilizes channel hopping. Both schemes are able to prevent or detect exposed wormholes but are vulnerable to adaptive wormholes.

5.2 Untrusted Relays

Most prior work on key generation with relaying channels considered only trusted relays. However, end-nodes (or their data) often have higher levels of security clearance than the infrastructure, e.g., gateways, routers, and relays. Therefore, the generation of secret keys using untrusted relays is required. He et al. [16] introduced the first PHYSEC key establishment scheme using untrusted relays. To do so, the authors introduced a helper that performs cooperative jamming to establish a secret-key rate larger zero. Unfortunately, jamming capabilities are not provided by today's transceiver modules and, therefore, not considered.

A secret key generation scheme with multiple untrusted relays has been proposed by Lai et al. [25]. The scheme broadcasts the result of the XOR of two keys k_{AR} and k_{RB}, which are generated based on the channels between a relay and two nodes. Both are than able to derive a shared secret key by XORing the broadcast key with their own key. However, to be untrusted the scheme can only work with multiple non-colluding relays, and therefore cannot work with either a single relay or multiple colluding relays.

Thai et al. [35, 36] proposed a novel scheme for generating a secret key between two legitimate nodes and the help of several untrusted relays, all equipped with multiple antennas. The numbers of antennas at the legitimate node should be at least 4, which is not achievable with today's low-resource sensor platforms.

Other approaches were introduced in theory and, further, have serious drawbacks. Our scheme in contrast works with a single untrusted relay (like a central gateway) and low-end sensor devices (such as single-antenna SoC solutions). Furthermore, our proposed scheme is thoroughly evaluated through both theoretical and experimental studies.

6. CONCLUSIONS

In this paper, we demonstrated that AWOAs are real-world threats. We demonstrated on 12 (10 CRKE, 2 AWOA detection) different PHYSEC protocols that RSSI-based systems are vulnerable to AWOAs. The attacks allow the attacker to learn the key or to perform attacks with hidden wormholes. Given the generality of the relay attack, it is likely that CRKE systems based on similar designs, e.g., using amplitude values of CIR or CTF, are also vulnerable to the same attack. We proposed a simple countermeasure that minimizes the risk of AWOAs.

We implemented a testbed based on the IEEE802.15.4 standard, which resembles the real-time capabilities of future 5G network with its short acknowledgement frames (RTT of 1 ms) and narrow bandwidth. We introduced the idea of generating artificial random small-scale fading to ensure that the channel profiles without mean are stationary random processes. We analysed critical coherence time characteristics in order to better quantify the systems' behavior.

Further, the AWOUR protocol for low-end wireless platforms is presented. We demonstrate that fresh key material can be extracted securely over a single untrusted relay. Using state-of-the-art mutual information estimation, we achieve secret-key rates of 0.5 bits per bidirectional communication step. Due to the precise adjustment of the reciprocal channel (and the corresponding random process), the ability to mutually derive key material implies distance bounding. This concept is novel and might have a larger impact in related areas, e.g., remote key-less entry systems or access control in general.

Security and connectivity of low-end platforms are basic requirements for the IoT. The paradigm shift from IoT to the Tactile IoT (TIoT) introduces further constraints such as low-latency communication which make efficient security solutions imperative. We believe that PHYSEC can open up new ways of realizing secure and cheap human tactile and visual feedback control systems.

Future work on this topic may include carrying out more measurements to recheck completeness of the coherence time results. Furthermore, a more formal model description of the introduced protocol is another connecting factor for the future.

7. ACKNOWLEDGMENTS

The authors would like to thank Prof. Dr.-Ing. Kreimeier and Benjamin Fleczok for allowing us to carry out the measurement in their production hall. Many thanks to Jürgen Förster for helping us with the graphics. The authors would also like to thank the anonymous reviewers for the thorough reviews and helpful suggestions.

8. REFERENCES

[1] R. Ahlswede et al. Common randomness in information theory and cryptography. I. Secret sharing. *IEEE_J_IT*, 1993.

[2] S. T. Ali et al. Zero reconciliation secret key generation for body-worn health monitoring devices. In *Conference on Security and Privacy in Wireless and Mobile Networks*, 2012.

[3] A. Ambekar et al. Improving channel reciprocity for effective key management systems. In *Signals, Systems, and Electronics*, 2012.

[4] J. G. Andrews et al. What will 5g be? *IEEE Journal on Selected Areas in Communications*, 2014.

[5] T. Aono et al. Wireless secret key generation exploiting reactance-domain scalar response of multipath fading channels. *Antennas and Propagation*, 2005.

[6] B. Azimi-Sadjadi et al. Robust key generation from signal envelopes in wireless networks. In *Conference on Computer and Communications Security*, 2007.

[7] E. Barker et al. Recommendation for the entropy sources used for random bit generation. *Draft NIST Special Publication*, 2012.

[8] E. Biglieri et al. *MIMO Wireless Communications*. 2010.

[9] M. Bloch et al. *Physical-Layer Security - From Information Theory to Security Engineering*. 2011.

[10] C. Chen et al. Secret key establishment using temporally and spatially correlated wireless channel coefficients. *Mobile Computing*, 2011.

[11] H. Chen et al. On providing wormhole-attack-resistant localization using conflicting sets. *Wireless Communications and Mobile Computing*, 2015.

[12] S. Eberz et al. A practical man-in-the-middle attack on signal-based key generation protocols. In *European Symposium on Research in Computer Security*, 2012.

[13] G. Fettweis. The tactile internet: Applications and challenges. *Vehicular Technology Magazine, IEEE*, 2014.

[14] S. T. B. Hamida et al. An adaptive quantization algorithm for secret key generation using radio channel measurements. In *Conference on New Technologies, Mobility and Security*, 2009.

[15] T. Hayajneh et al. Secure neighborhood creation in wireless ad hoc networks using hop count discrepancies. *MONET*, 2012.

[16] X. He et al. Two-hop secure communication using an untrusted relay: A case for cooperative jamming. In *Global Communications Conference*, 2008.

[17] Y. Hu et al. Wormhole attacks in wireless networks. *Selected Areas in Communications, IEEE*, 2006.

[18] Y.-C. Hu et al. Rushing Attacks and Defense in Wireless Ad Hoc Network Routing Protocols. In *Workshop on Wireless Security*, 2003.

[19] S. Jain et al. Wormhole detection using channel characteristics. In *International Conference on Communications, IEEE*, 2012.

[20] S. Jana et al. On the effectiveness of secret key extraction from wireless signal strength in real environments. In *Conference on Mobile Computing and Networking*, 2009.

[21] F. I. Khan et al. Wormhole attack prevention mechanism for RPL based LLN network. In *Ubiquitous and Future Networks*, 2013.

[22] A. Kraskov et al. Estimating mutual information. *Phys. Rev. E*, 2004.

[23] K. Krentz et al. 6lowpan security: Avoiding hidden wormholes using channel reciprocity. In *Workshop on Trustworthy Embedded Devices*, 2014.

[24] K. Krentz and G. Wunder. 6lowpan security: Avoiding hidden wormholes using channel reciprocity. In *Trustworthy Embedded Devices, TrustED*, 2014.

[25] L. Lai et al. Cooperative key generation in wireless networks. *IEEE Journal on Selected Areas in Communications*, 2012.

[26] Z. Li et al. Securing wireless systems via lower layer enforcements. In *Workshop on Wireless security*, 2006.

[27] H. Liu et al. Collaborative secret key extraction leveraging received signal strength in mobile wireless networks. In *IEEE INFOCOM*, 2012.

[28] M. Madiseh et al. Applying Beamforming to Address Temporal Correlation in Wireless Channel Characterization-Based Secret Key Generation. *IEEE_J_IFS*, 2012.

[29] S. Mathur et al. Radio-telepathy: extracting a secret key from an unauthenticated wireless channel. In *Conference on Mobile Computing and Networking*, 2008.

[30] M. McGuire et al. Bounds on secret key rates in fading channels under practical channel estimation schemes. In *International Conference on Communications, IEEE*, 2014.

[31] N. Patwari et al. High-rate uncorrelated bit extraction for shared secret key generation from channel measurements. *IEEE Trans. Mob. Comput.*, 2010.

[32] A. Pierrot et al. Practical limitations of secret-key generation in narrowband wireless environments. *arXiv preprint arXiv:1312.3304*, 2014.

[33] G. S. Smith. A direct derivation of a single-antenna reciprocity relation for the time domain. *Antennas and Propagation*, 2004.

[34] S. Song et al. Statistical wormhole detection for mobile sensor networks. In *ICUFN*, 2012.

[35] C. D. T. Thai et al. Physical-layer secret key generation with untrusted relays. In *IEEE GLOBECOM Workshops*, 2014.

[36] C. D. T. Thai et al. Physical-layer secret key generation with colluding untrusted relays. *Wireless Communications*, 2016.

[37] M. A. Tope et al. Unconditionally secure communications over fading channels. In *Military Communications Conference*, 2001.

[38] W. Trappe et al. Low-energy security: Limits and opportunities in the internet of things. *IEEE Security & Privacy*, 2015.

[39] T. Tsao et al. A Security Threat Analysis for the Routing Protocol for Low-Power and Lossy Networks (RPLs). Technical report, IETF, 2015.

[40] J. W. Wallace et al. Automatic secret keys from reciprocal MIMO wireless channels: measurement and analysis. *Information Forensics and Security*, 2010.

[41] Q. Wang et al. Fast and scalable secret key generation exploiting channel phase randomness in wireless networks. In *Conference on Computer Communications*, 2011.

[42] J. WC Jr. Microwave mobile communications, 1974.

[43] M. Wilhelm et al. Secret keys from entangled sensor motes: implementation and analysis. In *Conference on Wireless Network Security*, 2010.

[44] R. Wilson et al. Channel Identification: Secret Sharing Using Reciprocity in Ultrawideband Channels. *IEEE_J_IFS*, 2007.

[45] C. Ye et al. Information-theoretically secret key generation for fading wireless channels. *Information Forensics and Security*, 2010.

[46] C. T. Zenger et al. A novel key generating architecture for wireless low-resource devices. In *Workshop on Secure Internet of Things*, 2014.

[47] C. T. Zenger et al. Exploiting the physical environment for securing the internet of things. In *New Security Paradigms Workshop*, 2015.

[48] C. T. Zenger et al. On-line entropy estimation for secure information reconciliation. In *Workshop on Wireless Communication Security at the Physical Layer*, 2015.

[49] C. T. Zenger et al. Preventing Relay Attacks and Providing Perfect Forward Secrecy using PHYSEC on 8-bit µC. In *IEEE International Conference on Communications (ICC), Kuala Lumpur, Malaysia*, 2016.

[50] J. Zhang et al. Mobility assisted secret key generation using wireless link signatures. In *Conference on Computer Communications*, 2010.

9. APPENDIX

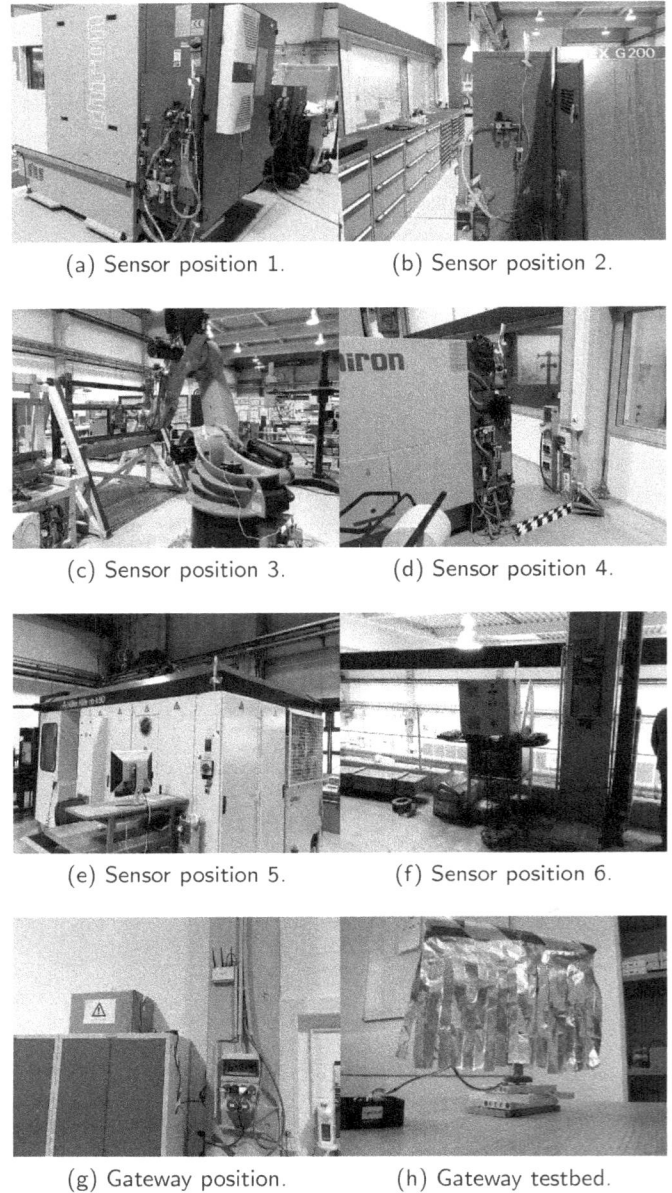

(a) Sensor position 1. (b) Sensor position 2.

(c) Sensor position 3. (d) Sensor position 4.

(e) Sensor position 5. (f) Sensor position 6.

(g) Gateway position. (h) Gateway testbed.

Figure 9: The testbeds consisting of six sensors and gateways as well as the aluminum strips based 'random process' generator.

A Prover-Anonymous and Terrorist-Fraud Resistant Distance-Bounding Protocol[*]

Xavier Bultel
University Clermont Auvergne
xavier.bultel@udamail.fr

Sébastien Gambs
UQAM, Montréal
gambs.sebastien@uqam.ca

David Gérault
University Clermont Auvergne
david.gerault@udamail.fr

Pascal Lafourcade
University Clermont Auvergne
pascal.lafourcade@udamail.fr

Cristina Onete
INSA/IRISA Rennes
cristina.onete@gmail.com

Jean-Marc Robert
ÉTS, Montréal
jean-marc.robert@etsmtl.ca

ABSTRACT

Contactless communications have become omnipresent in our daily lives, from simple access cards to electronic passports. Such systems are particularly vulnerable to *relay attacks*, in which an adversary relays the messages from a prover to a verifier. Distance-bounding protocols were introduced to counter such attacks. Lately, there has been a very active research trend on improving the security of these protocols, but also on ensuring strong privacy properties with respect to active adversaries and malicious verifiers.

In particular, a difficult threat to address is the *terrorist fraud*, in which a far-away prover cooperates with a nearby accomplice to fool a verifier. The usual defence against this attack is to make it impossible for the accomplice to succeed unless the prover provides him with enough information to recover his secret key and impersonate him later on. However, the mere existence of a long-term secret key is problematic with respect to privacy.

In this paper, we propose a *novel approach* in which the prover who wants to help his accomplice to authenticate does not leak his secret key but a reusable session key along with a group signature on it. This allows the adversary to impersonate him even without knowing his signature key. Based on this approach, we give the first distance-bounding protocol, called SPADE, integrating anonymity, revocability and provable resistance to standard threat models.

1. INTRODUCTION

With the accelerating convergence of our digital identities on our ubiquitous *smartphones*, developing secure authentication protocols is more important than ever. As an example, a virtual wallet including various personal credentials

[*]This work was partially supported by the "Digital trust" Chair from the University of Auvergne Foundation, by NSERC Discovery and Accelerator Supplement grants, and by the European Union through the European Regional Development Fund.

can be used for everyday life applications such as public transport, logistics and contactless-payment systems. Another crucial notion is to protect the privacy of the users against external eavesdroppers and legitimate entities. The canonical application for this concept is the contactless pass used for accessing public transport systems. In this context, privacy is a fundamental property in order for users to trust the system deployed.

Authentication protocols are among the most fundamental cryptographic primitives of the digital world. They enable an entity, called a *verifier*, to check the legitimacy of users (called *provers*) before giving access to a resource. The provers are assumed to possess cryptographic devices storing their secret credentials. To be secure, an authentication protocol must guarantee two properties: *correctness* and *soundness*. Correctness requires that a legitimate prover is always authenticated, while soundness demands that all illegitimate ones should be rejected by the verifier. Authentication protocols are often prone to *relay attacks* [6, 12], in which an adversary relays to the verifier the responses of a legitimate prover. This attack bypasses standard countermeasures such as encryption or digital signatures. Indeed, since the adversary forwards legitimate messages between the verifier and a legitimate prover, the verifier ends up authenticating the adversary.

Distance bounding (DB) was introduced by Brands and Chaum [8] to thwart relay attacks by allowing the verifier to estimate an upper bound on the distance between him and the prover using several *time-critical* challenge-response rounds. Assuming that trust requires physical proximity, if a prover is *outside* the close vicinity of the verifier, he should be rejected. Thus, in DB protocols, verifiers are equipped with a clock, and they measure the time between sending a challenge and receiving the corresponding response from the prover. Once the different *Round Trip Times* (RTTs) for all challenge-response rounds are measured, the verifier compares these values to a pre-existing bound t_{max} and accepts the prover if and only if: (a) the responses are correct and (b) all RTT values are below the threshold t_{max}.

To be secure, a DB protocol must resist at least to: (1) *Mafia fraud* (MF), (2) *Distance fraud* (DF) and (3) *Impersonation fraud* (IF). MF resistance requires that no illegitimate *Man-in-the-Middle* (MiM) adversary can authenticate to the verifier, even in the presence of a legitimate prover with whom he can interact. DF resistance demands that no legitimate but malicious prover, located outside the verifier's trusted vicinity, should be able to authenticate. A variant of this attack, in which a distant malicious prover uses an honest prover located in the verifier's vicinity to authenticate, is called *Distance Hijacking* (DH) [11]. Finally, the IF resistance addresses the simple situation in which the malicious adversary tries to fool the verifier without any help.

Another important threat against DB protocols is the *Terrorist Fraud* (TF), in which a malicious yet legitimate prover helps a cooperative MiM accomplice to authenticate. However, one of the assumptions is that the prover wants to retain control of his secret credentials. Thus, he is willing to help his accomplice, but without giving him a better chance to authenticate in latter attempts. Since this attack assumes that the prover *knows* his credentials, it could be prevented straightforwardly if a tamper-proof component is used to prevent the prover from learning this information. Unfortunately, relying only on tamperproofness is generally not sufficient [23]. In most payment systems relying on secure smartcards, back-end fraud detection mechanisms have been deployed to prevent any massive frauds. Thus, it is preferable to consider the most pessimistic scenario in which the adversaries are assumed to be given a *white-box* access to the secret keys. In this context, the usual countermeasure against TF is to force the prover to leak parts of his long-term key if he wants to give his accomplice a fair chance to succeed.

Since DB protocols were defined for RFID tags and readers, they use shared symmetric keys between provers and the verifier (*i.e.*, the prover is authenticated using his shared secret with the verifier). However, the seminal DB protocol of Brands and Chaum [8] was based on public-key cryptography. Improvements in RFID architectures as well as the emergence of NFC smartphones have motivated recent research in DB to consider public-key cryptography [16, 19, 27].

A recent concern in DB protocols is *privacy*. One of the first schemes to address this concept is the Swiss-Knife protocol [20]. However, its guarantee holds only if secret keys can never be leaked, and only with respect to an external eavesdropper but not against a legitimate verifier. Currently, no precise definition of this property is given and no formalized proof exists in the literature. Furthermore, as noted by Fischlin and Onete [14], the original protocol presents a flaw, since the same secret key is used both as input to pseudo-random function and to a function XORing it with one of the time-critical response strings.

Introducing privacy with respect to the verifier raises the question of the revocability of a prover by the registration authority. Hence, before the authentication succeeds, the verifier should check whether this prover has been revoked. Indeed, if this property is not taken into account, the corruption of a prover makes the whole system vulnerable, as there is no way to distinguish whether a prover uses stolen credentials or legitimate ones. In this paper, corrupting a user simply means that the adversary is able to obtain his secret keys. Building an anonymous protocol without any revocation mechanism is trivial: the same secret key is given to all provers who become indistinguishable. However in this case, one corruption forces the update of the keys of all users, which makes this solution impractical. Our aim is to fill this gap by proposing a provably TF-resistant, prover-anonymous, secure and revocable DB protocol.

A typical scenario for our secure and anonymous DB protocol can be described as follows. In a public transport system, users relying on their NFC-enabled phones may have access to buses or subway stations if they can properly authenticate. However, users must protect their identity with respect to legitimate verifiers trying to profile them. In such a context, a TF attack is simply a user ready to lend illegally his monthly pass to someone for a single trip while he is not using it. However, this user would not accept that his accomplice can impersonate him later at will to avoid being caught (if the same nonce N_p is used successfully numerous times). Thus, the presence of a backdoor in the verifiers can play in important role to deter such frauds. In an in-depth security approach, tamper-proof protection is not sufficient in this case. Indeed, it may protect the long term private key, but it would be useless to protect the two strings used in the time-critical phase implemented directly in the network access card for efficiency. The prover should answer the challenges as fast as possible, or otherwise the verifier can estimate that the prover is further than he really is. These strings are critical for the TF attacks and can therefore be easily obtained.

Another scenario could be the following one. Consider a research center, in which authorized personnel use experimental vehicles for both private and work-related purposes. In particular, they may use the vehicles *and* open the facility doors with a contactless (near-field) smartphone application. In this context, the following properties must be guaranteed. First, neither the vehicles, nor the buildings, must be accessible to someone who is not affiliated with the research center. Second, a vehicle or a building should only be unlocked by someone which is in its close proximity, as unlocking it remotely may leave the doors open to intruders. Next, the personnel should be held responsible if they unlock a facility door or a car that results in an unauthorized intrusion causing theft or damage. Finally, since the vehicles can also be used for personal purposes, their usage by someone should not be traceable ito respect his privacy. The protocol $SPADE$ fulfils all these requirements: namely MF and impersonation resistance, DF resistance, TF resistance and revocable anonymity.

Contributions. We propose SPADE (for *Secure Prover Anonymous Distance-bounding Exchange*), the first protocol to achieve prover-anonymity with respect to the strongest possible adversaries, provable TF resistance, and revocability of corrupted provers. A *wide-strong adversary* is the strongest that one can imagine. He can actively cheat during the protocol, corrupt entities and learn the result of the authentication.

For ensuring anonymity, our construction relies on the concept of group signatures [5], which enables a member of a group to sign anonymously on behalf of the group. New members can dynamically join the group or be revoked. This is managed by a central registration authority, which has to be involved in any signature verification. In case of dispute, a trusted authority can retrieve the identity of a signer.

In addition to privacy, our main contribution is to ensure TF resistance. Most TF-resistant DB protocols achieve this property by binding the responses of the time-critical phases to a long-term secret key. This forces the provers to reveal to their MiM accomplices some bits of their secret key to authenticate, thus allowing their accomplice to impersonate a prover in latter runs of the protocol. Our approach represents a radical change in the sense that it is based on a session key, chosen by a legitimate prover and signed with his group signature key, before being encrypted. To prevent replay attacks, the responses to the time-critical phases depend on a verifier-specific nonce. However, given a value that is reasonably close to the prover's session key, the adversary can replay the prover's signature to be authenticated on his behalf. The presence of a *backdoor*, which can be used to retrieve the information needed to impersonate a prover, should deter any prover to help potential accomplices. This was originally suggested by Fischlin and Onete [15].

Related Work. In a recent survey, Brelurut, Gérault and Lafourcade reviewed 42 DB protocols (ranging from 1993 up to 2015) [9]. Only nine of them are not broken yet, and none of them achieves at the same time provable TF resistance, prover anonymity and revocability. Lately, Gambs, Onete and Robert [16] introduced the concept of privacy against honest-but-curious and malicious verifiers that aim at profiling legitimate provers. They proposed a construction relying on the protocol proposed in [19], but in which the provers are managed as a group. Although they addressed MF, DF and IF, they did not tackle TF resistance, which is not easily compatible with privacy.

Recently, Vaudenay [28] introduced a generic construction to transform a DB protocol based on a symmetric-key scheme into one based on a public-key cryptography. His construction yields provable MF, DF and DH resistance against the strongest possible adversaries, but not TF resistance. Moreover, privacy is only limited to a MiM adversary and not with respect to a malicious verifier.

Ahmadi and Safavi-Naini [1] have proposed a privacy-preserving DB protocol that is claimed to be TF-resistant. Their protocol fixes the vulnerabilities [3] of the DBPK-log protocol [10], and provides prover anonymity. A new prover joining the system picks a secret key and obtains its blind signature from the registration authority. This signature is then used as a membership certificate. During a session of the DB protocol, the prover never reveals his secret key nor his certificate. Instead, he uses a zero-knowledge proof of knowledge to prove that he knows a valid certificate, and that its value was used to generate his responses during the protocol execution. Unfortunately, the security proofs are not yet available. Moreover, the mechanism used to ensure anonymity does not allow user revocation, which is a major limitation of this solution.

Three frameworks for analyzing the security of DB protocols have been published: Avoine, Ali Bingöl, Kardaş, Lauradoux and Martin [2], Dürholz, Fischlin, Kasper and Onete [13], and Boureanu, Mitrokotsa and Vaudenay [7]. In our analysis, the DFKO framework [13] and the compatible game-based TF resistance [15] are used. Though this framework is for a single prover and a single verifier, it can be extended to multiple provers and to capture DH attacks. Finally, the prover anonymity notion defined in [16] is used, which is compatible with the DFKO framework.

Outline. In Section 2, we review the notions necessary to understand our work such as the adversary models for DB protocols as well as the cryptographic primitives used in our protocol. Afterwards in Section 3, we describe SPADE. In Section 4, we define the security models and prove these security properties of our protocol in Section 5. Then in Section 6, we give an analysis on how to set the parameters of the protocol depending on the security goals before concluding in Section 7.

2. PRELIMINARIES

In this section, we review the security models for DB protocols before describing the tools used in SPADE.

2.1 Distance-Bounding Models

In this section, we briefly review the notion of distance-bounding authentication, as well as the DFKO framework, which we use to prove the security of our protocol. DB protocols involve two parties: a *prover* P and a *verifier* V. In the public-key setting, let $\{\mathsf{sk}_P, \mathsf{pk}_P\}$ denote the private and public keys of P and let $\{\mathsf{sk}_V, \mathsf{pk}_V\}$ represent the ones of V. All public keys are known by all parties. During the DB protocol, P and V interact with each other, yielding the bit $OutV = 0$ for *reject* or 1 for *accept* at the end of the verifier algorithm.

Adversary Model. In the DFKO model [13], an adversary $\mathcal{A}$ interacts with a prover and the verifier in three types of sessions: (1) *prover-verifier* sessions, in which $\mathcal{A}$ eavesdrops on an honest execution between a prover and a verifier, (2) *prover-adversary* sessions, in which $\mathcal{A}$ impersonates a verifier interacting with the prover, and (3) *adversary-verifier* sessions in which $\mathcal{A}$ impersonates a prover interacting with the verifier. Protocols are sequences of exchanges between a prover and the verifier. A message from the verifier to the prover and the subsequent response back is called a *round*. Successive rounds may be combined in *phases*. If the clock is used to measure the time elapsed from the beginning of the phase to its end, this phase is called *time-critical* while otherwise it is called *lazy*. Finally, sessions run by honest parties are associated with identifiers sid.

Adversaries are quantified in terms of their *computational resources*, the number of prover-verifier sessions q_{obs} eavesdropped, the number q_{v} of verifier-adversary and the number q_{p} of prover-adversary sessions initiated, as well as the adversary's winning advantage $\epsilon(n)$. In this paper, we consider the strongest possible adversaries against privacy, which are assumed to know the final result of an authentication session (*i.e.*, accept or reject), and to be able to corrupt provers (*i.e.*, get their keys) without any restriction. Such adversaries are called *wide-strong* in the literature [29].

Oracles. Adversaries are also classified depending on the oracles they may use. These oracles perform functionalities without giving any further details on their internal information unknown to their users.

Prover Anonymity. The PA concept due to Gambs, Onete and Robert [16] extends existing privacy models used in DB protocols [18, 19]. In this case, an adversary against the prover anonymity can be either a MiM adversary, an *honest-but-curious* or even malicious verifier. His objective is to link sessions involving a given prover. This game is characterized by a hidden bit b, and the goal of the adversary is to guess this bit.

The *PA game* is defined by an adversary $\mathcal{A}$ interacting with the provers through an oracle, which blinds their identity. The adversary $\mathcal{A}$ *wins* the game if he can identify with a non-negligible advantage which prover was selected by a challenger and hidden by the oracle. The adversary's advantage is simply given by the difference between his probability of guessing the identity of the selected prover among the set of potential provers and the trivial guessing probability of one over the cardinality of that set. A protocol is *PA-resistant* if there is no such a winning adversary.

Mafia-Fraud Resistance. MF attacks are defined with respect to an active MiM adversary $\mathcal{A}$, which can interact with a prover and the verifier in several sessions. His goal is to authenticate to the verifier, but without relaying information directly from the prover (since the verifier should detect relays). The DFKO framework rules out *pure relaying* attacks, which consist in an adversary forwarding the messages between two legitimate parties. A prover-adversary session sid' used concurrently with an adversary-verifier session sid to perform pure relays is called a *tainted* session.

An adversary $\mathcal{A}$ *wins* the MF game if there is at least one adversary-verifier session that is untainted by any other prover-adversary session, and in which the verifier accepts with a non-negligible probability the adversary as legitimate. A protocol is *MF-resistant* if there is no such adversary.

Terrorist-Fraud Resistance. In their extension of the DFKO framework, Fischlin and Onete [15] consider many variations of TF attacks. We use their game-based TF-resistance notion GameTF. Intuitively, the goal of the MiM adversary $\mathcal{A}$ colluding with a malicious prover is to be authenticated by the verifier. However, the prover also wants to control his accomplice's access in future sessions, in particular, by keeping his secret key as confidential as possible. This property is formalized as a two-phase game. First, the TF adversary $\mathcal{A}$ attempts to authenticate to the verifier with non-negligible probability. In the second one, an adversary $\mathcal{B}$ takes as input the $\mathcal{A}$'s complete view and runs a MF attack. If $\mathcal{B}$ authenticates with higher probability than in a regular MF attack, $\mathcal{A}$ is said to be *helpful* to $\mathcal{B}$.

An adversary $\mathcal{A}$ *wins* the TF game if he authenticates with a non-negligible probability, but is not helpful to anyone. A protocol is *TF-resistant* if there is no such adversary.

Intuitively, a protocol is TF-resistant if a malicious prover *cannot* help his accomplice authenticate with a non-negligible probability without losing control on his credentials. Thus, a *rational* prover will avoid to perform such an attack.

Impersonation-Fraud Resistance. IF resistance mainly concerns the lazy phases of the protocol. Here, the objective of the adversary $\mathcal{A}$ is to make the verifier accept his authentication in a session in which he does not relay the lazy phases from a honest session. $\mathcal{A}$ *wins* the IF game if there is at least one adversary-verifier session in which the verifier accepts with a non-negligible probability the adversary as legitimate, and such that no prover-verifier session shares the same lazy transcript. A protocol is *IF-resistant* if there is no such adversary.

Distance-Fraud Resistance. In the case of DF attacks, the adversary $\mathcal{A}$ is a malicious prover outside the proximity of the verifier. Since this adversary is not be able to beat the verifier's clock, an adversary-verifier session is defined as *tainted* if for any time-critical phase the adversary is unable to *commit* to that round's response *before* receiving the verifier's message for that phase. In this attack, the adversary usually sends the response before receiving the challenge. We omit from the adversary's quantification the number of sessions he creates with the prover.

An adversary $\mathcal{A}$ *wins* the DF game if there is at least one adversary-verifier session that is untainted by any other prover-adversary session, and in which the verifier accepts with a non-negligible probability the adversary as legitimate. A protocol is *DF-resistant* if there is no such adversary.

2.2 Cryptographic Primitives

First, we recall the definition of a public-key encryption scheme.

DEFINITION 1 (PUBLIC KEY ENCRYPTION). *A public key encryption scheme* PKE *is defined by:*

E.gen(1^λ) *returns a public and private key pair* (pk, sk).

E.enc$_{pk}(m)$ *returns the ciphertext* c.

E.dec$_{sk}(c)$ *returns* m *such that* E.dec$_{sk}$(E.enc$_{pk}(m)) = m$.

The related security game is defined as follows. An adversary receives a public key pk from the key pair (pk, sk) and has access to a decryption oracle. He sends two messages (m_0, m_1) to a challenger that computes the ciphertext $c = $ E.enc$_{pk}(m_b)$ for a random bit b. The adversary wins if he correctly guesses b. A PKE is IND-CCA2 secure [24], if there is no polynomial-time winning adversary.

Group Signature. In a group signature scheme [5,25], each member of the group has a personal signing key that he uses to sign a message on behalf of the group. An entity, called a *group manager*, adds new members to the group while another entity called the *opening authority* can open a signature to reveal the identity of the signer. Some schemes allow also dynamic group structures with revocation capabilities by the group managers.

DEFINITION 2 (REVOCABLE GROUP SIGNATURE). *A revocable group signature scheme* G–SIG *is defined by:*

G.gen(1^λ) *returns a group/master key pair* (gpk, msk) *and sets the user list* UL *and the revoked user list* RL.

G.join$_{msk}(i, gpk, UL)$ *is a protocol between a user* U_i *(using* gpk*) and a group manager* GM *(using* gpk *and* msk*). U_i interacts with GM to get his signing key* ssk$_i$*, while GM outputs a value* reg$_i$ *and adds* U_i *to* UL.

G.rev$_{msk}(i, RL, UL, gpk)$ *computes the revocation logs* rev$_i$ *for user* U_i*, using* reg$_i$*,* gpk *and* msk *and moves* U_i *to* RL.

G.sig$_{ssk_i}(m)$ *returns a group signature* σ.

G.ver$_{gpk}(\sigma, m, RL)$ *outputs 1 if and only if* σ *is valid for the message* m *and the key* ssk$_i$ *of a non-revoked user.*

G.ope$_{msk}(\sigma, m, UL, gpk)$ *outputs a user identity* U_i.

The essential security property required for a group signature is *unlinkability*. It captures the idea that no polynomial-time adversary should be able to distinguish with a non-negligible probability whether two signatures have been issued by the same signer or not. The adversary is assumed to have access to oracles that add new users (honest or corrupted), corrupt or revoke a user, sign with an user's signing key, and open a signature using the opening authority key (the oracle trivially rejects the challenge signature).

The second security property is *traceability*. It ensures that no polynomial-time adversary should be able to produce a valid signature for a revoked user or a honest user with non-negligible probability (using the same oracles as for the unlinkability experiment). An adversary breaks the traceability of a signature scheme if he is able to forge a valid signature on a message of his choice. For digital signature schemes, this property is known as EUF–CMA secure [17].

The last security requirement is *non-frameability*, which guarantees that no adversary is able to sign on behalf of a honest user even if he knows the key of the group manager. This property is rather strong since it protects the user against a corrupted group manager or opening authority.

Pseudorandom Function. A set PRF is a collection of polynomial-time pseudo-random functions $\{PRF_k\}_{k\in K}$ defined on a key set K, which is such that, for any polynomial-time adversary, the probability of distinguishing between outputs of PRF_k for a random key k and outputs of a truly random function is negligible.

In the random oracle model, defining $PRF_k(x) = H(k, x)$ is a simple way to construct PRF using a given cryptographic hash function H.

3. SPADE

We first describe the functionalities provided by an anonymous distance-bounding protocol, before detailing our proposition SPADE for such a protocol.

DEFINITION 3 (ANONYMOUS DB). *An anonymous distance-bounding protocol* DB *is defined by:*

DB.gen(λ) *sets a master key* MK *and a verification key* VK, *and sets the user list* UL *and the revoked-user list* RL.

DB.join$_{MK}(i, UL)$ *returns a prover secret key* psk$_i$ *for* P_i. *This algorithm also outputs a value* reg$_i$ *and adds* P_i *to* UL.

DB.auth(psk$_i$, VK, RL) *is an interactive authentication protocol between* P_i *(using* psk$_i$*) and* V *(using* VK *and* RL*). V returns 1 in case of success and 0 otherwise. This algorithm also outputs a transcript* trans.

DB.revoke$_{MK}(i, RL, UL)$ *computes the revocation logs* rev$_i$ *for* P_i, *using* reg$_i$ *and* MK, *and moves* P_i *from* UL *to* RL.

DB.open$_{MK}$(trans) *outputs the identity of prover* P_i.

Consider the scenario in which we have a group manager GM, a verifier V and a group of provers P_i, which can authenticate to V. During the initialization, GM uses DB.gen(λ) to produce a master key MK and a verifier key VK for V. Calling DB.join$_{MK}(i, UL)$, M also generates a secret key psk$_i$ for each prover P_i. Using these keys, P_i runs DB.auth(psk$_i$, VK, RL) to authenticate himself to V. Afterwards, GM can add new provers using DB.join and revoke a prover using DB.revoke. Finally, GM can lift the anonymity of a user by running the algorithm DB.open$_{MK}$(trans)"

The main idea behind SPADE is that the prover is authenticated anonymously as a member of an authorized group, ensuring anonymity due to the group signature scheme.

DEFINITION 4 (SPADE). *Let* $E = (E.gen, E.enc, E.dec)$ *be a PKE scheme,* $G = (G.gen, G.sig, G.ver, G.join, G.rev, G.ope)$ *be a* G–SIG *scheme and* PRF *be a pseudorandom-function set. The DB protocol* $(E, G, PRF)-SPADE$ *is defined by:*

DB.gen(λ) *sets the verifier keys* $(pk_V, sk_V) = E.gen(\lambda)$ *and the signature key pair* $(gpk, msk) = G.gen(\lambda)$. *It also returns the master key* MK $= (msk, gpk, pk_V, sk_V)$ *and a verification key* VK $= (sk_V, gpk)$, *and sets the user list* UL *and the revoked-user list* RL.

DB.join$_{MK}(i, UL)$ *runs the algorithm* G.join$_{msk}(i, gpk, UL)$ *to get* ssk$_i$ *and then constructs* psk$_i$ $= (pk_V, ssk_i)$ *for the prover i. This algorithm also returns a value* reg$_i$ *and adds* P_i *to* UL.

DB.auth(psk$_i$, VK, RL) *is described in Figure 1. The security parameter n, defining the number of rounds, is function of the security parameter λ.*

DB.revoke$_{MK}(i, RL, UL)$ *runs* G.rev$_{msk}(i, RL, UL, gpk)$.

DB.open$_{MK}$(trans) *computes* $(N_P, \sigma) = E.dec_{sk_V}(e)$, *in which e is the first message of the transcript. Afterwards, it outputs the prover* $P_i = G.ope_{msk}(\sigma, N_P, UL, gpk)$.

We now detail our protocol presented in Figure 1.

Initialization Phase. First, P generates a random n-bit string N_P and signs it $\sigma = G.sig_{ssk_P}(N_P)$. Then, he encrypts both values $e = E.enc_{pk_V}(N_P, \sigma)$, with the public key of V and sends the result to V. The verifier retrieves $(N_P, \sigma) = E.dec_{sk_V}(e)$ and checks the signature with G.ver$_{gpk}(\sigma, N_P, RL)$. If it is invalid, he aborts the protocol. Otherwise, V returns two new random n-bit strings m and N_V to P. Finally, both P and V compute $a = PRF_{N_P}(N_V)$.

Distance-bounding Phase. P and V perform n challenge-response rounds during a time-critical phase. This is the heart of the protocol as it is used to determine if the prover is in the verifier's vicinity. At round i, V sends a bit c_i and P answers with $a_i \oplus ((N_{Pi} \oplus m_i) \wedge c_i)$. The string m prevents a malicious prover from picking $N_P = 0^n$, which would allow him to respond with a_i even before receiving the challenges. At the end of each round, V stores the RTT denoted by Δt_i.

Verification Phase. P concatenates all the challenges C and the responses R, computes $\tau = PRF_{N_P}(N_V, m, C, R)$ and sends it to V. V checks $\tau \overset{?}{=} PRF_{N_P}(N_V, m, C, R)$ and verifies that the Δt_i are coherent with respect to the proximity threshold to ensure that P is within an authorized distance. If all these checks succeed and all the responses are correct, V returns $OutV = 1$ for acceptance, while otherwise he returns $OutV = 0$.

Novel Approach. In contrast to most protocols in the literature, our DB protocol does not rely on a long-term shared secret between a prover and the verifier, but on a session key N_P exchanged anonymously. Long-term shared secrets constitute a serious burden to overcome to provide anonymity for the prover as these secrets can be easily used to link different sessions of a user. The radical shift that we propose can be seen as the main contribution of this paper.

SPADE is built in such a way that an adversary can replay a session key if he gets access to it (*e.g.*, during a TF). To ensure that provers protect their session keys, we introduce a *stateless backdoor* in the verifier, allowing an adversary to recover the complete session key N_P provided that he knows enough bits about it. This sets a trade-off between the malicious prover and any potential accomplice. Indeed, providing too much information to an accomplice, he may eventually impersonate the prover, which is not desirable. At the other end of the spectrum, by not giving him enough information, he may not be helpful to the prover.

The backdoor is presented in Figure 2 and its analysis is given in Section 6. If V receives the bit $b = 1$, he gets afterwards e and N'_P. Then, he extracts $(N_P, \sigma) = E.dec_{sk_V}(e)$ and uses G.ver$_{gpk}(\sigma, N_P, RL)$ to verify the signature. If σ is valid, he returns N_P provided that the Hamming distance $d_H(N_P, N'_P)$ is smaller than a threshold t. Otherwise, he returns 0. Since a regular MiM adversary learns nothing about N_P, his probability to recover it using the backdoor

Prover P		**Verifier** V
$\text{pk}_V, \text{ssk}_P$		sk_V, gpk

Initialisation

$N_P \xleftarrow{\$} \{0,1\}^n, \sigma = \text{G.sig}_{\text{ssk}_P}(N_P)$ $\qquad$ $N_V \xleftarrow{\$} \{0,1\}^n, m \xleftarrow{\$} \{0,1\}^n$

$e = \text{E.enc}_{\text{pk}_V}(N_P, \sigma)$ $\xrightarrow{\quad e \quad}$ $(N_P, \sigma) = \text{E.dec}_{\text{sk}_V}(e)$

$a = PRF_{N_P}(N_V)$ $\xleftarrow{\quad m, N_V \quad}$ if $\text{G.ver}_{\text{gpk}}(\sigma, N_P, \text{RL}) = 0$ then abort

Distance Bounding

for $i = 1$ to n

$\qquad\qquad c_i \xleftarrow{\$} \{0,1\}$

$r_i = \begin{cases} a_i & \text{if } c_i = 0 \\ a_i \oplus N_{P_i} \oplus m_i & \text{if } c_i = 1 \end{cases}$ $\xleftarrow{\quad c_i \quad}$ **Start clock**

$\xrightarrow{\quad r_i \quad}$ **Stop clock**

Check timers Δt_i

Verification

$C = c_1 || \ldots || c_n$ and $R = r_1 || \ldots || r_n$ $\qquad$ $C = c_1 || \ldots || c_n$ and $R = r_1 || \ldots || r_n$

$\mathcal{T} = PRF_{N_P}(N_V, m, C, R)$ $\xrightarrow{\quad \mathcal{T} \quad}$ Check that $\mathcal{T} \stackrel{?}{=} PRF_{N_P}(N_V, m, C, R)$

If $\#\{i : r_i \text{ and } \Delta t_i \text{ correct}\} = n$

$\xleftarrow{\quad Out_V \quad}$ then $Out_V = 1$ else $Out_V = 0$

Figure 1: Anonymous TF resistant protocol from a public key encryption E, a pseudo-random-function set PRF and a group signature G, where $a||b$ is the concatenation of a and b, and $x \oplus y$ denotes the exclusive-or.

is negligible. However, the accomplice authenticating with the help of the prover should learn enough bits of N_P to use the backdoor. This new approach makes SPADE the first secure provable revocable and anonymous DB protocol.

4. SECURITY DEFINITIONS

In this section, we define the security properties of anonymous DB protocols as *games* between powerful adversaries and benign *challengers*. For more details, refer to [13, 16].

Initialization. The challenger uses DB.gen(n) to build the simulation environment (MK, VK, UL, RL) and sets four lists: two transcript lists TL_v for the verifier, TL_p for the prover P, a corrupted users list CU and a list HL representing the random oracle calls.

Oracles. The challenger can simulate these oracles:

- $\overline{\text{DB}}.\text{Join}^h(i)$ adds P_i by using $\text{DB.join}_{\text{MK}}(i, \text{UL})$.
- $\overline{\text{DB}}.\text{Join}^c(i)$ adds a corrupted P_i using $\text{DB.join}_{\text{MK}}(i, \text{UL})$. It also returns the secret key psk_i, and adds P_i to CU.
- $\overline{\text{DB}}.\text{Revoke}(i)$ runs $\text{DB.revoke}_{\text{MK}}(i, \text{RL}, \text{UL})$ on P_i.
- $\overline{\text{DB}}.\text{Corrupt}(i)$ simulates the corruption of P_i by returning his secret key psk_i and adding P_i to CU.
- $\overline{\text{DB}}.\text{Prover}(i)$ simulates a session by the honest prover P_i and adds the generated transcript to TL_p.
- $\overline{\text{DB}}.\text{Verifier}(d)$ simulates a session by a honest verifier V at a distance d by delaying messages appropriately. It then appends *tainted* $= 0$ at the end of the transcript and adds it to the list TL_v.
- $\overline{\text{DB}}.\text{Session}(i)$ simulates a session between a honest verifier V and a nearby honest P_i.
- $\overline{\text{DB}}.\text{Taint}(.)$ simulates an altered $\overline{\text{DB}}.\text{Verifier}(d)$ in which the time delay checks are bypassed. It then appends *tainted* $= 1$ to the transcript before adding it to TL_v.

- $H(\cdot)$ is a random oracle using a list HL. When receiving an input i such that $i \notin \text{HL}$, it draws a binary string r uniformly at random, adds an entry (i, r) in HL and returns r. If $i \in \text{HL}$, it returns the corresponding r.

4.1 Prover Anonymity

Let the anonymity experiment $\text{Exp}_{\mathcal{A},\text{DB}}^{\text{PA}}(\lambda)$ for an adversary $\mathcal{A}$ on a protocol DB be defined as follows.

DEFINITION 5 (PROVER ANONYMITY SECURITY).
$\mathcal{A}$ has access to the DB-oracles $\text{Join}^h(i)$, $\text{Join}^c(i)$, $\text{Revoke}(i)$, $\text{Corrupt}(i)$, $\text{Prover}(i)$, $\text{Verifier}(d)$, $H(\cdot)$ and $\text{Session}(i)$. First, $\mathcal{A}$ outputs (i_0, i_1). If i_0 or $i_1 \in \text{CU}$, the challenger aborts the experiment. Otherwise, he picks $b \xleftarrow{\$} \{0,1\}$. Then, $\mathcal{A}$ loses access to $\text{Corrupt}(i)$ and $\text{Revoke}(i)$ on identities i_0 and i_1 (the oracles return false if $\mathcal{A}$ tries). Finally, $\mathcal{A}$ has access to the DB-oracle $\text{Prover}_b(\cdot)$, which runs the DB protocol as the prover i_b using key psk_{i_b} interacting with $\mathcal{A}$.
$\mathcal{A}$ wins if and only if adv outputs b.
We define $\mathcal{A}$'s advantage on this experiment as $\text{Adv}_{\mathcal{A},\text{DB}}^{\text{PA}}(\lambda) = |\Pr[\text{Exp}_{\mathcal{A},\text{DB}}^{\text{PA}}(\lambda) = 1] - \frac{1}{2}|$ and the advantage on the PA experiment as $\text{Adv}_{\text{DB}}^{\text{PA}}(\lambda) = \max_{\mathcal{A} \in \text{Poly}(\lambda)}\{\text{Adv}_{\mathcal{A},\text{DB}}^{\text{PA}}(\lambda)\}$. DB is PA-resistant if $\text{Adv}_{\text{DB}}^{\text{PA}}(\lambda)$ is negligible[1].

In this game, the adversary has access to all the verifier-accessible information and he may interact with one of two provers chosen adversarially (the choice depends on a secret bit b). The adversary wins if he can identify the secret bit, which implies that he can distinguish transcripts produced by a given prover, thus linking the sessions of this prover.

4.2 Mafia Fraud

Let the mafia fraud experiment $\text{Exp}_{\mathcal{A},\text{DB}}^{\text{MF}}(\lambda)$ for an adversary $\mathcal{A}$ on a protocol DB be defined as follows.

---

[1]$\text{Poly}(\lambda)$ is the set of algorithms running polynomially in λ.

Prover P	Verifier V
$\mathsf{pk}_v, \mathsf{ssk}_p$	$\mathsf{sk}_v, \mathsf{gpk}$

	Initial message	
	$\xrightarrow{\quad b \quad}$	
if $b = 0$, run the protocol normally else		
	$\xrightarrow{\quad e, N_P' \quad}$	$(N_P, \sigma) = \mathsf{E.dec}_{\mathsf{sk}_v}(e)$
		if $\mathsf{G.ver}_{\mathsf{gpk}}(\sigma, N_P, \mathsf{RL}) = 1$ and $d_H(N_P, N_P') \le t$
	$\xleftarrow{\quad ret \quad}$	then $ret = N_P$ else $ret = 0$

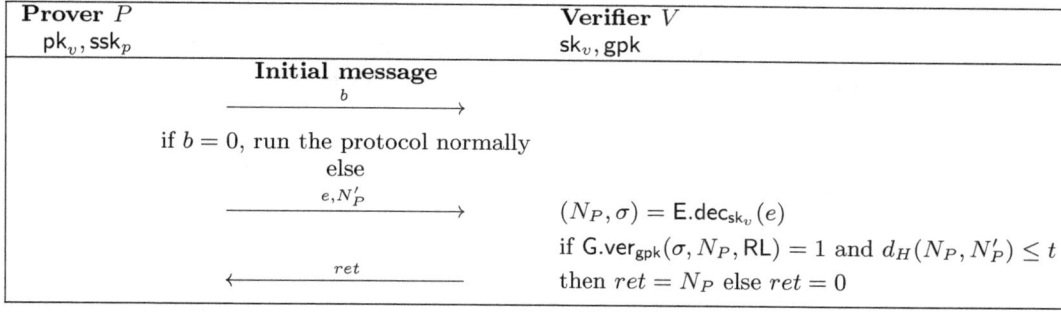

Figure 2: The backdoor mechanism. If the initial message is $b = 0$, the protocol is run normally. Otherwise, the verifier simply waits to receive a value e that he parses as (N_P, σ) and a string N_P'. If N_P and N_P' are close enough, he returns N_P.

DEFINITION 6 (MAFIA FRAUD SECURITY). *$\mathcal{A}$ has access to the DB-oracles $\mathsf{Join}^h(i)$, $\mathsf{Join}^c(i)$, $\mathsf{Revoke}(i)$, $\mathsf{Corrupt}(i)$, $\mathsf{Prover}(i)$, $\mathsf{Verifier}(d)$, $\mathsf{Session}(i)$, $\mathsf{H}(\cdot)$ and $\mathsf{Taint}(.)$.*

$\mathcal{A}$ wins if and only if $\exists$ $\mathsf{trans} \in \mathsf{TL}_v$ such that trans is the concatenation of all the messages exchanged during a DB session and the following conditions are satisfied:

- *$OutV = 1$, $tainted = 0$ is at the end of trans, and*
- *$\mathsf{DB.open}_{\mathsf{MK}}(\mathsf{trans}) \notin \mathsf{CU}$.*

We define $\mathcal{A}$'s advantage on this experiment as $\mathsf{Adv}_{\mathcal{A},\mathsf{DB}}^{MF}(\lambda) = \Pr[\mathsf{Exp}_{\mathcal{A},\mathsf{DB}}^{MF}(\lambda) = 1]$ and the advantage on the MF experiment as $\mathsf{Adv}_{\mathsf{DB}}^{MF}(\lambda) = \max_{\mathcal{A} \in \mathsf{Poly}(\lambda)} \{\mathsf{Adv}_{\mathcal{A},\mathsf{DB}}^{MF}(\lambda)\}$. DB is MF-resistant if $\mathsf{Adv}_{\mathsf{DB}}^{MF}(\lambda)$ is negligible.

In this game, the adversary is able to interact with provers and the verifier and wins if he authenticates to the verifier (in the presence of a prover) if, and only if, the attacker has not purely relayed information between the two legitimate parties.

4.3 Terrorist Fraud

A TF involves a legitimate but malicious prover and his accomplice interacting with the verifier.

First, we recall the definition of terrorist-fraud resistance given by Fischlin and Onete [15]. It is based on GameTF in which the accomplice (q_{obs}, q_v)-adversary $\mathcal{A}$ can eavesdrop q_{obs} honest prover-verifier sessions. He can also initiate q_v adversary-verifier sessions (and the matching adversary-prover sessions), in which he acts as a MiM adversary, forwarding information in the lazy phases. Then, $\mathcal{A}$ may act as the prover P in the time-critical phase. In all these sessions, the cautious P and V should select new values N_P and N_V for each session. Naturally, q_{obs} and q_v depend on the security parameter n. During these sessions, $\mathcal{A}$ can interact with P and V as specified in the MF game. In GameTF, the notion of a *tainted* session is defined as:

DEFINITION 7 (TAINTED SESSION - TF). *A TF adversary $\mathcal{A}$ taints an adversary-verifier session sid if there is a prover-adversary session sid' such that the following events occur: (i) $\mathcal{A}$ receives a message c from the verifier in sid, (ii) $\mathcal{A}$ sends a message c' in session sid' to the prover such that $c' > c^2$, and gets a response r such that $r > c'$, and (iii) $\mathcal{A}$ forwards a message r' in sid such that $r' > r$.*

[2] *i.e.*, c' can be sent only after c has been received.

Thus, relaying scheduling messages is ruled out, even if they are different. This is stronger than the pure relaying definition, which requires than the same messages are forwarded.

Let $\mathsf{view}_{\mathcal{A}}$ be the internal state of $\mathcal{A}$ colluding with P.

DEFINITION 8 (HELPFUL ADVERSARY). *A TF adversary $\mathcal{A}$ against a DB protocol DB is said to be helpful to an adversary $\mathcal{B}$ in the game Π if, given $\mathsf{view}_{\mathcal{A}}$, $\mathcal{B}$ wins the game Π with a probability greater than $\mathsf{Adv}_{\mathsf{DB}}^{\Pi}(\lambda)$, his original advantage without the help of his accomplice $\mathcal{A}$.*

In the $SPADE$ context, $\mathcal{B}$ may either want to play a MF attack or an IF attack. In both cases, a non-negligible help can be amplify to win these two games with probability one.

DEFINITION 9 (GameTF-SECURITY). *$\mathcal{A}$ has access to the DB-oracles $\mathsf{Join}^h(i)$, $\mathsf{Join}^c(i)$, $\mathsf{Revoke}(i)$, $\mathsf{Corrupt}(i)$, $\mathsf{Prover}(i)$, $\mathsf{Verifier}(d)$, $\mathsf{Session}(i)$ and $\mathsf{Taint}(.)$. A DB protocol DB is $p_{\mathcal{A}} - $ GameTF-secure if for any (q_{obs}, q_V) adversary $\mathcal{A}$ winning with probability $p_{\mathcal{A}}$, at least one of the two following conditions holds:*

- *$p_{\mathcal{A}}$ is negligible with respect to n,*
- *there exists a MF adversary $\mathcal{B}$ running $O(q_{\mathsf{obs}})$ prover-verifier sessions and $O(q_V)$ adversary-verifier sessions to which $\mathcal{A}$ is helpful.*

4.4 Impersonation Fraud

Let the IF experiment $\mathsf{Exp}_{\mathcal{A},\mathsf{DB}}^{IF}(\lambda)$ for an adversary $\mathcal{A}$ on a protocol DB be defined as follows.

DEFINITION 10 (IMPERSONATION FRAUD SECURITY). *$\mathcal{A}$ has access to the DB-oracles $\mathsf{Join}^h(i)$, $\mathsf{Join}^c(i)$, $\mathsf{Revoke}(i)$, $\mathsf{Corrupt}(i)$, $\mathsf{Prover}(i)$, $\mathsf{Verifier}(d)$, $\mathsf{Session}(i)$, $\mathsf{H}(\cdot)$ and $\mathsf{Taint}(.)$. $\mathcal{A}$ wins if and only if $\exists$ $\mathsf{trans} \in \mathsf{TL}_v$ such that trans is the concatenation of all the messages exchanged during a DB session, and the following conditions are satisfied:*

- *$OutV = 1$,*
- *$\nexists t \in \mathsf{TL}_p$ such that the lazy phases of t and trans are equal,*
- *and $\mathsf{DB.open}_{\mathsf{MK}}(\mathsf{trans}) \notin \mathsf{CU}$.*

Define $\mathsf{Adv}_{\mathsf{DB}}^{IF}(\lambda)$ as in Definition 6. DB is IF-resistant if $\mathsf{Adv}_{\mathsf{DB}}^{IF}(\lambda)$ is negligible.

4.5 Distance Fraud

Let the DF experiment $\mathsf{Exp}^{DF}_{\mathcal{A},\mathsf{DB}}(\lambda)$ for a distant adversary $\mathcal{A}$ on a protocol DB be defined as follows.

DEFINITION 11 (DISTANCE FRAUD SECURITY). $\mathcal{A}$ has access to the DB-oracles $\mathsf{Join}^c(i)$ and $\mathsf{Verifier}(d)$.

$\mathcal{A}$ wins if and only if $\exists$ trans $\in \mathsf{TL}_v$ such that trans is the concatenation of all the messages exchanged during a DB session, and the following conditions are satisfied:

- $OutV = 1$ and $d > d_{\max}$ (maximum distance allowed).

Define $\mathsf{Adv}^{DF}_{\mathsf{DB}}(\lambda)$ as in Definition 6. DB is DF-resistant if $\mathsf{Adv}^{DF}_{\mathsf{DB}}(\lambda)$ is negligible.

In this game, the adversary is a malicious prover, who can interact with the verifier in an arbitrary manner. He wins this game if and only if he is able to send all time-critical responses before receiving the respective challenges, for each time-critical round.

5. SECURITY RESULTS

Now that the models have been presented, we are ready to prove the main results of our paper.

In some of the theorems, the backdoor can be used to realize the attacks (e.g., a MF or an IF attack). In this case, let $p_{back}(n,t)$ denote the probability that a n-bit secret can be recovered through a polynomial number of queries to the backdoor with a threshold t. Theorem 6.1 gives the value of $p_{back}(n,t)$, for $t = \alpha n$, for some constant $\alpha > 0$.

5.1 Prover Anonymity

First, let us recall the security game for the anonymity of a revocable group signature. This generalizes the anonymity game described by Gambs, Onete and Robert [16].

Let the anonymity experiment $\mathsf{Exp}^{Anon}_{\mathcal{A},\mathsf{G-SIG}}(\lambda)$ for $\mathcal{A}$ on a revocable group signature G–SIG be defined as follows.

DEFINITION 12. **First phase:** The challenger creates $(\mathsf{UL}, \mathsf{RL}, \mathsf{msk}, \mathsf{gpk})$ using $\mathsf{G.gen}(1^\lambda)$, gives gpk to $\mathcal{A}$, and sets the lists CU and Σ. During this phase $\mathcal{A}$ has access to G-oracles:

$\overline{\mathsf{G}}.\mathsf{Join}^h(i)$ creates P_i using $\mathsf{G.join}_{\mathsf{msk}}(i, \mathsf{gpk}, \mathsf{UL})$.

$\overline{\mathsf{G}}.\mathsf{Join}^c(i)$ creates P_i using $\mathsf{G.join}_{\mathsf{msk}}(i, \mathsf{gpk}, \mathsf{UL})$ with $\mathcal{A}$ and adds him to CU.

$\overline{\mathsf{G}}.\mathsf{Revoke}(i)$ revokes P_i using $\mathsf{G.rev}_{\mathsf{msk}}(i, \mathsf{RL}, \mathsf{UL}, \mathsf{gpk})$.

$\overline{\mathsf{G}}.\mathsf{Corrupt}(i)$ returns the secret key of P_i. If $P_i \in \mathsf{UL}$, it sends ssk_i to $\mathcal{A}$ and adds P_i to CU.

$\overline{\mathsf{G}}.\mathsf{Sign}(i, m)$ returns a signature σ on behalf of P_i, using $\mathsf{G.sig}_{\mathsf{ssk}_i}(m)$ and adds the pair (m, σ) to Σ.

$\overline{\mathsf{G}}.\mathsf{Open}(\sigma, m)$ opens a signature σ on m and returns P_i to $\mathcal{A}$, using $\mathsf{G.ope}_{\mathsf{msk}}(\sigma, m, \mathsf{UL}, \mathsf{gpk})$.

Challenge: $\mathcal{A}$ selects (i_0, i_1). If i_0 and $i_1 \in \mathsf{CU}$, the challenger stops. Otherwise, he picks $b \xleftarrow{\$} \{0, 1\}$.

Second phase: $\mathcal{A}$ cannot use $\overline{\mathsf{G}}.\mathsf{Corrupt}(i)$ and $\overline{\mathsf{G}}.\mathsf{Revoke}(i)$ on i_0 or i_1. Moreover, $\mathcal{A}$ has access to the G-oracle:

$\overline{\mathsf{G}}.\mathsf{Sign}_b(i_b, m)$ simply returns $\mathsf{G.sig}_{\mathsf{ssk}_{i_b}}(m)$.

Afterwards, $\overline{\mathsf{G}}.\mathsf{Open}(\sigma, m)$ rejects all signatures produced by $\overline{\mathsf{G}}.\mathsf{Sign}_b(i_b, m)$.

Guessing phase: $\mathcal{A}$ outputs b' and the challenger returns the Boolean value $(b = b')$.

Define $\mathsf{Adv}^{Anon}_{\mathsf{G-SIG}}(\lambda)$ as in Definition 5. A group signature G–SIG is anonymous if $\mathsf{Adv}^{Anon}_{\mathsf{G-SIG}}(\lambda)$ is negligible.

THEOREM 5.1. Let G–SIG be a group signature scheme such that $\mathsf{Adv}^{Anon}_{\mathsf{G-SIG}}(\lambda)$ is negligible. Thus, SPADE is prover-anonymous and $\mathsf{Adv}^{PA}_{SPADE}(\lambda) \leq \mathsf{Adv}^{Anon}_{\mathsf{G-SIG}}(\lambda)$.

PROOF. Assume that there is a polynomial-time adversary $\mathcal{A}$ having a non-negligible advantage $\mathsf{Adv}^{PA}_{\mathcal{A},SPADE}(\lambda)$ on a challenger in $\mathsf{Exp}^{PA}_{\mathcal{A},SPADE}(\lambda)$. $\mathcal{A}$ can be used by an adversary $\mathcal{B}$, which is challenged in $\mathsf{Exp}^{Anon}_{\mathcal{B},\mathsf{G-SIG}}(\lambda)$. Thus, $\mathsf{Adv}^{Anon}_{\mathcal{B},\mathsf{G-SIG}}(\lambda) \geq \mathsf{Adv}^{PA}_{\mathcal{A},SPADE}(\lambda)$, contradicting the assumption on G–SIG.

Initially, the challenger in $\mathsf{Exp}^{Anon}_{\mathcal{B},\mathsf{G-SIG}}(\lambda)$ sends the key gpk and the revoked list RL to $\mathcal{B}$, which relays it to $\mathcal{A}$, as well as a function PRF and a PKE scheme E. Thus, $\mathcal{A}$ can initialize his own experiment $\mathsf{Exp}^{PA}_{\mathcal{A},SPADE}(\lambda)$ and return the public key pk_V to $\mathcal{B}$. Then, $\mathcal{B}$ creates the empty list CU. Having access to G–SIG-oracles from his challenger, $\mathcal{B}$ can simulate the DB-oracles for $\mathcal{A}$ as follows:

$\overline{\mathsf{DB}}.\mathsf{Join}^h(i)$: $\mathcal{A}$ creates P_i. $\mathcal{B}$ relays it to $\overline{\mathsf{G}}.\mathsf{Join}^h(i)$ and adds P_i to UL.

$\overline{\mathsf{DB}}.\mathsf{Join}^c(i)$: $\mathcal{A}$ creates P_i. $\mathcal{B}$ relays it to $\overline{\mathsf{G}}.\mathsf{Join}^c(i)$, obtains the signing key ssk_i, and adds P_i to UL and CU. $\mathcal{A}$ gets ssk_i.

$\overline{\mathsf{DB}}.\mathsf{Revoke}(i)$: $\mathcal{A}$ revokes P_i. $\mathcal{B}$ relays it to $\overline{\mathsf{G}}.\mathsf{Revoke}(i)$, which updates RL and sends it to $\mathcal{B}$. He relays it to $\mathcal{A}$.

$\overline{\mathsf{DB}}.\mathsf{Corrupt}(i)$: $\mathcal{A}$ corrupts P_i. $\mathcal{B}$ relays it to $\overline{\mathsf{G}}.\mathsf{Corrupt}(i)$ and gets ssk_i. $\mathcal{B}$ adds P_i to CU and returns ssk_i to $\mathcal{A}$.

$\overline{\mathsf{DB}}.\mathsf{Prover}(i)$: $\mathcal{B}$ simulates P_i for $\mathcal{A}$ as follows:

Initialization phase: $\mathcal{B}$ picks $N_P \xleftarrow{\$} \{0,1\}^n$, sends (i, N_P) to $\overline{\mathsf{G}}.\mathsf{Sign}(i, N_P)$ and gets back σ from $\mathcal{A}$. $\mathcal{B}$ then computes $e = \mathsf{E.enc}_{\mathsf{pk}_V}(N_P, \sigma)$ and sends e to $\mathcal{A}$ and receives (m, N_V). Afterwards, he computes $a = PRF_{N_P}(N_V)$.

Distance-bounding phase: $\mathcal{B}$ uses a, N_P and m to correctly answer to the challenges c_i sent by $\mathcal{A}$.

Verification phase: $\mathcal{B}$ builds (C, R) from the challenges and responses and sends to $\mathcal{A}$ the value $PRF_{N_P}(C, R)$.

Then, $\mathcal{A}$ picks two identities i_0 and i_1 and sends them to $\mathcal{B}$. If $i_0, i_1 \notin \mathsf{CU}$, $\mathcal{B}$ sends (i_0, i_1) to the challenger. In this phase, $\mathcal{B}$ simulates $\overline{\mathsf{DB}}.\mathsf{Prover}_b(\cdot)$ as follows. During the initialization phase, $\mathcal{B}$ picks $N_P \xleftarrow{\$} \{0,1\}^n$ sends it to $\overline{\mathsf{G}}.\mathsf{Sign}_b(i_b, m)$ and receives σ. He then computes $e = \mathsf{E.enc}_{\mathsf{pk}_V}(N_P, \sigma)$ and sends $(0, e)$ to $\mathcal{A}$. The objective of this prover simulation is the same as $\overline{\mathsf{DB}}.\mathsf{Prover}(i)$. Finally, during the guessing phase, $\mathcal{A}$ returns b' and $\mathcal{B}$ outputs the same b'.

The experiment is perfectly simulated for $\mathcal{A}$, and consequently, $\mathcal{B}$ wins his experiment with the same probability that $\mathcal{A}$ wins his and $\mathsf{Adv}^{Anon}_{\mathcal{B},\mathsf{G-SIG}}(\lambda) = \mathsf{Adv}^{PA}_{\mathcal{A},SPADE}(\lambda)$, contradicting the assumption on G–SIG. $\square$

5.2 Mafia Fraud

THEOREM 5.2. Let PKE be a IND-CCA2 secure encryption scheme such that $\mathsf{Adv}^{IND-CCA2}_{\mathsf{PKE}}(\lambda)$ is negligible and

G–SIG *a traceable signature scheme such that* $\mathsf{Adv}^{trace}_{\mathsf{G-SIG}}(\lambda)$ *is also negligible. Let q_p be the number of calls to the prover oracle, q_v the number of calls to the verifier oracle and $p_{back}(n,t)$ the probability to recover N_P through the backdoor. Thus, SPADE is MF-resistant in the random oracle model if the challenges are drawn uniformly at random by the verifier and*

$$
\begin{aligned}
\mathsf{Adv}^{MF}_{SPADE}(\lambda) \;\le\; & p_{back}(n,t) + \frac{q_\mathsf{p}^2 + q_\mathsf{v}^2 + 1}{2^n} + \\
& \mathsf{Adv}^{trace}_{\mathsf{G-SIG}}(\lambda) + q_\mathsf{p} \cdot \mathsf{Adv}^{IND-CCA2}_{\mathsf{PKE}}(\lambda).
\end{aligned}
$$

The proof of this result is given in Appendix A.

5.3 Terrorist Fraud

THEOREM 5.3. *Let $p_{back}(n,t)$ be the probability to recover N_P through the backdoor and r be the number of bits of N_P unknown to any potential accomplice. Thus, SPADE is $\max\left(p_{back}(n,t), \left(\frac{3}{4}\right)^r\right)$-GameTF-resistant.*

Remark, if there is an adversary $\mathcal{A}$ that knows all the bits of N_P, then there exists an adversary $\mathcal{B}$ to which $\mathcal{A}$ is helpful, and who wins with probability 1 (*i.e.*, in this case, SPADE is 1-GameTF-resistant). Similarly, SPADE is trivially 1-GameTF-resistant using insecure schemes. If an adversary can break the encryption scheme, he can find N_P encrypted in e and he can use it to authenticate himself. In addition, if an adversary can forge a signature, he can choose the nonce N_P himself, sign it and use it to authenticate. Finally, in a terrorist fraud scenario, the accomplice can authenticate himself even if he does not use the help of the malicious prover. Thus, a malicious prover cannot perform any efficient TF attacks while preserving his secret key.

PROOF. First, let us assume there is a polynomial-time $(q_\mathsf{obs}, q_\mathsf{v})$-adversary $\mathcal{A}$ that can win the TF game with a non-negligible probability with the help of his malicious prover. Then, we can construct an adversary $\mathcal{B}$ that can always win later on MF or IF games using $\mathcal{A}$'s view, contradicting Theorems 5.2 and 5.4. *A fortiori*, $\mathcal{A}$ can also do so.

To fool the verifier in a TF attack, $\mathcal{A}$ must get from P prior to the time-critical phase one of these two:

- Two n-bit strings $\mathbf{c}^0$ and $\mathbf{c}^1$ representing respectively the responses to the 0-challenges and the 1-challenges.

- An algorithm A to generate these strings.

If A is *stateless* (*i.e.*, the response to a challenge does not depend on the previous ones), these two are equivalent. For simplicity, the former case is used. Hence, $\mathcal{A}$ receives the strings $(\mathbf{c}^0, \mathbf{c}^1)$, representing his internal $\mathsf{view}_\mathcal{A}(\mathsf{sid})$. They are defined as:

$$
\begin{aligned}
\text{Case 1}: \quad & \mathbf{c}_i^0 = a_i \quad \text{and} \quad \mathbf{c}_i^1 = a_i \oplus (N_{Pi} \oplus m_i) \\
\text{Case 2}: \quad & \mathbf{c}_i^0 = a_i \quad \text{and} \quad \mathbf{c}_i^1 = \bot \quad \text{or} \\
& \mathbf{c}_i^0 = \bot \quad \text{and} \quad \mathbf{c}_i^1 = a_i \oplus (N_{Pi} \oplus m_i) \\
\text{Case 3}: \quad & \mathbf{c}_i^0 = \bot \quad \text{and} \quad \mathbf{c}_i^1 = \bot
\end{aligned}
$$

Under the assumptions that (1) the same values of N_P or N_V are never chosen twice by a cautious prover and an honest verifier, and that (2) the function PRF is pseudorandom, the values a_i can be seen as random values. Thus Case 2 cannot leak any information on N_P.

FACT 5.1. *For any round, the probability that $\mathcal{A}$ responds correctly to the challenge (let p_i denote such an event) is 1 in the first case, $\frac{3}{4}$ in the second one, and $\frac{1}{2}$ in the last one.*

If the objective of P and $\mathcal{A}$ is to fool the verifier, Case 2 should be preferred to Case 3, even though some bits of N_P may leak in the process. In fact, if Case 2 is chosen for r bits, half of them would leak during the time-critical phase for a winning session. These bits are the missing bits that had to be guessed successfully.

LEMMA 5.1. *Assume that a malicious prover P provides to his accomplice $\mathcal{A}$ two strings $(\mathbf{c}^0, \mathbf{c}^1)$ such that only one answer is known for r rounds (Case 2). Thus, $\mathcal{A}$ can fool a verifier in the time-critical phase of SPADE only with probability*

$$
\Pr(\mathsf{P}_0 \wedge \cdots \wedge \mathsf{P}_n | r) = 1^{n-r} \cdot \left(\frac{3}{4}\right)^r.
$$

This requires that the challenges are independent and identically distributed and that N_P has been randomly selected.

Other strategies can be used by P and $\mathcal{A}$ but they would leak more bits in the process.

First, remark that the trivial case in which $\mathcal{A}$ sends a successful query to the backdoor of V is discarded. This happens only with probability $p_{back}(n,t)$. Let suppose now that $\mathcal{A}$ has won the TF game with a non-negligible[3] probability $p_\mathcal{A}$. Consider the adversary-verifier session sid^* for which $\mathcal{A}$ has fooled V. This has happened with probability at least $\frac{p_\mathcal{A}}{q_\mathsf{v}}$. In such a case, $\mathcal{A}$ has successfully guessed the missing answers, which have been requested (*i.e.*, on average $\frac{r}{2}$ such queries). Since this happened, $\left(\frac{3}{4}\right)^r$ should be greater than the non-negligible $\frac{p_\mathcal{A}}{q_\mathsf{v}}$. Hence,

$$
\exists c, \forall n_c, \exists n > n_c, \left[\left(\frac{3}{4}\right)^r > \frac{n^{-c}}{q_\mathsf{v}} > n^{-c'}\right].
$$

since $q_\mathsf{v} \in n^{O(1)}$. Thus, r should be in $O(\log n)$.

If an adversary $\mathcal{B}$ gets the internal $\mathsf{view}_\mathcal{A}(\mathsf{sid}^*)$ and has eavesdropped to all the communications involving P, $\mathcal{A}$, and V, he would get e and N_P' such that $d_H(N_P, N_P') \in O(\log n)$. Thus, $\mathcal{B}$ (as well as $\mathcal{A}$ himself) would be able to retrieve N_P directly through the backdoor of V and eventually be able to do a MF or an IF on behalf of P with probability one. This concludes the proof that $\mathcal{A}$ is very helpful for $\mathcal{B}$! □

5.4 Impersonation Fraud

THEOREM 5.4. *Let PKE be a IND-CCA2 secure encryption scheme such that $\mathsf{Adv}^{IND-CCA2}_{\mathsf{PKE}}(\lambda)$ is negligible and G–SIG a traceable signature scheme such that $\mathsf{Adv}^{trace}_{\mathsf{G-SIG}}(\lambda)$ is negligible. Let q_p be the number of calls to the prover oracle, q_v be the number of calls to the verifier oracle, q be the number of (different) digests generated by H and $p_{back}(n,t)$ the probability to recover N_P through the backdoor. SPADE is IF-resistant in the random oracle model and*

$$
\begin{aligned}
\mathsf{Adv}^{IF}_{SPADE}(\lambda) \;\le\; & p_{back}(n,t) + \frac{q_\mathsf{p}^2 + q_\mathsf{v}^2 + q^2 + 1}{2^n} + \\
& \mathsf{Adv}^{trace}_{\mathsf{G-SIG}n}(\lambda) + q_\mathsf{p} \cdot \mathsf{Adv}^{IND-CCA2}_{\mathsf{PKE}}(\lambda).
\end{aligned}
$$

The proof is very similar to the one given in Appendix A.

---

[3]Formally, $p_\mathcal{A}$ is such that $\exists c, \forall n_c, \exists n > n_c, p_\mathcal{A} > n^{-c}$.

5.5 Distance Fraud

THEOREM 5.5. *If m is drawn from a uniform distribution by the verifier, then $SPADE$ is DF-resistant, and*

$$\mathsf{Adv}^{DF}_{SPADE}(\lambda) \leq \left(\frac{3}{4}\right)^n .$$

PROOF. To defeat the time-bound for each round i, the far-away prover must send r_i before receiving c_i. Since c_i is unpredictable, the prover cannot determine in advance whether he must respond a_i or $a_i \oplus N_{P_i} \oplus m_i$. Hence, if these two possible responses are different, he must guess c_i. On the other hand, if the two possible responses are equal, he succeeeds in passing the round with probability 1. Due to the uniform distribution of m, and the fact it is picked by V after the prover has committed to N_P with e, $Pr[a_i \oplus N_{P_i} \oplus m_i = a_i] = \frac{1}{2}$. From this, we deduce an upper bound on the probability of success for a given round: $\frac{1}{2} \cdot 1 + \frac{1}{2} \cdot \frac{1}{2} = \frac{3}{4}$. Since they are n independent rounds, the probability of success is at most $\frac{3}{4}^n$. □

5.6 Impersonation and Multiple Verifiers

Traditionally, security models for DB protocols assume that there is only one verifier. To extend these models to support numerous verifiers, we have mainly two options, which are to consider that verifiers are *honest-but-curious* or *malicious*. Unfortunately, in the latter case, SPADE as presented does not prevent the impersonation of a prover by a malicious verifier. Indeed, knowing N_P and its anonymous signature by P, the malicious verifier can simply reuse this information to another verifier. However, a simple modification can ensure that SPADE is secure in this broader context. Let assume that the verifier V_i has a public certificate with an identifier id_{V_i} and a public key sk_{V_i}. Thus, each nonce N_P can be associated to the appropriate identifier id_{V_i}. In fact, P would sign and encrypt $N_P||\mathsf{id}_{V_i}$.

If the malicious verifier ends up with the ciphertext e for another verifier, he cannot to retrieve N_P or its signature due to security of the encryption scheme. Furthermore, even if he is able to obtain a from P simply by sending only 0-challenges, the one-way property of the functions in PRF would prevent the verifier to retrieve N_P from N_V and a. Thus, the malicious verifier is limited to a classical MF against P and the legitimate verifier. The formal security model of this generalization is an important problem and will be addressed in future work.

6. THE PRESENCE OF THE BACKDOOR

The objective of the backdoor in the verifier is mainly to deter any prover to help potential accomplices. Remark that this mechanism is stateless for the verifier, as he simply has to decrypt the initial message of the protocol to retrieve the information needed to impersonate a prover. We further analyze the impact of the backdoor in this section.

The probabilities to detect MF or TF attacks depend on the proximity threshold t. There is clearly a trade-off between these two probabilities, as one increases and the other one decreases in function of t. Unfortunately, there is no *optimal* value for t, rather it depends of the security requirements – and the underlying threat models. At the end of this section, we review the main scenarios that we envision.

6.1 Querying the Backdoor

Let us assume that a verifier V_s, having a n-bit secret s, can be queried a polynomial number of times with strings $x \in \{0, 1\}^n$. If a query is *close* to s (*i.e.*, if $d_H(s, x) \leq t$, for some $t < \frac{n}{2}$), the verifier simply returns his secret. Otherwise, he simply outputs 0.

Since the number of potential queries is 2^n and the number of strings at Hamming distance at most t of s is simply $\sum_{k=0}^{t} \binom{n}{k}$,

LEMMA 6.1. *The probability that the ith random query is successful (let $\mathcal{Q}_i$ denote such an event) is*

$$\mathbf{p} = \Pr[\mathcal{Q}_i | n, t] = 2^{-n} \times \sum_{k=0}^{t} \binom{n}{k} .$$

6.2 Best Strategy to Retrieve the String s

As described in Section 5.3, the accomplice receives from a malicious prover two strings $(\mathbf{c}^0, \mathbf{c}^1)$ to help him to fool the verifier in a TF attack. These strings would clearly allow the accomplice to know the values of n and $r = \alpha n$. However, he can easily estimate the proximity threshold t by sending queries with increasing Hamming weight.

Let assume that $d_H(\mathbf{c}^0 \oplus \mathbf{c}^1, s) = r$ such that $t < r < \frac{n}{2}$. It can be shown that the best strategy for an adversary is to flip the minimal number of bits to transform $\mathbf{c}^0 \oplus \mathbf{c}^1$ into s. Thus, assume that the adversary selects $r - t$ bits, complements them and submits the result to V_s.

LEMMA 6.2. *Given n, t and r, the probability that the ith random query to retrieve s by flipping exactly $r - t$ bits of a given chain $\mathbf{c}^0 \oplus \mathbf{c}^1$ such tjat $d_H(s, \mathbf{c}^0 \oplus \mathbf{c}^1) = t$ is given by*

$$\Pr[\mathcal{Q}_i | \mathbf{c}^0 \oplus \mathbf{c}^1, n, t, r] = \frac{\binom{r}{r-t}}{\binom{n}{r-t}}, \text{ by symmetry } \frac{\binom{n-r+t}{t}}{\binom{n}{n-r}} .$$

6.3 Simple Case in which $t = \alpha n$ and $r = (\alpha + \epsilon)n$

Consider that the backdoor provided by the verifier is such that $t = \alpha n$, for some $\alpha > 0$. The probability of obtaining s with a query (Lemma 6.1) can be bounded by

$$\Pr[\mathcal{Q}_i | n, t] \approx \frac{O(1)}{2^{n(1-H(\alpha))} \cdot \sqrt{n}} ,$$

in which $H(\alpha) = \alpha \log \frac{1}{\alpha} + (1 - \alpha) \log \frac{1}{(1-\alpha)}$ (see [22], Prob. 9.42). This probability increases as α increases in $[0 \cdots \frac{1}{2})$.

THEOREM 6.1. *An adversary can achieve a MF or an IF with the involuntary assistance of the verifier V_s through $n^{O(1)}$ queries to V_s with probability*

$$\Pr[\cup_i \mathcal{Q}_i | n, t] \leq \sum_i \frac{O(1)}{2^{n(1-H(\alpha))} \cdot \sqrt{n}} = \frac{n^{O(1)}}{2^{n(1-H(\alpha))}} .$$

This follows from the union bound and the independence of queries.

An adversary can also get enough information to achieve a MF or an IF attack from the accomplice. Consider the situation in whcich the adversary has retrieved a string at Hamming distance $r = (\alpha + \epsilon)n$ of s, for some $0 < \alpha < (\alpha + \epsilon) \leq \frac{1}{2}$. Thus, the equation of Lemma 6.2 can be

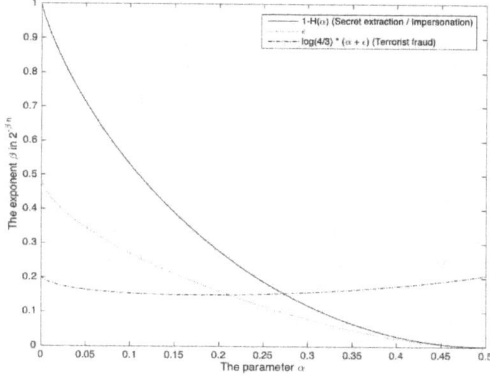

Figure 3: Plotting with respect to α the exponents of the probability in Lemma 5.1 ($\alpha+\epsilon$) and Theorem 6.1 ($1-H(\alpha)$), and the value of ϵ making $1-H(\alpha) = \nu(\alpha,\epsilon)$.

rewritten as

$$\Pr[\mathcal{Q}_i|\mathbf{c}^0 \oplus \mathbf{c}^1, n, \alpha n, (\alpha+\epsilon)n] = \frac{\binom{\alpha n + \epsilon n}{\alpha n}}{\binom{\epsilon n + (1-\epsilon)n}{\epsilon n}}$$

$$\approx \sqrt{\frac{(\alpha+\epsilon)(1-\epsilon)}{\alpha}} \left[\frac{(\alpha+\epsilon)^{\alpha+\epsilon}(1-\epsilon)^{1-\epsilon}}{\alpha^\alpha} \right]^n = \frac{O(1)}{2^{\nu(\alpha,\epsilon)n}},$$

in which $\nu(\alpha,\epsilon) = (\alpha+\epsilon)\log\frac{1}{\alpha+\epsilon} + (1-\epsilon)\log\frac{1}{1-\epsilon} - \alpha\log\frac{1}{\alpha}$ (see [21], Section 1.2.6).

THEOREM 6.2. *An adversary can achieve a MF or IF attack with the help of an accomplice of a TF attack through $n^{O(1)}$ queries to V_s with probability*

$$\Pr[\cup_i \mathcal{Q}_i|\mathbf{c}^0 \oplus \mathbf{c}^1, n, \alpha n, (\alpha+\epsilon)n] \leq \sum_i \frac{O(1)}{2^{\nu(\alpha,\epsilon)n}} = \frac{n^{O(1)}}{2^{\nu(\alpha,\epsilon)n}}.$$

6.4 Different Threat Models

In the following scenarii, the backdoor threshold t is set to αn (for some constant $0 < \alpha < 0.5$). An honest prover would like to have the lowest backdoor threshold as possible ($\alpha \to 0$) since it would ensure the protection of his secret and minimize the probability that an adversary retrieves some useful information directly from the verifier (as in Theorem 6.1). However, a malicious prover would take profit of such a small value. A relatively small value of $r = (\alpha+\epsilon)n$ would protect his secret while minimizing the probability of Lemma 5.1. Depending on the threats, the parameters (α,ϵ) are defined differently.

Honest prover. This prover will not attempt any TF attack and thus third parties represent the only adversaries. Hence, t can be set by the verifier to a small value such as $t = 0.01 \cdot n$, giving a probability in $O\left(\frac{n^{O(1)}}{2^{0.92n}}\right)$ of extracting the secret and having a successful MF or IF attack (as in Theorem 6.1).

Malicious and suspicious prover. This prover may attempt to do a TF attack while doing his best to protect his secret. His accomplice should not obtain any advantage over the backdoor, more precisely Theorems 6.1 and 6.2 probabilities should be equal (ϵ must be chosen accordingly). In

Figure 3, the intersection of the exponent $\alpha+\epsilon$ (terrorist fraud detection probability) and the exponent $1-H(\alpha)$ (secret extraction probability) gives the equilibrium. At this point, both probabilities are equal and in $O\left(\frac{n^{O(1)}}{2^{0.3715}}\right)$, for $t = 0.273 \cdot n$ (chosen by V) and $\epsilon = 0.0985$ (chosen by P). Notice that these intersection points have been obtained through numerical approximation.

Malicious prover having some trust in his accomplice. This prover may attempt to perform a TF. However, he accepts that his accomplice is able to impersonate him with a better probability than any other party. The prover may chose ϵ ten times smaller than expected in the previous scenario. This would increase the success probability of his TF attack. Hence, the verifier would have the responsibility to increase α, increasing implicitly all the success probabilities of the attacks. By plotting these curves as in Figure 3, we obtain $O\left(\frac{n^{O(1)}}{2^{0.3028}}\right)$, for $t = 0.2945 \cdot n$ (chosen by V).

7. CONCLUSION

Table 1: Summary of SPADE security properties.

Properties	Security probabilities
PA	$\mathsf{Adv}^{\mathsf{Anon}}_{\mathsf{G-SIG}}(\lambda)$
MF	$p_{back}(n,t) + \frac{q_p^2 + q_v^2 + 1}{2^n} + \mathsf{Adv}^{trace}_{\mathsf{G-SIG}}(\lambda)$ $+ q_p \cdot \mathsf{Adv}^{IND-CCA2}_{\mathsf{PKE}}(\lambda)$
TF	$\max\left(p_{back}(n,t), \left(\frac{3}{4}\right)^r\right)$
IF	$p_{back}(n,t) + \frac{q_p^2 + q_v^2 + q^2 + 1}{2^n} + \mathsf{Adv}^{trace}_{\mathsf{G-SIG}n}(\lambda)$ $+ q_p \cdot \mathsf{Adv}^{IND-CCA2}_{\mathsf{PKE}}(\lambda)$
DF	$\left(\frac{3}{4}\right)^n$

Considering the widespread development of contactless technologies, we believe that it is crucial to develop provably secure DB protocols, which address privacy issues to limit the ability of tracking users. In this paper, we have proposed SPADE, a provably TF-resistant prover-anonymous DB protocol, which uses group signatures to hide the prover's identity, even against a potentially malicious verifier. While our construction is provably resistant to all known attacks against DB protocols (see Table 1 for a summary), the backdoor introduced to obtain the TF-resistance lowers the resistance of the protocol to other threats. This is a frequent problem when designing provably TF-resistant protocols.

In addition to building the first protocol ensuring these properties, we have introduced a promising new approach to ensure TF resistance. In essence, the information leaked to an accomplice during a TF is no longer a long-term secret key but rather a temporary session key. Such a session key can then be used by the accomplice to authenticate. This novel approach opens the door for further research on terrorist fraud resistance.

Acknowledgments

We would like to thank the anonymous reviewers and our sheperd, Bart Preneel, who by their comments helped us to improve the quality of the paper.

8. REFERENCES

[1] A. Ahmadi and R. Safavi-Naini. Privacy-preserving distance-bounding proof-of-knowledge. In *ICICS 2014*, LNCS 8958, pages 74–88. Springer, 2015.

[2] G. Avoine, M. Ali Bingöl, S. Kardaş, C. Lauradoux, and B. Martin. A formal framework for analyzing RFID distance bounding protocols. *Journal of Computer Security - Special Issue on RFID System Security*, 19(2):289–317, 2010.

[3] A. Bay, Boureanu I, A. Mitrokotsa, I. Spulber, and S. Vaudenay. The Bussard-Bagga and other distance-bounding protocols under attacks. In *Inscrypt 2012*, LNCS 7763, pages 371–391. Springer, 2012.

[4] M. Bellare, A. Boldyreva, and S. Micali. Public-key encryption in a multi-user setting: Security proofs and improvements. In *EUROCRYPT 2000*, LNCS 1807, pages 259–274, 2000.

[5] M. Bellare, D. Micciancio, and B. Warinschi. Foundations of group signatures: Formal definitions, simplified requirements, and a construction based on general assumptions. In *EUROCRYPT 2003*, LNCS 2656, pages 614–629. Springer, 2003.

[6] S. Bengio, G. Brassard, Y. G. Desmedt, C. Goutier, and J.-J. Quisquater. Secure implementation of identification systems. *Journal of Cryptology*, 4(3):175–183, 1991.

[7] I. Boureanu, A. Mitrokotsa, and S. Vaudenay. Secure and lightweight distance-bounding. In *LightSec 2013*, LNCS 8162, pages 97–113. Springer, 2013.

[8] S. Brands and D. Chaum. Distance-bounding protocols. In *EUROCRYPT '93*, LNCS 765, pages 344–359. Springer, 1993.

[9] A. Brelurut, D. Gérault, and P. Lafourcade. Survey of distance bounding protocols and threats. In *FPS 2015*, LNCS 9482, pages 29–49. Springer, 2015.

[10] L. Bussard and W. Bagga. Distance-bounding proof of knowledge to avoid real-time attacks. In *Security and Privacy in the Age of Ubiquitous Computing*, IFIP, pages 222–238. Springer, 2005.

[11] C. Cremers, K. Rasmussen, B. Schmidt, and S. Čapkun. Distance hijacking attacks on distance bounding protocols. In *Symp. on Security and Privacy*, pages 113–127. IEEE, 2012.

[12] Y. G. Desmedt, C. Goutier, and S. Bengio. Special uses and abuses of the Fiat-Shamir passport protocol. In *Proc. of Advances in Cryptology – CRYPTO'87*, LNCS 293, pages 21–39. Springer, 1988.

[13] U. Dürholz, M. Fischlin, M. Kasper, and C. Onete. A formal approach to distance-bounding RFID protocols. In *Information Security*, LNCS 7001, pages 47–62. Springer, 2011.

[14] M. Fischlin and C. Onete. Subtle kinks in distance-bounding: an analysis of prominent protocols. In *WISec*, pages 195–206. ACM Press, 2013.

[15] M. Fischlin and C. Onete. Terrorism in distance bounding: Modeling terrorist fraud resistance. In *ACNS 2013*, LNCS, pages 414–431. Springer, 2013.

[16] S. Gambs, C. Onete, and J.-M. Robert. Prover anonymous and deniable distance-bounding authentication. In *AsiaCCS'14*, pages 501–506. ACM Press, 2014.

[17] S. Goldwasser, S. Micali, and R. L. Rivest. A digital signature scheme secure against adaptive chosen message attacks. *SIAM Journal on Computing*, 17(2):281–308, 1988.

[18] J. Hermans, A. Pashalidis, F. Vercauteren, and B. Preneel. A new RFID privacy model. In *ESORICS 2011*, LNCS 6879, pages 568–587. Springer, 2011.

[19] J. Hermans, Peeters R, and C. Onete. Efficient, secure, private distance bounding without key updates. In *WiSec 2013*, pages 207–218. ACM Press, 2013.

[20] C. H. Kim, G. Avoine, F. Koeune, F.-X. Standaert, and O. Pereira. The Swiss-Knife RFID distance bounding protocol. In *ICISC 2008*, LNCS 5461, pages 98–115. Springer, 2008.

[21] D. E. Knuth. *The Art of Computer Programming: Fundamental Algorithms*, 3^{rd}ed. Addison Wesley, 1997.

[22] D. E. Knuth, R. L. Graham, and O. Patashnik. *Concrete mathematics*, 2nd ed. Adison Wesley, 1994.

[23] S. Mangard, E. Oswald, and T. Popp. *Power analysis attacks: Revealing the secrets of smart cards*. Springer Science & Business Media, 2008.

[24] S. Micali, C. Rackoff, and B. Sloan. The notion of security for probabilistic cryptosystems. *SIAM Journal on Computing*, 17(2):412–426, 1988.

[25] T. Nakanishi, H. Fujii, Y. Hira, and N. Funabiki. Revocable group signature schemes with constant costs for signing and verifying. In *PKC 2009*, LNCS 5443, pages 463–480. 2009.

[26] V. Shoup. Sequences of games: a tool for taming complexity in security proofs. Cryptology ePrint 2004/332, 2004.

[27] S. Vaudenay. Proof of proximity of knowledge. Cryptology ePrint 2014/695, 2014.

[28] S. Vaudenay. Private and secure public-key distance bounding; application to NFC payment. In *Financial Cryptography*, LNCS 8975, pages 207–216. Springer, 2015.

[29] Serge Vaudenay. On privacy models for RFID. In *Proc. of Advances in Cryptology – Asiacrypt'07*, LNCS 4883, pages 68–87. Springer, 2007.

A. Mafia-Fraud Resistance Proof

Let the traceability experiment $\mathsf{Exp}^{trace}_{\mathcal{A},\mathsf{G-SIG}}(\lambda)$ for $\mathcal{A}$ on a revocable group signature scheme $\mathsf{G-SIG}$ be defined as:

DEFINITION 13. *The initialization is described in Def. 12.* **Guessing phase:** *$\mathcal{A}$ outputs a message m^* and a signature σ^*. Then, the challenger outputs 1 if and only if:*

- $(m^*, \sigma^*) \notin \Sigma$ and $\mathsf{G.ver}_{\mathsf{gpk}}(\sigma^*, m^*, \mathsf{RL}) = 1$,
- $\mathsf{G.ope}_{\mathsf{msk}}(\sigma^*, m^*, \mathsf{UL}, \mathsf{gpk}) \notin \mathsf{CU} \setminus \mathsf{RL}$.

i.e., $\mathcal{A}$ has been able to produce a valid and fresh signature for a message without using the key of a corrupted user. Define $\mathsf{Adv}^{trace}_{\mathsf{G-SIG}}(\lambda)$ as in Def. 6. A group signature $\mathsf{G-SIG}$ is traceable if $\mathsf{Adv}^{trace}_{\mathsf{G-SIG}}(\lambda)$ is negligible.

PROOF. OF THEOREM 5.2 This proof is built as a series of games [26]. The idea is to go from the initial security game $G0$ to a final game for which no successful polynomial-time adversary can exist. Each game Gi is associated with the probability $Pr[Gi]$ that an adversary wins the game. The proof makes small steps from one game to the next one, such that $|Pr[Gi] - Pr[G(i+1)]|$ is negligible. Proving the difference property for each step, and the fact that the winning probability for the last game is negligible prove that no adversary can win $G0$ with a non-negligible probability.

Proof strategy. We first rule out the use of the backdoor returning the provers' secret keys. Then, we force the verifier and the provers to never reuse their respective values N_V and N_P twice, and rule out a group signature forgery by the adversary. The last transition consists in replacing the initial message e by the encryption of a random message, completely independent from the actual value N_P used in the protocol. This game can be seen as the classical shared-secret DB protocol. The secret N_P is shared offline between the prover and the verifier, and the adversary $\mathcal{A}$ does not have any more access to a ciphertext containing this secret. This game $\mathcal{A}$ cannot be won with a non-negligible probability by any adversary. We build the following sequence of games, reducing progressively the capabilities of the adversaries. This follows from the difference lemma presented by Shoup [26].

In the following, WL denotes a list in which each $\mathsf{Prover}(i)$ stores every generated tuple (e, N_P, σ). It allows the provers and the verifier oracles to exchange their shared secrets.

Game $G1$. The backdoor is deactivated. $\mathcal{A}$ loses a (negligible) probability (Theorem 6.1) of recovering N_P from the backdoor. From the difference lemma [26], $|Pr[G1] - Pr[G0]| \leq p_{back}(n, t)$.

Game $G2$. The oracle $\mathsf{Prover}(i)$ uses different N_P values for each of the q_p calls. $\mathcal{A}$ loses an advantage of at most $q_p^2/2^n$. This follows from the binomial expansion of the probability that a given value has been selected zero or once and the union bound. Thus, $|Pr[G2] - Pr[G1]| \leq q_p^2/2^n$.

Game $G3$. The oracle $\mathsf{Verifier}$ uses different N_V values for each of the q_v calls. Thus, $|Pr[G3] - Pr[G2]| \leq q_v^2/2^n$.

Game $G4$. The oracle $\mathsf{Verifier}$ aborts if $\mathsf{G.ver}_{gpk}(\sigma, N_P, \mathsf{RL}) = 1$, no tuple of WL contains σ and $\mathsf{G.ope}_{msk}(\sigma, N_P, \mathsf{UL}, gpk) \notin \mathsf{CU}$. This happens if $\mathcal{A}$ produces a fresh signature σ on a value N_P without using the key of a corrupted user. Since G-SIG is a traceable group signature scheme, $|Pr[G4] - Pr[G3]| \leq \mathsf{Adv}_{\mathsf{G-SIG}}^{trace}(\lambda)$.

Game $G5$. The oracle $\mathsf{Prover}(i)$ sends an encrypted value N_{P0} unrelated to the actual value N_{P1} used in the protocol *by both parties*. The oracles are modified as follows:

- $\mathsf{Prover}(i)$ sets $N_{P0}, N_{P1} \xleftarrow{\$} \{0,1\}^n$, $\sigma_0 = \mathsf{G.sig}_{psk}(N_{P0})$, $\sigma_1 = \mathsf{G.sig}_{psk}(N_{P1})$, and $e = \mathsf{E.enc}_{pk_v}(N_{P0}, \sigma_0)$. It adds (e, N_{P1}, σ_1) to a list WL. It then sends e, but uses N_{P1}.
- $\mathsf{Verifier}$ acts as in $G4$, except for the N_P computation:
  - If $(e, N_{P1}, \cdot) \in \mathsf{WL}$, it uses N_{P1}. This is the main case, which corresponds to non-corrupted provers.
  - If $(e, \cdot, \cdot) \notin \mathsf{WL}$, it computes $(N_P^*, \sigma^*) = \mathsf{E.dec}_{sk_v}(e)$ and uses N_P^*.

Thus, $\mathcal{A}$ loses the possibility of recovering the value of N_P from the ciphertext e. However, this advantage is negligible since the PKE encryption scheme is IND–CCA2 secure.

Consider the extension of the IND–CCA2 security concept allowing a polynomially-bounded number q_p of challenges [4], with a single public/private key pair. During this experiment, the challenger picks a bit b and gives an oracle $\mathsf{LREnc}_b^{pk_v}(m_0, m_1)$, which returns the encryption of m_b. This oracle can be queried at most q_p times. The challenger also provides a decryption oracle that deciphers any ciphertext, except if it was generated by $\mathsf{LREnc}_b^{pk_v}(\cdot, \cdot)$. The distinguisher wins if he properly guesses b using the oracles.

Let us assume that there exists an efficient adversary $\mathcal{A}$ for the game $G5$. Thus, an efficient distinguisher $\mathcal{B}$ can be defined for the IND–CCA2 experiment using $\mathcal{A}$.

Initialization $\mathcal{B}$ sets up the environment (except the PKE setting). He creates two user lists UL and RL, and a group signature scheme setup with $\mathsf{G.gen}(1^\lambda)$, obtaining a couple (gpk, msk). He adds to UL n_p provers using $\mathsf{DB.join}_{msk}(i, \mathsf{UL})$.

Simulation $\mathcal{B}$ simulates a $SPADE$ environment for $\mathcal{A}$ with the DB-oracles of $G4$, with the following modifications to the prover and verifier oracles. When the oracle $\mathsf{Prover}()$ is called, it sets $e = \mathsf{LREnc}_b^{pk_v}(N_{P0}||\sigma_0, N_{P1}||\sigma_1)$, adds (e, N_{P1}, σ_1) to WL and uses N_{P1} internally. The oracle $\mathsf{Verifier}$ acts as in $G4$ if it receives e such that $(e, N_{P1}, \sigma_1) \in \mathsf{WL}$. Otherwise, it decrypts e with the provided decryption oracle. Finally, $\mathcal{B}$ returns the result of the authentication $OutV$ to the challenger, which is 1 if the verifier accepts, and 0 otherwise.

If $b = 1$, $e = \mathsf{E.enc}_{pk_v}(N_{P1}, \sigma_1)$, $(e, N_{P1}, \sigma_1) \in \mathsf{WL}$ and both parties use N_{P1} internally. This games corresponds exactly to the game $G4$. Otherwise, $e = \mathsf{E.enc}_{pk_v}(N_{P0}, \sigma_0)$ while the N_{P1} is used. This simulates the game $G5$.

Let $\mathcal{B}_0$ denote the event that the distinguisher outputs 0, and $\mathcal{B}_1$ the event that it outputs 1. Thus, $Pr[\mathcal{B}_1|b = 1] = Pr[G4]$ and $Pr[\mathcal{B}_0|b = 0] = 1 - Pr[G5]$, since $\mathcal{B}$ returns the result of the authentication to the distinguisher. The winning probability of $\mathcal{B}$ is then $Pr[\mathcal{B}_1 \wedge b = 1] + Pr[\mathcal{B}_0 \wedge b = 0]$, which is equal to $Pr[G4] \cdot \frac{1}{2} + (1 - Pr[G5]) \cdot \frac{1}{2} = \frac{1}{2} + \frac{Pr[G4] - Pr[G5]}{2}$. Now assume that $Pr[G4] - Pr[G5]$ is non negligible. Then $\mathcal{B}$ has a non-negligible advantage on the extended IND–CCA2 game. However, the advantage of $\mathcal{B}$ cannot be more than q_p times the advantage on the original IND–CCA2 experiment. Thus, $|Pr[G5] - Pr[G4]| \leq q_p \cdot \mathsf{Adv}_{\mathsf{PKE}}^{IND-CCA2}(\lambda)$, which is negligible by hypothesis.

The final game. The final step is to prove that the probability to win $G5$ is negligible. Since $\mathcal{A}$ cannot purely relay messages without using $\mathsf{DB.Taint}(.)$ and invalidating the session, for each round j,

- If $\mathcal{A}$ sends c_j' to $\mathsf{Prover}(i)$ before getting c_j from $\mathsf{Verifier}$, he would be wrong with probability $\frac{1}{2}$.
- If $\mathcal{A}$ sends c_j' to $\mathsf{Prover}(i)$ after receiving c_j from $\mathsf{Verifier}$, he must send r_j' before receiving r_j since pure relay is not allowed. He would be wrong with probability $\frac{1}{2}$.

In the first case, a wrongly guess challenge invalidates the final message τ. Hence, $\mathcal{A}$ must recompute this message to succeed. He cannot do so without guessing N_P, and his success probability is no more than $\left(\frac{1}{2}\right)^n$. In the second case, the authentication fails if $\mathcal{A}$ sends a single wrong response. Thus, his success probability is again no more than $\left(\frac{1}{2}\right)^n$. Since $a = \mathsf{H}(N_P, N_V)$ is a truly random value, during the time-critical phase, $\mathcal{A}$ cannot do better than guessing the answer of each challenging round. Thus, $Pr[G5] \leq \left(\frac{1}{2}\right)^n$. Finally, $\mathcal{A}$ cannot determine τ except with a negligible probability (because he would have to guess the value used as N_P).

From the sequence of games, let $\mathcal{A}^{MF} = 1$ denote the event that $\mathcal{A}$ wins the MF experiment, $Pr[\mathcal{A}^{MF} = 1] \leq p_{back}(n, t) + \frac{q_p^2 + q_v^2 + 1}{2^n} + \mathsf{Adv}_{\mathsf{G-SIGn}}^{trace}(\lambda) + q_p \cdot \mathsf{Adv}_{\mathsf{PKE}}^{IND-CCA2}(\lambda)$ $\quad\square$

Secure Motion Verification using the Doppler Effect

Matthias Schäfer[†]   Patrick Leu[‡]   Vincent Lenders[*]   Jens Schmitt[†]

[†]University of Kaiserslautern
Germany
{schaefer, jschmitt}@cs.uni-kl.de

[‡]trivo systems
Switzerland
patrick.leu@trivo.ch

[*]armasuisse
Switzerland
vincent.lenders@armasuisse.ch

ABSTRACT

Future transportation systems highly rely on the integrity of spatial information provided by their means of transportation such as vehicles and planes. In critical applications (e.g. collision avoidance), tampering with this data can result in life-threatening situations. It is therefore essential for the safety of these systems to securely verify this information. While there is a considerable body of work on the secure verification of locations, movement of nodes has only received little attention in the literature. This paper proposes a new method to securely verify spatial movement of a mobile sender in all dimensions, i.e., position, speed, and direction. Our scheme uses Doppler shift measurements from different locations to verify a prover's motion. We provide formal proof for the security of the scheme and demonstrate its applicability to air traffic communications. Our results indicate that it is possible to reliably verify the motion of aircraft in currently operational systems with an equal error rate of zero.

1. INTRODUCTION

Today's economy highly relies on the effectiveness of the transportation system. However, the capacity of the transportation system is pushed to its limits by the ever growing number of vehicles and airplanes. The solution to this problem lies in more autonomous means of transportation. Since machines can react faster and more accurately than humans, the minimum separation of vehicles can be reduced to increase the density, and, thus, the capacity of roads and airspace [1, 2].

To enable autonomous air and ground navigation applications such as collision avoidance, platooning, or automatic cruise control, new standards and technologies have been published to provide position, speed and direction of moving vehicles [3, 4]. However, as demonstrated in [5, 6, 7], integrity breaches due to malicious tampering with this data can result in life-threatening situations. Consequently, it is

essential for the safety of these systems to securely verify the integrity of the motion information.

A considerable body of work exists in the area of secure verification of locations, which could be used to verify motion in terms of changes in position over time, [8, 9, 10, 11, 12, 13]. These approaches, however, have been designed to verify *position* claims, not claims about speed and direction of movement, i.e., the *velocity*. As a consequence, such a point-wise verification of the velocity using location verification schemes only allows for verifying the average velocity between two positions. This is a fundamental drawback which renders this approach useless for time-critical applications (e.g. collision avoidance) since these applications often rely not only on the integrity of positions, but also on exact velocities of other vehicles at a particular instant in time. Such applications require solutions for securely verifying instantaneous velocity.

In this paper, we propose using the Doppler effect to securely verify the instantaneous velocity. The Doppler effect is a well-known technique to infer the relative speed of moving objects in classical radar systems [14]. It has also been used for passive emitter localization and motion estimation in [15, 16, 17, 18, 19].

Similarly, our approach relies on the Doppler shift, but uses it to verify the location and velocity of transmitters in a secure way. The key idea of our scheme is to measure the Doppler shift of a signal at multiple positions simultaneously. While an attacker may attempt to manipulate its transmission frequency to fool a single receiver, it cannot imitate the effect of motion in the frequency domain for more than two receivers at once.

We show that by using Doppler shift measurements from at least three different locations, we can securely verify all location and velocity claims. We provide formal proof for the security of our scheme, derive the theoretical requirements, and investigate the feasibility of verifying motion claims in operational real-world systems.

Our experimental results with air traffic control signals demonstrate that our approach can be used to significantly enhance the security of air traffic management systems. In particular, we provide means for measuring the Doppler shift of air traffic signals using off-the-shelf software-defined radios. Additional simulations using real air traffic motion data confirm that the accuracy of our setup is sufficient to securely verify the position and velocity of aircraft with an equal error rate of zero.

The rest of the paper is organized as follows. The next section introduces the problem of motion verification and our

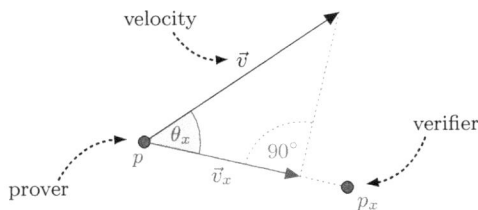

Figure 1: Notation and values used by our verification scheme to determine the Doppler shift.

basic verification scheme. It is then followed by a formal security analysis in Section 3. The feasibility of our scheme in the context of air traffic communication is evaluated in Section 4 and we provide a comparison with related solutions in Section 6. The transfer of our findings to other technologies such as vehicular networks and more sophisticated attacker models are discussed in Section 7.

2. MOTION VERIFICATION

Similar to the related problems of location verification [8] and track verification [13], we define the problem of motion verification as follows. A set of verifiers $\mathcal{V}$ wish to verify whether a moving prover's claimed motion in space C is true. A motion claim is a tuple $C = (p, \vec{v})$, where p denotes the prover's location and $\vec{v}$ its velocity vector. To differentiate the problem of motion verification from location verification, we demand that the prover claims to move with a speed that is not zero, i.e., $v = |\vec{v}| > 0$.

2.1 System Model

We consider a system in which a moving prover continuously broadcasts a wireless signal on a predefined center frequency f_0. The signal carries the prover's current motion claim $C = (p, \vec{v})$. A stationary receiver X is located at position p_x. As illustrated in Figure 1, we define $\vec{v}_x$ as the radial velocity of the prover towards X, and θ_x as the angle between $\vec{v}$ and $\vec{v}_x$. We can now calculate the change rate of the prover's distance to X, the so called *radial speed*, as

$$v_x = \cos(\theta_x) \cdot v .$$

Note that the radial speed becomes $v_x = v$ if the prover moves exactly towards X (i.e. $\theta_x = 0°$) and $v_x = -v$ if it moves away from X ($\theta_x = 180°$).

Due to the Doppler effect, X receives the signal with a frequency offset which depends on the radial speed. Accordingly, X receives the motion claim C on the frequency

$$f_x = \frac{f_0}{1 - \frac{v_x}{c}} ,$$

where c is the propagation speed of the prover's signal. The Doppler frequency shift (or simply Doppler shift) can then be calculated as

$$\delta_x = f_0 - f_x \ = \frac{f_0}{1 - \frac{c}{v_x}} .$$

2.2 Verification Method

The basic idea of our scheme is to measure the frequency of a prover's signal at different locations and cross-check its

conformance with the reported motion claim. From a protocol's viewpoint, as soon as one verifier detects a mismatch, it sends an alarm and we consider an attack detected.

To be more precise, each verifier $X \in \mathcal{V}$ located at (the known) position p_x measures the center frequency $\overline{f}_x$ of each motion claim $C = (p, \vec{v})$. It then checks the following verification condition:

$$\overline{f}_x \overset{?}{=} \frac{f_0}{1 - \frac{v_x}{c}} , \tag{1}$$

where the radial speed v_x is derived from C as explained in Section 2.1.

It is worth noting that our scheme neither relies on any sort of time synchronization among the nodes, nor does it require specialized hardware such as sectorized antennas. In addition, it is completely passive and does not require any additional communication. We conclude that our scheme is lightweight in the sense of verification speed (considers only single measurement), cost-efficiency, and scalability. As demonstrated in Section 4, the Doppler shift can be measured with simple commercial of-the-shelf hardware and there is no need to, e.g., allocate expensive RF spectrum bandwidth for dedicated verification communication. Except for the case of an attack, our scheme does in fact not require any exchange of control messages at all.

3. SECURITY ANALYSIS

For simplicity, we only consider two-dimensional Cartesian coordinates and vectors in our analysis. Extending our results to three dimensions is straightforward.

3.1 Attacker Model

We consider a single attacker A which is stationary and located at position p_a. By stationary, we mean that A's velocity vector $\vec{v}_a = \vec{0}$, where $\vec{0}$ denotes the null vector of length $|\vec{0}| = 0$. We further assume that the attacker only uses one antenna and cannot launch distributed attacks from multiple locations. However, it can arbitrarily adjust its transmission frequency and we do not impose any restrictions on the attacker's knowledge. In particular, A knows the exact locations of all verifiers. The attacker's goal is to successfully claim a motion different from its real one. This means, it broadcasts a false motion claim C_a with $C_a = (p, \vec{v}) \neq (p_a, \vec{0})$. *An attack is considered successful if Equation 1 is satisfied for all verifiers $X \in \mathcal{V}$.*

For ease of presentation, we start our security analysis with the trivial case of a single verifier and extend it step-by-step by adding more verifiers. We assume that due to the low system requirements of our scheme, cheap hardware enables deployments with large enough numbers of verifiers to achieve a coverage sufficient to provide security. As shown in the following analysis, our scheme already provides reasonable security if all positions of interest are covered by at least two verifiers.

3.2 Case $\mathcal{V} = \{X\}$

In case of a single verifier X, a stationary attacker has to imitate the Doppler effect with respect to X by adapting its transmission frequency f_a accordingly. In order to successfully claim C_a, it simply transmits C_a on the frequency expected by X according to Equation 1 (i.e. $f_a = f_x$). Since

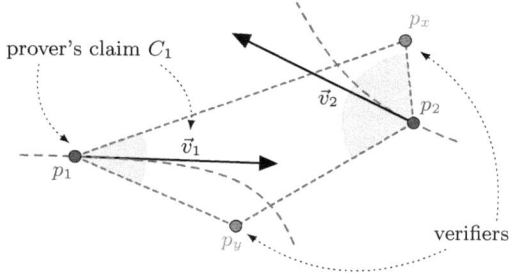

Figure 2: Example scenario with two verifiers at p_x and p_y and two motion claims $C_1 = (p_1, \vec{v}_1)$ and $C_2 = (p_2, \vec{v}_2)$ which are not verifiable using our scheme. Note that the velocity vectors always bisect the angle between the claimed position and the two verifiers when moving on a hyperbola.

the radial velocity of A and X is zero, X receives the signal on the expected frequency and the attack will not be detected. In this way, the attacker can successfully pretend arbitrary motions.

3.3 Case $\mathcal{V} = \{X, Y\}$

In order to delude two verifiers, the attacker has to find a false motion claim C_a and a transmission frequency which both match X's and Y's expectations at the same time. This means for a given motion claim C_a, the attacker's transmission frequency f_a must satisfy the following two equations:

$$f_a = \frac{f_0}{1 - \frac{v_x}{c}} \quad \text{and} \quad f_a = \frac{f_0}{1 - \frac{v_y}{c}}$$

It is easy to see that the two equations can only be satisfied if there is a motion claim C_a with $v_x = v_y$. In terms of physical effects, this means that the attacker can only claim motions where the Doppler effect observed by X equals that observed by Y (i.e. $f_x = f_y$). By replacing v_x and v_y by their definitions from Section 2.1, we can reduce the problem to finding a motion claim with

$$\theta_x = \theta_y \qquad (2)$$

This, in turn, holds only for $C_a = (p, \vec{v})$ where $\vec{v}$ bisects the clock- or counterclockwise angle between $\vec{v}_x$ and $\vec{v}_y$. An alternative, yet still geometric interpretation of this constraint is that the attacker can only claim motions where vector $\vec{v}$ is *tangential* to one arm of the hyperbola with focus points p_x and p_y and a semi-major axis length of half the difference of the distances from p to the foci. Figure 2 illustrates this for two verifiers and two motion claims C_1 and C_2.

We postulate that this constraint will already provide sufficient or even strong security for many scenarios since attackers are forced to claim motion along hyperbolas to stay undetected. Especially in the vehicular network scenario, it is rather unlikely that roads satisfy Equation 2. Even if the system faces hyperbolic roads, a proper positioning of the two verifiers can prevent legitimate occurrences of Equation 2. In addition to that, if we assume that X and Y know each other's positions, they can simply check Equation 2 in a first step. In case it is satisfied, they should consider the track claim suspicious. In case it is not satisfied, the verifiers can securely proceed with the normal verification procedure, i.e., they check Equation 1.

3.4 Case $\mathcal{V} = \{X, Y, Z\}$

Analogously to the previous case and assuming that the prover is not moving, we can conclude that an attacker facing three verifiers is limited to motion claims which result in equal Doppler shift at each verifier, i.e. $v_x = v_y = v_z$. It is clear that the attacker's options for p are now further reduced to positions on one of the extensions of the line segments $\overrightarrow{p_a p_b}$ with $p_a, p_b \in \{p_x, p_y, p_z\}$ and $p_a \neq p_b$. In other words, at least two verifiers must lie on a straight line from the perspective of the claimed location p.

Proof Let us assume that there are no verifiers $X, Y \in \mathcal{V}$ such that a straight line exists which intersects p_x, p_y, and p. This implies that the angle between $\vec{v}_x$ and $\vec{v}_y$ is different for all pairs of verifiers $X, Y \in \mathcal{V}$. We know from the previous case that the attacker has to bisect all these angles in order to satisfy Equation 1 for all three verifiers. As it is impossible to bisect two different angles which share one vector simultaneously, any velocity vector will violate Equation 1 for at least one verifier. $\square$

As explained above, subsequent motion claims have to comply with their predecessors in order to stay undetected for a certain period of time. Extending the considerations of Section 3.3 to three verifiers leads us to the conclusion that the attacker is now restricted to claiming motion along all three pairwise hyperbolas simultaneously and, thus, the pairwise hyperbolas must be equal. This, however, is only the case if all focus points (the verifiers) lie on one straight line since then, either $\theta_x = \theta_y = \theta_z = 0°$ or $\theta_x = \theta_y = \theta_z = 180°$ holds.

3.5 Conclusion

For any $\mathcal{V}$ with $|\mathcal{V}| > 1$, we can conclude from the analysis in the previous sections that our verification scheme is secure for *single* motion claims $C = (p, \vec{v})$ if there are two verifiers $X, Y \in \mathcal{V}$ with different expected radial speeds $v_x \neq v_y$.

It is worth noting that this condition can be guaranteed with an appropriate positioning of verifiers. For instance, covering any location of interest by at least four verifiers in a constellation different from a triangle or a straight line ensures that for every motion claim there is at least one verifier which expects a radial velocity different from the others. The same holds if all locations of interest are enclosed by at least three verifiers. The latter scenario is used in our simulations below (Section 5.4).

If historical motion claims are considered as well, we can additionally conclude that our scheme is secure if there are two verifiers $X, Y \in \mathcal{V}$ and the prover is not claiming to move along a hyperbola with foci p_x and p_y. If there are more than two verifiers it is secure.

4. FEASIBILITY STUDY

Real-world measurements are naturally prone to noise induced by hardware and the environment. We are specifically interested in whether we are able to build a real-world system with a sufficient accuracy to reliably detect violations of Equation 1. We have therefore selected the scenario of air traffic communication to test the applicability of our scheme in a real-world environment.

We are considering the Automatic Dependent Surveillance-Broadcast (ADS-B). The ADS-B protocol is a key component of the next generation air transportation system which is currently being deployed [20]. In ADS-B, aircraft determine their three-dimensional position and velocity using satellite navigation systems such as GPS. They periodically broadcast this information on the secondary surveillance radar frequency 1090 MHz.

As demonstrated in [5] and [6], ADS-B has serious security issues due to the lack of authentication mechanisms or encryption. More precisely, integrity of information provided by ADS-B cannot be guaranteed since it is possible to spoof ADS-B signals even with low-cost commercial off-the-shelf hardware. These security problems are aggravated by the long development, certification, and deployment cycles in aviation (usually 20-30 years) which render solutions requiring changes to the infrastructure useless in the short or even medium term [21]. Consequently, passive schemes (such as ours) are of special importance for aviation since they can run side by side with the existing infrastructure without any changes.

4.1 ADS-B Environment

As mentioned above, it is important to verify ADS-B data without requiring any changes to the standard or the infrastructure (including equipment in aircraft). Consequently, our scheme has to cope with ADS-B as it is. For this reason, we start our analysis with a short characterization of the ADS-B environment. We used dataset of air traffic positions from all over the world collected by the OpenSky Network[1]. The dataset was based on about 500 million recorded transponder messages.

In ADS-B, GPS-based velocity and position reports are each broadcast twice per second [3]. Since normal aircraft (e.g. airliners) usually move on quasi-linear tracks within short periods of time, we can interpolate missing velocity (or position) information for each received report. As demonstrated below, a simple linear interpolation achieves a sufficient accuracy for movements in the en-route airspace (altitudes above 9 km). Thus, we can consider both position and velocity reports as a motion claim and obtain an expected rate of about 4 claims per second.

Since the Doppler shift directly depends on the velocity of a target, we are particularly interested in typical speeds of aircraft. One thing we observed is that aircraft fly at different speeds depending on the altitude. For instance, the average velocity at altitudes below 9 km is 161 m/s while at higher altitudes, the so called en-route airspace, the average velocity is about 230 m/s.

The en-route airspace is of special interest to us since most aircraft are usually at high altitudes. In particular, the dataset from the OpenSky Network contained almost twice as many positions from the en-route airspace than from the lower airspace. That is because aircraft usually climb directly to the en-route airspace after the start and only descend to lower altitudes for landing. Hence, we can assume that velocities of about 230 m/s are typical for the air traffic scenario.

A second factor affecting our verification scheme with respect to expected Doppler shifts and number of verifiers required to cover a certain area is the range of a receiver. As shown in Figure 8, reception ranges are usually between 300-400 km if there is a clear line-of-sight. This allows for a large coverage of the en-route airspace with a relatively small numbers of receivers.

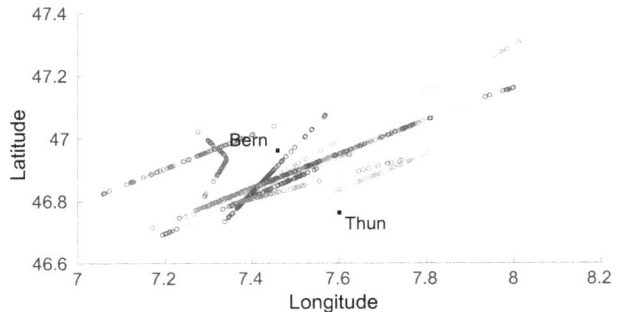

Figure 3: Tracks of the 17 flights observed with two USRPs located in Bern and Thun. Each USRP measured the frequency of incoming signals.

In the following sections, we show how off-the-shelf software-defined radios can be used as verifiers in this environment. Our results indicate that our scheme is a promising candidate for considerably improving the security of ADS-B .

4.2 Experimental Setup

In order to investigate the challenges and accuracy of Doppler shift measurements of ADS-B messages, we deployed two software-defined radios (Ettus USRP X300) at two sites in Switzerland (Bern and Thun) which are about 25 km apart. Both USRPs used a GPS-disciplined, oven-controlled crystal oscillator (GPSDO) as a clock source and a sample rate of 10 MHz. They provide I/Q samples with a resolution of 14 bit for both in-phase and quadrature component. The radio front-ends (SBX-120 daughterboards) were tuned to the center frequency of ADS-B (1090 MHz). Each setup recorded all ADS-B messages along with their raw I/Q samples using a modified version of the GNU Radio-based software receiver for transponder signals gr-air-modes[2].

After recording ADS-B signals for eight hours, we joined both datasets and identified all messages that were received by both USRPs based on their reception time and transponder ID. We then process the data with an ADS-B decoder based on the library provided by the OpenSky Network[3] to extract accurate three-dimensional position, velocity, and heading information from these messages. Figure 3 shows the position reports and the locations of the receivers. As a final processing step, we used linear interpolation to estimate the positions for non-position messages and velocity as well as heading for non-velocity messages.

With this setup and preprocessing steps, we collected over the course of about 8 hours a set of 2427 ADS-B messages from 17 different aircraft. Each message is assigned to a three-dimensional transmitter location (p), a velocity vector ($\vec{v}$) and the raw signal data as received by each of the receivers.

4.3 Results: Frequency of Arrival

The first step of our analysis was to investigate the noise level in frequency of arrival (FOA) measurements. A common approach to determine the FOA of a signal is to first translate it to its frequency domain representation using the discrete Fourier transform and then identify the peak frequency. This methodology requires evenly spaced samples

---

[1]https://opensky-network.org

[2]https://github.com/bistromath/gr-air-modes
[3]https://github.com/openskynetwork/java-adsb

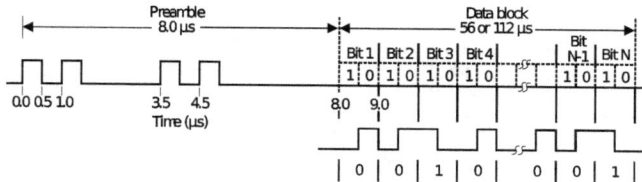

Figure 4: Pulse-position modulation of Mode S replies and ADS-B messages [22].

of the signal. In ADS-B, however, a pulse position modulation is used and the signal of interest arrives only in short bursts of 0.5 μs with either no, 0.5 μs spacing, or 1 μs spacing (see Figure 4). Since we are only interested in the peak frequency of these short bursts and not in the plain spectrum, we discard the samples between the pulses to reduce the spectral noise. This filtering results in an incomplete sample set. Unfortunately, algorithms for calculating the spectral representation of a signal based on incomplete samples have generally a higher computational complexity than the fast Fourier transform (FFT). The Lomb-Scargle periodogram, as a common approach, scales at $\mathcal{O}(N^2)$ whereas in contrast, the computational cost of the FFT only increases by $\mathcal{O}(N \log N)$ [23]. Hence, for efficiency reasons, we used a linear interpolation to fill the gaps and argue that it is sufficiently accurate since the expected Doppler shift is in the range of a few hundred Hertz while the gaps are at most 1 μs wide. To be more precise, if the aircraft moves directly towards the verifier at a speed of 230 m/s, the Doppler shift is 836 Hz. A gap of 1 μs corresponds to only 0.0836% of a complete oscillation of the Doppler shift frequency and the error caused by the linear interpolation is therefore assumed to be negligible. In summary, our FOA estimation is based on a continuous approximation of the original pulsed signal to amplify the signals spectral effect.

Let $x(n)$ be the n-th I/Q sample of the interpolated signal as received by X and $\mathcal{F}\{x\}$ its frequency domain representation that results from the discrete Fourier transform. We estimated the FOA by determining the peak frequency in the frequency domain representation of the interpolated signal:

$$\hat{f}_x = \arg\max_f |\mathcal{F}\{x\}(f)| \qquad (3)$$

By finally subtracting the expected Doppler shift from $\hat{f}_x$, we obtained the deviation of the measured from the expected FOA, corresponding to the measurement error when there is no attack.

The results are shown in Figure 5 and Table 1. Figure 5a shows the empirical cumulative distribution functions (ECDF) of the FOAs measured by the receiver in Bern and separated by aircraft. There are several notable observations.

First, while the messages of some aircraft vary around a central frequency within a range of less than 10 kHz, others cover the whole spectrum from -300 kHz to 300 kHz. We observed the same patterns for the respective aircraft in the FOAs of the second receiver in Thun. In fact, the outliers of both receivers (all values above the 10% percentile of the absolute error) coincide 90%. On the contrary, the standard deviation of the differences between the two receivers was less than 500 Hz for other aircraft (see Table 1). We conclude

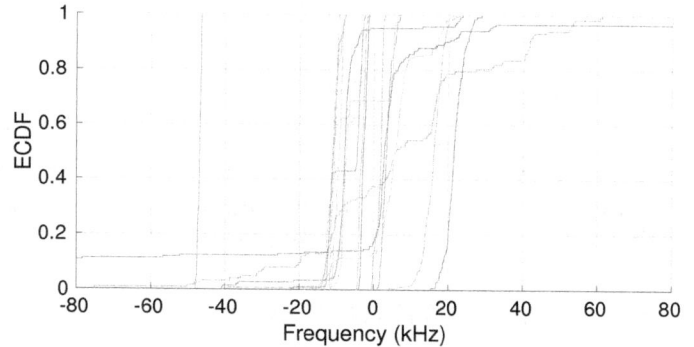

(a) ECDFs of the deviation of the measured FOA of the receiver in Bern from the expected frequency.

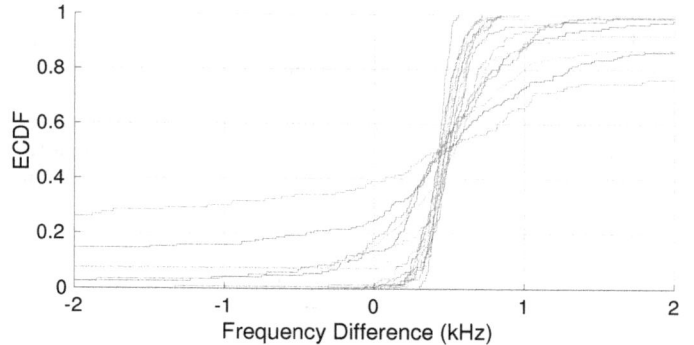

(b) ECDFs of the differences of the FOAs between the two receivers.

Figure 5: Aircraft-wise results of the frequency of arrival measurements desribed in Section 4.3.

that transponders installed in aircraft differ significantly in stability.

Secondly, the center frequencies of the transponders differ significantly as indicated by the horizontal difference of the ECDFs in Figure 5a. Consequently, we must assume that the actual transmission frequency is different from 1090 MHz as the transponders are obviously not calibrated or synchronized (e.g. using GPS).

Thirdly, the median difference of the FOAs of all transponders is always close to 500 Hz (see Figure 5b). Since this offset is independent of the transponder, we can assume that despite the use of the GPSDO, the radio front-ends of the receivers were not tuned to the exact same center frequency. In addition, as Table 1 shows, the median difference stays constantly around 450 ± 50 Hz for all flights and thus for the whole duration of our measurements (8h). This suggests that the frequency offset of the two receivers can be assumed to be constant over longer periods of time.

We can conclude from the above findings that directly applying our verification method (Equation 1) to transponder signals is not practical in the ADS-B scenario due to an unacceptably high noise level. Nevertheless, we can distinguish three kinds of noise that need to be addressed in order to achieve a sufficient accuracy. Therefore, we propose an adapted version of our verification scheme in the next section. It is specifically tailored to dealing with the special conditions of ADS-B signals.

A/C	1	2	3	4	5	6	7	8	9	10	11	12	13	14	15	16	17
min	302	-109e3	-229	-62	100	171	-35e3	-306	-1328	-18e3	-280e3	130	71	45	-33e3	25	-14e3
mean	434	-868	442	431	441	483	525	733	524	1413	-4117	490	473	479	-139	499	595
median	431	419	454	445	434	464	448	513	504	534	475	494	470	473	416	500	512
max	558	92e3	880	714	960	786	30e3	18e3	1499	18e3	265e3	819	1024	836	2094	844	19e3
std	53	28e3	131	131	134	121	5625	1979	322	8002	59e3	136	152	132	3899	132	5742

Table 1: Measurement results: minimum, mean, median, maximum, and standard deviation of the sets of differences $\hat{f}_x - \hat{f}_y$ per aircraft (A/C). All values are provided in Hz.

5. ADAPTED VERIFICATION SCHEME

In accordance with the above observations, we can model realistic frequency of arrival measurements with

$$\overline{f}_x = f_0 + \delta_x + \epsilon_x + \epsilon_t + \epsilon/2$$

where ϵ_x is a constant frequency offset of the receiver's radio front-end, ϵ_t is a constant frequency offset of the transmitter, δ_x the Doppler shift (see Section 2.1), and ϵ a random variable representing twice the random measurement noise. Under the assumption that the random measurement noise is additive, the frequency-difference of arrival (FDOA) at two verifiers X and Y is then

$$\begin{aligned}
\overline{f}_x - \overline{f}_y &= (f_0 + \delta_x + \epsilon_x + \epsilon_t) - (f_0 + \delta_y + \epsilon_y + \epsilon_t) + \epsilon \\
&= \delta_x - \delta_y + \underbrace{(\epsilon_x - \epsilon_y)}_{=\epsilon_{xy}} + \epsilon
\end{aligned} \quad (4)$$

The idea of our adapted scheme is to verify this FDOA instead of the FOA. As Equation 4 shows, this has the advantage that the actual transmission frequency $(f_0 + \epsilon_t)$ does not affect the verification. The sources of noise are reduced to the relative frequency offsets of the receivers ϵ_{xy} and the random noise ϵ.

As shown in the previous section, we can assume ϵ_{xy} to be constant over a sufficient amount of time. This allows us to learn ϵ_{xy} a priori in a calibration phase, for instance by exploiting signals from test transponders which are already widely deployed for the calibration of secondary surveillance radar infrastructures. We therefore assume ϵ_{xy} to be known at runtime.

The adapted FDOA-based verification scheme works as follows. For all pairs of verifiers X and Y which satisfy one of the conditions of Section 3.5, we check for each received ADS-B message

$$\left| (\overline{f}_x - \overline{f}_y) - (\delta_x - \delta_y) - \epsilon_{xy} \right| \overset{?}{<} \mathcal{T} \quad (5)$$

where $\mathcal{T}$ is a pre-defined threshold which depends on the measurement error and the expected FDOA. Note that if there is no measurement error ϵ and offset ϵ_{xy}, the left-hand side of Equation 5 becomes zero for legitimate motion claims.

5.1 Security

As we know from the previous analysis, if one of the requirements summarized in Section 3.5 is met, the verifiers expect different Doppler shifts, that is $\delta_x \neq \delta_y$ for at least two verifiers X and Y. Let f_a be the attacker's transmission frequency. The FDOA measured by X and Y then is

$$\begin{aligned}
\overline{f}_x - \overline{f}_y &= (f_a + \epsilon_x + \epsilon_t) - (f_a + \epsilon_y + \epsilon_t) + \epsilon \\
&= \epsilon_{xy} + \epsilon
\end{aligned}$$

Plugging this into Equation 5 yields

$$\begin{aligned}
\left| (\overline{f}_x - \overline{f}_y) - (\delta_x - \delta_y) - \epsilon_{xy} \right| \\
= \left| (\epsilon_{xy} + \epsilon) - (\delta_x - \delta_y) - \epsilon_{xy} \right| \\
= \left| \epsilon - (\delta_x - \delta_y) \right| \\
\overset{?}{<} \mathcal{T}
\end{aligned} \quad (6)$$

We analyze the security of the adapted scheme by considering the false acceptance and false alarm rate. Equations 5 and 6 show that, generally speaking, false alarms occur when ϵ exceeds $\mathcal{T}$ and fake claims become falsely accepted when the absolute difference of ϵ and the expected FDOA is below $\mathcal{T}$. We therefore say that $\mathcal{T}$ is optimal if it satisfies

$$\epsilon < \mathcal{T} < \left| \epsilon - (\delta_x - \delta_y) \right| \quad (7)$$

We can conclude that the adapted scheme is secure if $\mathcal{T}$ exists. In practice, however, such optimal $\mathcal{T}$ do often not exist since either the measurement error does not have an upper bound or the expected FDOA is not high enough to dominate the measurement error. The scheme can then only provide statistical guarantees based on the distribution of ϵ and the expected FDOAs. To analyze this further, the next section provides a realistic error model based on our real-world measurements.

5.2 Measuring the FDOA

The highest FDOA occurs if an aircraft moves exactly on the line between two verifiers. If we assume a speed of 230 m/s, the difference in radial speed is 460 m/s and the expected FDOA is about 1.6 kHz. Our previous measurements have shown that the accuracy of the above method is not sufficient. Since the maximum frequency difference exceeded 1.6 kHz (see Table 1), an optimal $\mathcal{T}$ does not exist. The goal of this section is to find a method to determine the FDOA accurately enough for secure verification real flights.

A common approach to estimate the FDOA directly from the I/Q samples is determining the offset with the maximum cross-correlation of the frequency domain representations $\mathcal{F}\{x\}(f)$ and $\mathcal{F}\{y\}(f)$ of X's and Y's signals [15]. An efficient way to find this offset (and thus the FDOA) is applying the convolution theorem:

$$\overline{f}_x - \overline{f}_y \approx \arg\max_f \left| \mathcal{F}\{x^* y\}(f) \right|$$

where * denotes the complex conjugate. In summary, we can estimate the FDOA by calculating the discrete Fourier transform of the product of the conjugated I/Q samples of one signal and the I/Q samples of the other signal.

The drawback of this method is that it requires the transmission of raw signal data to at least one node in the network. While exchanging I/Q samples at a sample rate of

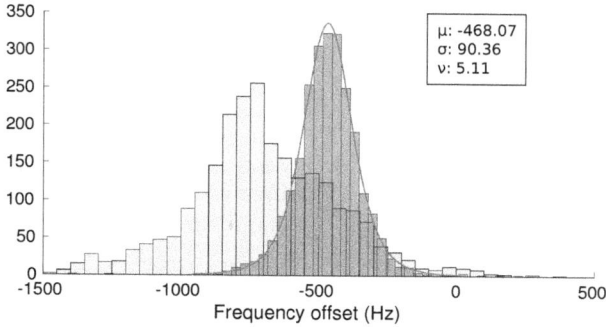

Figure 6: Histograms of the FDOA of all messages with (red; narrow) and without (blue; wide) Doppler compensation. The distribution is fitted by a t-location-scale distribution with location μ, scale σ, and shape ν.

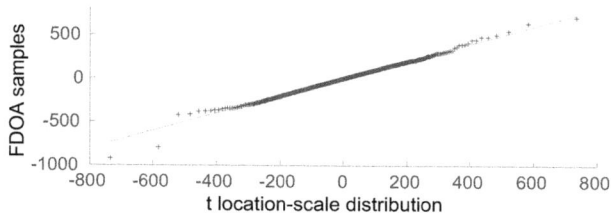

Figure 7: Q-Q plot comparing the random measurement error to the fitted t-distribution shown in Figure 6 after subtracting the estimated constant tuning offset.

10 MHz appears inefficient at first, we argue that this is not a problem for ADS-B messages. I/Q samples of USRPs are 32 bit wide[4]. Combined with a sample rate of 10 MHz, we obtain a total of 1200 samples per ADS-B packet. As a matter of fact, only about 580 of these samples actually convey information due to the pulse-based modulation used in ADS-B. Altogether, only 2320 bytes of signal data per verifier and message need to be exchanged to be able to use the above method.

5.3 FDOA Results

The measured frequency offsets according to this method are shown in Figure 6. After removing the estimated Doppler shift in the FDOA measurements, the left over error is distributed around $\epsilon_{xy} = -468.07$ Hz. Subtracting the constant offset ϵ_{xy} results in a random measurement noise ϵ which is well-fitted by a t-distribution with scaling $\sigma = 90.36$ Hz and $\nu = 5.11$ degrees of freedom (compare Figure 7).

The improvement achieved with this method is considerable. In particular, directly measuring the FDOA with the above method turns out to be much more robust in the presence of the highly unstable transponder signals. As the statistics in Table 2 show, some transponders are still more stable than others, but the variance dropped significantly. For example, if we consider the standard deviation as a measure of stability, aircraft 1 still performs best and aircraft 2

---

[4]In fact, it is only 28 bit wide since the ADC has an I/Q resolution of 14 bit but we skip this optimization for the sake of simplicity.

worst (compare Table 1) while the standard deviation of aircraft 2 is decreased by a factor of over 200. A closer look at the outliers below -345.45 Hz and above 374.8 Hz (99% were between these values) did not reveal any dependence on the signal-to-noise ratio or the bit confidence as defined in [3] and therefore rejects the hypothesis that temporal effects (e.g. higher noise levels) affects some flights more than others. We therefore confirm for our further analysis that the measurement error ϵ is independent and identically distributed for one transponder.

The highest error observed was $\max(|\overline{f}_x - \overline{f}_y|) = 918.82$ Hz. In terms of speed, a difference in the FDOA of 918.82 Hz corresponds to a difference in radial speed of 253 m/s. As mentioned above, the maximum difference in radial speed in the air traffic scenario is 460 m/s and the maximum expected FDOA 1.6 kHz. This combined with the result of our security analysis of the adapted scheme (Section 5.1) suggests, that our setup is not able to perfectly distinguish benign and fake motion claims without false alarms since

$$|\delta_x - \delta_y| \leq 2 \cdot \max(|\overline{f}_x - \overline{f}_y|)$$

and Equation 7 can therefore not be satisfied. However, the probability for such outliers is extremely low. In particular, the probability for a measurement error greater then $\mathcal{T}$ Hz is

$$P(|\epsilon| > \mathcal{T}) = 1 - \int_{-\mathcal{T}}^{\mathcal{T}} P(\epsilon = e)\,\mathrm{d}e \qquad (8)$$

If we assume that the underlying distribution of ϵ matches the fitted t-distribution above (compare Figure 7), the probability for errors, e.g, above 538 Hz (see results in Section 5.4) is

$$P(|\epsilon| > 538 \text{ Hz}) \approx 0.0018$$

Hence, if we use a threshold $\mathcal{T} = 538$ Hz, the expected false alarm rate is 0.16%. If we extend our scheme such that an alarm is only raised if Equation 5 is violated by two successive motion claims of an aircraft, the average false alarm rate drops quadratically to $P(|\epsilon| > \mathcal{T})^2 \approx 0.0003\%$.

The same holds for the probability of accepting an attacker's motion claim. A false location claim becomes accepted by the verifiers X and Y if $|\epsilon - (\delta_x - \delta_y)| < \mathcal{T}$. The probability for this inequality to be satisfied can be bounded as follows ($\mathcal{T} \geq 0$):

$$
\begin{aligned}
P(|\epsilon - (\delta_x - \delta_y)| < \mathcal{T}) &= P(||(\delta_x - \delta_y) - \epsilon| < \mathcal{T}) \\
&\leq P(|\delta_x - \delta_y| - |\epsilon| < \mathcal{T}) \\
&= P(|\epsilon| > |\delta_x - \delta_y| - \mathcal{T}) \\
&= 1 - \int_{\mathcal{T}-|\delta_x-\delta_y|}^{|\delta_x-\delta_y|-\mathcal{T}} P(\epsilon = e)\,\mathrm{d}e
\end{aligned}
$$

If we assume the expected FDOA of a fake motion claim is 1200 Hz and $\mathcal{T} = 538$ Hz, the probability of a false acceptance is lower than or equal to 0.0676%. If we require the acceptance of two successive motion claims for successful verification, the probability of an attacker not being detected drops to $4.5728 \cdot 10^{-5}\%$.

In order to strengthen these theoretical findings and to finally demonstrate that our setup is – despite the residual measurement error – capable of verifying real-world motions at reasonable false alarm/acceptance rates, we conducted simulations with real-world motion data and present the results in the next section.

A/C	1	2	3	4	5	6	7	8	9	10	11	12	13	14	15	16	17
min	-180	-390	-636	-707	-483	-246	-263	-312	-295	-415	-268	-263	-288	-448	-551	-319	-303
max	117	368	254	222	250	274	241	919	344	375	299	345	379	382	422	294	416
std	52	138	113	100	95	105	69	137	104	103	73	117	116	131	183	112	117

Table 2: Frequency-difference of arrival measurement results: minimum, maximum, and standard deviation of the FDOA per aircraft (A/C) minus the constant offset of $\epsilon_{xy} = -468.07$ Hz. All values are provided in Hz.

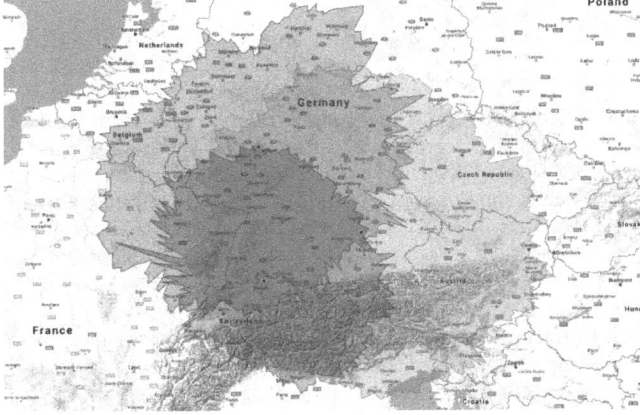

Figure 8: Locations and ranges of the three receivers used for our analysis.

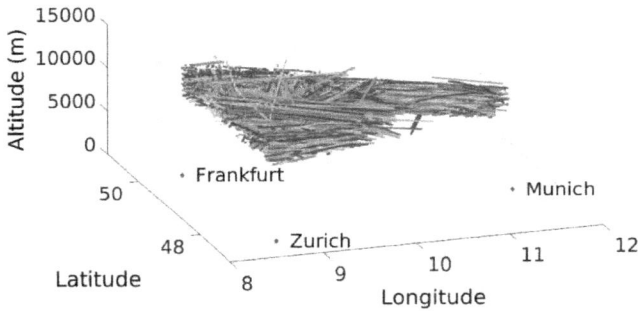

Figure 9: The receiver locations and the flights used for our simulations.

5.4 Performance in the Real World

While the previous sections concentrated on identifying and quantifying the challenges of the air traffic scenario and the capabilities of our USRP-based setup, this section aims at combining all our findings and investigates the performance of our setup in a realistic environment. We are particularly interested in the false acceptance rate and false alarm rate with real-world motion claims. For this purpose, we conducted the following simulations using real air traffic motion data.

We first selected three receivers of the OpenSky Network. Their locations and ranges are shown in Figure 8. They are located closely to major Central European airports (Frankfurt, Munich, and Zurich) and the triangle between them is fully covered by all three receivers. We have chosen them based on their constellation. The triangle constellation is generally good for our verification scheme as on the one hand, it produces high FDOAs of signals sent from within

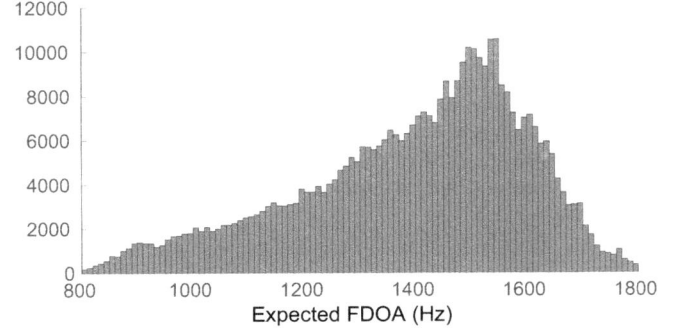

Figure 10: The expected frequency-difference of arrivals of our dataset from the OpenSky Network.

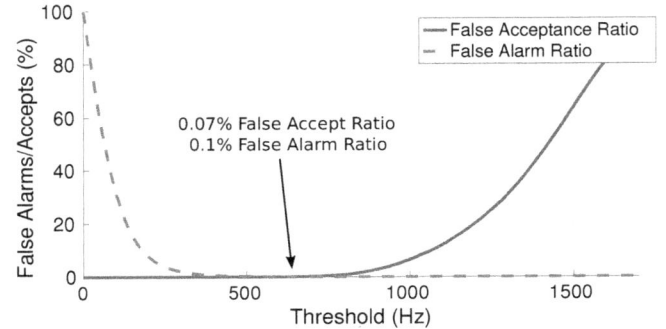

Figure 11: The false alarm and false acceptance ratios of our simulation for different thresholds. Each of the 402,627 motion claims was tested individually.

the triangle, and on the other hand, *there is always a pair of receivers which satisfies the verification requirements* (Section 3.5). We then fetched 24 hours (16/03/2016) of state vectors[5] from the en-route airspace (above an altitude of 9 km) of the triangle from the OpenSky Network's database. In total, we obtained 402,627 state vectors from 866 different aircraft. The total set of state vectors is shown in Figure 9. We refer to these state vectors as motion claims from here on.

For each motion claim and each pair of receivers, we calculated the expected FDOA. We know from the previous analysis that our verification scheme performs best when the expected FDOA is high. Therefore, we identified for each motion claim the pair of receivers with the highest expected FDOA and used this pair for verification. The FDOAs of the receiver pairs with the highest difference are shown in Figure 10. In the next step of our simulation, we

---

[5] A state vector consists of aggregated ADS-B position and velocity information within a second from one aircraft. See https://opensky-network.org/impala-tables.

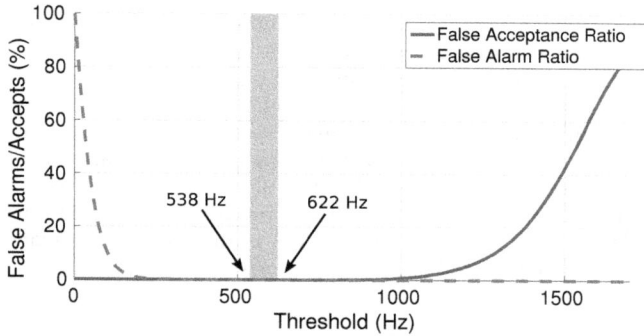

Figure 12: The false alarm and false acceptance ratios of our simulation for different thresholds using two successive motion claims. The gray interval marks the thresholds for which both false acceptance and false alarm ratio dropped to zero.

added to each FDOA value a random measurement error from the t-distribution with $\sigma = 90.36$ Hz and $\nu = 5.11$ and tested whether it would have been falsely accepted (dishonest prover) or falsely rejected (honest prover) for different thresholds. The results are shown in Figure 11. We can summarize that if the three verifiers verified each motion claim individually, the best performing threshold would have been $\mathcal{T} = 610$ Hz with a false alarm ratio of 0.1% and a false acceptance ratio of 0.07%. In absolute numbers, 304 of the 402,627 motion claims were falsely accepted and 366 falsely rejected.

We then repeated the simulation but instead of verifying each motion claim individually, we considered two successive motion claims at a time. In the simulation of an honest prover, we rejected a motion claim if Equation 5 was violated by both claims. Conversely, in the simulation of a dishonest prover, we accepted a claim if the claim and its preceding claim both satisfied Equation 5. The results for all thresholds are provided in Figure 12. Both rates dropped to zero for thresholds $\mathcal{T} \in [538, 622]$. In other words, by using two successive motion claims instead of one, *our scheme detected all attacks while producing no false alarms.*

6. RELATED WORK

Several methods have been proposed to securely verify the location of an emitter. Distance bounding protocols [24, 8, 9, 10] are two-way ranging protocols that rely on cryptographic techniques to enable a verifier to establish an upper bound on the physical distance to a prover. Mutlilateration is a passive localization technique based on the time difference of arrival (TDoA) of signals at geographically distributed stations that can be used for location verification [25, 26, 27]. However, these approaches only allow for verification of the position of a target, not its velocity and heading. In order to verify the motion of an object, multiple successive measurements are required to estimate the velocity and heading of the target. Thus, these approaches can only verify the *average* velocity and heading between the considered messages. In contrast, our scheme can be applied to single messages which allows for verification of the instantaneous motion.

Schäfer et al. have proposed a method to securely verify the track of an aircraft [13]. By validating the inter-arrival

times of successive location claims, their method can detect false track claims without requiring time synchronization among the sensors. While the requirements imposed on the hardware are equal to those of our scheme, secure track verification requires at least 40 ADS-B messages to reliably detect spoofing attacks in the presence of noise. In comparison, our evaluation showed that our approach can detect spoofing attacks with a single message in 0.07% of the cases and only needed a second message for an equal error rate of 0%.

Ghose and Lazos have proposed using Doppler shift measurements for verifying air traffic navigation information [19]. They proposed a scheme in which benign aircraft verify the velocity of other aircraft by estimating their radial velocity through Doppler shift measurements. However, they assume in their attacker model that an attacker cannot adjust the transmission frequency below the frequency tolerance of receivers for transponder signals of 312.5 kHz. In contrast, we do not put any limitations on the attackers frequency accuracy. It is worth noting here that an attacker using a commercial off-the-shelf software-defined radio (e.g. USRP) can achieve a frequency accuracy in the order of ± 0.01 Hz [28]. Therefore and in contrast to this work, our scheme is resistant to attackers which modify their center frequencies to mimic the Doppler effect.

7. DISCUSSION

7.1 A Look Ahead: Vehicular Networks

We have shown in the previous sections that motion verification based on FDOA measurements are not only feasible but also realistic for securely verifying motion of aircraft. However, ground vehicle scenarios consider much lower velocities. In vehicular networks, the expected radial speed of a car relative to a receiver located at the side of the road is about 15 m/s in cities and 35 m/s on highways. This means that Doppler shifts of radio waves in the vehicular scenario would be around 36 Hz in cities and 127 Hz on highways in the best cases. Measuring such a small Doppler shift accurately enough in the ultra high frequency (UHF) band would require extremely accurate hardware.

For that reason, we envision instead a system that relies on sound waves (e.g. ultra sound) for motion verification. The Doppler shift of sound waves is much higher than electromagnetic waves due to the low propagation speed (340 m/s). If we assume a transmission frequency of 19 kHz and a radial speed of 15 m/s, the frequency shift would be 922 Hz.

As a proof of concept, we conducted a simple experiment to analyze the accuracy of measuring the Doppler shift with sound waves. We used the built-in speakers and microphone of two off-the-shelf laptops as sender and receiver, and generated a tone with decreasing frequency from 20 kHz down to 2 kHz using the GNU Radio[6] toolkit. The receiving laptop used the method described in Section 4.3 to determine the FOA of the signal.

The results are shown in Figure 13. While half of the measurements experienced an error even below 1 Hz, the maximum absolute measurement error was 17.58 Hz. This corresponds to a radial speed of about 1 km/h. We can conclude that sound is a suitable medium for verifying velocities even below walking speed. It is worth noting that we used

---

[6]https://gnuradio.org

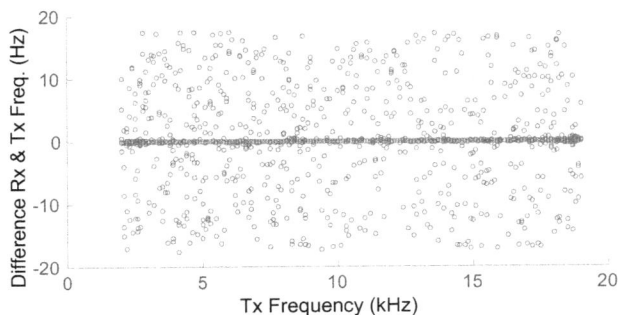

Figure 13: Measurement error of frequency of arrival measurements of sound waves with different frequencies. We used off-the-shelf laptops as transmitter and receiver.

here the FOA as opposed to the FDOA used in the air traffic scenario. Therefore, we could directly apply the basic verification scheme presented in Section 2.2 without calibration, synchronization, or communication between verifiers.

7.2 Limitations

Similar to location and track verification schemes which are based on signal arrival measurements, our motion verification scheme is not secure when faced with a mobile attacker or an attacker using several antennas (see e.g. [8, 13]). The reason is that the proof provided in Section 3 is based on the fact that all verifiers measure the same frequency. However, this assumption does not hold anymore if the attacker is either able to move or use multiple antennas to adjust the frequencies for each verifier individually.

In order to spoof a motion different from the real one, a mobile attacker needs to find a path and transmission frequency which results exactly in the expected received frequencies at all verifiers. Yet, such an attack can be considered rather unlikely in the air traffic scenario, because the attacker must be able to move at a speed of up to several hundred m/s to produce the same difference in received frequencies. Thus, a mobile attacker can only be realized by an extremely agile and fast aircraft which significantly reduces the feasibility of potential attacks. Similar attack limitations apply to vehicular networks as well since ground vehicles are forced to move along predefined paths (roads).

Attackers using several antennas remain an open problem. If the attacker is able to fully control the received frequency at each receiver, it can trivially spoof any motion. One way to defend against such attacks could be the use of *covered verifiers* which are located at positions unknown to the attacker [12]. When the verifier locations are secret, attackers have no means to determine the expected frequencies and are therefore limited to guessing with a low probability of success.

8. CONCLUSIONS

In this paper, we presented a method to securely verify the motion of a moving prover including the combination of position, speed, and direction of movement. Our scheme uses Doppler shift measurements from multiple positions. In our formal security analysis of the scheme, we proved the security of the underlying scheme and then adapted it to be able

to deal with realistic noisy measurement data. Finally, we demonstrated the practicality of our adapted scheme with simulations based on real-world air traffic motion data.

In our evaluation, we identified challenges specific to the air traffic scenario. In particular, we found that transponders used in aircraft generate extremely noisy signals which makes passively measuring Doppler shifts difficult. However, our measurements and simulations strongly suggest that our *adapted* scheme based on the FDOA is able to verify air traffic over a large area with an equal error rate of zero.

9. REFERENCES

[1] P. Varaiya, "Smart cars on smart roads: problems of control," *IEEE Transactions on Automatic Control*, vol. 38, no. 2, Feb 1993.

[2] E. A.Lester, "Benefits and incentives for ADS-B equipage in the National Airspace System," Sep. 2007, Massachusetts Institute of Technology.

[3] RTCA Inc., "Minimum Operational Performance Standards for 1090 MHz Extended Squitter Automatic Dependent Surveillance – Broadcast (ADS-B) and Traffic Information Services – Broadcast (TIS-B)," DO-260B with Corrigendum 1, Dec. 2011.

[4] J. Ploeg, B. Scheepers, E. V. Nunen, N. V. de Wouw, and H. Nijmeijer, "Design and experimental evaluation of cooperative adaptive cruise control," in *Proceedings of the International IEEE Conference on Intelligent Transportation Systems*, ser. ITSC 11, Oct. 2011.

[5] Andrei Costin and Aurélien Francillon, "Ghost is in the Air(traffic): On insecurity of ADS-B protocol and practical attacks on ADS-B devices," Black Hat USA, Jul. 2012.

[6] M. Schäfer, V. Lenders, and I. Martinovic, "Experimental Analysis of Attacks on Next Generation Air Traffic Communication," in *Applied Cryptography and Network Security (ACNS)*. Springer, Jun. 2013.

[7] B. DeBruhl, S. Weerakkody, B. Sinopoli, and P. Tague, "Is your commute driving you crazy?: A study of misbehavior in vehicular platoons," in *Proceedings of the 8th ACM Conference on Security & Privacy in Wireless and Mobile Networks (WiSec)*, ser. WiSec '15, Jun. 2015.

[8] N. Sastry, U. Shankar, and D. Wagner, "Secure verification of location claims," in *Workshop on Wireless Security (WiSe)*. ACM, 2003.

[9] D. Singelee and B. Preneel, "Location verification using secure distance bounding protocols," in *IEEE International Conference on Mobile Adhoc and Sensor Systems Conference (MASS)*. IEEE, Nov. 2005.

[10] S. Čapkun and J.-P. Hubaux, "Secure positioning of wireless devices with application to sensor networks," in *International Conference on Computer Communications (INFOCOM)*. IEEE, March 2005.

[11] L. Lazos, R. Poovendran, and S. Čapkun, "ROPE: Robust Position Estimation in Wireless Sensor Networks," in *ACM/IEEE International Symposium on Information Processing in Sensor Networks (IPSN)*, Apr. 2005.

[12] S. Čapkun, K. Rasmussen, M. Čagalj, and M. Srivastava, "Secure location verification with hidden and mobile base stations," *IEEE Transactions*

on Mobile Computing, vol. 7, no. 4, pp. 470–483, Apr. 2008.

[13] M. Schäfer, V. Lenders, and J. Schmitt, "Secure Track Verification," in *Proceedings of the IEEE Symposium on Security and Privacy*, Jul. 2015.

[14] M. I. Skolnik, "Radar Handbook," McMcGraw-Hill, 1970.

[15] A. Amar and A. J. Weiss, "Localization of narrowband radio emitters based on doppler frequency shifts," *IEEE Transactions on Signal Processing*, vol. 56, no. 11, pp. 5500–5508, 2008.

[16] Y. T. Chan and J. J. Towers, "Passive localization from Doppler-shifted frequency measurements," *IEEE Transactions on Signal Processing*, vol. 40, no. 10, pp. 2594–2598, 1992.

[17] C. Couvreur and Y. Bresler, "Doppler-based motion estimation for wide-band sources from single passive sensor measurements," *1997 IEEE International Conference on Acoustics, Speech, and Signal Processing*, vol. 5, pp. 3537–3540, 1997.

[18] B. Kusý, I. Amundson, J. Sallai, P. Völgyesi, A. Lédeczi, and X. Koutsoukos, "RF doppler shift-based mobile sensor tracking and navigation," *ACM Transactions on Sensor Networks*, vol. 7, no. 1, pp. 1–32, 2010.

[19] N. Ghose and L. Lazos, "Verifying ads-b navigation information through doppler shift measurements," in *IEEE/AIAA 34th Digital Avionics Systems Conference (DASC)*, Sep. 2015.

[20] M. Strohmeier, M. Schäfer, M. Fuchs, V. Lenders, and I. Martinovic, "Opensky: A swiss army knife for air traffic security research," in *Proceedings of the 34th IEEE/AIAA Digital Avionics Systems Conference*, ser. DASC, September 2015.

[21] M. Strohmeier, M. Schäfer, R. Pinheiro, V. Lenders, and I. Martinovic, "On perception and reality in wireless air traffic communications security," *arXiv:1602.08777 [cs.CR]*, Feb. 2016.

[22] *International Standards and Recommended Practices, Annex 10: Aeronautical Telecommunications*, 4th ed., International Civil Aviation Organization (ICAO), 2007, Volume IV: Surveillance and Collision Avoidance Systems.

[23] R. H. D. Townsend, "Fast calculation of the lomb-scargle periodogram using graphics processing units," *The Astrophysical Journal Supplement Series*, 2010.

[24] S. Brands and D. Chaum, "Distance-bounding protocols," in *Proceedings of the Workshop on the Theory and Application of Cryptographic Techniques (EUROCRYPT)*. Springer Berlin Heidelberg, May 1994.

[25] A. Smith, R. Cassell, T. Breen, R. Hulstrom, and C. Evers, "Methods to Provide System-Wide ADS-B Back-Up, Validation and Security ," in *IEEE/AIAA Digital Avionics Systems Conference*, Oct. 2006.

[26] K. Pourvoyeur and R. Heidger, "Secure ADS-B usage in ATC tracking," in *Tyrrhenian International Workshop on Digital Communications - Enhanced Surveillance of Aircraft and Vehicles (TIWDC/ESAV)*. IEEE, Sep. 2014, pp. 35–40.

[27] M. Strohmeier, V. Lenders, and I. Martinovic, "On the Security of the Automatic Dependent Surveillance-Broadcast Protocol," *IEEE Communications Surveys & Tutorials*, no. 99, 2014.

[28] *USRP X300 and X310 Configuration Guide*, Ettus Research, accessed March 2016. [Online]. Available: https://goo.gl/EqqLqE

More Semantics More Robust:
Improving Android Malware Classifiers

Wei Chen
University of Edinburgh, UK
wchen2@inf.ed.ac.uk

David Aspinall
University of Edinburgh, UK
david.aspinall@ed.ac.uk

Andrew D. Gordon
Microsoft Research
Cambridge, UK
University of Edinburgh, UK
andy.gordon@ed.ac.uk

Charles Sutton
University of Edinburgh, UK
csutton@inf.ed.ac.uk

Igor Muttik
Intel Security, UK
igor.muttik@intel.com

ABSTRACT

Automatic malware classifiers often perform badly on the detection of new malware, i.e., their robustness is poor. We study the machine-learning-based mobile malware classifiers and reveal one reason: the input features used by these classifiers can't capture general behavioural patterns of malware instances. We extract the best-performing syntax-based features like permissions and API calls, and some semantics-based features like happen-befores and unwanted behaviours, and train classifiers using popular supervised and semi-supervised learning methods. By comparing their classification performance on industrial datasets collected across several years, we demonstrate that using semantics-based features can dramatically improve robustness of malware classifiers.

Keywords

Mobile security; Android system; malware detection; machine learning

1. INTRODUCTION

The machine-learning-based classification plays an important role in automatic mobile malware detection. The main drawback is its poor robustness—the classification performance on the detection of new malware is bad [4]. Researchers have shown that well-trained classifiers can achieve good classification performance, e.g., precision as high as 99% and false positive ratio as low as 1% [3, 7, 42]. However, in these and most other studies, the training and testing data were collected in the same period and from the same source. These classifiers only presented good fits to training data. When these classifiers are applied in practice to detect new malware, the classification accuracy drops dramatically. A method adopted in industry to mitigate this problem is

to replace some old training data by new data and re-train classifiers to maintain good classification performance. But it is hard to decide how much old data should be removed and what kind of new data should be added.

In this paper we ask whether it is possible to improve robustness of classifiers over time, by using more general and abstract features, rather than simply substituting new data for old training data. We want to figure out the main factor which affects robustness of mobile malware classifiers and develop an approach to improve it. The main contributions of this paper are as follows.

- We show that the known best-performing classifiers, e.g., those using API calls as input features, perform badly on the detection of new malware; in particular, the precision and recall respectively drop from around 95% and 99% on the validation dataset to on average 55% and 26% on the testing dataset.

- We compare the classification performance of classifiers which were trained using popular supervised and semi-supervised learning methods, and conclude that the L1-Regularized Linear Regression is the most robust method, i.e., showing better and balanced performance on the validation and testing datasets.

- We demonstrate that semantics-based features improve robustness dramatically, in particular, increasing the precision and recall on the testing dataset respectively to as high as 73% and 67%, which are respectively 18 and 41 points better than those using syntax-based features.

We train and test using Android apps from several industrial datasets. They were collected and investigated between 2011 and 2014 by third-party researchers and malware analysts from anti-virus vendors.

- **Training and Validation.** We collected 3,000 malware instances, which were released and identified between 2011 and 2013, and 3,000 benign apps published in the same period. They include all malware instances from Malware Genome Project [45] and most from Mobile-Sandbox [34]. These malware instances have been manually investigated and organised into around 200 families by third-party researchers and malware analysts [1, 2, 27]. They were divided into a training

WiSec'16 , July 18-22, 2016, Darmstadt, Germany

© 2016 ACM. ISBN 978-1-4503-4270-4/16/07. . . $15.00

DOI: http://dx.doi.org/10.1145/2939918.2939931

dataset and a validation dataset. Each of them consists of $1,500$ malware instances across all families and $1,500$ benign apps.

- **Testing.** We test using a collection of $1,500$ malware instances, which were released and identified in 2014, and $1,500$ benign apps published in the same year. These malware instances were from Intel Security and have been investigated by malware analysts. The collection of benign appls is disjoint from those used for training and validation. They were randomly chosen from benign apps supplied by Intel Security.

We want to experiment on small datasets before testing on market-scale datasets in further work. We found that when the training dataset contained more than 1,000 apps, a well-trained classifier performed stably; so, datasets containing thousands of apps are enough for our purpose. Since the distribution of malware in real world is unknown, for each dataset we simply put in the same number of samples and kept malware and benign half-and-half.

We report performance of classifiers which were trained using the following machine learning methods:

- *trees:* decision trees [31], random forest [12], and the adaptive boosting [22] using decision trees as the base estimators;

- *linear:* the L1-regularized linear regression [37] and support vector machines [35];

- *semi-supervised:* the work by Zhou et al. [44];

- *others:* k-nearest neighbours [5] and naive Bayes,

and the following features:

- *syntax-based:* permissions, actions, API calls, and keywords;

- *semantics-based:* reachables, happen-befores, and unwanted behaviours.

These features were directly extracted from the bytecode of Android apps using static analysis. All semantics-based features are based on an abstract model called behaviour automata, which are collections of finite control-sequences of actions, events, and annotated API calls, to approximate the behaviours of Android apps. We adopt the approach proposed in [17] to construct behaviour automata and learn unwanted behaviours from them. More details on the feature extraction are given in Section 2.

A classifier is considered *robust* if its classification performance is good and balanced on the validation and testing datasets. Formally, we measure robustness of classifiers by calculating the F_β-measure [32] of F_1-scores of precision and recall on these two datasets. We trained 56 classifiers by using the above methods and features. The comparison between these classifiers demonstrates that semantics-based features improve robustness of malware classifiers. The details are given in Figure 3 and Table 3.

Malicious behaviours in a group of apps might be innocuous in another, e.g., sending text messages is normal for messaging apps but suspicious for E-reader apps; so, to further improve robustness we train and test cluster-specific classifiers. That is, apps are organised into small groups by using clustering methods; then, one classifier is trained for each group. The evaluation shows that robustness of these cluster-specific classifiers is better than general classifiers, especially, when semantics-based features are applied in the clustering process.

These evaluations confirm our intuition: semantics-based features capture general behavioural invariants in malware, which leads to better classification performance on the detection of new malware than that of classifiers using syntax-based features. We believe that by using more fine-grained semantics-based features better classification performance can be achieved.

Related Work.
Machine learning methods have been applied in Android malware detection for some time. Researchers have tested various supervised learning methods and different kinds of features. For example, the tool DroidAPIMiner [3] uses API calls as input features and relies on the KNN algorithm; the method Drebin [7] trains an SVM classifier using a range of syntax-based features; Yerima et al. applied naive Bayes [41] and ensemble learning [40] in training; Gascon et al. [23] proposed to use graph kernel of embedded call graphs; Zhang et al. [43] exploited the edit distance between API dependency graphs; behaviour graphs were used in DroidMiner [39]; Yuan et al. [42] designed a good deep-learning-based classifier; Narudin et al. [28] compared several methods and concluded that random forest and naive Bayes have the best classification performance. Clustering methods were applied as well. For instance, the tool Dendroid [36] uses the cosine similarity between call graphs to group malware instances into families; similar ideas were applied in DroidLegacy [18] to detect piggybacking. Among others, various probabilistic models were developed to rank risks in apps. For example, Peng et al. [30] built models on naive Bayes; the tool MAST [13] exploits the multiple correspondence analysis to figure out the most indicative features.

All of these tools and methods were trying to obtain good fits to training data by combining different methods and features. Robustness of malware classifiers, in particular, the classifier specifically designed to detect new malware, has received much less consideration. An early investigation of effects on classifiers caused by new malware has been done by Allix et al. [4]. They concluded that training on a random set of known malware could lead to significantly biased results. This discovery is also confirmed in our study, i.e., robustness of classifiers using syntax-based features is poor. Our research is beyond this primitive investigation and demonstrates a promising method to improve robustness of classifiers.

2. FEATURES

Syntax-based features are the most popular and the best-performing features known for malware classifiers, including: meta-information of an app, e.g. permissions, actions, intents, etc., and specific strings in code, e.g., API calls, commands, keywords appearing in UI elements, URLs, fragments of bytecode, etc. We call features "semantics-based" when they start to relate syntax-based features using dependency relations, e.g., an API method is invoked before another, the data-flow from a variable to another, a call-back is triggered by an event, call-graphs, etc. In this section, we will discuss and compare several syntax-based and semantics-based features.

2.1 Syntax-Based Features

An Android app consists of the manifest file *AndroidManifest.xml*, the bytecode *classes.dex*, the developer's signatures, libraries, and resources including: layouts, pictures, strings, etc. The manifest file specifies permissions requested by the app and components defined in the app. A component is often associated with actions which are requests or events it can deal with. By using the platform tool `aapt` we extract permissions and actions from the manifest file, and all strings defined in resources, from which we will choose keywords. We decompile the bytecode into assembly code by using the platform tool `dexdump`, from which we extract API calls.

2.1.1 Permissions

Permissions reflect resource requirements from an app. Although the developer can define their own permissions, we only care about system permissions which are pre-defined in the Android framework. We extract system permissions from the manifest file, e.g., INTERNET, ACCESS_FINE_LO CATION, CAMERA, etc. Around 200 system permissions govern more than 32,000 API methods [9]. To invoke a permission-governed API method, the developer has to specify its corresponding permission in the manifest file; otherwise, the app will crash at runtime. However, an app might request more permissions than it actually needs, so-called over-privileged [19, 21]. Thus, the list of system permissions requested by an app is a lightweight but very coarse characterisation of its behaviour.

2.1.2 Actions

Actions denote what kind of requests or events an app can deal with. For example, the following fragment of the manifest file tells us: a receiver component is defined in this app; it can deal with the action SMS_RECEIVED.

```
<receiver android:name="com.example.Receiver" >
  <intent-filter>
    <action android:name=
      "android.provider.Telephony.SMS_RECEIVED"/>
  </intent-filter>
</receiver>
```

We are interested in actions because a lot of identified malware instances will exploit specific actions. For example, an instance in the malware family Zitmo [27] will intercept an incoming SMS message to obtain the user's online transaction number, i.e., the unwanted behaviour is triggered by the action SMS_RECEIVED; the unwanted behaviours in the malware families Arspam [34] and Ginmaster [45] are triggered by the action BOOT_COMPLETED, i.e., the device finishes the booting; some instances in the malware families Anserverbot and Basebridge [45] load classes from hidden payloads when a USB mass storage is connected, i.e., the action UMS_CONNECTED.

Developers are allowed to define their own actions to implement communications between components within the same app. Since these developer-defined actions are too specific to be used as training features, we only extract from the manifest file system actions which are pre-defined in the Android framework. Around 800 system actions were collected from more than 10,000 sample apps.

2.1.3 API Calls

API calls appearing in code tell us what an app can possibly do. We collected more than 52,000 API calls by going through the assembly code of more than 10,000 sample apps. For example, from the following assembly code,

```
#1 : (in Lcom/example/main/Main;)
name : 'getPhoneNumber'
type : '()Ljava/lang/String;'

|0000: invoke-virtual {v3},
  Lcom/example/main/Main;.getBaseContext
|0003: move-result-object v1
|0004: const-string v2, "phone"
|0006: invoke-virtual {v1, v2},
  Landroid/content/Context;.getSystemService
|0009: move-result-object v0
|000a: check-cast v0,
  Landroid/telephony/TelephonyManager;
|000c: invoke-virtual {v0},
  Landroid/telephony/TelephonyManager;.getLine1Number
|000f: move-result-object v1
|0010: return-object v1
```

we extract the API calls `Context.getSystemService` and `TelephonyManager.getLine1Number` by looking for the instructions `invoke-*`.

The list of API calls is the best-performing feature known for malware classifiers. By carefully selecting salient API calls, combining with other syntax-based features, and choosing suitable machine learning methods, the precision of classifiers can usually reach as high as 99% and the false positive ratio is maintained as low as 1% [3, 7]. However, API calls have two drawbacks.

- It contains "noise" caused by the dead code and libraries, in particular, advertisement libraries [3].

- It can't characterise more sophisticated app behaviours. This is needed in practice: some malicious behaviours only arise when some API methods are called in certain orders [16, 25, 39].

These drawbacks will result in overfitting to training data. Accordingly, the performance on the detection of new malware is poor, as we will show later.

2.1.4 Keywords

We extract nouns from strings which are defined in resources of Android apps, so-called keywords. These keywords will be presented to the user in UI elements at runtime. They reflect what an app declares to do. For instance, the keywords "photo", "gallery", and "camera" often appear in a Photo Editor app and the keywords "weather", "city", and "temperature" are often seen in a Weather Forecast app.

These keywords are more precise than those extracted from the descriptions of apps. For each app on the official Android market—Google Play, a description explaining its functionality is supplied by its developer. Researchers have studied how to organise Android apps into groups by using the keywords extracted from these descriptions and how to identify the outliers in each group, e.g., abnormal usages of APIs [24]. However, most malware instances were collected from alternative Android markets. Their descriptions might not exist or are not written in English. They often contain a lot of redundant words, which are added to boost the appearance in search results.

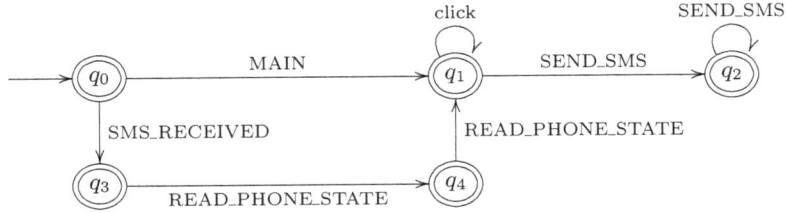

Figure 1: An example behaviour automaton.

Human-authored description	Learned unwanted behaviours in regular expressions
Arspam. Sends spam SMS messages to contacts on the compromised device.	1. BOOT_COMPLETED . SEND_SMS
Anserverbot. Downloads, installs, and executes payloads.	1. UMS_CONNECTED . LOAD_CLASS* . (ACCESS_NETWORK_STATE | READ_PHONE_STATE | INTERNET) . (ACCESS_NETWORK_STATE | READ_PHONE_STATE | INTERNET | LOAD_CLASS)*
Basebridge. Forwards confidential details (SMS, IMSI, IMEI) to a remote server. Downloads and installs payloads.	1. UMS_CONNECTED . (INTERNET | LOAD_CLASS | READ_PHONE_STATE | ACCESS_NETWORK_STATE)$^+$
Cosha. Monitors and sends certain information to a remote location.	1. MAIN . click . (click | ACCESS_FINE_LOCATION | DIAL)* . DIAL . (click | ACCESS_FINE_LOCATION | DIAL)* . (INTERNET | ϵ) 2. SMS_RECEIVED . (INTERNET | ACCESS_FINE_LOCATION)$^+$
Droiddream. Gains root access, gathers information (device ID, IMEI, IMSI) from an infected mobile phone and connects to several URLs in order to upload this data.	1. PHONE_STATE . (ACCESS_NETWORK_STATE | READ_PHONE_STATE$^+$. INTERNET) . (ACCESS_NETWORK_STATE | INTERNET)*
Geinimi. Monitors and sends certain information to a remote location. Introduces botnet capabilities with clear indications that command and control (C&C) functionality could be a part of the Geinimi code base.	1. ϵ | MAIN . click$^+$. VIBRATE . (click | VIBRATE)* . RESTART_PACKAGES . (MAIN . (click | VIBRATE)* . RESTART_PACKAGES)* 2. BOOT_COMPLETED . (ACCESS_NETWORK_STATE | click | INTERNET | RESTART_PACKAGES | ACCESS_FINE_LOCATION)$^+$
Ggtracker. Monitors received SMS messages and intercepts SMS messages.	1. MAIN . READ_PHONE_STATE 2. SMS_RECEIVED . SEND_SMS
Ginmaster. Sends received SMS messages to a remote server. Downloads and installs applications without user concern.	1. BOOT_COMPLETED . LOAD_CLASS 2. MAIN . SEND_SMS
Spitmo. Filters SMS messages to steal banking confirmation codes.	1. NEW_OUTGOING_CALL . READ_PHONE_STATE . INTERNET . (INTERNET | ϵ)
Zitmo. Opens a backdoor that allows a remote attacker to steal information from SMS messages received on the compromised device.	1. SMS_RECEIVED . SEND_SMS 2. MAIN . READ_PHONE_STATE 3. MAIN . SEND_SMS

Table 1: Human-authored descriptions versus learned unwanted behaviours.

2.2 Semantics-Based Features

We approximate an app's behaviour by an automaton, i.e., a collection of finite control-sequences of events, actions, and annotated API calls. Some API calls might indicate the same behaviour, for instance, `getDeviceId`, `getLine1 Number`, and `getSimSerialNumber` are all related to the behaviour of reading phone state; so we aggregate API calls into permission-like phrases and abstract automata by substituting phrases for API calls, so-called *behaviour automata* [17].

An example behaviour automaton is given in Figure 1. It tells us: this app has two entries which are respectively specified by the actions MAIN and SMS_RECEIVED; it will collect information like the phone state, then send SMS messages out; it can deal with the interaction from the user, e.g., clicking a button, touching the screen, long-pressing a picture, etc., which is denoted by the word "click". All states in this automaton are accepting states since any prefix of an app's behaviours is one of its behaviours as well.

We have designed and implemented a static analysis tool to construct behaviour automata. This tool models complex real-world features of the Android framework, including: inter-procedural calls, callbacks, component life-cycles,

inter-component communications, multiple threads, multiple entries, nested classes, and runtime-registered listeners. We don't model registers, fields, assignments, operators, pointer-aliases, arrays or exceptions. The choice of which aspects to model is a trade-off between efficiency and precision. In our implementation, we use an extension of permission-governed API methods generated by PScout [9] as the annotations. The Android platform tool `dexdump` is used to decompile the bytecode into assembly code, from which we construct automata.

From behaviour automata we produce the following features: reachables, happen-befores, and unwanted behaviours.

2.2.1 Reachables

Reachables denote the labels on edges which can be reached along a path from one of the entries in a behaviour automaton. For instance, all labels on the edges of the automaton in Figure 1 are reachables. They are more precise than permissions, actions, and API calls appearing in code. This semantics-based feature removes the "noise" caused by dead code and libraries. It reflects what an app can actually do but no order.

2.2.2 Happen-Befores

The happen-before denotes that something happens before another in a behaviour automaton. For example, the following pairs:

```
(MAIN, click), (SMS_RECEIVED, SEND_SMS),
(MAIN, SEND_SMS), (SMS_RECEIVED, click),
(SMS_RECEIVED, READ_PHONE_STATE),
(READ_PHONE_STATE, SEND_SMS),
(READ_PHONE_STATE, click), (click, SEND_SMS),
```

are happen-before features extracted from the automaton in Figure 1. These pairs characterise some interesting malicious behaviours which the reachables can't capture. For instance, the pair (SMS_RECEIVED, SEND_SMS) is a characterisation of a common malicious behaviour shared by malware instances in the family Zitmo [27]: obtaining the online transaction number from the incoming messages then sending it out by SMS messages to a specific phone number, to finish the online transaction instead of the real user.

In general, one can extract n-tuples as features from behaviour automata, i.e., things happening in certain orders. But, this will introduce a lot of redundant sequences, e.g., a "click" list, which waste the space for other more indicative features. Also, we found that constructing triples was already too expensive.

The happen-befores are less precise than pairs of sources and sinks produced by the data-flow analysis tools like Flow-Droid [8] or Amandroid [38]. However, compared with generating data-flow models, it is much easier to produce happen-befores for a large number of apps.

2.2.3 Unwanted Behaviours

An unwanted behaviour is a common sub-automaton which is shared by malware instances but rarely identified in benign apps. As an example, let us consider a malware family called Ggtracker [2]. A brief human-authored description of this family produced by Symantec is as follows.

> It sends SMS messages to a premium-rate number. It monitors received SMS messages and intercepts SMS messages. It may also steal information from the device.

One unwanted behaviour we have constructed from malware instances in this family can be expressed as the regular expression: SMS_RECEIVED.SEND_SMS. It denotes the behaviour of sending an SMS message out *immediately* after an incoming SMS message is received without the interaction from the user.

To construct unwanted behaviours from malware instances and benign apps, we generate sub-automata by calculating the intersection and difference between the behaviour automata of sample apps, and select the sub-automata which are strongly associated with and largely cover malware instances. Since this combinatorial construction and selection process is expensive, we adopt the approach proposed in [17] to accelerate it by exploiting the behavioural difference between malware instances and benign apps, and the family names of malware instances. This approach combines machine learning methods and text-mining techniques, and proceeds as follows.

1. Malware instances are organised into small groups according to their family names. Benign apps are added into each group to form a balanced training dataset.

2. For each group, we generate sub-automata by computing the intersection and difference between behaviour automata of apps in the same group, then train a linear classifier by taking these sub-automata as input features—checking whether a feature is a sub-automaton of the behaviour automaton of an app.

3. Those features which are actually used by the linear classifier are called *salient features*, i.e., their weights assigned by the linear classifier are not zero. We combine two groups by computing the intersection and difference between their salient features, then training a linear classifier on sample apps from these two groups to produce new salient features. This process continues until all groups are combined into a single group with a collection of salient sub-automata.

4. From these salient sub-automata an optimal subset is selected as *unwanted behaviours*. We apply text-mining techniques, e.g., subset-searching, weight ranking, and TF-IDF (term frequency - inverse document frequency) optimisation, etc., to help choose this subset, i.e., taking the salient features of the malware instances belonging to the same family as a document.

It took around two weeks to generate unwanted behaviours from apps in the training dataset using a multi-core desktop computer. We use the classification accuracy as the threshold to decide whether all features or only salient features are kept for each group. It was set to 90% in our implementation. At the end of computation, around 200 salient sub-automata are chosen as unwanted behaviours.

We list human-authored descriptions and learned unwanted behaviours for 10 prevalent families in Table 1. These descriptions for families were collected from their online analysis reports [2, 27, 34, 45]. A subjective comparison shows that unwanted behaviours compare well to human-authored descriptions. Also, they reveal the trigger conditions of some behaviours, which were often lacking in human-authored descriptions. For example, the expression BOOT_COMPLETED.SEND_SMS denotes that after the device finishes booting, this app will send a message out; the expression UMS_CONNECTED.LOAD_CLASS means that when a USB mass storage is connected to the device, this app will load some code from a library or a hidden payload; and the unwanted behaviour for Droiddream shows that if the phone state changes (the action PHONE_STATE), this app will collect some information then access Internet. In Table 1 only two behaviours are not captured by unwanted behaviours: "gain root access" for Droiddream and the behaviour of Spitmo.

Some behaviours of sample apps are not the same as unwanted behaviours, but, they often contain some unwanted behaviours as sub-sequences. For example, the behaviour SMS_RECEIVED.READ_PHONE_STATE.SEND_SMS contains the unwanted behaviour SMS_RECEIVED.SEND_SMS as a subsequence. To capture behaviours sharing the same patterns with the unwanted behaviours, if a behaviour contains an unwanted behaviour as a sub-sequence, we consider this behaviour as unwanted as well. We call them *extended unwanted behaviours*. For instance, we can generalise from the above unwanted behaviour and construct the automaton in Figure 2 as an extended unwanted behaviour. Here, we use the symbol Σ to denote the collection of events, actions, and permission-like phrases.

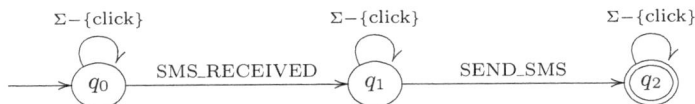

Figure 2: An example extended unwanted behaviour.

3. GENERAL CLASSIFIERS

We check whether a target app has any unwanted behaviour ψ by testing whether $A \cap \psi = \emptyset$, where A is the behaviour automaton of the target app. These testing results will be used as input features in further training. Another usage of unwanted behaviours is to test whether $\psi \subseteq A$. This will result in high false negatives because A might not contain all unwanted behaviours specified in ψ.

3. GENERAL CLASSIFIERS

In this section, we will investigate robustness of general mobile malware classifiers. These classifiers were trained by applying supervised learning methods, including: decision trees [31], naive Bayes, L1-regularized linear regression [37], support vector machines [35], random forest [12], adaptive boosting [22], and k-nearest neighbours [5], and a semi-supervised learning method [15]. For each machine learning method, we trained using different syntax-based and semantics-based features which have been discussed in previous section, and tested on the validation and testing datasets which are described in Section 1. We will demonstrate that the best-performing features on the validation dataset, which are often syntax-based features, have poor classification performance on the testing dataset. We will show that semantics-based features dramatically improve the classification performance of the detection of new malware and achieve the best classification performance on the testing dataset for most machine learning methods we will compare.

The methods KNN (k-nearest neighbours), SVM (support vector machines) and NB (naive Bayes) are included in our study, because these methods have been successfully applied in the Android malware classification, e.g., DroidAPIMiner [3], Drebin [7], Yerima et.al. [41], etc. We will compare their classification performance, combine them with the semantics-based features and test on new malware.

The L1LR (L1-regularized linear regression) was deliberately designed to train classifiers on sparse data, i.e, only a small part of features is responsible for a decision. This assumption coincides with our intuition: features like API calls and happen-befores contain a lot of redundant information and most API calls or happen-befores are actually useless for the classification. Thus, we choose the L1LR as a candidate method to improve the classification performance.

The RF (random forest) is an ensemble learning method. It was designed to mitigate the overfitting problem in the DT (decision trees). Instead of training a single decision tree, it trains several trees respectively on random subsets of samples using random subsets of input features, and makes decisions by taking majority votings. This leads to a better model by decreasing the variance without increasing the bias, which is needed in our experience to obtain better robustness. Except for the RF, as a baseline, we include the DT in our comparison as well.

The AdaBoost (Adaptive Boosting) is another supervised learning method we have tested. It is an iterative process to produce stronger learners from weak learners. It improves the performance of a weak learner by adjusting the weights assigned to samples in favour of those misclassified by weak learners.

The SEMI (semi-supervised learning) is applied on a collection of labelled and unlabelled samples. It makes use of unlabelled samples for training to achieve a better classifier than doing supervised learning on the labelled samples or doing unsupervised learning on the unlabelled samples. This matches with our goal to detect new malware.

We use the tools *liblinear* [20] and *libsvm* [14] respectively to train L1LR and SVM classifiers. As for other methods, we use their implementations in *scikit-learn* [29]. We use the decision trees as the base estimators in the AdaBoost classifiers. For the semi-supervised learning, we adapt the model LabelSpreading to label unlabelled samples, which is an implementation of Zhou et al.'s work [44].

We report performance of general classifiers on the testing dataset in Figure 3. It shows that semantics-based features have better classification performance than syntax-based features. In particular, the best F_1-score of precision and recall is achieved by the classifier using unwanted behaviours and L1-Regularized Linear Regression. The precision and recall are calculated as follows:

$$ \text{precision} = \frac{tp}{tp+fp} \quad \text{and} \quad \text{recall} = \frac{tp}{tp+fn}, $$

where tp, fp, and fn respectively denote the true positives, false positives, and false negatives.

The detailed classification performance is reported in Table 2. We summarise the main results as follows.

- *API calls achieve the best classification performance on the validation dataset.* The precision and recall of the classifiers using API calls as input features are respectively as high as 95% and 99%, e.g., in DT, RF, and SEMI classifiers.

- *The best-performing methods on the validation dataset are: DT, L1LR, RF, and SEMI, by using syntax-based features.* In particular, the average precision and recall for syntax-based features are respectively as high as 90% and 98%.

- *Syntax-based features have better classification performance on the validation dataset than semantics-based features.* The average precision and recall for syntax-based features on all tested methods are respectively 88% and 98%, while for semantics-based features these numbers are respectively 86% and 82%. That is, classifiers using syntax-based features have higher recall.

- *Syntax-based features perform badly on the testing data.* The average precision and recall on all tested methods are respectively 55% and 26%. In the worst case, the

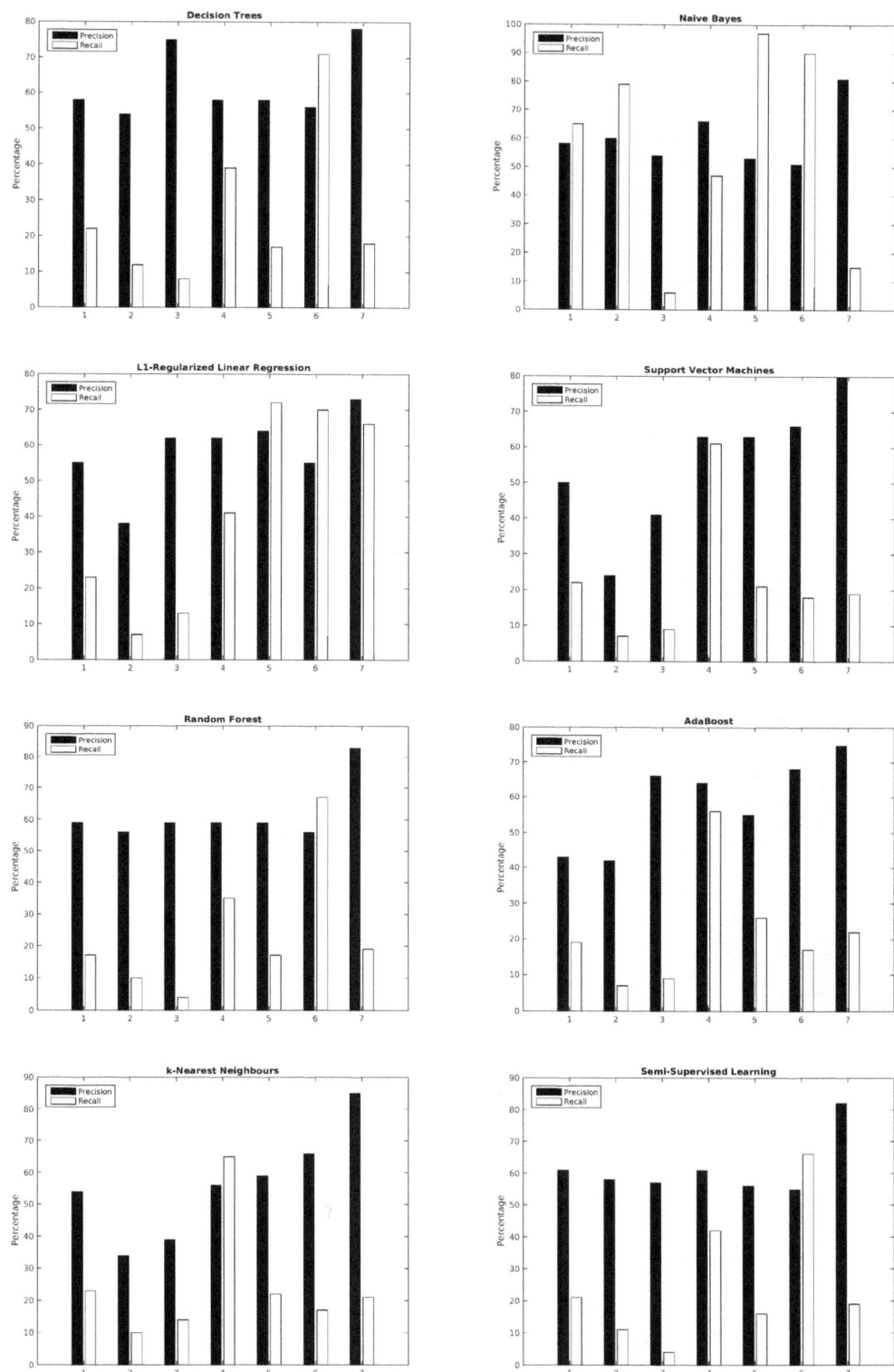

1: permissions; 2: actions; 3: API calls; 4: keywords;
5: reachables; 6: happen-befores; 7: unwanted.

Figure 3: The classification performance of general classifiers on the testing dataset.

Decision Trees	validation		testing	
	precision	recall	precision	recall
signature-based features				
permissions	90%	99%	58%	22%
actions	91%	99%	54%	12%
API calls	95%	99%	75%	8%
keywords	86%	93%	58%	39%
average	91%	98%	61%	20%
semantics-based features				
reachables	93%	86%	58%	17%
happen-befores	68%	92%	**56%**	**71%**
unwanted	95%	73%	78%	18%
average	85%	84%	64% ↑	35% ↑

Naive Bayes	validation		testing	
	precision	recall	precision	recall
signature-based features				
permissions	74%	100%	58%	65%
actions	74%	99%	60%	79%
API calls	93%	99%	54%	6%
keywords	87%	91%	66%	47%
average	82%	97%	60%	49%
semantics-based features				
reachables	61%	99%	**53%**	**97%**
happen-befores	61%	98%	51%	90%
unwanted	96%	47%	81%	15%
average	73%	81%	62% ↑	67% ↑

L1-Regularized Linear Regression	validation		testing	
	precision	recall	precision	recall
signature-based features				
permissions	89%	99%	55%	23%
actions	90%	99%	38%	7%
API calls	93%	98%	62%	13%
keywords	88%	94%	62%	41%
average	90%	98%	54%	21%
semantics-based features				
reachables	73%	90%	64%	72%
happen-befores	68%	92%	55%	70%
unwanted	72%	72%	**73%**	**66%**
average	71%	85%	64% ↑	69% ↑

Support Vector Machines	validation		testing	
	precision	recall	precision	recall
signature-based features				
permissions	88%	99%	50%	22%
actions	88%	99%	24%	7%
API calls	91%	100%	41%	9%
keywords	82%	97%	**63%**	**61%**
average	87%	99%	45%	25%
semantics-based features				
reachables	93%	86%	63%	21%
happen-befores	93%	77%	66%	18%
unwanted	96%	71%	80%	19%
average	94%	78%	70% ↑	19% ↓

Random Forest	validation		testing	
	precision	recall	precision	recall
signature-based features				
permissions	91%	100%	59%	17%
actions	92%	99%	56%	10%
API calls	95%	99%	59%	4%
keywords	89%	92%	59%	35%
average	92%	98%	58%	17%
semantics-based features				
reachables	94%	87%	59%	17%
happen-befores	69%	92%	**56%**	**67%**
unwanted	96%	73%	83%	19%
average	86%	84%	66% ↑	34% ↑

AdaBoost	validation		testing	
	precision	recall	precision	recall
signature-based features				
permissions	87%	99%	43%	19%
actions	91%	99%	42%	7%
API calls	94%	99%	66%	9%
keywords	84%	94%	**64%**	**56%**
average	89%	98%	54%	23%
semantics-based features				
reachables	90%	89%	55%	26%
happen-befores	94%	78%	68%	17%
unwanted	94%	72%	75%	22%
average	93%	80%	66% ↑	22% ↓

k-Nearest Neighbours	validation		testing	
	precision	recall	precision	recall
signature-based features				
permissions	89%	99%	54%	23%
actions	89%	99%	34%	10%
API calls	87%	99%	39%	14%
keywords	77%	97%	**56%**	**65%**
average	86%	99%	46%	31%
semantics-based features				
reachables	92%	85%	59%	22%
happen-befores	94%	77%	66%	17%
unwanted	95%	70%	85%	21%
average	94%	77%	70% ↑	20% ↓

Semi-Supervised Learning	validation		testing	
	precision	recall	precision	recall
signature-based features				
permissions	91%	100%	61%	21%
actions	91%	99%	58%	11%
API calls	95%	99%	57%	4%
keywords	87%	93%	61%	42%
average	91%	98%	59%	20%
semantics-based features				
reachables	94%	85%	56%	16%
happen-befores	69%	92%	**55%**	**66%**
unwanted	95%	72%	82%	19%
average	86%	83%	66% ↑	34% ↑

Table 2: The classification performance of general classifiers.

154

Training method	Training feature	ρ_1	$\rho_{0.5}$ ↓
NB	actions	76	71
L1LR	reachables	74	70
NB	reachables	72	70
L1LR	unwanted	71	70
NB	happen-befores	70	67
SVM	keywords	73	66
DT	happen-befores	70	65
AdaBoost	keywords	71	64
KNN	keywords	71	64
NB	permissions	71	64
L1LR	happen-befores	69	64
RF	happen-befores	69	64
SEMI	happen-befores	68	63
NB	keywords	68	59

Training method	Training feature	ρ_1	$\rho_{0.5}$ ↑
SEMI	API calls	14	9
RF	API calls	14	9
NB	API calls	19	13
SVM	actions	19	13
L1LR	actions	21	14
AdaBoost	actions	21	15
DT	API calls	25	17
SVM	API calls	26	18
KNN	actions	27	19
AdaBoost	API calls	27	19
RF	actions	29	20
SEMI	actions	31	22
DT	actions	33	23
L1LR	API calls	35	25

Table 3: The most and the least robust general classifiers.

precision and recall are respectively 24% and 7%, i.e., those of the SVM classifier using actions as input features; in the best case, these numbers are respectively 60% and 79%, i.e., those of the NB classifier using actions as input features.

- *Semantics-based features have better classification performance on the testing dataset than syntax-based features.* The average precision and recall for semantics-based features on all tested methods are respectively 67% and 38%. In the worst case, the precision and recall are respectively 56% and 16%, i.e., those of the SEMI classifier using reachables as input features; in the best case, these numbers are respectively 73% and 66%, i.e., those of the L1LR classifier using unwanted behaviours as input features.

- *The best-performing method on the testing dataset is L1LR, by using semantics-based features.* In particular, the average precision and recall for L1LR classifiers using the semantics-based features are respectively 64% and 69%.

- *Unwanted behaviours achieve the best classification performance on the testing dataset.* The L1LR classifier using unwanted behaviours as input features performs best on the testing dataset, in particular, the precision is 73% and the recall is 66%.

A *robust classifier* is required to perform well on the validation dataset as well as on the testing dataset. To achieve more robust classifiers, we want to pick up suitable features and machine learning methods according to the classification performance of 56 trained classifiers reported in Table 2. For this purpose, we introduce the following measure:

$$
\begin{aligned}
\rho_\beta &= (1+\beta^2)\frac{F_t \times F_v}{\beta^2 \times F_t + F_v} \\
F_t &= 2 \times \frac{P_t \times R_t}{P_t + R_t} \\
F_v &= 2 \times \frac{P_v \times R_v}{P_v + R_v}
\end{aligned}
$$

Here, the symbols P_t, R_t, P_v and R_v respectively denote the precision and recall of a classifier on the testing and the validation dataset. It is actually the F_β measure of two F_1-scores. The parameter β is usually set to 1 to get the harmonic mean of the classification performance on the testing and the validation datasets. By setting it to 0.5 we put more emphasis on the classification performance on the testing dataset. Table 3 displays the most robust 14 and the least robust 14 classifiers out of 56 general classifiers. We rank them by their $\rho_{0.5}$ values. From this table, we conclude:

- semantics-based features dramatically improve robustness of mobile malware classifiers;

- robustness of L1LR and NB classifiers is better than that of other classifiers.

This study reveals that syntax-based features usually lead to overfitting to training data. This is why their classification performance is good on the validation dataset but poor on the testing dataset. This drawback limits applications of classifiers trained using syntax-based features.

Since semantics-based features capture general behavioural invariants in malware, they can better characterise unwanted patterns in new samples. This leads to better classification performance on the testing dataset than syntax-based features. This success convinces us that semantics-based features have the potential to cope with zero-day malware.

4. CLUSTER-SPECIFIC CLASSIFIERS

A malicious behaviour in a group of mobile apps might be normal or innocuous in another group. For instance, sending SMS messages is normal for messaging apps, but unwanted for an E-reader app; accessing location is expected in a jogging tracer app but abnormal for a wallpaper app.

This observation motivates us to train using fine-grained groups of apps instead of the whole training dataset. The approach proceeds as follows.

1. Apps in the training dataset are orgranised into small groups by applying a clustering method. In our implementation, we use the method k-means [26] to cluster apps by computing the Euclidean distance between the binary vectors of features.

Clustering feature	Training method	Training feature	ρ_1	$\rho_{0.5}$ ↓
reachables	L1LR	unwanted	74	72
-	NB	actions	76	71
keywords	L1LR	reachables	74	71
reachables	KNN	keywords	75	70
-	L1LR	reachables	74	70
happen-befores	L1LR	unwanted	72	70
-	NB	reachables	72	70
-	L1LR	unwanted	71	70
happen-befores	L1LR	reachables	73	69
unwanted	L1LR	reachables	73	69
reachables	L1LR	reachables	72	69
unwanted	L1LR	unwanted	70	69
keywords	KNN	keywords	73	68

Clustering feature	Training method	Training feature	ρ_1	$\rho_{0.5}$ ↓
reachables	NB	reachables	71	68
unwanted	KNN	keywords	72	67
keywords	L1LR	unwanted	70	67
happen-befores	NB	reachables	70	67
-	NB	happen-befores	70	67
-	SVM	keywords	73	66
happen-befores	KNN	keywords	72	66
keywords	SVM	keywords	72	66
reachables	SVM	keywords	72	65
happen-befores	SVM	keywords	72	65
-	DT	happen-befores	70	65
happen-befores	SEMI	happen-befores	69	65
happen-befores	RF	happen-befores	68	65

Table 4: The most robust general and cluster-specific classifiers.

2. We train a classifier for each group by using the machine learning methods and features which lead to the most robust general classifiers, e.g., L1-Regularised Linear Regression and unwanted behaviours, naive Bayes and reachables, decision trees and happen-befores, etc., so-called *cluster-specific classifiers*.

3. We select a group for each target app. In particular, we compute the Euclidean distance between the binary vectors of features and adopt the average-linkage [33] to measure the distance between a group and the target app. The closest group is chosen.

4. The cluster-specific classifier for the chosen group is applied to decide whether the target app is malware.

We trained 60 cluster-specific classifiers using top combinations of methods and features in Table 3. We evaluated their robustness and compared to that of general classifiers. The most robust (general and cluster-specific) classifiers are listed in Table 4. The detailed classification performance of cluster-specific classifiers is reported in appendix. We conclude:

- robustness of cluster-specific classifiers is better than general classifiers, especially, when the method L1LR, KNN, RF, AdaBoost, or SEMI is applied in training and semantics-based features are used for clustering;

- except for keywords, using syntax-based features for clustering will result in less robust cluster-specific classifiers than general classifiers;

- the most robust cluster-specific classifier is achieved by using the L1LR as the training method and semantics-based features for clustering and training.

By using semantics-based features in clustering, we organise apps based on their behaviours rather than signatures. This is why using semantics-based features to group apps leads to more robust classifiers than using syntax-based features. It confirms our intuition: an unwanted behaviour is a common behavioural pattern shared by malware within a group of apps which have similar behaviours.

5. CONCLUSION AND FURTHER WORK

We investigate robustness of machine-learning-based mobile malware classifiers. We apply supervised and semi-supervised learning methods, and extract syntax-based and semantics-based features to train general classifiers. By comparing the classification performance of these classifiers on the validation and testing datasets, we conclude: semantics-based features improve robustness of malware classifiers, in particular, it dramatically improves the classification performance on the testing dataset. A similar study on clustering-specific classifiers supports this argument as well.

However, semantics-based features might lead to under-fitting to training data, i.e., their classification performance is not as good as syntax-based features on the validation dataset. A potential improvement is to add more fine-grained semantics-based features to achieve better fits to training data. Another is to combine syntax-based and semantics-based features in training. We will test these potential improvements in further work.

Extracting semantics-based features from apps is more expensive than extracting syntax-based features. It takes around 1 hour on average per app. But this effort is worthwhile. It will not only improve robustness of malware classifiers but also offer potential to understand and predict malicious behaviours in mobile apps.

In future, we want to further improve robustness of mobile malware classifiers by: (a) refining semantics-based features; (b) making use of the similarity between identified patterns and their variants in new unlabelled samples; (c) training and testing on market-scale datasets. It is also interesting to test the same argument on classifiers trained using the cutting-edge machine learning methods, e.g., deep learning [10, 42].

To efficiently learn unwanted behaviours from apps, we also want to develop a novel approach to combine machine learning methods and learning automata techniques [6, 11], such that semantics-based features can be applied in industry to obtain more robust classifiers over time.

6. REFERENCES

[1] Malware Genome Project. http://www.malgenomeproject.org/, 2012.

[2] Symantec security response. http://www.symantec.com/security_response/, 2015.

[3] Y. Aafer, W. Du, and H. Yin. DroidAPIMiner: Mining API-level features for robust malware detection in Android. In *SecureComm*, 2013.

[4] K. Allix et al. Are your training datasets yet relevant? In *ESSoS*, 2015.

[5] N. S. Altman. An introduction to kernel and Nearest-Neighbor nonparametric regression. *The American Statistician*, 46(3):175–185, 1992.

[6] D. Angluin. Learning regular sets from queries and counterexamples. *Inf. Comput.*, 75(2):87–106, 1987.

[7] D. Arp et al. Drebin: Efficient and explainable detection of Android malware in your pocket. In *NDSS*, pages 23–26, 2014.

[8] S. Arzt et al. FlowDroid: Precise context, flow, field, object-sensitive and lifecycle-aware taint analysis for Android apps. In *PLDI*, pages 259–269, 2014.

[9] K. W. Y. Au et al. PScout: Analyzing the Android permission specification. In *CCS*, pages 217–228, 2012.

[10] Y. Bengio. Learning deep architectures for ai. *Found. Trends Mach. Learn.*, 2(1):1–127, 2009.

[11] A. W. Biermann and J. A. Feldman. On the synthesis of finite-state machines from samples of their behavior. *IEEE Trans. Comput.*, 21(6):592–597, June 1972.

[12] L. Breiman. Random forests. *Mach. Learn.*, 45, 2001.

[13] S. Chakradeo et al. Mast: Triage for market-scale mobile malware analysis. In *WiSec*, pages 13–24, 2013.

[14] C.-C. Chang and C.-J. Lin. Libsvm: A library for support vector machines. *ACM Trans. Intell. Syst. Technol.*, 2(3):27:1–27:27, 2011.

[15] O. Chapelle, B. Schlkopf, and A. Zien. *Semi-Supervised Learning*. The MIT Press, 2010.

[16] K. Z. Chen et al. Contextual policy enforcement in Android applications with permission event graphs. In *NDSS*, 2013.

[17] W. Chen et al. On robust malware classifiers by verifying unwanted behaviours. In *12th International Conference on integrated Formal Methods*, 2016.

[18] L. Deshotels, V. Notani, and A. Lakhotia. DroidLegacy: Automated familial classification of Android malware. In *PPREW*, 2014.

[19] W. Enck et al. A study of Android application security. In *USENIX Security Symposium*, 2011.

[20] R.-E. Fan et al. Liblinear: A library for large linear classification. *J. Mach. Learn. Res.*, 9, 2008.

[21] A. P. Felt et al. Android permissions demystified. In *CCS*, pages 627–638, 2011.

[22] Y. Freund and R. E. Schapire. A decision-theoretic generalization of on-line learning and an application to boosting. *J. Comput. Syst. Sci.*, 55(1), 1997.

[23] H. Gascon et al. Structural detection of Android malware using embedded call graphs. In *AISec*, pages 45–54, 2013.

[24] A. Gorla et al. Checking app behavior against app descriptions. In *ICSE*, 2014.

[25] J.-C. Kuester and A. Bauer. Monitoring real android malware. In *Runtime Verification 2015*, 2015.

[26] J. MacQueen. Some methods for classification and analysis of multivariate observations, 1967.

[27] McAfee Threat Center. http://www.mcafee.com/uk/threat-center.aspx, 2015.

[28] F. A. Narudin et al. Evaluation of machine learning classifiers for mobile malware detection. *Soft Computing*, 20(1):343–357, 2016.

[29] F. Pedregosa et al. Scikit-learn: Machine learning in python. *J. Mach. Learn. Res.*, 12:2825–2830, 2011.

[30] H. Peng et al. Using probabilistic generative models for ranking risks of android apps. In *CCS*, pages 241–252. ACM, 2012.

[31] J. R. Quinlan. *C4.5: Programs for Machine Learning*. Morgan Kaufmann Publishers Inc., 1993.

[32] C. J. V. Rijsbergen. *Information Retrieval*. Butterworth-Heinemann, 2nd edition, 1979.

[33] R. R. Sokal and C. D. Michener. A statistical method for evaluating systematic relationships. *University of Kansas Science Bulletin*, 38:1409–1438, 1958.

[34] M. Spreitzenbarth et al. Mobile-sandbox: combining static and dynamic analysis with machine-learning techniques. *International Journal of Information Security*, 14(2):141–153, 2015.

[35] I. Steinwart and A. Christmann. *Support Vector Machines*. Springer, 2008.

[36] G. Suarez-Tangil et al. Dendroid: A text mining approach to analyzing and classifying code structures in Android malware families. *Expert Systems with Applications*, 41(4, Part 1):1104 – 1117, 2014.

[37] R. Tibshirani. Regression shrinkage and selection via the lasso. *Journal of the Royal Statistical Society, Series B*, 58:267–288, 1994.

[38] F. Wei et al. Amandroid: A precise and general inter-component data flow analysis framework for security vetting of Android apps. In *CCS*, pages 1329–1341. ACM, 2014.

[39] C. Yang et al. Droidminer: Automated mining and characterization of fine-grained malicious behaviors in Android applications. In *ESORICS*, 2014.

[40] S. Yerima, S. Sezer, and I. Muttik. High accuracy android malware detection using ensemble learning. *IET Information Security*, 9(6), 2015.

[41] S. Y. Yerima et al. A new Android malware detection approach using Bayesian classification. In *AINA*, pages 121–128, 2013.

[42] Z. Yuan, Y. Lu, and Y. Xue. Droiddetector: android malware characterization and detection using deep learning. *Tsinghua Science and Technology*, 21(1):114–123, Feb 2016.

[43] M. Zhang et al. Semantics-aware android malware classification using weighted contextual api dependency graphs. In *CCS*, 2014.

[44] D. Zhou et al. Learning with local and global consistency. In *Advances in Neural Information Processing Systems 16*, pages 321–328, 2004.

[45] Y. Zhou and X. Jiang. Dissecting Android malware: characterization and evolution. In *IEEE Symposium on Security and Privacy*, pages 95–109, 2012.

APPENDIX

A. THE CLASSIFICATION PERFORMANCE OF CLUSTER-SPECIFIC CLASSIFIERS

Decision Trees and Happen-Befores

clustering	validation		testing	
feature	precision	recall	precision	recall
-	68%	92%	**56%**	**71%**
permissions	84%	98%	38%	19%
actions	86%	99%	34%	12%
keywords	69%	91%	54%	69%
reachables	93%	86%	68%	20%
happen-befores	65%	91%	54%	72%
unwanted	95%	80%	75%	17%

Naive Bayes and Actions

clustering	validation		testing	
feature	precision	recall	precision	recall
-	74%	99%	**60%**	**79%**
permissions	85%	99%	63%	38%
actions	69%	100%	52%	73%
keywords	76%	99%	55%	63%
reachables	83%	100%	61%	54%
happen-befores	79%	100%	58%	57%
unwanted	79%	100%	54%	45%

Naive Bayes and Reachables

clustering	validation		testing	
feature	precision	recall	precision	recall
-	61%	99%	**53%**	**97%**
permissions	95%	85%	79%	20%
actions	80%	81%	45%	29%
keywords	90%	68%	60%	15%
reachables	66%	90%	57%	80%
happen-befores	64%	94%	53%	84%
unwanted	63%	89%	52%	79%

L1-Regularized Linear Regression and Unwanted

clustering	validation		testing	
feature	precision	recall	precision	recall
-	72%	72%	73%	66%
permissions	71%	99%	54%	55%
actions	73%	99%	59%	51%
keywords	64%	91%	54%	81%
reachables	74%	86%	**73%**	**67%**
happen-befores	74%	78%	74%	63%
unwanted	72%	71%	74%	64%

L1-Regularized Linear Regression and Reachables

clustering	validation		testing	
feature	precision	recall	precision	recall
-	73%	90%	64%	72%
permissions	71%	99%	56%	60%
actions	71%	99%	56%	55%
keywords	68%	93%	**65%**	**74%**
reachables	71%	88%	64%	69%
happen-befores	74%	86%	64%	70%
unwanted	74%	86%	69%	65%

Support Vector Machines and Keywords

clustering	validation		testing	
feature	precision	recall	precision	recall
-	82%	97%	63%	61%
permissions	86%	98%	47%	24%
actions	87%	99%	47%	20%
keywords	79%	91%	**61%**	**64%**
reachables	83%	92%	65%	57%
happen-befores	81%	93%	62%	60%
unwanted	84%	92%	52%	37%

Random Forest and Happen-Befores

clustering	validation		testing	
feature	precision	recall	precision	recall
-	69%	92%	56%	67%
permissions	83%	99%	45%	26%
actions	87%	99%	26%	8%
keywords	74%	90%	57%	64%
reachables	90%	87%	56%	23%
happen-befores	66%	84%	**56%**	**71%**
unwanted	95%	81%	77%	16%

AdaBoost and Keywords

clustering	validation		testing	
feature	precision	recall	precision	recall
-	84%	94%	**64%**	**56%**
permissions	86%	98%	55%	33%
actions	86%	99%	49%	24%
keywords	85%	87%	59%	40%
reachables	90%	93%	66%	32%
happen-befores	88%	90%	64%	41%
unwanted	85%	92%	63%	47%

k-Nearest Neighbours and Keywords

clustering	validation		testing	
feature	precision	recall	precision	recall
-	77%	97%	56%	65%
permissions	82%	99%	38%	23%
actions	85%	99%	51%	30%
keywords	73%	97%	**54%**	**83%**
reachables	73%	96%	61%	76%
happen-befores	74%	97%	56%	72%
unwanted	74%	96%	57%	73%

Semi-Supervised Learning and Happen-Befores

clustering	validation		testing	
feature	precision	recall	precision	recall
-	69%	92%	55%	66%
permissions	85%	98%	42%	19%
actions	87%	98%	44%	18%
keywords	73%	89%	54%	66%
reachables	93%	84%	70%	20%
happen-befores	67%	87%	**56%**	**71%**
unwanted	96%	80%	73%	16%

Evading Android Runtime Analysis Through Detecting Programmed Interactions

Wenrui Diao
The Chinese University of Hong Kong
dw013@ie.cuhk.edu.hk

Xiangyu Liu
The Chinese University of Hong Kong
lx012@ie.cuhk.edu.hk

Zhou Li
ACM Member
lzcarl@gmail.com

Kehuan Zhang
The Chinese University of Hong Kong
khzhang@ie.cuhk.edu.hk

ABSTRACT

Dynamic analysis technique has been widely used in Android malware detection. Previous works on evading dynamic analysis focus on discovering the fingerprints of emulators. However, such method has been challenged since the introduction of real devices in recent works. In this paper, we propose a new approach to evade automated runtime analysis through detecting programmed interactions. This approach, in essence, tries to tell the identity of the current app controller (human user or automated exploration tool), by finding intrinsic differences between human user and machine tester in interaction patterns. The effectiveness of our approach has been demonstrated through evaluation against 11 real-world online dynamic analysis services.

Keywords

Android malware; dynamic analysis; programmed interaction

1. INTRODUCTION

With the evolution of mobile computing technology, smartphone has experienced enormous growth in consumer market, among which Android devices have taken the lion's share. Unfortunately, Android's open ecosystem also turns itself into a playground for malware. According to a recent report [9], on average, 8,240 new Android malware samples were discovered in a single day.

To combat the massive volume of Android malware newly emerged, automated detection techniques (static and dynamic) were proposed and have become the mainstream solutions. Dynamic analysis frameworks monitor the behaviors of the app samples executed in a controlled environment under different stimuli. Compared with static analysis, dynamic analysis does not have to understand the complicated logic in malicious code and is immune to code obfuscation and packing. Moreover, less noticeable runtime malicious behaviors could be discovered.

The traditional dynamic analysis platforms were largely built upon emulators to enable fast and economic malware analysis.

WiSec'16, July 18–20, 2016, Darmstadt, Germany.

© 2016 Copyright held by the owner/author(s). Publication rights licensed to ACM. ISBN 978-1-4503-4270-4/16/07. . . $15.00

DOI: http://dx.doi.org/10.1145/2939918.2939926

To evade dynamic analysis, a broad spectrum of *anti-emulation* techniques have been proposed [21, 28, 14, 17] and adopted by malware authors. In general, these techniques were designed to fingerprint the runtime environment and look for artifacts that can tell physical device and emulator apart. Though effective at first, countermeasures have been developed by the security community to diminish the efficacy of anti-emulation. Recently, researchers proposed to use physical devices [19] and morph artifacts unique to emulators [12, 11, 13]. These methods wrecked the base of anti-emulation techniques, but we believe the arms race between dynamic analysis and evasion has not yet ended.

Automated Exploration. Different from the traditional desktop malware, Android malware are event-driven, meaning that malicious behaviors are usually triggered after certain combinations of user actions or system events. Therefore, the simple install-then-execute analysis model is not effective to trigger malware's runtime behaviors. To solve this issue, automated exploration techniques are integrated into dynamic analysis frameworks, including event injection, UI element identification, etc. The ultimate goal of them is to achieve good coverage of app's execution paths in a limited period.

New Evading Techniques. In this paper, we propose a new approach to evade Android automated runtime analysis through detecting programmed interactions. The core idea of this approach is to determine the identity of the party operating the app (a human user or an automated exploration tool) by monitoring the interaction patterns. To malware analysis, the goal of interaction is different from that of a real user. For efficiency, exploration tool injects simulated user events and avoids accessing the underlying devices. Such simulated events and hardware generated ones are inconsistent in most cases. Also, to achieve high coverage of execution paths, exploration tool tends to trigger all valid controls, among which some are not supposed to be triggered by human. We leverage these insights and built an evasive component `PIDetector`, which monitors the event stream and identifies the events unlikely coming from a real user. The malicious payload will be held from execution if a dynamic analyzer is identified.

Compared with the previous anti-emulation techniques, our approach exploits the gap between human and machine in runtime behaviors, instead of relying on features regarding execution environment. One prominent advantage of our approach is its robustness against any testing platform, even one composed of physical devices.

We implemented a proof-of-concept app and submitted it to 11 online dynamic analysis services screening samples submitted from all sorts of sources. The preliminary results have already demonstrated the effectiveness of our approach: nearly all (available) surveyed services exhibit at least one pre-defined pattern of programmed interactions. As a recommendation, the design of the current dynamic analysis platforms should be revisited to defend against such new type of evasion.

Contributions. We summarize this paper's contributions as below:

- *New Technique and Attack Surface.* We propose a new approach to evade Android runtime analysis: programmed interaction detection, which provides a new venue for evading dynamic analysis other than existing anti-emulation works.

- *Implementation and Evaluation.* We implemented a proof-of-concept app and tested it on several real-world Android dynamic analysis platforms. The experimental results demonstrate our approach is highly effective.

2. RELATED WORK

Most Android dynamic analysis frameworks are built upon emulators [20], which is easier to be deployed and more economical, as the cost of purchasing mobile devices is exempted. Besides, the app behaviors on emulators are easier to be monitored and controlled. Such frameworks, however, are not robust against evasive malware, and anti-emulation techniques have been widely discussed. In this section, we review these techniques and describe the countermeasures proposed by security community.

2.1 Anti-Emulation

Nearly all previous anti-emulation techniques [21, 28, 14, 17] exploit the unique features of the virtualized environment and refrain from executing the core malicious payload (e.g., sending SMS to premium number) when the host is found as an emulator. The features that differentiate emulators from real mobile devices and are leveraged for anti-emulation are listed below:

Firmware Features. The mobile devices manufactured by vendors are assembled from distinctive firmware, which embeds unique ID or information reflecting the hardware specification. On the contrary, emulators tend to use fixed dummy values to fill firmware features. For example, `null` and `android-test` are fed to firmware-query APIs like `Build.SERIAL` and `Build.HOST` by emulators.

Device Features. A lot of peripheral devices, especially sensors, have been integrated into mobile devices, like accelerometer and gyroscope. Not all the sensors are supported by emulators, which can be exploited for emulator identification. For the sensors simulated by emulators, the data stream produced differs significantly (usually constant) from what is generated from real devices (randomly distributed) [28].

Performance Features. Performance, particularly processing speed, is a disadvantage for emulators. Though modern desktop PC has more processing power, such improvement is overwhelmed by penalty from instruction translation. As shown in [28], adversary could measure CPU and graphical performance, and then determine the existence of emulator.

It also turns out that there exists a huge number of heuristics can be employed for emulator detection. Jing et al. [14] proposed a framework which can automatically detect the discrepancies between Android emulators and real devices, and more than 10,000 heuristics have been discovered. Fixing these discrepancies on emulators needs tremendous efforts by all means.

2.2 Countermeasures

The anti-emulation techniques surveyed above are quite effective but not impeccable. They all look for observable artifacts produced from *virtualization*, which turns out to be the Achilles' heel. We describe two types of countermeasures for obscuring running platform below:

Using Physical Devices. Building analysis platform on physical devices could thwart anti-emulation behaviors naturally. Vidas et al. [29] proposed a hybrid system named A5, which combines both virtual and physical pools of Android devices. More recently, Mutti et al. [19] proposed BareDroid, which runs bare-metal analysis on Android apps. The system is built solely upon off-the-shelf Android devices and applies several novel techniques like fast restoration to reduce the performance cost. The evaluation results of these works prove that malware are not able to discern the analysis platform with users' devices.

Changing Artifacts. Another direction is to change the observable artifacts to masquerade the emulators as real devices. Hu et al. [13], Dietzel [11] and Gajrani et al. [12] followed this trail. They customized the emulator framework and hooked runtime APIs (in both Java and Linux layer) to feed fake values to the probing functions of malware. The malicious behaviors could be revealed when the checks for real devices are all passed.

3. BACKGROUND AND MOTIVATION

From the perspective of the adversary, pursuing the direction of fingerprinting execution environment would lead to a dead-end in the trend that more and more analysis platforms are driven by real devices or tailored emulators. In this work, we explore a new direction: instead of sensing *what* environment runs the app, we inspect the behaviors of dynamic analyzer and focus on *how* it interacts with the app. We first briefly overview the current dynamic analysis techniques and then introduce the concept of *programmed interaction* to motivate our research.

3.1 Dynamic Analysis

Different from static analysis tools, which scrutinize the source code or binary code of the program to identify the malicious payload, dynamic analysis frameworks execute the program to capture the malicious behaviors in the runtime. In particular, the execution environment for dynamic analysis is instrumented, and various system or user inputs (e.g., clicking UI buttons) are injected to trigger all sorts of app's behaviors. If certain malicious I/O patterns or behaviors are identified (e.g., sending SMS to premium numbers), the app is considered as malware. Though static analysis avoids the cost of running app and is usually more efficient, it could be thwarted when obfuscation or packing techniques are employed. As shown in the work by Rastogi et al. [23], common malware transformation techniques could make malicious apps evade popular static analysis tools at high success rate. On the other hand, dynamic analysis is robust against code-level evading techniques and is suitable for processing apps with complicated program logics. A corpus of frameworks have been developed and proved to be effective, including DroidScope [31], AppsPlayground [22], CopperDroid [26], etc. Google also developed its dynamic analysis framework, Bouncer [16], to check every app submitted to Google Play.

3.1.1 Input Generation and Automated Exploration

Since app's runtime behaviors often depend on the inputs from the user or system, the effectiveness of the dynamic analysis framework highly depends on the strategy of input generation.

Comparing to the traditional PC malware, which tend to take malicious actions (e.g., controlling the system) once executed, mobile malware tend to delay the malicious actions till a sequence of events are observed (e.g., hijacking the legitimate app and stealing the received messages). Therefore, the testing platform should be able to generate the input in a context-aware manner and explore the execution paths automatically. Below, we describe two widely adopted strategies in automated path exploration:

Fuzzing-based Exploration. Fuzzing is a black-box testing technique in which the system under test is stressed with invalid, unexpected or random inputs transmitted from external interfaces to identify the bugs in programs [25]. On the Android platform, Google provides an official fuzzer Monkey [8], which generates pseudo-random streams of user events such as clicks, touches, or gestures, as well as a number of system-level events and injects them into the framework through Android Debug Bridge (ADB). Several dynamic analysis frameworks have incorporated Monkey as the exploration engine, such as VetDroid [32] and Andrubis [15].

Model-based Exploration. On the contrary, model-based testing aims at injecting events aligning with a specific pattern or model which could be derived by analyzing the app's code or UI. The test cases generated are usually more effective and efficient in discovering malicious activities. To support this testing mode, Google has developed an exploration tool named MonkeyRunner [5] which allows testing platform to interact with an app in pre-defined event sequences. MonkeyRunner has been adopted by several testing platforms including Mobile-Sandbox [24], CopperDroid [26], etc.

In the course of automated UI interactions, a large number of invalid actions could be triggered if the properties of UI structure is disregarded. As a solution, Google developed UI Automator [7], which inspects the layout hierarchy and device status to decide the meaningful UI actions. Besides, AppsPlayground [22] leveraged a number of heuristics to customize inputs for certain UI controls (e.g., login box). CuriousDroid [10] decomposes the on-screen layout and creates context-based model on-the-fly. SmartDroid [33] uses a hybrid model which extracts call graphs through static analysis and initiates actions leading to sensitive APIs.

3.2 Motivation: Programmed Interaction

The main design goal of the above frameworks is to explore *all* potential paths leading to malicious behaviors *efficiently*. As such, the input events they generated are usually predictable, fired at regular and short interval, and massive for good coverage, which significantly differ from what are produced by human users. Hence, leveraging this insight, we design a new mechanism to capture such *programmed interactions* and distinguish human users from testing platforms. We envision our approach could be implemented as a component (we call it PIDetector), embedded within Android malware and monitoring the system events of its interests. Before the execution of malicious payload, the collected event sequence will be analyzed by PIDetector, and the execution only proceeds when the event sequence is determined to be produced by human user.

Compared with anti-emulation techniques, our approach offers another layer of protection to malware even analyzed on bare-metal platforms. It is also robust against the upgrades which alter the observable artifacts by analysis frameworks. At the high level, our approach can be considered as a variant of CAPTCHA [30] – humans can pass, but computer programs can't pass. In fact, the state-of-art text or image based CAPTCHA schemes may achieve the same or even better accuracy in distinguishing human and computer. However, asking user to solve CAPTCHA before using the app would drive away many users and reduce the infection rate. In contrast, such issues are not embodied in our approach.

3.3 Assumptions

Our approach intends to evade the detection by dynamic analysis. Evading static analysis is out of the scope of our work. In fact, such task could be fulfilled by off-the-shelf obfuscators and packers.

We also assume the dynamic analysis platforms interact with the testing app through events injection, and the execution logic of the app cannot be forcefully altered, i.e., bypassing PIDetector and directly invoking malicious payloads. This strategy is in theory possible but requires precise analysis on app's code to identify the critical branches, which is quite challenging and again vulnerable to obfuscation and packing techniques. This setting is also adopted by all previous works on evading dynamic analysis [21, 28, 14, 17].

4. ATTACK VECTORS

In this section, we elaborate several attack vectors that can be leveraged to detect programmed interactions. Overall, the qualified attack vectors should fulfill the three requirements below:

- *Reverse Turing Test* – humans can pass, but current exploration tools can't pass.

- *Passive* – hard to be discovered by end-users.

- *Lightweight* – easy to be built and deployed.

Given these constraints, we design two classes of attack vectors targeting the vulnerabilities underlying event injections and UI element identification in dynamic analysis. To notice, some testing platforms built upon Monkey can be trivially identified through invoking the isUserAMonkey() API [3] and inspecting the returned value. We do not include it into the attack vectors as the returned value can be easily manipulated (e.g., it can be bypassed by UI Automator through calling setRunAsMonkey(false) [18]). We elaborate each attack vector in the following subsections.

4.1 Detecting Simulated Event Injections

We found the data attached to two types of user events, MotionEvent [6] for touchscreen tapping and KeyEvent [4] for key pressing, can be leveraged for detection. It turns out the both individual event and event sequence reveal distinguishable patterns.

4.1.1 Single Event

When a user operates a mobile device, the events are initiated by the onboard hardware and the information regarding the hardware is attached. To the opposite, the events injected by dynamic testing tools, like Monkey, are passed from external interfaces and most of the parameters are filled with dummy values. Specifically, while the core parameters (e.g., coordinates of input location) are filled with real values, the auxiliary parameters (e.g., keyboard type) are not filled similarly.

Table 1 and Table 2 list differences between the values generated from real-world usage and Monkey testing for MotionEvent and KeyEvent. Clearly, Monkey fills the values in a distinctive pattern that can be identified. For example, the ToolType parameter of KeyEvent generated by Monkey is always TOOL_TYPE_UNKNOWN, which cannot be used if this event is produced by hardware.

4.1.2 Event Sequence

To reach the high coverage of app behaviors in limited time, dynamic analyzers tend to inject events at high frequency which

Table 1: MotionEvent: real vs. simulated (by Monkey)

Parameter	Real	Simulated
ToolType	1: TOOL_TYPE_FINGER	0: TOOL_TYPE_UNKNOWN
DeviceId	[non-zero value]	0
Device	valid	null

Remarks: 1) DeviceId: zero indicates that the event does not come from a physical device and maps to the default keymap.

Table 2: KeyEvent: real vs. simulated (by Monkey)

Parameter	Real	Simulated
ScanCode	[non-fixed value]	0
DeviceId	[non-fixed value]	-1
Device.Name	[non-fixed value]	Virtual
Device.Generation	[non-fixed value]	2
Device.Descriptor	[non-fixed value]	af4d26ea4cdc857cc0f1 ed1ed51996db77be1e4d
Device.KeyboardType	1: non-alphabetic	2: alphabetic
Device.Source	[non-fixed value]	0x301: keyboard dpad

Remarks: 1) ScanCode: the hardware key id of the key event; 2) Generation: the number is incremented whenever the device is reconfigured and therefore not constant; 3) Descriptor: the unique identifier for the input device; 4) KeyboadType: the value is "non-alphabetic" as the nowadays smartphone models do not integrate hardware keyboards.

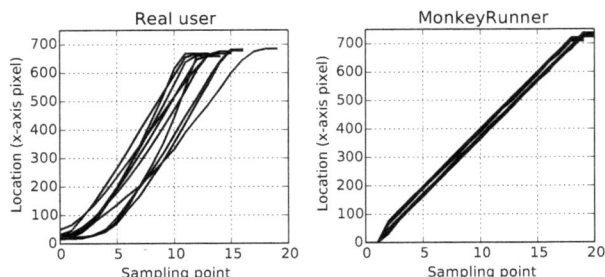

Figure 1: Swiping trajectory: real user vs. exploration tool

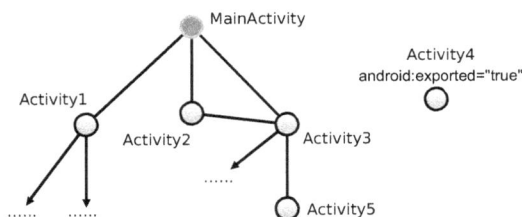

Figure 2: Example of isolated Activity

cannot be performed by human users. Therefore, by measuring the frequency of the events the dynamic analyzers could be identified. Also, the distribution of events along time series is also unique for dynamic analyzers, and we show how this observation could be leveraged for our purposes. As one example, the key presses are usually issued at changing speed when a user types text in EditText while the interval is fixed for dynamic analyzers. IME partially causes this: an IME will show up when a user taps EditText and due to the variance of the distances between characters on IME, the interval between key presses fluctuates.

From the aspect of MotionEvent series, Android provides standard APIs for an app to recognize touch gestures inputted by user. At the same time, a series of screen touching events (MotionEvent) can be observed, and the events are issued much more regular if from dynamic analyzers. As an example, we asked a participant to swipe the touch screen on Samsung Galaxy S III from far left to far right and directed MonkeyRunner for the same action. The test was ran 10 times and we draw the tap locations in x-axis (float x field of MotionEvent) against 20 sample points at the same interval in Figure 1. The trajectories of the swipes from the user are rather dispersed, and displacements at the start and end of the action are smaller. In contrast, Monkey's swipes are highly similar and are moved at constant speed. Such difference could be modeled through time series similarity measure related algorithms.

4.2 Implanting UI Traps

To increase the chance of triggering malicious activities, especially the ones associated with user behaviors, dynamic analyzers have to explore and interact with as many UI elements as possible. Such design, however, leads to a dilemma that can be exploited: the adversary could implant UI traps that are inaccessible to human users and unable to be distinguished by dynamic analyzers. Below we elaborate the designs of two such attack vectors:

4.2.1 Isolated Activity

An Android app defines the UI interface and routines for event processing in *Activity* component, which is also declared in the Manifest file. An app usually contains one main Activity and subsequent Activities that can be transitioned to, as shown in Figure 2. In addition, developers could export an Activity that can be launched by other apps (Activity4 in Figure 2), through setting android:exported="true". Common dynamic analyzers tend to parse the Manifest file and visit Activities in both cases while the users follow the defined interaction logic to visit Activities. This motivates us to create an *isolated Activity* which could not be reached through interaction as a trap: if an unused and exported Activity is invoked, the party behind should be dynamic analyzer. Such trap is hard to be detected ahead, as the interaction logic is defined in app's code and can be obfuscated.

4.2.2 Invisible UI Elements

We demonstrate another attack vector here which manipulates the visual effects of UI elements. A human user normally taps the UI elements she can see to input information. On the other hand, dynamic analyzers could invoke system APIs (such as parseViewHierarchy under DeviceBridge class) to identify *valid* elements and simulate the interaction. Therefore, we could leave a valid but *"invisible"* control in Activity as a trap, and use it to detect the dynamic analyzer falling in.

In fact, Android UI library provides a set of highly customizable UI controls for developers, including Button, TextView, Switch, etc. and they can be easily configured to be invisible. One such control is ImageButton that displays image as a button and accepts clicks. If the image is filled with the same color as the nearby pixels of background, it would not be discovered by the human user. Moreover, we could change the layout and location of the controls for the same purpose. For instances, we could set the control to be tiny (e.g., 1 pixel) or fall out of the screen.

Figure 3 explains this idea. From human's view, only a button (Test) and a sentence (Hello World) can be identified. Actually, 5 UI controls are embedded in the layout: ❶ text view, ❷ image button, ❸ switch, ❹ image button, and ❺ button. They are all valid to dynamic analyzers. For example, we ran Google UI Automator to parse the UI layout and it recognizes all controls and extracts the information listed below:

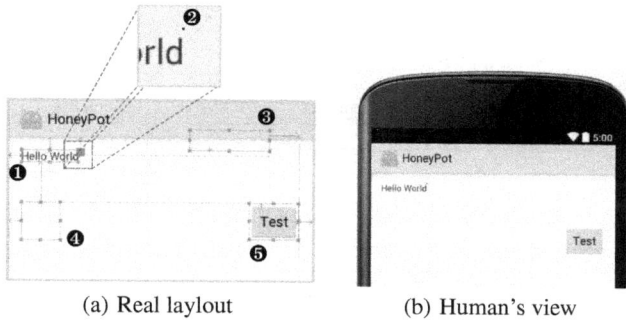

(a) Real laylout   (b) Human's view

Figure 3: Invisible UI elements: real layout vs. human's view

```
(0) FrameLayout[0,0][720,1280]
  (0) View[0,50][720,146]
  (1) TextView:Hello World[32,178][178,216]
  (2) ImageButton[176,178][178,180]
  (3) Switch:ON[408,124][614,180]
  (4) ImageButton[32,318][132,418]
  (5) Button:Test[560,318][688,414]
```

All these controls will be exercised by dynamic analyzers, but only ❶ and ❺ could be noticed by human. Therefore, events fired on other controls could indicate the existence of dynamic analyzers. To escape from this type of traps, dynamic analyzers have to accurately determine the visibility of UI controls (to human eyes), which remains an open problem.

5. EVALUATION

In this section, we present the experimental results on the effectiveness of `PIDetector`. The testing methodology is introduced first, and the results are discussed after.

Testing Methodology. We developed a testing app integrating `PIDetector` as an internal component. Our goal is to examine whether `PIDetector` can correctly detect dynamic analyzers through one or more attack vectors. Therefore, the testing app only has basic UI and functionalities, and we did not include malicious payload into the testing app to reduce the impact to the operationalized platforms. When the app is loaded, `PIDetector` starts to collect raw logs regarding fired events (details are provided below). The raw logs were sent to an HTTP server set up on Amazon Elastic Beanstalk [1] and analyzed through the models implemented by us. We decide to exfiltrate the event data to gain a better understanding of the behaviors of testing platforms. All analysis can be done locally when adopted by adversary's real app.

Raw Logs. The collected raw logs include the following information: the parameters of captured MotionEvent and KeyEvent objects, invoked Activities, visited UI elements. Every returned log is padded with a unique ID to distinguish different testing platforms and times of running. Only the first 100 logs are transmitted to the server to obtain enough data and avoid excessive network connections, which might be considered as anomaly activities by testing platforms. We also collected the configuration information of every tested service, such as Android ID, IMEI, `Build.SERIAL` and `Build.MANUFACTURER`, to see if countermeasures against anti-emulation are deployed.

Testing Platforms. We tested 10 dynamic analysis services built for malware analysis, among which four come from the academia while the others come from the security companies. In addition, we upload our testing app to Google Play to test its official dynamic

analyzer, Google Bouncer. These 11 services are listed in Table 3. The experiments were conducted in January and March 2016.

We were able to obtain valid raw logs from 7 services, and the final results are summarized in Table 3. Among the remaining ones, A5 and CopperDroid refused to analyze our app, since the processing queue has been fully occupied. No raw logs or informative messages are returned for Payload Security and Malwr, and we speculate the causes are: 1) they only launch static analysis on our app; 2) The outbound network connections from app are blocked.

Finding 1. *Nearly all (available) analysis services are vulnerable to at least one attack vector.* Most of them could be identified by analyzing single event parameter, except TraceDroid for lacking enough parameters and Google Bouncer for filling valid values. For example, the Input Device parameter of the KeyEvent from SandDroid was always "-1". Isolated Activity feature is also quite effective, and half of these online services fell into this trap. On the other hand, only Tecent Habo hit invisible elements, and no service was found to generate continuous event sequence (e.g., swipe). We suspect that these interactions are missed because complex UI analysis and interactions are not performed.

Finding 2. *Emulator camouflaging or physical device has been deployed by online analysis systems.* For example, we found the platform configuration of Google Bouncer is quite like physical device – Google Nexus 5 or 6, as showing below:

```
Version: 6.0.1              SDK_INT: 23
MODEL: Nexus 6             BRAND: google
BOARD: shamu               DEVICE: shamu
HARDWARE: shamu            SERIAL: ZX1G22HMB3
ID: MMB29K                 PRODUCT: shamu
DISPLAY: MMB29K            MANUFACTURER: motorola
HOST: wped2.hot.corp.google.com
BOOTLOADER: moto-apq8084-71.15
FINGERPRINT: google/shamu/shamu:6.0.1/MMB29K
    /2419427:user/release-keys
```

To notice, emulator camouflage has been used for other purposes on Android platform. BlueStacks [2], a popular emulator designed for running Android games on Windows and Mac platforms, camouflages itself as certain models of Samsung devices to evade emulator detection performed by apps. Hence, we believe our techniques for programmed interaction detection is meaningful even in the short term to attackers.

6. DISCUSSION

Limitations. As countermeasures, the developers of dynamic analyzers could change the UI interaction pattern and make the testing process closer to human beings. For example, the dummy parameter values of the injected MotionEvent and KeyEvent could be changed to use real data. On the other hand, how to hide against the more complicated attack vectors we devised (e.g., event sequence) is unclear. Though user's interactions on App UI can be recorded and replayed, challenges have to be addressed on how to automatically adjust the recorded actions to different apps.

7. CONCLUSION

In this work, we propose a new approach to evade Android runtime analysis. This approach focuses on detecting programmed interactions to determine whether an app is under analysis, instead of relying on the traditional emulator detection. The preliminary experimental results have demonstrated the effectiveness of our methods. We believe the evasive techniques leveraging subtleties of human-computer interaction should be seriously considered by

Table 3: Experimental results for online dynamic analysis services

Service Name	URL	Simulated Events			UI Traps	
		MotionEvent Paramters	KeyEvent Parameters	Event Sequence	Isolated Activity	Invisible UI Elements
NVISO ApkScan	https://apkscan.nviso.be	√	√	−	−	−
SandDroid	http://sanddroid.xjtu.edu.cn	√	√	−	√	−
TraceDroid [27]	http://tracedroid.few.vu.nl	×	×	−	√	−
Anubis [15]	http://anubis.iseclab.org	×	√	−	√	−
Tecent Habo	https://habo.qq.com/	√	√	−	−	√
VisualThreat	https://www.visualthreat.com	√	√	−	−	−
Google Bouncer	N/A – no public link	×	−	−	−	?
A5 [29]	http://dogo.ece.cmu.edu/a5/	The upload process always reported error.				
CopperDroid [26]	http://copperdroid.isg.rhul.ac.uk	Too many submitted samples were queued.				
Malwr	https://malwr.com	No raw log was returned.				
Payload Security	https://www.hybrid-analysis.com	No raw log was returned.				

Remarks: 1) "√": Judged as programmed interaction. 2) "×": Judged as human interaction. 3) "−": Not triggered or found. 4) "?": Google Bouncer clicked all buttons on the main Activity but ignored the image button which was camouflaged as a normal button by us. We speculate Bouncer only triggers the UI controls with the `Button` property by design. Since this is indirect evidence, so we label it as "?".

security community and call for further research on closing the gap between machine and human in runtime behaviors.

8. ACKNOWLEDGEMENTS

We thank anonymous reviewers for their insightful comments. This work was partially supported by NSFC (Grant No. 61572415), and the General Research Funds (Project No. CUHK 4055047 and 24207815) established under the University Grant Committee of the Hong Kong Special Administrative Region, China.

9. REFERENCES

[1] AWS Elastic Beanstalk. http://aws.amazon.com/elasticbeanstalk/.
[2] BlueStacks. http://www.bluestacks.com/.
[3] isUserAMonkey(). http://developer.android.com/reference/android/app/ActivityManager.html#isUserAMonkey().
[4] KeyEvent. http://developer.android.com/reference/android/view/KeyEvent.html.
[5] MonkeyRunner. http://developer.android.com/tools/help/monkeyrunner_concepts.html.
[6] MotionEvent. https://developer.android.com/reference/android/view/MotionEvent.html.
[7] Testing Support Library. https://developer.android.com/tools/testing-support-library/index.html.
[8] UI/Application Exerciser Monkey. http://developer.android.com/tools/help/monkey.html.
[9] G DATA Mobile Malware Report - Threat Report: Q4/2015. https://secure.gd/dl-us-mmwr201504, 2016.
[10] P. Carter, C. Mulliner, M. Lindorfer, W. Robertson, and E. Kirda. CuriousDroid: Automated User Interface Interaction for Android Application Analysis Sandboxes. In *Financial Cryptography and Data Security - 20th International Conference, FC 2016, Revised Selected Papers*, 2016.
[11] C. Dietzel. Porting and Improving an Android Sandbox for Automated Assessment of Malware. Master's thesis, Hochschule Darmstadt, 2014.
[12] J. Gajrani, J. Sarswat, M. Tripathi, V. Laxmi, M. S. Gaur, and M. Conti. A Robust Dynamic Analysis System Preventing SandBox Detection by Android. In *Proceedings of the 8th International Conference on Security of Information and Networks (SIN)*, 2015.
[13] W. Hu and Z. Xiao. Guess Where I am: Detection and Prevention of Emulator Evading on Android. *XFocus Information Security Conference (XCon)*, 2014.
[14] Y. Jing, Z. Zhao, G. Ahn, and H. Hu. Morpheus: Automatically Generating Heuristics to Detect Android Emulators. In *Proceedings of the 30th Annual Computer Security Applications Conference (ACSAC)*, 2014.
[15] M. Lindorfer, M. Neugschwandtner, L. Weichselbaum, Y. Fratantonio, V. van der Veen, and C. Platzer. ANDRUBIS-1,000,000 Apps Later: A View on Current Android Malware Behaviors. In *Proceedings of the 3rd International Workshop on Building Analysis Datasets and Gathering Experience Returns for Security (BADGERS)*, 2014.
[16] H. Lockheimer. Android and Security. http://googlemobile.blogspot.com/2012/02/android-and-security.html, 2012.
[17] D. Maier, M. Protsenko, and T. Müller. A Game of Droid and Mouse: The Threat of Split-Personality Malware on Android. *Computers & Security*, 54:2–15, 2015.

[18] A. Momtaz. Allow for setting test type as a monkey. https://android.googlesource.com/platform/frameworks/base/+/8f6f1f4%5E!/, 2013.
[19] S. Mutti, Y. Fratantonio, A. Bianchi, L. Invernizzi, J. Corbetta, D. Kirat, C. Kruegel, and G. Vigna. Baredroid: Large-scale Analysis of Android Apps on Real Devices. In *Proceedings of the 31st Annual Computer Security Applications Conference (ACSAC)*, 2015.
[20] S. Neuner, V. van der Veen, M. Lindorfer, M. Huber, G. Merzdovnik, M. Mulazzani, and E. R. Weippl. Enter Sandbox: Android Sandbox Comparison. In *Proceedings of the 2014 IEEE Mobile Security Technologies Workshop (MoST)*, 2014.
[21] T. Petsas, G. Voyatzis, E. Athanasopoulos, M. Polychronakis, and S. Ioannidis. Rage Against the Virtual Machine: Hindering Dynamic Analysis of Android Malware. In *Proceedings of the Seventh European Workshop on System Security (EuroSec)*, 2014.
[22] V. Rastogi, Y. Chen, and W. Enck. AppsPlayground: Automatic Security Analysis of Smartphone Applications. In *Proceedings of the Third ACM Conference on Data and Application Security and Privacy (CODASPY)*, 2013.
[23] V. Rastogi, Y. Chen, and X. Jiang. Catch Me If You Can: Evaluating Android Anti-Malware Against Transformation Attacks. *IEEE Transactions on Information Forensics and Security (TIFS)*, 9(1):99–108, 2014.
[24] M. Spreitzenbarth, F. C. Freiling, F. Echtler, T. Schreck, and J. Hoffmann. Mobile-Sandbox: Having a Deeper Look into Android Applications. In *Proceedings of the 28th Annual ACM Symposium on Applied Computing (SAC)*, 2013.
[25] A. Takanen, J. DeMott, and C. Miller. Fuzzing Overview. In *Fuzzing for Software Security Testing and Quality Assurance*. Artech House, 2008.
[26] K. Tam, S. J. Khan, A. Fattori, and L. Cavallaro. CopperDroid: Automatic Reconstruction of Android Malware Behaviors. In *Proceedings of the 22nd Annual Network and Distributed System Security Symposium (NDSS)*, 2015.
[27] V. van der Veen. Dynamic Analysis of Android Malware. Master's thesis, VU University Amsterdam, 2013.
[28] T. Vidas and N. Christin. Evading Android Runtime Analysis via Sandbox Detection. In *Proceedings of the 9th ACM Symposium on Information, Computer and Communications Security (ASIACCS)*, 2014.
[29] T. Vidas, J. Tan, J. Nahata, C. L. Tan, N. Christin, and P. Tague. A5: Automated Analysis of Adversarial Android Applications. In *Proceedings of the 4th ACM Workshop on Security and Privacy in Smartphones & Mobile Devices (SPSM)*, 2014.
[30] L. von Ahn, M. Blum, N. J. Hopper, and J. Langford. CAPTCHA: Using Hard AI Problems for Security. In *Advances in Cryptology - EUROCRYPT 2003, International Conference on the Theory and Applications of Cryptographic Techniques, Proceedings*, 2003.
[31] L. Yan and H. Yin. DroidScope: Seamlessly Reconstructing the OS and Dalvik Semantic Views for Dynamic Android Malware Analysis. In *Proceedings of the 21st USENIX Security Symposium*, 2012.
[32] Y. Zhang, M. Yang, B. Xu, Z. Yang, G. Gu, P. Ning, X. S. Wang, and B. Zang. Vetting Undesirable Behaviors in Android Apps with Permission Use Analysis. In *Proceedings of the 2013 ACM SIGSAC Conference on Computer and Communications Security (CCS)*, 2013.
[33] C. Zheng, S. Zhu, S. Dai, G. Gu, X. Gong, X. Han, and W. Zou. SmartDroid: an Automatic System for Revealing UI-based Trigger Conditions in Android Applications. In *Proceedings of the 2012 ACM Workshop on Security and Privacy in Smartphones and Mobile Devices (SPSM)*, 2012.

Detecting SMS Spam in the Age of Legitimate Bulk Messaging

Bradley Reaves, Logan Blue, Dave Tian, Patrick Traynor, Kevin R. B. Butler
{reaves, bluel, daveti}@ufl.edu {traynor, butler}@cise.ufl.edu
Florida Institute for Cybersecurity Research
University of Florida
Gainesville, Florida

ABSTRACT

Text messaging is used by more people around the world than any other communications technology. As such, it presents a desirable medium for spammers. While this problem has been studied by many researchers over the years, the recent increase in legitimate bulk traffic (e.g., account verification, 2FA, etc.) has dramatically changed the mix of traffic seen in this space, reducing the effectiveness of previous spam classification efforts. This paper demonstrates the performance degradation of those detectors when used on a large-scale corpus of text messages containing both bulk and spam messages. Against our labeled dataset of text messages collected over 14 months, the precision and recall of past classifiers fall to 23.8% and 61.3% respectively. However, using our classification techniques and labeled clusters, precision and recall rise to 100% and 96.8%. We not only show that our collected dataset helps to correct many of the overtraining errors seen in previous studies, but also present insights into a number of current SMS spam campaigns.

1. INTRODUCTION

Text messaging has been one of the greatest drivers of subscriptions for mobile phones. From the simplest clamshells to modern smart phones, virtually every cellular-capable device supports SMS. Unsurprisingly, these systems have been targeted extensively by spammers. The research community has, in turn, responded with a range of filtering mechanisms. However, this ecosystem and the messages it carries have changed dramatically in the past few years.

The most significant change in this ecosystem is the widespread interconnection with non-cellular services. Specifically, a wide range of web applications now use text messaging to interact with their customers. From second factor authentication (2FA) to account activation, the volume of legitimate messages with very little variation in their content is on the rise [2]. While a critical part of overall security for users, this shift in the makeup of traffic is having a major

impact on the efficacy of SMS spam filtering. Because legitimate bulk messages have characteristics similar to spam, including the ubiquity of a number (like a short code or one-time password) or a URL, as well as a call to action ("click here"), we hypothesize that SMS spam filters will need to change to account for a new messaging paradigm.

In this paper, we leverage a dataset of nearly 400,000 messages collected over the course of 14 months. We obtain such data by crawling public SMS gateways. Users rely on these public gateways to receive legitimate SMS verification messages as well as to avoid having their actual phone numbers exposed to lists that receive spam. We rely on this data to make the following contributions:

- **Release Largest Public Dataset:** We release a labeled dataset of bulk messaging and SMS spam, which is larger than any previously published spam dataset by nearly an order of magnitude.
- **Weaknesses in Previous Datasets:** We show that existing SMS spam/ham corpora do not sufficiently reflect the prevalence of bulk messages in modern SMS communications, preventing effective SMS spam detection. Specifically, we demonstrate that previously proposed mechanisms trained on such datasets exhibit extremely poor results (e.g., 23% recall) in the presence of such messages.
- **Characterization of SMS Spam Campaign:** We provide deeper insight into ongoing SMS spam campaigns, including both topic and network analysis. We find that the number of messages sent in a campaign is best explained by the volume of sending numbers available to the campaign.

2. RELATED WORK

Text messaging has become the subject of a wide range of security research. For instance, many services now rely on SMS for the delivery of authentication tokens for use in 2FA systems [1,5,9,23]. Recent work has demonstrated that many such systems are vulnerable to attack for a range of reasons including poor entropy [12,25] or susceptibility to interception [16]. Text messaging has also been analyzed as the cause of significant denial of service attacks [17,28–30] and a medium for emergency alerts [27].

SMS spam has received significant attention from the community. Researchers have developed a range of techniques for detecting such spam, with significant focus on message content [4,6,8,10,13,21,22,26,31,33]. This class of mitigation has by far been the most popular in the research commu-

DOI: http://dx.doi.org/10.1145/2939918.2939937

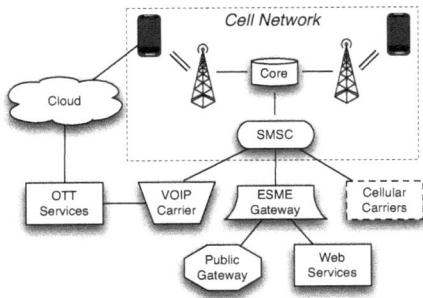

Figure 1: A high-level overview of the SMS ecosystem.

nity as collecting SMS spam can be done without special access to carrier-level data. The research community has relied almost exclusively on publicly available datasets, like those made available by Chen and Kan [7] or Almeida et al. [4]. Unfortunately, these datasets are quite limited, with only a few hundred actual spam messages. Other efforts have instead focused on network behaviors, such as volumes, sources and destinations [11,14,15,18–20,32]. Unfortunately, this latter class of analysis is generally limited to network providers, making independent validation difficult.

3. BACKGROUND

Text messaging within the traditional closed telephony ecosystem works as follows: a user generates a message on their phone and transmits it to their local base station, which delivers the SMS to the Short Messaging Service Center (SMSC). With the aid of other nodes in the network, the SMSC forwards the SMS to its destination for delivery.

Modern telephony networks accept text messages from a far larger set of sources. In addition to the SMSC receiving text messages from users served by other cellular providers, many VoIP providers (e.g., Vonage, Google Voice) also allow their users to send text messages. Messaging apps transported by Over the Top (OTT) connections now deliver messages via the public Internet. Lastly, a wider range of External Short Messaging Entities (ESMEs) such as web services used for two-factor authentication (e.g., Google Authenticator, Duo Security). Within this class also lies entities known as Public Gateways. These public websites allow anyone to *receive* a text message online by publishing telephone numbers that can receive text messages, and posting such messages to the web when they are received. These services are completely open — they require no registration or login, and it is clear to all users that any message sent to the gateway is publicly available.

It is through these Public Gateways that we are able to conduct our measurement study. Because these interfaces publish text messages for destinations that span a range of providers and continents, our work provides the first global picture into SMS spam (especially that which bypasses the spam filters of providers).

4. DATA CHARACTERIZATION

This paper makes use of several previously compiled datasets. First, we use two existing SMS spam and ham corpora. We use a spam corpus compiled by Almeida and Hidalgo [4] that contains 747 messages. For legitimate messages, we use a corpus of 55,835 messages collected by Chen and Kan [7] from submissions of personal text messages from volunteers.

We refer to these two corpora as the "public corpus." To the best of our knowledge, these messages are the largest publicly available collection of SMS ham and spam.

Many of the insights of this paper are made possible by a collection of SMS from another source: public SMS gateways. Public SMS gateways are websites that purchase a public phone number and post all text messages received by that number to a public website visible to anyone. These websites claim to exist for various reasons, including to avoid SMS spam by not revealing a user's true phone number, but the majority of messages (over 67.6%) received by these gateways consist of account verification requests or one-time passwords (i.e., legitimate bulk SMS). This means that the message type distribution of our data may not be representative of messages seen by a traditional mobile carrier. Even though this data may have fewer personal messages than typical, it is still a valuable data source for understanding the effects of bulk messaging on SMS spam classification. These gateways provide complete message content, sender and receiver numbers, and the time of message. The message data that we use was collected by scraping these websites, resulting in a dataset of 386,327 messages sent to over 400 numbers in 28 countries over a period of 14 months. Many of these messages are duplicates, or are syntactically or semantically identical (e.g., "Hello Alice" and "Hello Bob").

In a prior study [25], this data was grouped by ordering messages lexically and identifying boundaries where Levenshtein distance fell below 90%. The largest of these groups were manually labeled to identify message intent, including indicating if a message appeared to be unsolicited bulk advertising (i.e., spam). Only 1.0% of this labeled data consisted of spam messages. Note that messages sent by individuals are systematically excluded from analysis because they are not self-similar and do not form large groups.

For our experiments, we carved the gateway data into two distinct datasets. The first was one message from every labeled group (called "labeled gateway data"). This dataset is intended to train a machine learning classifier, and accordingly overwhelmingly similar messages are removed to avoid overfitting the classifier. This dataset consists of 754 messages, including 31 (4.1%) spam messages. The second dataset was all messages that were previously unlabeled, called the "unlabeled gateway data". This dataset consists of 99,363 messages of an unknown mixture of personal messages, legitimate bulk messages, and spam.

We have released both the labeled gateway training data and confirmed spam discovered in the unlabeled gateway dataset (details provided in subsequent sections). This dataset contains 1316 unique bulk messaging ham messages and 5673 spam messages. It is available at http://www.sms-analysis.org.

Ethical Considerations We note that there are ethical questions that must be considered in collecting this data. First, the data is publicly available, and therefore under United States regulations an institutional review board does not need to oversee experiments that collect or use this data. Furthermore, we note that users who expect to receive messages at these messages are aware that they will be publicly available, and accordingly must reasonably have low privacy expectations. However, senders of messages may not be aware that these messages will be public. Because of this, we seek to focus our use of this data on bulk messaging, where message content is unlikely to be confidential to either

Table 1: Classifier Performance

Training	P	P	P + LGW	P + LGW
Testing	P	LGW	LGW	UGW
Precision	94.1%	23.8%	100%	84.6%
Recall	88.8%	61.3%	96.8%	—
FP	0.1%	8.1%	0.0%	1.3%
FN	0.1%	1.6%	0.1%	—

Key: P — Public Corpora, LGW — Labeled Gateway Data, UGW — Unlabeled Gateway Data

the sender or recipient. Our methods are designed so that we systematically exclude messages between individuals, and in the event that any personally identifiable information (PII) is disclosed, we do not further analyze, extract, or make use of that information in any way. We note that any PII in this data was *already publicly leaked* before we collect and analyze it, so our use of this data does not further damage any individual's privacy. Finally, our corpora have been scrubbed of personally identifiable information by replacing sensitive information with fixed constants. We replaced every instance of names, physical addresses, email addresses, phone numbers, dates/times, usernames, passwords, and URLs that contain potentially unique paths or parameters. Every released message was examined by two researchers.

5. EVALUATING SMS SPAM CLASSIFIERS

As discussed in earlier sections, prior SMS spam corpora were collected by researchers who solicit volunteers to provide examples of SMS spam or legitimate messages. We believe that these corpora, under which the bulk of SMS spam research has been conducted, are fundamentally limited. For example, SMS has increasingly become a means of contact for many online services to provide information to users and to provide security related services like two-factor authentication. However, the existing corpora for SMS spam research do not account for such messages. Accordingly, we hypothesize that existing SMS spam detection research based on the corpora available will fail to accurately classify legitimate messages as benign.

We designed several experiments to test this hypothesis. The following subsections detail these experiments and their findings. Existing literature on machine learning for content-based SMS spam classification has exhaustively examined choices of machine learning algorithm [8] and feature selection [26], finding that while there is an optimal-accuracy design, other choices lead to only minor degradations in performance. We then implement and evaluate this classifier against gateway data to evaluate the effect of the spam corpus on the detection of SMS spam in the face of legitimate bulk messaging. *Our aim in doing so is demonstrate the impact on spam classification of changes in legitimate SMS messaging, not to establish an empirically optimal classifier.*

We conclude by retraining and applying this classifier to identify SMS spam in unlabeled gateway data.

5.1 Classifier Selection and Implementation

To evaluate the question of how bulk SMS would be classified, we needed to implement an SMS spam classifier. After reviewing the literature, we found that the best performing classifiers (taking into account accuracy, precision, and recall on cross-validated evaluation) use a support vector machine (SVM) [8]. SVM classifiers permit the use of kernels that allow an expansion of input data into a higher-dimensional

space to improve classification performance. The kernels used in prior work were unspecified, so we use a linear kernel as it is the simplest possible kernel. We confirmed this provided the best performance compared to other kernels, but omit a full analysis for space reasons. Regarding features, prior work has investigated a naive binary bag-of-words model, using only counts of keywords common in spam, n-grams, and more complicated feature sets. Prior work found that a simple binary vector indicating the presence of a word in the message performed best [26], so we also use this approach. Like Tan et al. [26], we preprocess the data to remove features that could induce classification on non-semantically meaningful features, including making all words lower case and replacing all URLs, email addresses, stand-alone numbers, and English days of the week with a fixed string. As in prior work, we do not remove stop words[1] from the feature vector. We use the scikit-learn Python library [24] for feature analysis and classifier implementation. Several other classifiers were evaluated using a variety of feature selection techniques. We found that results were consistent with those found in prior work, and omit further discussion for space.

With this classifier implemented, we train the classifier and evaluate its performance on the existing public corpora, then train and test the classifier using 5-fold cross validation to ensure consistency with previous work. The vocabulary in this dataset results in a feature vector with 39,558 words. After training, we see an overall accuracy of 99.8%. Precision (a measure of how many messages identified as spam are actually spam) was 94.1%, while recall (a measure of how much spam was correctly identified) was 88.8%. These results are consistent with the findings of Tan et al. [26], who found an F1 score of 93.6%, comparable to our classifier's F1 score of 91.4%. In summary, the classifier performance seems quite good.

5.2 Evaluating Classifier with Training Data

Having trained and validated a classifier, we can test our hypothesis that the classifier will fail to properly categorize legitimate bulk SMS messages, instead labeling it as spam. After classifying the data, we find that the classifier's performance significantly declines, confirming our hypothesis. Precision falls from 94.1% to 23.8%. Recall also declined from 88.8% to 61.3%. The practical impact of this classifier's poor performance on the user is best reflected by the overall false positive rate. In total, 8.1% of legitimate bulk messages would be miscategorized by the classifier, providing a frustrating user experience. In particular, dropping account verification messages will make new services inaccessible, and dropping SMS authentication messages would make services effectively unavailable for users.

To understand these results, we investigated the feature weights learned by our classifier. Feature weights indicate the relative importance of a particular feature in determining if a message is spam; positive weights indicate that a feature is indicative of spam, while weights close to 0 do not strongly indicate spam or ham. For example, the feature indicating the presence of a number has a weight of 0.637, while the word "rain" has a weight of -0.628. This indicates that the presence of a number (like a phone number or a price) is a strong indicator of "spamminess."

---

[1]Stop words are extremely common words, like "the", "and", etc., often removed during natural language data analysis.

To better understand our false positives, we examined the weights of the 20 most frequent words in our false positives. We find that words that are prevalent in legitimate bulk SMS like "code" or "verify" have weights with low absolute value (0.046 and 0.000 for these words). The words that are frequently used in these messages have weights that contribute almost nothing to the decision of the classifier.

As a result, the following message from the GW dataset is mislabeled as spam due to the effect of large positive weights provided by the features "has number" and "has URL."

```
WhatsApp code 351-852.  You can also tap on
this link to verify your phone:
v.whatsapp.com/351852
```

5.3 Evaluating Classifier on Labeled Data

Machine learning classifier performance is governed by many factors regarding model selection; however, experience shows that small datasets are often a bottleneck for classifier performance [3]. We hypothesized that better data, not a better model, was required to rectify the performance issues we found. To test this hypothesis, we retrain the classifier mentioned above to include the labeled gateway messages.

After running a cross validation analysis, we find that classifier performance increases to numbers comparable or better than those in the first experiment. We see an overall accuracy of 99.9%, with precision and recall of 100% and 96.8%. It is thus possible to distinguish legitimate and unsolicited bulk messages, at least in a cross-validation setting.

We again examined the feature weights of our messages, and we found that the features like "code" and "verify" have acquired strong weights: -0.402 and -0.706 respectively. This shows that the public corpus fails to provide enough data samples to fully cover the domain of legitimate messages, but this can be rectified using gateway data.

5.4 Evaluating classifier on unlabeled data

While cross validation is a standard technique for evaluating a classifier given a finite data set, it loses predictive value compared to using a true testing data set. To further evaluate our new retrained-classifier, we apply it to 99,363 unlabeled gateway messages. Because our gateway labeling data focused on messages that were highly similar or repeated to a high degree, we felt confident that there was spam in the unlabeled data as well.

To evaluate the new retrained classifier, we classified these messages, finding 8179 messages of unlabeled gateway data (8.2%) labeled as spam by the classifier. However, this does not tell us how many messages are legitimate bulk messages (i.e. false positives) and many are actually unsolicited. To answer this question, we manually label the messages marked as spam by our classifier.

Fortunately, many of these messages are similar in content, so they can be grouped together to label them. To facilitate clustering, we describe each message using a common technique in text data known as latent semantic analysis (LSA). LSA describes high dimensional text data as a low-dimensional feature vector that groups semantically similar messages together. LSA computes a term frequency – inverse document frequency matrix of the corpus, then applies a singular value decomposition to select the most important singular vectors, reducing the document space. We then cluster documents using the DBSCAN clustering

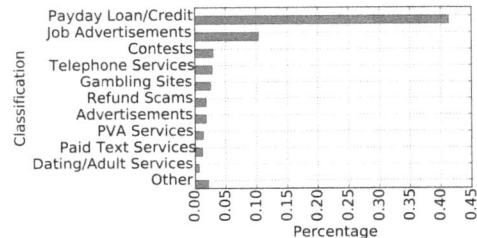

Figure 2: The top spam categories in gateway data

algorithm. DBSCAN identifies clusters by specifying a minimum cluster density and finding elements that form regions with density greater than the threshold. Unlike k-means, it does not make assumptions about cluster shape, or the number of clusters. After clustering, we identified 475 clusters of spam in the gateway data. We evaluate the effectiveness of our clustering algorithm by computing the average silhouette score of each message. Briefly, this score indicates the similarity of objects within each cluster (as opposed to a neighboring cluster), and our score of 0.644 indicates a good clustering structure. We characterize these clusters in more detail in the following section.

We then manually labeled these clusters for topic (e.g., pharma, payday loans, etc.) and whether the messages were actually spam (e.g., false positives). Unfortunately, determining if a message is solicited is not a perfect science, and there are some limitations to this approach. First and foremost, a message sent to some users may be solicited while the same message sent to others could be unwanted by others. Furthermore, we were not the intended recipients of these messages, and in some messages context is not always available to us when labeling. In situations where doubt was warranted, we erred on the side of assuming a message was indeed solicited (i.e. not spam). For example, we labeled any message as "not spam" if it seemed to be the response to a user inquiry or if it seemed to be part of an exchange in which a user could have prompted the message. Therefore, we believe that our reported results are conservative. Second, we ignore messages that were not clustered, so ground truth is unavailable for 13.1% of messages labeled as spam. Additionally, we did not have the resources to examine messages that were not classified as spam. Therefore, we cannot definitively measure recall or false negatives.

With labeled classification results, we can evaluate the performance of a SMS spam classifier trained with awareness of legitimate bulk messages. We found in total that 1261 messages appeared to be messages that could have been legitimate bulk messages. This corresponds to a corresponding precision of 84.6% – a substantial increase over the expected 23.8% that would be seen without training for legitimate bulk messages. This classifier also drastically reduces the false positive rate. We see a false positive rate of only 1.3% as opposed to the earlier 8.1%.

6. CLUSTERED SPAM DATA

The previous section described how it is necessary to include legitimate bulk messages in order to effectively classify messages from a modern SMS corpus. Those experiments produced a labeled dataset of over 8179 labeled messages grouped into 475 clusters, and this set provides a great example of the utility of using public data to develop content-based SMS spam classifiers. In this particular case, this data set is unique because it spans many countries, carriers, and

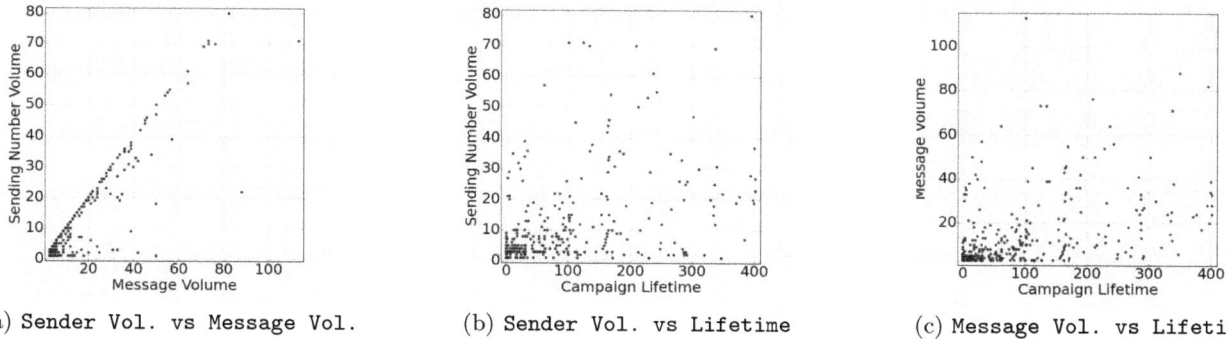

(a) Sender Vol. vs Message Vol.   (b) Sender Vol. vs Lifetime   (c) Message Vol. vs Lifetime

Figure 3: Campaign message volume is strongly correlated with sending message volume, while campaign lifetime is less related to the amount of messages sent or numbers used by a campaign.

months of time, unlike prior works that have studied only victim-submitted messages or spam in a single network.

6.1 Content Analysis

The gateway data included source and destination phone numbers. We used the Twilio phone number lookup service to provide information on the destination phone numbers (i.e. numbers controlled by the gateways), including the destination country and carriers. The United Kingdom received an overwhelming majority of the spam messages — 72.1%. This is even a disproportionate share considering that the UK received only 11.4% of the total messages in the gateway dataset. Australia, China, and Belgium also had disproportionally high spam message volumes as well.

These clusters were categorized into 18 distinct categories, and the top 10 categories are also shown in Figure 2. Messages offering payday loans or other forms of credit comprised 41.3% of all labeled spam in this message — dwarfing all other categories. Following loan spam was job advertising messages. 97.5% of these messages — 827 — were sent from a single number in a 7 hour period. Each message was personalized with a unique name and address; we believe that these messages were sent to a gateway as a test run for a bulk messenger service before sending the messages to their intended recipients. Because gateways collect a number of account verification requests, it was unsurprising to find advertising for telephony services ("obtain a phone number") or phone verification services. We also found the standard contests, online gambling opportunities, and a small number (57) of adult-oriented services common in spam data. However, we did find some more interesting schemes. One example was messages claiming to offer refunds or payouts for reasons as varied as unclaimed tax refunds, unclaimed injury settlements, or unfairly levied bank fees.

6.2 Network Analysis

By combining content analysis with network features like sending numbers, we can gain additional insights into SMS spam activity not available to earlier studies. In particular, we can study the activity of a given spam *campaign* — messages that may come from many different phone numbers but delivering a similar message to many users. For our analysis, we treat each spam cluster as a campaign. These campaigns are extensive in scope. They can have lifetimes of over a year (402 days) with a median lifetime of 53 days,

transmit messages to up to 12 countries, and send from up to 80 numbers with a median of 5.

We hypothesized that if networks take any sort of proactive measure to prevent nuisance bulk messaging, that spam campaigns with high message volumes and long lifetimes would need to use many sending numbers to deliver high message volumes over time. We also hypothesized that long-lived campaigns would have have high message volumes. Figure 3c visualizes the relationship between these variables, with each data point representing a single spam campaign. We also compute the Spearman correlation coefficients[2] between these variables. As expected, we found that the message volume and the number of sending phone numbers was strongly correlated ($\rho = 0.761$), as shown in Figure 3a. Surprisingly, we found a lower correlation ($\rho = 0.530$) between message volume and campaign lifetime; as shown in Figure 3b, low-volume campaigns are present across the lifetime range. Finally, we see that while many short-lived campaigns have low numbers of sending messages, many long-lived campaigns are successful using a small number of messages. These variables also share a weak correlation ($\rho = 0.473$). Overall, this data implies that spammers who want to send at high volumes must use many numbers to do so, but apart from many campaigns that send only a few messages over a short time scale, campaign lifetime seems unrelated to either the sending number volume nor the messaging volume.

7. CONCLUSION

As text messaging has evolved from a closed system where every message was generated within the cellular network to one where a wide variety of non-cellular services can send these messages, the nature of SMS data has substantially changed. The rise of legitimate bulk messages, which may syntactically resemble spam but provide valuable services such as two-factor authentication to users, means that traditional approaches to characterizing SMS spam are no longer adequate for classification. We address these problems in this paper by releasing the largest corpus of publicly available labeled bulk messages and SMS spam. Based on our classification techniques, we demonstrate that compared to

---

[2]Spearman correlations, represented as ρ, measure with a value from -1 to 1 whether a monotonic function (not a strictly linear function, as in the case of a Pearson correlation) relates two variables.

previous work, we raise precision across the public corpus from 23.8% to 100%, and raise recall from 61.3% to 96.8%. Even in the absence of manual labeling, we raise precision to 84.6% with a 1.3% false positive rate compared to 8.1% using previous techniques. We also find substantial amounts of SMS spam are related to finance, and certain countries are disproportionately targeted by spam. Our results demonstrate that new approaches to spam classification, and adequately sized SMS corpora, are essential to ensure the accurate classification of text messages as their form and function evolve and diversify.

Acknowledgments

The authors thank our shepherd, Emiliano De Cristofaro, and our anonymous reviewers for their helpful guidance. This work was supported in part by the National Science Foundation under grant numbers CNS-1526718, CNS-1464087, CNS-1540217, CNS-1542018, and CNS-1464088. Any opinions, findings, and conclusions or recommendations expressed in this material are those of the authors and do not necessarily reflect the views of the National Science Foundation.

8. REFERENCES

[1] Mobile Authentication. https://www.duosecurity.com/product/methods/duo-mobile.

[2] Massive growth in A2P SMS expected. http://www.telecompaper.com/news/ massive-growth-in-a2p-sms-expected-dimoco--1129833, 2016.

[3] Y. S. Abu-Mostafa, M. Magdon-Ismail, and H.-T. Lin. *Learning From Data*. AMLBook, United States, Mar. 2012.

[4] T. A. Almeida, J. M. G. Hidalgo, and A. Yamakami. Contributions to the Study of SMS Spam Filtering: New Collection and Results. In *Proceedings of the 11th ACM Symposium on Document Engineering*, DocEng '11, pages 259–262, New York, NY, USA, 2011. ACM.

[5] F. Aloul, S. Zahidi, and W. El-Hajj. Two factor authentication using mobile phones. In *IEEE/ACS International Conference on Computer Systems and Applications, 2009. AICCSA 2009*, pages 641–644, May 2009.

[6] L. Aouad, A. Mosquera, S. Grzonkowski, and D. Morss. SMS Spam — A Holistic View. In *Proceedings of the 11th International Conference on Security and Cryptography*, 2014.

[7] T. Chen and M.-Y. Kan. Creating a live, public short message service corpus: the NUS SMS corpus. *Language Resources and Evaluation*, Aug. 2012.

[8] G. V. Cormack, J. M. Gomez Hidalgo, and E. P. Sanz. Spam filtering for short messages. In *Proceedings of the Sixteenth ACM Conference on Information and Knowledge management*. ACM, 2007.

[9] D. DeFigueiredo. The Case for Mobile Two-Factor Authentication. *IEEE Security & Privacy*, Sept. 2011.

[10] S. J. Delany, M. Buckley, and D. Greene. SMS Spam Filtering. *Expert Syst. Appl.*, Aug. 2012.

[11] S. Dixit, S. Gupta, and C. V. Ravishankar. Lohit: An Online Detection & Control System for Cellular SMS Spam. *IASTED Communication, Network, and Information Security*, 2005.

[12] A. Dmitrienko, C. Liebchen, C. Rossow, and A.-R. Sadeghi. On the (In)Security of Mobile Two-Factor Authentication. In *Financial Cryptography and Data Security*. Springer, Mar. 2014.

[13] J. M. Gomez Hidalgo, G. C. Bringas, E. P. Sanz, and F. C. Garcia. Content Based SMS Spam Filtering. In *Proceedings of the 2006 ACM Symposium on Document Engineering*, New York, NY, USA, 2006. ACM.

[14] N. Jiang, Y. Jin, A. Skudlark, and Z.-L. Zhang. Understanding SMS Spam in a Large Cellular Network. In *Proceedings of the ACM SIGMETRICS/International Conference on Measurement and Modeling of Computer Systems*, SIGMETRICS '13, New York, NY, USA, 2013. ACM.

[15] A. Mosquera, L. Aouad, S. Grzonkowski, and D. Morss. On Detecting Messaging Abuse in Short Text Messages using

Linguistic and Behavioral patterns. *arXiv preprint arXiv:1408.3934*, 2014.

[16] C. Mulliner, R. Borgaonkar, P. Stewin, and J.-P. Seifert. SMS-based One-Time Passwords: Attacks and Defense. In *Detection of Intrusions and Malware, and Vulnerability Assessment*. Springer, 2013.

[17] C. Mulliner, N. Golde, and J.-P. Seifert. SMS of Death: From Analyzing to Attacking Mobile Phones on a Large Scale. In *Proceedings of the USENIX Security Symposium (SECURITY)*, 2011.

[18] I. Murynets and R. P. Jover. Analysis of SMS Spam in Mobility Networks. *International Journal of Advanced Computer Science*, May 2013.

[19] I. Murynets and R. Piqueras Jover. Crime Scene Investigation: SMS Spam Data Analysis. In *Proceedings of the 2012 ACM Conference on Internet Measurement Conference*, IMC '12, New York, NY, USA, 2012. ACM.

[20] Nan Jiang, Yu Jin, A. Skudlark, and Zhi-Li Zhang. Greystar: Fast and Accurate Detection of SMS Spam Numbers in Large Cellular Networks using Grey Phone Space. In *Proceedings of the 22nd USENIX Security Symposium.*, Washington DC, USA, 2013. USENIX Association.

[21] A. Narayan and P. Saxena. The Curse of 140 Characters: Evaluating the Efficacy of SMS Spam Detection on Android. In *Proceedings of the Third ACM Workshop on Security and Privacy in Smartphones & Mobile Devices*, SPSM '13, New York, NY, USA, 2013. ACM.

[22] M. T. Nuruzzaman, C. Lee, and D. Choi. Independent and Personal SMS Spam Filtering. In *2011 IEEE 11th International Conference on Computer and Information Technology (CIT)*, Aug. 2011.

[23] F. S. Park, C. Gangakhedkar, and P. Traynor. Leveraging Cellular Infrastructure to Improve Fraud Prevention. In *Proceedings of the Annual Computer Security Applications Conference (ACSAC)*, 2009.

[24] F. Pedregosa, G. Varoquaux, A. Gramfort, V. Michel, B. Thirion, O. Grisel, M. Blondel, P. Prettenhofer, R. Weiss, V. Dubourg, J. Vanderplas, A. Passos, D. Cournapeau, M. Brucher, M. Perrot, and E. Duchesnay. Scikit-learn: Machine Learning in Python. *Journal of Machine Learning Research*, 2011.

[25] B. Reaves, N. Scaife, D. Tian, L. Blue, P. Traynor, and K. Butler. Sending out an SMS: Characterizing the Security of the SMS Ecosystem with Public Gateways. In *Proceedings of the IEEE Symposium on Security and Privacy (S&P)*, 2016.

[26] H. Tan, N. Goharian, and M. Sherr. $100,000 Prize Jackpot. Call Now!: Identifying the Pertinent Features of SMS Spam. In *Proceedings of the 35th International ACM SIGIR Conference on Research and Development in Information Retrieval*, SIGIR '12, New York, NY, USA, 2012. ACM.

[27] P. Traynor. Characterizing the Security Implications of Third-Party EAS Over Cellular Text Messaging Services. *IEEE Transactions on Mobile Computing (TMC)*, 11(6):983–994, 2012.

[28] P. Traynor, W. Enck, P. McDaniel, and T. La Porta. Exploiting Open Functionality in SMS-Capable Cellular Networks. *Journal of Computer Security (JCS)*, 16(6):713–742, 2008.

[29] P. Traynor, W. Enck, P. McDaniel, and T. La Porta. Mitigating Attacks On Open Functionality in SMS-Capable Cellular Networks. *IEEE/ACM Transactions on Networking (TON)*, 17(1), 2009.

[30] P. Traynor, P. McDaniel, and T. La Porta. On Attack Causality in Internet-Connected Cellular Networks. In *Proceedings of the USENIX Security Symposium (SECURITY)*, 2007.

[31] A. K. Uysal, S. Gunal, S. Ergin, and E. S. Gunal. A Novel Framework for SMS Spam Filtering. In *2012 International Symposium on Innovations in Intelligent Systems and Applications (INISTA)*, July 2012.

[32] Q. Xu, E. W. Xiang, Q. Yang, J. Du, and J. Zhong. SMS Spam Detection Using Noncontent Features. *IEEE Intelligent Systems*, 27(6):44–51, 2012.

[33] K. Yadav, P. Kumaraguru, A. Goyal, A. Gupta, and V. Naik. SMSAssassin: Crowdsourcing Driven Mobile-based System for SMS Spam Filtering. In *Proceedings of the 12th Workshop on Mobile Computing Systems and Applications*, HotMobile '11, pages 1–6, New York, NY, USA, 2011. ACM.

DARPA: Device Attestation Resilient to Physical Attacks

Ahmad Ibrahim[*]
TU Darmstadt
Ahmad.Ibrahim@cased.de

Ahmad-Reza Sadeghi
TU Darmstadt
Ahmad.Sadeghi@cased.de

Gene Tsudik
UC Irvine
Gene.Tsudik@uci.edu

Shaza Zeitouni
TU Darmstadt
Shaza.Zeitouni@cased.de

ABSTRACT

As embedded devices (under the guise of "smart-whatever") rapidly proliferate into many domains, they become attractive targets for malware. Protecting them from software and physical attacks becomes both important and challenging. Remote attestation is a basic tool for mitigating such attacks. It allows a trusted party (verifier) to remotely assess software integrity of a remote, untrusted, and possibly compromised, embedded device (prover).

Prior remote attestation methods focus on software (malware) attacks in a one-verifier/one-prover setting. Physical attacks on provers are generally ruled out as being either unrealistic or impossible to mitigate. In this paper, we argue that physical attacks must be considered, particularly, in the context of many provers, e.g., a network, of devices. Assuming that physical attacks require capture and subsequent temporary disablement of the victim device(s), we propose DARPA, a light-weight protocol that takes advantage of absence detection to identify suspected devices. DARPA is resilient against a very strong adversary and imposes minimal additional hardware requirements. We justify and identify DARPA's design goals and evaluate its security and costs.

1. INTRODUCTION

In addition to traditional computing devices that come in various shapes and sizes (e.g., laptops, desktops, smartphones and tablets), so-called *smart* embedded computing devices are increasingly percolating into many spheres of everyday life. Such devices include household appliances, industrial machinery, automotive and avionic components, as well as many kinds of personal gadgets. In general, these smart devices differ from traditional computers in that their mission is not general-purpose computing. Hence, their capabilities and purposes are limited to supporting the goals of the device as a whole, e.g., sensing or actuation. These de-

vices represent attractive attack targets and their proliferation poses a formidable security challenge, for three reasons: **First**, they communicate via wired or wireless interfaces, which means that they can be accessed remotely. **Second**, in order to keep costs low and/or to conserve power, they lack necessary resources to defend themselves against attacks in the manner of general-purpose computers, e.g., via sophisticated OS security features or anti-malware tools. **Third**, because they are used to control (or interface with) physical equipment, a successful attack can cause actual real-world damage.

To address the aforementioned challenge, a lot of effort has been invested into both prevention and mitigation of attacks, especially, remote malware infestations, exemplified by the well-known Stuxnet episode [55]. The most popular approach is to verify the current state of a remote embedded device in order to establish that it behaves as it should, i.e., operates correctly. This translates into verifying device's software integrity, which is typically achieved using *remote attestation*, a distinct security service that provides a proof to a trusted entity (verifier) of software integrity of an untrusted – and possibly compromised – remote embedded device (prover).

Problem Description. Prior remote attestation results consider only remote software attacks, wherein the adversary's power is limited to manipulating prover's software from afar. This is in line with the need to protect the prover against remote malware infestations, under the assumption that the adversary never has physical access to the prover. Furthermore, prior schemes focus on the setting with a single prover. This was a natural first step.

In the single-prover setting, it is reasonable to assume that physical attacks on the prover are either impossible or very unlikely, especially, if the device is physically protected or unreachable, e.g., located on secure premises. Also, in case of multiple stand-alone (not inter-connected) provers, each can be attested individually and no-physical-attack assumption might still hold. However, there are current and emerging scenarios that involve multiple inter-connected devices, e.g., automotive, building, office, and factory automation environments. They differ from the single-prover setting in two important ways:

1. Faced with potentially numerous provers, attesting them individually can become expensive and unscalable, regardless of whether attestation is performed locally or remotely. This motivates a need to perform collective or aggregated attestation of the entire set of provers.

2. Provers might be heterogeneous and distributed over a

---

[*]Authors' names are listed in alphabetical order.

WiSec'16 , July 18-22, 2016, Darmstadt, Germany

© 2016 ACM. ISBN 978-1-4503-4270-4/16/07. . . $15.00

DOI: http://dx.doi.org/10.1145/2939918.2939938

large physical area, e.g., a factory floor. Consequently, the prior assumption about no physical attacks is no longer valid: some provers could remain physically unreachable while others might be within adversary's grasp. For example, in an office building, devices in public spaces might be easily accessible, in contrast to those inside individual private offices.[1]

The second issue has not been considered at all in the context of remote attestation. In contrast, the first issue has been noticed and progress has been made, to some extent, by Asokan et al. [4] in the design of SEDA– a technique for efficient and scalable attestation of a network of provers. This is attained by distributing the attestation burden across the entire network. However, SEDA focuses on so-called "device swarms". It does not attest topology and merely reports the number of devices that pass attestation. Also, SEDA's threat model only considers remote software-based attacks.

Goals and Contributions. If some devices can be captured and physically attacked, remote attestation techniques must define a stronger adversary model that allows physical attacks, and devise a means of mitigating such attacks. This paper represents the first step towards this goal and makes two main contributions. **First,** it defines the adversary model for collective attestation that allows physical attacks. **Second,** it constructs a collective attestation technique DARPA, that is secure in the presence of the strongest version of the adversary. Specifically, DARPA can detect both software-based and physical attacks. However, our main goal is to detect whether an attack has occurred, rather than identifying malicious devices. DARPA can be extended with a majority voting protocol in order to detect such devices. Finally, due to the dynamic nature of the targeted networks, we acknowledge the possibility of *false positives*, due to device failures, unreachablity, network partitioning or message loss. However, the main focus of this paper is security, i.e., to avoid *false negatives*.

The main premise for our work is that, in order to physically attack a device, the adversary must make it inaccessible for a certain non-negligible amount of time, e.g., to take it apart for the purpose of extracting secrets [5]. (Inaccessibility implies either physical removal of the device or switching it off *in situ*.) Therefore, detecting device's absence can be a sign of capture. In designing DARPA, we take advantage of prior work in Wireless Sensor Networks (WSN) literature [13, 14, 15, 23, 24, 25, 26, 53].

2. BACKGROUND AND OBJECTIVES

Physical Attacks. We consider unattended networks of embedded devices that are infrequently inspected physically. Some devices might be physically protected, while others can be subject to physical attacks, perhaps due to their type and/or location. This paper focuses on physical attacks that require disablement or disconnection of the device(s) from the network for a non-negligible amount of time. We refer to this event as device *capture*.

Physical attacks can be classified into invasive, non-invasive, and semi-invasive.

Invasive attacks [48] aim to extract information from a device by trying to directly access internal components using sophisticated and expensive specialized equipment, e.g., Focused Ion Beam (FIB) and micro-probing stations. Such attacks start with full or partial de-capsulation (i.e., removal of packaging using mechanical or chemical means, or mixture of both), followed by de-processing.

Non-invasive attacks [58], such as *side-channel* (e.g., power, time or electromagnetic radiation) attacks aim to stealthily extract cryptographic keys during normal device operations. They mainly use low-cost electrical engineering tools. Several countermeasures have been proposed to mitigate side-channel attacks at physical, technological and/or algorithmic levels [38, 58]. Examples include: shielding circuits, using analog isolation to hide the correlation between secret key and power consumption, or making execution path independent of cryptographic keys.

Semi-invasive attacks [49] are less expensive and less complicated than invasive attacks, since they involve cheaper equipment (e.g., laser microscopes) and only require decapsulation. Examples include: ultra-violet attacks, laser scanning, thermal imaging and optical fault injections.

Both invasive and semi-invasive attacks require detaching the device for some time (e.g., anywhere from several hours to weeks [47, 48]) using specialized tools. Even micro-probing, which can be performed while the device is operating, requires switching-off the device for at least the duration of de-capsulation and de-processing operations (which is non-negligible) before getting access to internal wiring and signals buried under passivation layer, using a micro-probing station. On the other hand, although side-channel attacks may require as little as few minutes and up to one day (if mounted *in-field* by an insider) they are very likely to be detected since they require bulky physical tools (e.g., an oscilloscope or EM-receiver/demodulator) to be attached to the victim device, or installed in close proximity.

Prevention *vs*. Detection: Attack prevention is clearly more appealing than attack detection. However, we recognize that the former is very difficult to achieve in the envisaged general setting of large distributed networks of heterogeneous devices. We believe that the only means of attack prevention are physical, e.g., placing all devices inside a secure perimeter, protecting them with other types of devices (e.g., alarm sensors that are themselves subject to attack), putting them inside protective containers or encasing them in various hard-to-penetrate materials, such as cement or metal. Besides being expensive and hampering mobility, all these approaches are simply not general. An alternative is to assume that each device is equipped with tamper-resistant components, which can be problematic since tamper-resistant hardware involves extra costs: monetary, power consumption, weight and volume. This motivates our focus on detection, rather than prevention, of physical attacks.

Objectives. We believe that, ideally, a secure *collective* attestation protocol should:

1. Verify collective integrity of the network.
2. Detect (and, ideally, identify) compromised devices.
3. Offer better efficiency than attesting devices individually.
4. Detect absent and thus possibly captured devices.
5. Attest network topology.

Properties (1–3) pertain to scalable attestation of groups (or swarms) of devices. The recently proposed SEDA proto-

---

[1]Similar examples include factory automation or perimeter monitoring scenarios where devices on the edges of the network are naturally more vulnerable than those in the middle.

col [4] aims at addressing (1–3), in a weaker (remote software-only) adversary model. SEDA does not address either (4) or (5). Property (4) is needed to mitigate a stronger adversary that can physically capture and fully compromise devices – it forms the crux of this paper's contribution. Property (5) is optional; it is important if the topology is a part of overall network's integrity. Our goal is a protocol that satisfies all these properties.

3. DARPA: PRELIMINARIES

3.1 System Model and General Idea

We consider a network of many, possibly heterogeneous, devices with either static or dynamic topology, e.g., automotive networks, industrial control systems, prospecting robots or IoT devices in smart home/office environments. There are s devices in total and each device D_i is uniquely identifiable, i.e., has a distinct id_i. The set of the id_i-s is denoted by $\mathcal{ID}$. We denote the verifier by $\mathcal{Adm}$.

The general idea of DARPA is that the network is mostly left unattended, i.e., in the time between successive attestations. During that time, each D_i periodically monitors all other $s - 1$ devices. This is achieved using the heartbeat protocol, executed at regular time intervals t_{hb}. Each D_i broadcasts a secure heartbeat to its immediate neighbors, thereby proving its presence. Each neighbor, in turn, forwards the received heartbeat to its own neighbors, and so on. Each D_i collects all heartbeats, verifies and logs them. At the time of next attestation, $\mathcal{Adm}$ performs a collective attestation protocol (e.g., SEDA) with the entire network and gathers, from each device, a set of logs – one for each heartbeat protocol instance executed since the previous attestation. This is done via a separate collect protocol.

3.2 Adversary Model

Similar to all other attestation techniques, we assume that the verifier is trusted. In the context of the prover, we consider three types of adversaries:

1. **Software** – $\mathcal{Adv}_{v,0}$ can remotely compromise (i.e., via software attacks) up to $v \leq s$ devices. This is the usual adversary model in prior attestation protocols.
2. **Physical** – $\mathcal{Adv}_{0,w}$ can capture (i.e., physically attack) up to $w < s$ devices.
3. **Hybrid** – $\mathcal{Adv}_{v,w}$ can compromise up to v, and capture up to, w devices.

We use v and w to refer to maximum numbers of devices that $\mathcal{Adv}$ can subvert – by software and physical means, respectively – within a certain time interval T_{att}. This interval corresponds to the longest period of time between successive instances of network attestation performed by $\mathcal{Adm}$, i.e., longest inter-attestation time gap. We assume $\mathcal{Adv}$ requires a non-negligible amount of time T_{cap} to physically attack a device. T_{cap} is expected to be appreciably longer than any communication delay within the network. We also limit $\mathcal{Adv}$'s scope of attacks as follows:

1. **No omnipotent adversary:** Given s devices total, we claim that $\mathcal{Adv}_{0,s}$ is impossible to mitigate. However, we consider the next most powerful adversary – $\mathcal{Adv}_{s,s-1}$, which can compromise all devices and capture all-but-one, without making any assumptions about the single uncaptured device.
2. **No noninvasive physical attacks:** $\mathcal{Adv}$ might exploit hardware side-channels (time, power, optical) to

extract devices secrets. Such attacks – which do not require switching off a device for a minimum amount of time – represent an orthogonal problem that is beyond the scope of this paper.
3. **No denial-of-service (DoS):** We consider DoS attacks to be out of scope, assuming that the envisaged $\mathcal{Adv}$ wants to remain stealthy and undetected while attempting to compromise and/or physically attack devices.

4. MITIGATING PHYSICAL ADVERSARY

For now, we assume that $\mathcal{Adv}$ can capture all devices – except one D_z – in a single T_{att} interval. However, we also assume that $\mathcal{Adv}$ can not compromise any device that it does not first capture. Hence, "0" in the first subscript of $\mathcal{Adv}_{0,s-1}$.

The intuition behind our approach is as follows: If the lower bound on the time needed to capture a device – T_{cap}– is known, the network can regularly run a collective heartbeat (absence detection) protocol, at intervals t_{hb}, shorter than T_{cap}. Therefore, if the following two conditions hold:

1. Each uncaptured device's heartbeat is unforgeable and uniquely tied to the particular instance (time) of the heartbeat protocol,
   and:
2. Each device periodically (every t_{hb} interval) emits its own time-based heartbeat and collects/records heartbeats of all other present devices

Then, it is safe to make the following assertion:

> **Assertion 1:** [**Alert**] If $0 < k < s$ devices are captured within a given T_{att}, then, by the next attestation instance, the log of at least one uncaptured device (D_z) will lack at least one other device's heartbeat, for at least one heartbeat protocol instance.

Assuming that D_k is absent for longer than T_{cap}, D_z's log would be missing at least one of D_k's heartbeats corresponding to a particular instance of the heartbeat protocol. This is because $T_{cap} > t_{hb}$, where t_{hb} is the interval between successive runs of the heartbeat protocol. Of course, after capturing D_k, $\mathcal{Adv}$ might extract its secrets and later attempt to forge the missing heartbeat(s). However, by that time, it is too late since this would take at least $T_{cap} > t_{hb}$ time and D_z would record D_k's absence. Note that, in practice, the inverse of **Alert** does not hold: a discrepancy between devices' logs at attestation time does not imply that any devices were captured. Indeed, a log discrepancy might occur due to lost heartbeat messages, device failures or (even temporary) unreachability. Thus, we readily acknowledge that *false positives* are possible. However, our main goal is to avoid *false negatives*.

Furthermore, we assert that:

> **Assertion 2:** [**Normalcy:**] At any attestation instance, if logs of all s devices match and contain every device's heartbeat for each heartbeat protocol instance, then no devices were absent for longer than T_{cap} time.

Normalcy implies that no device was captured since none were absent for at least T_{cap}. Therefore, the heartbeat log of D_z contains timely proof of every other device's presence, for each heartbeat protocol instance since the last attestation. And, because D_z is (at least) the only uncaptured device and its log agrees with all other devices' logs, no device was absent for $\geq T_{cap}$. (We emphasize that D_z's identity, id_z, is unknown to $\mathcal{A}dm$.) Consequently, no physical attacks took place.

4.1 DARPA:heartbeat Protocol

We first introduce some assumptions. The first two correspond to individual devices and the rest apply to the network:

1. **Reliable Clocks:** Each D_i has a reliable clock, loosely synchronized with $\mathcal{A}dm$'s clock. δ_t denotes the maximum clock skew between any two devices.

2. **Secret Keys:** Each D_i has a unique private signing key SK_i, which is assigned and installed (perhaps by $\mathcal{A}dm$) before deployment.

3. **Public Keys:** Each D_i knows the set of all id_i-s – $\mathcal{ID}$, and, for each D_j – the public key PK_j, as well as $\mathcal{A}dm$'s public key – $PK_{\mathcal{A}dm}$. For better efficiency, signatures can be replaced by message authentication codes (MACs). This variant is discussed in Section 6.

4. **Connectivity:** there always exists a path between any two devices, i.e., the network is always connected.

5. **Mobility:** devices might be mobile, i.e., network topology is subject to change. However, during DARPA's execution, topology is assumed to be static.

heartbeat is initiated in a distributed manner: D_i either receives a heartbeat message from one of its neighbors, or wakes up based on a timer, indicating that t_{hb} has passed since the last run of the protocol. In either case, D_i generates its own heartbeat, timestamped and signed with SK_i, and broadcasts it to neighbors. Whenever D_i receives a heartbeat from D_j, it verifies the timestamp and the signature. If both are valid, D_i logs the heartbeat as part of the current protocol and re-broadcasts it to the neighbors. Once D_i receives heartbeats from all peers, it terminates the protocol. Alternatively, D_i terminates the protocol based on a time-out – t_{acc} (see Table 1). Non-receipt of a valid heartbeat from some D_j within t_{acc} from the protocol start indicates that, from D_i's perspective, D_j is absent. The detailed description of the heartbeat protocol is shown in Figure 1. Table 1 summarizes our notation. In it, t_{tx} denotes the global upper bound for a network delay. However, since the time T_{cap} needed to physically attack a device is expected to be considerably greater than any other delay, a tight upper bound on network delay is not necessary. As mentioned earlier, the heartbeat protocol for D_i can start based on a timeout or a received heartbeat message. However, for the sake of clarity, we illustrate the protocol as starting only upon a timeout, assuming that heartbeat messages received prior to step 0 are queued in a buffer.

4.2 DARPA:collect Protocol

Periodically (at intervals upper-bounded by T_{att}), $\mathcal{A}dm$ initiates the collect protocol. We make no assumptions about $\mathcal{A}dm$'s location at that time: it could be local or remote. $\mathcal{A}dm$ generates a request: $Ch = N, t_{\mathcal{A}dm}, SIG_{\mathcal{A}dm}$ where: N is a random challenge, $t_{\mathcal{A}dm}$ is a timestamp, and $SIG_{\mathcal{A}dm}$ is $\mathcal{A}dm$'s signature over N and $t_{\mathcal{A}dm}$.

Upon receipt of Ch, D_i verifies the timestamp and the signature. If both are valid, D_i replies with the set of all logs collected since the last attestation instance – $LOG_i =$

s	total number of devices
i, j, z, k	device indexes $\in [1, s]$
v, w	max #-s of devices $\mathcal{A}dv$ can compromise or capture
id_j	identifier of D_j
$\mathcal{ID}$	set of all device id-s: $\{id_1 ... id_s\}$
SK_i, PK_i	dev_i's public and private keys, respectively
k_{ij}	symmetric key shared between D_i and D_j
K_i	symmetric key shared between D_i and $\mathcal{A}dm$
T_{att}	maximum interval between two consecutive attestations
T_{cap}	minimum time needed by $\mathcal{A}dv$ to capture a device; $T_{cap} < T_{att}$
δ_t	maximum clock skew between any two devices
t_{tx}	maximum time to transmit a message between any two devices. (includes processing time at intermediate devices)
t_{acc}	acceptance interval; $t_{acc} = \delta_t + t_{tx}$
t_{hb}	interval between successive heartbeat instance; $2 \cdot t_{acc} < t_{hb} < T_{cap} - t_{acc} - \delta_t$
$\#hb$	number of heartbeat protocol runs between successive attestations; $1 \leq \#hb = \lfloor \frac{T_{att}}{t_{hb}} \rfloor$
p	heartbeat protocol index; $0 < p \leq \#hb$
$hb_{i,p}$	D_i heartbeat message for p-th heartbeat protocol instance; $hb_{i,p} = \{p, t_{i,p}, id_i\}$
$SIG_{i,p}$	signature, computed by D_i, using SK_i over $hb_{i,p}$
$time()$	returns current time
$t_{i,p}$	D_i clock when $hb_{i,p}$ is created
$log_{i,p}$	D_i's log of all valid received heartbeats for p-th protocol instance
$present[s]$	bitmap indicating which devices were ever absent, $present[i] = 0$ implies that D_i was absent (at least once)
OK	flag indicating if any device was ever absent, $OK = 0$ implies that (at least) one device was absent at least once

$accept(t_{start}, t_{j,p}) = 0 \vert 1$	timestamp verification; returns "true" if $t_{j,p} = t_{start}$
$sign(SK, MSG)$	signature generation: using SK and MSG, yields a signature on MSG
$verify(PK, MSG, SIG)$	signature verification: using PK, checks SIG on MSG; yields $0 \vert 1$
$mac(k, MSG)$	computes MAC of MSG using k
$vermac(k, MSG, MAC)$	MAC verification: using k, checks MAC on MSG; yields $0 \vert 1$

Table 1: Notation

$\{log_{i,p}, ; 0 < p \leq \#hb\}$ – timestamped and signed with SK_i. Once $\mathcal{A}dm$ receives LOG_i, it verifies the timestamp and D_i's signature. If both are valid, it stores the corresponding log set. Having received LOG_i-s from all devices,

Figure 1: DARPA: heartbeat Protocol (as viewed by D_i)

$Timeout(timer_{hb})$

Start-timer($timer_{acc} = t_{acc}$)

$t_{i,p} = t_{start} = time()$, $hb_{i,p} = \{p, t_{i,p}, id_i\}$

$SIG_{i,p} = sign(SK_i, hb_{i,p})$

Set $log_{i,p} = hb_{i,p}$, Start-timer($timer_{hb} = t_{hb}$)

$D_i \xrightarrow{hb_{i,p},\ SIG_{i,p}}$ all neighbors

while $\left(\neg\ Timeout(timer_{acc}) \wedge sizeof(log_{i,p}) < s\ \right)$ **do**

  $D_i \xleftarrow{hb_{j,p},\ SIG_{j,p}}$ neighbor (D_j)

  if $(accept(t_{start}, t_{j,p}) \wedge hb_{j,p} \notin log_{i,p})$ **then**

    if $Verify(PK_j, hb_{j,p}, SIG_{j,p})$ **then**

      $Append(\{hb_{j,p}, SIG_{j,p}\}, log_{i,p})$

      $D_i \xrightarrow{hb_{j,p},\ SIG_{j,p}}$ all neighbors

    else

      Discard $hb_{j,p}$

    end

  else

    Discard $hb_{j,p}$

  end

end

$p = p + 1$

Figure 2: DARPA: collect Protocol (as viewed by $\mathcal{Adm}$)

---

for $0 < i \leq s$ **do**

  $t = time()$, $N \in \{0, 1\}^{\ell_N}$,

  $SIG_{\mathcal{Adm}} = \mathsf{sign}(SK_{\mathcal{Adm}}, t|N)\}$

  $\mathcal{Adm} \xrightarrow{Ch=\{t,N,SIG_{\mathcal{Adm}}\}} D_i$

  $\mathcal{Adm} \xleftarrow{resp_i=\{LOG_i,SIG_i\}} D_i$

  if $(verify(PK_i, LOG_i|Ch, SIG_i))$ **then**

    Store LOG_i

  else

    Discard $resp_i$

  end

end

Figure 3: DARPA: collect Protocol (as viewed by D_i)

$D_i \xleftarrow{Ch=\{t,N,SIG_{\mathcal{Adm}}\}} \mathcal{Adm}$

if $If\ (verify(PK_{\mathcal{Adm}}, t|N, SIG_{\mathcal{Adm}}))$ **then**

  $SIG_i = \mathsf{sign}(SK_i, LOG_i|Ch)$

  $D_i \xrightarrow{resp_i=\{LOG_i,SIG_i\}} \mathcal{Adm}$

else

  Discard Ch

end

$\mathcal{Adm}$ can easily determine whether any devices were absent for one or more heartbeat protocol instances since last attestation. Furthermore, $\mathcal{Adm}$ can identify the devices that were absent at each heartbeat protocol instance. According to the **Normalcy** assertion, if all logs match and contain all devices' heartbeats, then no device has been absent. The collect protocol is shown, in more detail, in Figure 2 and 3.

4.3 Efficiency Improvements

Several aspects of the above protocols involve some potentially impractical assumptions and costly operations. This is done mainly in order to simplify presentation; substantial cost reductions and simplifications can be made, as follows:

Communication Model: The collect protocol in Figures 2 and 3 is shown in an idealized communication setting, where each $\mathcal{Adm}$ "talks" *directly* to every D_j. While plausible, this is not a realistic assumption. However, recall that $\mathcal{Adm}$'s attestation request (Ch) is signed and so is D_i's reply — $resp_i$. These signatures essentially result in an authentic channel between $\mathcal{Adm}$ and D_i. Consequently, protocol's security is the same, regardless of whether $\mathcal{Adm}$ and D_i communicate directly, or through a sequence of intermediate hops, i.e., one or more D_j-s.

Public Key Signatures: Both heartbeat and collect protocols involve heavy use of signatures. This is done mainly for illustration purposes, as it makes the protocol more concise, though also more expensive. In the heartbeat protocol, it is easy to replace signatures with hop-by-hop MACs, assuming that a key shared is by every pair of neighboring devices. It is equally easy to replace signatures with MACs in collect, as long as each device shares a unique key with $\mathcal{Adm}$. In our context, MACs are no less secure than signatures, since our $\mathcal{Adv}_{0,s-1}$ is purely physical and can not capture *all* devices. Thus, as long as at least one D_z remains always present (uncaptured), it would accurately log at least one absent device (see Section 6 for details). One obvious downside of using MACs is the need for a separate key establishment protocol between adjacent devices, or a key pre-distribution scheme, to let each device share a symmetric key with every neighbor.

Heartbeat Logs: Figures 2 and 3 show each D_i collecting, and later sending to $\mathcal{Adm}$, accumulated logs (of the form $log_{i,p}$) bundled into LOG_i at collect time. Once again, this is done for ease of illustration. Instead, it is sufficient for each $log_{i,p}$ to contain a list of either absent or present devices, whichever is smaller. At the very minimum, we simply use a binary flag indicating whether at least one device was absent during any heartbeat instance. An optimized MAC-based implementation of DARPA is described in Section 6.

4.4 heartbeat: Correctness and Security

Correctness of the heartbeat protocol means that, if no device is absent, then all log sets (LOG_i-s) of all devices must match and contain every other device's heartbeat.

We assume that D_i is present and functional during the entire inter-attestation time gap T_{att}. Thus, D_i periodically emits an authenticated heartbeat $hb_{i,p} = \{p, t_{i,p}, id_i, \}$, and $SIG_{i,p}$ to all its neighbors. Since all devices have reliable clocks loosely synchronized with $\mathcal{Adm}$, the clock of every neighbor D_j deviates from $t_{i,p}$ by at most δ_t. Consequently, D_j receives $hb_{i,p}$ at $t \in [t_{i,p} - \delta_t, t_{i,p} + \delta_t + t_{tx}]$. Recall that t_{tx} is the maximum time to transmit a message between any two devices. Since $hb_{i,p}$ is a genuine heartbeat of D_i for the current heartbeat interval, i.e., $accept(p, t_{i,p}) = 1$, and $verify(PK_i, SIG_{i,p}) = 1$; and is received within the acceptance interval $t_{acc} = t_{tx} + \delta_t$, D_j appends $hb_{i,p}$ to its $log_{j,p}$ and forwards $hb_{i,p}$ it to all its neighbors. Similarly, each neighbor of D_j appends $hb_{i,p}$ to its $log_{j,p}$ and forwards it onwards. Since the network is always connected and its topology is static only for the duration of heartbeat instance, all heartbeat messages are received by all devices, within t_{tx} time. Thus, every D_k appends $hb_{i,p}$ to its $log_{k,p}$. It follows that LOG_j of every D_j matches and contains $hb_{i,p}$ of every other D_i for all p heartbeat instances.

Security of heartbeat means that, if $0 < w < s$ devices are absent, then logs of present devices lack at least one heartbeat of each absent one.

We again assume D_i is present, i.e., not captured. According to the definition of $accept()$ in Table 1, every uncaptured D_k only logs the heartbeat $hb_{i,p}$ (of D_i at p-th heartbeat interval) in its log if it was received in the same interval. We derive the upper and lower-bound on the time when $hb_{i,p}$ can be logged in $log_{k,p}$ (log time). Let t_1 be the expiration time of the p-th $timer_{hb}$ on any present D_k, i.e., at t_1, D_k generates its heartbeat $hb_{k,p}$, and logs in $log_{k,p}$ all heartbeats received either before t_1 or within $t_{acc} = t_{tx} + \delta_t$. However, since present devices (such as D_i) only generate correct heartbeats (i.e., based on the current timestamp), the acceptable $hb_{i,p}$ can be generated no earlier than $t_1 - \delta_t$. Consequently, log time is lower-bounded by $t_1 - \delta_t$, and upper bounded by $t_1 + t_{tx} + \delta_t$. Similarly, if $t_2 = t_1 + t_{hb}$ is the expiration time of $(p + 1)$-th $timer_{hb}$, log time of $hb_{i,p+1}$ is in $[t_2 - \delta_t, t_2 + t_{tx} + \delta_t]$. Therefore, D_i can be absent (and undetected) for at most: the time between sending $hb_{k,p}$ at the earliest time possible and emission of $hb_{k,p+1}$ at the latest time possible:

$$t_2 + t_{tx} + \delta_t - (t_1 - \delta_t) = t_1 + t_{hb} + t_{tx} + \delta_t - t_1 + \delta_t = t_{hb} + 2 \cdot \delta_t + t_{tx}$$

Since $T_{cap} > t_{hb} + 2 \cdot \delta_t + t_{tx}$, the log of every uncaptured D_k will lack at least one heartbeat of every captured D_i (either $hb_{i,p}$ or $hb_{i,p+1}$).

5. MITIGATING SOFTWARE ADVERSARY

In contrast to a physical adversary $\mathcal{Adv}_{0,s-1}$, a purely software $\mathcal{Adv}_{s,0}$ can not capture devices. However, it can remotely compromise any device's software, which is subject to attestation. In this section, we assume that the adversary can software-compromise *all* devices.

To guarantee security under $\mathcal{Adv}_{s,0}$, the attestation protocol must remotely verify overall software integrity of the network and, thus, of each D_i. To achieve this, we need to make some minimal assumptions about hardware security features of the underlying devices. In particular, the integrity measurement mechanism (attestation code) residing on D_i must be immune to software attacks. This condition can be satisfied by assuming availability of minimal hardware protection on each D_i, as done in the attestation literature for low-end embedded devices [4, 8, 19, 29]. In brief, minimal requirements/features are: Read-only Memory (ROM) for storing attestation code and associated cryptographic key(s) and a simple memory protection unit (MPU). The MPU has several tasks: (i) grants access to cryptographic key(s) **only** to attestation code, (ii) ensures non-interruptibility of execution of attestation code, and (iii) cleans up (flushes all registers and other temporary storage) at the end of attestation code execution.

Based on the above, compromised devices can be detected. Indeed, this is exactly what is achieved by a collective attestation protocol as recently proposed in SEDA [4]. In SEDA, $\mathcal{Adm}$ chooses an arbitrary device (initiator), and sends it an attestation request. The initiator forwards the request to its immediate neighbors who repeat the process. The request propagates over the entire network forming a spanning **tree** rooted at the inititator. Next, each leaf sends its parent an integrity report. The parent verifies each child's report and aggregates them (along with its own) into a single report, which includes the number of correctly attested devices. Reports are then propagated and aggregated, in reverse, along the spanning tree towards the initiator, and on to the verifier.

6. MITIGATING HYBRID ADVERSARY

The strongest adversary $\mathcal{Adv}_{s,s-1}$ can compromise all devices by software means, and physically attack all-but-one devices – D_z, within a single inter-attestation time gap T_{att}. To mitigate this adversary we integrate a secure collective attestation protocol (such as SEDA) which detects compromised devices, with DARPA:collect and combine it with DARPA:heartbeat to detect absent devices.

This requires the same hardware assumptions as in Section 5 to secure both the attestation and DARPA protocols. Most importantly, we assume that ROM-resident attestation code now includes heartbeat and collect protocols. Also, cryptographic keys used by heartbeat and collect are stored in ROM and accessible only to that attestation code. Private intermediate data, on the other hand is stored in access-protected RAM.

Figure 4 shows our implementation of the integrated protocol over a generalization of the SMART architecture [19] introduced in [8, 29]. In it, a Memory Protection Unit (MPU) controls access to the part of memory (ROM and RAM) storing secret keys and private protocol data. Access is controlled according to hardware-based access control rules in the table of Figure 4. For example, rule # 1 states that: *only code residing at address a_0 to a_3 (i.e., attestation, heartbeat, and collect) has read access to keys residing at addresses a_4 to a_5*. Similarly, heartbeat and collect have protected read and/or write access to their private intermediate data.

6.1 Protocol

The integrated protocol is shown in Figure 5; it is based entirely on symmetric cryptography. Every D_i is assumed to share a key K_i with $\mathcal{Adm}$, and k_{ij} – with each direct neighbor D_j.

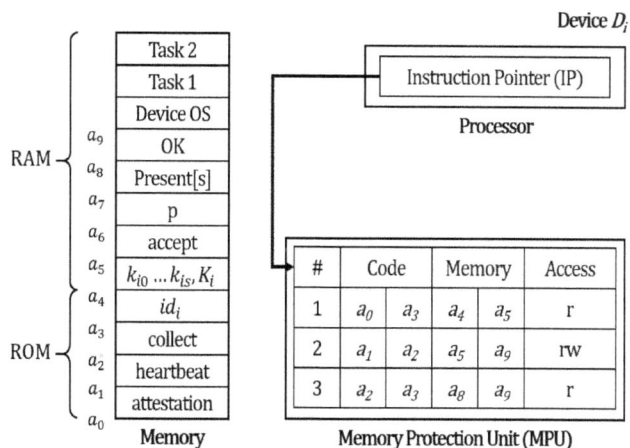

Figure 4: Implementation of DARPA

The protocol operates as follows: every t_{hb} interval, each D_i (D_w and D_k in the figure) generates a timestamped authenticated heartbeat $hb_{i,p}$ and σ_{ij} and broadcasts it to all neighbors D_j. Upon receiving an authenticated heartbeat from a neighbor D_j, D_i checks that:

1. $hb_{j,p}$ is not a duplicate.
2. $hb_{j,p}$ is received within acceptable time, i.e., $accept = true$.
3. $hb_{j,p}$ corresponds to current expected heartbeat instance, i.e., p.
4. the MAC σ_{ij} on $hb_{j,p}$ (re-computed with k_{ij}) verifies correctly.

If all checks succeed, D_i marks D_j as present ($present[j] = 1$), generates a new MACs on $hb_{j,p}$, and forwards it to its neighbors. After a fixed period of time ($t = 2 \cdot \delta_t + t_{tx}$), D_i checks whether all devices were present during the current heartbeat instance. If at least one D_j was absent, D_i sets $OK = 0$.

At attestation time, $\mathcal{A}dm$ randomly picks an initiator device – D_w – which serves as the interface to the rest of the network, see Figure 5. $\mathcal{A}dm$ creates a random challenge N, authenticates it along with the current time $t_{\mathcal{A}dm}$ with a MAC based on a shared key K_w. $\mathcal{A}dm$ then sends the authenticated challenge CH_w to D_w. This triggers both attestation and collect. Once D_w verifies CH_w, it creates a separate CH_j (authenticated with k_{wj}-based MAC) and forwards it to each neihboring D_j. Upon receiving CH_j, each neighbor authenticates the request and forwards an authenticated copy to each of its neighbors, and so on. This way, the challenge securely propagates throughout the network along a spanning tree rooted at D_w. Each leaf D_i creates a reply which includes:

1. $resp_i$, indicating whether a single device was absent at any heartbeat interval ($resp_i = \mathsf{mac}(K_i, OK|N)$). $resp_i$ is authenticated in an end-to-end manner.
2. its attestation response $attest_i$ to its parent D_j. $attest_i$ depends on the integrated collective attestation protocol. In SEDA, it represents the number of successfully attested devices.

The parent accumulates $attest_i$ and XORs $resp_i$ (along with its own) and propagates the result upstream, towards D_w. Finally, D_w forwards the accumulated reply to $\mathcal{A}dm$. $\mathcal{A}dm$

re-generates all MACs, XORs them, and compares the result to $resp_w$. If they match, $\mathcal{A}dm$ decides that no device has been captured and can now trust the attestation results in determining compromised devices, if any. The protocol is shown in Figure 5.

A distinct session identifier is needed to avoid double-counting benign devices. This identifier is sent along with the challenge and each device includes it in the attestation response. However, to allow devices to attest their neighbors and account for software updates, every device is initialized with its own software certificate, i.e., its software configuration signed by $\mathcal{A}dm$. Upon joining the network, each device sends its software certificate to its neighbors, each of whom verifies and stores it for future attestation. Further information about session management and distribution of software configurations for collective attestation can be found in [4].

6.2 Correctness and Security

Somewhat surprisingly, the integrated protocol is actually **not secure** against the strongest hybrid adversary. The main (and only) reason is due to the fact that the *Reliable Clocks* assumption is insufficient to mitigate $\mathcal{A}dv_{s,s-1}$. Consider the following attack scenario:

> *First $\mathcal{A}dv_{s,s-1}$ captures D_i during $p - th$ heartbeat instance and extracts its keys. Concurrently, $\mathcal{A}dv_{s,s-1}$ compromises (via software) all devices: $D_1, ..., D_s$ and infects them with malware, which tampers with their clocks, and extends the time a received heartbeat is accepted to $\geq T_{cap}$. After capture, D_i runs the p-th heartbeat instance. On each compromised device, D_i's heartbeat is accepted by the ROM-resident code running the* **heartbeat** *protocol, since it appears to be correct.*

Other similar attack scenarios are possible, where the common feature is the ability of malware (which is resident on compromised devices) to manipulate their clocks.

This insecurity leads us towards an additional requirement that we claim to be both necessary and sufficient to mitigate a hybrid adversary: the need for a **Reliable Read-Only Clock (RROC)** on each device. We use this terminology in order to stress the fact that each device's clock must be non-malleable, i.e., not modifiable by software from either ROM or RAM. However, we do not require the clock to be *secure* in terms of any kind of physical protection, i.e., no tamper-resistance or tamper-evidence is needed. An RROC can be realized with an inexpensive commercially available Real-Time Clock (RTC), such as [1].[2]

One alternative to the RROC requirement is **secure writable memory**. Such memory must be writeable only from ROM. It is not hard to see that, if each D_i has just a tiny amount of such memory, it can securely record the timestamp of the last heartbeat protocol. This way, once malware resets the D_z's clock to a prior heartbeat protocol instance, it would attempt to introduce backdated heartbeat messages from previously absent devices, ROM-resident attestation code would recognize stale timestamps, detect the inconsistency and take appropriate action. At the very least, D_z can ignore backdated heartbeats.

---

[2]Note that integrity of any intermediate software that reads the RROC is assumed to be assured, similar to attestation code in Figure 4.

Figure content:

Verifier Adm	Device D_w	D_j	D_k
$K_0 \ldots K_s$	$K_w, k_{wj}, \mathcal{ID}$	$K_j, k_{wj}, k_{jk}, \mathcal{ID}$	$K_k, k_{jk}, \mathcal{ID}$

$t = 0$

$p = 0$ $p = 0$ $p = 0$

$t_{hb} - \delta_t$

$accept = true$ $accept = true$ $accept = true$

t_{hb}

At D_w:
$hb_{w,p} = \{p, t_{w,p} = time(), id_w\}$
$\sigma_{wj} = \mathsf{mac}(k_{wj}, hb_{w,p})$

$\xrightarrow{HB_{w,p,wj} = \{hb_{w,p}, \sigma_{wj}\}}$

At D_j:
if $accept = true$ **and** $p_w = p_j$ **then**
  if $\mathsf{vermac}(k_{wj}, hb_{w,p}, \sigma_{wj})$ **then**
    $present[w] = 1$
    $\sigma_{jk} = \mathsf{mac}(k_{jk}, hb_{w,p})$

$\xrightarrow{HB_{w,p,jk}, \ HB_{j,p,jk}}$

$\xleftarrow{HB_{k,p,jk}}$

$\xleftarrow{HB_{k,p,wj}}$

$t_{hb} + \delta_t + t_{tx}$

At D_w:
$accept = false$
$p = p + 1$
$OK = OK \wedge (\wedge_i^s present[i])$
$\forall\, i \ present[i] = 0$

At D_j:
$accept = false$
$p = p + 1$
$OK = OK \wedge (\wedge_i^s present[i])$
$\forall\, i \ present[i] = 0$

At D_k:
$accept = false$
$\forall\, i \ present[i] = 0$

$t_{att} \leq \#hb \cdot t_{hb}$

At Adm:
$t_{Adm} = time(), \ N \in_R \{0,1\}^{\ell_N}$
$\theta_w = \mathsf{mac}(K_w, \{t_{Adm}, N\})$

$\xrightarrow{CH_w = \{\{t_{Adm}, N\}, \theta_w\}}$

At D_w:
if $\mathsf{vermac}(K_w, \{t_{Adm}, N\}, \theta_{Adm})$ **then**
  $\theta_{wj} = \mathsf{mac}(k_{wj}, \{t_{Adm}, N\})$

$\xrightarrow{CH_j = \{\{t_{Adm}, N\}, \theta_{wj}\}}$ $\xrightarrow{CH_k}$

$resp_w = \mathsf{mac}(K_w, OK|N)$
$p = 0$

$resp_j = \mathsf{mac}(K_j, OK|N)$
$p = 0$

$resp_k = \mathsf{mac}(K_k, OK|N)$
$p = 0$

$\xleftarrow{resp_k, attest_k}$

$resp_j = resp_j \oplus resp_k$

$\xleftarrow{resp_j, attest_j}$

$\xleftarrow{resp_w, attest_w}$

At Adm:
if $\oplus_i^s \mathsf{mac}(K_i, 1|N) = resp_w$ **then**
  $check(attest_w)$

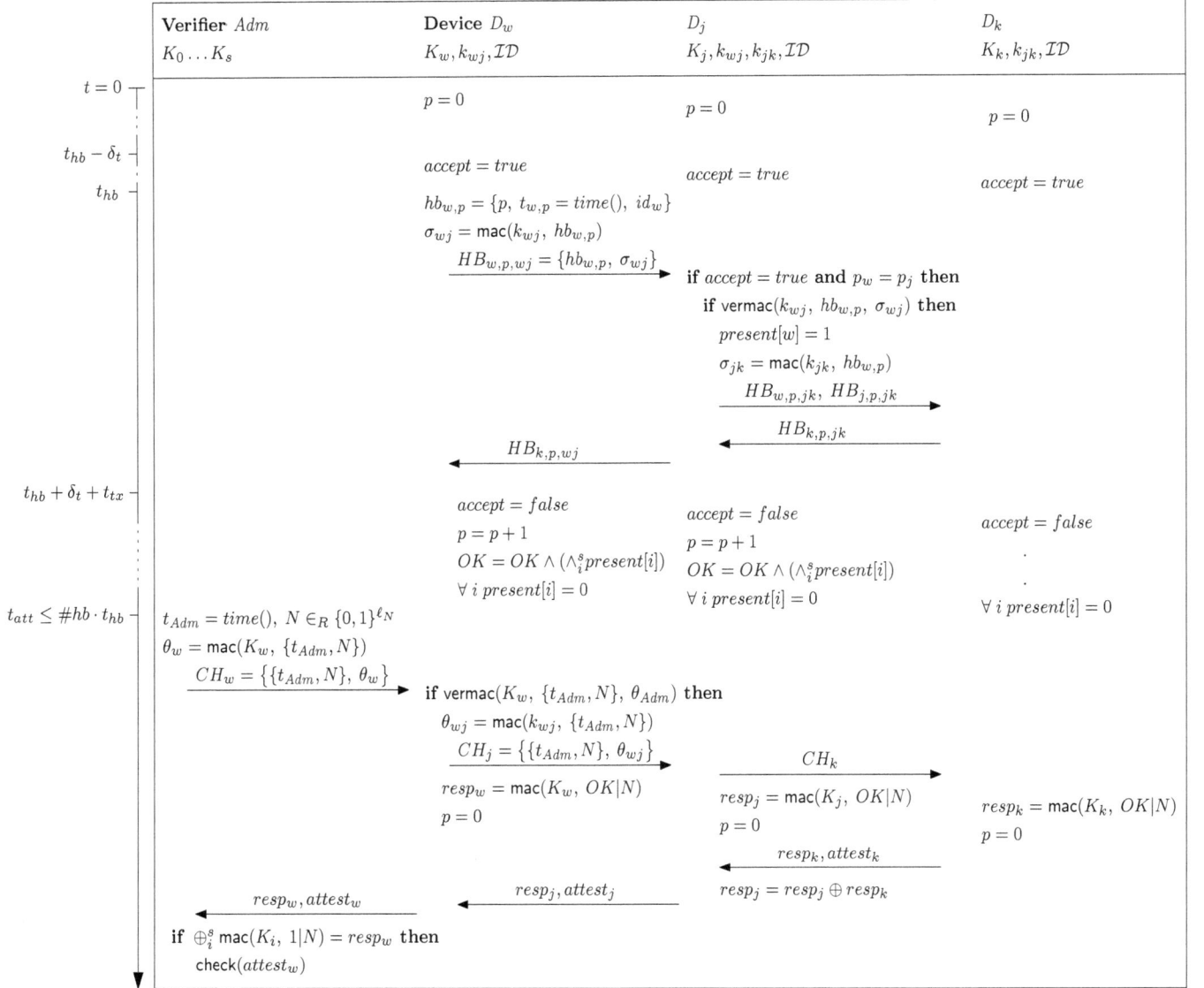

Figure 5: The complete DARPA protocol

Correctness of the integrated protocol means that, if no device was absent or compromised, then: (1) $attest_w$ indicates that no device is compromised, and (2) $resp_w$ matches $\oplus_i^s \mathsf{mac}(K_i, 1|N)$.

(1) follows directly from correctness of the collective attestation protocol. According to correctness of heartbeat, all devices receive valid heartbeats for all heartbeat instances, within T_{att}. Consequently, at each heartbeat instance and for every D_i, $present[i]$ is set to 1. Thus, at attestation time OK at D_i is also 1 ($OK = OK \wedge (\wedge_i^s present[1]) = 1 \wedge \cdots \wedge 1 = 1$), and $resp_i$ is initially set to $\mathsf{mac}(K_i, 1|N)$. Therefore, since all devices receive and accept CH, $resp_w = \oplus_i^s \mathsf{mac}(K_w, 1|N)$.

Security of the integrated protocol means that: (1) if no device was captured, then $attest_w$ correctly indicates the number of compromised devices; and (2) if at least one device is captured, $resp_w$ reflects that.

(1) follows directly from security of the collective attesta-

tion protocol. Furthermore, if no device is captured, hop-by-hop MACs and digital signatures are equally secure, since (due to SMART-like device architecture) malware has no access to keys. Thus, based on security of heartbeat, capture of (at least) one D_j is detected by all other devices. Of course, D_j can later forge heartbeats of absent devices, thus helping them evade detection. However, it can not reset an OK flag of an uncaptured device to 1 once it is set to 0 ($OK = \mathbf{OK} \wedge (\wedge_i^s present[i])$). Meanwhile, since keys shared with Adm and digital signatures are equally secure, $resp_w$ correctly indicates that at least one device (say, D_j) was captured. Consequently, Adv can try to evade detection of D_j's capture in several ways: (1) modifying heartbeat or collect protocol code, (2) extracting K_j before capturing D_j, (3) extracting K_z or modifying OK for every uncaptured D_z within the same T_{att}, or (4) fooling every uncaptured D_z into extending the time a received heartbeat is accepted, as illustrated in the attack example above. However, (1) is impossible since heartbeat and collect are part of ROM-resident attestation code. (2) and (3) are prevented since cryptographic keys and private data are accessible only to the attestation code. Finally, (4) is ruled out since D_z has a Reliable Read-Only Clock (RROC) which can not be modified by any software. Therefore, $Adv_{s,s-1}$ can not evade detection of D_j by software compromise. Consequently, $resp_w$ will correctly indicate that at least one device (i.e., D_j) was captured.

7. PERFORMANCE ANALYSIS

We evaluated computation, communication, and energy costs of both variant of DARPA We also compared, via simulations, performance of MAC- and signature-based implementations, for varying numbers of devices.

Computation Overhead: In the signature-based implementation, every D_i generates one and verifies s signatures in heartbeat. In collect, D_i generates one and verifies $(c_i + 1)$ signatures. Let c_i be the number of children of D_i in the spanning tree rooted in D_w. In the MAC-based implementation, D_i verifies s and generates $(N \cdot s)$ MACs in heartbeat. In collect, D_i verifies $(c_i + 1)$, and generates $(N + 1)$ MACs, where N is the number of D_i's neighbors.

Communication Overhead: In the digital signature-based implementation, D_i receives and sends at most N heartbeats in heartbeat. D_i, also receives N challenges and c_i responses; meanwhile, it sends 1 challenge and 1 response. The number of log sets in received and sent responses depends on D_i's position in the spanning tree. It is upper bounded by $s - 1$ and s respectively. In the MAC-based implementation, D_i receives s and sends s heartbeats as well as $N \cdot s$ MACs in heartbeat. D_i also receives N authenticated challenges and c_i MACs, while it sends 1 challenge and N MACs.

Energy Costs: Our estimate of DARPA's energy consumption is shown in Figure 6 and 7. We base it on energy costs of cryptographic operations and communication reported for TelosB sensor node [16]. We also set the number of heartbeat protocol instances to 20. As the results show, energy consumption is quadratic in the network size in the signature-based implementation, and linear in the MAC-based version. This significant improvement is mainly due to the significant reduction in communication. Moreover, on low-end embedded devices MACs are obviously much cheaper energy-wise than digital signatures. Figure 11 also shows an increase in energy consumption as a function of number of neighbors for the MAC-based version. This is due to the hop-by-hop MAC verification and re-generation.

Simulation Results: DARPA was evaluated using omnet++ simulator [40] with several topologies: chain, star, tree (with fan-out degrees: 2, 4, 8 and 12), and networks with fixed number of neighbors (4, 8 and 12). We emulated cryptographic operations as delays based on measurements from TyTAN [8]. Simulation uses 20-kbps as the communication rate for links between devices. It corresponds to the minimum bandwidth provided by ZigBee – a common protocol for IoT devices. We simulated collect and heartbeat based on digital signatures, described in Section 4, and the optimized MAC-based implementation described in Section 6. Results are shown in Figure 8, 9, 10, and 11. Results for networks with fixed number of neighbors are very similar to those for trees and are hence omitted, due to space limitations.

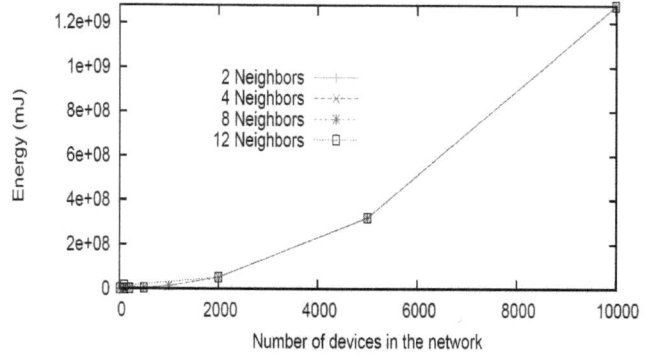

Figure 6: Energy consumption of signature-based DARPA

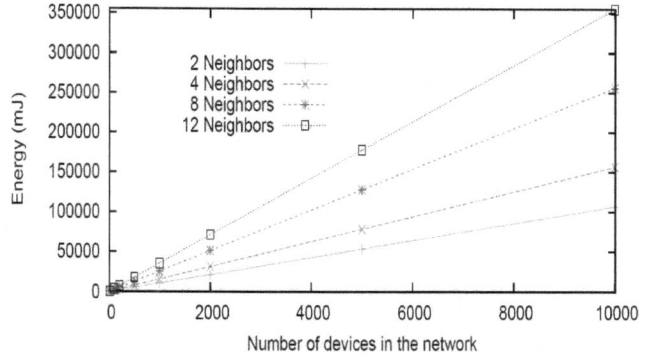

Figure 7: Energy consumption of MAC-based DARPA

As shown in Figure 8 and 9, for both implementations, and aforementioned topologies, run-time of heartbeat is linear in network size. However, the MAC-based implementation performs better, particularly in a chain topology. Computational overheard of heartbeat is linear (in network size) in chain and star, while logarithmic in tree topologies. Its communication overhead is always linear in network size. For this reason, the effect of replacing digital signatures with MACs is reduced. On the other hand, Figure 9 shows that run-time of heartbeat in $1,000 - node$ networks is about 13 seconds. This number is less than T_{cap}, and is therefore realistic.

Figure 10 and 11 show run-times of collect with digital signatures and MACs, respectively. The quadratic run-time of collect in the signature-based implementation is due to the quadratic communication overhead, since each of the s devices has to communicate its s log lists to Adm. Meanwhile, in the MAC-based implementation, only a constant size XOR-ed MAC is communicated. Consequently, this significant difference in run-times between the two implementations is due to the reduction in communication overhead from sending concatenated logs to sending XOR-ed constant size MACs. Note that the run-time of collect in the MAC-based implementation consequently converges to the computational overhead, which is linear in chain and star (and logarithmic in tree) topology.

Finally, as shown in the figures, chain is the worst-performing topology for collect, since responses are always sent through s hops, compared to $log(s)$ hops for trees and 1 hop for

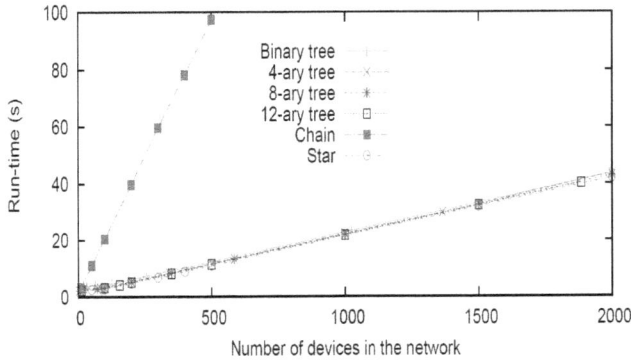

Figure 8: DARPA:heartbeat signature-based performance

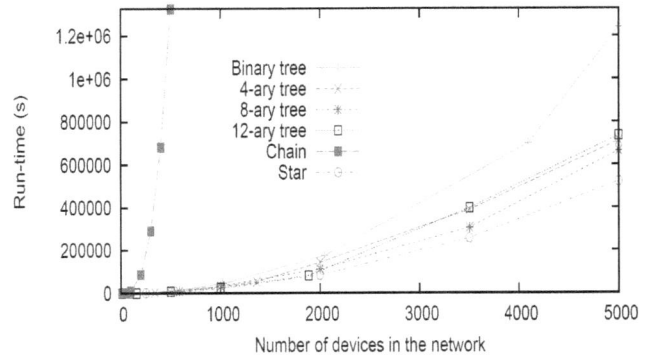

Figure 9: DARPA:heartbeat MAC-based performance

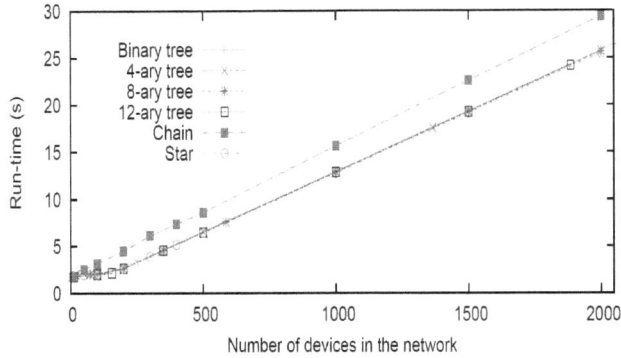

Figure 10: DARPA:collect signature-based performance

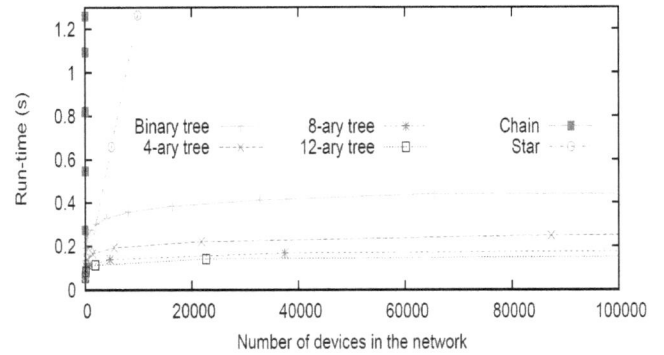

Figure 11: DARPA:collect MAC-based performance

star. On the other hand, star topology performs best in protocols where communication overhead dominates, i.e., in signature-based implementation of collect, and worst when computation overhead is dominant, i.e., in MAC-based. In the latter case, the central node in the star has to verify s MACs.

8. RELATED WORK

Remote Attestation is a popular research topic and many schemes have been proposed in the literature. They all share a scenario where the prover sends to the verifier a status report of its current software configuration. Authenticity of the report is typically assured by some form of secure hardware [19, 30, 31, 43, 44, 52] and/or trusted software [2, 22, 28, 31, 34, 45, 46, 54]. Attestation based on secure hardware is often too complex and expensive for low-end embedded systems. Software-based attestation [22, 28, 34, 45, 46] does not require any hardware and involves no cryptographic keys. However, its security relies on strong assumptions that are hard to achieve in practice [3], e.g.: adversarial silence while the attestation protocol runs, optimality of the attestation algorithm and its implementation, and fixed round-trip prover-verifier delay. Hence, common wisdom implies that secure and practical remote attestation requires at least a few security features in hardware [19, 21, 29].

Current attestation schemes consider only a single prover and do not accommodate groups thereof. Moreover, they consider only (remote) software attackers, with no physical access to provers. Only the recent SEDA [4] scheme performs collective attestation of interconnected devices by distributing attestation burden across the entire network. However, SEDA considers only remote software attacks, while DARPA identifies both compromised and captured devices.

Absence Detection is used (particularly, in sensor networks) to detect node failures and captures. Detecting failures by absence detection has been studied for static [50] and dynamic topologies [13, 23]. However, since these schemes are not designed with security in mind, they are ineffective in our adversarial setting.

A physical attack on a device requires expert knowledge, costly equipment, and most importantly, in most cases, removal of the device(s) from the network for a non-negligible amount of time [5]. Therefore, absence detection has been used to detect node capture attacks, by letting each device keep track of the time it needs to re-encounter a predetermined subset of peer devices [14, 15]. This time is then compared to a predetermined threshold. In static networks, each device simply measures absence time for each neighbor, and compares it to the minimal time needed to capture a device [24]. Techniques for dynamic networks allow a certain number of false negatives, depending on the threshold. However, static network techniques can not be extended to dynamic networks. Moreover, all proposed schemes are vulnerable to remote software attacks. In contrast, DARPA, besides being applicable to static and dynamic networks, can detect both remote software and physical attacks.

Secure data aggregation is a fundamental communication primitive in wireless sensor networks. It reduces communication overhead considerably, through combining data received from distinct sensor nodes, while preserving its security (secrecy and/or integrity). Several approaches have been proposed for integrity-preserving data aggregation. Some are based on cryptographic techniques [10, 11, 27, 32, 37, 42, 57], while others rely on trust relations [41] or witness-based solutions [17]. Integrity-preserving data aggregation can be combined with DARPA to provide security against physical adversary. However, these approaches involve computationally expensive asymmetric cryptography [32], or require globally shared keys [37]. Moreover, they have high computation and communication complexity [12, 17, 39]. They also mainly focus on detecting integrity breaches, rather than the identification of misbehaving nodes. Schemes that are able to detect captured nodes require a number of rounds which is at least logarithmic in the size of the network [51]. Moreover, such schemes are unable to detect captured nodes, unless they misbehave (i.e., alter with the aggregation result).

Key management protocols aim to achieve a trade-off between storage requirements, key connectivity, and resilience to node compromise. Most of proposed schemes aim at decreasing the number of keys each node needs to store. Storage reduction is achieved on the expense of connectivity, i.e., by leveraging knowledge of the network topology [56], or the probability of every two nodes communicating [20]. In such schemes, two nodes share a key if they consider each other reachable [35], or can not rely on other node(s) to provide a secure path [33]. It can also be achieved at the expense of resilience to node compromise. This is done using various mathematically flavored key distribution techniques [6, 7, 9, 18, 36]. While such schemes do not aim to detect captured nodes, they try to minimize the effect of node capture in terms of compromise of communication links. Moreover, some enable revocation of leaked credentials. DARPA requires either one private (signing) key per device or several symmetric keys shared between neighbors, and between every device and the verifier. Thus, its storage requirement is minimal. However, end-to-end authenticity is maintined due to attestation code's exclusive access to keys.

9. SUMMARY AND FUTURE WORK

This paper proposes DARPA – a scheme which mitigates a very powerful adversary capable of physical attacks, under reasonable assumptions. However, despite its benefits, DARPA has certain limitations that need to be addressed, including:

- False positives due to device failures and temporary unreachability, e.g., network partitioning.
- Lack of identification of potentially compromised devices.
- Relatively high communication overhead of the heartbeat protocol.

There are several concrete issues that we plan to tackle in the near-term:

- Use majority voting to identify compromised devices.
- Apply witness-based approach to mitigate network partitioning, i.e., if Adv physically attacks $\leq k$ devices within the inter-attestation gap, then each device must have at least $k+1$ witnesses for each heartbeat period.

- Lower heartbeat protocol overhead by sending heartbeats only to neighbors.
- Extend DARPA to support device mobility during heartbeat.

Acknowledgements

We thank anonymous reviewers for their useful comments, as well as Levente Buttyán for his insightful and constructive feedback. At TU Damstadt, this research was co-funded by the German Science Foundation, as part of project S2 within CRC 1119 CROSSING, EC-SPRIDE, the European Union's 7th Framework Programme, under grant agreement No. 609611, PRACTICE project, and Intel Collaborative Research Institute for Secure Computing (ICRI-SC). At UC Irvine, this research was supported by funding from the National Security Agency (H98230-15-1-0276) and the Department of Homeland Security (under subcontract from HRL Laboratories).

References

[1] Real-time clocks (rtc) ics. https://www.maximintegrated.com/en/products/digital/real-time-clocks.html.

[2] W. Arbaugh et al. A secure and reliable bootstrap architecture. In *IEEE S&P*, 1997.

[3] F. Armknecht et al. A security framework for the analysis and design of software attestation. In *ACM CCS*, 2013.

[4] N. Asokan et al. Seda: Scalable embedded device attestation. In *ACM CCS*, 2015.

[5] A. Becher et al. *Tampering with motes: Real-world physical attacks on wireless sensor networks.* Springer, 2006.

[6] R. Blom. An optimal class of symmetric key generation systems. In *EUROCRYPT Workshop*, 1984.

[7] C. Blundo et al. Perfectly secure key distribution for dynamic conferences. *Information and Computation*, 1998.

[8] F. Brasser et al. Tytan: Tiny trust anchor for tiny devices. In *DAC*, 2015.

[9] S. Çamtepe et al. Combinatorial design of key distribution mechanisms for wireless sensor networks. *IEEE/ACM Transactions on Networking*, 2007.

[10] H. Chan et al. Secure hierarchical in-network aggregation in sensor networks. In *ACM CCS*, 2006.

[11] H. Chan et al. SIA: Secure information aggregation in sensor networks. *JCS*, 2007.

[12] C.-M. Chen et al. RCDA: Recoverable concealed data aggregation for data integrity in wireless sensor networks. *TPDS*, 2012.

[13] W. Chen et al. On the quality of service of failure detectors. *IEEE TC*, 2002.

[14] M. Conti et al. Emergent properties: Detection of the node-capture attack in mobile wireless sensor networks. In *WiSec*, 2008.

[15] M. Conti et al. Mobility and cooperation to thwart node capture attacks in manets. *EURASIP WCN*, 2009.

[16] G. de Meulenaer et al. On the energy cost of communication and cryptography in wireless sensor networks. In *WiMob*, 2008.

[17] W. Du et al. A witness-based approach for data fusion assurance in wsn. In *GLOBECOM*, 2003.

[18] W. Du et al. A pairwise key predistribution scheme for wireless sensor networks. *ACM TISSEC*, 2005.

[19] K. Eldefrawy et al. SMART: Secure and minimal

architecture for (establishing a dynamic) root of trust. In *NDSS*, 2012.

[20] L. Eschenauer et al. A key-management scheme for distributed sensor networks. In *ACM CCS*, 2002.

[21] A. Francillon et al. A minimalist approach to remote attestation. In *DATE*, 2014.

[22] R. Gardner et al. Detecting code alteration by creating a temporary memory bottleneck. *IEEE TIFS*, 2009.

[23] N. Hayashibara et al. Failure detectors for large-scale distributed systems. In *SRDS*, 2002.

[24] J.-w. Ho et al. *Distributed Detection of Node Capture Attacks in Wireless Sensor Networks*. InTech, 2010.

[25] C. Hsin et al. Self-monitoring of wireless sensor networks. *Computer Communications*, 2006.

[26] C.-f. Hsin et al. A distributed monitoring mechanism for wireless sensor networks. In *ACM workshop on Wireless security*, 2002.

[27] L. Hu et al. Secure aggregation for wireless networks. In *SAINT Workshops*, 2003.

[28] R. Kennell et al. Establishing the genuinity of remote computer systems. In *USENIX*, 2003.

[29] P. Koeberl et al. TrustLite: A security architecture for tiny embedded devices. In *EuroSys*, 2014.

[30] J. Kong et al. PUFatt: Embedded platform attestation based on novel processor-based PUFs. In *DAC*, 2014.

[31] X. Kovah et al. New results for timing-based attestation. In *IEEE S&P*, 2012.

[32] V. Kumar et al. Secure hierarchical data aggregation in wireless sensor networks: Performance evaluation and analysis. In *IEEE MDM*, 2012.

[33] J. Lee et al. A combinatorial approach to key predistribution for distributed sensor networks. In *WCNC*, 2005.

[34] Y. Li et al. VIPER: Verifying the integrity of peripherals' firmware. In *ACM CCS*, 2011.

[35] D. Liu et al. Location-based pairwise key establishments for static sensor networks. In *SASN*, 2003.

[36] D. Liu et al. Establishing pairwise keys in distributed sensor networks. *ACM TISSEC*, 2005.

[37] A. Mahimkar et al. Securedav: A secure data aggregation and verification protocol for sensor networks. In *GLOBECOM*.

[38] S. Mansouri et al. An architectural countermeasure against power analysis attacks for fsr-based stream ciphers. In *COSADE*. 2012.

[39] S. Nath et al. Secure outsourced aggregation via one-way chains. In *SIGMOD*, 2009.

[40] OpenSim Ltd. OMNeT++ discrete event simulator. http://omnetpp.org/.

[41] S. Ozdemir. Secure and reliable data aggregation for wireless sensor networks. In *Ubiquitous Computing Systems*. 2007.

[42] S. Papadopoulos et al. Exact in-network aggregation with integrity and confidentiality. *TKDE*, 2012.

[43] B. Parno et al. Bootstrapping trust in commodity computers. In *IEEE S&P*, 2010.

[44] S. Schulz et al. Short paper: Lightweight remote attestation using physical functions. In *WiSec*, 2011.

[45] A. Seshadri et al. SWATT: Software-based attestation for embedded devices. In *IEEE S&P*, 2004.

[46] A. Seshadri et al. SAKE: Software attestation for key establishment in sensor networks. In *DCOSS*. 2008.

[47] S. Skorobogatov. Physical attacks on tamper resistance: Progress and lessons. In *Workshop on Hardware Assurance*, 2011.

[48] S. Skorobogatov. Physical attacks and tamper resistance. In *Introduction to Hardware Security and Trust*. 2012.

[49] S. P. Skorobogatov. *Semi-invasive attacks: a new approach to hardware security analysis*. PhD thesis, 2005.

[50] P. Stelling et al. A fault detection service for wide area distributed computations. *Cluster Computing*, 1999.

[51] G. Taban et al. Efficient handling of adversary attacks in aggregation applications. In *ESORICS*, 2008.

[52] Trusted Computing Group (TCG). Website. http://www.trustedcomputinggroup.org, 2015.

[53] R. van Renesse et al. A gossip-style failure detection service. In *Middleware*, 1998.

[54] A. Vasudevan et al. CARMA: A hardware tamper-resistant isolated execution environment on commodity x86 platforms. In *ASIACCS*, 2012.

[55] J. Vijayan. Stuxnet renews power grid security concerns, 2010.

[56] Z. Yu et al. A key management scheme using deployment knowledge for wireless sensor networks. *TPDS*, 2008.

[57] W. Zhang et al. Secure data aggregation in wireless sensor networks: A watermark based authentication supportive approach. *Pervasive and Mobile Computing*, 2008.

[58] Y. Zhou et al. Side-channel attacks: Ten years after its publication and the impacts on cryptographic module security testing. *IACR Cryptology ePrint Archive*, 2005.

Dissecting Customized Protocols: Automatic Analysis for Customized Protocols based on IEEE 802.15.4

Kibum Choi
Korean Advanced Institute of
Science and Technology
kibumchoi@kaist.ac.kr

Yunmok Son
Korean Advanced Institute of
Science and Technology
yunmok00@kaist.ac.kr

Juhwan Noh
Korean Advanced Institute of
Science and Technology
juwhan@kaist.ac.kr

Hocheol Shin
Korean Advanced Institute of
Science and Technology
h.c.shin@kaist.ac.kr

Jaeyeong Choi
Korean Advanced Institute of
Science and Technology
go1736@kaist.ac.kr

Yongdae Kim
Korean Advanced Institute of
Science and Technology
yongdaek@kaist.ac.kr

ABSTRACT

IEEE 802.15.4 is widely used as lower layers for not only well-known wireless communication standards such as ZigBee, 6LoW-PAN, and WirelessHART, but also customized protocols developed by manufacturers, particularly for various Internet of Things (IoT) devices. Customized protocols are not usually publicly disclosed nor standardized. Moreover, unlike textual protocols (e.g., HTTP, SMTP, POP3.), customized protocols for IoT devices provide no clues such as strings or keywords that are useful for analysis. Instead, they use bits or bytes to represent header and body information in order to save power and bandwidth. On the other hand, they often do not employ encryption, fragmentation, or authentication to save cost and effort in implementations. In other words, their security relies only on the confidentiality of the protocol itself.

In this paper, we introduce a novel methodology to analyze and reconstruct unknown wireless customized protocols over IEEE 802.15.4. Based on this methodology, we develop an automatic analysis and spoofing tool called WPAN automatic spoofer (WASp) that can be used to understand and reconstruct customized protocols to byte-level accuracy, and to generate packets that can be used for verification of analysis results or spoofing attacks. The methodology consists of four phases: packet collection, packet grouping, protocol analysis, and packet generation. Except for the packet collection step, all steps are fully automated.

Although the use of customized protocols is also unknown before the collecting phase, we choose two real-world target systems for evaluation: the smart plug system and platform screen door (PSD) to evaluate our methodology and WASp. In the evaluation, 7,299 and 217 packets are used as datasets for both target systems, respectively. As a result, on average, WASp is found to reduce entropy of legitimate message space by 93.77 % and 88.11 % for customized protocols used in smart plug and PSD systems, respectively. In addition, on average, 48.19 % of automatically generated packets are successfully spoofed for the first target systems.

Keywords

Wireless spoofing attacks; customized PAN protocol; automatic protocol reversing

1. INTRODUCTION

In an Internet of Things (IoT) environment, many devices communicate with one another using various wireless communication protocols. Because most applications operate in a personal area such as a home, office, or hospital, wireless personal area network (WPAN) technologies, such as ZigBee, Bluetooth, and Z-Wave, are essential for implementing IoT systems.

In particular, among various WPAN protocols, IEEE 802.15.4 has been widely used for lower layer protocol for several standards such as ZigBee, 6LoWPAN, WirelessHART, and MiWi. IEEE 802.15.4 is a standard that specifies the physical (PHY) layer and medium access control (MAC) layer for low-rate wireless personal area networks (LR-WPAN) [ ]. It operates on one of three frequency bands: 868–868.6 MHz, 902–928 MHz, or 2,400–2,483.5 MHz. It can provide up to 250 kbps at 10 m distance with low power and low cost. Because of the requirements of power and cost efficiency, IEEE 802.15.4 has a simple structure.

Notably, for many IoT systems and some safety-critical control systems, proprietary protocols (i.e., customized protocols) are used on top of IEEE 802.15.4. These include smart metering systems and platform screen door (PSD) systems. Although details of these customized protocols are unknown, they can be vulnerable to sniffing and spoofing attacks, because of the low power characteristics (i.e., simplicity and short message length) of IEEE 802.15.4 and the shared medium in wireless communication without message encryption and authentication. Through these attacks, private information such as electricity usage, life patterns, or medical records can be stolen, and overcharge of electricity bills, failure of power supply-and-demand control, wrong medical treatment or undesirable control of systems can occur. Furthermore, they can control target devices for their own purpose: for example, switching on and off, injecting malicious data into, and incapacitating the devices.

IEEE 802.15.4's MAC layer supports encryption that is one of big challenges for analyzing protocols. However, in this study, customized protocols using encryption are not considered because customized protocols do not usually use it for the low power characteristics. Even when no messages are encrypted, some challenges remain in analyzing and reconstructing customized protocols. First, obtaining and reverse engineering binary files that implement customized protocols are difficult. Unless the firmware of a target device is opened on the Internet, to obtain firmware, physical access to the device, and even in such a case, desoldering a memory or processor chip may be required. Even after obtaining the firmware, manual protocol reverse engineering is inefficient and time-consuming. While automatic reverse engineering has garnered considerable attention these days, it only supports popular architectures such as x86 or ARM. Second, wireless custom protocols use binary formats because of low-power consumption requirements, instead of using text data such as keywords. Because packet length is directly associated with power consumption, these protocols use fields that are as short as possible to represent various fields and commands. Finally, even after reverse engineering the protocol, evaluating analysis results is difficult due to the absence of ground truth.

The goal of this study is to analyze and reconstruct packet formats for customized protocols built on top of IEEE 802.15.4 standard. In addition, we aim to generate spoofing packets for the protocol. For these goals, we designed a novel methodology and developed an automatic analysis tool named WPAN automatic spoofer (WASp) based on the methodology. Our analysis and reconstruction methodology consists of four phases: packet collection, packet grouping, protocol analysis, and packet generation. Packet collection refers to the manual wireless channel sniffing process that must be conducted in carefully controlled conditions. This directly affects the effectiveness of analysis because critical factors such as the number of collected packets, the number of transceivers, and expected operations are bounded in this phase. The other three phases are fully automated. Initially, WASp groups packets according to crucial information from packet headers. For each packet group, the tool analyzes MAC layer data reuse (e.g., address field), byte-level entropy, the range of each byte column, and the existence of a cyclic redundancy check (CRC). In the second step, the tool combines results of all tests and generates scored analysis reports for every packet group using our scoring algorithm. Finally, for reports with a high score, it generates feasible packet lists for spoofing.

Our system is closely related to that of Netzob [ ], which aims to analyze and cluster the protocol by considering semantic information embedded in TCP/IP layer. While both Netzob and WASp target customized protocols, the main difference between them is the layer they are targeting. Netzob targets protocols on top of the TCP/IP layer, whereas WASp targets protocols built on top of the MAC layer of IEEE 802.15.4 which contains much less information then the TCP/IP layer. In other words, Netzob mainly relies on semantic information existing in TCP/IP. Therefore, we believe critical changes for Netzob are required to achieve the same goal as that of WASp.

To evaluate WASp, we used two commercial target systems, including a smart plug system for home use and a PSD system in a subway system. WASp automatically analyzes collected packets based on characteristics of customized protocols by deriving various parameters including n-gram and entropy. The results of our evaluation show that, for a smart plug system, the tool reduces an average of 93.77 % of the entropy for a customized protocol and provides possible rules to construct spoofing payload at a 48.19 % average success rate. In other words, we can control the power supply of devices connected to a smart plug using automatically generated spoofing packets. We could not perform our attack on a PSD system, because of legal and safety concerns. However, an average of 88.11 % of the entropy is reduced for PSD's customized protocol. Note that all vulnerabilities are responsibly disclosed to the agencies in advance. Our study contributes the following:

- We derive a general analysis methodology for customized protocols on top of IEEE 802.15.4, which is far different from that of typical network packet analysis.

- We build an automatic protocol analyzer and prove the possibility of automated protocol reverse engineering against wireless customized protocols.

- We show that taking control of applications using automatically generated spoofing packets by our tool is possible.

The remainder of the paper is organized as follows. Section 2 summarizes existing research related to automatic protocol analysis and compares these studies to our own. Section 3 provides information about customized protocols on top of IEEE 802.15.4. Section 4 explains the concept of our design to analyze target protocols and the basic concept of our automatic analysis. The detailed implementation and algorithms of our methodology are described in Section 5. In Section 6, we present the results of automatic analysis and spoofing on two commercial systems. We discuss limitations of this study in Section 7. We conclude the study in Section 8.

2. RELATED WORK

Because of the massive increase in the number of network protocols, including that of malware and botnets, security researchers have tried to automate protocol reverse engineering. Automated protocol reverse engineering has been used for deep packet inspection, intrusion detection or prevention, and automatic packet generation for fuzzing and replay attacks. We can classify it into two major categories: program-based and trace-based analyses. In addition to these two, protocol fuzzing is somewhat related to our automatic spoofing packet generation.

Studies on program-based analysis have attempted to analyze target protocols on a binary program and some of its input traces. For example, studies have analyzed processes that occur as a result of input messages to a server or client programs. By contrast, studies on trace-based analysis reverse engineer only with network traces of target protocols. Finally, studies on protocol fuzzing tests a target system by injecting many packets that resemble legitimate ones.

2.1 Program-Based Analysis

First, program-based research analyzes customized protocols based on program implementation. RolePlayer [ ] and AutoFormat [ ] attempt protocol parsing using a context-aware monitored execution. Polyglot [ ], Tupni [ ], Reformat [ ], Dispatcher [ ], and Prospex [ ] can be classified as a taint analysis using semantic program information. Because these programs use keywords or separators to identify fields, analysis is much simpler. In addition, they can monitor program flow according to specific message inputs. These cause the relation between parsed fields and their real meaning to be clearer than when employing network trace only approaches. This paper focuses on trace-based analysis, and program-based analysis is out-of-scope for this paper. Nonetheless, as we discussed in the introduction, program-based analysis is difficult and time-consuming.

2.2 Trace-based Analysis

Trace-based research analyzes network packet traces without any prior knowledge about the program that generates the packets, which can be divided into two types. The first type is reverse engineering against textual protocols such as HTTP or SMTP. Discoverer [ ], Reverx [ ], ProDecoder [ ], SANTaClass [ ], and ProWord [ ] fall into this type. These programs try to extract fields by parsing keywords. For example, keywords such as "GET" and "POST" in HTTP have specific delimiters or a similar interval. However, wireless customized protocols mostly use binary data for energy efficiency. Therefore, keyword parsing methods from these kind of

Table 1: Comparison studies closely related to WASp

	Target	Purpose	Characteristics
PROVEX [19]	Botnet C&C traffic	Botnet detection	• Byte value distribution • Signature creation
ProGraph [14]	General traffic	Analysis and classification	• Graph signature extraction
Netzob [4]	General traffic	Analysis and classification	• Need semantic information
FieldHunter [2]	General traffic	Analysis and classification	• Partial field extraction

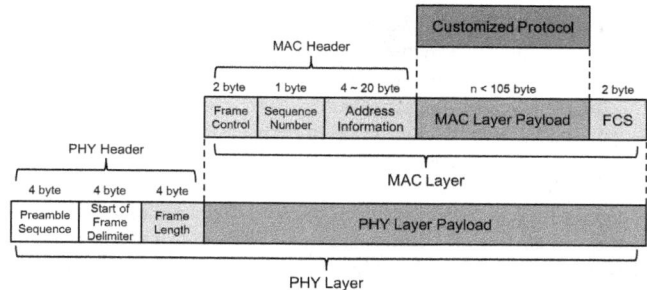

Figure 1: IEEE 802.15.4 data frame format (PHY and MAC layers) with customized protocol as an upper layer

textual protocol analysis are difficult to be used for reverse engineering wireless customized protocol.

The second type studies against binary protocols. PROVEX [19] extracts botnet C&C traffic signature based on byte distribution, and ProGraph [14] tries to infer protocol message formats by exploiting intra-packet dependency derived from constructing a graphical model. However, both of these programs passively analyze given network traces, and limit their application to either classification of network traces or generation of network signature for protocol detection. FieldHunter [2] and Netzob [4], can be used for both binary and textual formatted protocols by utilizing semantic information. However, FieldHunter extracts only partial fields such as message type and length, which can be distinguished by means of statistical characteristics, and skips unidentified fields.

As previously discussed, Netzob is closely related to our system, WASp. First, it uses not only syntactic information (e.g., encoding, checksums, and IP addresses), but also semantic information (e.g., file read/write and listing directories) to extract a message structure with high accuracy. Second, during analysis, it filters out samples considered to be noisy in order to improve clustering output. Finally, it clusters acquired target samples with available syntactic and semantic information, and infers important characteristics of sub-message fields such as value, offset, and size. However, Netzob is considerably different from WASp regarding the base information it uses and its output. First, Netzob depends on higher layer information (i.e., network and transport layers) compared to WASp. Specifically, it refers to well-known field values (e.g., IPv4 addresses, TCP port numbers) of specific implementations of such layers (i.e., IP and TCP) to infer the structure of the target protocol. Therefore, Netzob would require an overhaul to analyze IEEE 802.15.4 customized protocols that WASp targets. Second, Netzob infers only the structure of the target protocol and does not generate packets that can be directly spoofed to targets. It lacks the packet generation engine present in WASp, which automatically assembles spoofing packets based on analyzed field information. Table 1 summarizes comparison between these four systems.

2.3 Protocol Fuzzing

Protocol fuzzing is a type of fuzz testing that generates invalid or unexpected packets and injects them into a target system. An effective fuzzer for security testing must be designed with deep understanding of the target protocol as well as require automatic packet generation for security attacks.

For example, by collecting transmitted packets from a target system, SECFUZZ [21] tests known security protocols such as internet key exchange (IKE). It generates packets based on the assumption that the fuzzer has necessary information related to decryption such as encryption keys and nonces. In particular, it finds vulnerabilities automatically by attaching a dynamic memory analytical tool. AspFuzz [16] and regression finite state machine (RFSM) fuzzer [26] test state-aware complex protocols, and they establish their respec-

tive state machine models to represent the states and transitions of a target protocol. Thus, they can generate packets using anomalous data as well as the order of those packets. However, these fuzzers are not adequate to analyze customized protocols based on IEEE 802.15.4. They cannot analyze customized protocols because they require prior knowledge of target protocols. AutoFuzz [13] constructs a generic message sequence (GMS), an array list of static and variable data fields. It then generates packets by fixing data in static data fields and changing data in variable data fields. Although AutoFuzz does not require prior knowledge, its targets are textual protocols. Therefore, applying it to wireless binary-based customized protocols is difficult.

3. BACKGROUND

In this section, we explain the basic information of the IEEE 802.15.4 architecture and data frame format. We also define a customized protocol based on IEEE 802.15.4 as our target protocol.

3.1 IEEE 802.15.4

IEEE 802.15.4 is a standard that defines lower layer protocols for WPAN communications that use frequency bands of 868–868.6, 902–928, or 2,400–2,483.5 MHz. It mainly focuses on low-speed and low-power communication between wireless devices. Although WiFi offers high-speed solutions, IEEE 802.15.4 requires much less power and focuses on home-range devices. Essentially, it supports a communication range of 10 m, and a transfer rate of 250 kbps. Even if low power consumption is one of its main features, extremely low manufacturing and operation costs are also the chief features of IEEE 802.15.4. Furthermore, technological simplicity and flexibility make it adaptable to various wireless communication protocols. For example, well-known protocols, such as ZigBee, 6LoWPAN, WirelessHART, have been developed based on the IEEE 802.15.4 standard.

3.1.1 Architecture

The IEEE 802.15.4 architecture consists of only two layers: PHY and MAC. The PHY layer defines the physical specifications to transmit and receive radio frequency (RF) signals through a physical transmission medium. The MAC layer provides a reliable link between two nodes and is responsible for the following: encoding digital bits into packet frames for transmission, decoding them in order to receive frames, and controlling access to data in a network. This architecture is used not only for the lower layer of well-known wireless communication standards, but also for publicly unknown customized protocols designed by device manufacturers.

3.1.2 Data Frame Format

The data frame format of PHY and MAC layers of IEEE 802.15.4 is depicted in Figure 1. A PHY layer frame includes a PHY payload, which is a MAC layer frame that contains a MAC header, MAC payload, and frame check sequence (FCS). The MAC contains a frame control field (FCF), data sequence number, and address information. The MAC payload is the actual payload to be transmitted, and FCS is usually implemented as a CRC to detect common errors caused by noise in wireless communication channels.

As depicted in Figure 1, MAC payload is the real target field that contains a protocol customized by various manufacturers for their systems. To analyze this customized protocol, information in a MAC header and FCS is used. First, FCF in a MAC header contains important bitmap information such as packet type, security enabled status, acknowledgment (ACK) request status, and addressing mode. If the security enabled bit is not set, no encryption is applied to the upper layer, which means the protocol can be analyzed by an attacker. Address fields and FCS are utilized for address reuse detection and noise filtering, respectively.

3.2 Customized Protocol

The main target in this study is customized protocols designed by manufacturers themselves. Customized protocols can be identified by simply using deep packet inspection (DPI) tools such as Wireshark [12]. For example, if Wireshark indicates that an unknown protocol is a member of the IEEE 802.15.4 family of protocols (e.g., ZigBee and 6LowPAN) and payloads of their packets are abnormally parsed, then this unknown protocol can be considered as a customized protocol.

These customized protocols are widely used for various IoT devices. In this study, a customized protocol is defined as an upper layer protocol over well-defined PHY and MAC layers (i.e., IEEE 802.15.4). Because many wireless communication applications for IoT have several functionalities, complex protocols are not required. Thus, some manufacturers often use customized protocols instead of following existing standard protocols such as ZigBee and WirelessHART. In some cases, certain IoT devices seem to use ZigBee or some other standard WPAN protocols, but we found that they actually use customized protocols on top of IEEE 802.15.4. However, before capturing packets, recognizing whether a customized protocol is used in a wireless communication system is impossible. Therefore, finding proper target system for evaluation of WASp in Section 6 was difficult.

Customized protocols are not known publicly and vary according to devices or manufacturers. Therefore, analyzing customized protocols and generalizing them for automation are challenging. However, in many cases, customized protocols have several characteristics that enable unknown protocol analysis and spoofing attacks. These characteristics are as follows:

- MAC layer data such as source and destination addresses can be reused, because producing their own address system is burdensome.

- Common patterns such as ASCII bytes, periodically increasing or decreasing bytes, and sequential bytes are embedded.

- No authentication and poor packet integrity check are implemented. (e.g., using well-known CRC algorithms, checking only the increment of sequence numbers)

- Some bytes can be used without any alteration for spoofing attacks, because they are filled with fixed data regardless of the operation a target system.

Based on these characteristics, manually analyzing unknown customized protocols is possible. However, manual protocol reverse engineering is time-consuming and requiring new analysis for new targets.

Assumptions. To clarify the scope of our analysis, we assumed the following. First, the main purpose of protocol customization is neither flexibility nor convenience, but rather efficiency and low-power consumption. For example, a command field having textual data such as a keyword usually requires more than one byte, but a binary data field that corresponds to predefined commands can be represented in one byte. Second, packets are not encrypted. While some of the standards support encryption, customized protocols we have seen have not been using encryption. Third, packets are not fragmented, as fragmentation increases cost and the amount of power consumption. Finally, an attacker has no access privileges to the target system. From packet sniffing to spoofing attack, all processes are performed remotely.

4. ANALYSIS DESIGN

The final goal of this study is to analyze and reconstruct unknown wireless customized protocols over IEEE 802.15.4 for spoofing attacks at a high success rate. As a building block, we develop an analytical procedure for wireless spoofing attacks consisting of three phases inspired by the inductive approach. In this section, we provide an overview of our analytical procedure in three phases.

4.1 Overview

Figure 2 represents an overview of our analytical procedure to spoof wireless communication systems using the customized protocols mentioned in Section 3. Target devices employ IEEE 802.15.4 as PHY and MAC layers and an unknown customized protocol as an upper layer. Physical signals containing packets of a customized protocol are transmitted through a wireless channel (i.e., the air) that is publicly open. Because the target protocol is unknown, the starting point of analysis involves sniffing (i.e., collecting packets) by listening to RF signals in the proper wireless channel. For sniffing, we require an appropriate tool with an RF signal receiving and digital processing capability that can handle PHY and MAC layers such as KillerBee [24] and universal software radio peripheral (USRP) [11] with "gr-ieee-802-15-4" GNU radio module [3] that fully support the IEEE 802.15.4 standard.

After collecting enough packets, attackers can reverse-engineer the customized protocol. Protocol reverse engineering is the most important and challenging part. An attacker needs to distinguish each field and determine their meanings in raw byte sequences with logical evidence or intuition. This process is extremely tedious, time-consuming, and even prone to errors. The more that fields are revealed, the more efficient the spoofing attack is, because employing brute-force at every field is practically impossible.

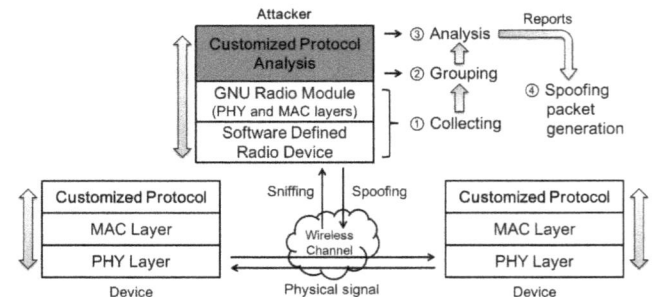

Figure 2: Overview of our analytical procedure for wireless communication sniffing and spoofing attacks against devices using customized protocols

In this study, we mainly focus on this protocol reverse engineering to generate possible spoofing packets efficiently. Therefore, our analytical procedure is built upon PHY and MAC layers as an lower layer. Generated spoofing packets can then be transmitted by the signal processing tool such as KillerBee and USRP.

4.2 Analytical Procedure

An inductive approach consists of observation, pattern, and theory. Similarly, protocol reverse engineering can be divided into three phases to make a spoofing attack possible for an IEEE 802.15.4-based customized protocol: collecting, grouping, and analysis as shown in Figure 2. To understand the meaning of each field in a customized protocol, controlling the variance of packets in predictable conditions in the first two phases is necessary. We strongly believe that this three-step procedure is a generic approach for IEEE 802.15.4-based customized protocol reverse engineering.

4.2.1 Collecting Phase

The first step in the collecting phase is to identify a communication channel. Because IEEE 802.15.4 has only 26 channels, by brute-forcing, we can identify the active channel that the target system uses. The collecting phase is usually considered as a simple process, as hardware supports this operation effectively. However, challenges in the subsequent phases totally depend on this packet collecting phase because any kind of contextual noises in this phase are hardly removed in the subsequent phases. Some variable factors or environments affect the variance of the packet data such as functionality, date, timing, and location. Note that all customized protocols utilize some of these data and their implementations can be somewhat different.

The functionality of a device is the most important factor to reverse engineer command related fields, and date and time are related to timestamps. The collecting phase has to run for sufficiently long time to clearly distinguish temporal information such as packet sequence number and time. The location is also highly related to the number of communication nodes. The number of nodes may complicate protocol reverse engineering. In other words, when the number of nodes is relatively small, the analysis become easier. By limiting the number of communication nodes, the entropy of address fields can be decreased. Therefore, if we can control these conditions, analysis becomes easier.

4.2.2 Grouping Phase

The second phase is a grouping process for the collected packets. Many types of packets exist in a typical digital communication protocol, such as request, response, command, and acknowledgment (ACK). The formats of these different types usually have different fields, and this difference causes the protocol analysis to be more complicated. By classifying the collected packets according to the source or destination addresses, we can obtain information about the request-response and command-ACK relationships. The length of the packet can provide useful information as well because different fields tend to have different packet lengths. For example, ACK packets are usually shorter than any other packets. Categorizing the collected packets according to the factors mentioned in the previous phase is also helpful.

4.2.3 Analysis Phase

The last step is the actual analysis of hex or ASCII-valued byte data in the grouped packets. The important data in the sequence of grouped packets are those that are repeated, periodic, monotonically increasing or decreasing, and otherwise meaningful. Repeated data can be related to the control features of the two previous phases

Table 2: Inferable information according to attributes of each byte

Data Attributes	Deducible Information
Repeatability	Source/destination addresses
Periodicity	Time stamp (data or time), Functional commands
Monotonic increment or decrement	Sequence number
Constant Field	Use the values of corresponding byte positions as fixed for spoofing attacks

including source or destination addresses, functional commands, and others. Periodic data can also be interpreted as having various meanings based on their timing characteristics such as time interval. Sequence numbers and timestamps of packets usually appear as monotonically increasing data, and they can be decoded according to their cycles. For example, the cycles of date or time data can be 12, 24, or 60 in decimal or hex, whereas those of a sequence number can be a full byte size. In particular, repeated data in every packet without any change are important because an attacker can use them as fixed values for a spoofing attack without knowing detailed information. Table 2 summarizes inferable information based on attributes of each byte previously mentioned.

Because one byte of data can have several of these attributes, multiple analysis results are possible. With some criteria or algorithms used for scoring different analysis results, we can choose one or some results to generate possible spoofing packets. According to the analysis results, the uncertainty of each field can be reduced. Therefore, we can generate possible spoofing packets more efficiently.

5. IMPLEMENTATION

Based on the design in Section 4, we implemented an automatic wireless customized protocol reverse engineering tool named WASp. As its final output, this tool generates scored analysis reports and possible spoofing packets by automatically analyzing input files containing captured packets.

In this section, we present details of the implementation of each module and byte-level analysis in WASp. The entire program flow of WASp is shown in Figure 3. WASp consists of four modules: parsing and grouping, byte-level analysis, report construction, and packet generation, which are marked Ⓐ, Ⓑ, Ⓒ, and Ⓓ in Figure 3, respectively. Essentially, packet capture (pcap) files containing captured packets in specific conditions (mentioned in Section 4.2.1) and context files describing those conditions for each pcap file are used as inputs for our tool. Captured packets in pcap files are parsed and then divided into several groups (Ⓐ). After the grouping, the analysis module performs byte-level tests in each byte position for every group. We designed five byte-level tests: CRC, n-gram, entropy, feature, and range (Ⓑ). The results of each test are merged and scored as a report that includes basic protocol format information (Ⓒ). Finally, based on scored results in the reports, our tool automatically generates possible spoofing packets (Ⓓ). Because a report is generated for each group, a user can select a report to generate spoofing packets or refer all reports according to one's purpose.

5.1 Parsing and Grouping

Our tool requires two kinds of inputs: pcap files and context files for each pcap file. Pcap files contain raw data of captured packets, and context files contain information concerning capturing conditions in (keyword, value) tuples designated by a user or attacker. Because those conditions can be combined with a byte or field in

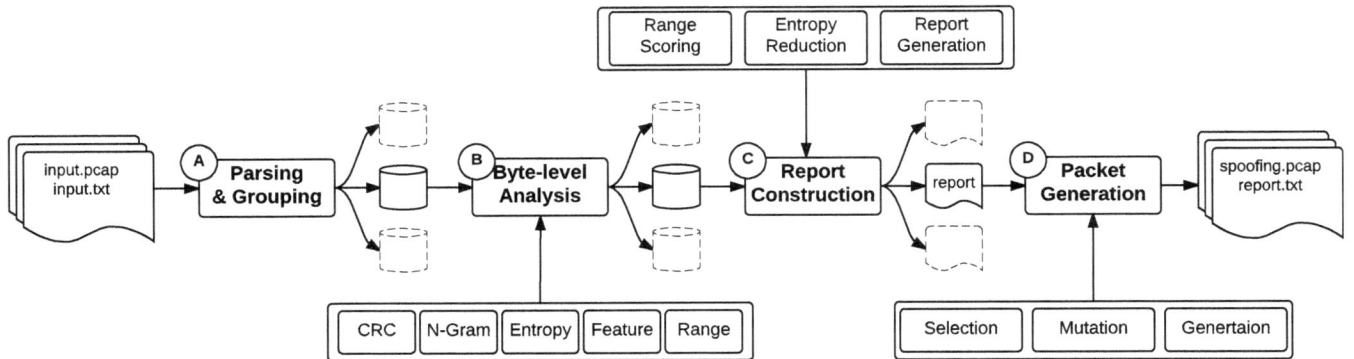

Figure 3: WASp: Automatic protocol reverse-engineering tool design

captured packets, context files can add information necessary for subsequent analyses.

For analyses, parsing and extracting MAC layer information from MAC headers of packets in pcap files are necessary. In this process, packets with wrong MAC layer CRCs are filtered out because they can be considered as broken packets in wireless transmission. After parsing, packets in pcap files are grouped into several groups according to packet length, and each group can be divided again into several subgroups according to (source address, destination address) tuples derived from MAC layer information. Because WPAN packets need to have minimal length to ensure low transmission power, customized protocols use a packet length that is as short as possible considering the purpose of each type of packet. In other words, the packet length is the easiest and most effective criterion to cluster packets according to type. By grouping and sub-grouping, we can reduce entropy related to address fields and even identify possible address byte positions and the values of given network nodes in a customized protocol.

Groups and subgroups classified in this module can also be used to produce a network diagram of a target system. Figure 4, which was automatically generated by WASp, shows an example of a network diagram for captured packets. Circles denote network nodes and their 2-byte hex values refer to MAC layer information in each node (i.e. addresses). Arrows refer to the direction of packet transmission, and next to each arrow, the byte length and number of corresponding packets are given. In addition, in Figure 4, packets contained in each arrow represent a subgroup and packets with the same byte length represent a group. This is helpful in understanding network structures or sender-receiver relationships of customized protocols, which have many communication nodes.

5.2 Byte-Level Analysis

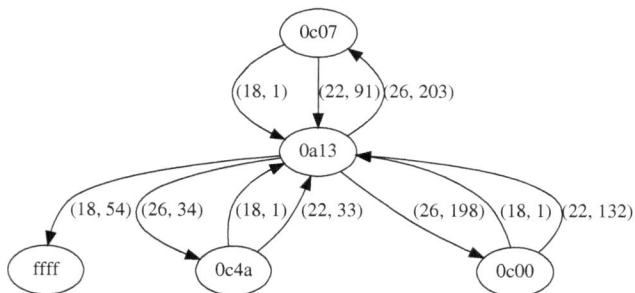

Figure 4: Example of network diagram for part of captured packets from PSD system as explained in Section 6

As previously mentioned, we essentially assumed that most data in the target protocols use a single-byte data format to reduce power consumption for each packet transmission. Because we do not know the target protocols at all, this is our best assumption at this point.

In the byte-level analysis module (ⒷⒷ in Figure 3), which is the main analysis process, we implemented five byte-level investigations. These investigations are based on characteristics of customized protocols explained in Section 3.2 for use in analyzing the formats of customized protocols.

CRC Test. CRC is one of the simplest methods for checking packet integrity. Thus, in customized protocols, well-known CRC algorithms are usually adopted. This test determines CRC existence using an n-gram method in customized payloads for each group or subgroup. For the CRC calculation, we adopted PyCRC module [ ], which supports nine common CRC methods including CRC-16, CRC-32, and CRC-CCITT. Because we consider packets that have the same length as a group, this test detects the CRC method for each group and identifies the most frequent CRC method and its byte positions. We considered captured packets with unmatched CRCs not only in MAC layer but also in customized protocol layer as noise data, and we filtered them out for subsequent analysis.

N-gram Test. The purpose of the n-gram test is to locate reused MAC header data such as source addresses, destination addresses, and network IDs in customized layer data. We built databases for every possible contiguous n-byte sequence (n-gram data) from both MAC header and customized layer data. By comparing both n-gram databases with the same length for all packets in a group or subgroup, this test detects byte positions and lengths of reused MAC header data fully or partially.

In cases in which a group contains multiple subgroups, MAC header data of packets in the subgroups may be more consistent than those in the group. Therefore, results of an n-gram test for each subgroup are merged to conduct an n-gram test for the group.

Entropy Test. To measure the variance of each byte, we applied entropy (i.e., Shannon entropy), which means the average of information contained in each set of data in our analysis. In this test, we calculated each byte position's entropy in packets of a group or subgroup and the entropy of each context in context files related to that group or subgroup.

If the entropy value of a byte position is zero, it means that the byte position is fixed, and thus, we can simply use the fixed value as it is for spoofing packet generation. Non-zero entropy values are used in the subsequent steps.

Feature Test. For each pcap file, (context, condition) paired context information is manually written in a context file. The context infor-

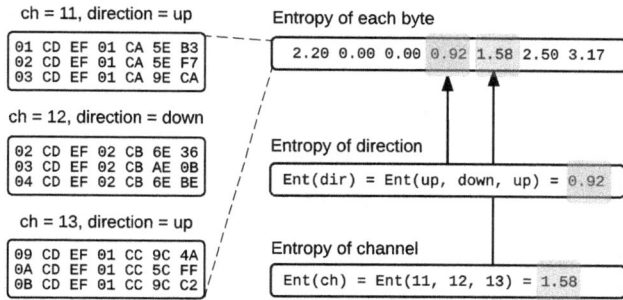

Figure 5: Example of feature test in byte-level analysis module

---

Data: Results of range and entropy tests
Result: Score list for multiple results of range test
$L \leftarrow$ the byte length of packets
$B_k[n] \leftarrow$ k-th result (bitmap) of range test $(0 \leq n < L)$
$H[n] \leftarrow$ a result of entropy test $(0 \leq n < L)$
$scoreList \leftarrow$ an empty list
foreach B_k **do**
    $score \leftarrow 0$
    $entropy_{range} \leftarrow$ the entropy of corresponding range
    for $i \leftarrow 0$ **to** L **do**
        $score \leftarrow score + \dfrac{B_k[i] \times H[i]}{entropy_{range}}$
    end
    $scoreList.\text{append}\,(score)$
end
return $scoreList$

Algorithm 1: Scoring algorithm for results of range test

---

mation describes conditions such as communication channel numbers among 26 physical communication channels in IEEE 802.15.4, specific operations that can be observed by an attacker (e.g., turning on/off or moving directions), capturing locations (for multiple sender-receiver pairs) when packets are captured in a pcap file. In the feature test, entropies for each byte position and each context calculated in the previous test are compared to identify context-related byte positions that have the same entropy value as that of context entropy. If the entropy of the n-th byte position is equal to that of the channel information, then we consider the n-th byte position related to the channel.

An example is given in Figure 5. Three pcap files are recorded in different conditions, and each pcap file contains three packets with a byte length of seven shown in the left side of the figure. In this case, the entities of corresponding context files are (channel, 11) and (direction, up) for the first pcap file, (channel, 12) and (direction, down) for the second, and (channel, 13) and (direction, up) for the last. Entropies of each byte position for nine captured packets and context information (i.e., channel and direction) are shown in the right side of Figure 5. Because the values of entropies are the same as those of channel and direction (0.92 and 1.58 in the fifth and fourth byte positions, respectively), our feature test contemplates that the fifth and fourth byte positions are meaningfully related to channel and direction, regardless of their byte values.

Range Test. To identify another useful piece of information in a group of unknown byte sequences, we classify each byte position by the range of changes of byte values into raw decimal, raw hexadecimal, ASCII decimal, ASCII hexadecimal, sexagesimal, printable, upper-case and lower-case-letter ranges. For example, if the changes in value of one byte position are bounded between 0x30 (character "0") and 0x39 (character "9") in a group or subgroup, then this byte position is classified as both ASCII decimal and printable ranges. In general, sequence number bytes use only decimal or hexadecimal values (both raw and ASCII formats), time stamp bytes are bounded in sexagesimal range, and the value of command bytes is in letters range. In this test, byte positions identified by CRC and n-gram tests as well as zero-entropy byte positions are excluded. As a result, a bitmap that contains ones at the same bit positions as the corresponding byte positions as well as zeros at other bit positions is generated for each range.

Because one range can be either a subset of or overlapped with other ranges, this test can generate multiple results. Therefore, to generate possible spoofing packets efficiently, scoring the multiple results with reasonable criteria is necessary. This scoring process is included in the next module.

5.3 Report Construction

The purpose of the report construction module (ⓒ in Figure 3) is to combine results of five tests in the byte-level analysis module to

reduce entropy, and score overlapped results for some byte positions. In the last stage of this module, reports summarizing all results of automatic analyses are generated for every group and subgroup.

Range Scoring. As explained in the previous subsection, the range test derives multiple results. To determine the results to be used for generating possible spoofing packets, we developed a scoring algorithm that couples the results of range and entropy tests. This algorithm is briefly summarized in Algorithm 1.

In the algorithm, entropies of each byte position bounded in a specific range are reflected in the score of a range test result, with the exception of byte positions identified by CRC and n-gram tests, as well as zero-entropy byte positions. In addition, scores are normalized with the maximum entropy of the specific range. Calculated scores are used to generate possible spoofing packets in the packet generation module.

Entropy Reduction. First, we mark fixed-value byte positions through whole packets in a group or subgroup (i.e., zero entropy). Second, even though actual values of byte positions are not fixed, we can regard them as fixed or limited-valued byte positions based on results of CRC, n-gram, and entropy tests. Therefore we can reduce entropies for some dynamic-value byte positions.

Our rules to reduce entropy are the following. Note that all threshold values in the rules are heuristically chosen.

- In a group or subgroup, if the number of packets that use the same CRC algorithm at the same byte positions in the CRC test is over 90 % of total number of packets, those byte positions are fixed as CRC bytes.

- In a group or subgroup, if the number of packets that reuse the same MAC layer information at the same byte positions in the n-gram test is over 80 % of total number of packets, those byte positions are fixed as the reused values.

- If the range of a byte position is specified by the range test, the values of the byte position are bounded in the specific range.

- If the actual entropy of one byte position is less than half the full entropy of a byte, the values of those byte positions are limited by their existing values in a group and subgroup.

Report Generation. Before spoofing packet generation, every result of previous analyses for each group and subgroup are integrated into a report. Because all tests except the entropy test can have multiple results, we merged results of those tests in order of priority based on the certainty and importance of each test. Byte positions identified in the CRC test are first locked, and then the results of n-gram and feature tests are applied in order. Finally, zero-entropy byte positions are fixed. The results of the range test are not merged exclusively. Instead, they are listed as scores in a report, and the results of the range test with the highest score is used for packet generation. In summary, for each byte position of customized protocol payloads in a group or subgroup, a single merged analysis result and the listed results of the range test are included in a report.

5.4 Packet Generation

Based on reports for each group and subgroup, the packet generation module (Ⓓ in Figure 3) automatically generates pcap files containing possible spoofing packets. Because reports show results based on byte position, we have to assign appropriate values to each byte position for spoofing attacks. Byte positions can be separated into two types: fixed and variable byte positions. From an attacker's point of view, he or she can simply duplicate fixed byte positions for spoofing attacks. By contrast, variable byte positions should be handled analytically based on analysis results rather than brute-forcing for efficient spoofing attacks. WASp generates spoofing packets based on the following three steps.

Selection. According to the number of groups and subgroups, dozens of reports are generated in the report construction module. WASp can generate possible spoofing packets for all reports, but it is considerably time-consuming and inefficient to verify the success or failure of spoofing attacks for every generated packet from all reports. However, because packets in subgroups are also contained in groups, generating possible spoofing packets for groups only is sufficient. In addition, a user can select specific reports for spoofing packet generation by considering contexts or spoofing conditions such as communication direction and target address.

Mutation. Our analysis approach is optimized to reduce entropy by finding meanings and bounding possible values of each byte or field. Naturally, the more we reduce entropy, the fewer the number of possible spoofing packets that are generated. This means excessive entropy reduction can reduce the chances of success in spoofing attacks. Therefore, we can trade entropy reduction for the chance of success. To increase the success rate, we can also mutate a report. For example, if adjacent byte positions with different entropies are in the same range, the maximum value among different entropies can be used for all of them, although one of them can be applied to entropy reduction rules mentioned in Section 5.3. This mutation can be enforced even for fixed byte positions.

Generation. After every process, all possible packets are generated according to the remaining entropies of each byte. These packets are used for spoofing attacks and in our evaluation.

6. EVALUATION

In this section, the performance of WASp is evaluated against two real-world targets: smart plug and PSD systems. Because of the unknown nature of customized protocols, we have no ground truth for our analysis results. Therefore, we use the amount of entropy reduction in our analyses and spoofing success rate in our experiments as evaluation metrics.

6.1 Target Systems

A smart plug system is an intelligent power metering system that basically consists of plug and controller units. The plug unit is controlled wirelessly by the controller unit and can turn the power of connected electrical devices on or off. In addition, it transmits the power usage information of the devices to the controller unit. For these functions, a customized protocol is used as wireless communication between the plug and controller units. We captured 217 packets in two contexts according to the functions of turning on/off and transmitting power usage information, to generate spoofing packets. The other target, a PSD system, prevents tripping and falling accidents at a platform, and it also reduces wind and dust caused by a train. Because the doors of both PSD and a train must be synchronized, PSD communicates with incoming trains wirelessly using a customized protocol. In our experiments, we captured 7,299 packets in 30 contexts which are combinations of five platforms, three trains, and both up and down directions.

We note that choosing target systems to evaluate WASp is limited because identifying whether a WPAN system uses a customized protocol before capturing packets is impossible.

6.2 Evaluation Metrics

For our evaluation, we used two evaluation metrics: the amount of entropy reduction and spoofing success rate. First, the amount of entropy reduction was used to demonstrate the efficiency of the automatic protocol analysis. Entropy is directly related to the number of generated spoofing packets, and too many spoofing packets cannot be transmitted in a reasonable time because of the limited speed of transceivers. For example, KillerBee, which in a SDR transceiver supporting IEEE 802.15.4, can ideally transmit as many as 500 packets per second, which means that nearly nine hours are required to transmit 3-byte brute-forced packets at least. Therefore, entropy must be reduced to a level sufficient to send in a limited time, especially for real-time spoofing attacks. In addition, the successful spoofing rate, which is the second metric, represents the accuracy of WASp. The high success rate proves that the formats and their values of spoofing packets generated by WASp (i.e., the report in Figure 3) are correctly constructed to approximate those of the actual customized protocol.

Therefore, both the amount of entropy reduction and the spoofing success rate must be considered to evaluate the performance of spoofing attacks. We note that although the main goal of this study is not to reveal the target protocol completely, WASp provides meaningful analysis results against the protocol. In addition, the results of WASp can be used to identify the most proper format of target protocols by analyzing successful and failed spoofing packets.

6.3 Evaluation Results

For our evaluation, we placed attacks on smart plug and PSD systems using automatically generated packets by means of WASp. Before actual analyses for generating spoofing packets, improper packets that contain wrong CRCs in MAC and custom layers were filtered out as noise packets through the process described in Section 5.1 and Section 5.2. The change in the number of packets by filtering is shown in Table 3. The numbers of packets that are used for actual analyses are given in the last row of Table 3.

6.3.1 Smart Plug System

For our evaluation, we performed spoofing experiments against a smart plug system because it is a commercial product and under our control. Therefore, for this target system, both metrics were measured by experiments.

Grouping. From the analysis results of packets collected from the smart plug system, we identified three packet formats (i.e., three groups) whose byte lengths were 23, 24, and 35, respectively, and the number of corresponding packets were 22, 135, and 43, respectively.

Table 3: Results of noise packet filtering with CRC in MAC layer and custom layer for both target systems (No custom layer CRC is implemented for the smart plug system.)

	# of Packets (Smart Plug)	# of Packets (PSD)
Originally Captured Packets without Filtering	217	7,299
Remaining Packets after Filtering Wrong MAC Layer CRC	200	6,986
Remaining Packets after Filtering Wrong Custom Layer CRC	200	6,963

These groups had no subgroups. This means that packets in each group are transmitted in only one direction.

Results. The plug unit is targeted for spoofing attack experiments because it is an actuator controlled by the controller unit. Accordingly, possible spoofing packets are generated based on the report of the group with 135 packets and a 24 byte length. From spoofing experiments, we determined that spoofing was successful if any response packet was detected for each spoofing packet.

By WASp (without mutation as described in Section 5.4), a series of possible spoofing packets (Type 1) that has maximally reduced entropy were generated. To enlarge the coverage of spoofing packets, Type 1 was mutated as Type 2 and 3. The last entropy reduction rule in Section 5.3 was not applied for Type 2, and the entropy was increased for Type 3 as the mutation example in Section 5.4. In other words, Type 1 is a subset of Type 2 and 3 for exclusively different byte positions. For each type, entropy reduction rates, the numbers of generated packets, and time duration to transmit all generated packets with a 0.2 seconds delay are shown in Table 4.

Type 1, which is the main type, showed 95.50 % reduced entropy compared to the original entropy. When each packet is transmitted every 0.2 seconds, 1.3 minutes are required to transmit all generated packets theoretically. By mutating Type 1, which increases entropy, the greater the number of spoofing packets that are generated and the more time is required proportionally. To test all packets for Type 3, over two hours are required.

In spoofing experiments, sending packets continuously for approximately two hours is nearly impossible, especially for a real-time spoofing attack. To avoid this practical limitation and for a fair comparison of the three types, we transmitted 100 spoofing packets that were randomly chosen for each type. In addition, we tested for different speeds to transmit packets from 0.002 to 0.9 seconds per packet. All experiments were repeated 100 times. The spoofing success rates were averaged for 100 times of identical experiments as shown in Figure 6.

The results show that the spoofing success rate increased from 0.002 to 0.1 seconds of the time interval according to the increased time interval per packet transmission and then stabilized after 0.2 seconds of the time interval. After stabilization, spoofing success rates for Type 1, 2, and 3 averaged 48.19 %, 5.52 %, and 47.09 %,

Table 4: Automatically generated spoofing packet types against a smart plug system (success rates are averaged over 10 identical experiments.)

	Entropy Reduction Rate	# of packets	Time to transmit all packets (0.2 seconds delay)
Type 1	95.50 %	400	1.3 minutes
Type 2	93.57 %	5,200	17.3 minutes
Type 3	92.04 %	40,000	133.3 minutes

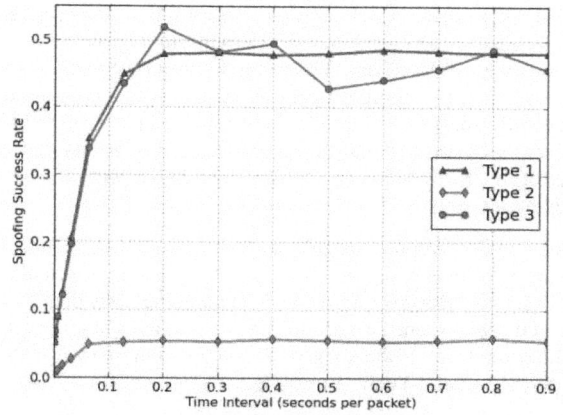

Figure 6: Spoofing success rate according to spoofing time interval from 0.002 to 0.9 seconds per packet (for 100 packets randomly chosen in possible spoofing packets generated by WASp)

respectively. Note that spoofing success rate of Type 1 and Type 3 are impressive results given the circumstances. Spoofing is performed without any internal system information such as current sequence number. Moreover, input datasets only contain limited number of packets during limited time span, making it impossible to guess the exact packet format.

When the time interval is too short, success rate is quite small, maybe because the device cannot handle packets in such a short time interval. Therefore, the graph shows the sharp increments of the spoofing success rate as the interval increases from 0 to 0.1 or 0.2 seconds. This means that for the spoofing test using spoofing packets generated by WASp, we cannot transmit spoofing packets and receive responses too quickly. Moreover, the total time for the spoofing test can be limited in some conditions, especially when a target system is not in our control. Hence, those packets should be generated efficiently. In other words, we have to lower the entropy of customized protocols during the analysis stage.

In the case of Type 2, the success rate significantly dropped compared to that of Type 1. Because the ratio of success rate drop between Type 1 and 2 (48.19 % and 5.52 %, respectively) is inversely proportional to the ratio of their packet numbers (400 and 5,200 in Table 4, respectively), this drop means that most of those additionally generated packets failed to spoof. Based on this comparison, we can remove useless values for a particular byte, which is also helpful in further protocol analysis. While it utilizes two orders of magnitude more spoofing packets, average success rates for Type 3 is lower than Type 1. This is due to the sampling effect. For each type, we choose 100 samples randomly as discussed above.

6.3.2 PSD System

In contrast to our evaluation of the smart plug system, we could use only the amount of entropy reduction as an evaluation metric in that of the PSD system. Because of legal and safety concerns, we could not perform spoofing attacks and were unable to obtain a spoofing success rate in this evaluation. However, the entropy reduction results suggest that our analysis is effective and that a spoofing attack in real-world situation is possible. Moreover, we strongly believe that packets generated by WASp can spoof a PSD system in a real-world situation because the entropy of PSD's customized protocol is reduced sufficiently.

Grouping. We clustered 7,299 packets into 15 groups according to packet length before noise packet filtering. After filtering, we excluded 336 packets, which represent only 4.6 % of the originally captured packets. However, among 15 groups, nine groups and two subgroups were filtered out. The removed groups consisted of a few packets and the number of these packets was not enough to automatically analyze. Therefore, those removed packets could be considered as noise for analysis. In addition, this means that the number of reports to which an attacker should refer was effectively reduced by filtering.

Results. Table 5 represents the results of entropy reduction by means of byte-level analysis (Ⓑ in Figure 3) and report analysis (Ⓒ in Figure 3). However, three of them contained less than 0.2 % of the total packets, and two groups only contained a single packet. After filtering, three of the six groups contained more than 99.8 % of captured packets. Their entropy reduction results are listed in Table 5.

Using WASp, the entropies of byte positions are decreased by anchoring those byte positions as CRC, reused MAC data, and context information, and then applying our entropy reduction rules (Section 5.3) to collected packets of the customized protocol. The amount of entropy reduction for each group is summarized in the last row of Table 5. The average entropy reduction rate is 88.11 % for three dominant groups.

7. DISCUSSION

Ground Truth. Customized protocols are proprietary protocols that have no accessible documentation related to protocol specification. We cannot know the exact protocol format. In other words, no ground truth exists to check whether packets are generated in the correct format. In addition, the target systems are a black box when an attacker has generally no privilege against program source code or firmware. Therefore, we evaluated our tool by performing spoofing attacks against the target system and measuring the attack success rate. As we mentioned in Section 1, the initial purpose of this research is to improve the security of wireless customized systems by automating spoofing attacks. Therefore, we infer the correctness of our analysis results through the success rate of spoofing attacks. In other words, if the spoofing attack with generated packets is effective, then we can explicitly evaluate the accuracy of our automatic analysis without the original packet format.

Selection Bias. Our tool requires sufficiently many packets to derive exact analytical results for a high success rate of spoofing attacks. For example, if we assume that our tool collects packets for only a single day and one field in the collected packets indicates the date, this date field will be considered as a fixed field. Therefore, packets that are generated based on this analysis result can counter a spoofing attack on another day if the target checks the packet generation date. Not only as in this case, but also entropy, range, and feature tests may be incorrect because of the selection bias of collected packets, and this will adversely affect the quality of reports and packets. Therefore, users must consider possible field cases and collect packets that can cover all cases with sufficient randomness to remove selection bias.

Table 5: Results of entropy reduction for the customized protocol used in a PSD system

	Group 1	Group 2	Group 3
Number of Packets	418	2,615	3,916
Custom Layer Packet Size	7 bytes	11 bytes	15 bytes
Enrtopy Reduction Rate	96.26 %	90.04 %	78.01 %

Incorrect Implementation of IEEE 802.15.4 CRC. Some vendors have implemented IEEE 802.15.4 CRC inaccurately on their IoT devices. For example, we collected IEEE 802.15.4 packets from a wireless parking space detection (WPSD) system in a hypermarket, and we found that they had wrong CRC values. Systems that possessed an extremely simple function and short wireless packet structure such as a WPSD system may work with CRC error. However, we could not analyze the protocol because we cannot guarantee that there is no error in the packets, as such errors will impair accurate analysis. Thus, this kind of system is out of scope for this study, and our tool filters packets that have a wrong MAC layer CRC or application layer CRC.

IEEE 802.15.4 Family Protocols. IEEE 802.15.4 defines only the PHY and MAC layers, and IEEE 802.15.4 family protocols such as ZigBee, Z-Wave, and WirelessHART have their own network layer on the MAC layer of IEEE 802.15.4. Although these protocols are based on IEEE 802.15.4, they are not within the scope of our tool. We assume that reusing the source and destination addresses and poor integrity checks are the characteristics of customized protocols. However, the family protocols do not have these characteristics. In particular, they support strong integrity checks such as keyed-hash message authentication code (HMAC), so generating spoofing packets is impossible.

8. CONCLUSION

The main purpose of this study is to analyze and reconstruct unknown wireless customized protocols over IEEE 802.15.4 automatically. For this purpose, we classify the characteristics of these protocols and develop a novel methodology to analyze and reconstruct these protocols based on those characteristics. In addition, applying the methodology, we implement an automated wireless customized protocol spoofer called WASp for analysis and spoofing packet generation. Compared to manual analysis, WASp is proved to be much faster and to generate efficient analysis reports with five kinds of byte-level investigation. In particular, results of byte-level statistical analyses including entropy and range tests revealed that WASp identifies meaningful byte positions, bounds their values, and narrows the coverage down for spoofing packet generation efficiently. For evaluation, possible spoofing packets are generated based on the analyses by WASp, and we apply those packets to real-world commercial applications such as smart plug and PSD systems. Results reveal that, on average, our tool could reduce approximately 90 % of entropies for both target systems, and approximately 48 % of generated packets could spoof one of them.

Although several previous works have studied automatic reverse engineering of network protocols for intrusion prevention and detection, they focused on application-level protocols as their targets. Thus, they are not fully applicable to our target protocols, which possess little context information because of low-power requirements. Consequently, to the best of our knowledge, this study is the first to implement an automated protocol reverse-engineering tool specialized for unknown customized protocols over IEEE 802.15.4. We believe that WASp is a useful tool to understand customized protocols with unknown structures that do not include textual data. In addition, WASp can be used to secure those protocols and prevent potential spoofing attacks for IoT networks that use WPAN.

9. ACKNOWLEDGMENT

This research was supported by Next-Generation Information Computing Development Program through the National Research Foundation of Korea (NRF) funded by the Ministry of Science, ICT & Future Planning (No. NRF-2014M3C4A7030648)

10. REFERENCES

[1] J. Antunes, N. Neves, and P. Verissimo. Reverse Engineering of Protocols from Network Traces. In *Proceedings of the 18th Working Conference on Reverse Engineering (WCRE)*, Limerick, Ireland, Oct. 2011.

[2] I. Bermudez, A. Tongaonkar, M. Iliofotou, M. Mellia, and M. M. Munafo. Automatic Protocol Field Inference for Deeper Protocol Understanding. In *Proceedings of the 14th IFIP Networking Conference (NETWORKING)*, Toulouse, France, May 2015.

[3] B. Bloessl, C. Leitner, F. Dressler, and C. Sommer. A GNU Radio-based IEEE 802.15. 4 Testbed. *12. GI/ITG FACHGESPRÄCH SENSORNETZE*, 2013.

[4] G. Bossert, F. Guihéry, and G. Hiet. Towards Automated Protocol Reverse Engineering Using Semantic Information. In *Proceedings of the 9th ACM Symposium on InformAtion, Computer and Communications Security (ASIACCS)*, Kyoto, Japan, June 2014.

[5] J. Caballero, P. Poosankam, C. Kreibich, and D. Song. Dispatcher: Enabling Active Botnet Infiltration using Automatic Protocol Reverse-Engineering. In *Proceedings of the 16th ACM Conference on Computer and Communications Security (CCS)*, Chicago, Illinois, Nov. 2009.

[6] J. Caballero, H. Yin, Z. Liang, and D. Song. Polyglot : Automatic Extraction of Protocol Message Format using Dynamic Binary Analysis. In *Proceedings of the 14th ACM Conference on Computer and Communications Security (CCS)*, Alexandria, VA, Oct.–Nov. 2007.

[7] P. M. Comparetti, G. Wondracek, C. Kruegel, and E. Kirda. Prospex: Protocol Specification Extraction. In *Proceedings of the 30th IEEE Symposium on Security and Privacy (Oakland)*, Oakland, CA, May 2009.

[8] W. Cui, J. Kannan, and H. J. Wang. Discoverer: Automatic Protocol Reverse Engineering from Network Traces. In *Proceedings of the 16th Usenix Security Symposium (Security)*, Boston, MA, Aug. 2007.

[9] W. Cui, V. Paxson, N. C. Weaver, and R. H. Katz. Protocol-Independent Adaptive Replay of Application Dialog. In *Proceedings of the 13th Annual Network and Distributed System Security Symposium (NDSS)*, San Diego, CA, Feb. 2006.

[10] W. Cui, M. Peinado, K. Chen, H. J. Wang, and L. Irun-Briz. Tupni: Automatic Reverse Engineering of Input Formats. In *Proceedings of the 15th ACM Conference on Computer and Communications Security (CCS)*, Alexandria, VA, Oct.–Nov. 2008.

[11] Ettus Research. USRP N2x0 Series Device Manual. http://files.ettus.com/manual/page_usrp2.html. [Online; accessed 12-March-2016].

[12] Gerald Combs and others. Wireshark. https://www.wireshark.org/. [Online; accessed 12-March-2016].

[13] S. Gorbunov and A. Rosenbloom. AutoFuzz: Automated Network Protocol Fuzzing Framework. *IJCSNS*, 10(8):239, 2010.

[14] Q. Huang, P. P. C. Lee, and Z. Zhang. Exploiting Intra-Packet Dependency for Fine-Grained Protocol Format Inference. In *Proceedings of the 14th IFIP Networking Conference (NETWORKING)*, Toulouse, France, May 2015.

[15] IEEE Computer Society. IEEE Standard for Local and metropolitan area networks - Part 15.4: Low-Rate Wireless Personal Area Networks (LR-WPANs), 2011.

[16] T. Kitagawa, M. Hanaoka, and K. Kono. AspFuzz: A State-aware Protocol Fuzzer based on Application-layer Protocols. In *Proceedings of the 15th IEEE symposium on Computers and Communications (ISCC)*, Riccione, Italy, June 2010.

[17] Z. Lin, X. Jiang, D. Xu, and X. Zhang. Automatic Protocol Format Reverse Engineering through Context-Aware Monitored Execution. In *Proceedings of the 15th Annual Network and Distributed System Security Symposium (NDSS)*, San Diego, CA, Feb. 2008.

[18] C. Năvălici. PyCRC 1.21-Python CRC Calculations Modules. https://pypi.python.org/pypi/PyCRC, 2015. [Online; accessed 12-March-2016].

[19] C. Rossow and C. J. Dietrich. PROVEX: Detecting Botnets with Encrypted Command and Control Channels. In *Detection of Intrusions and Malware, and Vulnerability Assessment*. Springer, 2013.

[20] A. Tongaonkar, R. Keralapura, and A. Nucci. SANTaClass: A Self Adaptive Network Traffic Classification System. In *Proceedings of the 12th IFIP Networking Conference (NETWORKING)*, Brooklyn, NY, May 2013.

[21] P. Tsankov, M. T. Dashti, and D. Basin. SECFUZZ: Fuzz-testing Security Protocols. In *Proceedings of the 7th International Workshop on Automation of Software Test (AST)*, Zurich, Switzerland, June 2012.

[22] Y. Wang, X. Yun, M. Z. Shafiq, L. Wang, A. X. Liu, Z. Zhang, D. Yao, Y. Zhang, and L. Guo. A Semantics Aware Approach to Automated Reverse Engineering Unknown Protocols. In *Proceedings of the 20th IEEE International Conference on Network Protocols (ICNP)*, Austin, TX, Oct.–Nov. 2012.

[23] Z. Wang, X. Jiang, W. Cui, X. Wang, and M. Grace. ReFormat: Automatic Reverse Engineering of Encrypted Messages. In *Proceedings of the 14th European Symposium on Research in Computer Security*, Saint Malo, France, Sept. 2009.

[24] J. Wright. KillerBee. https://code.google.com/p/killerbee/. [Online; accessed 12-March-2016].

[25] Z. Zhang, Z. Zhang, P. P. C. Lee, Y. Liu, and G. Xie. ProWord: An Unsupervised Approach to Protocol FeatureWord Extraction. In *Proceedings of the 33rd IEEE International Conference on Computer Communications (INFOCOM)*, Toronto, Canada, Apr. 2014.

[26] J. Zhao, S. Chen, S. Liang, B. Cui, and X. Song. RFSM: A Smart Fuzzing Algorithm Based on Regression FSM. In *Proceedings of the 8th International Conference on P2P, Parallel, Grid, Cloud and Internet Computing (3PGCIC)*, Compiegne, France, Oct. 2013.

Smart-Phones Attacking Smart-Homes*

Vijay Sivaraman
Univesity of New South Wales
Sydney, NSW, Australia
vijay@unsw.edu.au

Dominic Chan,Dylan Earl
Univesity of New South Wales
Sydney, NSW, Australia
dominiczchan@gmail.com,
dylan.earl@me.com

Roksana Boreli
National ICT Australia
Sydney, NSW, Australia
Roksana.Boreli@nicta.com.au

ABSTRACT

The explosion in Internet-connected household devices, such as light-bulbs, smoke-alarms, power-switches, and webcams, is creating new vectors for attacking "smart-homes" at an unprecedented scale. Common perception is that smart-home IoT devices are protected from Internet attacks by the perimeter security offered by home routers. In this paper we demonstrate how an attacker can infiltrate the home network via a doctored smart-phone app. Unbeknownst to the user, this app scouts for vulnerable IoT devices within the home, reports them to an external entity, and modifies the firewall to allow the external entity to directly attack the IoT device. The ability to infiltrate smart-homes via doctored smart-phone apps demonstrates that home routers are poor protection against Internet attacks and highlights the need for increased security for IoT devices.

1. INTRODUCTION

The Internet-of-Things (IoT) is growing at a rapid rate: Gartner predicts that deployments will grow from 5 billion in 2015 to 25 billion by 2020 [11]. The boom in Internet-connected household devices, such as light-bulbs, cameras, smoke-alarms, and door-locks, is fueling the growth of the "smart-home"; indeed surveys [14] indicate that 51% of people in the US are willing to pay in excess of $500 for a well-equipped smart-home, with family safety, property protection, lighting/energy management, and pet monitoring as top motivators. While the smart-home brings huge benefits to consumers, who can lock/unlock doors from miles away, get instant alerts when smoke is detected in the house, and control lighting systems remotely, it is accompanied by substantial risks to privacy and security: hackers have been known to intrude on the home via baby-monitor cameras [10], and even take control of light-bulbs [9] and power-switches [16] remotely.

*This work was funded by the Australian Research Council (ARC) grant DP150100564.

WiSec'16 , July 18-22, 2016, Darmstadt, Germany
© 2016 ACM. ISBN 978-1-4503-4270-4/16/07...$15.00
DOI: http://dx.doi.org/10.1145/2939918.2939925

Manufacturers have unfortunately been lax in embedding appropriate security protections in their consumer IoT devices, due to multiple reasons: business pressures force them to rush to market, revenues are derived from unit-sales rather than ongoing service, and security measures require skills and resources that add to costs. In spite of poor security on IoT devices shipping today, there is fortunately security at the perimeter of the network where they are deployed - a typical broadband router/gateway used in the home today, by virtue of its in-built NAT and firewall capability, prevents outside entities from launching gratuitous attacks on IoT devices inside the home network. For example, IoT devices like the Phillips Hue light-bulb and Belkin WeMo power-switch can be controlled with little or no authentication credentials [19], but are saved from being attacked openly on the Internet today by virtue of the home gateway behind which they sit; this is a consequence of the fact that an incoming packet would bear the public IP address assigned to the house, and the gateway would not know which of the multiple devices in the house, each with its own private IP address, to send the packet to. This "firewall" feature, a side-effect of network address translation (NAT) between the public and private IP addresses, protects IoT devices in the home from direct Internet attacks.

We believe that the inherent perimeter security provided by the home gateway is breeding complacency about the vulnerability of the smart-home to Internet attacks. In this paper we argue that the NAT/firewall protection is somewhat illusory, and can be easily penetrated by malware on users' smart-phones. We take an existing application from Apple's AppStore, instrument it to include malware, and get it approved as a legitimate app. We intentionally chose the Apple platform since it has tighter restrictions on what an app can do, and a more stringent approval process, than the Android platform. We then install and operate the instrumented app within selected homes (no human subjects were used for this trial, other than the members of this project team), and show how we can trigger it to scout for IoT devices in the home and report them to a server we operate in the cloud. The "reconnaissance" performed by our malware, which could not have been done from outside the home network, gives the attacker information about the IoT landscape within the house. Armed with this information, we then show how specific devices within the home can be attacked from outside. Our malware, when triggered appropriately, communicates with the home gateway (using Universal Plug-n-Play or UPnP) to modify firewall settings so that Internet traffic directed to a specific port is forwarded to the victim IoT device, thereby allowing arbitrarily crafted attacks to penetrate the home. Once done, the malware can restore firewall configuration to remove trace of the attack, or keep it open for future attacks.

We show that all the above are real, not hypothetical. Our instrumented app was on the Apple AppStore (for only a brief period due to ethical reasons), we used it to discover several IoT devices in multiple homes, we have used it to surreptitiously modify firewall configuration on home gateways from multiple vendors, and we have demonstrated how an attacker can compromise multiple IoT devices (including a Belkin WeMo power switch and a D-Link IP camera) previously thought secure behind NAT/firewall. Our attack method is general, in that it can be applied to a wide range of IoT devices, and can be evolved to exploit new vulnerabilities as they are discovered, without having to upgrade the app. Our demonstration of the "infiltration" of the smart-home via a smart-phone app raises the prospect that the security provided by home gateways may be illusory, and the threat to smart-home IoT devices from large-scale Internet attacks more real than thought before.

The rest of this paper is organized as follows: §2 reviews threats to smart-home IoT devices and current defense approaches. In §3 we outline the design and implementation of our attacks that bypass the home perimeter security, and demonstrate and evaluate its performance in §4. The paper is concluded in §5 with a discussion on the impact for emerging smart-homes.

2. BACKGROUND

2.1 IoT Security Threats

The vast heterogeneity in smart-home IoT devices makes their attack vectors large, and it very challenging to map out the entire threat space. Prior works have exposed serious security flaws in numerous smart-home devices: for example our earlier work [19] shows that Internet-connected smart-bulbs and power-switches are easily compromised because they have poor authentication controls, while [12] shows that digital photo-frames, cameras, and speakers transmit data in plain-text that is easy to snoop upon to compromise user privacy. In addition to the above security flaws that have been revealed in researchers' labs, there is growing evidence of large-scale real-world security breaches: in Jan 2014 it was reported that a smart-fridge was among 100,000 devices that were compromised to send out spam emails [17]. As the adoption of smart-homes increases, security of IoT becomes a growing concern.

2.2 IoT Security Defenses

The growing importance of IoT security has led to a flurry of activity to develop device-level solutions, both by large device manufacturers and by standards bodies: for example, security frameworks are being developed by the Online Trust Alliance [3], the M2I security framework [2], IEEE P2413 [1], and Google Brillo/Weave [5], to name but a few. While these are worthwhile efforts, they require the security solutions to be embedded in the IoT device, which will take a long time to mature and gain wide adoption. In the meantime, researchers are developing non-embedded solutions that can protect IoT devices by inspecting traffic at the network level [21, 22]. Such efforts are still in the early research stages and not ready for deployment.

The only thing that protects insecure devices like light-bulbs, power-switches, webcams, photo-frames, etc. in the smart-home today is the home router. As mentioned earlier, the home router, by virtue of its NAT functionality that translates between the public and private IP addresses, drops unsolicited traffic from the Internet entering the home. This not only prevents Internet attackers from accessing the device, but also hides them so an attacker does not even know what IoT devices are in the home. We will show in this paper that this over-reliance on the home router is dangerous; an attacker can infiltrate the smart-home using malware on the user's smart-phone, and once on the inside, can not only scout for vulnerable devices, but also expose them to external attack with ease.

3. ATTACK DESIGN & IMPLEMENTATION

The objective of our attack is to bypass the perimeter security in home routers. A home router typically translates between the single external-facing public IP address assigned to the house and multiple internal-facing IP addresses assigned to devices within the home. A side-effect of this network address translation (NAT) is that unsolicited traffic from the Internet cannot penetrate the house, thereby providing firewall perimeter security. Our approach to penetrating this perimeter security is to embed malware into smart-phone apps that the user unwittingly runs inside the home network.

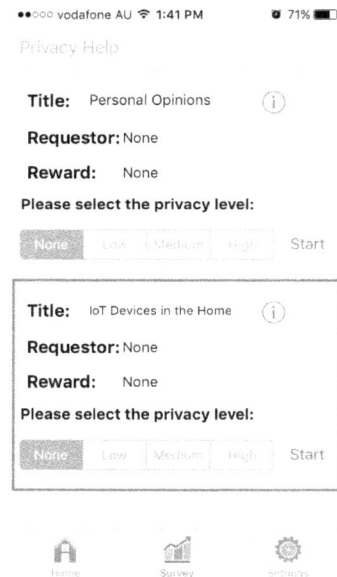

Figure 1: Survey app with malware trigger

3.1 The iPhone App

Mobile apps are susceptible to tampering, and App piracy is big business. We chose to work with iOS to demonstrate our attacks, since Apple operates a more secure ecosystem than Android; indeed independent analysis by MetaIntelli in 2015 found that over 90% of the 96,000 Android apps analyzed from the Google Play store had unprotected binary code [6], while Nokia's malware report for 2015 shows that 18 out of the 20 top smartphone infections were on the Android platform [18]. Our malware was inserted into an existing privacy-preserving survey app in the Apple AppStore, called Loki, resubmitted as a version upgrade, and was approved by Apple for release. We briefly describe the App and how it meets our design objectives.

Front end: We used a preexisting app to conceal our malware. This app has been on the AppStore for two years and was designed for users to take surveys. We chose this app as it had: (a) previously been released, so we could be sure that the underlying app itself would not affect the result of the app review process of our malware laden version, (b) legitimate uses of the networking APIs to fetch surveys, so that network activity by the malware would not arouse suspicion, and (c) no active user base so it was extremely unlikely that someone outside our group would download the malware laden app in the short period it was available on the AppStore. Our use of a preexisting app also demonstrates the ease with which our malware is embedded. As there is no tight integration between the user facing app and our malware it is feasible that our malware could be attached to apps en-masse, as has occurred with the case of the XcodeGhost malware [8].

Trigger: Packet sniffing of our modified survey app would reveal that our malware was scouting for devices, a functionality that is not typical in a survey app. In order to minimize the chance of detection by Apple in the app review process, we suppressed the malware from starting until a trigger condition had been met. Because our malware is embedded in a survey app we decided that an appropriate trigger condition would be the selection of a survey with the trigger phrase "IoT Devices", as illustrated in Fig. 1. By manipulating the list of surveys available at the server which delivers the surveys to the app, we are able to remote-control the triggering of the malware. Our use of the trigger phrase above is meant to target users who have some knowledge of the Internet of Things and hence more likely to own IoT devices, but any arbitrary trigger can be used in general.

Secrecy: Our malware performs network scans and transmissions, which can interfere with the responsiveness of the app, affecting user experience. We originally implemented the device discovery code in a synchronous manner, using POSIX sockets that blocked the user interface. Our initial experiments revealed that this did not scale well to a large number of IoT devices, and led to noticeable degradation in user experience. We therefore reimplemented our IoT device discovery process using the asynchronous `CocoaAsync-Socket` library, a socket wrapper that runs in a separate thread. This not only allows our app to scale to a large environment with many IoT devices, but also better decouples the front-end app from the malware, allowing the malware to be embedded more easily into other apps.

Generality: Our malware is designed to be a general tool that an attacker can use to target a multiplicity of IoT devices, not just one specific IoT device. This allows the attacker to target new IoT devices as they emerge in the market, or existing IoT devices with updated firmware, without requiring the user to upgrade the infected app. Our malware therefore has limited embedded intelligence; instead it works in conjunction with a cloud-hosted server that holds the attack logic for various IoT devices. This approach makes the attack many-fold more effective and scalable than a local attack on a specific IoT device from the app itself.

Functions: Our malware performs two functions. The first part, elaborated in §3.2, is able to scout the local net-

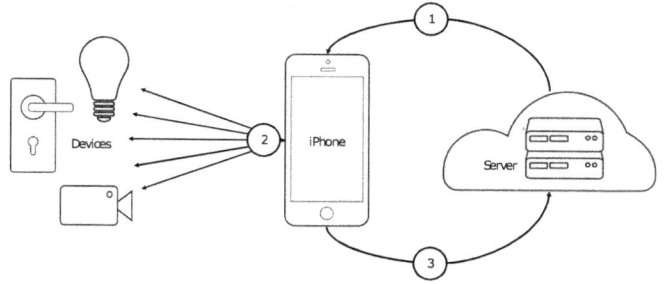

Figure 2: Malware scanning for IoT devices

work for IoT devices and relay this information back to our attack server. The scouting is done using Simple Service Discovery Protocol (SSDP), and information on discovered devices is uploaded to our server through an HTTP POST API. The second function, detailed in §3.3, is able to configure port mappings on the home router in order to give the external attack server direct access to a specific IoT device in the home. The malware fetches the appropriate instruction from our attack server using an HTTP GET request, and executes the port mapping on the home router by using a UPnP command that residential Internet gateway devices from most vendors support.

3.2 Scouting for IoT Devices

Fig. 2 shows the steps involved in scouting for IoT devices in the home. In step ① the malware is remotely triggered. In our case, the trigger happens when the server sends to the mobile app a survey containing the keyword "IoT Devices", as illustrated in Fig. 1.

Once triggered, in step ② our malware scans for IoT devices in the home. There is no "one" protocol for discovering IoT devices. A multitude of standards exist, including UPnP, Alljoyn, Bonjour, and IoTivity amongst others. For illustration, in this paper we have chosen to focus our efforts on UPnP, since it is also the most widely implemented. UPnP is a package of network protocols that allow devices to quickly and automatically establish their presence in the network. Devices which implement UPnP are designed to be able to interface with other networked devices straight out of the box with minimal configuration.

Simple Service Discovery Protocol (SSDP) is the protocol adopted by UPnP that facilitates the automatic discovery and identification of devices connected to the local network. Its widespread use by devices, including those which do not implement any other UPnP technologies, makes it an ideal choice for our malware to search for devices on the local network. We note that SSDP discovery on the home network can only be performed from within the home network; hence the app on the user's smart-phone can do so, but not any external entity on the Internet. SSDP searches are initiated by sending a multicast search packet (MSEARCH) over UDP to the multicast address 239.255.255.250 with default port 1900 as assigned by the Internet Assigned Numbers Authority (IANA), and as shown in Fig. 3. Devices reply to MSEARCH packets by sending a packet with basic information. A URL to a device description file is included in the packet under the location tag.

```
M-SEARCH * HTTP/1.1
HOST:239.255.255.250:1900
MAN:"ssdp:discover"
ST:ssdp:all
MX:3
```

Figure 3: An example of the body of an MSEARCH packet; to discover all devices we set the search target ST to ssdp:all

Our malware scouts for devices over both WiFi and bluetooth low energy (BLE). BLE devices send an advertisement packet periodically. Depending on the device the period between advertisements can be as short as 20ms or as long as 10.24 seconds. Other devices scanning for BLE devices can respond to these advertisement packets in order to connect and learn more information. As advertisements occur with a max period of 10.24 seconds, an 11-second interval sufficiently captures all BLE devices in the local environment. Since this is also a reasonable amount of time for the WiFi scouting to complete, we utilize the 11-second mark as a convenient time to halt the malware's discovery process.

In step ③, our malware packages and uploads the responses to the external server. We handle each response packet on a rolling basis. For each packet we locate the associated device description xml file and parse it to build a dictionary of device metadata and services offered by that device. Once parsing of the xml is finished we upload the dictionary as a JSON string to our server via an HTTP POST request. Examples of devices our malware discovers include light-bulbs, webcams, power-switches, and fitbits; specific devices of interest will be demonstrated in §4.

3.3 Attacking IoT Devices

Once our malware discovers the IoT devices in the home and reports them to the external server, an attack on any chosen IoT device can be initiated, following the steps shown in Fig. 4. In step ④, the server instructs the malware, using an HTTP GET request, on the parameters of the desired port-mapping so it can directly access the victim IoT device across the home router. The port-mapping mechanism configures the home router to map an incoming packet from the Internet, addressed to a specific transport-layer port at the home's public IP address, to a specific private IP address and port within the home; in other words, it allows specific unsolicited Internet traffic to enter the home.

Equipped with the parameters of the port-mapping, in step ⑤ our malware issues a UPnP command to set the desired port-mapping on the home router. Most off-the-shelf routers by default support automatic port-mapping via UPnP, in order to allow services such as peer-to-peer file sharing, user-hosted game servers, and video calling to function automatically without requiring manual configuration. Unfortunately, it is also what makes our attack vector a serious security threat for IoT devices. The UPnP protocol stack has no in-built security mechanism, and allows any host on the local network to issue commands without any authentication [13]; though there have been efforts to secure UPnP [20], such extensions are not implemented on common residential gateways (we have tried models from TP-LINK, Linksys and Netgear). Our app is therefore able

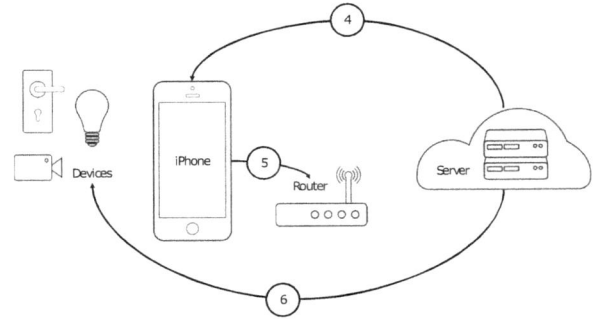

Figure 4: Malware setting up IoT attack

to create arbitrary port-mappings on the residential gateway. Our malware identifies the local IP address and port number of the home router from its earlier scan by looking for the `WANIPConnection` service that identifies a router. It therefore directs its port-mapping UPnP command to it, using a SOAP-based command sent over HTTP, as shown in Fig. 5. Here `remoteHost`, `externalPort`, `internalPort` and `internalClient` are the port-mapping parameters the malware obtains from our attack server.

```
<s:Envelope
xmlns:s="http://schemas.xmlsoap.org/soap/envelope/"
s:encodingStyle="http://schemas.xmlsoap.org/soap/encoding"\>
<s:Body>
<u:AddPortMapping xmlns:u="urn:schemas-upnp-org:
service:WANIPConnection:1"\>
<NewRemoteHost>{remoteHost}</NewRemoteHost>
<NewExternalPort>{externalPort}</NewExternalPort>
<NewProtocol>{protocol}</NewProtocol>
<NewInternalPort>{internalPort}</NewInternalPort>
<NewInternalClient>{internalClient}</NewInternalClient>
<NewEnabled>{enabled}</NewEnabled>
<NewPortMappingDescription>{mappingDescription}
</NewPortMappingDescription>
<NewLeaseDuration>{leaseDuration}</NewLeaseDuration>
</u:AddPortMapping>
</s:Body>
</s:Envelope>
```

Figure 5: The structure of an UPnP WANIPConnection AddPortMapping command.

Once the port-mappings have taken effect, the external server has direct access to the IoT device in the home. Depicted as step ⑥, it can now attack the device to exploit known vulnerabilities, such as poor authentication credentials. As we will demonstrate in the next section, these vulnerabilities which were earlier limited to the home network, have now been exposed to the Internet, allowing an outside entity to take control of the smart-home in spite of the perimeter security provided by the home router.

4. EXPERIMENTAL EVALUATION

4.1 Setup and Default Behavior

Our experimental setup is shown in Fig. 6. We emulate a home environment in our lab, comprising two IoT devices: a D-Link DCS5300G camera and a Belkin WeMo switch. Both have known vulnerabilities, in that they lack authentication

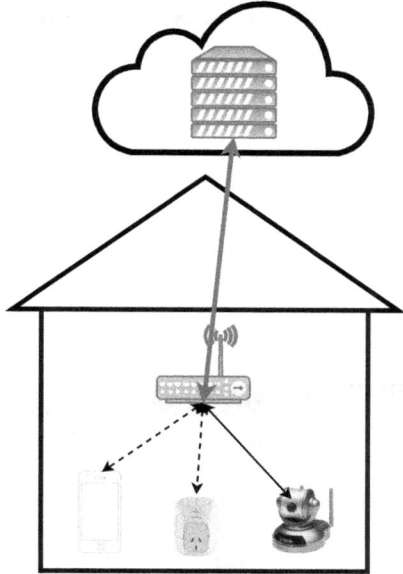

Figure 6: Experimental setup showing the cloud-based attack server, a Netgear R7000 wireless router, an iPhone, a Belkin WeMo switch and a D-Link camera.

credentials. The D-Link Internet camera comes out of the box with no credentials required to access the device, and similarly the WeMo switch will accept a `SetBinaryState` on/off command from any entity over its command port [15].

The IoT devices connect to the Internet via an off-the-shelf home router, the Netgear Nighthawk R7000 Wireless router in our case. The router is operated with default configurations, and assigns private IP addresses to the IoT devices. We operate an attack server in the cloud, that has scripts for attacking both IoT devices. We verified that attacks from the server do not reach the IoT devices (even if the server has all required information about the devices), since the home router by default drops all unsolicited incoming packets.

4.2 Enabling the Malware

We downloaded the survey app "Loki", containing the malware, from the Apple AppStore and installed it on an iPhone. We emphasize that no subjects other than the researchers in this project downloaded the app, and it was rapidly withdrawn from the AppStore once we had verified its functionality. We then created a survey questionnaire on the app server that contained our trigger phrase, as shown in Fig. 1. We then took the trigger survey on the iPhone, which caused our malware to begin scouting for WiFi and BLE devices in the home. We could see the HTTP POST messages coming to the server. Our server takes the body of these requests with the information of the discovered devices and stores it in a database. This is reflected by the server's front-end webpage, as shown in Fig. 7 depicting the uuid of the devices seen in the scans. Fig. 7(a) shows the D-Link camera details, including the manufacturer, model number and description, public IP address of the house, and the URL of the device including its private IP address. Fig. 7(b) shows similar details of the Belkin WeMo switch. We tested the malware in multiple homes, and found the reconnaissance by the malware to detect many kinds of devices, including the

home router itself, which has the `WANIPConnection` device-type. This ability to discover household devices would have been nearly impossible without the infiltration of the home by the malware.

4.3 Attacking the IoT Devices

Once the malware thread in the app has completed the discovery process, it begins sending GET requests to the server to fetch port-mapping parameters in order to punch holes through NAT and expose the selected local devices. In our experiment the server, having detected the WeMo switch amongst the detected devices, instructs the malware to map traffic to port 49154 (the port on which the WeMo is listening to commands, as shown in Fig. 7(b)) to Internal IP address 192.168.1.128 (the private address of the WeMo switch). The malware sends a UPnP message to the home router to do so, and this succeeds. Thereafter, the attack server is able to send appropriately formatted commands to the home's public IP address on port 49154, which get forwarded by the router to the WeMo switch. Since the WeMo switch does not implement any authentication, the attack server is able to control it remotely, turning it off and on at will. Similarly, we were able to instruct the malware to configure port-mapping on the home router to redirect traffic from our attack server addressed to port 80 to the D-Link DCS5300G Internet Security Camera. With this, the camera's web interface was available via the Internet, and the attack server was able to exercise full control over the camera.

5. DISCUSSION AND CONCLUSIONS

We have demonstrated in this paper that it is possible to release malware-laden smart-phone apps that can circumvent the firewall protection offered by home routers. Specifically, the malware can scout the home network for IoT devices, and expose them at will to external attack. This has far-reaching implications. An attacker can use such malware to build a database of household IoT devices, while also creating port-mappings on the home routers in readiness for a future attack. An attacker can thus launch a large-scale attack against these households at a time of their choosing, or worse yet, offer this as a service to other malicious entities. In some ways this parallels the large-scale DDoS attacks prevalent today (such as the DD4BC extortion scheme [4]) that abuse the SSDP, DNS, and NTP protocols to amplify attacks on victims, with significant economic costs.

Fixing the security problems demonstrated in this paper is not easy. Security extensions to the UPnP protocol, though available [7], are unlikely to be implemented by home router manufacturers, since their incentive is limited to making it simple for non-technical users to run peer-to-peer applications and game-servers that need to discover network presence and establish network services. Screening mobile Apps to identify malware is also non-trivial, since Apps may legitimately access UPnP services, or change behavior via a trigger (like ours) once they have passed through the screening process. Ideally, IoT device manufacturers should be embedding better security in their devices and reducing reliance on perimeter security; however, this may take a long time to eventuate. In the intermin, it might be worthwhile investing in security solutions that analyze network traffic to deduce illegitimate access, along the lines of the proposals in [21, 22].

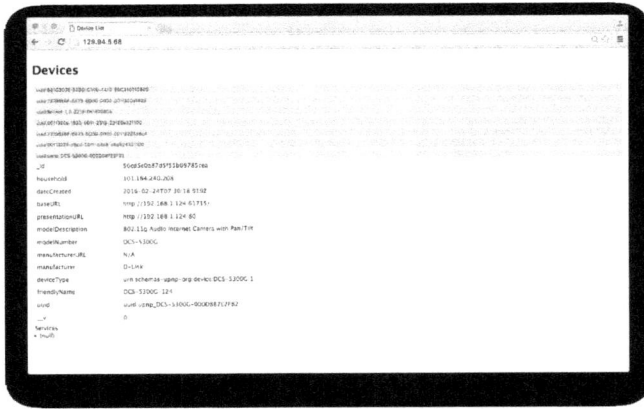

(a) D-Link webcam   (b) WeMo switch

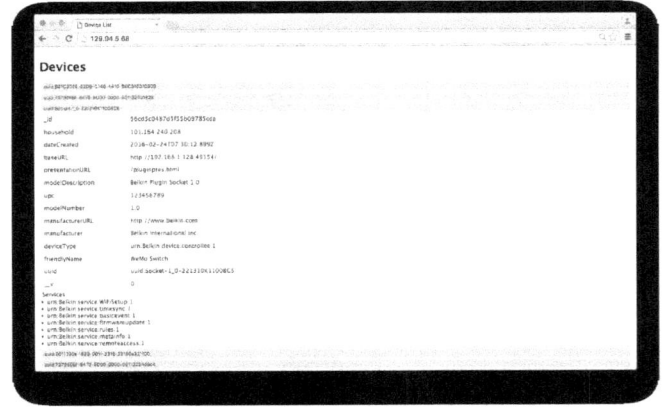

Figure 7: Detecting the (a) D-Link webcam and (b) WeMo switch inside the home

6. REFERENCES

[1] . IEEE P2413 Standard for an Architectural Framework for IoT. http://grouper.ieee.org/groups/2413/Intro-to-IEEE-P2413.pdf.

[2] . M2I Security Framework. http://www.m2isf.com/.

[3] . Online Trust Alliance. https://otalliance.org/.

[4] . DD4BC Group Targets Companies with Ransom-Driven DDoS Attacks. http://www.tripwire.com/state-of-security/security-data-protection/cyber-security/dd4bc-group-targets-companies-with-ransom-driven-ddos-attacks/, Jun 2015.

[5] . Google's first Brillo and Weave partners introduced at CES. http://www.digitaltrends.com/home/google-iot-brillo-weave-partners/, Jan 2016.

[6] Arxan Technologies. State of Application Security Report. https://www.arxan.com/wp-content/uploads/2015/06/State-of-Application-Security-Report-Vol-4-2015.pdf, Jun 2015.

[7] C. Ellison. UPnP Device Security: Service Template. http://upnp.org/specs/sec/UPnP-sec-DeviceSecurity-v1-Service.pdf, Nov 2003.

[8] Claud Xiao. More Details on the XcodeGhost Malware and Affected iOS Apps. http://researchcenter.paloaltonetworks.com/2015/09/more-details-on-the-xcodeghost-malware-and-affected-ios-apps/, Sep 2015.

[9] ExtremeTech. Philips Hue LED smart lights hacked, home blacked out by security researcher. http://www.extremetech.com/electronics/163972-philips-hue-led-smart-lights-hacked-whole-homes-blacked-out-by-security-researcher, 2013.

[10] Forbes. Baby Monitor Hacker Still Terrorizing Babies And Their Parents. http://www.forbes.com/sites/kashmirhill/2014/04/29/baby-monitor-hacker-still-terrorizing-babies-and-their-parents/#7784ae4817e2, 2014.

[11] Gartner. Gartner Says 4.9 Billion Connected "Things" Will Be in Use in 2015. http://www.gartner.com/newsroom/id/2905717, Nov 2014.

[12] S. Grover and N. Feamster. The Internet of Unpatched Things. In *Proc. FTC PrivacyCon*, Jan 2016.

[13] A. A. M. M. Haque. UPnP Networking: Architecture and Security Issues. In *Proc. TKK Seminar on Network Security*, Nov 2007.

[14] iControl. State of the Smart Home. http://www.icontrol.com/docs/pdf/2014_State_of_the_Smart_Home_-_Final.pdf, 2014.

[15] Isaac Kelly. Hacking the WeMo Switch. https://github.com/issackelly/wemo, 2012.

[16] NetworkWorld. 500,000 Belkin WeMo users could be hacked; CERT issues advisory. http://www.networkworld.com/article/2226371/microsoft-subnet/500-000-belkin-wemo-users-could-be-hacked--cert-issues-advisory.html, 2014.

[17] B. News. Fridge Sends Spam Emails as Attack Hits Smart Gadgets. http://www.bbc.com/news/technology-25780908, 2014.

[18] Nokia. Threat Intelligence Report. http://resources.alcatel-lucent.com/asset/193174, H2 2015.

[19] S. Notra, M. Siddiqi, H. H. Gharakheili, V. Sivaraman, and R. Boreli. An Experimental Study of Security and Privacy Risks with Emerging Household Appliances. In *Proc. International Workshop on Security and Privacy in Machine-to-Machine Communications (M2MSec)*, Oct 2014.

[20] T. Sales, L. Sales, H. Almeida, and A. Perkusich. A UPnP extension for enabling user authentication and authorization in pervasive systems. *Journal of the Brazilian Computer Society*, 16(4):261–277, Nov 2010.

[21] V. Sivaraman, H. H. Gharakheili, A. Vishwanath, R. Boreli, and O. Mehani. Network-Level Security and Privacy Control for Smart-Home IoT Devices. In *Proc. IEEE WiMoB Workshop on Internet of Things Communications and Technologies (IoT-CT)*, Oct 2015.

[22] T. Yu, V. Sekar, S. Sheshan, Y. Agarwal, and C. Xu. Handling a Trillion (Unfiable) Flaws on a Billion Devices: Rethinking Network Security for the Internet-of-Things. In *Proc. ACM HotNets*, Nov 2015.

DEMO: Demonstrating Practical Known-Plaintext Attacks against Physical Layer Security in Wireless MIMO Systems

Matthias Schulz
Secure Mobile Networking Lab
TU Darmstadt, Germany
mschulz@seemoo.de

Adrian Loch
IMDEA Networks Institute
Madrid, Spain
adrian.loch@imdea.org

Matthias Hollick
Secure Mobile Networking Lab
TU Darmstadt, Germany
mhollick@seemoo.de

ABSTRACT

After being widely studied in theory, physical layer security schemes are getting closer to enter the consumer market. Still, a thorough practical analysis of their resilience against attacks is missing. In this work, we use software-defined radios to implement such a physical layer security scheme, namely, orthogonal blinding. To this end, we use orthogonal frequency-division multiplexing (OFDM) as a physical layer, similarly to WiFi. In orthogonal blinding, a multi-antenna transmitter overlays the data it transmits with noise in such a way that every node except the intended receiver is disturbed by the noise. Still, our known-plaintext attack can extract the data signal at an eavesdropper by means of an adaptive filter trained using a few known data symbols. Our demonstrator illustrates the iterative training process at the symbol level, thus showing the practicability of the attack.

1. INTRODUCTION

Physical layer security schemes claim to be time-proof. In contrast to conventional security schemes, security at the physical layer does not rely on cryptographic mechanisms which may be broken in the future. In such conventional schemes, attackers may record protected frames in the hope of being able to decrypt them later. Physical layer security prevents this by not allowing attackers to successfully receive protected frames at all. In other words, attackers cannot even decode the data at the physical layer. This idea has quickly evolved from theory to practice and is getting closer to become a product. For instance, start-up companies have recently started to offer physical layer security solutions for key establishment and secure pairing.

Following the above evolution, orthogonal blinding was first proposed in theory [4] but quickly became a practical mechanism [2]. The underlying idea is to transmit artificial noise to prevent eavesdroppers from successfully decoding protected frames. To this end, the transmitter Alice uses multiple antennas—this allows her to transmit signals in multiple spatial dimensions. In particular, she transmits

data into one of the dimensions, and artificial noise on all other orthogonal dimensions. The intended receiver Bob records the transmission using a single antenna. Hence, he only receives one of the dimensions. Alice precodes the data based on the unique channel state information (CSI) of her link to Bob such that it falls exactly into the dimension Bob can receive. As a result, Bob does not receive any of the orthogonal noise. An eavesdropper Eve with one antenna also receives one dimension. However, since she is located at a different position than Bob, Eve receives a combination of data and noise, and thus cannot decode.

Orthogonal blinding is based on two strong assumptions, namely, that Eve (a) only has one antenna, and (b) does not know any part of the protected frames. In earlier work [3], we have shown that orthogonal blinding is vulnerable if (a) and (b) do not hold. Intuitively, if Eve has as many antennas as Alice, she can receive all dimensions. Further, if Eve knows a certain amount of plaintext, such as frame headers, she can determine which of the dimensions contains the data. To this end, she trains an adaptive filter based on the known-plaintext, which she can then use to decode the rest of the frame. In [3], we perform a thorough analysis on how much known-plaintext is needed to train such a filter, and show the feasibility of the approach based on practical testbed traces. Recent work in this area improves our attack on orthogonal blinding even further. For instance, the training of the adaptive filter can converge faster when exploiting the similarity of adjacent subcarriers in an orthogonal frequency-division multiplexing (OFDM) system [5]. Moreover, instead of only exploiting known plaintext, an attack on orthogonal blinding can also guess the content of low entropy fields in wireless packets, thus enabling ciphertext-only attacks [6].

In this demonstration, we show the above attack interactively using the Wireless Open-Access Research Platform (WARP) software-defined radio (SDR) [1]. That is, in contrast to our trace-based study in [3], we run the attack online on the actual wireless channels at the conference location. This allows conference attendees to experiment with the positioning of the antennas of each of the three parties in our scenario, that is, Alice, Bob, and Eve. Moreover, attendees can observe the performance of our attack on orthogonal blinding on an intuitive graphical user interface. This includes detailed physical layer information, such as CSI and quadrature amplitude modulation (QAM) constellations. For more details, see the Appendix. In the remainder of this demo proposal we explain our attack in detail and provide more details on our interactive implementation.

WiSec'16 , July 18-22, 2016, Darmstadt, Germany

© 2016 Copyright held by the owner/author(s).

ACM ISBN 978-1-4503-4270-4/16/07.

DOI: http://dx.doi.org/10.1145/2939918.2942418

2. SYSTEM OVERVIEW

Our system consists of three nodes: (1) Alice who intends to securely communicate with (2) Bob and an eavesdropper (3) Eve, who passively listens on the wireless communication between Alice and Bob. To protect the communication between Alice and Bob, Alice makes use of orthogonal blinding, a physical layer security scheme that hampers correct signal decodings at non-intended receivers while allowing Bob to only receive the data signal. To make it work, Alice needs at least one more transmit antenna than Bob to be able to use an additional spatial dimension to transmit artificial noise into the null space of the channel between Alice and Bob. Receiving the same transmission over a different channel destroys the orthogonality between the spatial streams containing data and artificial noise. Hence, an unintended receiver always gets a superposition of artificial noise and data as thoroughly described in [2] and [3]. In our demo, we set the number of Bob's receive antennas to one, Alice has two, what allows her to transmit up to two spatial streams. To be able to receive all of Alice's spatial streams, Eve also requires two antennas. An exemplary demonstrator setup is illustrated in Fig. 1.

3. IMPLEMENTATION

Our demonstrator is implemented using WARPLab, which is an interface between MATLAB and the WARP SDR. It allows to generate and analyse baseband signals in MATLAB and only use the WARP nodes as radio interfaces to transmit signals on a WiFi channel in the 2.4/5 GHz bands. For transmission, WARPLab loads baseband signals into buffers in the WARP nodes and triggers a transmission over Ethernet. The receiving WARP nodes trigger a reception at the same time and store the received signals in buffers from which WARPLab picks up the signals for further processing in MATLAB. Even though, this implementation is real-time incapable, the delay between receptions and transmissions is low enough to stay below the coherence time of the wireless channel in static environments. This is important as Alice first measures the channel state information between her and Bob by transmitting an empty frame whose preamble is used for the measurement. Then, she generates a transmit filter based on the measurement, filters data and artificial noise with this filter and transmits the resulting frame. If the wireless channel had changed between the two transmissions, the null space of the channel would have changed, too, resulting in Bob's reception being disturbed by artificial noise. Eve's attack performance, however, is not influenced, if the channel changes as she only requires to receive the second frame containing the disturbed data.

Our baseband filter implementation is done according to [3]. As we use OFDM as underlying physical modulation scheme, we separate each of our frames into OFDM symbols in the time domain. Each of these symbols splits a 40 MHz wide band into 128 subcarriers of which 110 are usable for data transmissions. For each of these 110 subcarriers Alice generates separate transmit filters using the Gram-Schmidt algorithm [2, 3]. Those filters are fed with uniformly distributed random 4-QAM data symbols and uniformly distributed artificial noise symbols. To separate the noise from the data at the eavesdropper, she separately trains normalized least mean squares (NLMS) filters on each subcarrier. In each training iteration, Eve accesses an additional set of

Figure 1: Exemplary setup of the demo with WARP nodes for Alice (two antennas), Bob (one antenna) and Eve (two antennas) and a monitor displaying the user interface.

110 of Alice's data symbols (one per subcarrier) and uses it as known plaintext to train the adaptive filter. The filter convergence is mainly influenced by the step-size μ, the wireless channel conditions and Eve's signal-to-noise ratio.

4. ACKNOWLEDGMENTS

This work has been funded by the German Research Foundation (DFG) in the Collaborative Research Center (SFB) 1053 "MAKI – Multi-Mechanism-Adaptation for the Future Internet", by LOEWE CASED, and by BMBF/HMWK CRISP.

5. REFERENCES

[1] Rice university WARP project, 2016.

[2] N. Anand, S.-J. Lee, and E. Knightly. Strobe: actively securing wireless communications using zero-forcing beamforming. In *Proceedings of the 31st Annual IEEE International Conference on Computer Communications (IEEE INFOCOM 2012)*, 2012.

[3] M. Schulz, A. Loch, and M. Hollick. Practical known-plaintext attacks against physical layer security in wireless MIMO systems. In *Proceedings of the Network and Distributed System Security Symposium (NDSS 2014)*, 2014.

[4] Y. Yang, W. Wang, H. Zhao, and L. Zhao. Transmitter beamforming and artificial noise with delayed feedback: secrecy rate and power allocation. *IEEE Trans. Commun., Netw.*, 14:374–384, 2012.

[5] Y. Zheng, M. Schulz, W. Lou, Y. Hou, and M. Hollick. Highly efficient known-plaintext attacks against orthogonal blinding based physical layer security. *IEEE Wireless Communications Letters*, 4(1):34–37, Feb 2015.

[6] Y. Zheng, M. Schulz, W. Lou, Y. Hou, and M. Hollick. Profiling the strength of physical-layer security: A study in orthogonal blinding. In *Proceedings of the 9th ACM Conference on Security and Privacy in Wireless and Mobile Networks (ACM WiSec 2016)*, 2016.

APPENDIX

Our demonstrator consists of three WARP SDR nodes. Each represents one communication party, in this case: Alice, Bob and Eve. All three nodes are connected by Ethernet to a computer that coordinates the experiments. It generates the baseband signals for the transmitters and analyzes the received baseband signals of the intended receiver and the eavesdropper. For the latter, the computer trains the adaptive filter.

The experiment is controlled by a graphical user interface illustrated in Fig. 2. On the left side, there is the transmitter, Alice, who generates 4-QAM data symbols and artificial noise symbols illustrated in the corresponding plots. All symbol plots contain all symbols of one OFDM frame at one subcarrier. The illustrated subcarrier can be selected in the control panel. Alice combines both symbols in the transmit filter ("TX FILTER") to generate symbols for each of her two antennas. After OFDM modulation, the antenna signals are either transmitted using WARP SDRs (mode set to "WARP Testbed" in the control panel) or simulated channels ("Simulation" mode) that do not require any radio hardware. The channel state information—measured between each of Alice's and each of the receivers' antennas—is illustrated as amplitudes over subchannel numbers in the plots labeled with "Channel ...". The red "x" marks the subcarrier used for the symbol plots. Right of the channel plots are either time-domain signals (currently not shown, as "Display" is set to "Symbol" instead of "Time-domain" in the control panel), or received symbol plots. One observes that Bob's symbols

are very similar to Alice's data symbols with a small amount of additive white Gaussian noise (AWGN). In simulation, the amount of noise can be adjusted with the signal-to-noise ratio ("SNR") setting. Bob's receive filter "RX FILTER" just adjusts amplitude variations introduced by attenuation on the channel. Unlike Alice's symbols, Eve's symbols are additionally affected by artificial noise and cannot be correctly mapped to the transmitted 4-QAM symbols. To get out the transmitted symbols, Eve trains an adaptive filter with known-plaintext symbols. The filter output after a preselected number of training iterations is animated in the figure labeled with "Iterations: ..." indicating the currently displayed training iteration. The red lines are error vectors and point to the locations, where the symbols are supposed to be, when filtering succeeds. How fast the filter adjusts its weights can be controlled by the step-size μ. In this example, it takes roughly 5 training iterations to be able to correctly decode the 4-QAM constellation.

One can control the experiment execution in the control panel in the lower left corner. The settings are already mentioned in the previous paragraph. Using the buttons, one can start and stop repeating experiment runs ("Start" and "Stop" buttons) or only run one experiment per button click ("Run once" button). Each run updates the graphs in the user interface. The "Replot" button restarts the plot function for the last experiment, which will reanimate the "Iterations ..." plot and use updated settings regarding the analyzed subcarrier, the iterations to be plotted and the step-size.

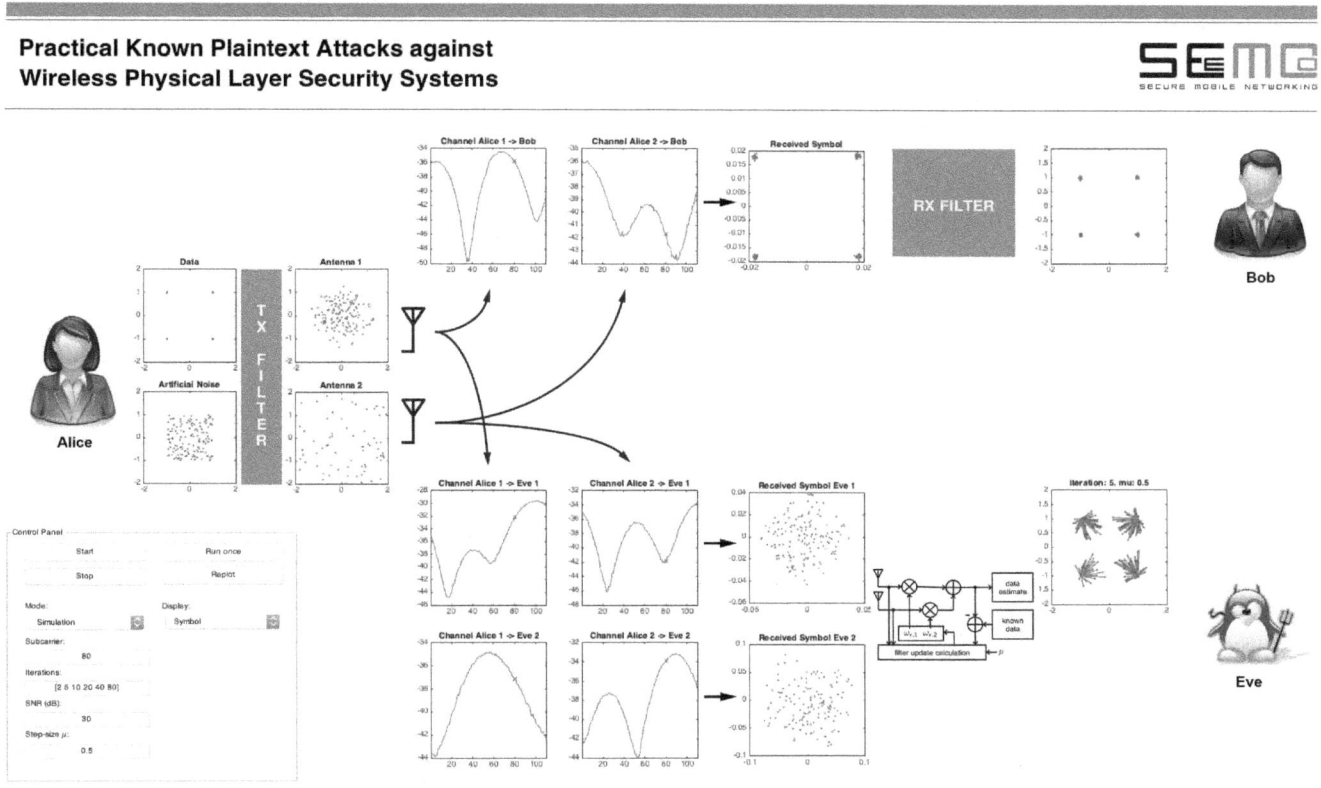

Figure 2: Screenshot of the graphical user interface used to control the experiments.

DEMO: Far Away and Yet Nearby - a Framework for Practical Distance Fraud on Proximity Services for Mobile Devices

[Extended Abstract]

Tobias Schultes, Markus Grau, Daniel Steinmetzer, and Matthias Hollick
Secure Mobile Networking Lab, TU Darmstadt, Germany
{tschultes, mgrau, dsteinmetzer, mhollick}@seemoo.tu-darmstadt.de

ABSTRACT

Proximity services are widely used in mobile applications for fast and easy data transfer and control of various systems within a defined range. Authorization is achieved by proximity detection mechanisms that surrogate extensive pairing processes. In this work, we present our Nearby Distance Fraud Framework (NeDiFF) to investigate distance fraud on various proximity services. NeDiFF cheats on proximity checks in services as Google Nearby Messages, Chromecast guest mode and Android device location. Our results emphasize that proximity services currently used for mobile devices are prone to relay attacks and should not be used in security-sensitive applications.

Keywords

Android; Chromecast; Distance Fraud; Google Nearby Messages; Location Spoofing; Proximity Detection; Relay Attack

1. INTRODUCTION

Proximity services for mobile devices are used to identify possible communication partners in a defined range without extensive pairing processes. Based on proximity detection, mobile devices are authorized to exchange messages, control systems or access location dependent information. Such systems provide great advantages, but often are vulnerable to distance frauds [2].

In this work, we investigate the necessary effort to successfully cheat on common proximity services for mobile devices. We practically investigate the feasibility of forging proximity detection in three popular application scenarios. We consider exemplary services that allow (1) message and data exchange with devices in proximity, (2) control of entertainment systems, and (3) access to location dependent information. Our Nearby Distance Fraud Framework (NeDiFF) demonstrates the practicality of distance fraud with

WiSec'16 July 18-22, 2016, Darmstadt, Germany
© 2016 Copyright held by the owner/author(s).
ACM ISBN 978-1-4503-4270-4/16/07.
DOI: http://dx.doi.org/10.1145/2939918.2942416

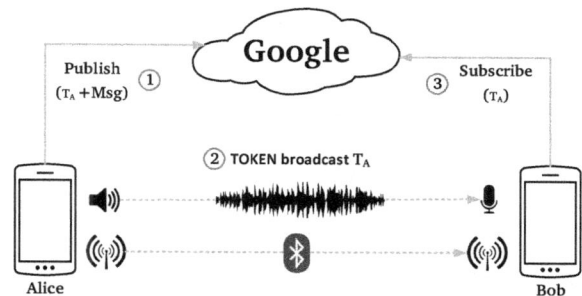

Figure 1: Nearby Messages operation principle

common resources: our tool-set only consists of laptop, Android devices and custom software. The results show that neither services guarantees proximity: all investigated scenarios are prone to distance frauds.

The remainder of this paper is structured as follows. In Section 2, we describe the proximity services considered in this work. We propose NeDiFF and evaluate the feasibility of distance fraud in Section 3. We discuss our results in Section 4 and finally conclude this work in Section 5.

2. PROXIMITY SERVICES

To address various application scenarios, we investigate distance fraud on different popular proximity services. In particular, we consider (1) Google Nearby Messages, (2) Chromecast guest mode, and (3) Android device location. Each of these services is described in the following.

2.1 Google Nearby Messages

Google Nearby Messages [1] is a publish/subscribe API for devices in proximity, which is part of Google APIs for Android. Figure 1 shows the operation principle with Alice publishing a message ①. The proximity detection is achieved by local transmissions of tokens over Bluetooth or ultrasonic audio ②. Bob receives Alice's token and sends it to Google to perform the subscription ③. The messages itself are always delivered through the Google cloud.

2.2 Chromecast Guest Mode

Chromecast is a media streaming device from Google, which can be plugged into TV to e.g. stream movies from a smartphone. In guest mode, the streaming device must be in the same room but not necessarily connected to the same network. Location checks are performed with a combination of WiFi and ultrasound signals. The smartphone receives WiFi beacons from the Chromecast and its associated access point to identify Chromecasts in proximity. Further, the smartphone must receive an ultrasonic audio token transmitted over the TV to approve that both devices are in the same room. If the latter check fails, a backup solution is to enter a PIN on the smartphone.

2.3 Android Device Location

A different approach is the usage of absolute positions for proximity estimation as typically performed on Android devices. A lot of mobile applications like Google Maps or Ingress[1] utilize this to determine the distance to points of interest. On Android, the position can be resolved with GPS and also by WiFi. The latter uses databases of MAC addresses, SSIDs and GPS positions of known access points. Scanning all WiFi networks in range allows to query respective positions.

3. DISTANCE FRAUD FRAMEWORK

In this section, we describe NeDiFF, our distance fraud framework and explain the identified methods that allow to perform distance fraud on the aforementioned proximity services. This incorporates token relaying on the audio and Bluetooth channel in Google Nearby Messages, location spoofing for Chromecast guest mode and Android device location as described in the following.

3.1 Google Nearby Messages

In Google Nearby Messages, we assume one device to share a message within a bounded area. To access this message from outside this area, the token can be recorded in range, transfered to a remote location and replayed again. This allows other devices at the remote location to pass the proximity check and retrieve the message from Google. This is a classical relay or wormhole attack (similar to [3]) that in Google Nearby Messages can performed on two mediums: the audio and the Bluetooth channel as described in the following.

Google Nearby Messages uses inaudible ultrasonic frequencies for token transmission on the audio channel. The sound can be recorded with a common microphone (as available in every phone) and transmitted to a remote place. There, the sound is replayed again using a common smartphone speaker. Our evaluations did not indicate any significant quality losses in this amplify-and-forward approach. Remote devices were able to retrieve the shared message.

On the Bluetooth channel, the token is published by setting its value as device name. The relay just needs to scan for Bluetooth devices in range and forwards their names. This follows the decode-and-forward approach as the remote end simply changes the Bluetooth interface name. Remote devices cannot distinguish, whether a certain device is the original or relayed one. As the transmitted amount of data is lower as in the audio relay, this approach performs faster, comes to the same result and was therefore used in NeDiFF.

3.2 Chromecast Guest Mode

Our framework supports remote devices to gain access to a Chromecast in guest mode without having physical access. However, to achieve this, several steps are necessary. As a

prerequisite it has to be known to which WiFi access point the Chromecast is connected to. This knowledge can for example be obtained by eavesdropping WiFi communication near the site of the Chromecast. MAC address and SSID of this access point have to be replayed at the remote location. Chromecast compatible applications attempt to connect as soon as a WiFi beacon with a Chromecast MAC is received. To accomplish the pairing, an audio token or four-digit PIN is required. The first can be achieved similar to the audio relay method in the Google Nearby Messages, the later can be guessed. Brute-forcing four-digits is assumed to be feasible with low effort but out-of-scope of this work. As Chromecasts do not punish failed connection attempts, this task becomes non time-critical. Using this approach, adversaries become able to stream arbitrary content to any Chromecast, even when the TV is in standby.

3.3 Android Device Location

The authors of [4] showed that Skyhook, a WLAN-based positioning system is prone to location spoofing. We used their approach against the positioning service integrated in Android and revealed that it is not protected against this kind of attacks, too. To perform location spoofing on such services, a WiFi fingerprint of the desired position is needed. The single access points can be cloned at a remote location by impersonating the particular MAC addresses and SSIDs. We integrate the scanning and relaying of access points in NeDiFF. Hence, we can pretend devices to be at completely different locations where we only scanned once for available networks. As all received access points are taken into account for position resolving, this method has higher success rates at remote locations with low WiFi density.

4. DISCUSSION

Our investigations with NeDiFF have shown that all three proximity services can be fooled by low-cost relay attacks. Unauthorized users at remote locations might stream videos onto any Chromecast connected TV with guest mode enabled or access Google Nearby Messages based application data (e.g. voting for tracks in Edjing playlists). They can also trick devices with spoofed locations to access location dependent information without residing at the right position. While cheating on the approach used in Google Nearby Messages requires a device within the intended range permanently, WiFi access points provide static information with long validity, which have to be obtained only once. Additionally WiFi beacons can easily be cloned and therefore are no proper method for proximity detection.

5. CONCLUSION

Distance fraud is a known threat on localization systems. Despite the fact that no suitable solutions exist, billions of devices makes use of proximity services for mobile devices. The advantages of delivering location aware content often dissolve the risks of location spoofing. However, the threat is no longer theoretical. We aim to increase awareness of this risk and propose NeDiFF, a low-cost framework to practically perform distance fraud on different proximity services. Our results show that neither service withstands distance fraud and should not be used in security-sensitive applications.

---

[1]https://www.ingress.com

6. ACKNOWLEDGMENT

This work has been funded by the DFG within CROSSING, the BMBF and the State of Hesse within CRISP-DA, and the Hessian LOEWE excellence initiative within CASED.

7. REFERENCES

[1] Google Nearby Messages API. https://developers.google.com/nearby/messages/overview. Accessed: 2016-05-13.

[2] J. Clulow, G. P. Hancke, M. G. Kuhn, and T. Moore. So near and yet so far: Distance-bounding attacks in wireless networks. In *Security and Privacy in Ad-hoc and Sensor Networks*, pages 83–97. Springer, 2006.

[3] M. Maass, U. Müller, T. Schons, D. Wegemer, and M. Schulz. NFCGate: an NFC relay application for Android. In *Proceedings of the 8th ACM Conference on Security & Privacy in Wireless and Mobile Networks*, page 27. ACM, 2015.

[4] N. O. Tippenhauer, K. B. Rasmussen, C. Pöpper, and S. Čapkun. Attacks on public WLAN-based positioning systems. In *Proceedings of the 7th international conference on Mobile systems, applications, and services*, pages 29–40. ACM, 2009.

8. APPENDIX: DEMONSTRATION

During the demonstration, we show distance fraud on the three proximity services: (1) Google Nearby Messages, (2) Chromecast guest mode, and (3) Android device location. In particular, we extend the operation range in Google Nearby Messages and Chromecast guest mode and spoof location of Android devices. In the following, we first describe the basic environmental setup for the demonstration and then discuss the individual distance frauds on each of the proximity services.

8.1 Environmental Setup

To demonstrate distance fraud, we need to spread our setup over different locations. We place devices at (1) the conference booth, (2) a shielded area at the conference booth and (3) a remote location far away from the conference location. Doing so, we become able to show that the operation range of proximity services can be extended to locations different than the intended area. At the conference booth, we place devices for interaction with conference participants. The shielded area is used for smartphones at the conference booth to emulate spatial distance by blocking the WiFi and Bluetooth frequency bands. At the remote location, we place devices that require no user interaction and use a webcam to monitor the outcome. All together, we use four Android devices, a laptop, a Chromecast and a common TV.

8.2 Google Nearby Messages

The first demonstration shows how to fool the proximity detection of Google Nearby Messages with NeDiFF. Therefore, a setup of four Android devices is necessary, as illustrated in Figure 2. Initially, a simple Android application called Nearby Devices is used to show the normal publish/subscribe behavior of Google Nearby Messages. At this point the proximity check for the shielded area will fail and no messages be delivered. Unshielded devices indeed receive the messages. The developed Android application NeDiFF

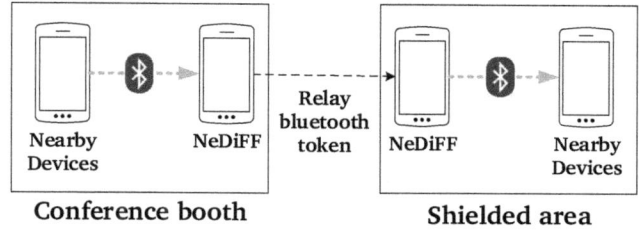

Figure 2: Google Nearby Messages demonstration

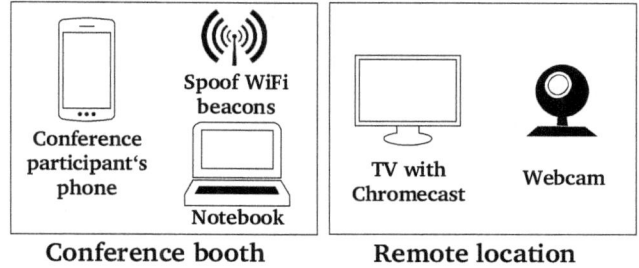

Figure 3: Chromecast demonstration

extends the range by relaying the Bluetooth channel into the shielded area. Doing so, the proximity check passes and the remote device becomes able to subscribe and receives the messages.

8.3 Chromecast Guest Mode

The second demonstration extends the operation range and fools Google Chromecast's guest mode built-in proximity check. As shown in Figure 3 the conference participant is directly involved with his own Android smartphone at the conference booth. He can use an application which implements the Google Cast API (e.g. Youtube) to stream content to the remote location. At the remote location, a Chromecast is connected to a TV and observed by an installed webcam. The participant can first try to establish a connection to the remote Chromecast, which initially fails. After unsuccessful tries, a laptop is started to broadcast previously captured WiFi beacons from Chromecast's location. Doing so, the conference participant becomes able to connect and stream arbitrary content to the remote Chromecast.

8.4 Android device location

The last demonstration shows how easy Android device locations can be spoofed. This involves conference participants' Android devices. First, the phone's GPS positioning is turned off to rely on WiFi localization only. Then, the current position of the device is checked with e.g. Google Maps. We use a setup similar to the left part of Figure 3. Both devices are located at the conference booth, but placed in a shielded area to suppress beacons of local WiFi networks. The phone will receive the spoofed beacons broadcasted by the laptop and update its position on Google Maps subsequently. In advance, an exemplary list of fingerprints to fake was captured with NeDiFF. These contain the MAC addresses and SSIDs of all access points at a specific location.

DEMO: Panoptiphone: How Unique is Your Wi-Fi Device?

Célestin Matte
Univ Lyon, INSA Lyon, Inria, CITI, France
celestin.matte@insa-lyon.fr

Mathieu Cunche
Univ Lyon, INSA Lyon, Inria, CITI, France
mathieu.cunche@inria.fr

ABSTRACT

MAC address randomization [5] in Wi-Fi-enabled devices has recently been adopted to prevent passive tracking of mobile devices. However, Wi-Fi frames still contain fields that can be used to fingerprint devices and potentially allow tracking. *Panoptiphone* is a tool inspired by the web browser fingerprinting tool Panopticlick [2], which aims to show the identifying information that can be found in the frames broadcast by a Wi-Fi-enabled device. Information is passively collected from devices that have their Wi-Fi interface enabled, even if they are not connected to an access point. *Panoptiphone* uses this information to create a fingerprint of the device and empirically evaluate its uniqueness among a database of fingerprints. The user is then shown how much identifying information its device is leaking through Wi-Fi and how unique it is.

CCS Concepts

•Networks → **Network privacy and anonymity;** •**Security and privacy** → *Mobile and wireless security;*

Keywords

Security; Privacy; 802.11; Information Elements; Probe Requests

1. INTRODUCTION

Tracking people through their mobile devices has become common despite being controversial. Tracking individuals using Wi-Fi signals emitted by their portable device is being used by surveillance [3] and commercial organizations [4]. Wi-Fi tracking is possible because Wi-Fi-enabled devices routinely transmit probe requests to search for nearby networks, and these requests contain the unique MAC address of the device [7]. An attacker can easily capture and track these requests using off-the-shelf hardware.

In response to these privacy violations, most Operating Systems (OSs) have now implemented different variants of

This work is partially funded by Région Rhône-Alpes's ARC7.

WiSec'16 July 18-22, 2016, Darmstadt, Germany

ACM ISBN 978-1-4503-4270-4/16/07.

DOI: http://dx.doi.org/10.1145/2939918.2942417

MAC address randomization [5]. While it is a necessary step towards increased privacy, it has been shown that MAC address randomization may not be sufficient in itself to provide adequate privacy [8]. Indeed, among other things, probe requests include valuable information for device fingerprinting, in the form of Information Elements (IEs) [6, §7.2.3], also called tagged parameters, or tags. These IEs are not mandatory and are used to advertise the support of various functionalities. They are generally composed of several subfields whose size can range from one bit to several bytes. The previous paper [8] showed that a subset of these IEs do not change over time, and can bring up to 7 bits of entropy. With our tool, we extend this work by listing all IEs handled by `libpcap` and provide a user-friendly way to display them, along with a calculation of their impact on privacy.

2. UNIQUENESS EVALUATION

The goal of *Panoptiphone* is to exhibit the trackability of a device by evaluating its uniqueness. This evaluation is based on the fingerprint built using the IEs found in the probe requests sent by this device. The uniqueness is evaluated with regard to a database of fingerprints. Following the approach of Panopticlick [2], we consider two metrics to evaluate this uniqueness: the anonymity set size that corresponds to the number of devices that are sharing the same fingerprint, and the entropy that quantifies the amount of identifying information provided by information elements.

The entropy of an IE or a set of IEs is computed as follows:

$$H_i = -\sum_{j \in E_i} f_{i,j} * \log f_{i,j} \tag{1}$$

where E_i is the domain of possible values for element i and $f_{i,j}$ is the frequency (i.e., probability) of the value j for the element i in the database. We consider the absence of an element as a possible value.

3. THE PANOPTIPHONE TOOL

The *Panoptiphone* tool is based on a three-step process. First, radio signals emitted by a device are captured through a Wi-Fi interface in monitor mode, then the resulting data is analyzed to evaluate the uniqueness of the device, and finally the result is displayed as a feedback to the user. The architecture of the tool is presented on figure 1.

To capture data, our tool only requires a Wi-Fi card supporting monitor mode. On a modern Linux system, this is the case for most basic off-the-shelf cards. Using an external dongle can simplify the estimation of proximity of users'

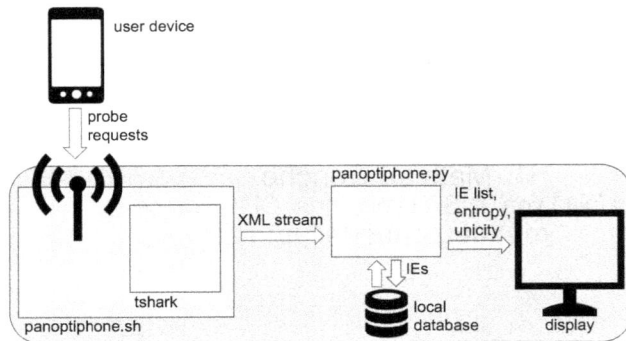

Figure 1: Architecture of the system

devices, but is not necessary. Adjacent devices are detected using RSSI.

The tool is composed of two scripts. The first one, `panoptiphone.sh`, is a small bash script configuring the Wi-Fi interface and launching `tshark` with appropriate options. The latter can output exhaustive information in a XML stream, which can then be parsed in real time by the second script, `panoptiphone.py`. The latter is a python script making the computations using and storing information in a local database, and displaying results. The display includes the list of Information Elements, which are presented using their `libpcap` name, along with metrics for each element.

We rely on a database of fingerprints obtained from the Sapienza dataset [1], composed of 8 millions of probe requests from 160 000 devices. Pending on the user consent, our tool can add a fingerprint of tested devices to the database.

The only information captured by our tool (in its current form) is the IEs contained in probe requests, sent by devices having an enabled Wi-Fi interface. Traffic data sent by associated devices, timing information or physical-layer information are not considered.

Once the fingerprint is captured, the privacy metrics (anonymity set size and entropy) are computed for each IE as well as for the whole fingerprint. The result of this analysis is then displayed to the user.

4. PRIVACY-PROTECTION MEASURES

It is often non-trivial to manipulate private data while disclosing privacy breaches. In order to guarantee the privacy of our tool's users, we keep as little necessary information as possible. In particular, we do not keep association between the different IEs, except for the global fingerprint, which is kept SHA256-hashed. Thus, the only information that can be obtained out of it is whether a full global fingerprint has already been seen. Furthermore, we encrypt elements which are direct identifiers or contain private information: MAC addresses, WPS's UUIDs, SSIDs.

In real-time mode, the tool only detects devices in a range close to the antenna (a few centimeters), to ensure only agreeing participants will have their data collected.

5. INTERACTION WITH PARTICIPANTS

During the demonstration, conference participants will be able to interact with *Panoptiphone* by testing the uniqueness of their Wi-Fi-enabled device. By bringing their device close to the antenna of *Panoptiphone*, they will trigger a capture event that will capture the fingerprint of their device, which will be processed by the tool to compute the uniqueness of the device. The result of this process will be displayed as a feedback to the user on a screen. Figure 2 presents an example of several commands and their output, starting with an example output of the real-time mode.

In addition, participants will be able to contribute by giving their data providing they agree to the storage of their fingerprint. The tool has several additional features such as the display of the global statistics of the fingerprints stored in the database as well as specific informations elements.

6. CONCLUSION

We introduce Panoptiphone, a user-friendly tool to shed light on the trackability of Wi-Fi-enabled devices, even when they are using industry-standard techniques such as MAC address randomization. We hope that this will raise awareness on the necessity to make deeper modifications on the Wi-Fi 802.11 protocol regarding information contained in probe requests that simple identifier randomization. We also aim to raise public concern on the trackability of devices carried by almost anyone at any time.

7. REFERENCES

[1] M. V. Barbera, A. Epasto, A. Mei, S. Kosta, V. C. Perta, and J. Stefa. CRAWDAD dataset sapienza/probe-requests (v. 2013-09-10). Retrieved 10 November, 2015, from, http://crawdad.org/sapienza/probe-requests/20130910, Sept. 2013.

[2] P. Eckersley. How unique is your web browser? In *Privacy Enhancing Technologies*, 2010.

[3] B. Gellman and A. Soltani. NSA tracking cellphone locations worldwide, Snowden documents show. *The Washington Post*, 2013.

[4] D. Goodin. No, this isn't a scene from minority report. This trash can is stalking you. *Ars Technica*, 2013.

[5] M. Gruteser and D. Grunwald. Enhancing location privacy in wireless LAN through disposable interface identifiers: A quantitative analysis. *Mobile Networks and Applications*, 10(3):315–325, 2005.

[6] IEEE Std 802.11-2012. *Wireless LAN Medium Access Control (MAC) and Physical Layer (PHY) Specifications*, 2012.

[7] A. B. M. Musa and J. Eriksson. Tracking unmodified smartphones using wi-fi monitors. In *Proceedings of the 10th ACM Conference on Embedded Network Sensor Systems*, SenSys '12, pages 281–294, New York, NY, USA, 2012. ACM.

[8] M. Vanhoef, C. Matte, M. Cunche, L. Cardoso, and F. Piessens. Why MAC Address Randomization is not Enough: An Analysis of Wi-Fi Network Discovery Mechanisms. In *AsiaCCS*, May 2016.

```
$ ./panoptiphone.sh wlan0 # Live capture
Capturing on 'wlan0'
MAC address: c0:ee:fb:75:0d:59 (OnePlus Tech (Shenzhen) Ltd)
One in 13654.92 devices share this signature
Field                            | Entropy | One in x devices have this value | value
wps.uuid_e                       | 0.528   |                       5606.000   |
wlan_mgt.tag.number              | 0.483   |                     163812.000   | 0,1,50,3,45,221,127
wlan_mgt.supported_rates         | 0.304   |                     163793.000   | 2,4,11,22
wlan_mgt.extended_supported_rates | 0.302  |                     162962.000   | 12,18,24,36,48,72,96,108
wlan_mgt.ht.capabilities.psmp    | 0.301   |                     162962.000   | 0x0000012c
wlan_mgt.ht.ampduparam           | 0.000   |                          1.000   | 0x00000003
[...]
total                            | 3.489   |

$ python panoptiphone.py -d # dump database
163858 devices in the database
Information element | Entropy | Aff dev | Number of values
wlan_mgt.tag.length | 3.959   | 99.97   | 417
wlan_mgt.tag.number | 3.046   | 99.97   | 414
wlan_mgt.ssid       | 3.695   | 99.97   | 20592
[...]
total               | 5.834   |  -      | 163858
29171 devices (17.80%) are unique in the database

$ python panoptiphone.py -v wlan_mgt.txbf.txbf # list possible values of a field
Value      | Number of times seen
0;0        | 115512
0          | 17353
FFFFFFFF   | 4
```

Figure 2: Example output of several commands

DEMO: Using NexMon, the C-based WiFi firmware modification framework

Matthias Schulz
Secure Mobile Networking Lab
TU Darmstadt, Germany
mschulz@seemoo.de

Daniel Wegemer
Secure Mobile Networking Lab
TU Darmstadt, Germany
dwegemer@seemoo.de

Matthias Hollick
Secure Mobile Networking Lab
TU Darmstadt, Germany
mhollick@seemoo.de

ABSTRACT

FullMAC WiFi chips have the potential to realize modifications to WiFi implementations that exceed the limits of current standards or to realize the implementation of new standards, such as 802.11p, on off-the-shelve hardware. As a developer, one, however, needs access to the firmware source code to implement these modifications. In general, WiFi firmwares are closed source and do not allow any modifications. With our C-based programming framework, NexMon, we allow the extension of existing firmware of Broadcom's FullMAC WiFi chips. In this work, we demonstrate how to get started by running existing example projects and by creating a new project to transmit arbitrary frames with a Nexus 5 smartphone.

1. INTRODUCTION

WiFi chips are mainly offered in two variants: SoftMAC chips that outsource time uncritical tasks into the driver and FullMAC chips that implement the complete medium access control (MAC) layer in the WiFi chip and only exchange Ethernet frames with the driver. In this work, we focus on the second category. These chips are mainly used in smartphones. They pursue the goal to relieve the main processor from handling and processing every received frame. The firmware not only offers to exchange Ethernet and WiFi frame headers, it also supports automatic address resolution protocol (ARP) responses and transmission control protocol (TCP) offloading.

Even though, WiFi manufacturers may offer a larger range of capabilities to developers and open up their firmwares similarly to existing open source SoftMAC drivers, such as bcrmsmac, manufactures keep firmwares locked and do not even provide datasheets that fully describe their internal chip architectures. The latter missing information includes the internal memory layout with memory mapped peripherals such as direct memory access (DMA) controllers, debug registers and other chip control registers.

In previous works, such as monmob [1] and bcmon [2], de-

WiSec'16 , July 18-22, 2016, Darmstadt, Germany

© 2016 Copyright held by the owner/author(s).

ACM ISBN 978-1-4503-4270-4/16/07.

DOI: http://dx.doi.org/10.1145/2939918.2942419

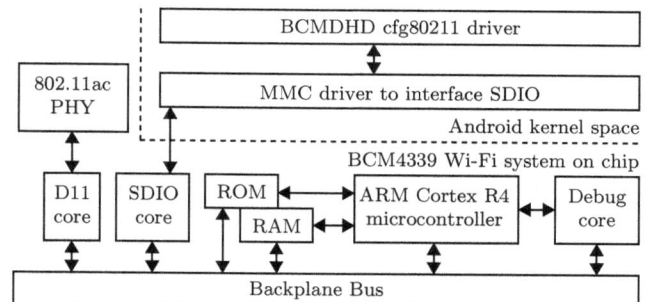

Figure 1: All Broadcom WiFi system-on-chips have a similar architecture. On SoftMAC chips, the D11 core is directly accessible by the driver, while on FullMAC chips an ARM processor arbitrates between driver and D11 core.

velopers patched parts of existing WiFi firmwares of Broadcom's BCM432x and BCM4330 chips to enable monitor mode and frame injection on iPhones and Android smartphones. Their works are currently not only used for WiFi penetration testing using mobile devices, but also in the research community to try out new MAC-layer communication protocols on smartphones. Even though, monmob and bcmon opened up access to the MAC-layer on smartphones, the patches them-selves are closed source and, hence, not easily extensible. For example, a new mesh implementation may rather focus on mesh frames than on processing all received frames of a WiFi receiver running in monitor mode. Using the latter requires to drop many received frames in the operating system which is less energy efficient than dropping them directly in the firmware.

With NexMon [3] we offer a framework to modify the WiFi firmware of Nexus 5 smartphones with Broadcom BCM4339 chips (but are not limited to this platform). As illustrated in Fig. 1, all of Broadcom's WiFi chips have a similar architecture. It consists of an interface to the driver (here SDIO), a physical layer core and a D11 core which is a real-time capable programmable state machine. Modifications to the D11's firmware are illustrated in [4]. Compared to SoftMAC chips, FullMAC chips also include an ARM processor that runs a firmware similar to the bcrmsmac driver on Linux. It is used to process received frames from the D11 core and forward them as Ethernet frames to the driver, as well as to process frames from the driver and send them out using the D11 core. In this work, we demonstrate how to use the NexMon framework to modify a chip's firmware.

In the following section, we first introduce the framework and then present some examples that are also available on our project website[1]. In the appendix, we describe how a conference participant can interact with our demonstrator.

2. PATCHING FRAMEWORK

The NexMon patching workflow is illustrated in Fig. 2. The patch code resides in the *patch.c* file. The compiler is instructed to create separate sections for each symbol, that means functions and global variables. The linker uses the *patch.ld* file to place the patch functions at defined locations. Symbols we intend to place by ourselves result in separate sections, other symbols are gathered in the *text* section. To call other functions existing in the firmware, the linker needs to know their locations to create correct branch instructions. To define those locations, we use the *wrapper.h* file, which contains function prototypes and addresses of the locations of those functions. From the header file, we create a *wrapper.c* file containing dummy function stubs and a *wrapper.ld* file to place the dummy functions using the linker. When linking the *patch.o* file to the *wrapper.o* file, the resulting *wrapper.elf* file contains the correct branch instructions as well as symbols from the wrapper and the patch files at the correct addresses. To only insert the sections of our patch into the resulting firmware, we need to extract each section from the elf-file into separate binary files. Then, we integrate those files into the original firmware binary using a Python script called patcher.py.

3. EXAMPLE PATCHES

On our project website, we offer multiple example projects that one can test on Nexus 5 smartphones. The

---

[1]NexMon project: https://dev.seemoo.tu-darmstadt.de/bcm/bcm-public

hello_world_example project simply illustrates how to print on the chip's console and read the result in Android user space. The *monitor_mode_example* shows how to activate promiscuous mode and forward each received WiFi frame directly to the driver without further processing. To analyze firmware code in RAM and ROM, we offer the *debugger_example*. It sets hardware breakpoints to redirect program execution at a breakpoint into a handler function that can read and change register values. This can, for exmaple, be used to analyze function arguments of functions residing in ROM or to perform single-step debugging to figure out, where errors occur during execution.

4. ACKNOWLEDGMENTS

This work has been funded by the German Research Foundation (DFG) in the Collaborative Research Center (SFB) 1053 "MAKI – Multi-Mechanism-Adaptation for the Future Internet", by LOEWE CASED, LOEWE NICER, and by BMBF/HMWK CRISP.

5. REFERENCES

[1] A. Blanco and M. Eissler. One firmware to monitor 'em all., 2012.
[2] O. Ildis, Y. Ofir, and R. Feinstein. Wardriving from your pocket – Using wireshark to reverse engineer broadcom wifi chipsets, 2013.
[3] M. Schulz, D. Wegemer, and M. Hollick. NexMon: A Cookbook for Firmware Modifications on Smartphones to Enable Monitor Mode. *arXiv:1601.07077*, 2015.
[4] I. Tinnirello, G. Bianchi, P. Gallo, D. Garlisi, F. Giuliano, and F. Gringoli. Wireless MAC processors: Programming MAC protocols on commodity hardware. In *Proc. of the 31st Annual IEEE International Conference on Computer Communications (INFOCOM)*, 2012.

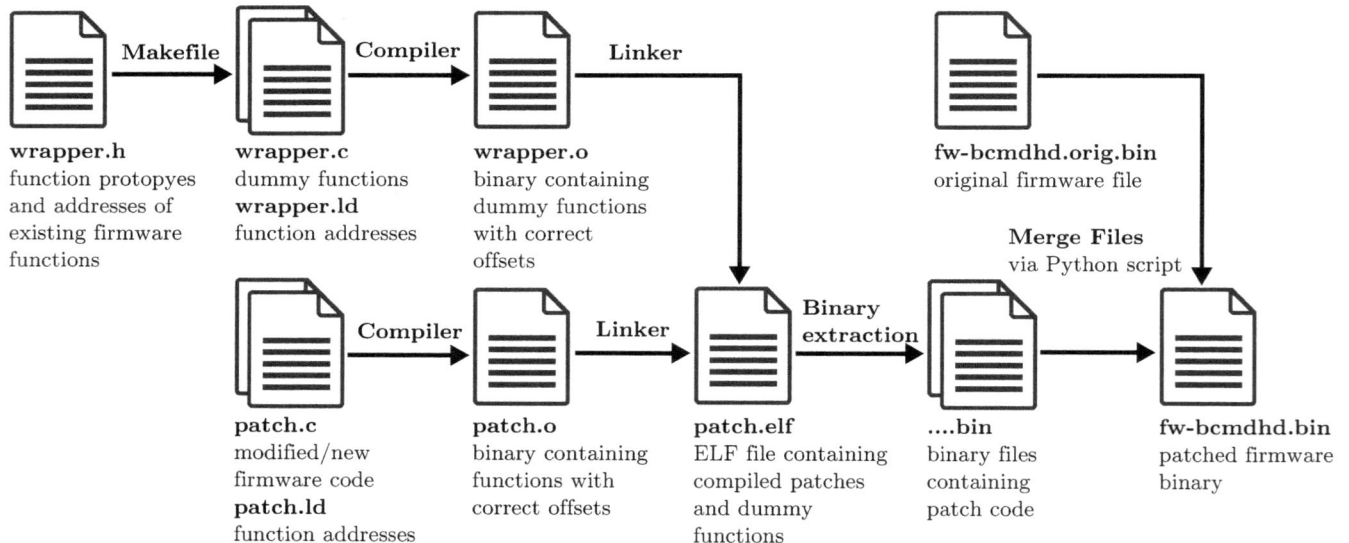

Figure 2: The NexMon firmware patching framework allows to write firmware patches in C or assember and to compile them into binary patches that can be linked to existing firmware functions.

APPENDIX

During the demonstration at the conference, we intend to show the participants how to get started with NexMon. Thereto, we bring a couple of Nexus 5 smartphones and laptops to program them. In addition, we intend to support participants who want to try out NexMon on their own smartphones. After creating a patched firmware file, it is combined with a driver and added to a *boot.img* file that also contains various binaries for penetration testing. A participant can use *fastboot* in bootloader mode to boot a Nexus 5 smartphone with the custom *boot.img*. This leaves the existing boot partitions in flash memory untouched and the phone can be rebooted into the original Kernel by a simple restart of the smartphone.

As a first test, the conference participants can take one of our example patches and execute them on the phone. The *monitor_mode_example* is a good starting point as it allows to run well known tools such as *tcpdump* or *airodump-ng* to observe and capture frames on the selected WiFi channel. The Nexus 5 supports single stream transmissions on channels with up to 80 MHz bandwidth in the 2.4 and 5 GHz WiFi bands following the 802.11ac standard and below.

To write a patch on their own, we instruct the conference participants to create their own "playground" project executing the following command in the *firmware_patching* directory:

```
make newproject NEWPROJECT=my_playground
```

This copies the *bcmdhd* driver as well as template *patch.c*, *patch.ld*, *Makefile*, and *patcher.py* files into a new *my_playground* directory. Then the conference participant has to select a function to hook so that our patch gets executed as soon as this function is called. We, therefore, propose the *wlc_radio_upd* function that sets up the physical layer core and activates the ability to transmit frames. We intend to overwrite the branch link instruction that calls *wlc_radio_upd* with a branch link instruction to our *wlc_radio_upd_hook* function that we insert into our *patch.c* file. The hook function should first call the original *wlc_radio_upd* function and then execute our own code before returning to the calling function. To achieve this, we write the *wlc_radio_upd_hook* function in assembler as it makes it easier to control how registers are used. We also need to save the link register before executing branch link instructions. Otherwise we cannot return to the calling function. The code looks as follows:

```
__attribute__((naked)) void wlc_radio_upd_hook(void) {
    asm("push {lr}\n"
        "bl wlc_radio_upd\n"
        "push {r0-r3}\n"
        "bl wlc_radio_upd_hook_in_c\n"
        "pop {r0-r3}\n"
        "pop {pc}\n");
}
```

This patch function should be placed in the free space starting at 0x180020 in the firmware. This is achieved by the following line in the *linker.ld* file:

```
.text.wlc_radio_upd_hook 0x180020: ↵
    { KEEP(patch.o (.text.wlc_radio_upd_hook)) }
```

This will only place the function in the object and elf-files. To extract the binary files, we need to set the *FUNCTIONS* variable in the Makefile to *wlc_radio_upd_hook*. To insert the binary file into the firmware, we need to insert the following line in the patcher.py file:

```
ExternalArmPatch(getSectionAddr( ↵
    ".text.wlc_radio_upd_hook"), ↵
    "wlc_radio_upd_hook.bin"),
```

As stated above, we intend to call our patch instead of the original function by replacing the branch link instruction at address 0x195B48 in the *WLC_UP* ioctl handler. Thereto, we insert the following line in the *patcher.py* file:

```
BLPatch(0x195B48, getSectionAddr( ↵
    ".text.wlc_radio_upd_hook")),
```

At this point, we can almost test, if the patch is working, but we are still missing the *wlc_radio_upd_hook_in_c* function called by our hook. As a start, we can simply insert a *printf* instruction as follows into the *patch.c* file:

```
void wlc_radio_upd_hook_in_c(void) {
    printf("hello world\n");
}
```

As we do not need to place this function at a specific address, the linker places it in the common *.text* section. To insert this section into the firmware, we need to uncomment the corresponding line in the *patcher.py* file. To test the new firmware, we run the following commands in the root directory of the NexMon project:

```
make boot
make reloadfirmware FWPATCH=my_playground
```

This reboots the smartphone with the built *boot.img* and copies the patched firmware as well as the corresponding driver module to the SD card. Here, it gets loaded as a kernel module. To load the firmware into the WiFi chip, we need to setup the *wlan0* interface and can then print the console of the chip using *dhdutil*:

```
adb shell "su -c 'ifconfig wlan0 up && ↵
    dhdutil -i wlan0 consoledump'"
```

In the output, one should see the hello world message. If it works, we continue to write the following code to create a new sk_buff, reserve space for additional headers, copy a beacon frame into the data variable and create a new station control block (SCB), which is required to transmit a frame through *wlc_sendctl*.

```
char pkt[] = {
    0x80, 0x00, 0x00, 0x00, 0xff, 0xff, 0xff, 0xff,
    0xff, 0xff, 0xcc, 0xcc, 0xcc, 0xcc, 0xcc, 0xcc,
    0xdd, 0xdd, 0xdd, 0xdd, 0xdd, 0xdd, 0x10, 0x00,
    0x00, 0x00, 0x00, 0x00, 0x00, 0x00, 0x00, 0x00,
    0x64, 0x00, 0x21, 0x05, 0x00, 0x06,
    'N', 'E', 'X', 'M', 'O', 'N' // SSID
};

void wlc_radio_upd_hook_in_c(void) {
    sk_buff *p; void *scb;
    struct wlc_info *wlc = WLC_INFO_ADDR;
    void *bsscfg = wlc_bsscfg_find_by_wlcif(wlc, 0);
    p = pkt_buf_get_skb(wlc->osh, sizeof(pkt) + 202);
    p->data += 202; p->len -= 202;
    memcpy(p->data, pkt, sizeof(pkt));
    scb = __wlc_scb_lookup(wlc, bsscfg, pkt, 0);
    wlc_scb_set_bsscfg(scb, bsscfg);
    wlc_sendctl(wlc, p, wlc->active_queue, scb,
        1, 0, 0);
}
```

Running this code sends out a beacon frame announcing the service set identifier (SSID) NEXMON. One can, for example, use *tcpdump* to receive this frame on a nearby device listening on WiFi channel 1 and filtering for the host address cc:cc:cc:cc:cc:cc.

POSTER: Assessing the Impact of 802.11 Vulnerabilities using Wicability

Pieter Robyns, Bram Bonné, Peter Quax, Wim Lamotte
iMinds - tUL - UHasselt
Expertise Centre for Digital Media
Wetenschapspark 2
3590 Diepenbeek, Belgium
{pieter.robyns, bram.bonne, peter.quax, wim.lamotte}@uhasselt.be

ABSTRACT

Wicability is an open platform created for researchers, that aims to provide insights into the spatial and temporal impact of both novel and past 802.11 security vulnerabilities. This is achieved through the automated collection and analysis of large datasets containing 802.11 Information Elements (IEs) transmitted by access points and stations. The results of this analysis are anonymized and provided free of charge to researchers through a web interface.

Keywords

802.11; vulnerability impact; open platform; Wicability

1. INTRODUCTION

When a novel vulnerability is discovered, it is desirable that its impact can be determined correctly. This impact assessment is based on the severity of the vulnerability itself and the number of affected devices. While the severity of the vulnerability is an arbitrary concept that may include properties such as exploitability, remediation level, impact on availability or confidentiality, etc., the number of affected devices can be objectively measured.

To measure the number of affected devices, several approaches can be considered depending on whether the vulnerability is caused by an implementation issue (vendor or operating system specific), a protocol design flaw, or a combination of both. In case of a vulnerability in a protocol such as WPS or WPA/TKIP for example, one could sample a number of Beacon frames from Access Points (APs) in a nearby city to approximate what percentage of APs supports the protocol. For vendor specific vulnerabilities, e.g. in a specific model of smartphone, it might be useful to look at sales reports[1] to see whether the device is prominent in the market or not. Unfortunately, such reports can be very expensive to obtain. Furthermore, the number of affected

---

[1] For example, Forrester or Gartner reports.

WiSec'16, July 18–22, 2016, Darmstadt, Germany.

© 2016 Copyright held by the owner/author(s).

ACM ISBN 978-1-4503-4270-4/16/07.

DOI: http://dx.doi.org/10.1145/2939918.2942421

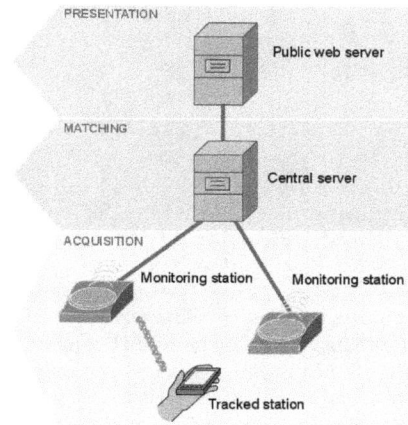

Figure 1: The three processing stages of Wicability

devices depends on geographical location and time: a given protocol could become deprecated (e.g. WEP), and some countries will adopt new protocols faster than others.

To help solve these problems, we introduce Wicability, an open platform created for researchers that aims to provide insights into the spatial and temporal impact of security vulnerabilities through the analysis of 802.11 Information Elements (IEs). We have performed an initial analysis on our own datasets, and welcome contributions from external researchers. Our tool distinguishes itself from other open databases such as WiGLE.net [1] and Crawdad [2] in that it can be used to determine the percentage of devices that supports a given protocol at a certain time and location. In the next sections, we will briefly discuss our platform.

2. CAPABILITY AGGREGATION

The protocols and capabilities supported by different devices are advertised in IEs. Such IEs are exchanged between STAs and APs prior to association through Probe Request, Probe Response and Beacon frames so that both parties know which protocols, data rates, and crypto suites can be used for communication. Our approach for aggregating this information comprises an acquisition, matching and presentation stage as shown in Figure 1.

2.1 Acquisition

To obtain a representative set of IEs, we have deployed multiple monitoring devices at densely crowded locations.

Field popularity

Click on a vendor to add it to the filter

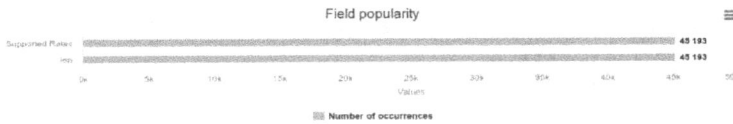

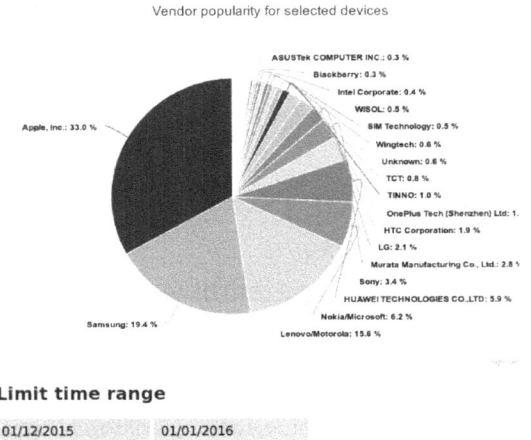

Vendor popularity for selected devices

Click on a value to add it to the filter

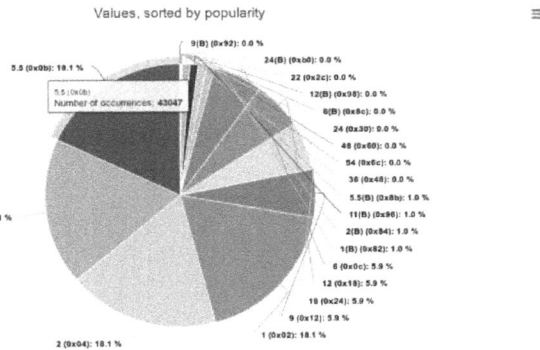

Values, sorted by popularity

Limit time range

01/12/2015   01/01/2016

Figure 2: Example use case where Wicability is queried for the `Supported Rates` IE of non-AP STAs. The left chart shows the distribution of the IE values. The vendor distribution for this IE is shown on the right.

Here, each monitoring device passively captured all management frames containing IEs using `libpcap` and a wireless interface configured in monitor mode. The captured frames were then forwarded to a central server over an SSH tunnel. No additional processing was performed at the monitoring devices in order to minimize their complexity. Alternatively, a `pcap` file can be provided to the server directly for analysis.

We are aware that the forwarded messages contain privacy sensitive data such as the MAC address and SSID list. However, no data frames are sent to the server, and no MACs or SSIDs will be accessible through the public platform.

2.2 Matching

In the matching stage, the captured IEs are grouped per MAC address and per dataset. The MAC addresses are only used to distinguish between different devices, and may therefore be anonymized as long as each real MAC address is consistently mapped to its corresponding pseudonym.

Observe that ideally, random MAC addresses should be excluded in order to prevent counting the same device multiple times. We offer two approaches to filter these random MACs. In a first approach, unknown OUIs or MACs that have the locally administered bit set are ignored. Our second approach utilizes MAC layer fingerprinting techniques to link similar IEs transmitted by random MAC addresses to their corresponding real MAC address. Finally, the dataset is labeled with the location, duration and timestamp of the capture.

2.3 Presentation

After the observed IEs have been matched with a specific device, each IE is parsed, converted to a queryable and human readable format, and stored in a public database. Privacy sensitive data such as the MAC / pseudonym and SSID names are excluded from this operation. The resulting dataset can be queried by researchers using the Wicability web interface. Figure 2 shows an example where the dis-

tribution of `Supported Rates` values is shown on the left, along with the vendor distribution for devices that transmit this IE on the right. The distribution of each possible field, field value or vendor in an IE can be queried.

3. CONCLUSION

We have introduced Wicability, an open platform that can be utilized as a tool to quantify the impact and remediation rate of protocol vulnerabilities. Additionally, the platform can be used to determine the number of devices observed from a specific (chipset) vendor or operating system, along with their supported capabilities. An overview of its core functionality was presented, which comprises the collection and analysis of IEs acquired through passive monitoring.

To complement our own collected data, we welcome submissions from external researchers to the Wicability platform. These submissions can be provided in the form of anonymized `pcap` files, i.e. where the SSID names and MAC addresses have been replaced with pseudonyms. As a result of these contributions, progressions such as the adoption of 802.11w amendment support for protected management frames in response to `Deauthentication` frame Denial of Service (DoS) attacks for example, can be studied in a spatio-temporal manner.

Acknowledgements

Research funded by a PhD grant of the Research Foundation Flanders (FWO).

4. REFERENCES

[1] WiGLE.net. *Wireless Network Mapping*, 2016 (accessed May 10, 2016). https://wigle.net/.

[2] J. Yeo, D. Kotz, and T. Henderson. CRAWDAD: a community resource for archiving wireless data at Dartmouth. *ACM SIGCOMM Computer Communication Review*, 36(2):21–22, 2006.

Poster: Design Ideas for Privacy-aware User Interfaces for Mobile Devices

Neel Tailor
De Montfort University
Leicester, LE9 1BH, UK
n.ee.l@live.co.uk

Ying He
De Montfort University
Leicester, LE9 1BH, UK
ying.he@dmu.ac.uk

Isabel Wagner
De Montfort University
Leicester, LE9 1BH, UK
isabel.wagner@dmu.ac.uk

ABSTRACT

Privacy in mobile applications is an important topic, especially when it concerns applications that gather and process health data. Using MyFitnessPal as an example eHealth app, we analyze how privacy-aware its user interface is, i.e. how well users are informed about privacy and how much control they have. We find several issues with the current interface and develop five design ideas that make the interface more privacy-aware. In a small pilot user study, we find that most of the design ideas seem to work well and enhance end users' understanding and awareness of privacy.

Categories and Subject Descriptors

H.5.2 [**Information Interfaces and Presentation**]: User Interfaces; K.4.1 [**Computers and Society**]: Public Policy Issues—*privacy*

Keywords

privacy awareness, mobile applications, user interface design

1. INTRODUCTION

With the increasing use of eHealth apps and their unprecedented access to sensitive data, eHealth privacy has become an important concern to the public. User interfaces (UIs) provide the point of contact between users and apps, and ideally allow users to express their privacy preferences towards apps. However, current eHealth app UIs have not been designed in a privacy-aware manner, which stops users from making informed and effective privacy choices [3]. Existing efforts to improve the privacy communication between apps and users focus on improving awareness of privacy policies and app permissions before an app is installed [1, 2]. In contrast, we consider the privacy-awareness of user interfaces while the user is using the app.

MyFitnessPal is an eHealth app that allows users to track food consumption, exercise and body weight, thus supporting users in achieving their dieting goals. We use MyFit-

WiSec'16, July 18–20, 2016, Darmstadt, Germany.

© 2016 Copyright held by the owner/author(s).

ACM ISBN 978-1-4503-4270-4/16/07.

DOI: http://dx.doi.org/10.1145/2939918.2942420

nessPal as an example to analyze weaknesses in the privacy awareness of current mobile user interfaces. Based on this analysis, we develop a privacy enhanced prototype UI and evaluate whether it helps users become more aware of their privacy and make more informed privacy decisions. While we developed the prototype to improve MyFitnessPal's UI, we are confident that our ideas are applicable to other mobile device UIs as well. Our research has implications for app designers who need to consider how to communicate privacy issues to their users throughout the design and development phases, building usable privacy into apps.

2. CRITERIA FOR UI DESIGN

We follow the three stages of the Inform–Alert–Mitigate (I-AM) cycle [3] to analyze MyFitnessPal's current user interface. The I-AM cycle is a user-centric approach to systematically assess and improve how privacy issues are addressed during app usage. The *inform* stage informs users of potential privacy issues, for example using privacy policies and app permission requests. The *alert* stage alerts users to ongoing privacy risks, for example caused by data transfers or sensor usage. The *mitigate* stage gives users options to mitigate ongoing privacy risks, for example by blocking data transfers or modifying sensor readings.

3. ANALYSIS OF CURRENT UI

For the *inform* stage, we find that lengthy privacy policies packed with legalese are not suitable for educating eHealth consumers on data collection, usage and sharing. In addition, links to privacy policies are presented so that users may not even notice them. For the *alert* stage, we find that users have no way to find out about ongoing data transfers or sensor usage. In addition, the on-screen alerts that ask users for specific permissions do not help users in deciding how much this permission will affect their privacy. For the *mitigate* stage, we find that users have no concrete mitigation options, other than uninstalling the app. Specifically, apps do not offer users to store data locally on the device, or to disable specific sensors.

4. DESIGN IDEAS TO ADDRESS GAPS

To overcome the issues with current user interfaces that we identified above, we developed a set of five design ideas that can be implemented into mobile user interfaces.

Privacy Policy. We re-structured the privacy policy by separating statements in the policy into different categories: in-

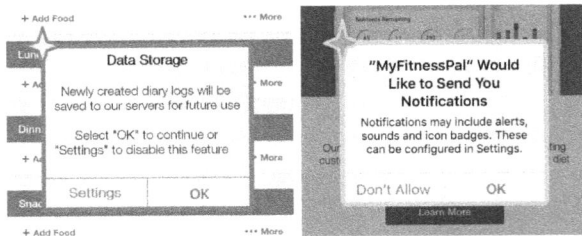

Figure 1: Traffic light alerts

formation collection, information use, information sharing, user control over stored information, service operation, and notification of policy changes. Each category is displayed with clear headings and icons that can be expanded by the user (Fig. 2). In addition to restructuring, we make display of the privacy policy mandatory before the app is first used. This is in contrast to how privacy policies are currently handled on app stores, where apps can be installed without ever seeing the privacy policy.

Icons for sensor usage. Icons for accelerometer usage and data transfers (top two items in Fig. 3) help to alert users to ongoing privacy risks. While using the app, these icons are displayed in the phone's status bar, similar to the already existing GPS icon, whenever data transfers are ongoing or sensors are being used.

Traffic light colors for alerts. We integrated a traffic light color scheme into on screen alerts that are displayed to the user (Fig. 1). The alerts are color-coded as red, amber, or green depending on the severity of the privacy notification. The color-coding enhances visual privacy awareness and ensures users pay more attention to more severe alerts.

Mitigation options. We designed an easily accessible mitigation options menu that the user can access during app usage (Fig. 3). The menu allows users to disable specific sensors the eHealth app uses, and to stop data transfers to the eHealth organization's remote servers. This concrete mitigation feature allows users to configure the data that eHealth apps acquire from them, thus giving users more control over their privacy, as well as increasing user trust and confidence in eHealth applications.

Incognito mode. The incognito mode ensures data is stored locally (bottom item in Fig. 3) by disabling data transfers to the app provider's servers and instead stores data locally on the device. This allows a person to freely use the eHealth app without having to worry that their data could be retrieved at a later date or shared with third parties.

5. EVALUATION

The user study involved providing the privacy enhanced prototype app as well as the original MyFitnessPal app to a sample of 16 people, who were then asked a series of questions about the new privacy features. The results show that the restructured privacy policy is easy to follow and more engaging than the current display of privacy policies. In addition, presenting the privacy policy before first use of the app increases the likelihood that it will be read. Almost all of our participants agreed that the new icons for data transfers and sensor usage made them more aware of the resources the

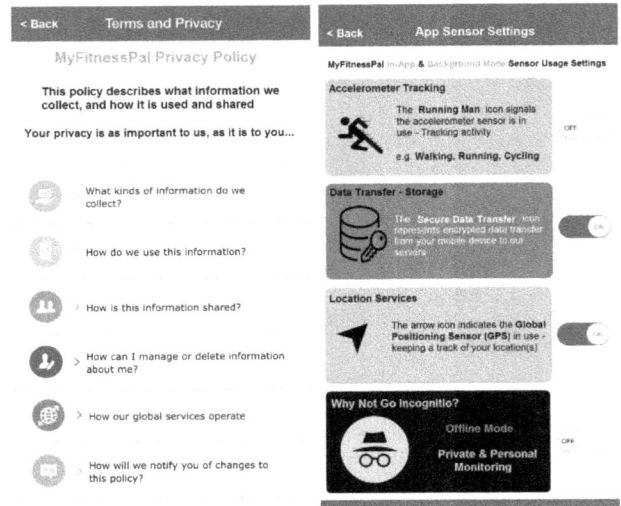

Figure 2: Privacy policy   Figure 3: Settings

app was using. More than 90% of the participants approved of our traffic light color scheme integrated into the on-screen alerts, and all agreed that they were better alerted to the severity of ongoing privacy risks. Over 80% of the participants found that the mitigation menu was easily accessible throughout the app, and the concept of having this menu gave almost all participants more control over their privacy and meant that they could tailor the app to their desires. The incognito mode was not as successful as the other ideas. Less than 50% of participants stated that they could use the app more confidently and felt their privacy would not be compromised. This may be caused by the wording we displayed when enabling incognito mode, because it did not clarify that data gathered during incognito mode would stay local and not be uploaded at any time.

6. CONCLUSIONS

This research found five issues with the current interface of the mobile eHealth app MyFitnessPal and developed five design ideas to address them. The results show that most of the design ideas help to enhance users' understanding and awareness of privacy. In our future research, we will seek to gather eHealth app providers' perspectives and involve more users in the evaluation for a further proof of concept. Our long term goal is to expand and refine our design ideas and integrate them into a fully functional application.

7. REFERENCES

[1] P. G. Kelley, L. F. Cranor, and N. Sadeh. Privacy As Part of the App Decision-making Process. In *CHI '13*, pages 3393–3402, Paris, France, 2013. ACM.

[2] J. Lin, S. Amini, J. I. Hong, N. Sadeh, J. Lindqvist, and J. Zhang. Expectation and Purpose: Understanding Users' Mental Models of Mobile App Privacy Through Crowdsourcing. In *UbiComp '12*, pages 501–510, Pittsburgh, PA, USA, 2012. ACM.

[3] I. Wagner, Y. He, D. Rosenberg, and H. Janicke. User Interface Design for Privacy Awareness in eHealth Technologies. In *CCNC '16*, pages 38–43, Las Vegas, NV, January 2016. IEEE.

POSTER: Experimental Analysis of Popular Anonymous, Ephemeral, and End-to-End Encrypted Apps

Lucky Onwuzurike
Computer Science Department
University College London

Emiliano De Cristofaro
Computer Science Department
University College London

ABSTRACT

As social networking takes to the mobile world, smartphone apps provide users with ever-changing ways to interact with each other. Over the past couple of years, an increasing number of apps have entered the market offering end-to-end encryption, self-destructing messages, or some degree of anonymity. However, little work thus far has examined the properties they offer. We present a taxonomy of 18 of these apps: we first look at the features they promise in their appeal to broaden their reach and focus on 8 of the more popular ones. We present a technical evaluation, based on static and dynamic analysis, and identify a number of gaps between the claims and reality of their promises.

1. INTRODUCTION

Following Edward Snowden's revelations, privacy and anonymity technologies have been increasingly often in the news, with a growing number of users becoming aware – loosely speaking – of privacy and encryption notions [2]. Service providers have rolled out, or announced they will, more privacy-enhancing tools, e.g., support for end-to-end encryption or HTTPS by default. At the same time, a number of smartphone apps and mobile social networks have entered the market, promising to offer features like anonymity, ephemerality, and/or end-to-end encryption (E2EE). While it is not that uncommon to stumble upon claims like "military-grade encryption" or "NSA-proof" in the description of these apps, little work thus far has actually analyzed the guarantees they provide.

This motivates the need for a systematic study of a careful selection of such apps. To this end, we compile a list of 18 apps that either offer E2EE, anonymity, ephemerality, or a combination of any two, focusing on 8 popular ones (Confide, Frankly Chat, Secret, Snapchat, Telegram, Whisper, Wickr, and Yik Yak). We review their functionalities and perform an empirical evaluation, based on *static* and *dynamic* analysis, aimed to compare the claims of the selected apps against results of our analysis.

Highlights of our findings include that "anonymous" social network apps Whisper and Yik Yak actually identify users with persistent distinct user IDs. Users' (previous) activities are restored

WiSec'16 July 18-22, 2016, Darmstadt, Germany

© 2016 Copyright held by the owner/author(s).

ACM ISBN 978-1-4503-4270-4/16/07.

DOI: http://dx.doi.org/10.1145/2939918.2942424

to their device after uninstalling and reinstalling the apps, and information collected by these apps could be used to de-anonymize them. We also find that the ephemeral-messaging app Snapchat does not always delete messages from its servers – in fact, "expired" chat messages are included in packets sent to the client. Then, we report that all actions performed by a user on Frankly Chat can be observed from the request URL, which is actually transmitted in the clear.

Note: An extended version of this poster abstract appears in [3].

2. BUILDING AN APP CORPUS

We build a list of smartphone apps that are categorized as "anonymous" on Product Hunt [1], and those popular among friends and colleagues. We then look at *similar apps* on Google Play, and focus on those described as offering end-to-end encryption, anonymity and/or ephemerality, as defined below:

Anonymity: is defined as the property that a subject is not identifiable within a set of subjects, known as the anonymity set [4]. In the context of this study, the term anonymity will be used to denote that users are anonymous w.r.t. other users of the service or w.r.t. the app service provider.

End-to-End Encryption (E2EE): Data exchanged between two communicating parties is encrypted in a way that only the sender and the intended recipient can decrypt it, so, e.g., eavesdroppers and service providers cannot read or modify messages.

Ephemerality: In cryptography, it denotes the property that encryption keys change with every message or after a certain period. Instead, here ephemerality is used to indicate that messages are not available to recipients from the user interface after a period of time [1]. For instance, in apps like Snapchat, messages "disappear" from the app (but may still be stored at the server) a few seconds after they are read.

First List. We initially select 18 apps, listed in Table 1, where we also report their first release date, number of downloads as reported by Google Play, the kind(s) of content that can be shared, and whether the apps create persistent social links.

Apps Selection. We focus on apps with the most downloads that offer ephemerality, anonymity, E2EE, or, preferably, a combination of them. We reduce our selection to the top 8 apps (bold entries in Table 1) with most downloads, selecting an app with more than one of our desired property when there is more than one app with same number of download. We exclude Silent Circle and TigerText as they require paid subscription and registered company email respectively.

---

[1] http://www.producthunt.com/e/anonymous-apps

App	Launch	#Downloads	Type	Content	Anonymity	Ephemerality	E2EE	Social Links
20 Day Stranger	2014	Unknown	Temporary OSN	Photos and location	Yes	No	No	No
Armortext	2012	50–100K	Chat (Enterprise)	Text and files	No	User-defined	Yes	Yes
BurnerApp	2012	100–500K	Temporary numbers	Call and SMS	N/A	N/A	No	Yes
Confide	2014	100–500K	Chat	Text, documents, photos	No	**After message is read**	**Yes**	Yes
CoverMe	2013	100–500K	Chat	Text, voice, photos, videos	No	User-defined	Yes	Yes
Disposable Number	Unknown	100–500K	Temporary numbers	Call and SMS	N/A	N/A	No	Yes
Frankly Chat	2013	500K–1M	Chat	Text, pictures, videos, voice	Optional for group chat	**10s**	No	Yes
Secret	2014	5–10M	Anonymous OSN, Chat	Text, photos,	**Yes**	No	No	Yes/No
Seecrypt SC3	2014	10–50K	Chat	Text, voice, files	No	No	Yes	Yes
Silent Circle	2012	100–200K	Encrypted Phone	Call, SMS, files	No	User-defined	Yes	Yes
Snapchat	2011	100–500M	Transient OSN	Photos, videos	No	**1 – 10s**	No	Yes
Telegram	2013	50–100M	Chat	Text, photos, audio, videos, files, location	No	**Optional**	**Optional**	Yes
TextSecure	2010	500K–1M	Chat	Text, files	No	No	Yes	Yes
TigerText	2010	500K–1M	Chat	Text, files	No	User-defined	Yes	Yes
Vidme	2013	50–100K	Video Sharing	Videos	Yes	No	No	No
Whisper	2012	1–5M	Anonymous OSN, Chat	Text, photos	**Yes**	No	No	No
Wickr	2012	100–500K	Chat	Text, files, photos, audio, videos	No	**User-defined**	**Yes**	Yes
Yik Yak	2013	1–5M	Local Bulletin	Text	**Yes**	No	No	No

Table 1: Our first selection of 18 smartphone apps providing at least one among ephemerality, anonymity, or end-to-end encryption. N/A denotes 'Not Applicable'. Apps in bold constitute the focus of our analysis.

3. ANALYSIS

Static Analysis. We perform static analysis of the 8 apps using dex2jar and JD-GUI to decompile them, aiming to analyze SSL/TLS implementations and look for potential information leakage. We inspect the `TrustManager` and `HostnameVerifier` interfaces used to accept or reject a server's credentials.

We find Frankly Chat, Whisper, and Wickr all contain `TrustManager` and `HostnameVerifier` that accept all certificates or hostnames. Alas, this makes it possible for an adversary to perform *Man-in-The-Middle (MiTM)* attacks and retrieve information sent on the sockets that use the vulnerable `TrustManager` and/or `HostnameVerifier`.

Dynamic Analysis. We conduct our experiments on a LG Nexus 4 running Android 5.1, that connects to a Wi-Fi access point under our control. We perform actions that include: sign-up, login, profile edit, send/read messages, while at the same time, monitoring traffic transmitted and received by the apps. We collect traffic using Wireshark and analyze unencrypted traffic to check for sensitive information transmitted in the clear. We also rely on HTTP proxies such as Fiddler and SSLSplit to mount Man-in-The-Middle (MiTM) attacks and decrypt HTTPS traffic. We used two different proxies because some Android apps are programmed to ignore proxy settings, hence, we used Fiddler as a regular proxy and SSLSplit as a transparent proxy.

When no proxy is used, traffic captured by Wireshark show that Frankly Chat leaks the Android advertising ID (a unique identifier) and Secret leaks Google Maps location requests (and responses). A summary of the results when a proxy is used is shown in Table 2. We found that anonymous social networks Whisper and Yik Yak actually identify their users with distinct IDs that are persistent as previous activities like chats, *whispers* and *yaks* are restored to the device even if the user uninstalls and reinstalls the app. This behavior shows that, although they do not require users to provide their email or phone number, they can still persistently link – and possibly de-anonymize – users. Also, while Snapchat promises that messages will "disappear" after 10 seconds, they are not immedi-

App	Fiddler	SSLSplit
Confide	No connection	No connection
Frankly Chat	TLS traffic is decrypted but packets containing chat messages not routed through proxy	TLS traffic is decrypted but there is no connection to the server when chat is attempted
Secret	All packets decrypted	Not Available (discontinued before we started using the transparent proxy)
Snapchat	All packets decrypted	All packets decrypted
Telegram	Connects but traffic does not pass through proxy	TLS traffic is decrypted but E2EE is enabled
Whisper	No connection	No connection
Wickr	Connects but traffic does not pass through proxy	TLS traffic is decrypted but E2EE is enabled
Yik Yak	All packets decrypted	All packets decrypted

Table 2: Summary of Dynamic Analysis Results.

ately deleted from its servers, as old messages are actually included in responses sent to the clients even though not always.

Acknowledgments. We wish to thank Balachander Krishnamurthy for motivating our research. This research is partly supported by PRESSID, a Xerox's University Affairs Committee award, and EU grants H2020-MSCA-ITN-2015 "Privacy&Us" and H2020-MSCA-RISE "ENCASE."

4. REFERENCES

[1] N. Bilton. Why I Use Snapchat: It's Fast, Ugly and Ephemeral, New York Times. http://nyti.ms/1jBMZrQ, 2014.

[2] P. H. O'Neill. The state of encryption tools, 2 years after Snowden leaks. http://www.dailydot.com/politics/encryption-since-snowden-trending-up/, 2015.

[3] L. Onwuzurike and E. De Cristofaro. Experimental Analysis of Popular Smartphone Apps Offering Anonymity, Ephemerality, and End-to-End Encryption. In *NDSS Workshop on Understanding & Enhancing Online Privacy*, 2016.

[4] A. Pfitzmann and M. Hansen. A Terminology for Talking about Privacy by Data Minimization. https://dud.inf.tu-dresden.de/literatur/Anon_Terminology_v0.34.pdf, 2010.

POSTER: Exploiting Dynamic Partial Reconfiguration for Improved Resistance Against Power Analysis Attacks on FPGAs

Ghada Dessouky
TU Darmstadt, Germany
ghada.dessouky@trust.cased.de

Ahmad-Reza Sadeghi
TU Darmstadt, Germany
ahmad.sadeghi@trust.cased.de

ABSTRACT

FPGA devices are increasingly deployed in wireless and heterogeneous networks in-field due to their re-programmable nature and high performance. Modern FPGA devices can have part of their logic partially reconfigured at run-time operation, which we propose to exploit to realize a general-purpose, flexible and reconfigurable DPA countermeasure that can be integrated into any FPGA-based system, irrespective of the cryptographic algorithm or implementation. We propose a real-time dynamic closed-loop on-chip noise generation countermeasure which consists of an on-chip power monitor coupled with a low-overhead Gaussian noise generator. The noise generator is reconfigured continuously to update its generated noise amplitude and variance so that is sufficiently hides the computation power consumption. Our scheme and its integration onto an SoC is presented as well as our proposal for evaluating its effectiveness and overhead.

1. INTRODUCTION AND MOTIVATION

Side-channel analysis (SCA) attacks constitute a major threat to the security of embedded devices and sensor nodes. Exploiting information leakage of a cryptographic implementation such as power consumption or timing or electromagnetic radiation can break the theoretic security of the implementation and enable successful key recovery rendering the cryptography useless. It is safe to assume that devices and sensors designed to function autonomously and in-field can easily get into the hands of an adversary, which motivates the necessity of hardening SCA attacks. Hence, this area of research has received plenty of attention and interest over the years, with an outcome of a wide range of potential countermeasures to defeat, or at least harden such SCA attacks.

We focus in this work on counteracting power analysis attacks on FPGA-based systems and network devices. Power analysis attacks are categorized as either simple power analysis (SPA) which is carried out by directly observing of a power trace, where instantaneous power consumption depends on a part and value of the secret key being processed. Differential power analysis (DPA) attacks, as first introduced in [2] rely on the relationship between the switching activities of transistors (due to bits flipping) of a cryptographic module and its instantaneous power consumption. These bit flips depend on the data being processed which may also depend on the secret cryptographic key which establishes a relationship between the secret key and the instantaneous power consumption. Such an attack is carried out by an adversary observing the target's power dissipation during the encryption by targeting an intermediate result of the computation which depends on both a portion of the message and a portion of the secret key. The adversary has to perform multiple measurements and statistical tests to determine if a correlation exists between the power consumption measured and the secret key. Therefore, in designing a secure cryptography module, it is necessary to incorporate countermeasures against SPA and DPA attacks. Such countermeasures aim at making an attack more difficult, and the effectiveness of a countermeasure is measured by the number of power trace samples required to establish a correlation between them and the secret key. In [4] and [3], these countermeasures are divided into mainly two groups: masking and hiding. Masking is usually at the algorithmic level and aims at randomizing the intermediate values processed by the cryptographic module. These have been successfully applied to several encryption algorithms such as in [7]. Hiding aims at removing the relation between the secret data and power consumption. Several hiding countermeasures exist such as power supply filtering, on-chip noise generation [1], wave dynamic differential logic (WDDL) [5] and symmetrical routing [6] and on-chip power regulation, insertion of dummy cycles, random order execution, and on-chip noise generation. In practice, no one countermeasure can guarantee the resistance of the cryptographic system against power attacks, and several countermeasures are often used simultaneously.

In this work, we focus our proposed DPA countermeasure to FPGA-based devices. The re-programmable nature, yet high performance, of FPGA devices have made them increasingly attractive as a choice of platform for embedded devices and an integral component of heterogeneous and wireless networks. Their increasingly wireless interfaces also enable their flexible in-field deployment and remote update and control. Being in-field however, they can easily fall in the hands of an adversary. Various countermeasures and hardening mechanisms against DPA attacks have been pro-

WiSec'16, July 18 - 20, 2016, Darmstadt, Germany
© 2016 ACM ISBN 978-1-4503-4270-4/16/07.
DOI: http://dx.doi.org/10.1145/2939918.2942426.

posed as described above. However, most of them require modifications to the cryptography module itself, its algorithm or implementation technology making them inflexible and specific to a certain cryptography implementations.

1.1 Contribution

We present a generic DPA countermeasure for FPGA-based devices that is both reconfigurable and re-usable with any cryptography module. We exploit the dynamic partial re-configurability of modern FPGA devices to implement a closed-loop real-time Gaussian noise generator which gets configured dynamically to vary the amplitude and variance of noise generated such that it is sufficient to hide the current power consumption. On-chip real-time power consumptions measurements are collected and used to guide the corresponding remote reconfiguration of the Gaussian noise generator. Our scheme is general-purpose, requires no modifications to the cryptographic algorithm or implementation that is to be secured, and therefore incurs no additional overhead on the performance of the cryptography, and aims to harden DPA attacks dynamically by continuously varying the noise amplitude and variance generated. Its estimated area overhead does not exceed 15% of the actual system area.

2. PROPOSED SCHEME

Our scheme extends one of the countermeasures proposed by Güneysu et al. in [1]. Toggling the input signal of a gate is the simplest and most effective way to impacts a gate's power consumption. Extending this to many gates can generate sufficiently high noise to hide the power consumption that is correlated with the current computation. A matrix of rows r and columns c of FPGA look-up tables (LUTs) configured as shift-registers can be implemented as simple Gaussian noise generator. The parameters r, c, the initial random bit patterns input to the matrix, as well as the configuration of the LUTs impact the amount of noise variance and amplitude generated. We propose to exploit the dynamic partial re-configurability of an FPGA device and allow that these parameters are dynamically reconfigured at run-time depending on continuous and real-time power measurements collected from an on-chip power monitor. This ring-oscillator based on-chip monitor measures the on-chip power consumption of the FPGA device at run-time and feeds these into a reconfiguration controller that determines the amplitude and variance of noise level required to sufficiently hide the current power consumption. It then fetches the corresponding bitstream from external memory and re-configures the noise generator with the newly computed parameters r, c, the initial bit pattern input to the matrix, and the LUT configuration values. This real-time dynamic closed-loop on-chip noise generation countermeasure aims to continuously harden the DPA attack by generating noise amplitude and variance that is continuously changing depending on the current power consumption measured by the on-chip monitor.

3. SYSTEM ARCHITECTURE

Our power measurement and noise generation framework are integrated onto a typical System-on-Chip consisting of one or more cryptographic modules among others for prototyping. A system bus is usually used for the cores to communicate, whether security-critical or not. Along with the Gaussian noise generator matrix and on-chip monitor, a reconfiguration controller is required to receive power measurements from the monitor and compute the required noise amplitude and variance. It then fetches the nearest-match bitstream from external DRAM and reconfigure the Gaussian noise generator via the Internal Configuration Access Port (ICAP) with this bitstream.

4. IMPLEMENTATION AND EVALUATION

We integrate our countermeasure core into an open-core SoC, such as Amber or Sparc-V8 Leon and implement our SoC onto a Xilinx Virtex-7 FPGA board for prototyping our countermeasure and evaluating its effectiveness in resisting DPA attacks and the area and power costs incurred. An oscilloscope operating at a sampling rate of at least 2.5 GS/s and a bandwidth of at least 500 MHz is used to collect the power measurements in order to assess the effectiveness of our countermeasure.

5. CONCLUSIONS

We present a countermeasure against side-channel DPA attacks for FPGA-based embedded devices which exploits dynamic and partial logic reconfiguration of an FPGA. The parameters of an LUT-based Gaussian noise generator are updated continuously at run-time to match real-time on-chip power measurements collected to ensure that a sufficiently high and varying noise is constantly generated. This countermeasure is general-purpose, non-specific to any cryptography implementations, requires no inflexible modifications to the algorithm or its implementation and incurs no overhead on the performance of the cryptographic module.

6. REFERENCES

[1] T. Güneysu and A. Moradi. *CHES 2011 Proceedings*, chapter Generic Side-Channel Countermeasures for Reconfigurable Devices, pages 33–48. 2011.

[2] P. C. Kocher, J. Jaffe, and B. Jun. Differential power analysis. In *Proceedings of the 19th Annual International Cryptology Conference on Advances in Cryptology*, CRYPTO '99, pages 388–397. Springer-Verlag, 1999.

[3] S. Mangard, E. Oswald, and T. Popp. *Power Analysis Attacks: Revealing the Secrets of Smart Cards (Advances in Information Security)*. Springer-Verlag New York, Inc., 2007.

[4] N. Mentens, B. Gierlichs, and I. Verbauwhede. *CHES 2008 Proceedings*, chapter Power and Fault Analysis Resistance in Hardware through Dynamic Reconfiguration, pages 346–362. 2008.

[5] K. Tiri and I. Verbauwhede. A logic level design methodology for a secure dpa resistant asic or fpga implementation. In *Design, Automation and Test in Europe Conference and Exhibition, 2004. Proceedings*, volume 1, Feb 2004.

[6] P. Yu and P. Schaumont. Secure fpga circuits using controlled placement and routing. In *(CODES+ISSS), 2007 5th IEEE/ACM/IFIP International Conference on*, pages 45–50, Sept 2007.

[7] Z. Yuan, Y. Wang, J. Li, R. Li, and W. Zhao. Fpga based optimization for masked aes implementation. In *2011 IEEE 54th MWSCAS*, pages 1–4, Aug 2011.

Poster: Friend or Foe? Context Authentication for Trust Domain Separation in IoT Environments

Markus Miettinen
TU Darmstadt, Germany
markus.miettinen@trust.tu-
darmstadt.de

Jialin Huang
TU Darmstadt, Germany
jialin.huang@trust.tu-
darmstadt.de

Thien Duc Nguyen
TU Darmstadt, Germany
ducthien.nguyen@trust.tu-
darmstadt.de

N. Asokan
Aalto University and University
of Helsinki, Finland
asokan@acm.org

Ahmad-Reza Sadeghi
TU Darmstadt, Germany
ahmad.sadeghi@trust.cased.de

1. MOTIVATION

The Internet of Things (IoT) is rapidly emerging, resulting in a growing demand for guaranteeing its security and privacy. Imagine the following scenario: In a not so distant future you have just purchased a number of Internet-of-Things (IoT) appliances for your smart home. You are standing in your living room and would like to have these new devices wirelessly connect to each other and your home network. The set of your own devices in your network constitute your *trust domain*. Most IoT devices are equipped with environmental sensors, e.g., for monitoring ambient luminosity, audio, or temperature. A breach in your trust domain could leak such sensor data, and hence potentially sensitive private information about your behavior and habits, to outsiders.

Therefore, you want to make sure that none of your devices accidentally connect to your neighbor's home network. You also want to make sure that *only your own* devices are granted access to your trust domain. The devices could use appropriate service discovery and key exchange protocols to establish secure communication links with each other and other devices like the home WiFi router. But how can your devices distinguish between other devices that belong to your trust domain and devices of your neighbors that happen to lie within wireless communication range? That is, how can devices in a trust domain (e.g., your home) authenticate each other?

2. PREVIOUS APPROACHES

One approach is to ask user's interaction to facilitate authentication as in Bluetooth Secure Simple Pairing [4]. However, user-mediated "manual authentication" is not appropriate for IoT scenarios for two reasons. First, even a simple interaction requirement quickly becomes burdensome if users have to repeat it separately for dozens or hundreds of devices in their IoT domains such as smart homes. Second, many IoT devices lack the necessary hardware (such as user I/O or NFC peripherals) for manual authentication.

Another approach which is common practice today for admitting a new WiFi-enabled IoT device into a user's domain is to involve a smartphone to assist in the process. The user downloads an app from the device vendor and uses it to connect to the new device over an ad-hoc WiFi connection and transmit WiFi network access credentials thereby allowing the new device to join his trust domain. This approach, however, is vulnerable to an active man-in-the-middle.

One may also try to authenticate IoT devices using similar approaches as done in wireless sensor networks [1]. These approaches are, however, based on pre-distributing key material to devices before deployment. In future IoT environments such key pre-distribution is not feasible. First, IoT devices will be manufactured and shipped by hundreds of different device vendors all over the world. It is not likely that all of them would share mutual security associations required for establishing a common key pool from which to draw pre-distributed keys. Second, different users might be using devices coming from the same vendor, thus sharing the same key pool. It is impossible to distinguish different users' devices based on their pre-distributed keys.

The idea of using shared entropy extracted from ambient context of two co-located devices provides potential solutions for IoT devices authentication [2, 3]. However, existing context-based authentication schemes have limitations that make them unsuitable for IoT settings. They are either distance-critical, or lack a clear feasibility analysis. For example, practical constraints related to the entropy loss incurred by the error-correcting codes were not considered in previous work, and these constraints turn out to be quite strict in these context-based designs.

3. OUR CONTRIBUTION

To overcome the above limitations we propose a scalable context authentication approach for trust domain separation for IoT devices leveraging ambient context information, like audio, sensed by on-device sensors. Our scheme can assist users to securely admit IoT devices into their trust domains with minimal user interaction. Our main contributions are:

WiSec'16 July 18-22, 2016, Darmstadt, Germany

© 2016 Copyright held by the owner/author(s).

ACM ISBN 978-1-4503-4270-4/16/07.

DOI: http://dx.doi.org/10.1145/2939918.2942422

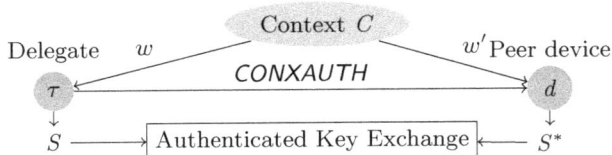

Figure 1: Context authentication and key exchange

- Context authentication approach for trust domain separation in IoT environments utilizing the error correcting capability of fuzzy extractors. Our approach is implemented on Android.

- Security analysis showing strict limits for context entropy and bit similarity. We evaluate our scheme based on empirical data and demonstrate its feasibility.

4. SYSTEM DESIGN

We use context authentication to allow devices to determine that they are co-located in a context C of the user's trust domain $\mathcal{D}$, which is composed of all the user's IoT devices d. By context C, we mean a distinct subspace of $\mathcal{D}$ where the sensed ambient environment like luminosity and audio is similar, e.g., a room in the user's apartment.

We utilize two kinds of devices: context-specific *delegates* τ and a *domain master* M, e.g., the user's smartphone, that is used to manage IoT devices in $\mathcal{D}$. The user assigns delegate τ for each context C of $\mathcal{D}$ by setting up a strong security association between τ and M, e.g., by traditional manual pairing. This is done only once for each context, so the user burden remains manageable. The main adversary of concern are external devices that do not belong to trust domain $\mathcal{D}$ but are located in close proximity of the devices in C so that they can communicate over a proximity channel in the same way as legitimate peer devices.

The key part of our solution is a *context authentication* protocol as depicted in Fig. 1. First, delegate τ and peer device d derive context fingerprints w and w', respectively, from their observations of the ambient context like changes in the noise level or luminosity in C. Since τ and d are co-located in the same context C, these fingerprints will be similar. This similarity is used to authenticate the mutual context by running the CONXAUTH protocol over the wireless channel (e.g., WiFi or Bluetooth). CONXAUTH, uses fuzzy extractors for correcting errors between w and w' caused by inevitable variations in sensing. Delegate τ publishes error-correcting information which d uses to correct its fingerprint w' to be identical with w, given that w and w' are similar, i.e., if their Hamming distance $\mathsf{dist}(w, w')$ is below a given threshold t. Delegate τ and d then use their (corrected) fingerprints to derive context authentication secrets S and S^*, respectively. If $\mathsf{dist}(w, w') \leq t$, the authentication secrets will be identical, i.e., $S = S^*$.

Delegate τ and d then use S in an authenticated key exchange protocol run over the wireless channel to confirm the authentication and to agree on a secure link key. Admission to the trust domain is then granted by the domain master M, e.g., after requesting confirmation from the user.

5. EVALUATION

The error-correction-capable fuzzy extractor is applied as a main primitive in our context authentication protocol.

Table 1: Average min-entropy rate and number of extracted bits of fingerprints during active times of day.

Exp.	Entropy rate	Bit rate/h	Active time
Home 1	0.92	122.61	08:00–22:00
Home 2	0.95	194.46	08:00–22:00
Home 3	0.97	239.65	08:00–22:00
Office 1	0.92	225.22	10:00–18:00
Office 2	0.89	101.46	10:00–18:00
Office 3	0.96	203.99	10:00–18:00
Office 4	0.93	149.08	10:00–18:00
Office 5	0.91	96.41	10:00–18:00

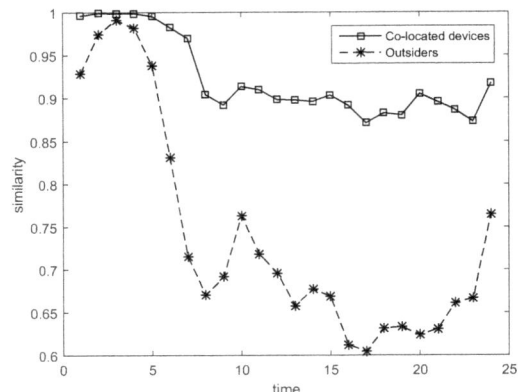

Figure 2: Average similarity of fingerprints of co-located and non-co-located devices in a domestic context

Here, two factors are critical for security: 1) the entropy rate and 2) the similarity of the sensed context fingerprints. The security properties of fuzzy extractors impose tight constraints on these factors. Our analysis shows that the similarity of context fingerprints should be at least 80%, and have an entropy rate of at least 0.85.

To evaluate the feasibility of our protocol, we collected context measurements in several different contextual settings, including domestic and office environments. Results of the entropy rate of and similarity of fingerprints between co-located devices are shown in Tab. 1 and Fig. 2. As we can see, they also fulfil the above requirements.

6. ACKNOWLDEGMENTS

This work was supported in part by the German Science Foundation (project S2, CRC 1119 CROSSING), the European Union's Seventh Framework Programme (609611, PRACTICE), and the German Federal Ministry of Education and Research within CRISP.

References

[1] D. Liu, P. Ning, and R. Li. Establishing pairwise keys in distributed sensor networks. *ACM Trans. Inf. Syst. Secur.*, 2005.

[2] M. Miettinen, N. Asokan, T. D. Nguyen, A.-R. Sadeghi, and M. Sobhani. Context-based zero-interaction pairing and key evolution for advanced personal devices. In *ACM Conference on Computer and Communications Security*, 2014.

[3] D. Schürmann and S. Sigg. Secure communication based on ambient audio. *IEEE Transactions on Mobile Computing*, 12, 2013.

[4] J. Suomalainen, J. Valkonen, and N. Asokan. Standards for security associations in personal networks: a comparative analysis. *IJSN*, 4, 2009.

Poster: Security Design Patterns With Good Usability

[Poster Abstract]

Hans-Joachim Hof
Muse - Munich IT Security Research Group
Munich University of Applied Sciences
Lothstrasse 64
80335 Munich, Germany
hof@hm.edu

Gudrun Socher
Department for Computer Science and
Mathematics
Munich University of Applied Sciences
Lothstrasse 64
80335 Munich, Germany
gudrun.socher@hm.edu

ABSTRACT

This poster presents work-in-progress in the field of usable security. The usability of security mechanisms is crucial to avoid unintended misuse of security mechanisms which lowers the security level of a system. It is the goal of the work presented in this poster to identify security design patterns with good usability. Requirements for security design patterns with good usability stem from existing usable security design guidelines. A collection of security usability failures is presented as well as examples of how misuse anti-patterns can be derived from these failures. Misuse cases will be used in future work to identify security design patterns with good usability.

Keywords

Usability, Security Design Patterns, Design Patterns, Usable Security;

1. INTRODUCTION

Previous works in the field of usable security have focused on the compilation of a design guide for usable security mechanisms [2, 3]. While these guidelines are of great help during the high-level design process of a product, there is still the need for more technical help for software developers during the fine-grain design and implementation processes.

Design patterns are a well-known approach for reusable solutions of common problems within a given context. They come in the form of a description or a template on how to solve a class of problems. They are an established way to formalize best practices in software design.

Security design patterns are reusable solutions to the problem of controlling a set of specific threats through some security mechanism, defined in a given context. Refer to [1, 4] for an overview of security design patterns. Usability design patterns as collected in [5] are great for effective interaction

design. The goal of the work presented in this poster is to extend security design patterns in the usability dimension to patterns for usable security.

To identify security design patterns with good usability, a collection of security usability failures is used as well as the usable security design guidelines described above. Examples of misuse anti-patterns are identified for some of the usability failures. Based on these misuse anti-patterns, future work will identify security design patterns with good usability.

2. REQUIREMENTS FOR DESIGN PATTERNS FROM SECURITY DESIGN GUIDELINES

Previous work includes security design guidelines [2, 3]. These guidelines are general advises on how to design systems. The guidelines are:

- Understandability for all users,
- Empowered users,
- No jumping through hoops,
- Efficient use of user attention and memorization capabilities,
- Only informed decisions,
- Security as default,
- Fearless System,
- Security guidance, educating reaction on user errors, and
- Consistency.

These guidelines are used as requirements for the design patterns to be identified.

3. EXAMPLE SECURITY USABILITY FAILURES

The poster shows a collection of security failures that are used to identify misuse cases and that will be the input to the design of the security design patterns with good usability in future work.

Categories of the security failures presented in the poster include:

WiSec'16 July 18-22, 2016, Darmstadt, Germany

© 2016 Copyright held by the owner/author(s).

ACM ISBN 978-1-4503-4270-4/16/07.

DOI: http://dx.doi.org/10.1145/2939918.2942423

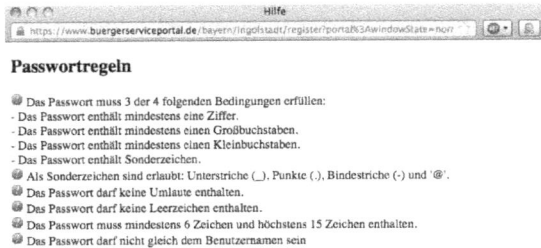

Figure 1: Password policy of the citizen portal of the city of Ingolstadt, Germany: unnecessarily complicated password rules, which are hard to understand, frustrate users rather than motivating them to choose strong passwords.

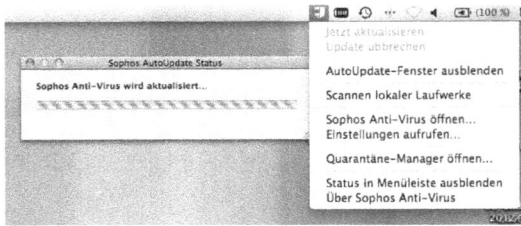

Figure 2: Forced update of virus scanner: no possibility to stop or postpone the update (see greyed out option in the drop-down menu).

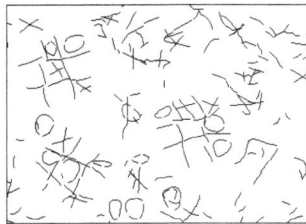

Figure 3: Complicated Captcha: Complicated Security measures annoy users.

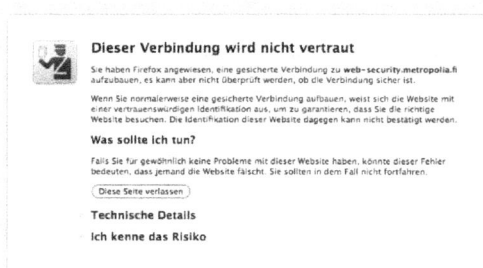

Figure 4: Example of an unacceptable security choice: The explaination is too long. Given choices are difficult to understand. The given choice voids the security of the certificate system.

- Authentication usability failures: Password-based authentication often comes with bad usability. Figure 1 shows an example. In the example, a complicated password policy is enforced on the user without helping the user to use a strong password.

- Strict security enforcement usability failure: Figure 2 shows an example of a forced update that cannot be stopped or postponed by a user (greyed out option).

- Anti-Bot usability failure: Several services use so-called captchas (Completely Automated Public Turing test to tell Computers and Humans Apart) to hinder automated scripts (bots) to use this service. However, automated captcha solving algorithms get better and better, so captchas get more and more complicated, resulting in captchas like the one in Figure 3 that are extremely annoying for human users.

- Security decisions with unacceptable choices usability failure: Figure 4 shows an error message of the Firefox browser when it encounters a certificate of an unknown certificate authority (e.g. a self-signed certificate). As a user cannot verify such a certificate, a safe option would be to block the site. However in this case, many sites would be inaccessible. Firefox allows to add an exception to the security check, hence voids the security of the certificate system.

More categories are shown on the poster. The poster shows examples of misuse anti-patterns for these categories of security usability failures. For example, one of the misuse anti-patterns is called "Enforcing a complicated password policy for password-based authentication".

4. CONCLUSION

The poster shows several requirements for usable security mechanisms. A collection of examples for security usability failures are shown. The poster shows examples of how misuse anti-patterns can be derived from the security usability failures. These misuse cases will be used to identify security design patterns with good usability in future work.

5. REFERENCES

[1] E. Fernandez-Buglioni. *Security Patterns in Practice: Designing Secure Architectures Using Software Patterns.* John Wiley and Sons, 2013.

[2] H.-J. Hof. User-centric it security – how to design usable security mechanisms. In *The Fifth International Conference on Advances in Human-oriented and Personalized Mechanisms, Technologies, and Services (CENTRIC 2012)*, pages 7–12. IARIA, November 2012.

[3] H.-J. Hof. Towards enhanced usability of it security mechanisms – how to design usable it security mechanisms using the example of email encryption. *International Journal On Advances in Security*, 6(1&2):78–87, 2013.

[4] C. Steel, R. Nagappan, and R. Lai. *Core Security Patterns.* Prentice Hall, 2012.

[5] J. Tidwell. *Designing Interaces.* O'Reilly Media, Inc., 2nd edition, 2010.

POSTER: Toward a Secure and Scalable Attestation

[Extended Abstract]

Moreno Ambrosin[1], Mauro Conti[1], Ahmad Ibrahim[2], Gregory Neven[3],
Ahmad-Reza Sadeghi[2], and Matthias Schunter[4]

[1]University of Padua, Italy   [2]Technische Universität Darmstadt, Germany
[3]IBM Zurich Research Laboratory, Switzerland   [4]Intel Labs, Portland, OR, U.S.A.

{ahmad.ibrahim, ahmad.sadeghi}@trust.tu-darmstadt.de,
{Ambrosin, Conti}@math.unipd.it, matthias.schunter@intel.com,
NEV@zurich.ibm.com

ABSTRACT

Large numbers of smart devices are permeating our environment to collect data and act on the insight derived. Examples of such devices include smart homes, factories, cars, or wearables. For privacy, security, and safety, ensuring correctness of the configuration of these devices is essential. One key mechanism to protect the software integrity of these devices is attestation.

In this paper, we analyze the requirements for efficient attestation of large numbers of interconnected embedded systems. We present the first collective attestation protocol which allows attesting an unlimited number of devices. Simulation results show a run-time of 5.3 seconds in networks of 50, 000 low-end embedded devices.

1. INTRODUCTION

Smart devices are rapidly proliferating into every domain of our life. These devices range from tiny wearables to large industrial installations such as, smart factories. Unlike traditional computers, smart devices usually lack the necessary security capabilities which protect them against attacks. Today, an adversary can easily attack such devices and compromise both privacy and safety [5]. One key mechanism to prevent such attacks and ensure the safe and secure operation of a device, is *remote software attestation*.

While today attestation can be performed on individual smart devices, there is no viable approach to securely scale attestation to *a very large number* of devices. Indeed, the first attempt in this direction, SEDA [1], assumes a software-only attacker, i.e., all the devices in the network are not physically tampered. This assumption is not realistic, in the envisioned large scale deployments.

In this paper we present the first collective attestation scheme for large networks of embedded devices that is: *secure*, *scalable*, and *publicly verifiable*.

2. RELATED WORK

Individual Device Attestation is a well-established research area. The purpose of an attestation protocol is to enable a verifier to verify

the software integrity of remote device (denoted by prover). We distinguish three main approaches of attestation: (1) software-based attestation, which requires no secure hardware and does not rely on cryptographic secrets, making it particularly attractive for low-end devices with limited resources. Unfortunately, the security of software-based attestation has been challenged; (2) co-processor-based attestation, which offers improved security guarantees. However, due to their high cost and complexity, they are not suitable for low-end embedded devices; and (3) hardware/software co-design [3], which aims at minimizing the hardware security features required for enabling secure remote attestation. Such security features can be as simple as a Read Only Memory (ROM), and a simple Memory Protection Unit (MPU).

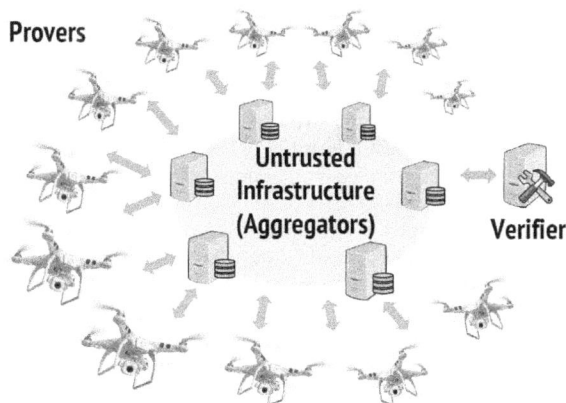

Figure 1: Representation of our system model

Collective Attestation. SEDA [1], made a first step towards a *collective attestation*. However, The main focus of SEDA is efficiency and applicability to low-end embedded devices, rather than security in the presence of a realistic adversary. SEDA is based on neighbors verification and hop-by-hop MACs for authentication. Consequently, every device in SEDA is supposed to be equipped with the minimal hardware required for attestation. Moreover, an adversary which compromises the software of a large number of devices can be evade detection by SEDA through physically tampering with one single device in the network. Our proposed solution, which is based on multi-signatures, allows devices with no security hardware to participate in the protocol. Physically tampered devices, on the other hand, can only evade their own detection.

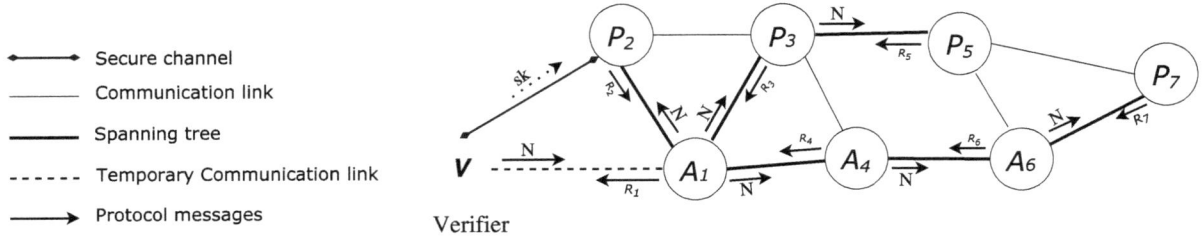

Figure 2: Collective attestation in a network of seven devices (three aggregators and four provers)

Multi Signature. A multi-signature scheme [2] allows n different signers to sign the *same* message m in a constant-size signature, i.e., with signature length independent of n. Most multi-signature schemes also have verification time quasi-independent of n, meaning that the number of core cryptographic operations (e.g., exponentiations or pairing computations) is independent of n.

3. REQUIREMENTS

A collective attestation protocol should satisfy the following requirements:

- *Security:* The protocol should be secure in the presence of a strong adversary capable of physical tampering, i.e., the attestation result of one devices should not be dependent on the hardware security of any other device.
- *Scalablity,* The protocol should efficiently verify the integrity of a large collection of devices. The run-time of the protocol should be at most logarithmic in the size of the network.
- *Public Verifiablity,* i.e., the produced attestation report should be publicly verifiable

4. NETWORK ATTESTATION

Our protocol combines attestation trees with a Boldyreva's multi-signature scheme [2]. It thus provides secure collective attestation with *constant* overhead on the verifier and logarithmic overall run-time. This allows even low power verifier devices, such as a smartphone, to verify the integrity of very large industrial or IoT setups. The collected result is publicly verifiable, and ensures that every devices that is not physically tampered, is also not software-compromised.

The proposed protocol is executed between the following entities: *prover* (P), *aggregator* (A), and *verifier* ($\mathcal{V}$). As shown in Figure 2, each device is initialized before deployment (by $\mathcal{V}$) with a multi-signature secret key, to which $\mathcal{V}$ stores the public key. At attestation time, $\mathcal{V}$ randomly chooses an aggregator device A_1 and sends it a random challenge N. Upon receiving the challenge, each device forwards it to its neighbors, until the challenge is received by every device in the network. Consequently, a spanning tree rooted at A_1 is formed. Finally, starting at leaf nodes in the tree, every prover P_i composes a proof of integrity of its software configuration, (e.g., hash of its binary). It then generates a multi-signature over the software configuration and the received challenge. P_i sends the generated signature to its parent node as an attestation response R_i. Upon receiving all responses from its child nodes, an aggregator A_j aggregates the received multi-signatures according to the definition in [2]. The generated multi-signature R_j is then forwarded to the parent node. As a result, the final multi-signature R_1 is generated by A_1 and then forwarded to $\mathcal{V}$. Having the public keys of all devices in the network, $\mathcal{V}$ can verify the received multi-signature in constant time. If the signature verifies correctly, $\mathcal{V}$ concludes that every (physically untampered) device in the network is not software-compromised.

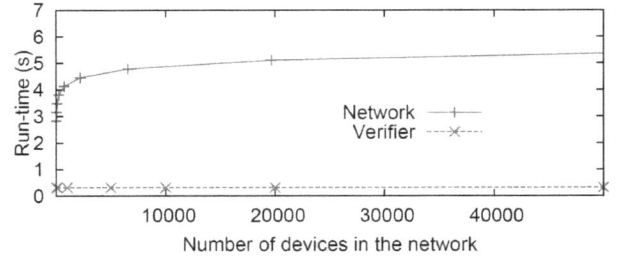

Figure 3: run-time in networks with 4 neighbors per device

5. PERFORMANCE ANALYSIS

We simulated our protocol using the OMNeT++ [4] simulation environment for networks with up to $50,000$. Each device in the network has four neighbors. We based our simulation on measurement of the real execution time on both TyTAN [3] security architecture as prover devices and an Intel Galileo board as the verifier. The run-time of the protocol at both ends (i.e., network and verifier) is shown in Figure 3. As shown in the figure the run-time of the protocol (as function of the network size) is logarithmic at the network's end and constant on the verifier. The overall time required to attest a network of $50,000$ devices is about 5.3 seconds.

6. CONCLUSIONS

Collective attestation is a building block for securing the Internet of Things. For very large numbers of devices, to enables enterprises to validate the configuration and software and ensure that all devices are indeed up-to-date. In this paper, we have proposed the first practical and secure collective attestation scheme. It substantially improves the state of the art (e.g. SEDA [1]) by allowing aggregators that are not equipped with security hardware. our protocol is also resilient to a strong adversary, which is capable of physical tampering. Unfortunately, it only allows collective attestation of homogeneous networks with constant run-time. For future work, we aim to design a collective attestation protocol which enables secure, and efficient attestation of heterogeneous networks.

Acknowledgement

This work has been co-funded by the German Science Foundation as part of project S2 within the CRC 1119 CROSSING, EC-SPRIDE, the European Union's Seventh Framework Programme under grant agreement No. 609611, PRACTICE project, and the Intel Collaborative Research Institute for Secure Computing (ICRI-SC).

7. REFERENCES

[1] N. Asokan et al. Seda: Scalable embedded device attestation. In *ACM CCS'15*.
[2] A. Boldyreva. Threshold signatures, multisignatures and blind signatures based on the gap-diffie-hellman-group signature scheme. In *PKC '03*.
[3] F. Brasser et al. Tytan: Tiny trust anchor for tiny devices. In *DAC'15*.
[4] OpenSim Ltd. OMNeT++ discrete event simulator. http://omnetpp.org/, 2015.
[5] J. Vijayan. Stuxnet renews power grid security concerns, 2010.

Author Index